Time Out
Prague

Penguin Books

PENGUIN BOOKS

Published by the Penguin Group
Penguin Books Ltd, 27 Wrights Lane, London W8 5TZ, England
Penguin Books USA Inc., 375 Hudson Street, New York, New York 10014, USA
Penguin Books Australia Ltd, Ringwood, Victoria, Australia
Penguin Books Canada Ltd, 10 Alcorn Avenue, Toronto, Ontario, Canada M4V 3B2
Penguin Books (NZ) Ltd, 182-190 Wairau Road, Auckland 10, New Zealand

Penguin Books Ltd, Registered Offices: Harmondsworth, Middlesex, England

First published 1995
Second edition 1997
Third edition 1998
Fourth edition 2000
10 9 8 7 6 5 4 3 2 1

Colour reprographics by Westside Digital Media, 9 Bridle Lane, London W1
and Precise Litho, 34-35 Great Sutton Street, London EC1
Printed and bound by Cayfosa-Quebecor, Ctra. de Caldes, Km 3 08 130 Sta, Perpètua de Mogoda, Barcelona, Spain

Edited and designed by
Time Out Guides Limited
Universal House
251 Tottenham Court Road
London W1P 0AB
Tel + 44 (0)20 7813 3000
Fax + 44 (0)20 7813 6001
Email guides@timeout.com
www.timeout.com

Editorial
Editor Will Tizard
Listings Editor Katka Šuranská
Copy Editing Desmond McGrath
Proofreader Ronnie Haydon
Indexer Cathy Heath

Editorial Director Peter Fiennes
Series Editor Ruth Jarvis
Managing Editor Dave Rimmer
Deputy Series Editor Jonathan Cox
Editorial Assistant Jenny Noden

Design
Art Director John Oakey
Art Editor Mandy Martin
Senior Designer Scott Moore
Designers Benjamin de Lotz, Lucy Grant
Scanning/Imaging Dan Conway
Picture Editor Kerri Miles
Deputy Picture Editor Olivia Duncan-Jones
Picture Admin Kit Burnet
Ad Make-up Glen Impey

Advertising
Group Advertisement Director Lesley Gill
Sales Director Mark Phillips
International Sales Manager Mary L. Rega
Advertisement Sales (Prague) Creative Partners
Advertising Assistant Catherine Shepherd

Administration
Publisher Tony Elliott
Managing Director Mike Hardwick
Financial Director Kevin Ellis
Marketing Director Christine Cort
General Manager Nichola Coulthard
Production Manager Mark Lamond
Production Controller Samantha Furniss

Features in this guide were written and researched by:
Introduction Will Tizard. **History** Jonathan Cox, Paul Lewis, Will Tizard. **Prague Today** René Jakl, Will Tizard. **Architecture** Jonathan Cox, Siegfried Mortkowitz, Damon McGee. **Literary Prague** Jenny Smith. **Beer** Mark Baker. **Accommodation** Ky Krauthammer, Anthony Maes. **Sightseeing** Carole Cadwalladr, Jonathan Cox, Lacey Eckl, Jeremy Hurewitz, Rick Jervis, Ky Krauthammer, Dave Rimmer, Will Tizard. **Restaurants** Will Tizard **Cafés** Will Tizard. **Pubs & Bars** Will Tizard. **Shops & Services** Emma McClune, David Newman, Sandra Tuma. **By Season** Will Tizard. **Children** Sandra Tuma. **Film** Joseph Cahill, Raymond Johnston. **Galleries** Joseph Cahill, Ky Krauthammer. **Gay & Lesbian** Jean-Jacques Soukoup. **Music: Rock, Roots & Jazz** Will Tizard. **Music: Classical & Opera** Micheal Halstead, Will Tizard. **Theatre & Dance** Theodore Schwinke. **Sport & Fitness** František Bouc, Julia Gray. **Trips Out of Town** Jonathan Cox, Julia Gray, Dave Rimmer, Anna Sutton, Will Tizard. **Directory** Mark Baker, Theodore Schwinke, Jenny Smith, Sasha Štěpán, Katka Šuranská, Will Tizard. **Further Reference** Dave Rimmer, Will Tizard.

The Editor would like to thank:
Kevin Ebbutt, Jennifer and Radek Helia, Ky Krauthammer, Karel Krofta, Hanka Kučerová, Barbara and Bill Tizard, and Sasha Štěpán. Extra-special thanks to Katka Šuranská.

Maps by JS Graphics, 17 Beadles Lane, Old Oxted, Surrey RH8 9JG.

Photography by Matt Carr and Julie Denesha except: pages 7-23 and 250-254 AKG London; page 26 Associated Press; page 265 Jerry Driendl/Telegraph Colour Library; page 266 Liba Taylor/Hutchison Picture Library; pages 158, 182, 203, 240 and 256 Will Tizard. The following pictures were provided by the featured establishments: pages 39, 115, 122, 188, 196, 199, 202, 217, 233 and 235.

The following photographs were supplied by the featured establishments: pages 217, 233, 235.

Contents

Introduction

It's the beauty of Prague that hits you first. It's almost overwhelming – angels and gargoyles, domes and arches, spires and façades from every architectural style of the last millennium surround you in Staré Mĕsto, the city's ancient heart. Prague's endless string of invaders each contributed a style, it seems, and, miraculously, only the Swedes ever did much physical damage.

If Prague has a museum-like quality, though, it's anything but dry. True, there's a moroseness and a kind of fatalism about the Czechs, just as in much of Central Europe (another contribution down to the invaders of the city, perhaps). And building a free-market democracy on the ruins of a communist dictatorship is, as you'd expect, a messy and painful process at times, even more than a decade after the Velvet Revolution. But the newness of the independent Czech state can be very liberating. Especially when mixed with ancient Bohemian rituals such as drinking beer. Here is where the inherent hedonism of Praguers can be witnessed – and usually sampled liberally. Young Czechs without enough take-home pay to buy a metro pass every month just ride without paying and spend their crowns at the Roxy dancing to deep house from DJ Pierre.

It's a sexy city, too, for such a Gothic one. Marital infidelity rates are among the highest in the world, the nation is obsessed with beauty pageants and there's definitely something about moonlight over Malá Strana. The left bank district huddled beneath Prague Castle is indescribably gorgeous by night.

Perhaps 'sensuousness' is closer to the mark than 'hedonistic'. The curving lines of Prague's baroque cathedrals sometimes almost seem to blend in to the strains of classical recitals, without which it's simply impossible to imagine Prague.

For the average visitor, it's awfully hard not to fall in love, one way or the other, even if it's just with the beer. Many never do tear themselves away. You could be next.

ABOUT THE TIME OUT CITY GUIDES

This is the fourth edition of the *Time Out Prague Guide*, one of an expanding series of *Time Out* City Guides produced by the people behind London and New York's successful listings magazines. Our team of writers and researchers, all experts in their fields and residents of Prague, have plumbed the deepest cellar bars and peered from the highest spires to update this guide with all the information you'll need to explore the Golden City.

THE LOWDOWN ON THE LISTINGS

Above all, we've tried to make this book as useful as possible. Addresses, telephone numbers, transport information, opening times, admission prices and credit card details are all included in our listings. And, as far as possible, we've given details of facilities, services and events, all checked and correct at the time we went to press. However, owners and managers can change their arrangements at any time. Before you go out of your way, we'd strongly advise you to phone and check opening times, dates of events and other particulars. While every effort has been made to ensure the accuracy of the information contained in this guide, the publishers cannot accept responsibility for any errors it may contain.

PRICES & PAYMENT

We have noted whether venues such as shops, hotels and restaurants accept credit cards or not, but have only listed the major cards – American Express (**AmEx**), Diners Club (**DC**), MasterCard (**MC**) and Visa (**V**). Some businesses may accept other cards, but generally speaking credit cards are still not common in the Czech Republic. It's rare, but not inconceivable, that small businesses will take travellers' cheques.

For every restaurant we have given the price range for main courses, as well as set menus where relevant. Accommodation prices take seasonal fluctuations into account.

The prices we've supplied should be treated as guidelines, not gospel. Fluctuating exchange rates and inflation can cause charges, in shops and restaurants particularly, to change rapidly. If prices vary wildly from those we've quoted, ask whether there's a good reason. If not, go elsewhere. Then please write and let us know. We aim to give the best and most up-to-date advice, so we always want to know if you've been badly treated or overcharged.

There is an online version of this guide, as well as weekly events listings for over 30 international cities, at **www.timeout.com**.

THE LIE OF THE LAND

Prague is divided into both numbered postal districts and into areas with names. Sometimes these correspond and sometimes they don't, so in our listings we have provided both. After the street name and address, we supply the name of the district and then its basic postal code. The main central areas of Prague are Hradčany, Malá Strana, Staré Město and Nové Město (all of which, bar part of Nové Město, fall into Prague 1) and these are also the main divisions we have used in our Sightseeing section and in chapters that are organised by area.

TELEPHONE NUMBERS

To phone Prague from outside the Czech Republic, first dial the international code 00, then 42 (the code for the Czech Republic) then 02 (the area code for Prague) and finally the local number (anything from four to eight digits). From within the relevant area, dial only the local number.

Mobile phone numbers in Prague are preceded by four digits, beginning with 06. To call them from anywhere outside the Czech Republic, dial 00, then 42, then the mobile number.

ESSENTIAL INFORMATION

For all the practical information you might need for visiting Prague – including visa and customs information, disabled access,

emergency telephone numbers, a list of useful websites and the lowdown on Prague's transport network – turn to the Directory section at the back of this guide. It starts on page 268.

MAPS

At the back of this guide you'll find a series of fully indexed colour maps to the city of Prague and the major highways of the Czech Republic – they start on page 304. Every place listed in this guide that falls within the street maps will have a map reference against it to aid location.

LET US KNOW WHAT YOU THINK

We hope you enjoy the *Time Out Prague Guide*, and we'd like to know what you think of it. We welcome tips for places that you feel we should include in future editions and take notice of your criticism of our choices. There's a reader's reply card at the back of this book – or you can email us on pragueguide@timeout.com.

Advertisers

We would like to stress that no establishment has been included in this guide because it has advertised in any of our publications and no payment of any kind has influenced any review. The opinions given in this book are those of *Time Out* writers and entirely independent.

In Context

Feature boxes

Vyšehrad – home for national heroes.

History

Czechs versus Germans, Hussites versus Jesuits, underground resistance versus Nazis, dissidents versus communists – the history of Prague is a story of conflict.

In around 400 BC, a Celtic tribe called the Boii occupied the region where the Czech Republic now lies and gave it the name Bohemia. The Boii successfully repelled attacking armies for the best part of 1,000 years, but they were eventually driven out by the Germanic Marcomanni and Quadi tribes who in turn were wiped out by Attila the Hun in AD 451. Slavic tribes are believed to have moved into the area sometime during the seventh century. They were ruled over by the Avars whose harsh regime provoked a successful Slavic rebellion.

THE PŘEMYSLID DYNASTY

The Czechs had to wait until the eighth century and the founding of the **Přemyslid dynasty** for real independence. The dynasty's origins are shrouded in myth. One relates that, in the absence of a male heir, **Čech** tribe leader Krok was succeeded by his soothsaying daughter Libuše. But the men of the tribe, indignant at being ruled over by a woman, told her to go and

find a husband. Libuše went into a trance and sent her white horse over the hills. The horse, she foretold, would find a ploughman with two spotted oxen and he would become their leader. Her horse quickly located the farmer, whose name was **Přemysl**.

Prague, too, is supposed to have been founded following a similar trance-induced vision. This time Libuše declared from the hilltop at Vyšehrad that 'a city whose splendour will reach to the stars' would be created nearby. Everyone then went into the woods again, this time to search for a craftsman making a door sill (*práh*), for, as Libuše said, 'mighty Lords bend before a low door'. When the craftsman was found, the site of the city was determined.

In the ninth century, Charlemagne briefly occupied the region and a Slavic state was created in Moravia under Prince Mojmír. In 860 Mojmír's successor, Rostilav, appealed to the Pope for Christian apostles with a knowledge of the Slavic language to help him put an end to the

In Context

worship of sun gods. The Byzantine Emperor sent two Greek monks, **Cyril** and **Methodius** (designers of the Cyrillic alphabet) but Frankish and German priests objected and, following Methodius's death in 885, the Slavonic liturgy they had established was made illegal.

Rostilav's nephew **Svatopluk** (871-94) had sided with the Germans over the liturgical issue and with their assistance ousted his uncle. Svatopluk built an empire encompassing Moravia, Bohemia and Slovakia. After Svatopluk's death the Magyars grabbed a chunk of Slovakia. They were to hold on to it right up until the early 20th century and their presence there was to disrupt all attempts to unite Slovaks and Czechs.

Over the next four centuries, Bohemia rode a rollercoaster that alternately descended into chaos and rose to the heights of political supremacy in Central Europe. Things continued peacefully in the early tenth century under the humane rule of Prince **Václav** or **Wenceslas** (921-9). Although Christmas carols still sing his praises, many Czech nobles felt that 'Good King' Wenceslas had sold out to the Germans and neglected Slavic interests. The nobles sided with Wenceslas's brother **Boleslav** (the Cruel, 935-67), who had Wenceslas murdered in 929. Boleslav then fought the Germans for 14 years.

Bohemia was briefly united with Moravia. Prague was made a Bishopric in 973 and the process of bringing Christianity to Bohemia was soon completed. By the end of the 12th century, however, internal bickering over succession had become so bad that, as the historian Palacký put it, 'in the storm of ages the Czechs were about to drown as a state and a nation'. The turning point

'Good King' **Wenceslas**... looks out.

came in 1197 when **Otakar I** confronted his brother Vladislav outside Prague in a showdown for the throne. Diplomatic negotiations on the night before the battle resulted in the two princes agreeing a deal that made Otakar I Bohemian King and Vladislav Margrave of Moravia. By Otakar's death in 1230 a period of peace and prestige had been achieved. His son and successor **Václav I** was made one of the seven electors of the Holy Roman Empire.

With national prestige reaching new heights, **Přemysl Otakar II** (1253-78) made his territorial claims. He snatched Cheb from the Germans and won and lost Slovakia twice. For a while his empire stretched from Florence to Poland, gaining him the title 'King of Gold and Iron'. But then Otakar challenged Rudolf of Habsburg for the throne of the Holy Roman Empire – and Rudolf won. In 1276 Rudolf invaded Bohemia, leaving Otokar with only a rump empire – Bohemia and Moravia. Otakar's successor Václav II (1278-1305) was forced to look east and south for conquests in Poland, Hungary, Croatia and Romania. His son Václav III was assassinated in 1306, allegedly by Habsburg agents. Since he left no heir, the Přemyslid dynasty came to an end.

THE GERMANS ARE COMING

During this period the demographic nature of Bohemia changed significantly. The Přemysls encouraged German immigration and German women married Czech nobles. German clerics filled top positions in the Church, and German merchants gave life to the towns, introducing new laws and administration methods. Prague was reorganised into three autonomous areas: Malá Strana, Hradčany and Staré Město (Old Town). The Jewish community of Malá Strana was forced into a ghetto in the Old Town to give the Germans more *Lebensraum*.

Successive kings drew upon the economic power of the towns to counterbalance the rural nobility. The Prague Germans demanded an ever greater voice and by the 14th century Czech and German nobles had begun a conflict that was to underlie much of Czech history.

In 1310 **John of Luxembourg**, the 14-year-old son of the Holy Roman Emperor, was elected King of Bohemia. The first years of his reign were marked by tussles with the Czech nobles over the extent of royal power. He was married to the second daughter of Václav II in order to give him proper Přemyslid credentials, but his loyalties went no further.

John's interest in Prague was ephemeral and obscure. He once attempted to recreate the Knights of the Round Table by inviting all the great knights of Europe to the city, but none of them turned up. John spent most of his time wheeling and dealing in the diplomatic circles of Europe. Back home the nobles' power grew. Prague gained a town hall and became the dominant centre of Bohemia. It was raised from a Bishopric to an Archbishopric in 1344.

THE GOLDEN AGE OF CHARLES IV

John died in a kamikaze charge against Welsh archers at the Battle of Crécy. His son **Charles IV** was elected Holy Roman Emperor in 1346, making his position as King of Bohemia unassailable. His plans for the development of Prague had the full force of Empire behind them and ushered in a golden age. Charles (1346-78) brought to Bohemia the stability that his father John had failed to achieve. Prague escaped the Black Death that ravaged Europe in 1348 and under Charles emerged as one of the most dazzling centres in Europe.

Charles had been educated at the French court and was fluent in several languages , including Czech. Through his mother he laid claim to Přemyslid lineage. Thus he became known as 'Father of his Country' and the 'Priest Kaiser'.

Charles brought the 23-year-old Swabian architect **Peter Parler** to Prague to build the **Charles Bridge** (*see page 94*) and to work on **St Vitus's Cathedral** (*see page 71*), a Gothic masterpiece that would reflect Prague's spiralling glory.

In 1348 Charles established Central Europe's first university, declaring that Bohemians should 'no longer be obliged to beg for foreign alms but find a table prepared for them in their own kingdom'. In a far-sighted move, he founded the **Nové Město** (New Town), which was constructed around wide streets, relieving the Old Town of the stress created by the concentration of artisans' workshops. Charles also undercut the power of the nobility in 1356 by reorganising the electoral system.

Availing himself of his omnipotent position in the Holy Roman Empire, Charles declared the union of Bohemia, Moravia, Silesia and Upper Lusatia indissoluble, and grafted chunks of Germany on to Bohemia. He abandoned claims to Italian territories but refused to accept Papal dictates north of the Alps.

> ' **Jan Milíč stunned crowds by declaring their beloved Charles was the Antichrist.** '

Charles was a devout Christian. Under his rule the clergy came to own half the land in the kingdom. But at the same time Charles was intensely conscious of the growing corruption in the Church and often sided with the fiery preachers whose sermons condemned its excesses. These included the rabble-rousing **Jan Milíč** of Kroměříž, who had a tendency to go a little over the top. He stunned crowds by declaring their beloved Charles was really the Antichrist, then urged his followers to prepare for the imminent apocalypse. Since he preached in Czech rather than German, the anti-clerical hysteria he inspired became closely identified with Czech nationalism. It was an explosive mix.

INCORRIGIBLE KING WENCESLAS

The seeds of religious indignation were sown under Charles but the bitter fruits were not tasted until the reign of his incorrigible son **Wenceslas IV** (1378-1419). When the Archbishop of Prague ordered all of the writings of English Protestant reformer John Wycliffe to be burnt, Wenceslas forced the Archbishop to compensate the owners of the manuscripts. A champion of the common man, he would go out shopping dressed in commoners' clothing, but if shopkeepers cheated him he would have them executed. Despite (or because of) notorious displays of temper such as roasting the chef who had spoilt his lunch, there was supposedly a virtual absence of crime in Prague during his reign.

Wenceslas and quiet piety never sat easily together. At his christening he was alleged to have urinated into the holy water and he was still unable to control himself at his coronation. He was perhaps closest to God the morning after a pub crawl and is said to have spent most of his last years in a drunken stupor. The nobles were unimpressed and formed a 'League of Lords' to have him imprisoned, but he escaped while in the royal bathhouse, seducing the beautiful bath attendant and persuading her to row him down the Vltava to safety.

JAN HUS – OBSTINATE PREACHER

Wenceslas lacked the moral and intellectual authority to steer Bohemia through the dangerous religious waters ahead. In 1403 the Rector of Prague University, **Jan Hus**, influenced by Wycliffe's reformist doctrines, took up the campaign against Church corruption. The battleground moved to the university where Czech supporters of Hus squabbled with the Germans. The King decreed in favour of the Czechs and the German academics left for Leipzig to found their own university. The Church establishment was quick to launch a counter-offensive. Hus's arguments were deemed heretical, although he was actually something of a moderate compared to those who would subsequently campaign in his name. Even so, Hus was persuaded by Wenceslas, under pressure from the Church, to leave Prague in 1412. The obstinate preacher continued his crusade in the countryside.

Jan Hus pays the penalty for refusing to recant – do fries go with that stake?

In November 1414, Hus was summoned by Wenceslas's brother Sigismund, King of Hungary, to appear before the General Council at Constance. Hus went in good faith carrying a safe conduct pass granted by Sigismund. But on arrival he was thrown in jail. The Council ordered Hus to recant his teachings and accused him of portraying himself as a fourth addition to the Holy Trinity. He challenged the Council to prove from the Scriptures that what he preached was false, but was told that he should recant simply because his superiors told him to do so. He refused and on his 46th birthday, 6 July 1415, Hus was burnt at the stake.

Hus embodied two vital hopes of the Czech people: reform of the established Church and independence from German dominance. It was not, therefore, surprising that he was to become a martyr. His motto 'truth will prevail' and the chalice, which represented lay participation in the Sacrament, became rallying symbols for his followers. The main tenets of Hussitism were contained in the Four Articles of Prague. These demanded unrestricted preaching of the word of God; communion in both kinds ('sub utraque specie' – his followers were known as Utraquists), allowing congregations to partake in not just the bread, but also the wine of the Eucharist; removal of property from monks and clergy; and strict punishment of sins committed by members of the Church.

BRAZEN HUSSITES

A few weeks after Hus's death, several hundred nobles in Bohemia sent a protest to the Council of Constance, declaring their intention to defend Hus's name and promote his teachings. The groundswell of popular feeling soon engulfed Wenceslas IV. Under pressure from the Church, he suppressed the Hussites. Then, on 30 July 1419, an angry Hussite crowd stormed the Town Hall protesting at the detention of prisoners who had been arrested for creating 'religious disorder'. The mob threw the Mayor and his councillors through the window to their deaths. Prague's first defenestration finally shattered all hopes for peace.

'Radical Hussites arrived in force and burnt alive nine monks at the stake.'

Wenceslas withdrew his decrees and died in an apoplectic fit a few days later. Hussite mobs marked the occasion by rioting and sacking the monasteries. Sigismund, who had been complicit in the burning of Hus, elbowed his way on to the Bohemian throne, and moderate Utraquist nobles, keen to find a compromise, greeted him with sycophantic deference. But radical preachers like Jan Želivský furiously denounced

General Jan Žižka – one eye on repelling Catholics from Vitkov hill.

Sigismund and Rome, prompting the Pope to call for a holy crusade against Bohemia.

Prague was almost under siege but the Hussites were undaunted. Again the Utraquists approached Sigismund, only to report back that he swore to destroy all heresy by fire and sword. Meanwhile, radical Hussites arrived in the city in force and, as a sign of their seriousness, burnt alive nine monks in front of the Royal Garrison.

THE VATICAN STRIKES BACK

Rome's call to arms against the heretic nation was taken up all over Europe and the Czechs soon found themselves surrounded. They were united, however, behind a powerful moral cause and had a freshness and zeal that came from being independent and free. They also had in their ranks a brilliant one-eyed general called **Jan Žižka**. He not only repelled the enemies from Vitkov hill in what is now Žižkov in Prague, but, by 1432, he and his 'Warriors of God' (as the Czechs called themselves) were pillaging all the way up to the Baltic coast. Women fought and died equally alongside men.

The Hussites were united during times of greatest danger but as the battle turned in their favour, old divisions re-emerged. The majority, known as **Praguers**, were moderate and middle class and their leaders were based at the University of Prague. The more extreme group, known as **Táborites**, were based on a fortified hillside called Tábor. They banned all class divisions, shared their property and held religious services only in Czech.

Once the Pope realised that the holy war had failed, he reluctantly invited the Czechs to discuss a peace settlement. The Táborites were cynical about the Pope's overtures whereas the Praguers had never wanted to break with Rome and viewed their Hussite allies in Tábor as a little too revolutionary. In 1434, the Prague nobles marched their army down to confront the Táborites and wiped out 13,000 of them at the **Battle of Lipany**, thereby settling the issue of negotiations with Rome.

> ### 'The Táborites' lack of trust in Rome proved well founded.'

In 1436 the Pope and the Utraquists signed the Basle Compacts, which recognised the Czechs as 'faithful sons of the Church', and accepted Utraquist demands for communion in both kinds. But there was no agreement on the issue of corruption in the Church. The Táborites' lack of trust in Rome was to prove well founded. A Papal envoy was sent to Prague to cool things down. On his arrival he reproached the Praguers for conducting religious services that diverted from Roman practice. It was pointed out to the envoy that the Pope had agreed to this in the Basle Compacts. When the envoy denied any knowledge of the Compacts, he was shown the original document as proof, whereupon he and the document disappeared. Troops pursued the envoy across Bohemia and retrieved the document from his suitcase.

WANTED: STRONG KING

Without a strong king, Prague was descending into national, religious and class anarchy. The King, Ladislav the Posthumous of Habsburg, was dependent on the Utraquist noble, **George of Poděbrady** (Jiři z Poděbrad). George was formally elected to the throne in 1458. From the outset he was hemmed in by hostile opponents. He eliminated the rump of the radical Táborites and suppressed a separatist pacifist Christian movement called the Unity of Czech Brethren, which was becoming immensely popular. He also fought and defeated a confederacy of plotting nobles. He kept the reactionary Catholics at bay while trying not to antagonise Rome, and resisted the German population's demands for more power. George feared another holy crusade against his country and as a diversionary tactic he tried to form a League of Christian Kings and Princes against the Turks. The idea was pooh-poohed by princes and bishops as an impertinence against the Pope and the Holy Roman Emperor. For his part, the Pope reneged on the Basle agreement and excommunicated George.

The Hussite wars had altered the political balance in the land. The Church's power was devastated and the vacuum filled by the nobles who seized Church property and ruled mercilessly over the peasants. A hard-fought power struggle between the King and the nobles forced George to look abroad to the Polish **Jagellon** dynasty for a successor. Following his death in 1471, Vladislav II became the King of Bohemia, to be followed by Ludvik in 1516.

> ## 'A new constitution reduced the peasants to serfdom and stripped the towns of their power.'

The two Jagellon monarchs, ruling in absentia, failed to keep the nobles in check. In 1500 the nobility extracted a new constitution confirming their status, reducing that of the peasants to serfdom and stripping the towns of their power. Lutheran ideas, which were close to Hussitism, seeped in from Germany and religious tensions soon flared up again. Anxious Utraquists, fearing a reproach from Rome, tried to keep the lid on these developments. They redirected all their efforts to suppressing the Unity of Czech Brethren, but the Brethren only grew in strength.

THE HABSBURGS MOVE IN

When the second Jagellon King, Ludvík, was drowned in a swamp while running away from the Turks at the Battle of Mohács in 1526, the Estates of Bohemia elected the Habsburg Duke

Ferdinand I as King of Bohemia; the dynasty was to last until 1918. Ferdinand knew how precarious his status was as a foreign Catholic monarch in a fiercely anti-Catholic country. At first he was sensitive to his new subjects, and refrained from persecuting the growing number of Lutherans. In 1546 he called upon the Estates to raise finance and an army to fight the Turks. When it transpired that he intended to use the army against Protestants in Germany, the Bohemian army refused to cross the Saxon border. The Estates, outraged at being tricked, sent a list of 57 demands to the King.

Ferdinand sent troops into Prague and began a systematic suppression of Protestant dissidents. He appointed Catholics to key official posts and in 1556 invited the Jesuit Order to Bohemia. The Jesuits, organised on quasi-military lines, spearheaded the Counter-Reformation. They were put in control of higher education throughout the kingdom and became tutors to the sons of leading nobles.

Ferdinand's Habsburg successors understood the importance of Bohemia. It was one of the Electors of the Holy Roman Emperor and was also extremely wealthy. Bohemia was already footing most of the bill for the disastrous war against the Turks, who by now had taken Budapest. Until 1618 the Habsburgs engaged in a game of religious brinkmanship with Bohemia's mostly Protestant population.

When **Maximilian II** became King in 1562 he hoped to divide and rule Bohemia by supporting the conciliatory Utraquist movement (middle class and nominally Catholic) and suppressing the Unity of Czech Brethren. Instead, in a series of rearguard concessions he allowed Bohemia to unhook itself from the Roman Church and gave his approval, albeit verbally, to the adoption of the 'Confessio Bohemica', which set out the key elements of Hussite and Lutheran practices.

RUDOLF'S SURREAL REIGN

The Estates were pleased with their gains. They duly voted through new taxes for the Turkish wars and approved Maximilian's choice of successor, **Rudolf II** (1576-1611). In 1583 Rudolf moved his court from Vienna to Prague and for the first time in 200 years, the city became the centre of an empire. The Empire badly needed a man of action, vision and direction to deal with the Turkish invaders and the demands of Bohemia's Protestants. What it got was a dour, eccentric and melancholic monarch who was engrossed in alchemy and astrology and tended to ignore everyone except Otakar his pet lion. While Europe headed inexorably towards the Thirty Years' War, Prague drifted slowly into a surreal fantasy world.

'As news of the Emperor's hospitality spread, scores of geniuses, eccentrics and fraudsters rolled into town.'

While political life was frustrated by the Emperor's political inertia, Rudolfine Prague was experiencing a dazzling confluence of artistic, scientific and mystical experimentation. Rudolf played host to scores of international artists, including the painters Spranger and Von Aachen, and scientists, including astronomers Tycho Brahe and Johannes Kepler. Mystics and alchemists were welcomed with lodgings and a royal salary and, as news of the Emperor's hospitality spread, scores of geniuses, eccentrics and fraudsters rolled into town. Intellectual debates raged through the city on subjects ranging from the possibility of squaring a circle to the existence of ancient giants.

Rudolf had a staunch sense of Habsburg and Catholic destiny, but little stomach for a fight. He was more interested in developing a higher religious synthesis to heal the divisions in European Christendom than in adopting the proselytising approach of the Jesuits. In later years, in a state of semi-secluded insanity, he would issue violent threats against his Protestant nobles. But by then the Papacy had long since written him off as a liability to the Counter-Reformation.

But as Turkish armies thrust northwards, the Habsburgs relied more than ever on the military and financial support of the Protestant Estates. Protestantism may have been considered undesirable, but it was clearly preferable to Islam. An attack on Vienna was looming, and Protestant support was by no means assured. Rudolf dealt with the crisis by hiding away in Prague Castle, and a flabbergasted coterie of Archdukes concluded that he had to go. His brother Matthias picked up the reins.

CATHOLICS OUT THE WINDOW

Despite their promises to Bohemia, Matthias and his successor **Ferdinand II**, both strong Counter-Reformation Catholics, turned out to be more formidable than expected. The Bohemian Estates found themselves playing a frenzied game of threats, bluff, false promises and provocation with the new rulers. It would only be a matter of time before Bohemia (and as a result, Europe) would explode.

The fuse was lit in the towns of Broumov and Hrob, where Protestants had built chapels in accordance with the guarantees of the Letter of Majesty. When the Bishop of Prague ordered the destruction of one chapel and the Abbot of the Břevnov Monastery closed the other, fuming

Rudolf II – emperor of the eccentrics.

Protestants summoned an assembly of the Estates in Prague and issued a stinging rebuke to Vienna. The Emperor heightened the stakes by banning the Estates from further meetings.

'Miraculously, they survived, landing below in a pile of excrement.'

In Prague, anger was mounting. On 23 May 1618, the whole assembly marched to the Old Royal Palace. They were met by the Emperor's diehard Roman Catholic councillors, Slavata and Martinic, whom they accused of being behind the ban. After a fierce struggle, the two councillors and their secretary were dragged to the window and thrown out. Miraculously, they all survived, landing in a dung heap below.

Prague's most famous defenestration turned out to be the first violent act of the **Thirty Years' War** – and an emotive and symbolic event over which all Europe could take sides. But what actually made the difference in terms of 17th-century realpolitik was the election to the Bohemian throne of **Frederick of the Palatinate**, son-in-law of James I of England and Scotland and head of the Protestant Union of German Princes. His election tipped the balance of power between Protestant and Catholic Electors within the Holy Roman Empire four-three in favour of the Protestants.

Ferdinand II was ready to fight it out but, unfortunately for Bohemia, the likeable young Frederick had little notion of what a battlefield looked like. While Ferdinand was preparing for war, Frederick was swimming nude in the Vltava and enjoying courtly life. The Czechs nevertheless believed that their new man would rally all the powerful Protestant princes of Europe to defend Bohemia.

By November 1620 the combined forces of the Roman Catholic League, consisting of Spain, Italy, Poland and Bavaria, were massing in support of Ferdinand. Frederick had failed to rally anyone except the Protestants of Transylvania. On 8 November 1620 the two armies faced each other at White Mountain (Bílá Hora) on the outskirts of Prague. Many expected the Czechs to fight with the same bravery and skill as their Hussite forebears. But on the second Imperial charge the Protestant infantry fled with their officers in pursuit yelling at them to come back and fight.

PROTESTANTS LOSE THEIR HEADS

On the first anniversary of the infamous defenestration a large crowd gathered in Prague's Old Town Square to witness the beheading of 27 leading Protestant nobles and scholars. The less privileged also had their tongues ripped out, hands chopped off and their heads skewered on the towers of Charles Bridge. While the Thirty Years' War raged on in Europe, Ferdinand settled once and for all the Habsburg's hereditary claim to Bohemia.

> **'Bohemia lost three-quarters of its native nobility, its eminent scholars and any vestige of independence.'**

Ferdinand made no bones about his plan for Bohemia when he confided that it was 'better to have no population than a population of heretics'. In the ensuing years Bohemia lost three-quarters of its native nobility, along with its eminent scholars and any vestige of national independence. The country was ravaged by the war, which reduced its population from three million to 900,000. Three-quarters of the land in Bohemia was seized and used to pay war expenses. All Protestant clergy and anyone refusing to abandon their faith were driven from the country or executed. Thirty thousand wealthy Protestant families had their possessions confiscated and were sent into exile. While the depopulated towns and villages filled up with another influx of German immigrants, the peasants were forced to stay and work the land. The slightest opposition was suppressed

ruthlessly and Jesuits swarmed into the countryside to 're-educate' them.

Ferdinand moved his court back to Vienna in 1624. In 1627 he formally cancelled all significant powers of the Bohemian Diet (Parliament). He ruled virtually by royal decree, maintaining Bohemia as a separate entity so that the Habsburgs could cast an extra vote in the election of the Holy Roman Emperor. The Czechs were taxed to the hilt and the money used to prettify Vienna and pay off war debts. Confiscated Protestant estates were handed over to subservient Catholics.

During the Thirty Years' War, Prague was invaded by Saxon Protestants but then retaken by **General Wallenstein**. The Bohemian-born Wallenstein (or Valdštejn) was a convert from Protestantism who rose from obscurity to become leader of the Imperial Catholic armies of Europe. He totted up a spectacular series of victories but was hugely disliked by the Emperor's Jesuit advisors who conspired to have him dismissed. Wallenstein, who had been secretly negotiating with the Swedish enemy, switched sides back to the Protestants.

When he entered Bohemia in 1634, the Czech exiles pinned their hopes on a Wallenstein victory. He didn't get far. Later that year a band of Irish mercenaries burst into his Cheb residence where the general was recovering from gout. He was gagged, stabbed and dragged down the stairs to his death. The Thirty Years' War, which had begun in Prague Castle, petered out on Charles Bridge in 1648, as Swedish Protestants scuffled with newly Catholicised students and Jews from the ghetto.

SPRECHEN SIE DEUTSCH?

By the mid 17th century, German had replaced Czech as the official language of government. Czech nobles sent their sons to German schools, Charles University was renamed Charles-

Don't hesitate – defenestrate!

In Context

Ferdinand University and handed over to the Jesuits, who taught in Latin. The lifeline of Czech heritage now rested almost entirely with the enslaved and illiterate peasantry. In 1650, at the nadir of Bohemia's despair, the exiled leader of the Unity of Czech Brethren, Jan Comenius, exhorted his people to keep hope alive: 'I believe that after the tempest of God's wrath shall have passed, the rule of thy country will again return unto thee, O Czech nation.'

Paradoxically, this period of oppression produced some of Prague's most stunning baroque palaces and churches. Infused with the glorification of God and Rome, the baroque served to overwhelm and seduce Prague's citizens. Czech writer Milan Kundera has called the baroque explosion 'the flower of evil' and 'the fruit of oppression', but it did its job; before the century was out the vast majority of the population had reverted to Catholicism.

The 18th century was a dull time for Prague. Empress **Maria Theresa** lost Silesia to the Prussians and woke up to the fact that unless the Empire was efficiently centralised more of the same was going to happen. A new wave of Germanisation in schools and government was soon under way and the small Prague cog turned within the grand Viennese machine. Life occasionally brightened up when Mozart rolled into town to conduct a new opera, but the Czechs felt that they could do little but merely survive and wait for better times.

Maria Theresa's successor, the enlightened despot **Joseph II**, had little patience with the Church. He kicked out the Jesuits, closed monasteries, nationalised the education system, freed Jews from the ghetto and vastly expanded the Empire's bureaucracy. In 1775 there had been a peasants' revolt and a spate of reforms meant that they could now get married without their masters' permission. Internal tolls were abolished and the industrial revolution was getting under way. It was all good news for the Czechs except for one thing: the reforms were taking place in the German language.

CZECHS ASSERT THEMSELVES

For the first 75 years of the 18th century, Czech virtually became extinct as a literary language. It was practised, rather than spoken, as the quaint hobby of eccentric intellectuals. But gradually Czechs began asserting themselves culturally with a vigour that recalled the good old Hussite days. It started with the revival of the Czech language, and ended in 1918 with political independence.

The peasants had never abandoned the Czech language, though scholars were obliged to teach and write their history in German. By the end of the 18th century a number of suppressed works

were published, notably Balbín's *Defence of the Czech Language* with its rallying cry, 'Do not let us and our posterity perish'. The Bohemian Diet began to whisper in Czech; the Church, seeing rows of empty pews, started to preach in Czech; and Emperor Leopold II even established a chair in Czech Language at Prague's university. However, Napoleon's conquests made it harder for Czech leaders to claim it was all just a harmless cultural development.

Emperor **Francis I** (1792-1835) was taking no chances with liberal nationalist nonsense. In his will he had only two words of advice for his successor, **Ferdinand V** (1835-1848): 'Change nothing!' But the cultural revival continued. Philologist Josef Dobrovský produced his *Detailed Textbook of the Czech Language* in 1809; Jungmann reconstructed a Czech literary language; František Palacký wrote a *History of the Czech Nation*; František Škroup composed the Czech national anthem; Prague's theatres staged patriotic dramas; and Čelakovský had the nation singing Czech verses.

1848 AND ALL THAT

The cultural revival inevitably took a political turn. The Czechs demanded equal rights for their language in government and schools. Then in 1848, revolution once again swept through Europe. A pan-Slav Congress was held in Prague during which a conservative scholarly group led by Palacký clashed with the radicals. Copycat demonstrations were multiplying throughout the Empire, finally bringing down the previously impregnable Viennese government of Prince Metternich. Shaken, Emperor Ferdinand V bought time by tossing promises in Prague's direction.

'The new Emperor Franz Josef came to the throne riding a wave of terror.'

In Prague the force of reaction came in the sinister figure of Prince Windischgrätz. He fired on a peaceful gathering in Wenceslas Square, intentionally provoking a riot in order to give himself an excuse for wholesale suppression. The new Emperor **Franz Josef** (1848-1916) came to the throne on 2 December 1848 riding a tidal wave of terror. In 1849 he issued the March Constitution, which declared all the Habsburg territories to be one entity ruled from the Imperial Parliament in Vienna.

NATIONHOOD BECKONS

After taking a bashing from Bismarck in 1866, the Habsburgs introduced a new constitution that codified some basic civil rights. But Czech

TG Masaryk – saddled with independence.

claims for independence were ignored in the new Austro-Hungarian structure. Francis Joseph refused even to take a coronation oath as King of Bohemia.

The old-guard Czech deputies, led by Palacký, battled on for concessions in the Imperial Parliament. They threw in their lot with the conservative Polish and Austro-German deputies, and won concessions on language. But it meant accepting an electoral system in Bohemia that favoured the German population. A group known as the **Young Czechs** attacked the establishment for pursuing a 'policy of crumbs'. There was in fact little alternative, but national passions were running high.

The Young Czechs adopted Jan Hus as their hero and were supported by Realist Party leader Professor **Tomáš Garrigue Masaryk**. Masaryk focused attention on the moral traditions of Czech history, pointing to the Hussite and National Revival movements as beacons for the nation. In 1891 elections to the Diet, the Young Czechs swept the board.

The Czechs began to forge the political, social and economic infrastructure of a nation. Rapid industrialisation transformed the region with highly successful industries such as brewing, sugar production, metalworking, coal mining and textiles. An efficient rail network criss-crossed Bohemia and Moravia and linked the Czech lands to the European economy. Industrialisation gave rise to working-class political movements; Catholic parties also emerged.

Czech arts also flourished. The era produced composers Smetana, Dvořák and Janáček, and painters such as Mucha. Literature blossomed in the writings of such as Mácha, Neruda and Vrchlický. The Czech Academy of Sciences and Arts achieved renown. Only the political expression of nationhood remained frustrated.

WORLD WAR I

The outbreak of World War I broke the stalemate. At first the Czechs assumed that they could win concessions on a federal constitution in return for Czech support for the war. However, mere mention of a constitution provoked repression from Vienna. It would prove a costly policy for the Empire. The Czechs soon realised that their hopes lay in the downfall of the Empire itself and, along with millions of soldiers from other minority groups, deserted en masse to the other side. Six divisions of Czechs were soon fighting for the Allies while in Prague an underground society known as the Mafia ceaselessly carried out a campaign of agitation against the regime.

Meanwhile, Masaryk and **Edvard Beneš** were trying to drum up Allied support for an independent state. They found, however, that the Habsburgs were often viewed more as misguided conspirators than as evil warmongers such as the Kaiser. In fact, many diplomats had no wish to see the Austro-Hungarian Empire pulled apart. Europe's crowned heads and nobles were certainly opposed to the destruction of a powerful member of their club.

Even so, the United States took the lead, granting de jure recognition to a provisional Czechoslovak Government under Masaryk. On 18 October 1918 Masaryk declared 'the Habsburg dynasty unworthy of leading our nation' and the provisional National Committee agreed upon a republican constitution. But their power was only theoretical. The key to actual power lay in controlling the Empire's food supplies. Bohemia was the breadbasket of the Empire and Habsburg generals, fearing a revolution if food did not get to the population, gave the nod to the Provisional Council.

'The population of Prague spilled on to the streets in triumphant celebration.'

On 28 October a National Committee member, Antonín Švehla, marched into the Corn Institute and announced that the Committee was taking over food production. Later that day the Habsburg Government sent a note to American President Woodrow Wilson acquiescing to Czechoslovak independence. The population of Prague spilled on to the streets in triumphant celebration. Not a shot was fired in opposition.

THE FIRST REPUBLIC

The new Republic of Czechoslovakia had a positive start. It had suffered hardly any destruction during the war; it was highly industrialised, with generous reserves of coal and iron ore; and it had an efficient communications infrastructure and a well-trained and educated bureaucracy. Its workforce was literate and politically represented. The national leadership, in particular Masaryk and Beneš, were internationally respected diplomats, and the new nation bloomed into a liberal democracy.

Ethnic rivalry was the biggest strain on the new nation. The Pittsburgh Agreement, which had promoted the concept of a new state, referred to a hyphenated Czecho-Slovakia in recognition of the two different histories. The Slovaks were predominantly agricultural people and had been ruled by Hungarians rather than Habsburgs and, unlike Bohemia and Moravia. Unlike the Czechs, they looked upon the Catholic Church as a symbol of freedom. The Slovaks resented what they felt was a patronising air from Prague, but until the late 1930s only a minority of voters backed the separatist Slovak People's Party under pro-fascist leaders Hlinka and Tiso.

In Prague ethnic tensions were characterised more by rivalry than by jealousy. The Jews, who comprised only 2.5 per cent of the country's population, were mainly concentrated in Prague and formed a significant part of the intelligentsia. That most Jews spoke German also created some Czech resentment.

The Germans, who formed 23 per cent of the population and had their own political parties, presented the biggest obstacle to a united nation. Educated, professional and relatively wealthy, they were spread throughout the Czech lands, although Prague and the Sudeten area near the German border had the greatest concentration. The Czechs were sensitive, if perhaps also a little sanctimonious, towards minority rights and permitted the Germans to run their own schools and universities.

Only a few years earlier, however, the German language had dominated the region and the Germans were not pleased with their minority status. They had lost out in the land reforms, had suffered disproportionately from the 1930s depression, and Sudeten savings kept in Weimar Republic bank accounts had gone up in inflationary smoke.

'A FARAWAY COUNTRY'

The economic and ethnic resentments found a political voice in young German gymnastics teacher **Konrad Henlein**, who vaulted to prominence as head of the pro-Hitler Sudeten German Fatherland Front. By 1935 the Sudeten Party was the second largest parliamentary bloc.

The infamous Reinhard Heydrich. See p17.

But the sizeable Czech communist party was ordered by Stalin to back the liberal Beneš in the presidential elections to counter the Henlein threat, and Beneš took an easy victory.

'Czechoslovakia was encircled, outnumbered, abandoned.'

In March 1938 Henlein told Hitler, 'We must always demand so much that we can never be satisfied.' In 1938 after intimidating their rivals, the Sudeten Nazis won 91 per cent of the German vote and demanded union with Germany. British Prime Minister Neville Chamberlain was not wholly unsympathetic to their claim. For him the Sudeten crisis was a 'quarrel in a faraway country between people of whom we know nothing'. Chamberlain went to Munich with the French premier to meet both Mussolini and Hitler. All of the parties involved in the crisis (except Czechoslovakia, which wasn't invited) agreed that Germany should take the Sudetenland. In return Hitler guaranteed that he would make no further trouble, and even signed his name on a piece of paper saying as much, which naïve Neville waved to the world promising 'peace in our time'.

The announcement was met with demonstrations in Prague. Czechoslovakia had a well-armed, well-trained army but was in a hopeless position. With Poland and Hungary also eyeing her borders, Czechoslovakia found herself encircled, outnumbered, abandoned by her allies and attempting to defend a region that did not want to be defended. Beneš capitulated. Six months later Hitler took the rest of the country, with Poland snatching Těšín and Hungary grabbing parts of southern Slovakia. On 14 March, 1939 a day before Hitler rode into Prague, the Slovaks declared independence and established a Nazi puppet government. Hitler dubbed the remnants of Czechoslovakia the Reich Protectorate of Bohemia and Moravia.

THE LIGHTS GO OUT

Except for its Jews and Gypsies, Czechoslovakia survived occupation better than most European countries. German was made the official language of government (Hitler wanted to reduce Czech to a patois within a generation) and a National Government of Czechs was set up to follow Reich orders. Hitler had often expressed his hatred of 'Hussite Bolshevism' but he needed Czech industrial resources and skilled manpower for the war. Almost all of Czechoslovakia's military hardware was taken over by Germany.

Many Czechs avoided acts of defiance, sitting out the war and hoping for Allied victory. Hitler lost no time in demonstrating the ferocity of his revenge on those who did resist. When a student demonstration was organised, nine of its leaders were executed, 1,200 students were sent to concentration camps and all Czech universities were closed. **Reinhard Heydrich**, later to chair the infamous Wannsee Conference on the Final Solution, was appointed Reichsprotektor. Aiming to wipe out further resistance, he instituted rounds of calculated terror against the intelligentsia while enticing workers and peasants to collaborate.

Beneš had fled to London where he had joined Jan Masaryk (son of Tomáš) to form a provisional Czechoslovak government in exile. There they were joined by thousands of Czech soldiers and airmen who fought alongside the British forces. Czech intelligence agents passed approximately 20,000 messages on to London, including the details of Germany's ambitious planned invasion of the Soviet Union.

'The Germans went on an orgy of revenge.'

Fearful that the accomplishments of the Polish resistance were overshadowing Czech resistance activities, Beneš approved a plan for the assassination of Heydrich. Underground leaders in Prague doubted its effectiveness and advised against it. But they were overruled, and British-trained Czech parachutists were dropped into Bohemia. On 27 May 1942, **Jan Kubiš** and **Josef Gabčik** ambushed Heydrich's open-top Mercedes, botching the job but fatally injuring the Reichsprotektor, who died several days later.

German reprisals were swift and terrible. The assassins and their accomplices were hunted down to the crypt of the **Orthodox Cathedral of Sts Cyril and Methodius** (see page 107). The Germans then went on an orgy of revenge. Anyone with any connection to the paratroopers was murdered. The villages of **Lidice** and **Ležáky** were mistakenly picked out for aiding the assassins and razed to the ground. The adult males of the villages were murdered, the women were sent to concentration camps (in Ležáky they were shot) and the children were either 're-educated', placed with German families or killed. The transportation of Jews to concentration camps was stepped up.

Occasional acts of sabotage continued. But the main resistance took place in the Slovak puppet state where an uprising began on 30 August 1944 and lasted four months. The Czechs' act of defiance came in the last week of the war. In May 1945, 5,000 died during a four-day uprising in Prague.

The US forces that had just liberated Pilsen (Plzeň) to the west were only a few miles from Prague. But Allied leaders at Yalta had agreed other plans. Czechoslovakia was to be liberated by the Soviets, and General Eisenhower ordered his troops to pull back. General Patton was willing to ignore the order and sent a delegation to the leaders of the Prague uprising asking for an official request for American troops to liberate the capital. The communist leaders refused. Although communist power was not consolidated until 1948, the country had found itself inside the Soviet sphere of influence.

THE LAST POGROM

More than 300,000 Czechs and Slovaks perished in the war, most of them Jews. The Jewish population of Czechoslovakia was destroyed. Most of them were rounded up and sent to the supposedly 'model' **Theresienstadt** (Terezín; see page 253) ghetto, 64 km (40 miles) north of Prague. Many died there, but the remainder were transported to Auschwitz and other concentration camps.

Around 90 per cent of Prague's ancient Jewish community had been murdered. It had been one of the oldest Jewish communities in Europe, arriving at least 1,000 years earlier and possibly even before the Czechs themselves. For most of this period the community had been walled into a ghetto in the Old Town and life there was characterised by pogroms, poverty and mysticism. Between the late 18th century, when

Theresienstadt/Terezin –
model of terror. *See p17.*

they left the ghetto, and the arrival of the Nazis, Jews had dominated much of Prague's cultural life. Now the rich literary culture that had produced Franz Kafka had been wiped out. Indeed, Kafka's family also perished in Auschwitz. The only thing that saved some of Prague's synagogues and communal Jewish buildings from Nazi destruction was the Germans' morbid intention to use them after the war to house 'exotic exhibits of an extinct race'.

The Czech government under the Reich Protectorate actively supported the extermination of its Romany citizens and helped to run dozens of concentration camps for Gypsies in Bohemia and Moravia. An estimated 90 per cent of the Czech Romany population was to die in Nazi concentration camps, mostly in Germany and Poland.

STALIN PULLS THE STRINGS

Beneš's faith in liberalism had been dented by the way the Western powers had ditched his country. He began to see the political future of Czechoslovakia as a bridge between capitalism and communism. His foreign minister Jan Masaryk was less idealistic, stating that 'cows like to stop on a bridge and shit on it'.

Beneš needed a big power protector and believed that if he could win Stalin's trust, he could handle the popular communist party of Czechoslovakia while keeping the country independent and democratic. During the war he signed a friendship and mutual assistance treaty with the Soviet Union, and later established a coalition government comprising principally communists and socialists. In 1945 Stalin knew that a straightforward takeover of a formerly democratic state was not politically expedient. He needed Beneš as an acceptable front in order to buy time. For all his tightrope diplomacy, Beneš was effectively shuffling his country into Soviet clutches.

> ### 'Beneš's diplomatic skill was no match for the brutal tactics of Moscow-trained revolutionaries.'

The Soviets and Czech communists were widely regarded as war heroes and won a handsome victory in the 1946 elections. **Klement Gottwald** became Prime Minister of a communist-led coalition. Beneš, still hoping that Stalinist communism could co-exist in a pluralistic democracy, remained President. The communists made political hay while the sun shone. They set up workers' militias in the factories, installed communist loyalists in the

1948 – the working-class falls into line.

police force and infiltrated the army and rival socialist coalition parties.

One of the first acts of the government, approved by the Allies, was to expel more than 2.5 million Germans from Bohemia. It was a popular move and, as Klement Gottwald remarked, 'an extremely sharp weapon with which we can reach to the very roots of the bourgeoisie.' Thousands were executed or given life sentences, and many more were killed in a wave of self-righteous revenge.

In 1947 Czechoslovakia was forced to turn down American economic aid under the Marshall Plan. Stalin knew that aid came with strings and he was determined to be the only puppetmaster. In February 1948, with elections looming and communist popularity declining, Gottwald sent the workers' militias on to the streets of Prague. The police occupied crucial party headquarters and offices, and the country was incapacitated by a general strike. Beneš's diplomatic skill was no match for the brutal tactics of Moscow-trained revolutionaries. With the Czech army neutralised by communist infiltration and the Soviet army casting a long shadow over Prague, Beneš capitulated and consented to an all-communist government. Gottwald now became Czechoslovakia's first 'Working Class President'.

Shortly after the coup, **Jan Masaryk** fell to his death from his office window. The communists said it was suicide. But when his body was found, the window above was tightly fastened. The defenestration had a distinctly Czech flavour but the purges that followed had the stamp of Moscow. They were directed against resistance fighters, Spanish Civil War volunteers, Jews (often survivors of concentration camps) and anyone in the party hierarchy who might have posed a threat to Moscow. The most infamous trial was of **Rudolf Slánský**, a loyal sidekick of Gottwald who had orchestrated his fair share of purges. After being showered with honours, he was arrested a few days later. In March 1951, Slánský and ten senior communists (mostly

1968 – the people and the Soviets fall out.

Jews) were found guilty of being Trotskyite, Titoist or Zionist traitors in the service of US imperialists. They 'confessed' under torture, and eight were sentenced to death. The country had descended into a mire of fear and lunacy.

PRAGUE SPRING

Gottwald dutifully followed his master, Stalin, to the grave in 1953 and the paranoia that had gripped Prague took a long time to ease. By the 1960s, communist student leaders and approved writers on the fringes of the party hierarchy began tentatively to suggest that, just possibly, Gottwald and Stalin might have taken the wrong route to socialism. A drizzle of criticism turned into a shower of awkward questions. On 5 January 1968 an alliance of disaffected Slovak communists and reformists in the party replaced Antonín Novotný with the reformist Slovak communist, **Alexander Dubček**.

'Prague was infused with a fresh air of freedom.'

For the next eight months, the world watched developments in Prague as Dubček rehabilitated political prisoners and virtually abandoned press censorship. Moscow was alarmed and tried to intimidate Dubček by holding full-scale military manoeuvres in Czechoslovakia, but the reforms

continued. On 27 June, 70 leading writers signed the widely published *Two Thousand Word Manifesto* supporting the reformist government. Suppressed literature was published or performed on stage, Prague was infused with the fresh air of freedom. Dubček called it 'socialism with a human face'.

Soviet leader Leonid Brezhnev, following 'full and frank' discussions, failed to influence the Czechoslovak leader. On the night of 20 August 1968, nearly half a million Warsaw Pact troops entered the country, took over the Castle and abducted Dubček and his closest supporters. The leaders fully expected to be shot, but Brezhnev needed an acceptable front for a policy of repression with a human face.

Meanwhile on the streets of Prague, thousands of people confronted the tanks. Free radio stations using army transmitters continued to broadcast, and newspapers went underground and encouraged Czechs to refuse any assistance to the occupiers. Street signs and house numbers were removed, and the previously Stalinist workers' militia defended a clandestine meeting of the national party conference.

RESISTANCE IS FUTILE

The resistance prevented nothing. Dubček stayed in power for eight more months and watched his collaborators being replaced by pro-Moscow ministers. In April 1969 Dubček, too, was removed in favour of **Gustav Husák** who was eager to push Moscow's 'normalisation'. Husák purged the party and state machinery, the army and the police, the unions, the media, every company and every other organ of the country that might have a voice in the nation's affairs. Anyone who was not for Husák was assumed to be against him. Within a short time every aspect of Czechoslovak life was filled with Husák's mediocre yes-men. Husák was able to subdue the nation into apathy by permitting a limited influx of consumer goods.

On 16 January 1969, a 21-year-old philosophy student called **Jan Palach** stood at the top of Wenceslas Square, poured a can of petrol over himself and set himself alight. He died four days later. A group of his friends had agreed to burn themselves to death one by one until the restrictions were lifted. On his deathbed Palach begged his friends not to go through with it, though some of them did.

> '**Jan Palach's death symbolised, with malicious irony, the extinguishing of the flame of hope.**'

The newsreader who announced his death was in tears. Some 200,000 people went to Wenceslas Square to place wreaths at the spot where Palach fell; and a vast procession made its way to Charles University. Palach's coffin was taken to the Old Town Square where 100,000 people heard the bells of Týn Church ring out and a choir sing a Hussite chorale.

Palach's death symbolised, with malicious irony, the extinguishing of the flame of hope. As Václav Havel wrote: 'People withdrew into themselves and stopped taking an interest in public affairs. An era of apathy and widespread demoralisation began, an era of grey, everyday totalitarian consumerism.'

CHARTER 77

Instead of mass arrests, tortures and show trials, the communists now bound up the nation in an endless tissue of lies and fabrications, and psychologically bludgeoned all critical thought by rewarding people for not asking awkward questions and punishing them for refusing to spy on their neighbours. Punishment could mean spells in prison and severe beatings, but for most it meant losing a good job and being forced into menial work. Prague possessed an abnormally high percentage of window cleaners with PhDs, and was probably the only city where professors became street sweepers.

There were some, however, who refused to be bowed. A diverse alternative culture emerged in

which underground (*samizdat*) literature was painstakingly copied and circulated around a small group of dissidents. In December 1976 a group led by **Václav Havel** issued a statement demanding that the Czechoslovak authorities observe human rights obligations, and specifically those contained in the Helsinki Agreement of 1975, which the government had signed. **Charter 77** became a small voice of conscience inside the country, spawning a number of smaller groups trying to defend civil liberties. In 1989 it had 1,500 signatories. But there seemed little hope for real change unless events from outside took a new turn. Then, in the mid-1980s, Mikhail Gorbachev came to power in the Soviet Union and initiated his policy of perestroika.

THE VELVET REVOLUTION

The Soviet leader came to Prague in 1988. His spokesman was asked what he thought the difference was between the Prague Spring and glasnost. He replied, '20 years'. In the autumn of 1989 the Berlin Wall came down and the communist regimes of Eastern Europe began to falter. The Czechoslovak government, one of the most hardline regimes in Eastern Europe, seemed firmly entrenched until 17 November. When police violently broke up a demonstration on Národní třída commemorating the 50th anniversary of the closure of Czech universities by the Nazis, a rumour, picked up by Reuters news agency, said that a demonstrator had been killed. Another demonstration was called to protest against police brutality.

On 20 November 200,000 people gathered in Prague to demand the resignation of the government. The police behaved with restraint and the demonstrations were broadcast on television. The government then announced that the man who had allegedly been killed on the 17th was alive and well, but many were sceptical. Some months after the revolution it emerged that the KGB had probably been behind the rumour as part of their masterplan to force out the government and replace it with something more in line with Soviet glasnost.

That, in the end, there had not been a death made little difference ultimately. A committee of opposition groups formed themselves into the **Civic Forum** (Občanské fórum), led by Václav Havel, who addressed the masses in Wenceslas Square. On 24 November some 300,000 people assembled there to see him joined by Dubček, who had already spoken to crowds in Bratislava. The government had lost control of the media, and millions watched the scenes on television. Students from Prague raced out to factories and farms to galvanise the workers into supporting a general strike for the 27th. Workers' militias had put the communists into power in 1948; it was crucial that they not stand by communism in its final hour.

> **'Given the KGB's involvement, it might as well have been called the Velvet Putsch.'**

Acting communist Prime Minister Adamec also appealed to the crowds, and further purges within the communist party followed. The party then declared that the 1968 Soviet invasion had been wrong, promising free elections and a multi-party coalition. It was all too late. A new government of reform communists was proposed, but rejected by Civic Forum. Negotiations continued between the communists and Civic Forum until 27 December, when a coalition of strongly reformist communists and a majority of non-communists – mainly from Civic Forum – took power with Havel as President. Not a single person died. Havel's co-revolutionary Rita Klimová called it the Velvet Revolution. But in some ways, given the KGB's involvement in the handover of power, it might as well have been called the Velvet Putsch.

THE POST-COMMUNIST CHALLENGE

Czechoslovakia entered the last decade of the 20th century a free country. On New Year's Day Havel spoke to the reborn nation: 'For the past 40 years on this day you have heard my predecessors utter different variations on the same theme, about how our country is prospering, how many more billion tons of steel we have produced, how happy we are, how much we trust our government and what beautiful prospects lie ahead of us. I do not think that you put me into office so that I, of all people, should lie to you. Our country is not prospering. The great creative and spiritual potential of our nation is not being used to its full potential… We have become morally ill because we have become accustomed to saying one thing and thinking another… all of us have become accustomed to the totalitarian system accepting it as an unalterable fact… None of us is merely a victim of it, because all of us helped to create it together.'

For months after the revolution Prague floated in a dream world. The novelty of the playwright President captured the world's imagination. But the serious issues of economic transformation and the relationship between Czechs and Slovaks loomed as formidable challenges. In the summer of 1992 the right-of-centre Civic Democratic Party (ODS), led by **Václav Klaus**, a no-nonsense free marketeer, was voted into power. But just as Klaus got down to the business of

privatisation and decentralisation, calls for Slovak independence grew to a deafening roar. Nationalist sentiments had grown in Slovakia but remained a fringe issue until the electoral rise of **Vladimír Mečiar**'s Slovak separatist HZDS party.

Slovaks had always resented what they had felt was a benign neglect by Prague, and Havel had never been hugely popular among them. One of his first acts as President was to abandon the arms trade. Unfortunately, his pacifist intentions took the heart out of the Slovak economy. Slovaks complained that economic reforms were going too fast. But Klaus would not compromise, and had a mandate from Czech voters to press on. Mečiar upped his separatist threats until, with Machiavellian manoeuvring, Klaus called Mečiar's bluff and announced that he would back Slovak independence.

The two leaders divided up the assets of the state, and the countries peacefully parted ways on 1 January 1993 without so much as a referendum. Havel was elected President of the new Czech Republic, but Klaus had also outmanoeuvred him, forcing Havel into a predominantly ceremonial role.

Klaus indicated that he had little time for a policy of flushing out communists from responsible positions (known as 'lustration'). Thus communists successfully dodged the spotlight amid a blizzard of accusations and counter-accusations. A significant number of Czechs seemed to have skeletons in their cupboards, and it became impossible to untangle the good from the bad. As dissidents watched helplessly, communists remained in charge of the country's largest factories.

The first four years of the Czech Republic under Klaus's leadership produced massive economic changes, which helped make the Czechs the envy of the East and the pride of the West. Foreign investors and businesses quickly capitalised on the massive opportunities for profit and development. The Czech Republic moved to the head of the queue for accession into the European Union.

THE VELVET HANGOVER

Economic differences between the haves and have-nots have increased drastically since 1992. Klaus's Pragocentric policies and the decision to prioritise macroeconomic issues backfired in the 1996 elections, when his ODS party barely managed to keep power. A year later, with the boom days of foreign investment clearly over and headlines alleging secret ODS campaign funding from interested parties, Klaus shocked the nation by stepping down. Miloš Zeman and his Czech Social Democratic Party gained the most votes but not an absolute majority. Zeman

Vaclav Havel –
conscience, stricken.

agreed to become Prime Minister with Klaus and his party in charge of Parliament. This pact of political opposites was called absurd by everyone including Havel, who was also alarmed by the duo's next move: a proposal to limit the power of smaller parties.

Czech membership in NATO, announced just before the start of the bombing campaign against Serbia in 1999, was followed almost immediately by further embarrassment. Zeman, in typically bombastic style, announced that he was all for NATO membership but had no intention of providing Czech ground troops for UN patrols in Kosovo. It soon became apparent that leadership from the left deserved no more credibility than had Klaus's government. Cynicism and apathy began to take root.

Where once the hot issues were civic questions such as lustration and privatisation, these days attention is focused more on the private world of salaries, family and home. Industrial workers, doctors, farm labourers and teachers – just about anyone whose wages are falling far behind prices, the majority of the Czech population – have not benefited from Prague's new wealth. Businesses are run under the table from residential apartments while the government is

largely ignored. Even Zeman's appointment of communists to high-ranking positions in the spring of 2000 didn't register much of a response, and nobody now expects delivery on his early promises to solve the crises in health care, education and housing.

Havel, the symbolic conscience of the nation, has been stricken not just by power politics, but also by failing health. Frequently hospitalised, he has forced the public to consider the possibility of life without their moral leader – and that there's no obvious heir to the role. One source of comfort for the President (apart from his remarriage to Czech actress Dagmar Veškrnová) was the 1998 Winter Olympics. For the first time in nearly two decades, the Czech ice-hockey team defeated the Russians and struck gold. Old Town Square had not held such cheering mobs since the Velvet Revolution.

As Prague fills out with designer coffee shops and international hotels, at least Havel can see the Czech Republic returning to its old status as the most Western of East European nations. But as long as the electorate remains alienated, economic appearance belies a political reality which is still far from true democracy.

Key events

c400 BC Celtic Boii tribe occupies Bohemia.
7th century AD Slavic tribes settle in the region.
c700 The Přemyslid dynasty begins.
863 Cyril and Methodius bring writing and Christianity to Great Moravia.
929 'Good King' Wenceslas is killed by his brother and becomes a martyr and the Czech patron saint.
973 Prague is made a bishopric.
1235 Staré Město gets a Royal Charter; Jews forced into the ghetto.
1253 Otakar II becomes king and conquers half of Central Europe.
1306 Přemyslid dynasty ends with the murder of Václav III.
1346 Charles IV becomes Holy Roman Emperor and King of Bohemia; founds Central Europe's first university, in Prague.
1352 Swabian architect Peter Parler begins work on St Vitus's Cathedral.
1357 Foundations laid for Charles Bridge .
1378 Charles's son becomes king Wenceslas IV.
1389 3,000 Jews killed in pogrom.
1403 Jan Hus, Rector of Prague University, begins preaching against Church corruption.
1415 Hus, having been excommunicated and declared a heretic, is burned at the stake.
1419 Hussite mob throws the Mayor out of the New Town Hall window; the Hussite wars begin.
1420s-1430s Hussites repel all attacks.
1434 Moderate Hussites wipe out the radicals and the Pope agrees to allow them considerable religious freedom.
1458 Czech noble George of Poděbrady becomes the 'People's king' but is soon excommunicated by the Pope.
1471-1526 The Jagellon dynasty rules in Bohemia.
1526 Habsburg rule begins with Ferdinand I.
1556 Ferdinand invites the Jesuits to Prague to counter fierce anti-Catholicism in Bohemia.
1583 Habsburg Emperor Rudolf II moves the court to Prague, where it remains for the next two decades.
1609 Astronomer Johannes Kepler publishes his Laws of Planetary Motion; Rudolf concedes religious rights to Bohemia's Protestants.
1618 Protestants throw two Catholic councillors from a window in the castle, thus starting the Thirty Years' War.
1620 Protestants lose the Battle of White Mountain.

1621 27 Protestant leaders executed in Old Town Square.
1648 The Thirty Years' War ends on Charles Bridge as the citizens of Prague repel the Swedes.
1740 Maria Theresa becomes Empress.
1743 French attack Prague.
1757 Prussians attack Prague.
1781 Emperor Joseph II abolishes the Jesuits and closes monasteries.
1848 Revolutions in Europe; unsuccessful uprisings in Prague against Austrian troops.
1893 Clearing of the Jewish ghetto begins.
1914 Outbreak of World War I; Habsburgs refuse concessions on federalism and Czech soldiers desert to the Allies.
1918 Czechoslovak Republic founded with Tomáš Masaryk as its first President.
1938 Chamberlain agrees to let Hitler take over the Sudetenland.
1939 Hitler takes all Czechoslovakia.
1942 Czech paratroopers assassinate Reichsprotektor Reinhard Heydrich. Nazis destroy villages Lidice and Ležáky in revenge.
1945 Prague uprising; the Red Army arrives.
1948 The communist party assumes power under Klement Gottwald.
1951 The Slánský show trials and mass purges against the regime's enemies.
1968 Reformist communist Dubček becomes First Secretary and promotes 'socialism with a human face', but the Prague Spring is crushed by Warsaw Pact troops.
1969 Philosophy student Jan Palach immolates himself in protest.
1977 The underground movement Charter 77 is established to monitor human rights abuses.
1989 Student demos turn into full-scale revolution and the communist regime falls.
1990 Václav Havel elected President of Czechoslovakia.
1992 Václav Klaus elected Prime Minister.
1993 The Slovak Republic and Czech Republic become separate, independent states.
1996 Michael Jackson's statue briefly takes up the spot vacated by Stalin's in Letná Park, as part of his HIStory tour.
1998 Largest demonstrations since Velvet Revolution sweep city to celebrate Czech hockey team winning Olympic gold.
2000 Largest demonstrations since Olympics fill Wenceslas Square to demand the ouster of Prime Minister Miloš Zeman and ODS head Václav Klaus.

JEDNO
MARTINI PRO
TU DÁMU
NAPROTI!

Prague Today

Metamorphosis – or just a case of *plus ça change*?

Leave it to a Slovak rock star to pen the most apt summation of modern Prague society. For a while there seemed to be nothing else wailing from stereos all over the Golden City but Richard Müller's song 'Nina Ricci':

'We used to have the smell of stables, with flies
and spilled beer, and it made us pretty happy
Now what makes you happy?'
Under every skirt is the same Sabatini
In the trash lies Lancôme
And constantly from Šumava wafts sweet
Nina Ricci.'

Could it be that Czechs can finally afford to live in a future they dreamed of under communism? Indulge a glossy Martini-ad lifestyle?

Well, they're trying.

If you are a foreign investor asking the Czech Finance Ministry that question, staff will nod and smile and hand you a mound of charts and tables extolling the suitability of Prague as a destination for your money. Among its advantages are a cheap, well-educated workforce and a convention facility known as the Congress Centre that's undergone a 2.2 billion Kč revamp since communist times.

But if you ask a recent Charles University graduate – a potential component of that cheap, well-educated workforce – you'll hear a different kind of tune. If the early 1990s were a time of unleashed freedom, improvisation and massive changes, today is the time when Prague could use some stability, they will argue. People have tired of hearing about banks going belly-up while Parliament bickers back and forth over whether the puppeteers of the Spejbl and Hurvínek Theatre (*see page 239*) deserve a state subsidy of 23 million Kč.

DEMOCRATIC DOWNSIDES

To many Czechs witnessing the work of their first freely elected leaders, the pre-1989 concept of strong state control is beginning to look good again by comparison. Unpredictable, anarchic freedom and the sluggish democratic decision-making process obviously have their downside. The communists have now become the second strongest political party in the country.

Realistically, Czechs don't have as many reasons for cynicism as they imagine. Western democracies are often just as corrupt and inefficient. One survey, conducted by Transparency International and hopefully brandished by the current administration, places the Czech Republic 37th among 85 countries ranked for corruption. This puts it slightly behind Hungary but a bit ahead of Poland. And, if nothing else, Parliament can proudly say that it is officially vastly more honourable than its counterparts in Cameroon, Paraguay and Honduras.

'Czechs are proving remarkably adept at making capitalism work for them.'

And anyway, if corruption is a given, this is something that can also be used to ordinary people's advantage. Czechs are proving

remarkably adept at making capitalism work for them. Nearly every family now has a car, a cottage in the country and very often an under-the-table business providing a nice little tax-free earner. And even legal wages have almost doubled since 1989, while unemployment has risen only to rates that many Western nations would envy (*see page 27* **Prague by numbers**).

In part, both near-full employment and the tendency to operate in the grey market are a legacy of communism. But Czechs are hardly stuck for contemporary role models when it comes for ideas of how to fiddle. The governing left-wing Social Democrats of Prime Minister Miloš Zeman came into power in 1998, surfing a wave of discontent with the failings of former premier Václav Klaus and his right-wing Civic Democratic Party. The Thatcherite Klaus presided over the privatisation of all the property nationalised by the communists, but his friends grew suspiciously rich during the

Prime Minister **Miloš Zeman** – on a two-year turnaround from election to rejection.

Prague by numbers

Population of Prague **1.2 million**
Population of Czech Republic **10.3 million**

Ethnic divisions
Czech **94.4 per cent**
Slovak **3 per cent**
Polish **0.6 per cent**
German **0.5 per cent**
Gypsy **0.3 per cent**
Hungarian **0.2 per cent**
Other **1 per cent**

Religions
Atheist **39.8 per cent**
Roman Catholic **39.2 per cent**
Protestant **4.6 per cent**
Orthodox **3 per cent**
Other **13.4 per cent**

72: average life expectancy for a Czech male
78: average life expectancy for a Czech female

£7,000 ($11,300): GDP per capita

Nine per cent: unemployment rate

11,709 Kč: average monthly wage in the Czech Republic

1,183 Kč: average monthly rent

1st: ranking of taxes and insurance among the expenses of an average Czech family

26.8 days: average duration of one sick leave from work

2:1: ratio of people to cars in Prague

628,000: average number of cars and trucks that daily pass through the centre of Prague

110: number of new Prague Metro cars ordered from the CKD-Siemens-ADtranz consortium in 1995

1 Number of new Prague Metro cars delivered as of 2000

5,000: number of the 23,000 people held in Czech prisons as of July 2000 who had yet to be convicted

84: Percentage of the public who believe that embezzlers in the Czech Republic use bribery and inside connections to escape justice

26: percentage of all crimes committed in the Czech Republic that occur in Prague

28: percentage of people surveyed by *Reflex* magazine who regularly sneak on to the Prague metro without a ticket

1: approximate number of students admitted to Charles University out of every 400 who apply

50: percentage by which the sale of legal CD recordings fell over the last three years

510 Kč: typical price difference between legal Western CD and a high-quality Czech copy

370: number of medieval Jewish graves discovered during construction of the Česká Poijišťovna insurance building on Vodičkova

45 million Kč: Amount it cost to reconfigure the building to allow the graves to remain undisturbed

70: percentage of Czech women who are 'unfaithful and happy' according to Czech *Cosmopolitan*

1st: world ranking of Czechs as consumers of beer per capita

30 billion: annual amount of cigarettes produced by Phillip Morris's factories in the Czech Republic

significant profits while employees were laid off. Meanwhile banks made easy loans to fund new business ventures without making realistic assessments, losing billions in the process.

Thus Zeman, promising that government was finally going to pay attention to pensioners, students and the environment, won the most votes – but not quite enough to form an absolute majority. So he turned to Klaus, who was still popular enough to do well. Prague's conservative voter base, said to be so loyal to Klaus that they would elect his tennis racket were it only to run, was going to be needed by Zeman if he hoped to hang on as Prime Minister. So Zeman, whose cabinet of 17 ministers includes 15 former

communist party members, struck a power-sharing deal with arch capitalist Klaus.

This 'opposition agreement' produced a new administration that might have featured in one of Václav Havel's absurdist plays. Virtually the first move of Klaus and Zeman's was to propose revisions to the constitution that would limit the powers of President Havel and smaller parties.

The public appears finally to have had enough. They turned out in the hundreds of thousands on Wenceslas Square (*see page 102* **Be there, be (Wenceslas) square**) in early 2000 to demand the resignations of both Klaus and Zeman. They were roundly ignored by the government and have since abandoned their protests and their popular slogan, which runs: 'Děkujeme, odejděte' – 'Thank you, now get out.'

But not all public demonstrations are complaining about something. The nation's frustrations with evolving democracy can at least occasionally be released more joyfully at the spontaneous street parties which salute each Czech sporting victory. The entire city seems to turn out whenever the Czech national ice hockey team bags some silverware. From the 1998 Winter Olympics on, the Czechs have grabbed every hockey title within reach, most recently the May 2000 World Cup in Moscow. And when they win, the normally docile Czechs go nuts.

Thus the Czech Republic is finally earning some kind of place in the world through sport, if not through political or economic prowess.

PROMISED YOU A MIRACLE

In March 1999, the Czech Republic's accession into NATO finally shook off the last of the Soviet legacy. But though nearly every Czech political party supports the Czech Republic's proposed entry into the European Union, Brussels is beginning to drag its feet. While the EU dawdles and considers offering some sort of limited, conditional membership, Václav Klaus tries to dismiss the EU as a bunch of meddlesome bureaucrats. But his bravado is seen by many as a thin smokescreen for an awareness that the Czech Republic does not, perhaps, represent the economic miracle it was once hoped and purported to be.

The slide began in 1997 and was highlighted in the biting 1999 European Commission report on the progress of EU applicant countries that threw cold water on the Czech Republic's image of itself as a sort of central European economic tiger. Instead the Commission warned that the country was seriously lagging behind the other so-called 'first wave' candidates in its introduction of EU laws and harmonisation of standards. Other important points cited were the country's glacially slow and inconsistent courts and the unacceptable situation of tension and discrimination regarding Czech Romanies.

The Justice Ministry has promised to reform sluggish courts and weed out incompetent judges but it's anyone's guess when the public will see any results. There has been a little more progress in relations between the overwhelmingly Slavic Czech majority and the republic's various minority groups. A few months after the international news crews filmed the town of Ústí nad Labem's pathetic attempt to build a wall that segregated its white and Gypsy residents, the town finally caved in and tore the thing back down.

Opinion polls show that the attitudes of most Czechs toward minorities are steadily, if slowly, improving. A Romany news presenter on the respected state broadcaster, Czech Television, has actually proven a boost to the station's ratings. Prague Jews are also beginning to feel confident enough to sound off (*see page 97* **Jewish community finds its voice**), and gays

Bisexual business mogul **Václav Fischer**'s political career is taking off.

Welcome to democracy and can I see those papers again? Gypsies still endure suspicion.

and lesbians are now more out than ever. Recently elected conservative senator Václav Fischer, an openly bisexual travel business mogul, is gaining in popularity on Václav Klaus. But the richer mix of lifestyles and tolerance in Prague is not appreciated by all.

AN ANXIOUS AGE

Older Czechs, who find their pensions buying less and less, along with workers whose jobs are no longer guaranteed for life, are beginning to cry out for more stability and order. The groundswell of anxiety has not been lost on government and police, who are responding by flexing their muscles. And since it's a lot simpler to pass laws cracking down on obvious targets than to root out corruption in high places, Prague is now host to a paper storm of laws against drug use and illegal immigrants.

> **'Perhaps recalling his own youthful days in jail as a dissident, Havel pardoned 19-year-old Stanislav Pobuda.'**

Alcohol sales continue to go through the roof, as do related road accidents, and children watch Marlboro ads at the cinema before every new Hollywood action cruncher. But since 1 Jan 1999, the possession of what the law defines as 'more than a small amount' of contraband is legal grounds for two years in prison. And that's after going to trial, which often takes months while the accused languishes in jail.

One of the few national leaders to consistently demonstrate a commitment to civil society,

President Václav Havel in February 2000 made a gesture expressing his confidence in the new drug law. Perhaps recalling his own youthful days in jail as a dissident, Havel pardoned 19-year-old Stanislav Pobuda, releasing him from a four-year prison sentence he had landed for selling a few joints to a friend.

The chief criticism of the law is that arrest and charging is completely up to the discretion of the police. Czech police are not particularly respected or known for their consistency. Once an important tool of the communist regime, they are now known mostly for ineptitude and corruption. At press time, serious concern was being expressed over the likelihood that Czech cops could be easily drawn into splitting heads before news cameras during protests at the forthcoming IMF convention in Prague.

Not exactly the stuff of a Martini commercial, the Finance Minister's assurances notwithstanding. And as for that Charles University graduate?

Well, like most Czechs, she likes fashion well enough but she's also a realist. She'll find a job in Prague that pays better than any available in the village where she grew up, keep it if it suits her, otherwise move on. After work, you'll find her at the local street cafe, perhaps resigned for now to sipping the world's finest beer – the cheap Czech stuff – rather than the cosmopolitan Martini she might aspire to.

And if the government can keep its nose out of her dreams of buying an apartment and starting a family, that'll suffice. Foreign luxuries will come when they come.

But perhaps she might just one day drop a few hints to her boyfriend. There's this one little bottle, nicely wrapped, and a bit more intriguing than any she's noticed in Prague shops before. Nina Ricci, she thinks it's called.

Cubist apartments. *See p33.*

Architecture

A thousand years of building has left Prague with examples of everything from Romanesque to deconstructivism. But just what is cubist architecture?

In few cities do so many diverse means of architectural expression exist side by side, or co-exist so harmoniously, as in Prague. Largely spared the destruction of two world wars, the city contains virtually every major style from Romanesque to deconstructivism, and stands as a living example of how Europeans have shaped and decorated their living spaces over the last thousand years. Here, history has been transformed into a single statement of beauty.

Take the city's most recent, and most controversial, showpiece, the deconstructivist **'Fred and Ginger'** building by Frank Gehry and Vladimír Milunič. It's the indirect result of 'collateral damage' from World War II: an errant US bomber, whose crew mistook Prague for Dresden, created a prime vacant lot for it on the New Town bank of the Vltava River.

Václav Havel, during his playwright-dissident days before taking the oath of President, lived next door and owned the cleared land. In the late 1980s, he and Croatian-born neighbour Milunič often discussed what to build on the site once the Communist regime fell. They decided on an arts centre at first, but an office building won out in the end. The result ingeniously reflects the more staid historic buildings around it, yet instantly revived Prague's reputation as a city of visual daring and distinction.

BEGINNINGS

The city lies in a basin encircled by seven hills. Though inhabited continuously for 250,000 years, it was not established as a town until the seventh century, when Slav tribes came down from the safety of the highlands to settle on the banks of the Vltava. At first they built wooden structures, none of which survives. Then, in the second half of the ninth century, a stone fortress was built on a rocky outcrop on the left bank, and, in the early tenth century, another castle was constructed on the right bank a little upstream.

Around these structures – **Prague Castle** (*see page 69*) and Chrasten Castle (now **Vyšehrad**; *see page 110*) respectively – the settlements began to develop that eventually grew into the city of Prague.

From the 11th to the 13th century, architecture in Prague was characterised by the simple forms, heavy, rounded arches, tunnel and cross vaults and thick columns of the Romanesque. Few complete buildings from the period remain, but the style can be most clearly observed in the three surviving rotunda, all of which are small, vaulted and have a conical roof with a lantern. The **Rotunda of St Martin** (second half of the 11th century, Vyšehrad, Vyšehrad, Prague 2) is the oldest. Less conspicuous are the **Rotunda of St Longinus** (late 11th century, Na rybníčku, Nové Město, Prague 2, map p309 K7) and the **Rotunda of the Holy Cross** (early 12th century, corner of Karoliny Světlé & Konviktská, Staré Město, Prague 1, map p306 G5).

The most extensive surviving Romanesque building in the city is **St George's Basilica** (10th century; rebuilt 11th century) in the Castle complex (*see page 74*).

The marshy right bank of the river, less densely populated than the area around the Castle and more liable to flood, began expanding with the creation of a market place (now **Old Town Square**) in 1100 and saw a profusion of Romanesque buildings. By 1170 the two settlements were linked by the Judith Bridge (later replaced by **Charles Bridge** *see page 94*), and the Old Town was established by decree in 1287. A later decree raised the level of the city by about ten feet to avoid flooding, leaving many Romanesque rooftops at the street level of new Gothic buildings. Romanesque structures made perfect foundations and many Romanesque basements still exist, such as that in the **House of the Lords of Kunštát and Poděbrady** (*see page 96*).

GOTHIC

Gothic architecture, imported from France around 1230, offered greater spatial dynamism through ribbed vaulting, pointed arches and buttressing. As a construction technique, it also made possible taller, wider and more delicate buildings, allowing for complex tracery and stained glass. The **Old-New Synagogue** (*see pages 31 and 98*) is one of the best-preserved medieval synagogues in Europe. Two pillars in the centre of its vaulted hall-nave support six bays of ribbed vaulting reaching heights of up to nine metres (30 feet). Its portal, one of the oldest in Prague, features a beautifully carved decoration in the tympanum. The oldest Gothic complex in Bohemia is **St Agnes's Convent** (*see pages 99, 116 and 222*) now part of the National Gallery.

The heydey of Gothic architecture in Prague came during the reign of Charles IV (1346-78). The Emperor summoned German Peter Parler to implement his grand design for a new, fortified city. This New Town, planned in four geometric sections, with a central axis on **Wenceslas Square** (*see page 100; see also page 102* **Be there, be (Wenceslas) square**.) doubled the size of the city. Construction began in 1348, the year Charles University was founded. Parler was responsible for **Charles Bridge** (*see page 94*) and the seamless, innovative additions to the French-inspired **St Vitus's Cathedral** (*see page 71*). Parler's vault in the cathedral's Chapel of St Wenceslas is a masterpiece.

Many townhouses in Prague contain Gothic elements, but few retain an original Gothic façade and plan. An exception is the **House of the Stone Bell** (*see page 222*) on Old Town Square, next to the **Kinský Palace** (*see page 204*). Across the narrow way from it is the more typically masked **Church of Our Lady before Týn** (*see page 92*). The larger, 'masculine' spire on the right shields its 'feminine' partner from the afternoon sun, though not from the garish spotlights at night.

A fascinating hybrid of Gothic and modern is the **Emmaus Monastery** (*see page 106*). Rebuilt in the baroque style in the 17th century,

Gehry's **'Fred & Ginger'** building. *See p30.*

Rotunda of St Martin. *See p31.*

its spires and vaults were destroyed in the same World War II air raid that made space for the 'Fred and Ginger' building. Lost, too, were beautiful frescoes and most of the neo-Gothic façade added in the 17th century. New spires made of reinforced concrete shell plates designed by František Černý were added in 1967. Viewed from the riverbank, they seem to have been placed there as a prank. A closer look reveals an organic blend of diverse art forms.

RENAISSANCE

Bricks and mortar took on a pivotal role under the first Habsburg ruler of Bohemia, Ferdinand I (1526-64). Cheaper, easier and more conducive to rapid construction than raw stone, brick facilitated the Renaissance renovation of Malá Strana after the fire of 1541. Where new buildings were not put up, Renaissance façades were tacked on to surviving Gothic ones. The period saw a move towards more human-scale, horizontal spaces – simpler masses and clearer forms, punctuated by columns and pillars.

The Renaissance arrived in earnest with the construction of Paolo della Stella's extraordinary **Belvedere** (*see pages 77 and 202*) in the Royal Gardens by the Castle. In the same gardens is Bonifác Wohlmut's **Ball Game Court** (*see page 78*), a marvellous display of 16th-century

sgraffito. A technique of scratching through black or brown mortar to create a pattern or picture, this was particularly suited to *trompe l'oeil* effects such as imitation stonework, as seen in the **Schwarzenberg Palace** on Hradčanské náměstí, now home of the Military Museum (*see page 120*).

Perhaps the period's most striking and unusual building is the **Hvězda Hunting Lodge** (in the Obora Hvězda park, Břevnov) built in the form of a six-pointed star. Odd as it is, its design faithfully honours the Renaissance principle of placing a central structure above a regular geometric figure. The stucco work decorating the vaults was created by Italian craftsmen over a period of four years.

BAROQUE

Prague's first baroque edifice, designed by Giovanni Pieronni, was the titanic **Wallenstein Palace** (*see page 84*), which was constructed for and named after the megalomaniac commander of the Imperial Catholic armies. This building prefigured the dominance of the baroque after the Thirty Years' War, which was fuelled in part by the need to rebuild much of war-damaged Prague. After 1648, the city had enormous city-wide baroque fortifications built, dwarfing the old Gothic ones.

> **'Czech baroque flitted between the plainer French and the more sensual Italian high baroque in its effort to seduce the city back into the Catholic fold.'**

With Bohemia now securely within the Habsburg empire, the task of consolidating the Counter-Reformation was handed to the Jesuits, who promptly started their own building programme. The most significant result was the **Church of St Saviour** in the **Clementinum** (*see page 94*), an elegant and more austere example of early baroque. Czech baroque flitted between the plainer French and the more sensual Italian high baroque in its effort to seduce the city back into the Catholic fold. The baroque penchant for excess led to elaborate decoration, scale, curves and complexity, as seen in Prague baroque's magnum opus, the extravagant **Church of St Nicholas** (*see pages 85 and 221*). The father-and-son team of Christoph and Kilian Ignaz Dientzenhofer trotted out every trick in the baroque book for this one: imitation marble, *memento mori* motifs, lashings of gold, *trompe l'oeil*, layered vistas, sensuously curved façades.

Origami in stone

In the rest of the world the term 'cubist architecture' will elicit a wry grin. Dadaist joke, perhaps? Do be serious. How could you possibly translate into stone the revolutionary painting style of Picasso and his cohorts?

Leave it to the Bohemians of the wild First Republic days. In 1911-13 they happily set about making Prague into the first – and still the only – city in the world with cubist architecture.

Perhaps it was the city's architectural diversity and abundance that drew Czech architects to such a radical form of expression at a time when everyone else was turning to functional logic in construction. Or maybe, as the architect Vladimír Miluniç speculates, they were simply nuts. Miluniç, who co-designed the daring 'Fred and Ginger' building, views cubism as a model for his own work and a precursor of the deconstructivism of the late 20th century.

When painter Bohumil Kubišta introduced cubism from Paris, artists in all fields saw in it a chance to forge a new, unified mode of expression. Cubism's oblique lines, breaking the flat surface into a profusion of planes, call to mind Japanese origami creations. Czech architects translated the technique by creating highly dynamic façades composed of broken surfaces of varying complexity that dress a building in dramatic plays of light and shadow.

The most radical examples were designed by Josef Chochol as **apartment buildings** and **family homes** below Vyšehrad (see page 110). The house at Neklanova 30, Prague 2, with its wedge-shaped surfaces, brilliantly mirrors the acute angles of the streets around it. More extreme still is the villa at Libušina 3, Prague 2, almost baroque in its depth and profusion of angular surfaces. The surrounding garden and wall are themselves exuberantly cubist. More of Chochol's light tricks can be seen on the riverbank, at Rašínovo nábřeží 6-10, Prague 2.

The movement's most often overlooked achievement is the world's only cubist lamp-post (pictured above; 1912, Jungmannovo náměstí, Nové Město, in front of the **Church of Our Lady of the Snows**; see page 106). And conveniently situated for inebriated art appreciation is the **Diamant House** (see page 106), as all-night trams pass before it. It's now a car dealership.

But Prague's first plunge into cubist architecture was Josef Gočár's **House of the Black Madonna** (pictured left; see page 117), currently housing a collection of Czech cubist paintings and furniture. Viewed from the former fruit market in front, it's remarkable how this completely avant-garde building manages not only to co-exist with, but also to enhance its 300-year-old neighbours.

It's a harmony only a nut could have foreseen.

The War of the Austrian Succession and the Seven Years' War brought yet more extensive damage to the city, and yet another rebuilding programme. Niccolo Pacassi restored the south side of the **Castle** for Empress Maria Theresa and gave it the late baroque unity that we see today from Charles Bridge. None of it can touch the opulence of the **Loreto** (*see page 80*), which represents the first wave of aesthetic assault on Protestant Bohemia and the inspiration for all subsequent baroque churches, espeically later epic works such as the Church of St Nicholas (*see page 32*).

The **Vrtbovská Garden** (*see page 86* **Unseen green**) in Malá Strana is a little-known treasure of baroque design and a beautiful example of Italian terracing. Built in 1715-20 and decorated with statues by sculptor Matthias Bernard Braun, it was reopened in June 1998, following renovations that took as long as its original construction.

The new Habsburg-friendly gentry also caught the baroque wave, visible in some of the city's finer townhouses. In some instances, however, a baroque façade has merely been superimposed on to an older structure.

REVIVALISM

The end of baroque and the beginning of revivalist architecture came in 1780, when newly crowned Joseph II issued a decree of religious tolerance and another specifying the height, materials and construction methods of new buildings. One year later, Antonín Haffenecker built the neo-classical **Estates Theatre** (*see pages 222 and 236*) for Count Nostitz. It drew on new materials, such as cast iron, which lent themselves to the neo-classical forms that expressed the no-nonsense rationality of the Enlightenment.

The manufacturing middle classes, rather than the church or nobility, now began to call the tune. Prague's first suburb, Karlín, was constructed within a generous, rational grid plan that even included factories. Blocks of flats with common water facilities and dry toilets began to appear. Austrian influence, revival movements (neo-classicism and romanticism) and growing democratisation began to dominate the city. Municipal construction responded to newly recognised social needs – schools, houses and hospitals, rather than churches and palaces. The spread of railways and growing engineering expertise gave rise in 1845 to the first train station, **Masarykovo nádraží** (Havlíčkova, Nové Město, Prague 1, map p307 L3). A massive undertaking, employing 4,000 workers, it was one of the most impressive stations in Europe when completed.

On 16 May 1868, 50,000 people walked in procession behind the foundation stone for the **National Theatre** (*see pages 105, 222 and 237*), designed by Josef Zitek. The project

Paolo della Stella's extraordinary **Belvedere** – the Renaissance in earnest. *See p32.*

Figures prefiguring the baroque at **Wallenstein Palace**. *See p32.*

employed a generation of artists and designers – called, in fact, the National Theatre Generation. Sadly, their collective effort burnt to the ground shortly after opening. Within two months, money was raised by public subscription to rebuild it, this time according to the designs of one of Zitek's colleagues, Josef Schulz. He went on to build the **National Museum** (*see pages 100 and 120*).

The National Theatre answered the Czech population's thirst for grand municipal symbols, and became a focal point for the emerging Czech national identity. Neo-Renaissance and neo-baroque were the order of the day: heavy, monumental, civic, grand. Architectural decoration leant on Czech folklore and historical motifs – as seen on the painted façade of the **Wiehl House** (corner of Vodičkova and Wenceslas Square, Nové Město, Prague 1, map p307 K5). However, this approach did leave Prague looking somewhat parochial by the turn of the century.

ART NOUVEAU
As banking wealth and investment changed from Viennese to Czech hands, the rise of a business class and the desire to discard historicism demanded a new direction. The move towards decorative style, symbolism and decadence found inspiration in art nouveau (called secessionism in the Austro-Hungarian Empire). Viennese-trained architect Friedrich Ohmann introduced the style to Prague with his Café Corso of 1898, now destroyed.

Ohmann's next project, the **former Hotel Central** (1902, Hybernská 10, Nové Město, Prague 1, map p307 L3), was an art nouveau facsimile with glass cornice and floral motifs. Its debt to the French style is indicative of the sensibility of the era. Rodin's 1902 exhibition and visit to Prague enthused Czechs with the notions of individualism, universality and democracy implicit in Republican French culture. Municipal and residential art nouveau buildings spread across the city, many still visible in neighbourhoods such as Vinohrady and Vršovice.

> **'Polívka helped bring about the culmination and possibly the death of art nouveau in the extraordinary Municipal House.'**

One of Ohmann's collaborators, Osvald Polívka, built both the heavily ornamented **Prague Insurance Building** (the windows below the cornice spelling out 'Prague') and the much more restrained **Topič Building** next door (1903-5, Národní třída 7&9, Staré Město, Prague 1, map p306 H5). The stylistic opposition was intentional. Polívka helped bring about the culmination and possibly the death of art nouveau in the extraordinary **Municipal**

House (*see pages 149 and 221*). Nine years in construction under Antonín Balšánek's plans, with Polívka designing the interior, this project brought together artistic luminaries of the day, including Alfons Mucha. Its excessive ornamentation was already something of an anachronism at its opening in 1912. It now houses the Prague Symphony Orchestra, a café, an exhibition hall and a French restaurant. During concerts, audiences' eyes wander from Bohemian oak trim to cut-glass skylights and ceiling dome mosaics of old Czech myths.

The most tenacious art nouveau edifice in Prague is surely the **Grand Hotel Evropa** (*see page 61*), which clings to its original purpose. Though its interiors have never really recovered from communist neglect, the gilt in its grand façade gleams brightly in the morning sun on Wenceslas Square.

More typical was the fate of Josef Fanta's train station **Hlavní nádraží** (*see pages 103 and 268*) in decay since communist times. The last remnants of its original grandeur are visible only from inside the Fantova kavárna restaurant on the otherwise closed upper level, or from a car whizzing along the motorway in front of the entrance towers.

CZECH MODERNISM

As Viennese influence waned and aspirations of independence grew, Czech architects began to make their mark on the city. Even before the birth of Czechoslovakia, Jan Kotěra, a pupil of Vienna's

Otto Wagner, planted the seeds of Czech modern architecture. He concentrated on geometric functionalism – an approach that was to influence the later modernist movement. His **Urbánek Publishing House** (1911-12, Jungmannova 20, Nové Město, Prague 1, map p306 J5) used planes of brick to create a pared-down, singular façade.

After the collapse of the Austro-Hungarian Empire ushered in the First Republic, new sensibilities prevailed. In 1920, President Tomáš Garrigue Masaryk asked Slovenian Josip Plečnik to renovate and modernise **Prague Castle**. His sensitivity, innovation and expert craftsmanship greatly enhanced the ancient structure; the classically inspired Columned Hall, in particular, is sublime. In contrast, the clashing styles of Plečnik's **Church of the Sacred Heart** (Náměstí Jiřího z Poděbrad, Žižkov, Prague 3, map p311 C3), ugly and beautiful by turns, anticipates the stylistic upheavals of postmodernism.

The colourful, but heavy and awkward style of the short-lived rondo-cubism (also known as National Style) can be seen at the former **Bank of the Czechoslovak Legions** (1921-3, Na Poříčí 24, Nové Město, Prague 1, map p307 L3), designed by Josef Gočár. Russian constructivism and the influence of Adolf Loos (*see below* '**I don't do ground plans**') had a major impact on modernist buildings. The constructivist icon of the Veletržní palác in Holešovice, now housing the **National Gallery Collection of 19th-**

'I don't do ground plans'

In mid-2000 the doors were finally opened to a house that embodies the ultra-modernism of designer Adolf Loos. Born in Brno in 1870, Loos first sprung his rational, anti-ornamental style on the world in 1910 with the Steiner House in Vienna. The revolutionary free-flowing interior was his mantra made manifest: 'I don't design ground plans, façades or sections. I design spaces.' By 1928, when such ideas were becoming trendy, an adventurous developer named Müller commissioned Loos and Karel Lhota to build him a veritable temple of modernism. The spatial relationships of its interior were to be completely alien to the bourgeois mansions of the past, except in the lavish use of costly materials. Eventually the house was purchased by the city and delivered into the care of the Museum of the City of Prague. The whole place then underwent two years of renovation said to have cost nearly 50 million Kč.

The villa is set in a quiet neighbourhood of trees and family homes of past Czech presidents, ministers, artists and intellectuals – the very bourgeois Loos was trying to instruct. Whether they would have learned will never be known, but the Müller villa makes it plain that Czech design would have put a very different face on the city had the heavy hand of history not fallen again.

Müller Villa

Nad Hradním vodojemem 14, Střešovice, Prague 6 (2431 2012/ vila.muller@muzeum.mepnet.cz). Tram 1, 2, 18. **Open** *Guided tours 9am, 11am, 2pm and 4pm Tue, Thur, Sat, Sun (booking required). Office 9am-6pm Tue, Thur, Sat, Sun; closed Mon, Wed, Fri.* **Admission** 300 Kč; 200 Kč concessions; 100 Kč per person for English or German-speaking guide.
Opening hours may change in wintertime.

National Style: the rondo-cubist **Bank of the Czechoslovak Legions**. *See p36.*

and 20th-Century Art (*see page 115*) used reinforced concrete liberally. Its huge atrium is wonderful. The shabby but elegant functionalist riverfront **Mánes Building** (1928, Masarykovo nábřeží 250, Nové Město, Prague 1, map p308 G7) typified the spirit of the interwar republic, attracting every major artistic heretic of the period. It is resuming that role today as a contemporary art gallery.

> **'Prague was quickly surrounded by gargantuan and soulless housing estates, where shoddy blocks now degenerate into suburban slums.'**

COMMUNISM

On the whole, communism was an architectural disaster. The overbearing Stalinist bulk of the **Holiday Inn Prague** (*see page 62*) admittedly holds a grim fascination, but it's readily apparent that it was planned by a team from the Military Design Institute. Further out, Prague was quickly surrounded by gargantuan and soulless housing estates, where shoddy blocks of flats (*paneláky*) built for workers now degenerate into suburban slums. The laughable **Congress**

Centre (*see page 212*) squats across from the banal **Corinthia Towers** (*see page 62*), which was intended to counterbalance the horizontal tedium of the 'palace'. Between them juts the brutal, vast span of the **Nusle Bridge** (Nuselský most, 1965-9, Nusle), which helped link many of the southerly and easterly housing estates to the city centre.

The arrogance and tastelessness characteristic of the era is manifest in the lower halls of **Hlavní nádraží** (*see pages 103 and 268*). Cowering under the regal, secessionist structure above, they are an eyesore even for loitering drunks, let alone for transient travellers who must wonder if they've come to the right place.

At the **National Theatre** (*see page 237*) Communist design nearly accomplished what fire could not. In 1962, a competition was held to expand the building, but the winning architect died before his design could be built. Changes were made during construction, and other architects were invited to add their two shillings' worth. The result, the **Nová Scéna**, a two-part monstrosity clad in glass and completed in the 1980s, continues to inspire debate: some claim that it is the ugliest building in the world; others say it might not be.

But the masterpiece of communist design is surely the **Žižkov TV Tower** (*see page 113*). This structure dominates the entire city and seems set to blast off into space at any moment.

Ready for blast-off! **Žižkov TV Tower** is a masterpiece of communist design. *See p37.*

BEYOND THE VELVET REVOLUTION

Since 1989, Prague and its citizens have been preoccupied with restoration and enrichment. Enormous infrastructure investments are being made and countless complex state and private renovations are taking place. But not all that glitters here is gold. Incensed by the garish and historically inaccurate colours that have been applied to the city's façades, Prague architect Daniel Špička managed to get the historic centre placed on the World Monuments Fund's List of 100 Most Endangered Historic Sites. The city was being transformed into a theme park for tourists, he complained, because local preservationists were choosing colours according to their whims. A perfect example of 'the Disneyland effect' are the façades of the complex of baroque palaces, now a part of the Czech Parliament, forming the northern side of Malostranské náměstí. The belfry tower of the **Church of St Nicholas** (*see page 32*), just a stone's throw away, represents restoration at its best. Its muted golden façade recalls what most of Prague looked like centuries ago and why it was dubbed 'the Golden City'.

The most eyecatching new addition to Prague's skyline remains Vladimír Milunič and Frank Gehry's **'Fred & Ginger'** building (as in Astaire & Rogers), also known to Czechs as 'Tanečni dům', or 'Dancing House' (corner of Rašínovo nábřeži and Resslova, Nové Město, Prague 2, map p308 G8). It depicts the tangoing couple as a glass-clad 'feminine' vertical held close by a contrastingly rigid 'masculine' tower, playing with a tradition in spire construction dating back to the Middle Ages and the **Church of our Lady before Týn** (*see page 92*). The office and restaurant project is the most significant postmodern building in Prague since the Velvet Revolution.

> **'The Myslbek Centre so incensed President Havel that he went on national radio to denounce it.'**

Crass commercialism has also left its mark in the city. The **Myslbek Center** (*see page 180*), for example, destroyed in one fell swoop the elegant lines and scale of the entire historic promenade and blocked forever the sight-line to the Týn Church. It so incensed President Havel that he went on national radio to denounce it.

Less controversial is the grand-scale **Zlatý Anděl** office, residential, and shopping complex currently being built in the working-class district of Smichov. Designed by renowned French architect Jean Nouvel, it will drastically and irrevocably alter both the neighbourhood's landscape and character.

The rampant commercial forces unleashed since 1989 may well prove a bigger threat to the city's architecture than all of its turbulent past. But Prague has survived wars, floods, fires, Nazis and Bolsheviks with its splendour and soul intact. With luck, these may also withstand the upheavals of globalisation.

Literary Prague

An abundance of magazines, readings and would-be
Hemingways, plus a living tradition of dark Czech writing,
make Prague eastern Europe's most literary city.

Prague's international literary scene is
extraordinarily vital for a city its size. More
than any other city of the former East Bloc it has
translated new freedoms into a cross-fertilisation
of international literary work. The fructifying
process that results ensures that what's
published here has a freshness and raw quality
that makes it exciting.

Except when it's dreadful. A large expat
vanity publishing sector was encouraged by the
media blitz hailing Prague as the 'Left Bank of the
'90s', an image the city has yet to live down. But
the continuing absence of a young Ernest
Hemingway or Gertrude Stein has allowed a
relaxed and unhurried literary scene to develop,
in which expats grapple with a new world of
possibilities while Czech writers struggle for
identity in the absence of censors. Now that the
spotlight has moved on, the international literary
scene is thriving.

The new generation of Czech writers is typified
by poet and novelist **Jáchym Topol**, whose *City,
Sister, Silver* explores a gritty world of free-market
sleaze and opportunism. **Lukáš Tomin**'s
introspective *Ashtrays, The Doll and Kye* are open-
ended poetic collections, whose sombre mood is
true to the perpetually tangled life of a Prague
intellectual. Tomin's death by accident so early in
his career will diminish 21st-century Czech
literature. The vivid prose of **Evald Murrer**,
collected in *The Diary of Mr. Pinke* and *Dreams at
the End of the Night*, is an instance of the best post-
revolutionary writing being translated into
English by imprints such as Twisted Spoon Press
(*see page 40* **Bent on publishing**). Other
anthologies of strange and experimental modern
Prague writing include *Daylight in Nightclub
Inferno* (Catbird Press, 1997) and *This Side of
Reality* (Serpent's Tail, 1996).

The surrealist vein running through much of
this work is a survivor from the pre-war First
Republic. Its source can be traced to poet
Vítězslav Nezval, who founded the Czech
Surrealists in the 1930s. He was also a member of
the Devětsil avant-garde movement, as was
Nobel laureate poet **Jaroslav Seifert**.

Expat and international publications also owe much to the writerly traditions of Prague. English-language literary publications have increased in number and improved in depth since the media circus of a few years ago. Prague's longest-running English-language literary mags are *Optimism*, a Czech and expat monthly, and *Jejune*, a quarterly of unorthodox new writing from varied tongues.

Trafika and *The Prague Revue* are both annuals that publish Czech and international writing, much of it never before seen in print. *Semtext* is a free magazine featuring mostly poetry, while *One Eye Open*, a Czech and English magazine of poetry, fiction, and essays, focuses on women's issues and writing. All of these publications can usually be found at **The Globe Bookstore and Coffeehouse** (*see pages 41, 150 and 165*).

Digging into the classics at a clean, well-lit café is one of Prague's most satisfying pursuits and a far less risky one for the reader. Modern Czech literature emerged in the middle of the 19th century, as part of the wider Czech nationalist movement. The first novel of this linguistic revival, **Božena Němcová**'s *Babička* (*Grandmother*), published in 1855, inaugurated a new era for writing in colloquial Czech. Němcová remains a much-loved figure – her face can be found on the 500 Kč note – and her fairy tales are still read to children today.

Franz Kafka, arguably Prague's most famous native son, was also an admirer of Němcová. Of all the writing to emerge from Prague's German-speaking Jewish community, his is by far the best known, though his contemporaries, poet **Max Brod** and novelists **Paul Leppin** (*Severin's Journey into the Dark*) and **Gustav Meyrink** (*The Golem*), were far more famous during his lifetime. That culture was nearly wiped out by the Holocaust, but two survivors, **Jiří Weil** and **Arnošt Lustig**, wrote accounts of life behind the barbed wire.

Jaroslav Hašek made a major contribution to Czech literary history with *The Good Soldier Švejk*, a rambling novel whose protagonist never misses an opportunity to get an order wrong, a strategy that gets him through World War I intact. Whether his subversion is mischievously purposeful or merely idiotic is never clear, giving rise to a philosophical school of survival under occupation. This near mysticism is quintessentially Czech, and makes *Švejk* required reading for anyone who wants to penetrate the national character. Hašek himself bore no small resemblance to his creation, a rotund merrymaker with an unquenchable thirst for beer.

Bent on publishing

Any non-Czech looking to explore the nation's literature beyond the established works will find the way cleared for them by Prague-based **Twisted Spoon Press**. Going where no publisher has gone before, it brings a range of new Czech writing to an English-language audience in lovingly produced books that are consistently beautiful outside and in. Twisted Spoon is responsible for the first translations of significant contemporary Czech authors such as **Evald Murrer**, as well as historically important works. Its edition of *The Arsonist* by **Egon Hostovský**, a 1935 novel considered a masterpiece of Czech prose, stands next to new translations of Czech greats: **Franz Kafka**'s *Contemplation*, *A Hunger Artist* and *A Country Doctor* and **Bohumil Hrabal**'s *Total Fears* are highlights of their catalogue.

The unifying theme of Twisted Spoon's books is a deep interest in the absurd, the grotesque and the avant-garde. The strong Prague tradition in these areas is rarely available to English-speaking readers in anything but Kafka stories, as bigger publishers consider other writers too risky. Twisted Spoon likes to defy market concerns with books like *Baradla Cave*, a striking new novella by leading Czech surrealist **Eva Švankmajerová**.

Translations of older Prague literature from both Czech and German complement the modern repertoire. **Ladislav Klíma**'s writing is an example, particularly *The Sorrows of Prince Sternenboch*, an influence on dissident writers of the 1970s and 1980s. The edition of **Paul Leppin**'s bizarre *Severin's Journey Into the Dark* also filled a major gap in the English translations of pre-war Prague literature. The macabre and spooky Prague found in Kafka's work is explored with equal richness by Leppin.

In recent years, Twisted Spoon has begun publishing work written in English, and literature in translation from all over Central Europe. Among the most intriguing of their many books by Prague expat writers are *Seances* by **Louis Armand** and *Amuwapi* by **Christopher Lord**.

Twisted Spoon editions are available at **The Globe Bookstore and Coffeehouse** (*see pages 41, 150 and 165*), at the publisher's website, (www.twistedspoon.com) or directly from: Twisted Spoon Press, PO Box 21, Preslova 12, 150 21 Prague 5.

Ian McEwan navigates **The Globe**.

After the communists seized power in 1948, independent-minded writers were banned, jailed, forced into menial jobs or exiled. Those who continued to write were obliged to publish *samizdat* manuscripts, illicitly distributing individually typewritten pages between themselves. **Václav Havel** was part of that network while penning his satirical and absurdist plays *The Memorandum*, *The Garden Party* and *Audience*, among others, some of which are still sporadically performed. Other dissident writers worth discovering are **Zdeněk Urbánek** (*On the Sky's Clayey Bottom*), whose short stories offer a fantastic and often absurd view of everyday life under communism, and the scientist-poet **Miroslav Holub**. The novels of **Bohumil Hrabal** (*Closely Observed Trains*, *I Served the King of England*) are masterpieces of Czech literature, and his writing remains popular. Hrabal died in 1997 after a fall from a fifth-floor window while feeding pigeons. Though this was officially ruled an accident, many readers still wonder – a character in one of his books written decades earlier met exactly the same fate.

This rich literary tradition is celebrated in Prague by numerous international writing and literary festivals. In summer, a month doesn't go by without an important writers' gathering. The action starts in April with the **Prague Writer's Festival**, a star-studded series that has brought the likes of Harold Pinter, William Styron, and EL Doctorow to town. See their web page (www.pwf.globalone.cz) for details. July sees the **Prague Summer Seminars**, run by the University of New Orleans (details at www.uno.edu/prague). Both hold readings open to the public, sometimes featuring well-known Czech writers with simultaneous English translation. August 2000 saw the first **Prague School of Poetics' annual festival**, with a focus on avant-garde international writing and performance. (For info, contact the school at 0603 762 910 or prazskaskola@hotmail.com.)

Readings

Circus Magica
Ježkova 14, Žižkov, Prague 3 (no phone). Metro Jiřího z Poděbrad/11 tram. **Admission** free. **No credit cards.** Map p308 B2.
An international artists' space that hosts readings along with various strang events such as 'Darkness night', an evening of music and socialising where speech is forbidden and the room is pitch-black, or 'Animals night' when everybody brings their pets. The kind of venue that may not be around for long.

The Globe Bookstore & Coffeehouse
Pštrossova 6, Nové Město, Prague 1 (2491 7230/ www.ini.cz/globe). Metro Národní třída/6, 9, 18, 21, 22, 23 tram. **Open** 10am-midnight Mon-Thur; 10am-1am Fri, Sat; 10am-midnight Sun. **No credit cards.** Map p308 G7.
Hosts an infrequent but wonderful programme of readings. If a well-known writer is in town, it's more than likely that he or she will make an appearance here. The Globe has presented readings by Allen Ginsberg, Robert Creeley, Amy Tan, Ian McEwan and scores of other literary luminaries. *See also p150 and p165.*

Jazz Club Železná
Železná 16, Staré Město, Prague 1 (2423 9697). Metro Můstek/3, 9, 14, 24 tram. **Open** 3pm-midnight daily. **Admission** 70 Kč. **No credit cards.** Map p306 J3.
In One Voice, a slam at 4.30pm on the second and fourth Sunday of every month, is the best place to sample a mix of unpublished young foreign and Czech writers – admittedly a risky proposition. Performances consist of anything from two to seven musicians, generally of no small talent, playing background music that frequently drowns out the young poets they are accompanying. The music is often interesting. The poetry, when audible, tends to lapse into the tedious.

Literární Kavárna G+G
Čerchovská 4, Vinohrady, Prague 2 (627 3332). Metro Jiřího z Poděbrad/11 tram. **Open** 10am-10pm Mon-Fri; closed Sat, Sun. **Admission** free. **No credit cards.** Map p311 B2.
A writer's dream café, the G+G was opened by Slovak former dissident Fedor Gál and his son, poet Robert Gál. Their venture is a delightful combination of publishing house, bookshop and literary café with a widely varied calendar of events – expect anything from an international literary evening with musicians to a concert by Jim Čert, accordionist to President Havel.

Radost/FX Café
Bělehradská 120, Nové Město, Prague 2 (2425 4776). Metro IP Pavlova/4, 6, 11, 16, 22, 23 tram. **Open** 11.30am-4am daily. **Admission** free. **No credit cards.** Map p309 L8.
Sunday night Beefstew readings at 7pm, begun in 1993, are still going strong, though quality varies week to week. *See also p144, p159 and p228.*

Beer

Don't give *pivo* the heave-ho – Czech beers are almost certainly the best and cheapest in the world.

Czechs on average drink more beer than anyone else in the world. The official consumption figure is around 161 litres per person a year. That works out to no fewer than a bottle of beer a day for every man, woman and child in the country.

The figure is probably higher in the capital city, where every neighbourhood has at least two or three packed pubs. And it's not uncommon to see housewives at the pub filling the family jug (*džbán*) for home consumption. (Then again, a sign in one Prague 6 local where dedicated drinkers hang out night and day reassures patrons that: '*Kdo pije doma, je alkoholik*', 'One who drinks at home is an alcoholic.')

The simple answer to why beer drinking is so firmly engrained in Czech culture is that the beer is just that good. The soil and climate of west Bohemia are ideal for growing Žatec hops, the most crucial brewing ingredient. And traditional recipes are still followed religiously, usually allowing for only barley, malt, hops, yeast and water. No additives, no preservatives.

There's also the issue of prices. As they rise all around for everything else, beer remains relatively cheap. Czechs watch beer prices closely and brewers are loath to raise them even a crown for fear of alienating customers. It's also a political issue. The hero of Jaroslav Hašek's *The Good Soldier Švejk* says that any government which raises beer prices will fall within a year. The communists kept beer prices low for four decades. There was certainly never any economic reason not to drink.

Brewing in the Czech lands has over a 1,000-year tradition, the time of the oldest known records of hops cultivation and exports. Documents from the Middle Ages and later are filled with affectionate references to *pivo* and Bohemia. A popular European Renaissance rhyme went: *Unus papa Romae, una cerevesia Raconae* ('A pope in Rome, a beer in Rakovnik'). Beer is still brewed today in that Czech town, 50 kilometres (30 miles) west of Prague.

The beer has changed greatly in character over the centuries, mainly due to the influence of the Pilsener brewery in the west Bohemian city of Plzeň (Pilsen). It was there in the mid-19th century that modern Czech beer – bottom-fermented, amber-coloured, hoppy, with a slightly sweet aftertaste – was first developed and popularised. 'Pilsener' soon conquered the world, supplanting the heavier, darker, bitter brews that came before. To this day, the word Pilsener or pils is commonly used to describe any type of light lager.

> **'Draught beer is best, drinking out of bottles is a step down, and canned beer is strictly for tourists.'**

Most of the 80 or more breweries in the Czech Republic are small, serving surrounding towns and districts, while a handful of big brewers account for the bulk of national sales. Their names become familiar after a couple of days in Prague: Pilsner Breweries (makers of Pilsner Urquell and Gambrinus), Staropramen (Prague's largest brewer, owned by UK brewer Bass), Budvar (makers of Czech Budweiser), Radegast and Velké Popovice. (*See page 43* **Beer necessities**.)

Microbreweries have been slow to catch on, but a few have recently gained a foothold in Prague. The pub **U Fleků** (*see page 160*), technically a microbrewery since it makes its fine beer on-site, has been in business since the 15th century. Beer lovers come from around the world to sample its wonderful dark brew – and are routinely ripped off with charges for unordered shots of Becherovka.

You can buy beer just about anywhere, from cinemas to all-night grocers, and drink it on public streets until you can't stand up. But beer's true home is the neighbourhood pub (*pivnice* or *hospoda*), whose staff will usually know how to store and tap it properly. To order,

▶ For a guide to the best places for savouring Czech beer, see chapter **Pubs & Bars**.

Beer necessities

Characterising the tastes of Czech beers is a bit like trying to write music about wildflowers. The best way to learn one from another is through repeated tasting. But faced with all the beers in all the bars of Prague, the burning questions is: where on earth to start?

Well, **Gambrinus**, especially the 10-degree *světlé* (light) variety, is the nation's most popular beer, due in part to its comparatively low price. **Pilsner Urquell** has the best reputation among Czechs (and is the best-known Czech beer abroad), though some detect a distinctly bitter finish. **Radegast**, an upstart from Moravia with a crisp, clean bite, seems to win all the taste competitions. The newest dark horse is Brno's **Starobrno**, with its full, ruby-tinged **Červený drak** (Red Dragon), winner of the annual Pivex national beer trade fair. Many veteran beer drinkers swear by bitter **Kozel** (look for the goat on the label), brewed just south of Prague in **Velké Popovice**. **Budvar**, the original Budweiser from southern Bohemia, is deliciously sweet but probably owes at least part of its wide appeal to vastly favourable comparisons with its wholly unrelated American namesake.

A sizable Prague school is devoted to **Staropramen**, whose main brewery is the pride of the Prague district of Smíchov, though some connoisseurs consider it overly perfumed. Out in the Prague suburbs and beyond in the countryside, it's usually the small local brew that gets the nod, and indeed sampling these can redeem a trip to the bleakest corners of the republic. **Braník** and **Měšťan** are both Prague hinterland treats, while road trips to South Bohemia are vastly enriched by sampling **Regent** (from Třeboň) and the rare Budvar dark (*tmavé* or *černé*) or **Eggenberg** from Český Krumlov. The success story of humble Humpolec is **Bernard**, which claims to still use wooden vats throughout the brewing process.

The beer gem hidden among the better-known wines of Znojmo in south Moravia is **Hošťan**, with a 1720 pedigree and the thumbs-up from leading Czech pivologist, František Frantík (*see page 44* **Swallowing the bitterest pils**). You surely won't find it in Prague but it may just be worth the trip to the far southeast of the country.

tell the waiter '*pivo prosím*'. Most pubs stock only one or two kinds of beer, so you usually won't have to specify a brand. You might get a choice between 10- and 12-degree beers, the former a little lighter and with less alcohol. In more traditional pubs, once you have placed your first order, the waiter will continue bringing rounds until you wave him away. He marks each beer on a small slip of paper, then tots up the damage at the end of the session. Don't be the last at the table, as you may end up holding a bill that's sprouted a dozen more ticks for beers than anyone can remember drinking.

Draught beer is best, drinking out of bottles is a significant step down and canned beer is strictly for tourists. The alcohol level varies from brand to brand, but ranges from about 3.5 per cent to a little more than 5 per cent. Dark beer tends to be sweeter than the light, which has a full-bodied flavour but can be bitter. If you don't care for the hoppiness of the lights and the dark beer seems too sweet, ask for an *ezané*, a half-and-half mix (it literally means 'cut') of the two.

The price of beer depends on where you drink it, not on the brand or type. A half-litre in a decent pub shouldn't cost more than 20 Kč, but prices in the tourist-oriented city centre can rise to 50 Kč or higher. It's perhaps worth seeking out smaller, grimier neighbourhood pubs where your cash can go three or four times as far – and with an authenticity that no money could buy.

Swallowing the bitterest pils

Every country should have a guy like **František Frantík** (pictured) – someone whose only job is to monitor the quality of beer. 'Franta,' as his friends call him, works for the Czech Research Institute of Brewing and Malting, an august institution founded more than a century ago and still dedicated today to the pursuit of the perfect pint.

Most of Franta's day is spent on serious pursuits like developing new strains of yeast or ensuring that brewers use only homogenous barleys. He's also a writer for the highly respected publication *Kvasný průmysl*, (Fermentation Industry), but still finds ample time to slip out to the pub to sample the fruits of his labour.

A common Czech lament is that foreign concerns buying up local breweries and introducing new production methods are wreaking havoc in the industry. But Franta says the beer is actually getting better, not worse. Brewers now have access to better ingredients, he argues, and with more beer being exported, the standards have to be higher. He also points out that the deep pockets of foreign owners have given brewers more money to buy state-of-the-art equipment. The rate at which small breweries are going out of business is indeed alarming,

he concedes, but no more so than in any other industry.

Franta has been with the institute almost 20 years, after earning a degree in chemistry at Charles University. He calls his work at the institute the culmination of a boyhood dream. His only regret is that he didn't attend Prague's Technical University for Beer Studies, the ultimate education for beer-testers. 'I'm a mere chemist,' he says, as he lifts his glass to sample the molecules.

So, after all these years of tasting and testing, what does Franta look for in a beer?

'The first thing I consider is the foam on top,' he says. 'A good two or three centimetres is perfect.' Then there's the question of colour: 'not too dark, and not too light.'

'Fullness', a quality exhibited in the bitter Pilsner Urquell 12-degree, is another sought-after but difficult-to-translate beer concept that, according to Franta, basically means how much it resembles a loaf of bread. More bready, in both taste and texture, is preferred to less bready. Finally, the beer has to have what he calls 'vigour,' something he struggles to translate but finally renders as 'sharpness on the tongue.' Bitter, in his world, is definitely better.

Accommodation

Accommodation

Land in the lap of luxury or slum it in backpacker city, but be sure to book ahead.

The sense of adventure that once tinged the search for accommodation in Prague is, by and large, consigned to the past. You no longer have to worry that a party of roaring Danes has usurped your reservation in the one hotel with both hairdryer and fax machine, leaving you to trawl the main station for likely-looking old ladies holding *Zimmer frei* signs.

That's not to say that everything is now rosy, and especially not if you fall in between the two main categories of Prague visitors – the down-at-heel and the very well-heeled. Backpackers can choose from at least a hundred hostels or spare rooms, most of which sprout like dandelions every summer only to wither with the autumn. Those at the other end of the spectrum enjoy a wide choice of luxury hotels. The situation for the rest still needs improvement.

The good news is the growing number of hotels and pensions where, for less than 4,000 Kč, you can get a decent room for two with bath, breakfast and all the German TV you can watch. True, the room may have bright orange curtains, red plastic rotary phones and the smell of antiseptic, but think of it as a nostalgic throwback to those pre-1989 days when the customer was never right.

INFORMATION & BOOKING

Prague has a surprisingly diverse profusion of renovated or brand-new hotels, from medieval, family-run inns to giant, corporate-owned multi-star hotels. Though accommodation in Prague is still pricey compared with dining or entertainment, there are ways to beat the system: many hotels give discounts to groups and for longer stays (normally around ten days or more); rooms are generally 20-40 per cent cheaper in the off-season, roughly December to March; and many moderate and expensive hotels give 10-20 per cent discounts in July and August when business travel dwindles. Smaller places may offer a significant reduction for cash payment – or a massive credit card surcharge. Try to establish this, preferably with hard-copy confirmation, before you arrive.

Service is streets ahead of what it was a few years ago. That said, travellers are still prey for various scam artists. At the better class of hotel, you can get hit with ludicrous charges for both local and international telephone calls. Watch out for the taxis that cluster around the hotel entrances: for these hustlers, a taxi metre is a slot

machine that always pays off. If the hotel has its own fleet, it's a safe bet, although the charges are double those set for regular city taxis (*see page 271*). Prague's hotel star rating system is voluntary, so no official agency certifies that a four-star hotel is any better than a three-star.

As the number of rooms increases each year, so, it seems, does the demand. If you come to the city in peak months without reservations, expect to pound the pavement for hours before you find a clean, well-lit place. Even off-peak, it's still wise to book. Most of the more expensive hotels have English-speaking staff; those at cheaper establishments may struggle, though you can usually make yourself understood. Many hotels can arrange airport pick-ups for a fixed price, which will save you time, money and hassle.

PRICES & CLASSIFICATION

Hotels are classified below according to their cheapest double room; prices include breakfast, unless stated otherwise. Note that these prices are usually only available in the off-season and also be aware that some of the more upmarket hotels fix their room rates in German marks or US dollars. For ease of use we have converted all prices into Czech crowns, but exchange-rate fluctuations may affect these.

All rooms in the 'Luxury' and 'Expensive' categories have an en suite bathroom. This also applies to the 'Moderate' category, unless otherwise stated. Facilities in other categories vary – it's always best to check exactly what you'll be getting when you book. Longer-term accommodation (*see page 278* **Finding a flat**) as well as hotels particularly welcoming to gay people (*see page 207*) are listed in other chapters.

Accommodation agencies

Unless otherwise noted, the following agencies organise private accommodation in flats and also book hostel beds, pensions and hotels at no extra charge. Getting a flat outside the centre can cut the cost by around 35 per cent. Travellers' Hostel (*see page 58*) in the Old Town functions as a booking office for a whole network of hostels.

Ave

Hlavní nádraží, Wilsonova 8, Nové Město, Prague 2 (2422 3521/2422 3218/ fax 2422 3463/ avetours@avetours.anet.cz) Metro Hlavní nádraží. **Open** 6am-11pm daily. **Credit** AmEx, DC, MC, V. **Map** p307 M5.

In the main station, this is probably the most convenient option for those arriving by train or at a late hour with no place to go.

Branches: Na příkopě 16, Nové Město, Prague 1 (261 013); Ruzyně Airport, Prague 6 (316 4266); Nádraží Holešovice, Prague 7 (6671 0514); Old Town Bridge Tower (Staroměstská Mostecká věž), Křižovnické náměstí, Staré Město, Prague 1 (536 010)(summer only); Staroměstské náměstí 2, Staré Město, Prague 1 (2448 2018).

City of Prague Accommodation Service

Haštalská 7, Staré Město, Prague 1 (2481 3022). Metro Náměstí Republiky/5, 8, 14 tram. **Open** 10am-1pm, 2pm-7pm daily. **No credit cards. Map** p306 J2.
A reputable firm that offers good service.

Mary's Accommodation Service

Italská 31, Vinohrady, Prague 2 (2225 4007/2225 3510). Metro Náměstí Míru/11 tram. **Open** 9am-7pm daily. **Credit** AmEx, MC, V. **Map** p309 M7.
A friendly, English-speaking, low- to mid-priced agency that places visitors in pensions, hotels and private apartments throughout the city. The minimum rate is for two people, and reservations must be guaranteed with credit card (for which a surcharge is added). Generally, breakfast is not included in the prices.

RHIA Agency

Školská 1 (at Žitná 17), Nové Město, Prague 2 (2223 0858/2223 3190/fax 2223 2506). Metro IP Pavlova, Můstek or Národní třída/3, 9, 14, 16, 22, 23, 24 tram. **Open** 10am-8pm daily. **Credit** AmEx, MC, V. **Map** p308 J7.
A full-service travel agency offering great alternatives to hostels for just a bit more dosh. Staff can arrange accommodation with safe parking, and you can also change currency here.

Stop City

Vinohradská 24, Vinohrady, Prague 2 (2423 1233/fax 2422 2497/www.stopcity.com). Metro Muzeum or Náměstí Míru/11 tram. **Open** Apr-Oct 10am-9pm daily. Nov-Mar 11am-8pm daily. **Credit** AmEx, MC, V. **Map** p309 M6.
Stop City's helpful, incredibly patient staff will book you into a pension, hotel, private room or apartment starting at less than 500 Kč per person. They don't handle hostel bookings but are willing to make reservations for callers from abroad, provided a credit card number is given via fax.

Tom's Travel

Ostrovní 7, Nové Město, Prague 1 (2499 0990/2499 0991/fax 2499 0999/www.travel.cz). Metro Národní třída/6, 9, 18, 22, 23 tram. **Open** June-Aug 8am-10pm daily. Sept-May 8am-8pm daily. **Credit** AmEx, MC, V. **Map** p308 G6.
Tom's is a reputable and veteran Prague agency that can book two- to five-star hotels, pensions, apartments and hostels and offers free airport transfer with advance bookings. Also handy for booking rooms in other Czech cities.

Hradčany

Some of Prague's most romantic and atmospheric lodgings are nestled around Prague Castle in Hradčany, though budget options are scarce. Hotels round here tend to be small and may lack the gadgetry a business traveller needs. Hiking uphill to your bed on a Castle lane could be a bit of a bother – or it could be the best aid to digesting a heavy old-fashioned Czech dinner and putting a romantic finish on your day.

Deluxe (over 8,000 Kč)

Hotel Savoy

Keplerova 6, Prague 1 (2430 2430/fax 2430 2128/www.hotel-savoy.cz). Tram 22, 23. **Rooms** 61. **Rates** 8,800 Kč single/double; 9,800 Kč deluxe room; 2,220 Kč extra bed. **Credit** AmEx, DC, MC, V. **Map** p304 A3.
Stepping into the dignified lobby, complete with reading room and fireplace, it may seem hard to imagine this as a haven for celebs such as Tina Turner and Princess Caroline of Monaco. But the prima donnas aren't the only ones who know this as a peaceful bastion of first-class service and tasteful, modern rooms. Standard rooms are spacious, and the deluxes amount almost to a suite.
Hotel services Beauty salon. Disabled: access, room adapted. Gym. Interpreting services. Jacuzzi. No-smoking rooms. **Room services** Dataport. Fax. Room service. VCR.

Expensive (6,000-8,000 Kč)

Romantik Hotel U raka

Černínská 10, Prague 1 (2051 1100/fax 2051 0511/www.romantikhotels.com). Tram 22, 23. **Rooms** 6. **Rates** 6,200-6,900 Kč single; 6,900-7,500 Kč double. **Credit** AmEx, V. **Map** p304 A2.
Dating back to 1739, this small, rustic pension is a good choice for couples with time to spare. It's located a short stroll from the Castle and within earshot of the bells of the Loreto (see p80). There are just six rooms here – two in the main house and four adjacent cottages – plus a beautiful breakfast room/inn/café/reading room with brick hearth. Invariably booked, so reserve well in advance. No children under 12. No bar.
Hotel services Air-conditioning. Limousine service. Parking. Safe. **Room services** Room service.

Moderate (3,000-6000 Kč)

U krále Karla

Úvoz 4, Prague 1 (5753 2869/5753 3594/fax 5753 3591/www.romantichotels.cz). Metro Malostranská/12, 22, 23 tram. **Rooms** 19. **Rates** 4,250-5,800 Kč single; 4,600-6,300 Kč double; 6,200-6,900 Kč suite; 1,100 Kč extra bed. **Credit** AmEx, MC, V. **Map** p304 C3.

The solid oak furnishings, painted vaulted ceilings, stained-glass windows and various baroque treasures lend this hotel the feel of an aristocratic country house. In fact it was once owned by the Benedictine order. If the daily hike up the hill from the tram seems daunting, try U krále Karla's cousin, U páva (*see p51*), opposite the Vojanovy Gardens. Large discounts for payment in cash are sometimes available here.

Hotel services *Babysitting. Parking.* **Room services** *Room service. Safe. Trouser press.*

Malá Strana

Second only to Hradčany in views and atmosphere, Malá Strana is filled with evocative little inns and pensions much easier to ramble back to after a long day out – it's only a stroll across the Charles Bridge from all the entertainments of the Old Town. Although the district attracts a steady flow of tourists, many back streets remain blissfully untouched by modern times.

Expensive (6,000-8,000 Kč)

Hotel Hoffmeister
Pod Bruskou 7, Prague 1 (5101 7111/fax 5101 7100/www.hoffmeister.cz). Metro Malostranská/12, 18, 22, 23 tram. **Rooms** 42. **Rates** 6,000-7,100 Kč single deluxe; 6,900-8,400 Kč double deluxe; 8,400-

10,000 Kč suite; extra bed (only in some rooms) 1,300 Kč. **Credit** AmEx, DC, MC, V. **Map** p305 F1.
A good option for those more interested in exploring romantic Prague than in networking and closing the deal. It's on a busy junction, but the soundproofed windows triumph over the noise. The lobby and rooms are filled with original works by artist Adolf Hoffmeister, father of the present owner. Downstairs you'll find a superb wine bar with a cosy, 1920s speakeasy feel and a well-thought-out selection of Moravian and international vintages. Breakfast costs extra.

Hotel services *Air-conditioning. Babysitting. Business services. Disabled: room adapted. Garden. Limousine service. Parking. Safe.* **Room services** *Dataport. Room service.*

Moderate (3,000-6000 Kč)

The Blue Key
Letenská 14, Prague 1 (5732 7250/fax 5732 9062/ www.bluekey.cz). Metro Malostranská/12, 22, 23 tram. **Rooms** 28 **Rates** 2,950-4,250 Kč single; 3,230-5,450 Kč double; 5,350-8,600 Kč suite; extra bed 925-1,295 Kč; under-14s free with 2 adults. **Credit** AmEx, MC, V. **Map** p305 E3.
This 14th-century townhouse is the sort of place ordinary Praguers used to live in before the free market brought skyrocketing housing costs. In the refit rooms were kitted out in restrained Italian furnishings with, yes, a blue colour scheme. Most

A room with a view at
Na Kampě 15. *See p51.*

Residence Nosticova – classy nook. *See p52.*

rooms and suites come with kitchenettes. Ask for a room facing the courtyard rather than one overlooking busy Letenská. The lower rates apply from January to March.
Hotel services *No-smoking rooms.* **Room services** *Safe.*

Hotel Sax

Jánský vršek 328/3, Prague 1 (5753 1268/fax 5753 4101/hotelsax@bon.cz). Metro Malostranská/12, 22, 23 tram. **Rooms** 22. **Rates** 3,700 Kč single; 4,400 Kč double 5,100 Kč; suite; extra bed 1,000 Kč. **Credit** AmEx, DC, MC, V. **Map** p304 C3.
As crisp and comfortable as the lobby and rooms are, the real Sax appeal is its location, up the hill from Malostranské náměstí, perfect for those who want to be in one of Malá Strana's quieter corners. Reliable service.
Hotel services *Disabled: access, rooms adapted. Laundry. Parking.* **Room services** *Dataport. Room service.*

Hotel Pod Věží

Mostecká 2, Prague 1 (5753 2041/5753 2060/ fax 5753 2069/hotel@podvezi.com). Metro Malostranská/12, 22, 23 tram. **Rooms** 12. **Rates** 4,500-5,000 Kč single; 5,600-6,800 Kč double; 6,300-9,300 Kč suite. **Credit** AmEx, DC, MC, V. **Map** p305 E3.
Enthusiastically styling itself as 'a place of retreat for the visitor, service for the guest who – as we

know – is the messenger of joy', this is a good option for tourists who want to be in the thick of Malá Strana. The hotel is a few cobblestones further from Charles Bridge than U Tří pštrosů (*see p52*) and offers slightly lower prices, if less ye olde charm. The standard room, called a suite, is really a deluxe double; the two 'double' rooms have twin beds.
Hotel services *Babysitting. Garden (summer). Parking.* **Room services** *Room service. Safe. VCR.*

Kampa Hotel

Všehrdova 16, Prague 1 (5732 0508/5732 0837/ fax 5732 0262/www.euroagentur.cz). Metro Malostranská/12, 22 tram. **Rooms** 85. **Rates** 2,400-3,300 Kč single; 3860-4,680 Kč double; 4,860-5,940 Kč triple. **Credit** AmEx, DC, MC, V. **Map** p305 E5.
On a quiet backstreet in Malá Strana, the Kampa has retained its 17th-century architecture and style through recent renovations. Rooms are elegantly arranged. The vaulted 'Knights Hall' dining room and outdoor garden restaurant offer Czech and international cuisine. Small stylish salons are available for special events.
Hotel services *Garden. Laundry. Limousine service. Parking. Restaurant. Safe.* **Room services** *Mini-bar. TV: satellite.*

Hotel U páva

U Lužického semináře 32, Prague 1 (5732 0743/5731 5867/fax 533 379/www.romantichotels.cz). Metro Malostranská/12, 18, 22, 23 tram. **Rooms** 11. **Rates** 4,300-5,400 Kč single; 4,500-5,900 Kč double; 1,100 Kč extra bed; 6,500-6,900 Kč suite. **Credit** AmEx, DC, MC, V. **Map** p305 F3.
The dark oak ceilings and crystal chandeliers don't synthesise as well as the seamless elegance of U krále Karla (also owned by Karel Klubal; *see p47*), but the ideal location in a serene corner of Malá Strana makes one quite forgiving. Suites 201, 301, 401 and 402 look on to the Castle, but some other rooms are dark and viewless. The adjacent house is being converted into a 27-room annexe, due to open in September 2000.
Hotel services *Limousine service. Parking. No-smoking rooms.* **Room services** *Room service.*

Na Kampě 15

Na Kampě 15, Prague 1 (5753 1432/ www.nakampe15.cz). Metro Malostranská/ 12, 22, 23 tram. **Rooms** 26. **Rates** 3,600-5,400 Kč single; 4,000-5,800 Kč double; 5,400-7,200 Kč apartment. **Credit** AmEx, DC, MC, V. **Map** p305 F4.
This newish Kampa Island venture affords fine views of the Charles Bridge and Old Town, yet is far enough from the bridge to provide peace and quiet. The management has done a sensitive restoration job on what was once a 15th-century tavern that brewed one of the city's pioneering beers. Rooms feature exposed beams and garret windows, with modern furnishings. The cellar restaurant and back beer garden have a reasonably varied menu with a good assortment of Czech and French wines.
Hotel services *Bar. Garden. Restaurant.* **Room services** *TV: satellite. Safe.*

Pension Dientzenhofer

Nosticova 2, Prague 1 (531 672/fax 5732 0888/ dientzenhofer@volny.cz). Metro Malostranská. 6, 9, 12 ,22, 23 tram. **Rooms** 6. **Rates** 2,600 Kč single; 3,500 Kč double; 4,800 Kč suite. **Credit** AmEx, DC, MC, V. **Map** p305 E4.

Tucked away off a busy street, this 16th-century house is the birthplace of one of the greatest baroque architects, Kilian Ignaz Dientzenhofer (*see page 32*), whose work fills this quarter of the city. The quiet courtyard and back garden offer a lovely respite in the midst of Malá Strana while rooms are bright rooms and the staff friendly. Book well ahead, though as it invariably fills up for summer. **Hotel services** *Bar. Disabled: access. Laundry. Parking.*

Residence Nosticova

Nosticova 1, Prague 1 (5731 2513/fax 5731 2517/ nostic@bohem-net.cz). Metro Malostranská/12, 22, 23 tram. **Rooms** 10. **Rates** 4,700-5,600 Kč suite; 6,800-9,800 Kč large suite. **Credit** AmEx, DC, MC, V. **Map** p305 E4.

A classy little nook for those who plan to stay longer, this recently modernised baroque 'residence' is on a quiet lane just off Kampa Island. The suites range from ample to capacious and come with antique furniture, bathrooms big enough to swim in and, best of all, fully equipped kitchenettes. Two have working fireplaces. If you don't feel like cooking your own, continental breakfast is served in the elegant wine bar for an extra charge. No restaurant. **Hotel services** *Parking.* **Room services** *Kitchenettes. Safe.*

U Tří pštrosů

Dražického náměstí 12 at, Prague 1 (5753 2410/ fax 5753 3217/www.utripstrosu.cz). Metro Malostranská/12, 22, 23 tram. **Rooms** 18. **Rates** 4,000-5,050 Kč single; 5,400-6,900 Kč double; 6,800-9,900 Kč suite; 950-1,250 Kč extra bed. **Credit** AmEx, DC, MC, V. **Map** p305 E3.

The location at the foot of Charles Bridge may scare away some who fear the non-stop din of tourists shrieking 'This is just like Disney World!' in 34 different languages. Once inside, the noise factor turns out to be surprisingly minimal. Unfortunately, service has slipped several notches recently, so it about evens out. The 18 rooms are pretty, with original ceiling beams that provide a rustic feel. The stairs are steep, so this is not a good choice for the less agile. If you want a view of the bridge, ask for it. **Hotel services** *Babysitting. Parking.* **Room services** *Room service. Safe.*

Cheap (under 3,000 Kč)

Dům U velké boty

Vlašská 30/333, Prague 1 (5753 2088/5753 3234/rippl@mbox.vol.cz). Metro Malostranská/12, 22, 23 tram. **Rooms** 12. **Rates** 1,650 Kč single; 2,700-3,500 Kč double; 3,800 Kč suite. **No credit cards**. **Map** p304 B4.

This charming family-run house is hidden away in the thick of Malá Strana. Attentive service and loads of gorgeous period furniture make this a perfect nest from which to explore romantic Prague. The house dates back to 1470 and has recently had a thorough renovation from walls to furniture trim. It

Hostel Sokol – *See p53.*

Hotel Pařiž Praha – sky-high sumptuousness.

has also been frequented by many European writers, artists and actors. There's no big sign, so look for the 'Rippl' buzzer. Breakfast is an extra 150 Kč. **Hotel services** *Fax. Gym. Laundry.*

U červené sklenice

Na Kampě 10, Prague 1 (5753 2918/0602 357 700/ www.hotel-kampa.cz). Metro Malostranská/12, 22, 23 tram. **Rooms** 4. **Rates** 2,900 Kč-4,600 Kč double; 3,300-5,800 Kč apartment. **Credit** MC, V. **Map** p305 F2.

For the prices charged you'd expect more luxury at this tiny baroque house on Kampa Island, but if you're fascinated by parades of Charles Bridge walkers, this is the place to be. Two rooms face the bridge and two face the recently prettied-up Na Kampě Square. The outdoor café is handy, though the restaurant is cramped. Significant discounts from January to April.
Hotel services *Bar.* **Room services** *TV: satellite. Safe.*

Hostels

Hostel Sokol

Újezd 450; Prague 1 (5700 7397/fax 5700 7340). Metro Malostranská/12, 22 tram. **Beds** 90. **Open** 24 hours daily. **Rates** 270 Kč per person. **No credit cards.** **Map** p305 E5.

Supremely cheap lodging in an ideal location. Follow a labyrinth of halls through the Sokol sports centre to get to reception. Once you finally find the reception desk you've found budget travel paradise. Great terrace for sipping beer with a view. Not far from the Castle and Charles Bridge.
Hostel services *Bedding. Lock boxes at reception. Lockers in room. Kitchen access. Terrace.*

Staré Město

You can't do better for pubbing and clubbing than the Old Town but you do pay for the convenience in room rates, and at some locations in noise and crowds. Large, modern and central hotels abound in this this right bank district. Fine

restaurants and galleries are also most highly concentrated here, as is much of Prague's more alternative shopping.

Deluxe (over 8,000 Kč)

Casa Marcello

Řásnovka 783, Prague 1 (231 0260/231 1230/ fax 231 3323/www.casa-marcello.cz). Metro Náměstí Republiky/5, 8, 14 tram. **Rooms** 32 **Rates** 8,900 Kč single/double; 10,100 Kč junior suite; 11,300 Kč apartment. **Credit** AmEx, DC, MC, V. **Map** p306 J1.

This rambling hotel wedged into an untrafficked Old Town nook has a picturesque location almost impossible to find without a large map. They know how good it is, and charge accordingly. Although opened less than a decade ago, the hotel feels older, with clunky furniture and carpets in need of cleaning. There's no lift, and some rooms lack air-conditioning. Better-equipped rooms can be had more cheaply elsewhere, but for atmosphere, look no further.
Hotel services *Garden. No-smoking rooms.* **Room services** *Dataport.*

Hotel Pařiž Praha

U Obecního domu 1, Prague 1 (2219 5195/fax 2422 5475/www.hotel-pariz.cz). Metro Náměstí Republiky/5, 8, 14 tram. **Rooms** 95. **Rates** 8,000-10,000 Kč single/double; 14,000 Kč executive single/double. **Credit** AmEx, DC, MC, V. **Map** p306 K3.

A century-old, family-run Prague fixture immortalised in a bawdy chapter of Bohumil Hrabal's *I Served the King of England*, this sumptuous, art nouveau hotel has gone a long way toward raising quality to match its sky-high prices. The public spaces are as elegant as any in the city, and the replica fittings in the rooms, along with touches such as bathrobes and tiled bathroom floors, are reminders of a more genteel age. If it's sheer pampering and slavish service you're after, though, a more modern hotel may better fit the bill.
Hotel services *No-smoking floor.* **Room services** *Dataport.*

Inter-Continental

Náměstí Curieových 43/5, Prague 1 (2488 1111/ fax 2481 1216/www.interconti.com). Metro Staroměstská/17 tram. **Rooms** 364. **Rates** 11,000-13,000 Kč single; 11,900-14,000 Kč double; 15,200-28,500 Kč suite. **Credit** AmEx, DC, MC, V. **Map** p306 H2.

Once you get over the first impression of its 'brutalist' 1970s design, the Inter-Continental will charm the beast in you, from the shoe-shine service to the view from the terrace. All traces of communist design were expunged during a £32-milion ($50-million) refurbishment in the 1990s. The conference facilities leave nothing to be desired and the fitness centre is complete, although a curious island in the pool prevents lap swimming (almost impossible in Prague). Service is sometimes more grovelling than effectual. The spacious suites feature a full range of

Grand Hotel Bohemia.

electronic widgets for the professional business traveller. Excellent views on the river side.
Hotel services *Beauty salon. Disabled: access, room adapted. Gym. No-smoking floors. Putting green. Secretarial services. Swimming pool.* **Room services** *Dataport (some rooms). Fax (some rooms). Keyboard for Internet access (some rooms). Room service. Voicemail.*

Expensive (6,000-8,000 Kč)

Grand Hotel Bohemia
Králodvorská 4, Prague 1 (2480 4111/fax 232 9545/ austria-hotels.co.at). Metro Náměstí Republiky/5, 8, 14 tram. **Rooms** 78. **Rates** 5,700-7,850 Kč single; 7,560-11,400 Kč double; 16,000 Kč suite; 2,100 Kč extra bed (1,050 Kč for 7-12s; free for under-7s).* **Credit** AmEx, DC, MC, V. **Map** p307 K3.
Grand indeed, this gorgeous hotel under Austrian management makes an art deco counterpoint to the neighbouring art nouveau gem, the Municipal House (*see p35, 91, 104 and 221*). Even standard rooms are chock full of amenities, including a fax machine and trouser press. Most rooms on the sixth to eighth storeys have fabulous views over the red roofs of the Old Town. The Boccaccio Room doubles as a grand ballroom or an extravagant conference room for up to 140.

Hotel services *Beauty salon. Disabled: rooms adapted. No-smoking floor.* **Room services** *Dataport. Fax. Trouser press.*

Hotel Esprit Praha
Jakubská 5, Prague 1 (2287 0111/fax 231 5284/ www.pragueesprit.cz). Metro Náměstí Republiky/5, 8, 14 tram. **Rooms** 29. **Rates** 5,000 Kč single; 6,000 Kč double; 6,500 Kč junior suite. **Credit** AmEx, MC, V. **Map** p307 K3.
A newly renovated former strip club handily located in the heart of Old Town, now returned to the family that founded it in 1924. Individually decorated rooms are a hybrid of ubiquitous modern hotel decor and 1920s style. Art deco elements and wood trim add a nice touch and corner rooms offer great vantages for spying on street life and gables.
Hotel services *Disabled: access. Limousine service. Grill-bar. Non-smoking rooms. Restaurant.* **Room services** *Dataport. Mini-bar. TV: satellite.*

Moderate (3,000-6000 Kč)

Hotel Černá liška
Mikulášská 2, Prague 1 (2423 2250/fax 2423 2249). Metro Staroměstská/17, 18 tram. **Rooms** 12. **Rates** 2,500-4,000 Kč single; 3,100-4,800 Kč double; 4,000-

6,300 Kč suite; extra bed 1,000 Kč. **Credit** DC, MC, V. **Map** p306 H3.

Though a location right on Old Town Square is not for everyone, the recently opened Black Fox offers excellent value in the medieval centre of Prague. Wake up to the sound of the Týn church bells (and the rumble of tourist traffic) then stumble out into gallery-hopping, pubbing and clubbing central, without ever needing to risk your trip's budget on one of Prague's infamous crooked taxis. A welcoming staff oversees these dozen neatly furnished rooms with modern baths.

Hotel services *Concierge. Laundry. Limousine service. Restaurant. Safe. Secretarial services.* **Room services** *TV: satellite.*

Pension Metamorphosis

Malá Štupartská 5 (Ungelt Square) Prague 1 (2482 8387/fax 2482 6059/www.metamorphis.cz). Metro Náměstí Republiky/5, 14, 26 tram **Rooms** 12. **Rates** 3,010-6,020 Kč double; 3,430-6,860 Kč suite; 1,000-1,400 Kč extra bed. **Credit** AmEx, DC, MC, V. **Map** p306 J3.

The once-empty square on which this new pension stands has become a tourist mecca, jammed with craft shops, a respectable bookstore, and cafés – the largest of which is on the ground floor of the Metamorphosis itself. This supplies a constant low-grade din but the rooms here are tastefully done and far enough above it all to afford a respite. Great value and location with engaging service, though probably not ideal in high season. You're unlikely to wake up as a beetle.

Hotel services *Bar. Parking. Restaurant. No lift.* **Room services** *Mini-bar in suites. TV: satellite.*

U Medvídků

Na Perštýně 7, Prague 1 (2421 1916/ fax 2422 0930/ www.umedvidku.cz). Metro Národní třída/6, 18, 21, 22, 23 tram. **Rooms** 22. **Rates** 2,015 Kč single; 3,030 Kč double; 4,045 Kč triple. **Credit** AmEx, MC, V. **Map** p306 H5.

The Little Bears offers comfortable rooms and good service above one of a dying breed of Prague pubs – the sort that still attracts locals in search of great beer and food at good prices (*see p157*). The pension rooms with raftered ceilings could hardly be better located or better priced. They're not luxurious but are comfortable and charming and the staff is welcoming. Remarkably quiet despite being only one block from one of downtown's busiest streets.

Hotel services *Bar. Garden. Restaurant.* **Room services** *Mini-bar. TV.*

U zlaté studny

Karlova 3, Prague 1 (tel/fax 2222 0262/ www.hotel.cz/u_zlate_studny). Metro Staroměstská/17, 18 tram. **Rooms** 6. **Rates** 3,900-4,200 Kč double; 4,200 Kč-4,600 Kč suite; 500 Kč extra person (under 15s free). **Credit** AmEx, MC, V. **Map** p306 H4.

This 16th-century Renaissance structure stands on the Royal Path connecting Charles Bridge and Old Town Square. The four roomy suites and two doubles are decorated in Louis XIV antique and replica

The best Hotels

For reading Bohumil Hrabal's *I Served the King of England*
Hotel Paříž Praha (see page 53).

For mingling with rock stars
Hotel Savoy (see page 47).

For encountering Stalin's ghost
Holiday Inn Prague (see page 62).

For encountering Stalin's undelivered messages at reception
Grand Hotel Evropa (see page 61).

For a fab biz confab
Radisson SAS (see page 58).

For a relaxing mixed sauna
Hotel Axa (see page 59).

For brunching with the family
Renaissance Prague Hotel (see page 61).

For sampling a fine Moravian pinot
Hotel Hoffmeister (see page 49).

For the total workout
Marriott (see page 61).

For the total makeout
Romantik Hotel U raka (see page 47).

For business services on a budget
Don Giovanni (see page 62).

For stumbling home from the U Medvídků beerhall
U Medvídků (see page 57).

furnishing with painted vault ceilings. A perfect choice for exploring most of historic Prague on foot.
Hotel services *Restaurant. Fax. Laundry.* **Room services** *Mini-bar. Safe.*

Cheap (under 3,000 Kč)

Betlem Club

Betlémské náměstí 9, Prague 1 (2222 1574/fax 2222 0580/betlem.club@login.cz). Metro Národní třída/6, 9, 18, 22, 23 tram. **Rooms** 22. **Rates** 2,100-2,500 Kč single; 2,600-3,300 Kč double; 2,900-3,600 Kč suite; 400-600 Kč extra bed; under-5s free. **Map** p306 H4.

A homey hotel on an agreeable square, only a twist and a turn away from Charles Bridge or, in the other direction, Wenceslas Square. Fairly spacious

Accommodation

Accommodation

rooms are punctuated by a little too much brass, but are nevertheless clean, attractive and well stocked with necessities. At the price, this is one of the Old Town's best bargains, and there are small single rooms in the attic priced even lower. With the money you save here, treat yourself to dinner at nearby **V Zátiší** (*see p129*).

Cloister Inn

Konviktská 14, Prague 1 (2421 1020/fax 2421 0800/ www.cloister-inn.cz). Metro Národní třída/6, 9, 18, 22, 23 tram. **Rooms** 73. **Rates** 2,200-3,000 Kč single; 2,750-3,800 Kč double; 3,300-4,750 Kč triple. **Credit** AmEx, MC, V. **Map** p306 G5.

Resting behind the cheaper Pension Unitas run by the same people (*see below*), this three-star hotel has a lot going for it: attentive staff, great location, good prices and a nearby house full of nuns in case you are in need of redemption. The boxy rooms exude an institutional feel, but at this price in Old Town, it's hard to grumble.

Hotel services *Concierge. Disabled: access, adapted room. Interpreting service. Laundry. No-smoking rooms. Parking.* **Room services** *Safe.*

Pension Salieri

Liliová 18, Prague 1 (2222 0196/ PensionSalieri@atlas.cz). Metro Staroměstská/17, 18 tram. **Rooms** 8 **Rates** 530 Kč per person (shared bath); 730 Kč per person (private bath). **No credit cards.** **Map** p306 H4.

The pension Salieri is hidden in a courtyard just off the old coronation route leading from Old Town Square to the Charles Bridge. Its modest interior and small rooms call to mind a hippie guest house in a historic building, an image somehow not dispelled by the Internet café. Despite the pedestrian traffic out front, the passage to the street effectively keeps out the din. The location and price – same amount per person whether the room's a single or a quad – can't be beat.

Hotel services *Bar. Garden. Internet café.*

Pension Unitas

Bartolomějská 9, Prague 1 (2421 1020/fax 2421 0800/www.cloister-inn.cz/unitas). **Rooms** 35. **Rates** 1,020 Kč single; 1,200 Kč double; 1,650 Kč triple;. 2,000 Kč quad; 2,350 Kč 5-bed; 2,700 Kč 6-bed. **No credit cards. Map** p306 H5.

One floor has standard, comfortable hostel rooms, the basement has communist-era prison cells that once imprisoned playwright/dissident Václav Havel. Fine and clean, a genuine bargain.

Hotel services *Parking.*

U krále Jiřího

Liliová 10, Prague 1 (2222 0925/2424 8797/ fax 2222 1707/www.kinggeorge.cz). Metro Staroměstská or Národní třída/17, 18 tram. **Rooms** 9 (all en suite). **Rates** 1,700 Kč single; 2,900 Kč double; 3,800 Kč triple; 3,300-5,000 Kč apartment. **Credit** AmEx, DC, MC, V. **Map** p306 G4.

This pension above the James Joyce pub (*see p156*) has attic rooms with sloped ceilings and ancient

beams. On a picturesque but busy lane, walking distance to Charles Bridge and Old Town Square.

Hotel services *Fax. Garden. Safe. Wine bar.*

Hostels

Travellers' Hostel

Booking office: Dlouhá 33, Prague 1 (2482 6662/ 2482 6663/fax 2482 6665/www.travellers.cz). Metro Náměstí Republiky/5, 14, 26 tram. **Open** 24 hours daily (all branches). **Rates** (per person) 550 Kč doubles; 430 Kč triples; 400-380 Kč 4-6 bed rooms; 350 Kč dormitory. **No credit cards. Map** p307 K2.

This hostel, built over the Roxy club (*see p204*), also functions as a booking office connecting travellers to a whole network of hostels. The two constants are good value and English-speaking backpackers.

Hostel services *Bar. E-mail. Fax. Laundry.*

Nové Město

Prague's fast, cheap and clean pubic transport makes New Town a viable option for business travellers looking for better value and modern facilities without sacrificing easy motorway access or much proximity to the centre. The northerly areas of this district are within walking distance of Old Town and are undergoing an exciting renaissance.

Deluxe (over 8,000 Kč)

Hotel Palace Praha

Panská 12, Prague 1 (2409 3111/fax 2422 1240/ www.palacehotel.cz). Metro Můstek/3, 9, 14, 24 tram. **Rooms** 124 **Rates** 9,100 Kč single; 9,600 Kč double; 11,600 Kč junior suite; 1,850 Kč extra bed. **Credit** AmEx, DC, MC, V. **Map** p307 K5.

Quite possibly the best service in Prague, with an enthusiastic staff that insists the hotel should have six stars. Simple but comfortable rooms, two restaurants and a café, each with its own piano player, and a location just close enough – but thankfully not too close – to Wenceslas Square. Some more expensive rooms have fax machines.

Hotel services *Disabled: access, rooms adapted. Interpreting services. No-smoking floors.* **Room services** *Dataport. Keyboard for Internet access.*

Radisson SAS

Štěpánská 40, Prague 1 (2282 0000/fax 2282 0100/ www.radisson.com/praguecs). Metro Muzeum/3, 9, 14, 23 tram. **Rooms** 211. **Rates** 9,000 Kč single/ double; 1,700 Kč extra bed. **Credit** AmEx, DC, MC, V. **Map** p309 K6.

Originally constructed in 1930 as the Alcron Hotel, this stylish phantom has awakened as the Radisson SAS after a 10-year dormancy. Its restoration was one of the most extensive in modern Prague hotel history, involving liberal doses of art deco. Just off Wenceslas Square, it's now New Town's most luxurious business hotel with first-rate techno gadgets, five phone lines per room, infrared dataports, heated bathroom tiles and downstairs jazz bar. **Hotel Services** *Bar. Dining Room.Dry cleaning. Garage Parking. Gym. Laundry. Disabled: access.* **Room Services** *Dataport. Fax. voicemail. Internet access. TV: pay movies. Room service (24-hr).*

Expensive (6,000-8,000 Kč)

K+K Fenix

Ve Smečkách 30, Prague 1 (3309 2222/fax 2221 2141/www.kkhotels.com). Metro Muzeum/3, 9, 14, 23 tram. **Rooms** 130 **Rates** 5,500 Kč single; 7,400 Kč double. **Credit** AmEx, DC, MC, V. **Map** p309 K6.
The newly built, Austrian-owned K+K is a fresh and efficient business hotel situated off the top of Wenceslas Square. Professional, with standard conference amenities plus a bistro and small, streamlined fitness centre.
Hotel services *Bar. Conference rooms. Garage parking. Gym. No-smoking rooms. Sauna.* **Room services** *Dataport. TV: satellite. Safe.*

Grand Hotel Evropa – art nouveau time capsule. See p61.

Moderate (3,000-6000 Kč)

Best Western City Hotel Moráň

Na Moráni 15, Prague 2 (2491 5208/ fax 2492 0625/bw-moran@login.cz). Metro Karlovo náměsti/3, 4, 14, 16, 18, 22, 23, 24 tram. **Rooms** 57. **Rates** 3,700-5,220 Kč single; 4,650-6,200 Kč double; extra bed 825-1,000 Kč. **Credit** AmEx, DC, MC, V. **Map** p308 H8.
Clean, bright rooms in a comfortable hotel with a good location near the river, all within walking distance of the Old Town and Vyšehrad. Not great value, but the staff are friendly and capable.
Hotel services *Air-conditioning. Limousine service. No-smoking rooms. Safe.*

Hotel 16 U sv. Kateřiny

Kateřinská 16, Prague 2 (2492 0636/2491 9676/ fax 2492 0626) Metro IP Pavlova/16,22,23 tram. **Rooms** 11. **Rates** 2,300 Kč single; 3,100 Kč double; 3,500 Kč apartment. **Credit** MC, V. **Map** p309 K8.
This small family-run inn is located on a quiet street within walking distance of the Botanical Gardens. Tranquil and intimate, good value, but not central.
Hotel services *Bar. Disabled: access.* **Room services** *Mini-bar. Safe.*

Hotel Axa

Na Poříčí 40, Prague 1 (2481 2580/ fax 2421 4489/www.vol.cz/AXA). Metro Florenc or Náměsti Republiky/3, 8, 24, 26 tram. **Rooms** 131. **Rates** 2,200-2,600 Kč single; 3,100-3,600 Kč double; 3,700-4,300 Kč triple; 3,800-4,500 Kč suite; extra bed 600-700 Kč; 220 Kč pets. **Credit** AmEx, DC, MC, V. **Map** p307 M2.
Sorely needed renovation over the past five years has raised the Depression-era Axa out of the ranks of backpackerdom. The prices remain quite fair, there's a good range of services, and the location isn't bad – halfway between two downtown metro stations. If you're a light sleeper, ask for a room at the back of the hotel away from the tram tracks. There is a decent workout centre, pool and sauna, though these are not run by the hotel and cost extra.
Hotel services *Bar. Beauty salon. Business services. Disabled: access, rooms adapted. Fax. Gym. Laundry. Restaurant. Safe. Swimming pool.* **Room services** *Mini-bar (some rooms).*

Hotel Meteor Plaza Best Western

Hybernská 6, Prague 1 (2419 2111/2419 2130/ fax 2421 3005/www.hotel-meteor.cz). Náměsti Republiky/3, 5, 8, 14, 24, 26 tram. **Rooms** 88. **Rates** 2,720-4,900 Kč single; 3,300-6,000 Kč double; 3,740-6,400 Kč triple; 4,290-7,000 Kč suite. **Credit** AmEx, DC, MC, V. **Map** p307 L3.
Much like most Best Westerns anywhere in the world, meaning reasonable comfort at reasonable rates, this time just yards from Old Town. The 14th-century wine cellar and restaurant out back offer relief from the rather blighted street out front.
Hotel services *Babysitting. Beauty salon. Concierge. Gym. Limousine service. Parking. Restaurant.* **Room services** *Mini-bar. TV: satellite/VCR. Room service.*

One room, nice view, no running water

Every Friday evening, from the time the weather even hints at Spring until the last leaf has fallen, they pack the Smíchov metro station en route to buses and trains outbound from Prague: Mum, Dad, a kid or two, and Granny, all carrying bags of groceries and trying to keep the family Alsatian from breaking its lead. They're headed for the family *chata*. Czechs boast a rate of second-home ownership that may exceed that of any other European country. But before you agree to spend a lovely weekend at a Czech friend's country home, be aware of what you're letting yourself in for: the typical weekend cottage in Bohemia or Moravia is a tiny wooden hut amid a dense mass of identical huts clustering near a river or pond convenient to public transport.

If you're lucky enough to be invited along for the weekend, you might cautiously sound out your host on the conditions at the local *chata* estate. Is there electricity? (Generally not.) Running water? (If not, there's always the river.) Proper beds? (If you don't mind sharing Granny's.) On the other hand, you'll be treated to home cooking, better than anything you'll find in Prague, plenty of romps with Rover, and all the beer you can drink from the inevitable makeshift pub nearby.

Some weekend cottages are enchanting, and some are in the most scenic parts of the country. The flip side is, you'd be very hard-pressed to find a lovely hill or dale in Bohemia unspoiled by a colony of *chaty*. Favoured locales near the capital include the dramatically inclined banks of the Sázava River to the southeast and the gentler terrain of the Berounka River to the southwest. The latter rambles past Karlštejn Castle, among other fine attractions.

The *chata* craze took off during the last two decades of communist rule, when the average worker enjoyed a reasonable amount of disposable income but had few opportunities to dispose of it. After the sixth summer holiday to Bulgaria, the attractions of home began to look better, and many families invested their savings in a cosy little cottage, either building it themselves (Czechs are incorrigible DIYers) or going through the unofficial bartering network – you install my boiler, I'll take care of your parking ticket – that the authorities tolerated for the sake of domestic tranquillity. A lucky few got their hands on an old farmhouse, or maybe a hunting cabin, and converted it into a *chalupa*, or cottage in the more genteel sense.

Now that the Czech Republic once again has open borders and it's possible to visit the actual West, *chaty* are more popular than ever. After all, America's so far, everything's so expensive there, and have you tasted what they call beer?

Heading for the family *chata* – 'Your turn to sleep with granny!'

Hotel Opera

*Těšnov 13, Prague 1 (231 5609/fax 231 1477/
www.hotel-opera.cz). Metro Florenc/3, 26 tram.*
Rooms 67. **Rates** 3,500 Kč single; 3,890 Kč double;
6,500 Kč suite. **Credit** AmEx, DC, MC, V.
Map p307 M1.
This place has always been good value, just blocks
away from Old Town. A recent renovation means
guests no longer need to sacrifice comfort. The
rooms remain small and simply furnished and the
staff is helpful. The neo-Renaissance façade of this
1890s building is a sight in itself.
Hotel services *Bar. Limousine service. Restaurant.*
Room services *TV: satellite.*

Jerome House

*V Jirchářich 13, Prague 1 (2491 1011/2491 2127/
fax 2491 2128/www.bohemia-incoming.cz). Metro
Národní Třída/6, 18, 21, 22, 23 tram.* **Rooms** 25.
Rates 2,590 Kč single; 3,890 Kč double; 4,300-9,400 Kč
4-5 person apartment. **Credit** MC, V. **Map** p308 H6.
A combination travel agency and newly renovated
budget hotel. Tucked away on a side street near the
National Theatre, it's in a great location for getting
around on foot. The house is bright and modern, the
staff helpful but the rooms are basic dorm-style.
Room services *TV.*

Marriott

*V Celnici 8, Prague 1 (2288 8888/
fax 2288 8889/www.marriotthotels.com). Metro
Náměstí Republiky/3, 8, 24 tram.* **Rooms** 293.
Rates 5,500 Kč all rooms; 6,600 Kč executive suites.
Credit AmEx, DC, MC, V. **Map** p307 L3.
The recently built Prague Marriott set out to
become the epitome of modern conveniences for
both business and pleasure in Prague – and largely
succeeded. With built-in casino, shopping arcade,
fitness centre and its own metro entrance, you could
be tempted never to venture outside. That would be
a pity, as the hotel is just one block from Old Town.
Hotel services *Bar. Beauty salon. Garage Parking.
Gym. Restaurant. Swimming pool.* **Room services**
TV: satellite/pay movies. Voicemail. Safe.

Renaissance Prague Hotel

*V Celnici 7, Prague 1 (2182 1111/
fax 2182 2200/www.renaissancehotels.com).
Metro Náměstí Republiky/3, 5, 14, 24, 26 tram.*
Rooms 315. **Rates** 3,600-7,380 Kč standard
single/double; 5,150-8,280 executive; 6,475-11,700 Kč
suite. **Credit** AmEx, DC, MC, V. **Map** p307 L3.
This most central of Prague's giant luxury hotels
offers exemplary service for tourists and business
folk, while resisting the trend to raise prices to offset the decline in Czech currency. The Marriott
chain owns the Renaissance as well as operating its
flagship Prague hotel across the street (*see above*),
with even shinier brass-and-marble fittings and
slightly higher prices. Breakfast costs extra.
Hotel services *Babysitting. Business services.
Disabled: rooms adapted. Executive lounge. Gym. No-
smoking floors. Swimming pool.* **Room services**
Dataport. TV: VCR (extra charge).

Cheap (under 3,000 Kč)

Grand Hotel Evropa

*Václavské náměstí 25, Prague 1 (2422 8117/
fax 2422 4544). Metro Můstek/3, 9, 14, 24 tram.*
Rooms 93 (53 en suite) **Rates** 2,990 Kč single; 3,990 Kč
double; 4,990 Kč triple; 5,200 Kč quad; 5,000 Kč
apartment. **Credit** AmEx, MC. V. **Map** p307 K5.
A grandiose exemplar of art nouveau on the outside, the Evropa remains a time capsule of communism in the inside. Built in 1889, and given its
current cream and gold façade in 1905, it has witnessed a lot from its perch over Wenceslas Square.
So have the staff, and the changes seem to have
worn them all out thoroughly. Still, the frisson of
the bad old days can be a trip if taken with a sense of
humour – and it's an unquestionable bargain for its
location dead in the centre of things.
Hotel services *Bar. Laundry. Restaurant. Safe.*
Room services *Room service. TV: satellite.*

Hostels

Charles University Dorms

*Voršilská 1, Prague 1 (290 073/2491 3692/
fax 2431 1107). Metro Národní třída/6, 9, 17, 18, 21,
22, 23 tram.* **Open** 9am-1pm Mon, Tue; 1pm-4pm
Wed; 9am-1pm Thur, Fri; closed Sat, Sun. **Rates** 165-
295 Kč per person, double. **No credit cards.**
Map p308 H6.
One central office takes care of booking some 1,000
dorm rooms scattered throughout the city. They're
only available from late June to late September but
are an incredible value. Just don't expect a lot.

Klub Habitat

*Na Zderaze 10, Prague 2 (tel/fax 2492 1706/
2491 8252/www.euroagentur.cz). Metro Karlovo
náměstí/3, 6, 14, 18, 21, 22, 24 tram.* **Rooms** 4.
Rates 400 Kč per person (with breakfast). **No credit
cards.** **Map** p308 H7.
Watch for the easily missable sign and the
unscrupulous place around the corner that sometimes poses as Klub Habitat. The genuine article is
a friendly, owner-run spot in a handy downtown
location. Wood floors, clean shared bathroom,
munchies and lemonade at reception. Excellent
value and a step up from most hostels. All proceeds
go to Czech children's charities. Book well ahead as
there are just enough rooms for this place to have
full occupancy all year.
Hostel services *Bar. Kitchen access.*

Further afield

Žižkov is pubbing heaven, a magnet for young
bohemians, and home to some truly frightful
housing stock. Holešovice and Dejvice are leafy
northern boundaries just across the Vltava from
the city centre. Vyšehrad and neighbouring
Vinohrady offer classy, up-and-coming
residential streets.

Deluxe (over 8,000 Kč)

Corinthia

Kongresová 1, Vyšehrad, Prague 4 (6119 1111/ fax 6121 1673/www.corinthia.com). Metro Vyšehrad/7, 18, 24 tram. **Rooms** 544.
Rates 8,000 Kč single/double; 12,600-18,000 Kč suite. **Credit** DC, MC, V.

This 24-storey hotel is an unmissable if unlovely landmark on the southern skyline. It made headlines a couple of years ago in the Czech press when the US government declared it off-limits to Americans because of its new owners' alleged ties to Libya. The embargo remains technically in effect, so US citizens should consult the embassy in Prague before considering the Towers. The new owners have cranked the service up a notch, and the hotel continues to have a loyal following of business travellers. Although a bit out of the centre, it's right next to the metro, a major motorway and the city's biggest conference centre. Rooms are on the small side, but the views over the city are as expansive as any.
Hotel services *Beauty salon. Bowling. Disabled: access, rooms adapted. Gym. Interpreting services. No-smoking rooms. Squash court Swimming pool.* **Room services** *Dataport. Fax (some rooms).*

Expensive (6,000-8,000 Kč)

Holiday Inn Prague

Koulova 15, Dejvice, Prague 6 (2439 3111/ fax 2431 0616/reserv@prague.holiday-inn.cz). Tram 20, 25. **Rooms** 243. **Rates** 7,400 Kč single 7,750 Kč; double; 8,810 Kč suite/executive room; 1,070 Kč extra bed. **Credit** AmEx, DC, MC, V.

Modelled on Stalin's colossal Seven Sisters in Moscow and adorned with heroic socialist realist friezes, the 14-storey Holiday Inn is perfect if you want a communist nostalgia trip. Reconstruction in 1996-7 has left the rooms pleasant, modern and not at all like one of Uncle Joe's gulags. Prices are pretty high, even for a one-of-a-kind lodging experience. As the hotel is off the beaten path, guests either learn to get around on the tram or rely on taxis.
Hotel services *Beauty salon. Disabled: access, rooms adapted. Garden. Gym. Interpreting services. No-smoking floors.* **Room services** *Dataport. Fax (executive rooms).*

Prague Hilton

Pobřežní 1, Karlín, Prague 8 (2484 1111/ fax 2484 2378/www.hilton.com). Metro Florenc/8, 24 tram. **Rooms** 788. **Rates** 5,400-7,100 Kč single (6,800-8,500 Kč executive); 6,120-7,800 Kč double (7,800-9,500 Kč executive); extra bed free; 10,600 Kč junior suite; 13,000 Kč executive suite; 28,000 Kč family apartment. **Credit** AmEx, DC, MC, V.

This massive, mirrored cube frames the largest atrium in the Czech Republic. Huge leather armchairs, lots of greenery and gently bubbling fountains spell relaxation and recreation, as do the pool, sauna, salon and indoor tennis courts. Not for those

raring to grab a map and tramp through the city sights. That may be why the likes of Richard Nixon, Nelson Mandela and the Clintons chose this hotel's Presidential Suite. There is an abundance of services for both business guests and tourists, but only the executive rooms and suites include breakfast.
Hotel services *Beauty salon. Disabled: access, rooms adapted. Gym. Interpreting services. No-smoking floors. Putting green. Swimming pool.* **Room services** *Dataport (business-class rooms). Safe (business-class rooms). Voicemail.*

Diplomat Hotel Praha

Evropská 15, Dejvice, Prague 6 (2439 4111/ fax 2439 4215/www.diplomat-hotel.cz). Metro Dejvická/2, 20, 26 tram. **Rooms** 382.
Rates 5,700-6,500 Kč single; 6,850-7,600 Kč double; 7,600-8,600 Kč executive double; 11,100-15,900 Kč suite; free under-6s. **Credit** AmEx, DC, MC, V.

A 20-minute drive from the airport, the Diplomat is best suited for business people. Executive rooms go at premium prices, as they recently underwent the refurbishment that the other rooms are crying out for. There's a go-kart track in the basement for those who like to mix pleasure with duty. Use of the fitness centre is included in the room rates.
Hotel services *Air-conditioning. Beauty salon. Business services. Disabled: access, rooms adapted. Gym. Interpreting services. Limousine service. No-smoking floors. Parking. Safe.* **Room services** *Dataport (executive rooms). Room service. Safe (executive rooms).*

Moderate (3,000-6000 Kč)

Don Giovanni

Vinohradská 157a, Žižkov, Prague 3 (6703 1111/ fax 6703 6704/dongio@rogner.cz). Metro Želivského/10, 11, 16, 26 tram. **Rooms** 400. **Rates** 4,200-7,600 Kč single/double; 5,600-8,400 Kč suite. **Credit** AmEx, DC, MC, V. **Map** p311 E2.

This relative newcomer may be the best value in this class, especially for business travellers. The lobby contains impressive original art and sculpture; guests in a hurry may appreciate the stellar business services. Don't be put off by the location out of the centre; the hotel is right by the Želivského metro stop, so downtown is less than ten minutes away. It is adjacent to Franz Kafka's final resting place. Rock-solid value.
Hotel services *Air-conditioning. Business services. Concierge. Disabled: access, rooms adapted. Gym. Lift. No-smoking floors. Parking.* **Room services** *Dataport. Refrigerator. Room service. Safe.*

Hotel Praha

Sušická 20, Dejvice, Prague 6 (2434 1111/ fax 2431 1218/www.htlpraha.com). Metro Dejvická. **Rooms** 124. **Rates** 2,915-4,865 Kč single; 3,410-5,695 Kč double; 6,020-10,050 Kč suite; extra bed 1,575 Kč. **Credit** AmEx, DC, MC, V.

This showcase of 1970s flamboyance, with its bulbous lights and extravagant leather upholstery, used to be reserved exclusively for Communist

Recovering from last night's blow-out at **The Clown & Bard**.

Party officials and visiting dignitaries. Now mere mortals – albeit mortals with expense accounts – can relax in rooms that have hosted dignitaries such as Colonel Gadaffi and BB King. Access to a car (or lots of taxis) is a virtual necessity if you want to see the city but at least airport access is direct and fast. Children under 12 stay free.

Hotel services *Air-conditioning. Beauty salon. Billiards. Bowling. Business services. Concierge. Disabled: rooms adapted. Garden. Gym. Interpreting services. Limousine service. Parking. Safe. Swimming pool.* **Room services** *Room service. Safe (some rooms).*

Hotel Schwaiger

Schwaigrova 3, Bubeneč, Prague 6 (3332 0271/ fax 3332 0272). Metro Hradčanská/131 bus. **Rooms** 12. **Rates** 2,400-3,000 Kč single; 3,200-4,000 Kč double; 3,600-4,500 Kč suite; extra bed 600 Kč. **Credit** AmEx, MC, V. **Map** p310 A2.

Hanuš Schwaiger, one of the 'National Theatre Generation' of painters, once occupied this pale yellow villa. It's now a simple yet comfortable small hotel in the lush diplomatic quarter of Bubeneč, and not as hard to find as the village-like quality of the neighbourhood might make you think. The rooms are furnished for comfort rather than style, although some of them have handsome coffered ceilings. There's a garden restaurant on the premises and just down the road is a gate into Prague's prettiest park, Stromovka.

Hotel services *Garden. Parking. Restaurant (2). Wine bar.* **Room services** *Mini-bar.*

Hotel Sieber

Slezská 55, Žižkov, Prague 3 (2425 0025/ fax 2425 0027/www.johansen.com). Metro Jiřího z Poděbrad/11, 16 tram. **Rooms** 14. **Rates** 4,480 Kč single; 4,780 Kč double; 5,480 Kč suite. **Credit** AmEx, DC, MC, V. **Map** p311 C3.

An efficiently-run place close to both the raucous pubs of Žižkov and the upscale shopping of Vinohrady, the Sieber makes up in friendliness what it lacks in luxury amenities. No antique furnishings here, just solid, tasteful comfort and reliable business services. Note that the lift stops a half-flight from the room levels.

Hotel services *Air-conditioning. No-smoking rooms. Parking.* **Room services** *Bathrobes. Dataport.*

Cheap (under 3,000 Kč)

Hotel Anna

Budečská 17, Vinohrady, Prague 2 (2251 3111/ fax 2251 5158/www.hotel.cz/anna). Metro Náměstí Míru 16, 22, 34 tram. **Rooms** 23. **Rates** 2,170 Kč single; 2,970 Kč double; 3,700 triple; 4,100 Kč apartment. **Credit** AmEx, MC, V. **Map** p311 B3.

On a quiet, tree-lined street in Vinohrady, stained-glass windows, wrought-iron staircase and tall French windows make this an exceptional choice. Not terribly central, but the trade-off for clean air is reasonable enough. And it's only a short tram ride or a pleasant walk into town.

Hotel services *Air-conditioning. Bar. Fax. Laundry. Parking.* **Room services** *TV: satellite.*

Hotel City

*Belgická 10, Vinohrady, Prague 2 (2252 1606/
fax 2252 2386/web.telecom.cz/hotel.city). Metro
Náměstí Míru 4, 6, 11, 16, 22, 34 tram.* **Rooms** 19.
Rates 1,200-1,700 Kč single; 1,600-2,400 Kč double;
1,900-2,600 Kč triple; 2,100-2,800 Kč quad.
Credit AmEx, DC, MC, V. **Map** p309 M9.
In quiet Vinohrady, the Pension City has upgraded
itself to Hotel City. Still borderline, the hotel is good
value for the no-frills traveller. Reasonably central.
Hotel services *Fax. Safe.* **Room services** *TV:
satellite.*

Hotel Olšanka

*Táboritská 23, Žižkov, Prague 3 (6709 2202/
fax 2271 3315/www.olsanka.cz). Metro Flora/5, 9, 26
tram.* **Rooms** 200. **Rates** 1,600-2,300 Kč single; 2,200-
2,700 Kč double; 2,900-3,400 Kč triple; 3,500 Kč suite;
half-price for children aged 3-12; 250 Kč pets. **Credit**
AmEx, MC, V. **Map** p311 D2.
Within walking distance of the great hardcore pubs,
and clubs of Žižkov, the Olšanka is no beauty. But
it's modern, clean and affordable, with a sports centre, tennis court and pool.
Hotel services *Bar. Beauty salon. Gym. Massage.
Parking. Restaurant. Safe. Swimming pool (indoor).
Tennis court (indoor).* **Room services** *TV: satellite.*

Julian

*Elišky Peškové 11, Smíchov, Prague 5 (5731 1144/
fax 5731 1149/www.julian.cz). Tram 6, 9, 12.*
Rooms 31. **Rates** 2,120-2,980 Kč single; 2,480-3,280
Kč double; 700-900 Kč extra bed. **Credit** AmEx, DC,
MC, V. **Map** p306 H1.
On the edge of Smíchov, the Julian is slightly off the
beaten path, yet just ten minutes' walk or a quick
tram ride from Malá Strana. The fireside reading
room and reception area is the Julian's jewel. The
fourth floor is air-conditioned and all apartments
have kitchenettes. Pets welcome.
Hotel services *Bar. Disabled: access. Fax. Gym
(small). Laundry. Parking.* **Room services** *Safe.*

Pension Chaloupka

*Nad hradním vodojemem 83, Střešovice, Prague 6
(2051 1761/ www.web.telecom.cz/pensionchaloupka).
Metro Hradčanská/1, 2, 18 tram.* **Rooms** 8.
Rates 800 Kč single; 1,350 Kč double; 1,800 Kč triple;
2,200-2,500 Kč apartment. **No credit cards.**
A basic Czech pension, so only a half-step up from
dormitory life, but a good bargain 15 minutes' walk
from the Castle and on a night tram line.
Hotel services *Bar. Parking.*

Hotel Tříska

*Vinohradská 105, Žižkov, Prague 3 (627 5457/
fax 627 0662/www.link.cz/turist/triska). Metro Jiřího z
Poděbrad/11 tram.* **Rooms** 51. **Rates** 1,800 Kč single;
2,200 Kč double; 3,000 Kč triple; 3,800 Kč quadruple.
No credit cards. **Map** p311 C3.
A friendly hotel with bright and clean rooms in a
funky old building in the centre of Vinohrady. The
spare, all-white rooms – the best of which face away
from the noisy street – have high ceilings that tend
to dwarf the woodwork furnishings.

Hotel services *Parking. Restaurant.* **Room
services** *TV: satellite. Telephone.*

Pension Větrník

*U Větrníku 40, Břevnov, Prague 6 (2061 2404/
fax 3536 1406/milos.opatrny@telecom.cz). Metro
Hradčanská, then tram 1, 18.* **Rooms** 6 (all en suite).
Rates 2,000 Kč double; 3,000 Kč apartment; 500 Kč
extra bed. **Credit** MC.
Away from the centre but definitely a spot for those
who favour comfort over location. The six rooms in
this restored 18th-century windmill overlook a
large secluded garden with high walls, blocking the
less pleasant views beyond. Charming owners and
a private tennis court are further enticements.
Hotel services *Fax. Laundry. Garden. Parking.
Restaurant. Safe.* **Room services** *TV: satellite.*

Pension Vyšehrad

*Krokova 6, Vyšehrad, Prague 2, (4140 8455). Metro
Vyšehrad/8, 24 tram.* **Rooms** 4 (all en suite).
Rates 900 Kč single; 1,300 Kč double; 1,800 Kč triple.
No credit cards.
This beautiful and tranquil family home on a hill-
side with a wonderful garden and view has been a
pension for ten years. The family cat has the run of
the house and guests' pets are welcome.
Hotel services *Garden. Parking.*

Hostels

The Clown & Bard

*Bořivojova 102, Žižkov, Prague 3 (2271 6453). Metro
Jiřího z Poděbrad/5, 9, 11, 26 tram.* **Beds** 90.
Rates 250 Kč single in 35-bed room; 450Kč per person
double room; 350-400 Kč per person 4-6 person
apartments (with kitchen and private bath).
No credit cards. **Map** p311 B2.
This hostel and coffee bar is a great place for backpackers and locals alike, surrounded by numerous
pubs and restaurants in arty, working-class
Žižkov. The ground-floor pub features live music
several nights a week and attracts an eclectic mixture of guests, expats and hip Czechs (*see p161*). No
lockout and no reservations. Breakfast available.
Hotel services *Bar. Fax. Laundry.*

Hostel Boathouse

*Lodnická 1, Modřany, Prague 4 (tel/fax 402 1076/
boathouse@volny.cz). Tram 3, 17, 54.* **Beds** 56.
Open 24 hours daily. **Rates** 270-350 Kč per person.
No credit cards.
Seasonal regulars engage in first-name banter with
the friendly staff at this hostel set amid Vltava
riverbank meadows. It's a good 20-minute tram ride
south of Old Town but lines run 24 hours from the
Černý kůň stop 10 minutes' walk away. Boats are
available for rent, as are bikes when available and
there's even a driving range. Booking at least a
week ahead is recommended in summer, but they'll
try to find a place for anyone who turns up. A basic
breakfast and dinner are served (50 Kč and 70 Kč,
respectively).
Hotel services *Internet. Laundry. Parking.*

Sightseeing

Feature boxes

Introduction

More sights than a snipers' convention – and all of them just a stroll away.

The centre of Prague has more palaces, museums, cellar pubs and forgotten alleys than you could ever properly explore in a lifetime, but the whole area is walkable and can be covered fairly well in a weekend.

A bend of the Vltava arcs through the heart of the city, gracing it with nine dramatic bridges, all scaled perfectly for a stroll from one side of Prague to the other. The river eventually runs north to the Baltic after curling around Letná, the high country on the left bank that first provided a strategic vantage to Stone Age peoples. The neighbouring hill of **Hradčany** (*see page 69*) gave the first Czech princes, the Přemyslids, their castle foundations, which still exist today under the Prague Castle complex.

Below Hradčany, the **Malá Strana** district (*see page 81*) is a delightfully jumbled mix of its former histories as a craftsman's quarter, a prize granted to nobles supporting the crown, and a hotbed of poets bristling against foreign domination in coffeehouse cabals. Cottages, fabulous palaces and smoky cafés line up side by side on its narrow, twisting streets.

On the right bank, the river is also responsible for the unique underworld of flat **Staré Město**, the Old Town (*see page 90*), with its subterranean drinking holes, cinemas, music halls and galleries. These countless vaulted, stone-walled spaces were once at street level but constant medieval flooding of the Vltava prompted city fathers to raise the streets one storey to the level at which they lie today.

The city's layers are a good part of the reason people come here for a week and end up staying for years; no matter how deep you dig, you're constantly making new discoveries. Prague is, too, as it excavates itself from the more modern burial of Soviet fraternal protection.

Even a decade after the fall of communism, the buzz saws can still be heard and the scaffoldings are still being removed to reveal the new façades required for their new capitalist occupants: a French bank, a Czech real estate office or a designer dress shop. Half a dozen new courtyards have been opened and filled with curious little businesses in Old Town since the last edition of this guide and more are clearly on the way.

Surrounding Old Town to the south and east is **Nové Město**, the New Town (*see page 100*), the first area of the city to be laid out with broad modern streets, thoughtfully planned by Charles

IV in 1348. This is where the city's business gets done, as it has been for centuries. Much of it is of little interest to the visitor, but Wenceslas Square is very much the heart of modern Prague and the area south of the National Theatre is beginning to bloom as a fashionable gastronomic quarter.

To the east of the city centre lies the rough and tumble district of **Žižkov** (*see page 111*). This area of crumbling tenements proudly boasts the highest number of pubs per capita in the world – an obvious draw for the boho expats who are doing their best to make this traditionally working-class district their own.

WALK THE WALK

For a city whose fortunes have changed as often as the power balance of Central Europe, Prague is remarkably intact. Everything from Socialist Realist monstrosities to the relics of Prague's first tenth-century rotundas surround you, and most of these cost nothing to see.

But for visitors who'd like to immerse themselves in the stories of these places, the madcap folks at **Prague Walks** host eight daily walking tours of the old centre of town that depart (assuming decent weather) from the **Astronomical Clock** on Old Town Square.

These tours are: Prague Introduction at 10.30am and 12.30pm; Musical Prague at 11am; Castles and Cathedrals at 11am and 2pm; Jewish Quarter 1pm and 2.30pm; Architecture at 2pm; Mysterious Prague at 4pm; Franz Kafka's Prague at 4pm; and A Dramatic Century at noon. They have no office; just show up ten minutes before and look for the person holding up the Prague Walks poster. The tours cost between 100 Kč and 200 Kč

More conventional guided tours are also available through the following:

Pragotur

Old Town Hall, Staroměstské náměstí, Prague 1 (2448 2562/fax 2448 2380/www.prague-info.cz). Metro Staroměstská/17, 18 tram. **Open** 9am-6.30pm Mon-Fri; 9am-3.30pm Sat, Sun. **Rates** 2,684 Kč for 2-4 people; 3,928 Kč for up to 10. **No credit cards.** **Map** p306 H3.
Four-hour walking tours of the Old Town and Prague Castle led by informative, if conventional guides. Fax them to book ahead or arrange tours in person at their office, which can be found at the rear of the Prague Information Service bureau (*see p288*) in Old Town Hall.

Hradčany

Quiet, contemplative streets surround Prague's principal icon.

Maps p304 & p305

No single feature of Prague resonates with as much national identity as **Prague Castle,** centrepiece of the **Hradčany** district. That the Castle has been occupied by foreign powers for most of its 1,000-year history only increases its symbolic importance to Czechs now that it's been returned its creators. The castle gates have been literally thrown open since the Velvet Revolution and now invite midnight strolls and early-morning promenading.

The rest of **Hradčany** comprises the surrounding streets, which stretch north and west from the Castle across the hilltop. It's quiet, enchanting and less heavily touristed than the Castle itself. The Castle grounds demand lengthy strolling but there are a fair number of options for refuelling up here and a handful of terrace restaurants visible below. Otherwise, there are rich pickings down the hill in Malá Strana.

Prague Castle

Founded some time around 870 by Přemysl princes, the impressive, if somewhat sombre collection of buildings that make up the Castle – including a palace, three churches and a monastery – has been variuosly extended, torn down and rebuilt over the centuries. The final touches, including the present shape of St. Vitus's Cathedral, were not added until the early 20th century, thus the Castle resembles a vast museum of architectural styles stretching all the way back to the Romanesque.

The grandiose façade enclosing the complex is the result of the **Empress Maria Theresa**'s desire to bring some coherence to the jumble of mismatched parts that the Castle had become by the mid-18th century. But the result of **Nicolo Pacassi**'s monotonous design is uninspiring – 'an imposing mass of building in the factory style

Prague Castle – positively resonating with national identity.

of architecture', as one 19th-century commentator put it. After Maria Theresa's son, **Joseph II**, attempted to turn the Castle into a barracks, it was largely deserted by the Habsburgs. Václav Havel chose not to live here, although his presidential office was installed in the Castle. He did his best to enliven the palace, opening it to the public and hiring the costume designer from the film *Amadeus* to remodel the guards' uniforms. *See page 70* **Designer history**.

You really can't get away without spending at least half a day up here. Unfortunately, every visitor to Prague knows this. The result is a notable lack of any real city life, and an awful lot of chattering tour groups and whirring video cameras. To avoid the worst of the crush, come as early or as late in the day as you can.

The first & second courtyards

The grandest entrance to the Castle complex, through the Hradčanské náměstí gates, is now overseen from a discreet distance by an approving **Tomáš Garrigue Masaryk**, whose bronze likeness was added during the celebrations of Praha 2000. The gateway has been dominated since 1768 by Ignatz Platzer's monumental sculptures of battling Titans. They create an impressive, if not exactly welcoming,

entrance. The changing of the guard takes place in this courtyard, a Havel-inspired attempt to add some ceremonial pzazz to the Castle. Though the change is carried out hourly every day between 5am and 10pm, the big crowd-pulling ceremony, complete with band, takes place at noon (*see page 70* **Designer history**). The two tapering flagpoles are the work of Slovene architect **Josip Plečnik**, who was brought in by President Masaryk during the 1920s to create a more uniform look for the seat of the First Republic.

To reach the second courtyard go through the Matthias Gate (Matyášova brána), a baroque portal dating from 1614, topped by a German Imperial Eagle that pleased Hitler when he came to stay in 1939. The monumental stairway on the left leads up to the magnificent gold and white **Spanish Hall** (Španělský sál; open to the public only during occasional concerts), built in the 17th century for court ceremonies. The decor was redone in the 19th century when the trompe l'oeil murals were covered with white stucco, and huge mirrors and gilded chandeliers were brought in to transform the space into a suitably glitzy venue for the coronation of Emperor Franz Joseph I.

Franz Joseph, however, failed to show up and it was not until the 1950s that the hall was given a new use – it was here the Politburo came to discuss

Designer history

The noon changing of the guard at Prague Castle is a stirring sight with the semblance of an age-old ritual. And that's just what the 1990 administration ordered: the semblance. For the ceremony is a piece of confected theatre produced by master dramatist Václav Havel.

Havel once remarked that he did not believe democracy could be founded in a nation with 'grubby-looking troops'. With that in mind, he commisioned Theodor Pištěk, the Academy Award-winning costume designer for Miloš Forman's films *Amadeus* and *Valmont*, to design new outfits for the guards. Out went the ill-fitting, Soviet-style green uniforms and in their place appeared stately navy-blue tunics and tri-colour shoulder braiding, adorned with epaulets, collars and belt buckles emblazoned with insignia of Czech legionnaires from World War I. New caps were conceived with the help of a US Naval attaché who happened to be in town (creating an impression that will be oddly familiar to anyone who's ever lived near an American naval base).

Duty assignments were changed from keeping Castle visitors at bay to standing

benignly at attention before the entry gates, looking picturesque for tourist cameras, and putting up with the taunts of children trying to make them laugh. The newly outfitted troops were an unqualified success.

But there was still something missing. Enter Michal Prokop, Czech pop star extraordinaire, formerly of the Prague 1960s sensation Framus Five. A convincing fanfare for an elaborate changing of the guard ceremony was composed without much difficulty, but where to put the brass band? The first courtyard is awfully small, even without a crowd of onlookers. So the musicians play their sousaphones and trumpets out of a Castle window, standing on tables for acoustical reasons. And for the choreography, the head of the Castle Guard took a video camera to Buckingham Palace to record suitably ceremonial-looking steps.

Designer history? Perhaps, but then there's little in the historical record for Czechs to work with. A history of Bohemia and Moravia didn't even exist in Czech until the cultural revival of the 19th century. If the Castle Guard is guilty the success of their latest five-year plan, protected from assassins by a reinforced steel door. Behind the austere grey walls of the second courtyard lies a warren of opulent state rooms whose heyday dates from the time of **Rudolf II**. The state rooms of the second courtyard, which are rarely open to the public, housed Rudolf's magnificent art collection and such curiosities as a unicorn's horn and three nails from Noah's ark. The bulk of the collection was carried off in 1648 by Swedish soldiers, although the remnants are housed in the **Prague Castle Picture Gallery** (*see page 117*) on the north side of the courtyard by the **Powder Bridge** (U Prašného mostu) entrance. In the middle of the courtyard is a 17th-century baroque fountain, and the **Chapel of the Holy Rood**, rebuilt in neo-baroque style in the late 19th century.

Prague Castle

Pražský hrad

Hradčanské náměstí, Prague 1 (information in English and Czech 2437 3368/www.hrad.cz). Metro Malostranská/12, 22, 23 tram. **Open** *May-Oct* 9am-5pm daily. *Nov-Mar* 9am-4pm daily. **Admission** 120 Kč adults; 60 Kč children, students; 300 Kč guided tours for up to five people. Tickets are valid for three days. **No credit cards. Map** p304 C2.

There's no charge to enter the grounds of the Castle, but you'll need a ticket to see the main attractions. An audio guide (available in English) costs extra

and is available from the information centre in the third courtyard. One ticket covers entrance to the **Old Royal Palace**, the **Basilica of St George**, the **Powder Tower** and the choir, crypt and tower of **St Vitus's Cathedral**. Entrance to the art collection of **St George's Convent** (*see p116*) and the **Toy Museum** (*see p123*) costs extra.

It's a stiff walk up to the Castle from Malá Strana and Malostranská metro station. The least strenuous approach is to take the 22 tram, which snakes around the back of the hill, and get off at the Pražský hrad stop. There are several cafés within the Castle complex.

St Vitus's Cathedral

The third courtyard – the oldest and most important site in the Castle – is entirely dominated by the looming towers, pinnacles and buttresses of **St Vitus's Cathedral** (Katedrála sv. Vita). Although it was only completed in 1929, exactly 1,000 years after the murdered St Wenceslas was laid to rest on the site, the cathedral is undoubtedly the spiritual centre of Bohemia. This has always been a sacred place: in pagan times Svatovit, the Slavic god of fertility, was worshipped on this site, a clue perhaps to why the cathedral was dedicated to his near namesake St Vitus (*svatý Vít* in Czech) – a Sicilian

Guards! Stand to attention, look picturesque, and whatever happens, don't giggle.

of theatre, they surely aren't any more so than the architects who knocked down medieval chapels to put a neo-Gothic front on to the unfinished St Vitus's Cathedral a century ago.

And sentry parades are surely more innocent than the *Rukopis královédvorský*, an historical account of ancient Czech victories 'discovered'

by Václav Hanka in 1817, later pronounced a complete fraud by President Masaryk.

Besides, if the first non-violent revolution in the history of these lands isn't worthy of a little ceremony and spectacle, then what is? Now if the director could just get the guards to stop smirking on duty....

Sightseeing

Prague Castle

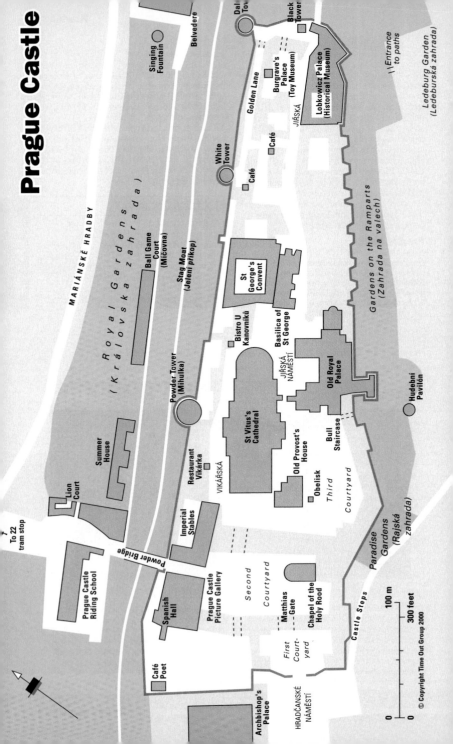

Café Poet

Archbishop's Palace

HRADČANSKÉ NÁMĚSTÍ

To 22 tram stop

Prague Castle Riding School

Spanish Hall

Prague Castle Picture Gallery

Imperial Stables

Powder Bridge

Matthias Gate

First Court-yard

Second Courtyard

Chapel of the Holy Rood

Lion Court

Summer House

Restaurant Vikárka

VIKÁŘSKÁ

Old Provost's House

Obelisk

Third Courtyard

St Vitus's Cathedral

Powder Tower (Mihulka)

Bistro U Kanovníků

Basilica of St George

JIŘSKÁ NÁMĚSTÍ

Bull Staircase

Old Royal Palace

Hudební Pavilón

St George's Convent

Paradise Gardens (Rajská zahrada)

Castle Steps

Gardens on the Ramparts (Zahrada na valech)

White Tower

Café

Café

JIŘSKÁ

Golden Lane

Burgrave's Palace (Toy Museum)

Lobkowicz Palace (Historical Museum)

Dal... Tower

Black Tower

Entrance to paths

Ledeburg Garden (Ledeburská zahrada)

MARIÁNSKÉ HRADBY

R o y a l   G a r d e n s   (K r á l o v s k á   z a h r a d a)

Ball Game Court (Míčovna)

Stag Moat (Jelení příkop)

Singing Fountain

Belvedere

0   100 m

0   300 feet

© Copyright Time Out Group 2000

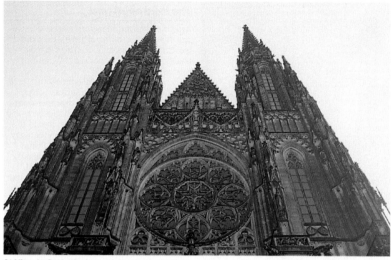

St Vitus's Cathedral – no spires loom higher.

peasant who became a Roman legionnaire before he was thrown to the lions. Right up until the 18th century young women and anxious farmers would bring offerings of wine, cakes and cocks. The cathedral's Gothic structure owes its creation to Charles IV's lifelong love affair with Prague. In 1344 he managed to secure an archbishopric for the city, and work began on the construction of a cathedral under the instructions of French architect Matthew of Arras. Inconveniently, Matthew dropped dead eight years into the project, so the Swabian Peter Parler was called in to take up the challenge. He was responsible for the 'Sondergotik' or German Late Gothic design. It remained unfinished until late 19th-century nationalists completed the work according to Parler's original plans. The skill with which the later work was carried out makes it is difficult to tell where the Gothic ends and the neo-Gothic begins, but a close look at the nave and the twin towers and rose window of the West end will reveal the tell-tale lighter-coloured stone from the 1920s.

From outside, as from anywhere in the town below, the **Great Tower** is easily the most dominant feature. The Gothic and Renaissance structure is topped with a baroque dome. This houses **Sigismund**, unquestionably the largest bell in Bohemia, weighing in at a hefty 15,120kg (33,333lbs). Getting Sigismund into the tower was no mean feat: according to legend it took a rope woven from the hair of the city's noblest virgins to haul it into position. Below the tower is the **Gothic Golden Portal** (Zlatá brána),

decorated with a mosaic of multicoloured Venetian glass depicting the Last Judgement. A Getty-funded project to restore it was a mere three years behind schedule at the time of going to press, but it is assuredly regaining its lustre. On either side of the arch are sculptures of Charles IV and his wife Elizabeth of Pomerania, whose talents allegedly included being able to bend a sword with her bare hands.

Inside, the enormous nave is flooded with multi-coloured light from the gallery of stained glass windows created at the beginning of this century. All 21 of them, during a period of nationalist fervour, were sponsored by financial institutions including (third on the right) an insurance company whose motto – 'those who sow in sorrow shall reap in joy' – is incorporated into the biblical allegory. The most famous is the third window on the left, in the Archbishop's Chapel, created by Alfons Mucha. It depicts the Christian Slavonic tribes; appropriately enough, it was paid for by Banka Slavia.

On the right is the **Chapel of St Wenceslas** (Svatováclavská kaple), on the site of the original tenth-century rotunda where 'Good King' Wenceslas was buried. Built in 1345, the chapel has 1,345 polished amethysts, agates and jaspers incorporated into its design, and contains some of the saint's personal paraphenalia, including armour, chain shirt and helmet. Unfortunately, it is closed to the public – too many sweaty bodies were causing the gilded plaster to disintegrate – but a glint of its treasure trove glory can be glimpsed over the railings.

Sightseeing

Golden Gothic mosaic at St Vitus's. *See p73.*

Occasionally, on state anniversaries, the skull of the saint is put on display, covered with a cobweb-fine veil. A door in the corner leads to the chamber that contains the **crown jewels**. A papal bull of 1346 officially protects the jewels, while popular legend unofficially prescribes death to anyone who uses them improperly. Reichsprotektor Reinhard Heydrich was the last person to test the legend, and was assassinated within a year of placing a crown upon his head. The door to the chamber is locked with seven keys held by seven people, after the seven seals of Revelations.

The most extraordinary baroque addition to the cathedral was the silver tombstone of **St John of Nepomuk**, the priest who was flung from Charles Bridge in 1393 as a result of King Wenceslas IV's anti-clericalsim. The tomb, designed by Fischer von Erlach the Younger in 1733-6, is a flamboyant affair. Two tons of silver were used for the pedestal, statue of the saint and fluttering cherubs holding up a red velvet canopy. The phrase 'baroque excess' scarcely does it justice. Close by is the entrance to the crypt. Below lie the remains of various Czech monarchs, including George of Poděbrady and Rudolf II. The most eyecatching tomb is Charles IV's modern, streamlined metal affair designed by Kamil Roškot (1934-5).

The third courtyard

After the cathedral, the second most noticeable monument in the third courtyard is the somewhat incongruous 17-metre (50-feet) high granite obelisk, a memorial to the dead of World War I erected by Plečnik in 1928.

Close to the Golden Portal is the entrance to the **Old Royal Palace** (Starý královský palác), which contains three levels of royal apartments. Six centuries of kings called the palace home and systematically built new parts over the old. In what is now the basement you can see the dingy 12th-century Romanesque remains of Prince Soběslav's residence. The top floor contains the highlight of the palace, the **Vladislav Hall**. Designed by Benedict Ried at the turn of the 16th century, its exquisitely vaulted ceiling was the last flowering of the Gothic, while the large, square windows are the first expressions of the Renaissance in Bohemia. It is here that the National Assembly elects its new president. The specially designed **Rider's Steps** allowed knights to enter the hall without dismounting. Higher up again (in the Louis Wing) is the **Bohemian Chancellery** and the window through which the victims of the defenestration of 1618 were ejected.

At the eastern end of the cathedral is Jiřské náměsti, named after **St George's Basilica** (Bazilika sv. Jiří). Stand far enough back from the Basilica's crumbling red and cream baroque façade to get a good look at the two Romanesque towers jutting out behind. The Italian craftsmen who constructed them in 1142 built a fatter male tower (Adam, on the left) standing guard over a more slender female one (Eve, on the right). The Basilica, founded by Prince Vratislav in 921, has burned down and been rebuilt over the centuries. Its first major remodelling took place 50 years after it was first erected when a Benedictine convent was founded next door. A major renovation in the early 20th century swept out most of the baroque elements and led to the uncovering of the original arcades, remnants of 13th-century frescoes and the bodies of a saint (Ludmila, who was strangled by assassins hired by Prince Wenceslas's mother Drahomira) and a saint-maker (the notorious Boleslav the Cruel, who martyred his brother Wenceslas by having him stabbed to death). The Basilica's rediscovered simplicity and clean lines seem far closer to godliness than the mammon-fuelled baroque pomposity of most Prague churches.

On the left of the main entrance is an opening built to give access for the Benedictine nuns from **St George's Convent** next door (now housing part of the **National Gallery**'s vast collections; *see page 116*) and to keep to a minimum their contact with the outside world.

St Vitus's – don't
defenestrate here.
See p73.

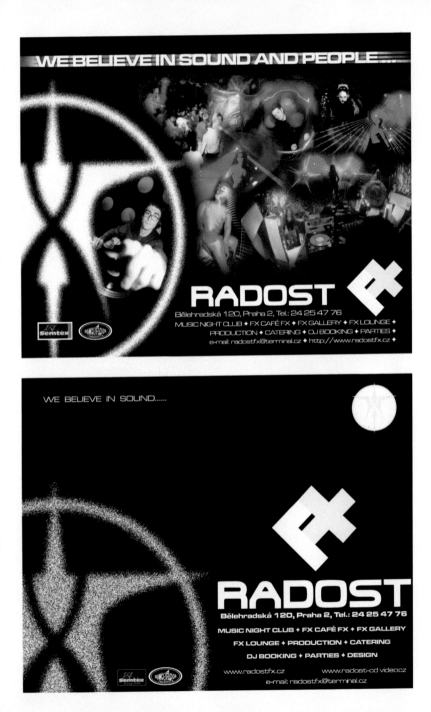

Vikářská lane, on the north side of the cathedral, is where Picasso and Eluard came to drink in the Vikářská tavern. It gives access to the 15th-century Mihulka or **Powder Tower** (Prašná věž). Here Rudolf II employed his many alchemists, who were engaged in attempts to distill the Elixir of Life and transmute base metals into gold. The tower now houses an exhibit about alchemy, bell- and cannon-forging and Renaissance life in the Castle.

Elsewhere on the Castle grounds

Going down the hill from St George's, signposts direct you to the most visited street in Prague, **Golden Lane** (Zlatá ulička). The tiny multi-coloured cottages that cling to the castle's northern walls were thrown up by the poor in the 16th century out of whatever waste materials they could find. Some allege that the name is a reference to the alchemists of King Rudolf's time, who supposedly were quartered here. Others contend that it alludes to a time when soldiers billeted in a nearby tower used the lane as a public urinal. In fact, the name probably dates from the 17th century, when the city's goldsmiths worked here. Houses used to line both sides of the street, with barely enough space to pass between them, until a hygiene-conscious Joseph II had some of them demolished in the 18th century. Although the houses look separate, a corridor runs the length of their attics and used to be occupied by the sharpshooters of the Castle Guard. The house at No.22 was owned by Kafka's sister Otla, and he stayed here for a while in 1917, reputedly drawing the inspiration for his novel, *The Castle*. If he rewrote it today, he'd call it *The Souvenir Shop*. Atmospheric at night, by day the lane is a traffic jam of shuffling tourists.

At the eastern end some steps take you under the last house and out to the **Dalibor Tower** (Daliborka), named after its most famous inmate, who amused himself by playing the violin while awaiting execution. According to legend (and Smetana's opera *Dalibor*), he attracted crowds of onlookers who turned up at his execution to weep en masse. Continuing down the hill takes you past another **Lobkowicz palace** (Lobkovický palác), one of several in the town. This one, finished in 1658, houses the **Historical Museum** (*see page 118*). Opposite is Burgrave House, now home of the **Toy Museum** (*see page 123*). The statue of a naked boy in the courtyard fell victim to Marxist-Leninist ideology when President Novotný decided that his genitals were not an edifying sight for the masses and ordered them to be removed. Happily the boy and his equipment have since been reunited.

The lane passes under the **Black Tower** (Černá věž) and ends at the **Old Castle Steps** (Staré zámecké schody), which lead to Malá Strana. Before descending, pause at the top for a view over the red tiled roofs, spires and domes of the 'Little Quarter'. An even better view can be had from the **Paradise Gardens** (*see page 86* **Unseen green**) on the ramparts below the Castle walls (enter from the Bull Staircase, or from outside the Castle, to the right of the first courtyard). This is where the victims of the second and most famous defenestration fell to earth. They were fortunate that it was a favoured spot for emptying chamber pots, as the dung heap surely saved the lives of the defenestrated Catholic counsellors. The site is now marked by an obelisk, signifying ground consecrated by the victorious Habsburgs after putting down the upstart Czech Protestants.

The gardens laid out in 1562 were redesigned in the 1920s by Josip Plečnik. The spiralling **Bull Staircase** leading up to the Castle's third courtyard and the huge granite bowl are his work. Their restoration looks to be at long last complete, and it is now possible to make the descent to Malá Strana by the terraced slopes of the beautiful Renaissance **Ledebour Gardens** (*see page 86* **Unseen green**).

The Royal Garden & the Belvedere

Crossing over the **Powder Bridge** (U Prašného mostu) back by the Castle's second courtyard, you reach the **Royal Garden** (Královská zahrada), on the outer side of the **Stag Moat** (*see page 86* **Unseen green**). It was laid out for Emperor Ferdinand I in the 1530s and included a maze and a menagerie, but was devastated by Swedish soldiers in the 17th century.

At the eastern end of the gardens is the **Belvedere** (open *summer* 10am-6pm daily; *winter* 10am-5pm daily. *Dec-Feb* closed) saved from French fire in the 18th century by a canny head gardener's payment of 30 pineapples. The stunning Renaissance structure was built by Paola della Stella between 1538 and 1564 (though construction work was interrupted by a fire at the Castle in 1541). The strangely shaped green copper roof is supported by delicate arcades and Ionic columns. The Belvedere was the first royal structure in Prague dedicated to pleasure-seeking rather than power-mongering – it was commissioned by Ferdinand I as a gift for his wife Anne – a loveshack one remove away from the skulduggery of life in the Castle. But the long-suffering Anne never got to see 'the most beautiful piece of Renaissance architecture north of the Alps' (as the city's tourist brochures invariably call it). She drew her last breath after producing the 15th heir to the throne. The royal couple are immortalised in the reliefs adorning the façade. The Belvedere went on to become the site of all sorts of goings-on: mad King Rudolf installed his astronomers here and the communists bricked up the windows of the upper level to prevent assassins from getting too close to the president. People come here today to see occasional art shows (*see page 202*). In front of the palace is the so-called **Singing Fountain**, cast in bronze by Bohemian craftsmen in the 1560s. It used to hum as water splashed into its basin, but sings no longer since extensive reconstruction.

On the southern side of the garden overlooking the Stag Moat is another lovely Renaissance structure, completed by Bonifác Wohlmut in 1563 to house the king's **Ball Game Court** (Míčovna). The elaborate black and white sgraffito has to be renewed every 20 years. The last time this was done some decidedly anachronistic elements were added to the allegorical frieze depicting Science, the Virtues and the Elements: look carefully at the lovely ladies on the top of the building and you'll see that the woman seated next to Justice (tenth from the right) is holding a hammer and sickle. On the same side of the garden, closer to the entrance, is the mustard-coloured Dientzenhofer Summer House (Zahradní dům), the presidential residence between 1948 and 1989. During this period, large sections of the Castle were closed to the public and huge underground shelters were excavated to connect the president's residence with the rest of the complex. No sooner were the shelters completed than it was seen that the subterranean passages might help to conceal counter-revolutionary saboteurs, and so the exit shafts were blocked off with enormous concrete slabs.

Hradčany

Hradčany owes its grand scale and pristine condition to the devastating fire of 1541, which destroyed the medieval district, and the frenzied period of Counter-Reformation building following the Protestant defeat at the Battle of White Mountain in 1620. Little has changed here in the last two centuries.

The area's focal point is **Hradčanské náměstí**, one of the grandest squares in the city, lined with imposing palaces built by the Catholic aristocracy, anxious to be close to the Habsburg court. It was nonetheless cut off from the Castle and its neurotic inhabitants by a complicated system of moats and fortifications, which remained until Empress Maria Theresa had a grand spring clean in the mid-18th century. Along with the moat went the tiny Church of the Virgin Mary of Einsedel,

which used to stand next to the castle ramp. Lovely as this was said to have been, it's hard to believe that it was lovelier than the superb panorama of Malá Strana, the Strahov Gardens and Petřín Hill that the demolition opened up.

On the north side of the square, next to the Castle, is the domineering 16th-century **Archbishop's Palace** (Arcibiskupský palác), tarted up with a frothy rococo façade in 1763-4. Next door, slotted in between the palace and a row of former canons' houses, stands the **Sternberg Palace** (Šternberský palác), which houses part of the **National Gallery**'s collection of European art (*see page 116*). Opposite stands the heavily restored **Schwarzenberg Palace** (Schwarzenberský palác), one of the most imposing Renaissance buildings in Prague. It was built between 1545 and 1563, the outside exquisitely decorated with 'envelope' sgraffito. It now contains the **Military Museum** (*see page 120*) that will reopen in 2001 with its comprehensive collection of killing instruments – perhaps an appropriate exhibit for the country which gave the world the words 'pistol' and 'Semtex'.

Further up Loretánská is the pub **U Černého vola** (*see page 154*), a simple Renaissance building with a crumbling mural on the façade. As a result of some direct action in 1991, it's one of the few places left in Hradčany where the locals can afford to drink. The regulars foiled several attempts at privatisation by forming a co-operative to run it in conjunction with the Beer Party, now downgraded from a political party to a civic association. You don't have to feel guilty about the amount you drink here – all profits go to a nearby school for the blind.

The pub looks out on to **Loretánské náměstí**, a split-level square on the site of a pagan cemetery. Half of it is taken up by a car park for the Ministry of Foreign Affairs in the monolithic **Černín Palace** (Černínský palác) – an enormous and unprepossessing structure; its long and imposing grey façade, articulated by an unbroken line of 30 pillars, is telling. Commissioned in 1669 by Humprecht Johann Černín, the Imperial ambassador to Venice, the construction of the palace financially ruined his family. As a result, the first people to move in were hundreds of 17th-century squatters. Gestapo interrogations were later conducted here during the Nazi occupation. Its curse surfaced again in 1948, when Foreign Minister Jan Masaryk, the last major political obstacle to Klement Gottwald's communist coup, fell from an upstairs window a few days after the takeover and was found dead on the pavement below. No one really believed the official verdict of suicide but no evidence of who was responsible has ever come to light.

The Loreto – full-on baroque. *See p80.*

Somewhat dwarfed by the Černín Palace is the **Loreto** (*see below*), a baroque testimony to the Catholic miracle culture that swept the Czech lands after the Thirty Years' War. The façade (1721) is a swirling mass of stuccoed cherubs, topped with a bell tower. Every hour the 27 bells ring out the cacophonous melody 'We Greet You a Thousand Times'.

The streets behind the Loreto are some of the prettiest and quietest in Hradčany. The quarter was built in the 16th century for the Castle staff; its tiny cottages are now the most prized real estate in the city. Going down Kapucínská, you pass the **Domeček** or 'Little House' at No.10, once home to the notorious Fifth Department – the counter-intelligence unit of the Defence Ministry. At No.5 on nearby Černinská is **Gambra** (*see page 206*), a quirky gallery specialising in surrealist art. Its owner, the world-renowned animator Jan Švankmajer, lives in the attached house (*see page 198* **Intimate pleasures of inanimate objects**). At the foot of the hill is **Nový Svět** ('New World'), a street of brightly coloured cottages restored in the 18th and 19th centuries which is all that remains of Hradčany's medieval slums. Most of the rest were destroyed in the Great Fire of 1541. Tycho Brahe, the Danish alchemist known for his missing nose (which he lost in a duel) and spectacular death (his bladder exploded), lived at No.1, called 'The Golden Griffin'.

Back up from Loretánské náměstí is Hradčany's last major square: **Pohořelec**. The passage at No.8 leads to the peaceful surroundings of the **Strahov Monastery** (*see below*). The monastery contains a magnificent libraries and fine collection of religious art.

The Loreto

Loreta
Loretánské náměstí 7, Prague 1 (2051 6740). Tram 22. **Open** 9am-12.15pm, 1-4.30pm Tue-Sun. Closed Mon. **Admission** 80 Kč adults; 60 Kč children, students. **No credit cards. Map** p304 B3.
The Loreto is probably the most outlandish piece of baroque fantasy in Prague. Its attractions include a sculpture of the bearded St Wilgefortis, the skeletons of another two female saints, an ecclesiastical extravagance, and the highest concentration of cherubs to be found anywhere in the city. It was built as part of a calculated plan to reconvert the masses to Catholicism after the Thirty Years' War.

At its heart is a small chapel, the **Santa Casa**, whose history is so improbable that it quickly gained cult status. The story goes that the original Santa Casa was the home of Mary in Nazareth until it was miraculously flown over to Loreto in Italy by angels, spawning a copycat cult all over Europe (there are 50 in Bohemia alone). This one, from 1626-31, boasts two beams and a brick from the 'original', as well as a crevice left on the wall by a

divine thunderbolt that struck an unfortunate blasphemer. The red colour scheme makes it look less like a virgin's boudoir and more like somewhere to hold a black mass.

The shrine was a particular hit with wealthy ladies who donated the money for baroque maestri Christoph and Kilian Ignaz Dientzenhofer to construct the outer courtyards and the **Church of the Nativity** (1716-23) at the back. They also sponsored the carving of St Wilgefortis (in the corner chapel to the right of the main entrance), the patron saint of unhappily married women, who grew a beard as a radical tactic to get out of marrying a heathen, and that of St Agatha the Unfortunate, who can be seen carrying her severed breasts on a meat platter (in the Church of the Nativity). The famous **diamond monstrance**, designed in 1699 by Fischer von Erlach and sporting 6,222 stones, is in the treasury.

Strahov Monastery

Strahovský klášter
Strahovské nádvoří 1, Prague 1 (2051 7451). Tram 8, 22/143, 149, 217 bus. **Open** 9am-12.30pm, 1-5pm Tue-Sun. Closed Mon. **Admission** 50 Kč adults; 30 Kč children. **No credit cards. Map** p304 A4.
The Premonstratensian monks set up house here in 1140, and embarked upon their austere programme of celibacy and silent contemplation. The complex still has an air of seclusion, a fragrant orchard stretching down the hill to Malá Strana and, since 1990, several cowled monks who've returned to reclaim the buildings nationalised by the communists in 1948. Their services are once again held in the Church of Our Lady, which retained its 12th-century basilica ground plan, after remodelling in the early 17th century.

The highlights of the complex are the superb libraries. Within the frescoed Theological and Philosophical Halls are 130,000 volumes (there are a further 700,000 in storage) forming the most important collection in Bohemia. Visitors can not, alas, stroll around the libraries, but are allowed to gawp through the doors. The comprehensive acquisition of books didn't begin until the late 16th century. When Joseph II effected a clamp-down on religious institutions in 1782, the Premonstratensians managed to outwit him by masquerading as an educational foundation, and their collection was swelled by the libraries of less shrewd monasteries. Indeed, the monks' taste in reading matter ranged far beyond the standard ecclesiastical tracts, including such highlights as the oldest extant copy of *The Calendar of Minutae or Selected Times for Bloodletting*. Nor did they merely confine themselves to books: the 200-year-old curiosity cabinets house a collection of deep-sea monsters that any landlocked country would be proud to possess.

In another part of the complex, the **Strahov Gallery** exhibits a small part of the monastery's considerable collection of religious art.

Malá Strana

Palaces and embassies, gardens and jazz bars, cathedrals and cottages –
Prague's 'Little Quarter' is large on attractions.

Map p305

Malá Strana, the traditional craftsman's quarter
hunkered down in the shadow of the Castle it
serves, is the more organic of Prague's two sides. Its
cathedrals, embassies, cafés and parks are strewn
around rising and falling land, forming irregular
vistas: jumbled rooftops, former royal orchards
and Old Town across the Vltava. The name Malá
Strana ('Little Quarter' or 'Lesser Town') is an
accurate reflection of its area but hardly of its
contents. Its streets are full of decorous details that
make it the setting for period film shoots – even the
lamp-posts sprout ornamental flourishes.

It was founded by the Přemyslid Otakar II in
1287, when he invited merchants from Germany
to set up shop on the land beneath the castle walls.
Very little remains of this Gothic town – the
present-day appearance of the quarter dates from
the 17th century. The area was transformed into a
sparkling baroque district by the wealthy Catholic
aristocracy, who won huge parcels of land in the
property redistribution that followed the Thirty
Years' War. When the fashionable followed the
court to Vienna in the 17th century, the poor
took back the area. It has been the home of poets,
drunks and mystics ever since, living cheek-by-
jowl with the ambassadors and diplomats who

also inhabit what is one of Prague's two diplomatic
quarters – the British, American, Irish, German,
Italian and French embassies, among many
others, are situated in Malá Strana.

Today, the character here is changing rapidly,
as accountancy firms, bankers and wine bars set
up shop. It's still remarkable, though, just how
few businesses there are in what is one of the
most central Prague districts. Malostranské
náměstí now throbs with life deep into the night,
but this is mostly down to the tourist trade, plus
its many bars, restaurants and music venues.
Apart from stores selling souvenirs and cut glass,
there is very little shopping in the area.

Malostranské náměstí & around

The main drag between Charles Bridge and
Malostranské náměstí is **Mostecká**. It's a
continuation of the Royal Route – the path taken
by the Bohemian kings to their coronation – and
is lined with elegant baroque dwellings. At
No.15 is the **Kaunitz Palace** (Kaunicův palác),
built in 1773 for Jan Adam Kaunitz, an advisor
to Empress Maria Theresa, who sycophantically
had the exterior painted her favourite colours –

Tourists come and tourists go but **Malá Strana** dawdles on.

Darkness and noon: **Malá Strana**'s narrow, winding backstreets.

yellow and white. It's now the embassy of the former Yugoslavia. Just off Mostecká are the **Blue Light** jazz pub (*see page 154*) and **U Patrona** restaurant (*see page 129*), both pricey establishments but oases of quality in a stretch too dominated by naff souvenir shops.

At the heart of the quarter is **Malostranské náměstí**, a lively square edged by large baroque palaces and Renaissance gabled townhouses perched on top of Gothic arcades. Here you'll find the 100-year-old **Malostranská kavárna** (*see page 148*), which, when it reopened a few years back, added a much-needed boost to Prague's once-vibrant café culture. Bang in the middle, dividing the square in two, is the **Church of St Nicholas** (*see page 85*), a monumental late baroque affair, whose dome and adjoining bell tower dominate the skyline of Prague's left bank. Built between 1703 and 1755, it's the largest and most ornate of the city's Jesuit-founded churches. During its construction, the Society of Jesus waged a battle against local residents loath to let go of the two streets, two churches and various other structures that had to be demolished to make room for the church.

The grim block next door at No.25 is another Jesuit construction, built as a college for their priests and now housing harassed-looking maths students. More appealing is the **Lichtenstein Palace** (Lichtenštejnský palác; *see page 222*) opposite, finished in 1791. The Lichtensteins used to be major landowners in Bohemia and the alpine principality has been waging a battle to regain the palace, which was confiscated in 1918. They have been unsuccessful so far, and the palace is currently used as a venue for classical

concerts. Also in the square, located in the former town hall at No.21, is the club **Malostranská beseda** (*see page 212*), home to music of a more raucous bent. Opposite the south side of St Nicholas is a parade of pubs and restaurants. The American backpacker hangout **Jo's Bar** (*see page 155*), its downstairs club, **Jo's Garáž** (*see page 227*) and the seafood restaurant **Circle Line** (*see page 143*) are all on this stretch. The tables outside this last, in the south-west corner of the square, are a grand spot for summer dining.

Nerudova heads up from the north-west corner of the square towards the Castle, and is a fine place to begin deciphering the ornate signs that decorate many Prague houses: there's the Three Fiddles at No.12, for example, or the Devil at No.4. This practice of distinguishing houses continued up until 1770, when that relentless modernist Joseph II spoiled all the fun by introducing numbered addresses.

The street, which is crowded with cafés, restaurants and shops aimed at the ceaseless flow of tourists to and from the Castle, is named after its famous son, 19th-century novelist **Jan Neruda**. He lived at No.47, the Two Suns (U dvou slunců). The house was turned into a pub and during the communist period was a favourite hang-out of the Plastic People of the Universe, the underground rock band who were later instrumental in the founding of Charter 77. The place is now a joyless tourist trap. Also to be ignored is the turquoise drinking establishment at No.13 where Václav Havel, in an uncharacteristic lapse of taste, took Yeltsin for a mug of beer. A better bet is **U Kocoura** at No.2. It's owned by the Friends of Beer, formerly a political party, now a civic association. Although their manifesto is a bit vague, their ability to pull a good, cheap pint is beyond question. The more recent **Bazaar Mediterranée** (*see page 139*) at No.40 offers enviable terrace views for lunch and ridiculous striptease and dragshow entertainments with dinner.

The alley next door leads up to the British Embassy at Thunovská 14, which a diplomatic wag christened 'Czechers'. Leading up from here are the **New Castle Steps** (Nové zámecké schody), one of the most peaceful (and least strenuous) routes up to the Castle, and a star location in the film *Amadeus*.

There are more embassies back on Nerudova, the Italians occupying the Thun-Hohenstein Palace (Thun-Hohenštejnský palác) at No.20, built by Giovanni Santini-Aichel in 1726 and distinguished by the contorted eagles holding up the portal, the heraldic emblem of the Kolowrats for whom the palace was built. The Italians were trumped for a while by the Romanians, however, who used to inhabit the even more glorious **Morzin Palace** (Morzinský palác) opposite at No.5. Also the work of Santini-Aichel (1714), the façade sports two hefty Moors, a pun on the family's name, who hold up the window ledge. Their toes have been rubbed shiny by passers-by who believe that touching them will bring luck.

Walking back down Nerudova, if you continue straight down the tram tracks in instead of veering off on to Malostranské náměstí, you'll see on your left the **Church of St Thomas** (*see page*

85). Its rich baroque façade is easy to miss, tucked into the narrow side street of Tomášská. Based on a Gothic ground plan, the church was rebuilt in the baroque style by Kilián Ignaz Dientzenhofer for the Augustinian monks. The symbol of the order – a flaming heart – can be seen all over the church and adjoining cloisters (now an old people's home) and even in the hand of St Boniface, a fully dressed skeleton who occupies a glass case in the nave.

On the corner of Josefská and Letenská is the **Church of St Joseph** (sv. Josef), a tiny baroque gem set back from the road and designed by Jean-Baptiste Mathey. Since 1989 it has been returned to the much-diminished Order of English Virgins, who were also one-time owners of the nearby **Vojan's Gardens** (*see page 86* **Unseen green**), one of the most tranquil spots in the city.

Running parallel to U lužického semináře is **Cihelná**, a street named after the former brick factory now being renovated into studios. The street provides an opening on to the river and an almost perfect view of the Vltava and Charles Bridge beyond. Back on Letenská, towards Malostranská metro station, is a door in a wall leading into the best-kept formal gardens in the city. The early 17th-century **Wallenstein Gardens** (*see page 86* **Unseen green**) belonged, along with the adjoining **Wallenstein Palace**, to General Albrecht von Wallenstein (Valdštejn), commander of theCatholic armies in the Thirty Years' War and a formidable property speculator. The palace (now the Ministry of

Malá Strana streets are full of decorous details – even the lamp-posts sprout ornamental flourishes.

Church of St Nicholas – dome of baroque.

Culture) is simply enormous. Designed by the Milanese architect Andrea Spezza between 1624 and 1630, it once had a permanent staff of 700 servants and 1,000 horses.

This area of Malá Strana, between Malostranská metro station and the square, is these days sprouting cosy little bars and cafés, one of the best being **Palffy Palác** (*see page 135*).

Church of St Nicholas

Chrám sv. Mikuláše
Malostranské náměstí, Prague 1 (536 983). Metro Malostranská/12, 22 tram. **Open** 9am-4pm daily. **Admission** 45 Kč adults; 15 Kč children, students. **No credit cards. Map** p305 D3.

The immense dome and bell-tower of St Nicholas, which dominate Malá Strana, are monuments to the money and effort that the Catholic Church sank into the Counter-Reformation. The rich façade by Christoph Dientzenhofer, completed around 1710, conceals an interior and dome by his son Kilián Ignaz dedicated to high baroque at its most flamboyantly camp – bathroom-suite pinks and greens, swooping golden cherubs, swirling gowns and dramatic gestures; there's even a figure coyly proffering a pair of handcuffs.

Commissioned by the Jesuits, it took three generations of architects, several financial crises and the demolition of much of the neighbourhood between presentation of the first plans in 1653 to final completion in 1755. Inside, a *trompe l'oeil* extravaganza created by the Austrian Johann Lukas Kracker covers the ceiling, seamlessly blending with the actual structure of the church below. Frescoes portray the life and times of St Nicholas, best known as the Bishop of Myra and the bearer of gifts to small children, but also the patron saint of municipal administration. Maybe this is why St Nicholas's was restored by the communists in the 1950s when the rest of Prague's baroque churches were left to crumble.

Church of St Thomas

Kostel sv. Tomáše
Josefská 8, Prague 1 (530 218/5731 3142). Metro Malostranská/12, 22 tram. **Open** 10.45-1pm, 2.30-6pm daily. **Admission** free. **Map** p305 E3.

It's worth craning your neck to get a good look at the curvy pink façade of St Thomas's. The lopsided structure is the legacy of an earlier Gothic church built for the Order of Augustinian hermits. After the structure was damaged by fire in 1723, Kilián Ignaz Dientzenhofer was employed to give it the baroque touch. The newly rich burghers of Malá Strana provided enough cash for the frescoes to be completed at breakneck speed (they took just two years) and for Rubens to paint the altarpiece *The Martyrdom of St Thomas*. They even bought the bodies of two saints. The original altarpiece is now part of the National Gallery's collection on show in the **Šternberg Palace** (*see p116*) and has been replaced by a copy, but the skeletons of the saints dressed in period costume are still on display. Next door are 17th-century cloisters, where the monks dabbled in alchemy before realising that transforming hops into beer was easier and more lucrative than trying to make gold out of lead. A door on Letenská leads to their former brewery, now a tourist-infested restaurant.

Kampa Island

The approach to Malá Strana from Staré Město via the Charles Bridge affords one of the best photo opportunities in the city: the twin towers of the bridge, framing an almost perfect view of the Church of St Nicholas and the Castle behind. Before continuing, however, take the flight of steps on the left, leading down to Na Kampě, the principal square of **Kampa Island**. Until 1770, it was known simply as Ostrov or 'island', which understandably led to confusion with the other islands of the Vltava – especially since Kampa's southern end looks as if it's attached to land. A fork of the Vltava, the narrow Čertovka, or Little Devil, runs briefly underground there but resurfaces to slice Kampa from the mainland. It went by the altogether unromantic name of the Ditch until it was cleaned up and rechristened in the 19th century. The communists proposed filling the Čertovka to create a major road but were thwarted by a sudden outbreak of good sense, and this singular place, with its medieval water wheels, has survived.

Kampa is an oasis of calm on even the most crowded August day. At the south end is one of the loveliest parks in the city. This was created in the 19th century when an egalitarian decision was made to join the gardens of three private palaces and throw them open to the public. Washerwomen once rinsed shirts on the banks – note the **Chapel to St John of the Laundry** near the southern end). Today it's taken up by snoozing office workers and bongo-beating hippies. The river and bridge views are as romantic as they come, while the chestnut trees make shady spots for reading and recharging. In spring the park is filled with

pink blossom. **Kampa Park** the restaurant (*see page 143*), one of Prague's classier and pricier places to eat, is at the other end of the island where the Čertovka runs back into the river, and offers the finest waterfront view of any dining establishment in town.

Between Kampa & Petřín Hill

Across the tiny bridge on Hroznová that leads to tranquil Velkopřevorské náměstí is the elegant **Buquoy Palace** (Buquoyský palác), a pink stucco creation dating from 1719, which now houses the French Embassy. Opposite is the **John Lennon Wall**. During the 1980s this became a

Unseen green

The Czech word for garden, *zahrada*, connotes ventures into unseen and sometimes forbidden refuges of delight. Malá Strana offers these in abundance, most hidden behind unremarkable entrances.

A decade of campaigning to restore formerly aristocratic gardens, left bedraggled and in ruins by the communists, is finally paying off, as the **Gardens Beneath Prague Castle/Ledeburg Gardens** demonstrate. Sweeping views and some delightfully sinuous landscaping grace the five miniature gardens on the southern slope of the Castle hill, all revived through the sponsorship of Václav Havel and the Prince of Wales.

At the Castle itself, the Bull Staircase (due south of St Vitus's Cathedral) leads to the Castle's 'other' gardens, **Paradise Gardens/Gardens on the Ramparts**, where Prague natives go while tourists tramp off to the Royal Gardens on Hradčany. Note the obelisks and urns of the First Republic makeover worked by Josip Plečnik.

Between the castle and the Royal Gardens is laid out the newly opened **Stag Moat**, last used as a royal hunting park in 1743. Actually a natural ravine of the trickling Brusnice stream, the 'moat' conceals a bench, the views from which were much admired by First Republic president TG Masaryk.

Vojan's Gardens, down below in Malá Strana proper, are an island of tranquillity only accessible by a small door in the street-side wall. These flower beds have been blooming ever since they wre created in 1248.

The **Wallenstein Gardens** on the next block were once the private pottering grounds of megalomaniac Catholic warlord Albrecht von

Wallenstein, but were reclaimed by the public long ago – a small compensation for the homes gobbled up in the first place. In grounds laid out by Milanese architect Andrea Spezza in 1624, occasional summer concerts here are blissful.

Czech novelist Ivan Klíma once declared that the sequestered 275-year-old **Vrtba Gardens** were his favourite spot. Swarming with classical giants and gods, courtesy of sculptor Matthias Braun, it also features a palace once inhabited by the legendary painter of Czech romanticism, Mikoláš Aleš. A mockup of his studio can be glimpsed through the French windows on the first terrace.

Gardens Beneath Prague Castle/Ledeburg Gardens

Ledeburská zahrada
Valdštejnské náměstí 3 (upper entrance from Gardens on the Ramparts). Metro Malostranská/12, 22 tram. **Open** *Apr-Oct* 10am-6pm daily. *Nov-Mar* closed. **Admission** 40 Kč adults; 25 Kč children, students. **No credit cards. Map** p305 E2.

Paradise Gardens/Gardens on the Ramparts

Rajská zahrada/Zahrada na valech
Prague Castle, third courtyard (2437 3368). Metro Malostranská/12, 22 tram. **Open** *Apr-Oct* 9am-5pm daily. *Nov-Mar* closed. **Admission** free. **Map** p305 D2.

Stag Moat

Jelení příkop
Prague Castle (2437 3368). Metro Malostranská/12, 18, 22, 23 tram. **Open** *Apr-Oct* 10am-6pm daily. *Nov-Mar* closed. **Admission** free. **Map** pp304-305 C/D/E1.

place of pilgrimage for the city's hippies, who dedicated it to their idol and scrawled messages of love, peace and rock 'n' roll across it. The secret police, spotting a dangerous subversive plot to undermine the state, lost no time in painting over the graffiti, only to have John's smiling face reappear a few days later. This continued until 1989 when the wall was returned to the Knights of Malta as part of a huge restitution package. The Knights proved even more uptight than the secret police and were ready to whitewash the graffiti when an unlikely Beatles fan, in the form of the French Ambassador, came to the rescue. Claiming to enjoy the strains of 'Give Peace a Chance' wafting through his office window, he sparked a

diplomatic incident but saved the wall. In the summer of 1998, the Knights had a change of heart, the graffiti and crumbling remains of Lennon's face were removed, the wall was replastered and the Beatle's portrait repainted by artist František Flasar. The John Lennon Peace Club is encouraging modest graffiti – preferably in the form of little flowers.

Just around the corner is the lovely **Maltézské náměstí**. The Knights of Malta lived here from the time that Vladislav II offered them a refuge in Prague until the communists dissolved the order. The eight-pointed cross has been all over the square since the Knights regained great swathes of property

Vojan's Gardens
Vojanovy sady
*U lužického semináře. Metro
Malostranská/12, 18, 22 tram.* **Open** *Apr-Sept*
8am-7pm daily. *Oct-Mar* 8am-5pm daily.
Admission free. **Map** p305 E/F3.

Vrtba Gardens
Vrtbovská zahrada
Karmelitská 25. Tram 12, 22, 23. **Open** *Apr-Oct*
10am-6pm daily. *Nov-Mar* closed. **Admission**
20 Kč. **No credit cards. Map** p305 D3.

Wallenstein Gardens
Valdštejnská zahrada
*Valdštejnské náměstí 4. Metro
Malostranská/12, 18, 22 tram.* **Open** *Mar-Apr*
10am-6pm daily. *May-Sept* 9am-7pm daily. *Oct-Feb* closed. **Admission** free. **Map** p305 E2.

Wallenstein Gardens –
former pottering grounds of
a megalomaniac warlord.

under the restitution laws. Round the corner on Prokopská, **U Maltézských rytířů** restaurant (*see page 127*) occupies a Gothic cellar that was once a hospice operated by the Knights. The baroque building on the corner of the square was once the Museum of Musical Instruments. It has suffered more than its fair share of misfortune: its priceless Flemish tapestries were given to Von Ribbentrop, Hitler's foreign affairs adviser, and its Stradivarius violins were stolen in 1990; now the museum is closed for good.

Although the museum is gone, the sound of students practising at the nearby conservatory provides a soundtrack for wandering around the area. The highlight of the square is the strange **Church of Our Lady Beneath the Chain** (Panny Marie pod řetězem), the oldest Gothic parts of which were built by a military-religious order to guard the Judith Bridge that spanned the Vltava close to where Charles Bridge stands today. Two solid towers still protect the entrance – they now contain the most unusual apartments in Prague. The Hussite wars interrupted the construction of the church and it was never completely finished. In place of a nave is an ivy-covered courtyard that leads up to a baroque addition (dating from 1640-50) built in the apse of the original structure. Inside, by the altar, are the chains from the original bridge that give the church its name.

At the foot of Petřín Hill runs **Újezd**, which becomes **Karmelitská** as it runs north before leading into **Malostranské náměstí**. There are peculiar diversions along the way. The first is at the intersection of Újezd and Vítězná, (the border between Malá Strana and Smíchov) where you'll find the popular **Bohemia Bagel** (*see page 148*) spilling rock music and American college kids on to the street. There they mix with Death Metal fans from Klub Újezd next door. Next is the **Michna Palace** (Michnův palác), a fine baroque mansion built in 1640-50. It was intended to rival the Wallenstein Palace, which was itself built to compete with the Castle. With these gargantuan ambitions, Francesco Caratti took Versailles as his model in designing the garden wing of Michna. Today the gardens contain little but tennis courts.

Just north up Karmelitská, at No.9, is the **Church of Our Lady Victorious** (*see below*), the first baroque church in Prague (1611-13). It belongs to the Barefooted Carmelites, an order that returned to the city in 1993 and has taken charge of the church's most celebrated exhibit: the doll-like, miracle-working **Bambino di Praga**. Porcelain likenesses of the wonderbaby fill shop windows for blocks around and pilgrims from around the world file into the church. Heading left up the hill from Karmelitská is Tržiště, on the corner of which stands **U Malého Glena** (*see page 155*), a convivial jazz pub owned by American Glen Spicker. A little further up is the hip **St Nicholas Café** cellar bar (*see page 155*). The 17th-century **Schönborn Palace** (Schönbornský palác), now the American Embassy, is at Tržiště 15. It was built by Giovanni Santini-Aichel, who, despite his Mediterranean-sounding name, was a third generation Praguer and one of the descendants of Italian craftsmen who formed an expat community on Vlašská just up the hill.

From here, Tržiště becomes a tiny lane that winds up the hill, giving access to some of the loveliest hidden alleys in Malá Strana. Developers have been busy converting most of the flats here into investment property but No.22 is a great survivor, **Baráčnická rychta** (*see page 154*). It's one of the most traditional – and certainly the most insalubrious – drinking establishments of the Little Quarter.

Vlašská runs on up the hill from Tržiště and contains the German Embassy, housed in the **Lobkowicz Palace** (Lobkovický palác) at No.19. This is one of four Lobkowicz Palaces in Prague and its design (1703-69) is based on Bernini's unrealised plans for the Louvre. You can get a glimpse of the gorgeous gardens through the gate, though access to the original aviary and bear pit is forbidden. In 1989 thousands of East Germans ignored the *verboten* signs and scaled the high walls, setting up camp in the garden until they were granted permission to leave for the West. The Lobkowicz family were major landowners in Bohemia until the nationalisation of property in 1948. They have succeeded in regaining five castles, and the wine bar next door serves a good selection from their estate in **Mělník** (*see page 252*).

Vlašská ambles on upwards, fading out as it passes a hospital and chapel founded in the 17th century by the area's Italian community, and eventually leading back on to Petřín Hill.

Church of Our Lady Victorious

Kostel Panny Marie Vítězné
Karmelitská 9, Prague 1 (530 752). Tram 12, 22. **Open** 9am-7pm Mon-Sat; 10am-8pm Sun. **Map** p305 D4.
The early baroque church is entirely eclipsed by its diminutive but revered occupant: Il Bambino di Praga (Pražské Jezulátko). This 400-year-old wax effigy of the baby Jesus draws pilgrims, letters and lots of cash from grateful and/or desperate believers the world over. The list of miracles that the Infant of Prague is supposed to have performed is long and impressive and over 100 stone plaques expressing gratitude attest to the efficacy of his powers. The effigy, brought from Spain to Prague in the 17th century, was placed under the care of the

Carmelite nuns just in time to protect them from the plague. It was later granted official miracle status by the Catholic Church.

A wardrobe of over 60 outfits befits this dazzling reputation: the baby Jesus is always magnificently turned out, and his clothes have been changed by the Order of English Virgins at sunrise on selected days for 200 years. While he is said to be anatomically correct, the nuns' blushes are spared by a specially designed wax undershirt. At the back of the church is a shamelessly commercial gift shop where tour groups jostle for miraculous souvenirs.

Petřín Hill

Rising up in the west of Malá Strana is **Petřín Hill** (Petřínské sady), the highest, greenest and most peaceful of Prague's seven hills. This is the largest expanse of greenery in central Prague – a favourite spot for tobogganing children in winter and canoodling couples in summertime. 'Petřín' comes from the Latin word for rock, a reference to the hill's past role as the source for much of the city's Gothic and Romanesque building material. The southern edge of the hill is traversed by the so-called **Hunger Wall** (Hladová zeď), an eight-metre (23-foot) high stone fortification that was commissioned by Charles IV in 1362 in order to provide some work for the poor of the city.

The lazy (and fun) way up to the top of the hill is to catch the funicular from Újezd (running roughly every ten minutes from 9:15am until 8:45pm, stopping halfway up by the pricey Nebozízek restaurant). At the top is a fine collection of architectural absurdities. Ascend the 299 steps of the **Petřín Tower** (see below), a fifth-scale copy of the Eiffel Tower, for spectacular views over the city. The tower was erected in 1891 for the Jubilee Exhibition, as was the neighbouring mock Gothic castle that now houses the **Mirror Maze** (see below), a fairground-style hall of wacky reflectors. There's a café at the base of the tower, and a basic refreshment hut nearby.

The third and least-frequented of the Petřín attractions is **Štefánik Observatory** (see below) at the top of the funicular. It's well worth a peek. On clear days you can look at sunspots and possibly a planet or two; on good nights there are views of craters on the moon.

While kids get the most out of the hilltop attractions, Petřín's meandering paths are the attraction for grown-ups. It's possible to wind through the apple, pear and rowan trees for hours, never quite working out when you will come across the statue of **Karel Hynek Mácha**, unofficial patron saint of lovers. The unlit bowers are a favourite of his disciples, who gravitate here

as soon as the first buds appear and linger until the last of the leaves has fallen.

Strahov Monastery (see page 80) and the 22 tram stop are a gentle downhill stroll away.

Mirror Maze
Zrcadlové bludiště
Petřín Hill, Prague 1 (531 362). Tram 12, 22, then funicular railway. **Open** *Apr-Oct* 10am-6.30pm daily. *Nov-Mar* 10am-4.30pm Sat, Sun; closed Mon-Fri and in bad weather. **Admission** 30 Kč adults; 20 Kč children. **No credit cards. Map** p304 C5.

Housed in a cast-iron mock Gothic castle complete with drawbridge and crenellations is a hall of distorting mirrors that still causes remarkable hilarity among kids and their parents. Alongside is a wax diorama of one of the proudest historical moments for the citizens of Prague: the defence of Charles Bridge against the Swedes in 1648.

Petřín Tower
Rozhledna
Petřín Hill, Prague 1 (5732 0112). Tram 12, 22, then funicular railway. **Open** *Apr-Oct* 10am-7pm daily. *Nov-Mar* 10am-5pm Sat, Sun; closed Mon-Fri and in bad weather. **Admission** 25 Kč adults; 10 Kč students; 5 Kč children. **Map** p304 B5.

While Parisians were still hotly debating the aesthetic value of their newly erected Eiffel Tower, the Czechs decided they liked it so much that they constructed their own version out of recycled railway tracks in a lightning 31 days for the 1891 Jubilee Exhibition. Its fiercest opponent was Adolf Hitler, who looked out of his room in the Castle and immediately ordered 'that metal contraption' to be removed. Somehow it survived. It's fairly tatty these days, but the stiff climb to the top is made worthwhile by phenomenal views of the city. This is about the only vantage point that gives a view of **St Vitus's Cathedral** as a complete building, and not just a set of spires poking over the top of the rest of the Castle. Just try not to think about the way the tower sways in the wind.

Štefánik Observatory
Hvězdárna
Petřín Hill, Prague 1 (5732 0540). Tram 12, 22, then funicular railway. **Open** *Mar* noon-5pm, 7-9pm Tue-Sun; closed Mon. *Apr-Aug* 2-7pm, 9-11pm Tue-Fri; 10am-noon, 2-7pm, 9-11pm Sat, Sun. Closed Mon. *Sept* 1pm-6pm, 8pm-10pm Tue-Sun; closed Mon. *Oct* noon-5pm, 7-9pm Tue-Sun; closed Mon. *Nov-Feb* 11am-4pm, 6pm-8pm Tue-Sun; closed Mon. **Admission** 20 Kč adults; 10 Kč children, students; under-6s free. **No credit cards. Map** p304 C5.

Prague is justly proud of its historical astronomical connections. Both the haughty Dane Tycho Brahe and his protégé Johannes Kepler resided in the city. The duo feature in the observatory's displays (which contain enough English labelling to be helpful), along with stellar information and a CD-Rom about famous space missions. Telescopes offer glimpses of sunspots and planets during the day and panoramas of the stars and the moon on clear nights.

Staré Město

The Old Town is a labyrinth of cellar bars, ancient churches, new restaurants, hidden squares, fashion shops and the Charles Bridge. Now get lost.

Map p306

It's almost impossible not to get lost in Staré Město – the 'Old Town' – and much the best way to get a true measure of the area's charm is to do exactly that. Settled in the tenth century, it has always been where the town's business got done. While the city's rulers plotted and intrigued up on the hill, the town's merchants got on with making a quick buck, a skill that has re-emerged in post-communist times as the natives learn to wash the tablecloths, smile at the customers and stick a few noughts on the bill.

The Powder Gate to the Old Town Square

The **Powder Gate** (see below), a Gothic gateway dating from 1475 at the eastern end of Celetná, marks the boundary between the Old and New towns and is also the start of the so-called Královská Cesta, or **Royal Route**, the traditional coronation path taken by the Bohemian kings and now a popular tourist track. The first stretch runs west down **Celetná**, a pleasant pedestrianised promenade lined with freshly restored baroque and Renaissance buildings. A more recent addition is the **House of the Black Madonna** ('U černé matky boží'), at No.34, the first cubist building in the city (built in 1913; see also page 33 **Origami in stone**), and now, appropriately enough, housing an exhibition of Czech cubist art, furniture and architecture (see page 117). The madonna herself, a treasured artefact that adorned the outside corner, has been moved indoors for safekeeping and a copy will replace it – hopefully reducing the need for protective bars.

On the other side of Celetná, an alley leads in to **Templová**, where you'll be immersed in a part of town where ancient façades are jumbled in with fresh new pastel paint jobs, and meticulous restoration has revitalised long-dormant lanes. Round here is the hub of expat nightlife, where backpackers, tourists and foreign residents disappear into a warren of bars, clubs and restaurants, most of which, for some reason, have French names: **La Provence** (see page 137), **Chateau Rouge** (see page 156), **Le Saint-Jacques** (see page 137) and the **Marquis de Sade** (see page 156) are all within a block of each

other, and the **Radegast** pub (see page 157) is around another corner. Late at night, the strip outside Chateau Rouge (which has the longest hours of all these places) is filled with youths of all nationalities, vomiting on the street, groping in corners, conducting minor drug deals, annoying the neighbours and squabbling with the Chateau's neanderthal bouncers.

Opposite is the **Church of St James** (see below) on Malá Štupartská – a typical baroque reworking of an older Gothic church. From here you can find a sharp contrast from the sleaze of the popular bars in this neighbourhood and stroll through the crisply restored, café- and restaurant-lined square of **Týn**, better known by its German name of **Ungelt**. This square now houses upscale businesses such as **Le Patio** (see page 150 and 179), the well-stocked English-language bookstore **Anagram** (see page 164), the popular sport bar **Legends** (see page 156), and the **Ebel Coffee House** (see page 148). Continuing through the square to the west will take you past the **Church of Our Lady before Týn** (see page 92), Staré Město's parish church since the 12th century, and on to Old Town Square. The Týn church is a scary structure, looming ominously over the square and somehow redolent of a Monty Python animation – you almost expect the building to uproot itself and set off squelching tour groups across the city.

Church of St James

Sv. Jakuba
Malá Štupartská. Metro Náměstí Republiky/ 5, 14, 26 tram. **Open** 9.30am-12.30pm, 2.30-4pm Mon-Sat; 2-3.45pm Sun. **Map** p306 J3.
St James's boasts a grand total of 21 altars, some fine frescoes and a desiccated human forearm hanging next to the door. This belonged to a jewel thief who broke into the church in the 15th century and tried to make off with some gems from the statue of the Virgin. The Madonna grabbed him by the arm and kept him captive until the offending limb had to be cut off. However, its appearance – it looks like a piece of dried up salami – could be explained by the fact that the church's most prominent worshippers were members of the Butchers' Guild.

Powder Gate

Prašná brána
U prašné brány, Prague 1. Metro Náměstí Republiky/5, 14, 26 tram. **Open** Apr-Oct 10am-6pm daily. Nov-Mar

Sightseeing

Old Town Square: even older than it looks.

closed. **Admission** 20 Kč adults; 10 Kč under-6s. **Map** p307 K3.

The Powder Gate, or Tower, is a piece of late 15th-century flotsam, a lonely relic of the fortifications that used to ring the whole town. The bridge that incongruously connects it to the art nouveau masterpiece of the Municipal House (*see p35, p204 and p221*) used to give access to the royal palace that stood on the same site during the tenth century. By the mid-14th century Charles IV had founded the New Town, and the city's boundaries had changed. The Powder Gate remained mouldering until it at last gained a purpose, and a name, when it became a store for gunpowder in 1575. This unfortunately made it a legitimate target for invading Prussian troops and it was severely damaged during the siege of 1757. It was once again left to crumble until the neo-Gothic master Josef Mocker provided it with a new roof and redecorated the sides in the 1870s. Today you can ascend a precipitous staircase to the top.

The Old Town Square

For centuries the beautiful **Old Town Square** (Staroměstské náměstí), edged by an astonishing jumble of baroque and medieval structures, has always been the natural place for people visiting Prague to gravitate. This was the medieval town's main market place and has always been at the centre of the action: criminals were executed here; martyrs were burnt at the stake; and, in 1948, huge crowds greeted the announcement of the communist takeover. Most of the houses are much older than they look, with Romanesque cellars and Gothic chambers hiding behind pastel-coloured baroque and Renaissance façades. If the effect seems somewhat toy-town today, especially in comparison to the crumbling structures in many of the surrounding streets, it should come as no surprise to learn that it was the communists who spent an unprecedented £6.25 million ($10 million) smartening up the formerly

grimy square for the 40th anniversary of the Czechoslovak Socialist Republic.

The west side is lined with stalls selling kitschy crafts and untempting souvenirs. The grassy area behind them was thoughtfully provided by the Nazis, who destroyed much of the **Old Town Hall** on 8 May 1945 when the rest of Europe was holding street parties and celebrating the end of World War II. The town lost most of its archives, though it gained a fine vista of the lovely **Church of St Nicholas** (sv. Mikuláš). Built in 1735 by Kilián Ignaz Dientzenhofer, this is an inside-out church: the exterior, with its white stucco and undulating façade, is even more ornate than the interior. An added attraction in winter is provided by the heated seats, installed to prevent your bottom freezing during organ concerts.

The **Old Town Hall** (*see page 92*) was begun in 1338, after the councillors had spent several fruitless decades trying to persuade the king to allow them to construct a suitable chamber for their affairs. John of Luxembourg finally relented, but with the bizarre proviso that all work was to be financed from the duty on wine. He obviously underestimated the high-living inhabitants of the Old Town, because within the year they had enough money to purchase the house adjoining the present tower.

You can go and look at what remains of the Old Town Hall after the Nazis' handiwork, although trying to decipher the extraordinary components of the **Astronomical Clock** (*see page 92*) is more rewarding. It was constructed in the 15th century, sometime before the new-fangled notion that Prague revolves around the sun and not vice versa. Undismayed, the citizens kept their clock with its gold sunburst swinging happily around the globe. One of Prague's most famous tourist rituals is waiting for the clock to strike the hour while souvenir sellers buzz around.

The brief appearance of figures of the apostles over the clock is remarkably short and laughably unspectacular. Far more entertaining is watching the embarrassed faces of the crowds as they exchange 'is that it?' looks with one another before shuffling away.

Perhaps the finest of the houses that make up what is left of the Old Town Hall is the **Minute House** (U minuty), the beautiful black and white sgraffitoed house on the corner, which dates from 1611. Franz Kafka lived here as a boy; opposite the Astronomical Clock is the **Café Milena** (*see page 148*), named after Milena Jesenská, the radical journalist who is best remembered for being Kafka's girlfriend. The area teems with other Kafka sites. The writer was born in a house at U Radnice 5 (the ground floor of the building that replaced it contains one of Prague's most informed and unpretentious classical CD outlets,

Music shop Trio; *see page 182*), lived for a while at Oppelt's House on the corner of Pařížská and the square (this is the house where *Metamorphosis* takes place), went to primary school on nearby Masná and later attended the strict German Gymnasium on the third floor of the Golz-Kinský Palace. This frothy stuccoed affair in the north-east corner of the square once contained Kafka's father's fancy goods shop; it's now the **Franz Kafka Bookshop** (Knihkupectví Franze Kafky). Adjoining the palace is the **House of the Stone Bell** (*see pages 31 and 222*), the baroque cladding of which was removed in the 1980s to reveal a 14th-century Gothic façade beneath.

The focal point of the square is the powerful Jan Hus Monument dedicated to the reformist cleric, designed by Ladislav Saloun and unveiled in 1915 (and received as a passé artistic flop). Here tourists and school groups pause to rest their feet, chat, consult their guidebooks and sing along with buskers. On the orders of the Pope, Hus was burnt at the stake in 1415 for his revolutionary thinking, although the Catholic Church, some 500 years after the fact, has finally formally apologised. Hus's fans may at last feel vindicated as they point to the quote on the side of his monument that reads 'Pravda vítězí' ('Truth will prevail'). Those words were also used by President Gottwald in the 'Glorious February' of 1948, accurately as it finally turned out in 1989.

Church of Our Lady before Týn

Kostel Matky boží před Týnem
Staroměstské náměstí 14, Prague 1 (232 2801). Metro Náměstí Republiky or Staroměstská/17, 18 tram. **Open** 30 min before services at 5.30pm Mon-Fri; 1pm Sat; 11.30am, 9pm Sun. **Map** p306 J3.
The twin towers of Týn topped by what look like witches' hats are one of the landmarks of the Old Town. The church nave is much lighter and more inviting than its foreboding exterior would lead you to believe. The church dates from the same period as St Vitus's Cathedral (late 14th century), but whereas St Vitus's was constructed to show the power of King Charles IV, Týn was a church for the people. As such it became a centre of the reforming Hussites in the 15th century, before being commandeered by the Jesuits in the 17th. They commissioned the baroque interior, which blends uncomfortably with the original Gothic structure. At the end of the southern aisle is the tombstone of Tycho Brahe, Rudolf II's personal astronomer, famous for his false nose-piece and his fine line in gnomic utterances. If you look closely at the red marble slab, you'll see the former, while the lines above provide evidence of the latter, translating as 'Better to be than to seem to be'. Lit up at night, the Týn looks like some kind of monstrous spacecraft. If you're lucky, you may see bats swooping around the steeples at dusk, completing the fairytale

Arch-Goth – **Church of Our Lady before Týn**.

Gothic image. At press time renovations were just beginning and these seemed likely to disrupt normal opening hours.

Old Town Hall & Astronomical Clock

Staroměstská radnice/Orloj
Staroměstské náměstí, Prague 1 (2448 2909). Metro Staroměstská/ 17, 18 tram. **Open** 9am-6pm daily. **Admission** 30 Kč adults; 20 Kč children. **Map** p306 H3.
The Old Town Hall, established in 1338, was cobbled together over the centuries out of several adjoining houses, but only around half of the original remains standing today. The present Gothic and Renaissance portions have been carefully restored since the Nazis blew up a large chunk of it in the last days of World War II. The Old Town coat of arms, adopted by the whole city after 1784, adorns the front of the Old Council Hall, and the clock tower, built in 1364, has a viewing platform that is definitely worth the climb. The 12th-century dungeon in the basement became the headquarters of the Resistance during the Prague Uprising in 1944 when reinforcements and supplies were spirited away from the Nazis all over the Old Town via the connecting underground passages. Four scorched beams in the basement (not open to the public) remain as a testament to the Resistance members who fell there. On the side of the clock tower is a plaque, marked by crossed machine guns, giving thanks to the Soviet soldiers who liberated the city in 1945. There's also a handful of soil from Dukla, a pass in Slovakia where the worst battle of the Czechoslovak liberation took place, resulting in the death of 84,000 Red Army soldiers.

The Astronomical Clock has been ticking, tocking and pulling in the crowds since 1490. Every hour on the hour between 8am and 8pm crowds gather to watch wooden statuettes of saints emerge from behind trap doors while below a lurid lesson in medieval morality is enacted by Greed, Vanity, Death and the Turk. The clock shows the movement of the sun and moon through the 12 signs of the zodiac as well as giving the time in three different formats: Central European Time, Old Czech

Time (in which the 24 hour day is reckoned around the setting of the sun) and, for some reason, Babylonian Time. A particularly resilient Prague legend concerns the fate of the clockmaker, Master Hanuš, who was blinded by the vainglorious burghers of the town to prevent him from repeating his horological triumph elsewhere. In retaliation Hanuš thrust his hands inside the clock and simultaneously ended both his life and (for a short time at least) that of his masterpiece. Below the clock face is a calendar painted by Josef Mánes in 1865, depicting saints' days, the astrological signs and the labours of the months.

Old Town Square to Charles Bridge

The simplest and most direct route from the Old Town Square to Charles Bridge is along Karlova, although twisting and curling as it does, the lane would not be particularly obvious were it not for the inevitable crowds proceeding along it. This is the continuation of the Royal Route and becomes an unrelenting bottleneck in the summertime when tour groups and souvenir hawkers jostle for supremacy on the narrow way.

To reach Karlova, walk past the Old Town Hall into Malé náměstí (Little Square). In the centre is a plague column enclosed by an ornate Renaissance grill and overlooked by the neo-Renaissance **Rott House**, built in 1890 and entirely decorated with murals of flowers and peasants by Mikoláš Aleš. Friday's American Bar is a newer addition to the square, which attracts weekending punters with impressive burgers and a total absence of Czechness. There's a branch of jeweller Mappin & Webb on the corner, evidence of the rapid upmarket trajectory of this area. (On the other side of the square, a block down Celetná, there's a large, glowing Versace shop, and Pařížská is crowded with designer outlets of all kinds.)

Buggy off out of **Old Town Square**.

The twists and turns of Karlova lead past a procession of souvenir shops and retailers of Bohemian glass. At the third twist it winds past the massive, groaning giants that struggle to hold up the portal of the **Clam-Gallas Palace** (Clam-Gallasův palác) on Husova. Designed by Fischer von Erlach and completed in 1719, the palace now houses the city's archives.

The vast bulk of the **Clementinum** (*see page 94*) makes up the right-hand side of Karlova's last stretch. After the Castle, it's the largest complex of buildings in Prague. The Jesuits, storm troopers of the Counter-Reformation, set up home here on the site and carried on the tradition of book-burning and brow-beating. Like much of the Old Town, Karlova is best viewed at night when most of the tour groups are safely back at their hotels. And if you get peckish along the way there are two all-night eateries: **U zlatého stromu** (*see page 228*) at Karlova 6, where there's a non-stop restaurant in a bizarre complex that also includes a hotel, disco and softcore strip show, and **Pizzeria Roma Due** (*see page 140*) at Liliová 18. Further up Liliová is the **James Joyce** (*see page 156*), Prague's principal Irish pub, and the **U krále Jiřího** (*see page 157*), which serves radically cheaper beer next door. The excellent **V Zátiší** (*see page 129*) restaurant is also along here at Liliová 1.

At the foot of Karlova, tourists have trouble crossing the road past the continuous stream of trams and cars that race through **Křižovnické náměstí** (Knights of the Cross Square). The eponymous Knights, an elderly bunch of neo-medieval crusaders, have come out of retirement and reclaimed the Church of St Francis (sv František). Designed by Jean-Baptiste Mathey in the late 17th century, the church, which has a massive red dome and has been described as looking as if it has been 'gouged out of so much Dutch cheese', is unusual for Prague, not least because its altar is facing the wrong way. The gallery next door houses a job-lot of religious bric-a-brac that the Knights extricated from various museums, and a subterranean chapel decorated with stalactites made out of dust and eggshells, an 18th-century fad that enjoyed unwarranted popularity in Prague.

On the eastern side of the square is the **Church of St Saviour** (sv Salvátor), which marks the border of the Clementinum. Opposite, guarding the entrance to Charles Bridge is the **Old Town Bridge Tower** (*see page 95*), a Gothic gate topped with a pointed, tiled hat. Climb the tower for a bird's-eye view of Prague's domes and spires, the wayward line of Charles Bridge and the over-the-top **Mlynec** (*see page 145*), the naff **Klub Lávka** (*see page 227*) and the newest major edition to Prague clubbing, **Karlovy Lázně** (*see page 227*), all below on the river and beyond.

Sightseeing

Clementinum

Klementinum

Mariánské náměstí 4, Staré Město, Prague 1 (2166 6311). Metro Staroměstská/17, 18 tram. **Open** *Library* 9am-7pm Mon-Sat; closed Sun. *Chapel of Mirrors* for concerts only. **Map** p306 G3/4.

In the 12th and 13th centuries this enormous complex of buildings was the Prague headquarters of the Inquisition, and when the Jesuits moved in during the 16th century, kicking out the Dominicans who had set up home there in the meantime, they carried on the tradition of fear, intimidation and forcible baptising of the city's Jews. They replaced the medieval Church of St Clement with a much grander design of their own (rebuilt in 1711-15 and now used by the Greek Catholic Church) and gradually constructed the building of today, which is arranged around five courtyards, demolishing several streets and 30 houses on the way. Their grandest work was the Church of St Saviour (sv. Salvátor), whose opulent but grimy façade faces the Staré Město end of Charles Bridge and was designed to reawaken the joys of Catholicism in the largely Protestant populace. It was built between 1578 and 1653 by the Jesuits and was the most important Jesuit church in Bohemia. The Jesuits' main tool was education and their library is a masterpiece. It was finished in 1727, and has a magnificent trompe l'oeil ceiling split into three parts, showing the three levels of knowledge, with the Dome of Wisdom occupying the central space. However, the ceiling started crumbling and to prevent the whole structure from collapsing the Chapel of Mirrors was built next door in 1725 to bolster the walls. The interior, decorated with fake pink marble and the original mirrors, is lovely. Mozart used to play here and it is still used for chamber concerts today, which is the only way you can get in to see it. At the centre of the complex is the Astronomical Tower, where Kepler, who lived on nearby Karlova, came to stargaze. It was used until the 1920s for calculating high noon: when the sun crossed a line on the wall behind a small aperture at the top, the Castle would be signalled and a cannon fired.

House of the Lords of Kunštát and Poděbrady

Dům pánů z Kunštátu a Poděbrad

Řetězová 3, Prague 1 (2421 2299 ext 22). Metro Staroměstská/17, 18 tram. **Open** *May-Sept* 10am-6pm Tue-Sun; closed Mon. *Oct-Apr* closed. **No credit cards. Admission** 20 Kč. **Map** p306 H4.

This house is one of the few accessible examples of Romanesque architecture in Prague. It was begun in 1250, originally built as a walled-in farmstead, but like its neighbours in the Old Town was partially buried in the flood-protection scheme of the late 13th century, which reduced the vaulted ground floor to a cellar. By the mid-15th century it was quite palatial, a suitably grand dwelling for George of Poděbrady, who set out from here for his election as king. The upper storeys were later greatly altered. Now it houses a modern art display and an interesting little exhibition in honour of George of Poděbrady whose well-meaning scheme for international co-operation is hailed as a forerunner of the League of Nations. During the summer months the courtyard hosts a trippy music bar called Kumštat (*see p212*).

Charles Bridge

Charles Bridge (Karlův most) is the most popular place in the city to come and get your portrait painted, take photos of the Castle, have your pocket picked or pick up a backpacker. The range of entertainment is always dodgy and diverse, from blind folk-singers through assorted dodgy portrait painters to the man who plays Beethoven concertos on finger bowls.

The stone bridge was built in 1357 (replacing the earlier Judith Bridge that collapsed in a flood in 1342) and has survived over 600 years of turbulent city life, although a large and embarrassing chunk of it tumbled into the Vltava in 1890. The **Old Town Bridge Tower** (*see page 95*) was added in 1373. The statues lining the bridge didn't arrive until the 17th century, when Bohemia's leading sculptors, including Josef Brokof and Matthias Braun, were commissioned to create figures to inspire the masses as they went about their daily business. The strategy proved more effective than an earlier Catholic decoration – the severed heads of Protestant nobles. More mundane statues were added in the 19th century.

The third statue on the right from the Old Town end is a crucifixion bearing a mysterious Hebrew inscription in gold. This was added in 1696 by a Jew found guilty of blaspheming in front of the statue, according to local lore; his punishment was to pay for the inscription 'Holy, Holy, Holy, Holy Lord' to be added. A plaque has recently been added by the Jewish community, telling the full story (*see page 97* **Jewish community finds its voice**).

St John of Nepomuk – perhaps the most famous figure – is eighth on the right as you walk towards Malá Strana and recognisable by his doleful expression and the cartoon-like gold stars fluttering around his head. According to popular belief, John was flung off the bridge after refusing to reveal the secrets of the queen's confession, but he was actually just in the wrong place at the wrong time during one of Wenceslas IV's anticlerical rages. A bronze bas-relief below the statue depicts the scene and people stop and rub it for luck. The statue – placed here in 1683 – is the bridge's earliest. It was cast in bronze and has survived better than the sandstone statues, which have been badly damaged by the elements and have mostly been replaced by copies.

Charles Bridge – the *most* with the mostest.

Further towards Malá Strana, fourth from the end on the left, is the Cistercian nun St Luitgard, made by Matthias Braun in 1710, and shown in the middle of her vision of Christ. The statue is considered by many, including Prince Charles, to be the finest statue on the bridge, and he has pledged the money to save her from the elements, which are threatening to wipe the look of wonder off her face. On the same side, second from the Malá Strana end, is the largest and most complex grouping on the bridge. It commemorates the founders of the Trinitarian Order, which built its rep by ransoming captured Christians: Saints John of Matha and Felix of Valois (accompanied by his pet stag) plus a rogue St Ivan, included for no obvious reason. Below them stand a lethargic figure of a Turk and his snarling dog framing three imprisoned true believers.

If you've fallen for the city, seek out the gold cross located halfway across the bridge, touch it, make a wish – and hey presto, it's guaranteed that you'll return. The best time to come is at night when the Castle is floodlit in various pastel shades and appears to hover overhead.

Old Town Bridge Tower

Staroměstská mostecká věž
Křižovnické náměstí, Staré Město, Prague 1
(no phone). Metro Staroměstská/17, 18 tram.
Open Apr-Oct 10am-7pm daily. Nov-Mar 10am-5pm
daily. **Admission** 30 Kč adults; 20 Kč children.
No credit cards. Map p306 G4.
Built in 1373, along the shadow line of St Vitus's Cathedral, the Old Town Bridge Tower was badly damaged in 1648 by marauding Swedes, but Peter Parler's sculptural decoration on the eastern side survives. There's a boring exhibit on the tower's history inside, but the real reason it's worth venturing in is to take in the splendid view. Most visitors miss the medieval groping of the figures on the tower's outer corners – just visible before you go under the tower, coming from the Old Town direction. Each depicts a buxom lass, clearly getting felt up by a gentleman friend.

Southern Staré Město

Canny German merchants were the first to develop the area south of the Old Town Square. They built a church dedicated to St Havel (more commonly known as St Gall) when Charles IV generously donated some spare parts of the saint from his burgeoning relic collection. The onion domes of the existing **Church of St Havel** (on Havelská) were added later in 1722 by the Shod Carmelites (the Barefooted Carmelites settled on the other side of the river). The opposite end of Havelská is lined with slightly bowed baroque houses precariously balanced on Gothic arcades. The merchants have at last returned, and the street now contains Prague's best market (*see page 180*). As well as handmade wooden toys, there are abundant piles of fruit and vegetables.

Between here and Celetná, in Ovocný trh, is one of Prague's finest neo-classical buildings: the **Estates Theatre** (*see pages 222 and 236*), unofficially dubbed 'The Mozart Theatre'. Unlike Vienna, Prague loved Mozart and Mozart loved Prague. During the composer's lifetime, the theatre staged a succession of his greatest operas, including the premiére of *Don Giovanni*, conducted by Wolfgang Amadeus himself. The building was paid for by Count Nostitz, after whom it was named when it opened in 1783 – aimed at promoting productions of works in the German language. But by the late 19th century most productions were being performed in Czech, and the name was changed to the Tyl Theatre, after the dramatist JK Tyl. His song 'Where Is My Home?' was played here for the first time and later adopted as the Czech national anthem.

The massive oriel window overlooking the theatre belongs to the **Carolinum**, the university founded by Charles IV. Charles never made a move without consulting the stars, and ascertained that Aries was an auspicious sign for the first university in central Europe, which was founded on 7 April 1348. It came to grief at the hands of another Aries, Adolf Hitler, when it was badly damaged in World War II.

Opposite the Estates Theatre is the **former Soviet House of Science and Culture**. Fancy boutiques have taken over most of the complex, although there's a permanent exhibition of gaudy Russian paintings and some Russian books and CDs on sale. Just around the corner on Michalská is the ominous shape of tourist attractions to come: **St Michael's Mystery** (*see below*).

St Michael's Mystery

Michalská 27-29, Staré Město, Prague 1 (2421 3253).
Metro Staroměstská/6, 9, 18, 22 tram. **Open** 10am-8pm
daily. **Admission** 355 Kč. **Credit** MC, V. **Map** p306 H4.
A massive cash infusion has transformed St Michael's Church from ruined baroque cathedral

Sightseeing

into the supremely kitsch St Michael's Mystery. Billed as a 'Kafka-esque' tour through Prague history, it assails visitors with 14 Disney-style scenes and audio in English, German and Czech, featuring talking file drawers, polystyrene figures from the Old Town clock tower, a souped-up special effects elevator and old newsreel footage. If all that fails to seduce visitors inside, there's still the culinary marvels of fries and coffee at the adjoining, subtly dubbed restaurant, 'Mike's'. *See also p192.*

Around Betlémské náměstí

Once the poorest quarter of the Old Town and a notorious area of cut-throats and prostitutes (their present-day sisters can be seen lining Perlova and Na Perštýně a few blocks away), this was the natural breeding ground for the radical politics of the late 14th century. On the north side of Bethlehem Square are the swooping twin gables of the ascetically plain **Bethlehem Chapel** *(see below)*, a reconstructed version of the 1391 building where Jan Hus and other independent-minded Czech preachers passed on their vision of the true church to the Prague citizenry. Across the courtyard is the **Galerie Jaroslav Fragnera** *(see page 204)*, with the **Klub Architektů** *(see page 131)* offering passable cheap eats in the vaulted basement and, in the summer, also at tables outside. The square's other refreshment station is the 'Keltic Bar' Boji, a pricey new sports drinking hole capitalising on the name of the earliest known tribe of Bohemians, believed to be Celts. The nextdoor gallery, **Galerie Jiřího a Běly Kolářových** *(see page 205)*, owned by the Czech legend of collage, Jiří Kolář, testifies to continuing advances in Old Town's art scene.

On the other side of the square is the **Náprstek Museum** *(see page 119)*. After making his fortune by inebriating the masses, Vojta Náprstek installed a collection of ethnological knick-knacks in the family brewery. A 19th-century do-gooder, he didn't just spend his time hunting down shrunken heads, but also founded the first women's club in the country. The room, untouched for 100 years, can still be seen, although the peep-hole he drilled through from his office perhaps draws into question the purity of his motives.

One of the three Romanesque rotundas in the city, the **Church of the Holy Rood** (Rotunda sv. Kříže), is on nearby Konviktská. The tiny, charming building, dating from the early 12th century, was built entirely in the round so that the devil had no corner to hide in. Today it's dwarfed by the surrounding tenement buildings. If you don't manage to get a look inside, try the Hostinec U rotundy. Covered with lovely sgraffito, it's as authentic a pub as you'll find in the Old Town,

with cheap beer and a contingent of locals who'll try to stare you out when you walk in.

On Husova, to the north-east, is the Church of St Giles (sv. Jiljí), a massive Gothic structure that looks like a fortress from the outside. It was built by the Dominicans in 1340-70, an order that has recently come back to reclaim its heritage and inhabit the monastery next door. Nearby is U Zlatého tygra *(see page 158)*, favourite watering hole of **Bohumil Hrabal** *(see page 41)*, the author and Nobel Prize nominee who spent half his life inside a pub and the other half writing about what goes on inside pubs. The irascible octagenarian died in 1997. If the snarling old-timers within make you feel unwelcome, go instead to the **House of the Lords of Kunštát and Poděbrady** *(see page 31)* on Řetězová. In the basement are the atmospheric remains of a Romanesque palace, and temporary exhibitions from the puppet faculty of Charles University, spookily spotlit against the crumbling vaults and pillars. In the courtyard is **Kumštát** *(see page 212)*, one of the best spots for summer drinking in the Old Town.

Parallel to Konviktská is the unnaturally quiet Bartolomějská. Czechs still avoid its environs – a legacy of the role it played in communist times. Police departments line the street and most dissidents of note did time in the StB (Secret Police) cells in the former convent. The building, now containing the **Pension Unitas** *(see page 58)*, has been restored to the Sisters of Mercy and you can stay the night in the cell where President Havel was once locked up to ponder the error of his ways. The river is only a few dozen yards away and from here you have a perfect view across it to Kampa, with the Castle high up on the hill. Turning right will take you past Novotného lávka, a cluster of buildings jutting into the river centred around a 19th-century water tower and a small cluster of bars, and back to Charles Bridge. Turn left to reach the National Theatre and the beginning of the New Town.

Bethlehem Chapel

Betlémská kaple
Betlémské náměstí, Staré Město, Prague 1 (no phone). Metro Národní třída/6, 9, 18, 22 tram. **Open** *Apr-Oct* 9am-6pm daily. *Nov-Mar* 9am-5.30pm, daily.
Admission 30 Kč adults; 20 Kč children, students.
Map p306 H4.
The Bethlehem Chapel, a huge, plain, barn-like structure dating from 1391, was where the proto-Protestant Jan Hus delivered sermons in the Czech language accusing the papacy of being, among other things, an institution of Satan. It is perhaps not surprising that he was burnt at the stake in 1415. His last request before being thrown to the flames was for 'history to be kind to the Bethlehem Chapel'. In response, the fanatical Jesuits bought up the site and promptly turned it into a woodshed. In

Jewish community finds its voice

For tourist legions strolling through the tumbled tombstones of Old Jewish Cemetery of Prague it takes a great deal of imagination to perceive their surroundings as a once-vibrant quarter. The squawking crows instead mark this place as one of acute melancholy. But outside the cemetery walls, the meditative mood disperses among the gaily dressed crowds of visitors who take the quarter as what Hitler meant it to be when he left it intact: a museum.

The true motives behind the Nazis' decision to accumulate plundered Jewish property in Prague and spare the city's synagogues may never be fully known. But the 1,500 or so active participants in the Jewish community today would take considerable exception to being thought of as exhibits. A half-century after the Holocaust and a decade after the end of atheist communism, the community is beginning to shed its quiet role in exchange for a more international spotlight. The controversy over a 17th-century crucifixion scene on the Charles Bridge, bizarrely draped with a chain of Hebrew lettering, made headlines all over Europe. The legend that a local Jew who blasphemed the Lord was forced to pay for the gold lettering has been debated by scholars but whatever its origins, Jews find the presence of an Old Testament verse on the Christian icon offensive and after 300 years of repression finally felt confident enough to kick up a fuss. Local and American Jewish groups successfully pushed for an explanatory plaque, which was installed early in 2000.

A more bitter controversy erupted into street demonstrations in early 2000 when orthodox Jews from around the world flew to Prague to protest the plans of the Czech insurance company, Česká Pojišťovna, to construct an office building over a 13th-century Jewish

graveyard discovered on Vladislavova during construction. The eventual uneasy compromise: the graves are to be encased in concrete and left to rest where they are, protected from archaeologists, sightseers and property developers.

The issue of restituting stolen land and property to its prewar owners has also brought out new voices within the community. To its shame, the Czech parliament dithered for a full decade after 1989 before agreeing, in principle, that most of the stolen Jewish property should be returned. A hint of the financial ramifications was the 150 million Kč the state then had to fork out for a couple of dozen paintings, including early abstracts by František Kupka. These had been stolen from a Jewish industrialist by the Nazis, and then later nationalised by the communists without their previous owners' consent.

In spite of, or because of, its growing visibility, Prague's official Jewish leadership maintains a rigid Orthodoxy and brooks no argument about a more flexible stance. That may be the result of the community's vulnerability during communist times (the present Chief Rabbi was a dissident writer who did jail time under the old regime), but members of the younger set sometimes chafe. After all, they say, during the First Republic, before the destruction of Czech Jewry, the city's Jewish community was among the most highly assimilated in Europe. Sadly, the fruits of their prosperity and creative spirit seem destined to remain under glass until new blood arrives. It will of necessity be blood from abroad, because young Czechs from Jewish families, despite a couple of post-revolutionary years when Judaism became trendy, no longer see much to attract them back into the fold.

the 18th century, German merchants moved in and built two houses within the walls. Hus's wish was finally fulfilled under the communists. They chose to look on him as a working-class revolutionary thwarted by the forces of imperialism and spared no expense in the extensive restoration of the chapel. Three of the original walls remain and still show the remnants of the scriptures that were painted on them to enable people to follow the service. A team of friendly ladies are happy to answer any queries. Upstairs is a small exhibition, captioned in spectacularly broken English, that chronologically runs through the development of Hussitism and the history of the chapel.

Josefov

The main street of Josefov is Pařížská, an elegant, tree-lined avenue of designer shops, flash restaurants, expensive cocktail bars and international airline offices, which leads from the Old Town Square down to the river. Here you'll find swish places like the **Intercontinental Hotel** (*see page 53*) and the river. Here you'll find swish places like the **Jewel of India** (*see page 141*), **Barock** (*see page 141*) and **Bugsy's** cocktail bar (*see page 155*). This is all, however, in sharp contrast to the rest of what was once Prague's Jewish quarter.

The spiritual heart of Josefov is the **Old-New Synagogue** (*see below*), which stands on a wedge of land between Maiselova and Pařížská. Built around 1270, this is the oldest synagogue in Europe. Legend has it that the foundation stones were flown over by angels from the Holy Temple in Jerusalem under the condition ('*al tnay*' in Hebrew) that they should be returned on Judgement Day, hence the name Alt-Neu in German or Old-New in English.

Next door is the former **Jewish Town Hall** (Maiselova 18), dating from the 1560s, with a rococo façade in various delicate pinks, and a Hebraic clock whose hands turn anti-clockwise. The money to build the Town Hall and neighbouring **High Synagogue** was provided by Mordecai Maisel, a contemporary of Rabbi Löw's and a man of inordinate wealth and discriminating taste. The Town Hall has been the centre of the Jewish community ever since. The High Synagogue, built at the same time as the Town Hall and attached to it, was returned to the community early in 1994 and is now, once again, a working synagogue serving the Jewish community (not open to sightseers).

Further down Maiselova you'll find the **Maisel Synagogue**. (This, with the Pinkas, Klausen and Spanish synagogues, and the Old Jewish Cemetery and Ceremonial Hall, comprise the extraordinary **Jewish Museum** (*see page 118* **The Jewish Museum**), also funded by the wealthy 16th-century money-lending mayor. Sadly, the current building is a reconstruction of the original (apparently the most splendid synagogue of them all), which burnt down in the great fire of 1689 when all 316 houses of the ghetto and 11 synagogues were destroyed. The present structure, sandwiched between tenement blocks, dates from 1892-1905, and houses a permanent exhibition of Jewish history from its origins in Bohemia to the 19th century.

On U starého hřbitova is the **Old Jewish Cemetery** (*see page 120*), a small, unruly patch of ground that contains the remains of thousands upon thousands of bodies. Forbidden to enlarge their burial ground, the Jews had to bury bodies on top of each other in an estimated 12 layers, so that today crazy mounds of earth are jammed with lopsided stone tablets.

To the left of the entrance is the **Klausen Synagogue** (*see page 119*), built in 1694 by the same craftsmen responsible for many of Prague's baroque churches. Inside, the pink marble Holy Ark could almost pass for a Catholic altar were it not for the gold inscriptions in Hebrew. Here you'll find displayed various religious artefacts and prints as well as explanations of Jewish customs and traditions. Facing the synagogue is the **Former Ceremonial Hall** (*see page 120*), designed in the style of a Romanesque castle at the beginning of this century, which hosts an exhibition of funeral ceremony and ornament.

On the other side of the cemetery is the **Pinkas Synagogue** (*see page 121*), built as the private house of the powerful Horowitz family in 1607-1625. The building is now primarily given over to a memorial to the more than 80,000 Jewish men, women and children who died in Nazi concentration camps according to German transport lists. A communist-era 'refurbishment' once obscured the names recorded on the Pinkas walls but every one was painstakingly repainted in a two-year project started in April 1997. Josefov's final synagogue, the **Spanish Synagogue** (*see page 121*), was built just outside the boundaries of the ghetto in 1868, on Dušní. It was constructed for the growing number of Reform Jews, and its façade is of a rich Moorish design. Since being returned to the community it has been meticulously restored and is now a working synagogue again. It features a permanent exhibition on Jewish history in the Czech lands up to the beginning of World War II.

Old-New Synagogue

Staronová synagoga
Červená 2, Prague 1 (232 1954). Metro Staroměstská/17, 18 tram. **Open** *Nov-Mar* 9am-4pm Mon-Thur, Sun; 9am-2pm Fri; closed Sat. *Apr-June* 9am-6pm Mon-Thur, Sun; 9am-5pm Fri; closed Sat. **Admission** 200 Kč adults; 140 Kč children, students; free under-6s. **No credit cards. Map** p306 H2.

A rather forlorn piece of medievalism. The oldest survivor of the ghetto and the spiritual centre of the Jewish community for over 600 years, it has now been returned to the community and is still used for services. The austere exterior walls give no clues to its peculiar Gothic interior. An extra rib was added to the usual vaulting pattern to avoid the symbolism of the cross. Instead the decor and structure

Leaning headstones of the **Old Jewish Cemetery**.

revolve around the number 12, after the 12 tribes of Israel: there are 12 windows, 12 bunches of sculpted grapes, and clusters of 12 vine leaves decorate the pillar bases. The interior was left untouched for 500 years as a reminder of the blood spilled here during the pogrom of 1389, when the men, women and children who sought sanctuary in the synagogue were slaughtered by Christians. The 19th-century neo-Gothic crusaders, however, couldn't resist the temptation to 'restore' the original look and slapped a fresh coat of paint over the top.

Oak seats line the walls facing the *bema*, or platform, protected by a Gothic grille, from which the Torah has been read aloud every day for more than 700 years, except during the Nazi occupation. The tall seat marked by a gold star belonged to Rabbi Löw, the most famous inhabitant of the ghetto. The rabbi lived to the age of 97, and a sculpture by Ladislav Saloun to the right of the New Town Hall in Mariánské náměstí depicts the manner of his death. Unable to approach the scholar, who was always absorbed in study of the scriptures, Death hid in a rose that was offered to Löw by his innocent granddaughter. The rabbi's grave is in the Old Jewish Cemetery, recognisable by the quantity of pebbles and wishes on scraps of paper that are placed upon the tomb to this day.

Despite its wealth of historical and religious significance, there's not much to see inside the synagogue and precious little explanation.

Precious Legacy Tours

Maiselova 16, Staré Město, Prague 1 (232 1951/ www.legacytours.cz). Metro Staroměstská/17, 18 tram. **Open** 9am-6pm Mon-Fri, Sun; closed Sat. **Credit** Amex, MC, V. **Map** p306 H3.

This Jewish travel agency purveys tickets for the various Jewish Museum sights, the Old-New Synagogue, tours of Prague and trips to Terezin (*see p253*). The English-speaking staff are also able to book boat tours, meals in kosher restaurants and accommodation.

Northern Staré Město

The site along the banks of the Vltava wasn't incorporated into the new design of Josefov, and the grandiose buildings have their backs turned upon the old ghetto. Going down Kaprova towards the river will bring you to Náměstí Jana Palacha, named in memory of **Jan Palach**, the first of the students who set themselves on fire in 1969 in protest at the Soviet invasion (the second was called Jan Zajic, who didn't get a square named after him, but does also feature in the memorial on Wenceslas Square). Dominating the square is the **Rudolfinum** (*see page 221*) or 'House of Arts', built between 1876 and 1884 (and named after Rudolf II) in neo-classical style and entirely funded by the Czech Savings Bank to display its 'patriotic, provincial feelings'. You can see the bank's corporate logo, the bee of thrift, in

the paws of the two sphinxes with remarkably ample breasts who guard the riverfront entrance. In 1918 the concert hall became home to the parliament of the new Republic.

When Chamberlain returned to England from meeting Hitler in 1938 disclaiming responsibility for the 'quarrel in a faraway country between people of whom we know nothing', it was here that 250,000 of these people came to take an oath and pledge themselves to the defence of the Republic. The Nazis, having little use for a parliament building, turned it back into a concert hall and called it 'The German House of Arts'. Legend has it that a statue of the Jewish composer Mendelssohn was ordered to be removed for obvious reasons, but the workmen, not knowing what Mendelssohn looked like, took their lessons in racial science to heart and removed the figure with the biggest nose – which turned out to be Richard Wagner. Opposite, with its back to the Old Jewish Cemetery, is the fine **Museum of Decorative Arts** (*see page 117*).

Few visitors make it over to the streets of semi-derelict art nouveau tenement houses in northern Staré Město, but they are well worth inspection, even without the attraction of **St Agnes's Convent** (Klášter sv. Anežky české; *see page 116*), the oldest example of Gothic architecture in the city. Its founder St Agnes died a full 700 years before the Pope deigned to make her a saint. Popular opinion held that miracles would accompany her canonisation, and sure enough within five days of the Vatican's announcement the Velvet Revolution was under way. The convent now hosts the National Gallery's Bohemian Gothic collection.

Nearby is Dlouhá or 'Long Street', which contained no less than 13 breweries in the 14th century when beer champion Charles IV forbade the export of hops. These days its main attraction is the **Roxy** at No.33 (*see page 215*). It's a thoroughly crumbling cinema that was once the headquarters of the Communist Youth Association and is now the city's most atmospheric club. Next door is the serene **Čajovna Duše** (*see page 152*) tea house, which moved out of the club itself to make way for, after seven years, the installation of the Roxy's first proper bar. In the enjoyably quiet streets between Dlouhá and the river lie several more convivial bars and cafés, including the French-style **Chez Marcel** (*see page 135*), the impossibly Irish **Molly Malone's** (*see page 157*), the always crowded and fashionable **Kozička** (*see page 156*), the neo-Bohemian **Blatouch** (*see page 148*), the Czech all-American **Žiznivý pes** (*see page 158*) and, on the other side of Revoluční, is **Terminal Bar** (*see page 152*), the wirehead hangout of choice among Prague's many Internet cafés and Prague's only pub with a bridge inside.

Nové Město

Beyond the picturesque Old Town precincts, Prague's real life begins.

Maps p307, p308 & p309

Nové Město, the New Town, is far from new and no longer a township. It was founded in 1348 by Charles IV, who'd had a premonition that the Old Town would be destroyed by fire and floods. Despite frequent fires and floods, the Old Town still stands, but the decision was a good one: his far-sighted urban planning led to the creation of wide boulevards and broad squares which have adapted well to the rigours of modern life. While tourists trawl the fantasy landscapes of Malá Strana and the Old Town, Nové Město is a reality check, though a charming one, of offices, shops, cinemas, theatres, fast-food outlets and banks.

Old and New Towns meet along the line of Národní třída, Na příkopě and Revoluční. Nové Město, bounded to the east by traffic-pounded Wilsonova, wraps around the Old Town and Josefov, stretching from the river to the north down to Vyšehrad in the south.

Wenceslas Square

Wenceslas Square (Václavské náměstí), once known as the Horse Market, is the hub of city life. You'll find yourself passing through it several times a day. More of a broad boulevard than a square, it was laid out over 600 years ago under Charles IV, and has always been a good place to check out the changing fortunes of the city. This century, Nazis, communists, anti-communists and a naked Allen Ginsberg have all paraded its length. *See page 102* **Be there, be (Wenceslas) square**.

The May Day parades have these days been replaced by a sleazy collection of drug dealers, pickpockets and crooked cab drivers. You'll be assailed by the smell of frying sausages and if you're a businessman, by any number of strip club promoters. The shops, which used to have dull names like House of Fashion or House of Food, have been privatised, glamorised and outfitted with McDonald's counters. All the designer names and discount chains from back home have now come here to stay.

The bottom end of the square is a pedestrian area, invariably thronging with tour parties, backpackers and Euro-teens heading for the last surviving disco (there used to be a clutch of them here) whose lights pulse out over the scene. The kiosks here are the place in town to buy foreign newspapers and magazines.

A tour of the square

Almost every architectural style of the last 150 years is represented somewhere on the square. Starting at the lower end by the newsstands, the revolutionary **Baťa** building (Ludvík Kysela, 1927-9) at No.6, with its massive expanses of plate glass, was an important functionalist structure. Pioneering cubist architect Emil Králíček, together with Matěj Blecha, built the asiatic-inspired **Adam Pharmacy** at No.8, giving it a cubist interior. Jan Kotěra's first building in Prague, **Peterka House**, stands a few doors up at No.12, signalling art nouveau's first moves towards more geometric forms. Unashamedly retro, the **Wiehl House** (1896) on the corner of Vodičkova was built by Antonín Wiehl in neo-Renaissance style and decorated with elaborate sgraffito. Beyond are the arcades of the Lucerna complex and Blecha's **Supich Building** (1913-16) at Nos.38-40, complete with likeably bizarre Assyrian-style masks adorning its façade. The second-floor balcony of the **Melantrich Building** (No.30) became the unlikely venue for one of the most astounding events of the Velvet Revolution: on 24 November 1989, in front of a crowd of over 300,000 people, Václav Havel and Alexander Dubček stepped forward here and embraced, signifying the end of 21 years of 'normalisation'. Within weeks the entire cabinet had resigned.

Up at the top end, and crowning the whole square, is Josef Schulz's massive neo-Renaissance **National Museum** (1885-90; *see page 120*), a swaggering, monumental 19th-century block, cut off from the rest of the square by a dual carriageway. Across the road is the ugly 1970s building that housed the Federal Assembly until the Czech-Slovak split in 1993. The building has now become the base of **Radio Free Europe**, which, after playing its part in the toppling of totalitarianism, moved in to take advantage of the cheap rent.

Also at the top end of the square are two of Prague's most symbolic sites – one ancient in inspiration, one modern. The former is Josef Václav Myslbek's huge equestrian **statue of St Wenceslas** (Václav). Although a monument to the Czech patron saint has stood here since the late 17th century, Myslbek's serene prince wasn't unveiled until 1912. The surrounding statues of saints Agnes, Adalbert, Procopius and Ludmila,

Wenceslas Square: boulevard of bustle.

Be there, be (Wenceslas) square

Stick around Wenceslas Square long enough and you're bound to see heads rolling.

Long before 250,000 people rang out communism here with jangling keys in November 1989, the square was well-versed in revolution. A generation earlier it witnessed throngs of student protestors who would not be so successful. In August 1968, the cries for Alexander Dubček's 'Socialism with a Human Face', were answered by Warsaw Pact tanks.

The seeds of that oppression had been planted by another capacity crowd on Wenceslas Square in February 1948 who listened quietly to the announcement that First Working-Class President Klement Gottwald and the Communist Party were assuming power in accordance with the wishes of the wise leadership of the Soviet Union.

A Czech Television documentary aired in the mid-1990s showed the square filled with just as many people during the Nazi occupation, all raising their arms in unison in a fascist salute to the Reichsprotektorat of Böhmen and Mähren. The same people had taken to these streets in 1938 to denounce the Munich Treaty, in which England, France and Italy surrendered a chunk of Czechoslovakia to Nazi Germany, as the affronted viewers of the documentary were at pains to point out in a deluge of angry letters.

Easier to swallow for Czechs is the memory of the thousands who wept for joy as TG Masaryk, the country's first president, stood on a balcony in the square and announced the dissolution of the Austrian-Hungarian Empire and the formation of the Czechoslovak Republic on October 28, 1918.

Nearly as treasured in popular memory was the turnout 70 years earlier for the 'národní obrození' or National Awakening revolution of 1848, which shook the Habsburg Empire to its foundations. Had that uprising not foundered on nationalist splits between Czech and German Praguers, some scholars theorise that

Wenceslas's grandmother, were added in the 1920s. Just down from the statue is the **memorial to the victims of communism**, commemorating the sacrifice of Jan Palach who burned himself alive on 16 January 1969 in protest against the Soviet invasion of the previous August.

Coming back down the north side, past the Soviet-style Jalta Hotel, one encounters perhaps the square's best-known building, the glittering art nouveau **Grand Hotel Evropa** (*see page 61*) at Nos.25-27, built by Alois Drýak and Bendřich Bendelmayer (1903-6). Passing the carbuncle that is the **Julius Meinl** department store (*see page 176*), at the bottom end of the square is Antonín Pfeiffer's **Koruna Palace** (1912-14), a fine example of the 'Babylonian'-inspired buildings that enjoyed a vogue at the time as a result of contemporary archaeological digs in Mesopotamia. Now it's a shopping mall.

Northern Nové Město

The pedestrianised **Na příkopě** runs from Wenceslas Square to Náměstí Republiky along the line of what was once a moat. It has been quaintly dubbed 'Prague's Wall Street' because of its concentration of banks, and the financial institutions range from the neo-Renaissance **Živnostenská banka** at No.20 to the art deco **Komerční banka** at No.28. With the opening of branches of **TGI Friday's** and **Carli Gry** it

seems clear which way the tone of the street is going. **Čedok** (*see page 288*), the national tourist office, is at No.18. Here, apart from picking up leaflets, you can also buy tickets to major events, as well as international train and bus tickets.

Dominating **Náměstí Republiky** is the luscious art nouveau **Municipal House** (*see pages 104, 203 and 221*), which stands on the border of the Old and New Towns. Built between 1905 and 1911, and lavishly restored in the mid-1990s, this extravagant combination of colour and curves was where Czechoslovakia was signed into existence in 1918. Incongruously attached to the Municipal House is the blackened Gothic **Powder Gate** (*see page 80*), predating it by half a millennium.

Facing the Municipal House is the neo-classical former customs house, **U Hybernů** (The Hibernians), now the site for occasional exhibitions. Running east from Náměsti Republiky is Hybernská, named after the Irish monks who settled here in the 16th century after falling foul of Elizabeth I. Their contribution to city life was to introduce the potato, an event from which Czech cuisine has never recovered. The street itself is unremarkable save for the presence of the **American Center for Culture and Commerce** in the baroque Lidový dům at No.7, a building which ironically used to house the Lenin Museum. At No.4 once stood the Café Arco, meeting place of the self-styled 'Arconauts' who included Franz Kafka and Max Brod. Across

true independence might have arrived in the Czech lands much earlier than it did.

If fortune smiles on the Czech Republic, the Velvet Revolution will be the last uprising played out on Wenceslas Square. But if the early months of 2000 were any indicator, that may be wishful thinking. The protest movement known as *Díky a odejděte* ('Thank you, now get out') most recently packed Wenceslas Square with demonstrators calling for the resignation of Prime Minister Miloš Zeman and the head of the leading ODS Party, Václav Klaus. Both have lost points in the polls since their Velvet Revolution glory days, after corruption scandals within ODS and Zeman's remarkable knack for offending his constituents with crass behaviour.

If this duo want their careers to last much longer they had better pray that Wenceslas Square remains filled with nothing more than its usual overpriced hotels and chain stores.

the road in the Masaryk railway station – Prague's first, built in 1845 – is the late-night buffet **Bistro Flip**, serving fried cheese until 11pm every night to the cream of the city's unsavouries (*see page 230*).

The largely anonymous streets south of here contain Prague's newest museum, the **Mucha Museum** (*see page 117*), on Panská, and the main post office, on Jindřišská. The latter is an extraordinary place – a covered courtyard filled with newly modernised booths, but still bustling with all the routine paperwork transactions of life in an extremely bureaucratic state.

Two buildings make it worth braving the streaming traffic of the Wilsonova expressway, bounding Nové Město in the east. The **State Opera** (*see page 222*), built by the Viennese architects Fellner and Helmer in 1888, was something of a last gasp assertion of identity by Prague's German community in the midst of the great Czech National Revival. More interesting, though, is the city's main station, **Hlavní nádraží**, also known as Wilsonovo nádraží (*see pages 36 and 268*). Smelly, crumbling, inhabited by lowlifes and one of Prague's main gay cruises, the station might seem an unlikely place to seek out the pleasures of Prague's bourgeois age. That it had been dedicated first to Emperor Franz Joseph and then to the American President Wilson gave the communists two very good reasons to plant a high-speed bypass outside its front door and create a modern soulless extension

beneath. The upper levels, which were left to rot in obscurity until the **Fantova kavárna** opened there in the mid-1990s, are an atmospheric remnant of a bygone age. The café contains some of the best art nouveau murals anywhere in Prague, with languorous women serving as a backdrop to the rent boys who now congregate beneath them. The cavernous lower levels are tacky, dirty, bustly and a must for fans of communist architecture.

Just north of Náměstí Republiky is the **Kotva** department store (*see page 169*). This was once one of the shopping showpieces of the Eastern Bloc, and 75,000 people a day would come from as far away as Bulgaria to snap up its fine selection of acrylic sweaters, orange plastic cruets and official portraits of Gustav Husák. It has now been overhauled and the communist idea of fashion replaced by the German one. There's another classic communist-era department store, **Bílá labuť**, not far away on busy Na Poříčí; its glass-curtain wall is a classic functionalist feature. Almost opposite is a rare example of the rondo-cubist style: Pavel Janák's Banka Legií from the early 1920s. On the other side of the Wilsonova flyover is the beleaguered neo-Renaissance block containing the **Museum of the City of Prague** (*see page 119*).

Further north, beyond the **Postage Stamp Museum**, on nábřeží Ludvíka Svobody next to the river, stands a monolithic structure, recognisable by a dome that glows orange at

Legionnaires' Bridge and the **National Theatre.** *See p105.*

night. This is the Ministry of Transport, built in the 1920s and for a spell the HQ of the Central Committee of the communist party. It was here that on 21 August 1968 tanks arrived to escort Alexander Dubček to be flown off to the Kremlin for 'fraternal discussions'.

Municipal House

Obecní dům

Náměstí Republiky 5, Prague 1 (2200 2111). Metro Náměstí Republiky/5, 14, 26 tram. **Map** p307 K3.

All the leading artists of the day were involved in the creation of the Municipal House or Obecní dům (1905-11), a masterpiece of stained glass, coloured mosaics, tiled murals and gold trimmings. Erected during the death throes of the Austro-Hungarian Empire, the building became a symbol of the aspirations of the new republic, representing a stylistic and structural break with the *ancien règime*. It was here that the proud and newly independent state of

Czechoslovakia was officially signed into existence in 1918, and a plaque on the side pays a tribute to a country that no longer exists.

Following a major renovation, it is once again possible to attend concerts in the spectacular Smetana Hall, and see the other magnificent civic rooms including, most splendid of all, the Lord Mayor's Salon, which is covered with murals by Alfons Mucha depicting heroes of Czech history. The façade is by Osvald Polívka who also designed the exquisitely ornamented Kavárna Obecní Dům (*see p149*); the monumental mosaic called 'Homage to Prague' above the main entrance, featuring languid ladies in an altogether un-urban setting, is by Karel Spillar. It is offset by Ladislav Šaloun's sculptural composition entitled 'The Humiliation and Resurrection of the Nation'. The café and restaurant, basement bars and gallery are all open to the public, though a guided tour provides access to the other splendid corners. *See also pages 203 and 221.*

Národní was the playground of generations of Czechs in the last century and the battleground of another generation this century. Standing proudly on the banks of the Vltava, topped by a crown of gold and with sculptures of bucking stallions lining the balustrade, the **National Theatre** (*see also page 237*) is a product and symbol of the fervour of 19th-century Czech nationalism. It took 20 years to persuade the general public to cough up the money to begin construction, and from 1868 to 1881 to build it. Then, just days before the curtain was to go up on the first performance, it was gutted by fire. An emotive appeal, launched immediately by the leading lights of the city's cultural institutions, raised enough money to start all over again in just six weeks. In 1883 the building finally opened with a gala performance of *Libuše*, an opera about the mythical origins of the Czech nation written especially for the occasion by Smetana. A bronze memorial halfway down on the south side (by No.20) pays tribute to the events of 17 November 1989, where the violent police suppression of a student demonstration sparked the beginning of the Velvet Revolution.

The department store on the corner of Spálená is a barometer of the changes that have occurred since then. It used to be called Máj after the most sacred date in the communist calendar, 1 May. These days it's owned by **Tesco** (*see page 169*).

By the memorial at No.20 is **Reduta** (*see page 216*), the venerable jazz club where Bill Clinton tested his saxophone skills before a global audience. Further down at No.7, through an exquisite wrought-iron entrance, is **Viola**, once a literary hangout that sports one of the three framed Václav Havel signatures to be found in various drinking holes around town. Next door, with a fine view across the river to the Castle, is the redoubtable **Slavia** (*see page 149*), once the centre of Prague's café life and, after a long closure, happily reopened and hoping to regain a little of its past glory.

The embankment running south contains a fine if not terribly remarkable collection of art nouveau apartment houses. At No.78 is the block containing Václav Havel's flat. In a deliberate break with tradition, Havel declined to move into the swanky presidential quarters at the Castle and stayed on in his own down-at-heel tenement across the river. Now the gesture has been made, admired and written about, he has purchased an altogether more upmarket residence in Prague 6. Not that he can necessarily be blamed, however, since the plot next door at the old place was for some time a building site while a controversial Frank Gehry construction was going up: the so-called **'Fred & Ginger' building**, the form of which supposedly resembles that pair of twirling Hollywood stars (*see page 38*).

Southern Nové Město

Just south of the Old Town end of Wenceslas Square is Jungmannovo náměstí, site of the world's only **cubist lamp-post** (*see page 33* **Origami in stone**). Tucked away in an obscure corner, Emil Králíček's bizarre and somewhat forlorn-looking creation, much derided when it was completed in 1913, has become something of a Prague cultural icon. It stands in front of the towering church of **Our Lady of the Snows** (*see page 106*), a sort of wannabe St Vitus's Cathedral. A path from here leads to the unexpected oasis of the **Franciscan Gardens** (Františkánská zahrada), a haven of clipped-hedge calm in the middle of the city.

From Jungmannovo náměstí, Národní třída (National Avenue) divides the Old and New towns, meeting the river at the most Legii.

The climax of this art nouveau promenade is **Palackého náměstí**, which is dominated by the monumental sculpture by Stanislav Sucharda of 19th-century historian František Palacký, who dedicated 46 years of his life to writing a history of the Czech people. Palacký looks pretty solemn, seated on an enormous pedestal, book in hand and utterly oblivious to the bevy of beauties and demons flying around him. Behind him rise the two modern spires of the altogether more ancient **Emmaus Monastery** or Monastery of the Slavs (klášter Na Slovanech), which was founded by Charles IV, the towers added after the baroque versions were destroyed by a stray World War II bomb.

The island closest to the embankment, at the bottom of Národni třída, is **Slovanský Island**. In the days before slacking was an art form, Berlioz came here and was appalled at the 'idlers, wasters and ne'er-do-wells' who congregated on the island. With a recommendation like that it's hard to resist the outdoor café or a few lazy hours in one of the rowing boats for hire. There's also a fine statue of Božena Němcová, as seen on the front of the 500 Kč note. She was the Czech version of George Sand, a celebrated novelist whose private life scandalised polite society. At the southern tip is the art gallery **Výstavní síň Mánes** (*see page 206*), a 1930s functionalist building incongruously attached to a medieval water tower. The left-wing intelligentsia used to gather here between the wars, while in 1989 Civic Forum churned out posters and leaflets from here. The island is also home to the newly restored cultural centre **Žofín** – a large yellow building dating from the 1880s that has long been associated with the Czech cultural psyche, and hosted tea dances and concerts until just before World War II. Today it hosts classical concerts and conventions and features one of the loveliest beer gardens in Bohemia out back (but avoid its restaurant side unless desperate).

Church of Our Lady of the Snows

Kostel Panny Marie Sněžné
Jungmannovo náměstí, Prague 1 (2224 6243). Metro Můstek. **Open** 6am-7.30pm daily. **Map** p306 J5.
Charles IV founded the church to mark his coronation in 1347, intending it to stretch more than 100m (330ft), but, after the 33-m (110-ft) high chancel was completed in 1397, funds dried up. What remains is a voluptuous, vertiginous affair that sweeps the eyes upwards, scaling the towering and typically over-the-top black and gold baroque altarpiece. Despite this oppressive presence, the church is a wonderfully light, tranquil space, with an interesting marbling effect on the walls. The church was erected 1,000 years after the Virgin Mary appeared to fourth-century Pope Liberius in a dream, telling him to build a church where the snow fell in August. He knocked off Santa Maria Maggiore in Rome.

Nové Město – secessionist façades.

Around Karlovo náměstí

There are some fine backstreets to explore between Národni třída and Karlovo náměstí, as well as some major thoroughfares. Jungmannova contains the **Bontonland** (**Supraphon**) (see page 181) and Popron music shops. The best-known fixture in this area is **U Fleků** (*see page 160*), at Křemencova 11, the world's oldest still-operating brew pub and the place to go if you want to unload some cash and meet a lot of Germans bellowing drinking songs (if you can put up with that, the beer tastes wonderful). Its entrance is marked by a picturesque old clock, hung like a tavern sign. At Spálená 82 is the **Diamant House**, designed by Emil Králíček in 1912, which takes its name from the broken-up prisms that constitute the façade (*see page 33* **Origami in stone**). The ground floor has now become a Škoda showroom and the neon strip lights that adorn it are a dubious aesthetic addition. A nice touch is the cubist arch which shelters a piece of baroque statuary and bridges the gap, literally and historically, between this building and the 18th-century Church of the Holy Trinity next door.

Karlovo náměstí is an enormous expanse that used to be a cattle market and the site of Charles IV's relic fair. Once a year he would wheel out his collection of saints' skulls, toenails and underwear, the townsfolk dutifully gawped, cripples would throw down their crutches and the blind would miraculously regain their sight. These days you're most likely to come across the square in a night tram, minor miracles in their own right. Its other attractions include the 14th-century **New Town Hall** (Novoměstská radnice). It was from here that several Catholic councillors were ejected from an upstairs window in 1419 – and the word 'defenestration' entered the language.

On the eastern side of the square is the splendidly restored Jesuit **Church of St Ignatius** (sv. Ignác), an early baroque affair in cream, pink and orange stucco, with gold trimmings. No.24 was once a restaurant used for training waiters employed by the secret police. The James Bonds of the catering world learnt how to plant bugs in dissidents' soup and dish up the sauce to their eager employers. In the south-west corner is the **Faust House** (Faustův dům), an ornate 17th-century building that has more than a few legends attached to it. Edward Kelly, the earless English alchemist, lived here, as apparently did the Prince of Darkness, who carried off a penniless student and secured the house a place in Prague's mythic heritage.

Halfway across the square on Resslova is the baroque **Cathedral of Sts Cyril & Methodius** (*see below*), scene of one of the most dramatic and poignant events of World War II – the last stand of the assassins of Reichsprotektor Reinhard Heydrich.

Going in the opposite direction up the hill is Ječná, where Dvořák died at No.14; but rather than staring at the plaque on the wall, go to the **Dvořák Museum** (*see page 121*) on nearby Ke Karlovu, where you can catch a chamber recital. It's quartered in a gorgeous summer house designed by Dientzenhofer – the Villa Amerika – these days surrounded by incongruous modern bits of concrete.

At the far end of the street is a museum of a very different sort – the **Police Museum** (*see page 121*). Brek, the stuffed wonder dog responsible for thwarting the defection of hundreds of dissidents, has been given a decent burial, but there's still plenty of gruesome exhibits to delight the morbid.

If it all gets too much, you can seek sanctuary in the unusual church next door, which is dedicated to Charlemagne, Charles IV's hero and role model. The octagonal nave of **Na Karlově** was only completed in the 16th century, although the superstitious townspeople refused to enter it for years, convinced that it would collapse. The ornate, gilt frescoed walls inside were restored after the building was partially destroyed in the Prussian siege of 1757, but bullets can still be seen embedded in them. From the garden there are extensive views across the Nusle Valley to Vyšehrad on the other side. Close by on Vyšehradská is the **Church of St John on the Rock** (sv. Jan na skalce), a fine Dientzenhofer structure built in the 1730s, perched at the top of an impressive double stairway; a little further to the south are the delightful but little-visited **Botanical Gardens**, where the hothouses have recently been rebuilt and the tranquil terraces retain a strong attraction for pram-wielding mothers and old folk.

Orthodox Cathedral of Sts Cyril & Methodius

Kostel sv. Cyrila a Metoděje
Resslova 9, Prague 2 (2492 0686). Metro Karlovo náměstí/4, 7, 9, 12, 14, 16, 18, 22, 24 tram. **Open** 10am-4pm Tue-Sun; closed Mon. **Admission** 30 Kč adults; 10 Kč children, students. **Map** p308 H8.
This baroque church, built in the 1730s, was taken over and restored by the Czech Orthodox Church in the 1930s. A plaque and memorial outside, together with numerous bullet holes, still attract tributes and flowers today, and are clues to what happened inside during World War II. In 1942, two Czech paratroopers trained in England were flown into Bohemia, together with five colleagues, to carry out the assassination of Reinhard Heydrich, Reichsprotektor of Bohemia and Moravia and the man who chaired the infamous 1942 Wannsee Conference on The Final Solution. Josef Gabčík, Jan Kubiš and their co-conspirators were given sanctuary in the crypt here after the event, until they were betrayed to the Germans. In the early hours of 18 June, 350 members of the SS and Gestapo surrounded the church and spent the night bombarding it with bullets and grenades. The men who managed to survive until dawn used their final bullets to shoot themselves.

The incident did not end there. Recriminations were swift, brutal and arbitrary. Hundreds of people, many of them Jews, were rounded up in Prague and shot immediately, while five entire villages and most of their inhabitants were liquidated, the most famous being Lidice. The events brought about a turning point. Britain repudiated the Munich Agreement and Anthony Eden declared that Lidice had 'stirred the conscience of the civilised world'. The story of the assassination and its aftermath is movingly told (in English) in the crypt of the church (entrance on Na Zderaze) where the Czech paratroopers made their last stand.

Further Afield

The place where Stalin stood, the castle where the town began, the district where beer is boss, plus galleries, monasteries and parks galore – even Prague's suburbs are something to see.

Holešovice, Letná & Troja

Map p310

At first glance, Holešovice is an unremarkable 19th-century suburb filled with grimy tenement blocks and factories, and containing one of Prague's two international train stations. However, this district to the north of the Old Town over the Vltava also contains two of Prague's finest green spaces and is rapidly throwing off its post-war torpor.

Down towards the river on Kostelní is the **National Technical Museum** (*see page 122*), a constructivist building dating from 1938-41. whose dull name belies a fascinating collection. Five minutes' walk east is Holešovice's main drag, Dukelských hrdinů. Here stands another constructivist building, the enormous **Veletržní palác**, built in the mid-1920s to house trade fairs which had outgrown **Výstaviště** (*see page 109*). It was gutted by fire in 1974 but has been splendidly restored; the stunning white-painted atrium rises up seven storeys lined with sweeping guard rails, giving it the feel of a massive ocean liner. Pop in to peak at the atrium even if you don't want to look around the new **National Gallery Collection of 19th- and 20th-Century Art** (*see page 115*) within. **The Globe Bookstore and Coffeehouse**, an expat institution once around here, has now moved to New Town (*see pages 40, 150 and 165*).

A couple of minutes' walk to the north is **Výstaviště** (*see page 109*), an unusual wrought-iron pavilion built to house the Jubilee Exhibition of 1891 and considered the first expression of art nouveau in the city. Here, in the **Lapidarium** (*see page 117*), you'll find an intriguing collection of reject monuments that once stood around the city. From the top of the ferris wheel in the nearby **Lunapark** there are fine views over the woody environs of Stromovka, a vast park laid out by Rudolf II in the 16th century, as a place where he could commune with nature. Rudolf's favoured companion here was English alchemist and mathematician John Dee, who got the job when he claimed to understand both the language of the birds and the one in which Adam conversed with Eve in Eden. Today, the leafy park makes a wonderful spot for a stroll or picnic.

If you still have the energy, take the half-hour walk back to the Old Town via the sedate embassy-land of Bubeneč, past the Sparta Stadium and through **Letná Park** (Letenské sady). This is where the biggest demonstration of 1989 took place, attended by nearly a million people. On the edge of the park, with a fine view overlooking the town, is the plinth, now housing a giant metronome, where the statue of Stalin used to stand. Below is the splashy new restaurant **Aqua** (*see page 145*) serving new-fangled fusion food on the banks of the Vltava.

Alternatively, a 20-minute walk north of Stromovka (or you can take the 112 bus from Nádraží Holešovice metro) brings you to **Troja Cháteau** (*see below*). Commissioned by Count Šternberg in the 1700s and built by a French architect and Italian craftsmen, it contains some stunning trompe l'oeil frescoes. Count Šternberg's horses were particularly fortunate, inhabiting a sumptuous stable block with marble floors and decorated with frescoes of their noble forebears. The inmates of **Prague Zoo** (*see page 192*) across the road can only curse their historical mis-timing, for, despite having found a new patron in Coca-Cola, their living conditions are altogether less salubrious.

Troja Cháteau

Trojský zámek

U trojského zámku 1, Holešovice, Prague 7 (688 5146). Metro Nádraží Holešovice/112 bus. **Open** *Apr-Sept* 10am-6pm Tue-Sun; closed Mon. *Oct-Mar* 10am-5pm Sat-Sun; closed Mon-Fri. **Admission** 120 Kč adults; 60 Kč children, students. **No credit cards.**

After winning huge tracts of land in the property lottery that followed the Thirty Years' War, Count Šternberg embarked upon creating a house worthy of his ego. A Czech nobleman, he was anxious to prove his loyalty to the Habsburg emperor and literally moved mountains to do so. The hillside had to be dug out to align the villa with the royal hunting park of Stromovka and the distant spires of the cathedral. The result is a paean to the Habsburgs, modelled on a classical Italian villa and surrounded by formal gardens in the French style. On the massive external staircase, gods hurl the rebellious giants into a dank grotto. In the Grand Hall the virtuous Habsburgs enjoy a well-earned victory over the infidel Turks. This, a fascinating though slightly ludicrous example of illusory painting, is

Troja's main attraction. To see it you have to don huge red slippers to protect the marble floors. An insensitive restoration programme has destroyed the villa's atmosphere, and the installation of a small collection of 19th-century Czech painting has done little to redeem it.

Výstaviště

Prague 7 (2010 3111/2010 3204). Metro Nádraží Holešovice/5, 12, 17 tram. **Open** 2-9pm Tue-Fri; 10am-9pm Sat, Sun; closed Mon. **Admission** *Tue-Fri* free. *Sat, Sun* 20 Kč, free under-6s. **Map** p310 D1.
Built out of curvaceous expanses of wrought iron to house the Great Exhibition of 1891, Výstaviště sig-

nalled the birth of the new architectural form in Prague. During the 1940s it became the site of various communist congresses, but today it is principally used to house car and computer expos. It's worth dodging past the salesmen to see the interior.

The industrial feeling of the wrought-iron structure is offset by vivid stained glass and exquisite floral decorations. The best view of the exterior is from the back, where a monumental modern fountain gushes kitschily at night in time to popular classics, accompanied by a light show. The grounds are filled with architectural oddities such as the Lapidárium (*see p117*), an open-air cinema

Letná Park metronome: where Stalin got ticked off. *See p108.*

and the delightfully dilapidated funfair, Lunapark, which nevertheless pulls in crowds of Czech families at the weekends.

Dejvice & further west

Some of the most exclusive residences in the city are located in Prague 6, the suburbs that lie beyond the Castle. You'd never guess this, though, from the rather desolate hub of the area, Vítězné náměstí, where a statue of Lenin used to stand. Nearby is the **U Cedru** restaurant (*see page 141*), serving up the some of the best Middle Eastern food in Prague.

Leading north from the square is the wide Jugoslávských partyzánů (Avenue of Yugoslav Partisans) at the end of which you'll find the **Holiday Inn Prague** (*see page 62*). This monumental piece of 1950s socialist realism is one of the last remaining bastions of Marxist-Leninist interior decoration in the city. The bars, which used to be frequented by morose party officials after a hard day inventing production figures, have now been taken over by morose mafioso types. Very much a sign of the times.

On the hill above the hotel are the **Baba Villas**, a colony of constructivist houses built after, and inspired by the huge success of, the 1927 Exhibition of Modern Living in Stuttgart. Under the guidance of Pavel Janák, all 33 of the houses were individually commissioned to provide simple but radically designed living spaces for ordinary families. However, they were quickly snapped up by leading figures of the Czech avant-garde, and many of them are still decorated with original fixtures and fittings. None, alas, is open to the public, but they are still a must-see for any fan of modern architecture. Take bus 131 to U Matěje and walk up Matějská to reach the estate.

On the western fringe of the city, just off Patočkova, is the **Břevnov Monastery**, inhabited by Benedictine monks since AD 993 and modelled on 'God's perfect workshop'. The monks celebrated their millennium with an enormous spring clean, sweeping out traces of the Ministry of the Interior, which for the last 40 years had used the **Basilica of St Margaret** (sv. Markéta) as a warehouse for its files on suspicious foreigners. This Romanesque church was remodelled by the Dientzenhofer father-and-son act in the early 18th century, and is one of their most successful commissions, with a single high nave and unfussy interior.

Close by, near the terminus of tram 22, a small stone pyramid marks the site of Bílá Hora, or White Mountain, where the decisive first battle of the Thirty Years' War took place in 1620. Within the park is the **Hvězda Hunting Lodge** (Letohrádek Hvězda), an extraordinary product of the Renaissance mind, its angular walls and roof arranged in the pattern of a six-pointed star (*hvězda* in Czech). It was built in the 1550s for Archduke Ferdinand of Tyrol who was obsessed with numerology, and the whole is conceived as an intellectual conundrum.

North of here, off Evropská, is the extensive and wonderfully wild **Divoká Šárka** (*see pages 193 and 243*), a fine place to stroll, swim or cycle away from the city crowds and fumes. There's a nude sunbathing area in summer.

Smíchov & Barrandov

Smíchov has undergone some changes since Mozart stayed here. Rapid industrialisation rather spoilt the ambience of the aristocracy's summer houses and the area has since been taken over by factories (including the Staropramen Brewery) and factory workers. Proletarian glories are still commemorated in the massive socialist realist murals in Anděl metro station. You can get an idea of what Smíchov was once like at **Bertramka**, the house with lilac-scented gardens that belonged to František and Josefina Dušek, now a museum devoted to their most famous house guest, Wolfgang Amadeus Mozart (*see page 122*).

South of Smíchov is **Barrandov**, the Czech version of Hollywood. On the cliffs below there are even white Hollywood-style letters that spell out B-a-r-r-a-n-d-e, although this is actually in homage to the 19th-century geologist after whom the quarter takes its name. Enormous studios were built here in the 1930s and the site has been the centre of the Czech film industry ever since.

Vyšehrad

Vyšehrad, the rocky outcrop south of Nové Město, is where all the best Prague myths were born. Here Libuše, the mother of Prague, fell into a trance and sent her horse out into the countryside to find her a suitable spouse. The horse returned with a strapping young ploughman called Přemysl, after whom the early Bohemian kings take their name. Alas, no evidence has been uncovered to back up the legend, but it has emerged that a castle was founded here in the first half of the tenth century, enjoying a period of importance when King Vratislav II (1061-92) built a royal palace on the rock. Within half a century, though, the Přemyslid rulers had moved back to Prague Castle and Vyšehrad's short period of political pre-eminence was over.

The easiest way to reach Vyšehrad is to take the metro to the Vyšehrad stop, under the enormous road bridge spanning the Nusle valley. Built in the 1970s, the bridge was hailed as a monument to socialism, an epithet hastily dropped when chunks of concrete began falling on passing pedestrians, and it became the most popular spot for suicides in the city. Walk away from the towering **Corinthia Towers** (*see page 62*) and past the unappealing, monolithic **Congress Centre** (*see page 212*), completed in 1980 as the supreme architectural expression of the 'normalisation' years, then through the baroque gateway into the park. The information centre to the right can provide maps of the area.

One of the first sights you will pass is the over-restored **Rotunda of St Martin**. Dating from the second half of the 11th century, it is the oldest complete Romanesque building in Prague.

There's been a church on the same site at Vyšehrad since the 14th century, but it was apparently irrevocably damaged when Lucifer, angered by an insubordinate cleric, threw three large rocks through the roof. The granite slabs (known as the Devil Pillars) can be found close to the Old Deanery, but the holes are gone and Joseph Mocker's neo-Gothic **Church of Sts Peter and Paul** (sv. Petr a Pavel) dates from the beginning of the 20th century. Restoration has brought out the best of the splendid polychrome interior, decked out with art nouveau-style saints and decorative motifs.

Next door is the Vyšehrad Cemetery, conceived by the 19th-century National Revival movement and last resting place of the cream of the country's arts worthies, including the composers Dvořák and Smetana, writers Karel Čapek and Jan Neruda and painter Mikoláš Aleš. The Slavín (pantheon), designed by Antonín Wiehl, jointly commemorates further artistic big cheeses such as painter Alfons Mucha and sculptor Josef Václav Myslbek. Surrounded by Italianate arcades, the cemetery contains an abundance of fine memorials, many of them displaying art nouveau influences.

On the south side of the church are four monumental sculptural groups by Myslbek depicting mythological heroes from Czech history; the couple nearest to the church are the legendary founders of Prague – Přemysl and Libuše. The park extends to the cliff edge overlooking the Vltava, from where there are fine views across the water to the Castle.

If you continue down the hill from Vyšehrad along Přemyslova, you'll find one of Prague's most outstanding pieces of cubist architecture, a corner apartment block designed by Josef Chochol at Neklanova 30 (1911-13; *see page 33* **Origami in stone**). Some way south is a railway bridge popularly known as 'The Bridge of Intelligence', because it was built by members of the intellectual élite who ended up working as labourers after losing their jobs during the purges of the 1950s.

Vinohrady & Žižkov

Map p311

Vinohrady came into existence in what the communist guidebooks called the period of Bourgeois Capitalism, and it's an area of magnificent, if crumbling, fin de siècle tenements. The heart of the neighbourhood is Náměstí Míru, with the twin spires of the neo-Gothic **Church of St Ludmila** (sv. Ludmila) and the opulent Vinohrady Theatre. The **Radost/FX** café, gallery and nightclub complex (*see pages 41, 144, 159 and 228*), still one of Prague's premier clubs, is nearby on Bělehradská. The **Medúza** café (*see page 151*) on quiet Belgická is one of the city's nicest daytime spots. The whole area south of Náměsti Míru has become a centre of Prague's gay community with several bars, clubs and pensions in the area.

The main artery of Vinohrady, however, is Vinohradská, a little further north. Formerly called Stalinova třída, it saw some of 1968's fiercest street battles against Warsaw Pact troops. Art nouveau apartment blocks line Vinohradská, looking out on to the **Church of the Sacred Heart** (Nejsvětější Srdce Páně), one of the most inspiring pieces of modern architecture in the city, dominated by its huge glass clock. It was built in 1928-32 by Josip Plečnik, the pioneering Slovenian architect.

Fans of ecclesiastical modernism might also like to look at Pavel Janák's 1930s **Hussite Church** (Husův sbor) on the corner of U vodárny and Dykova, and Josef Gočar's functionalist **Church of St Wenceslas** (sv. Václav) on náměstí Svatopluka Čecha.

Near Plečnik's church is the **Žižkov TV Tower** (*see page 113*), which was completed in 1989. Another nearby venue worthy of note is **Hapu** (*see page 161*), a contender for top mixed-drinks bar of the republic.

Tumbling down the hill to the north and east is Žižkov, a district notorious for its insalubrious pubs and whorehouses and for its large Romany population. Žižkov has always been a working-class district, so it's not surprising that the post-war presidents chose to be interred here, in the massive **National Memorial** (*see below*) on top of Vítkov Hill. Outside this mausoleum stands the largest equestrian statue in the world, a 16.5-ton effigy of Hussite hero **Jan Žižka**. The corpses were ejected from the mausoleum in 1990. It's an eerie, neglected place which these days occasionally hosts raves.

Further east on Vinohradská are two fine cemeteries. The first, **Olšany Cemetery** (*see page 112*), is the largest in Prague – a huge city of the dead. Since 1989 the cemetery has begun to suffer from the usual urban blights (graffiti) as well as some more unusual ones (grave-robbing).

Sightseeing

The people's republic of Žižkov

More beer per capita is consumed by Czechs than any other people, and the people of Žižkov work hard to ensure that it stays that way. Pop into a Žižkov pub and you'll often find an ancient, devastated man or woman sipping their *pivo* underneath a television playing the local hockey game. Breath in the blue smoke, sit down for a cheap (even by Prague standards) half-litre yourself, and soak in the Žižkov vibe. The waiter and fellow patrons will regard you with open contempt and suspicion. Stay strong, Žižkov can smell weakness. Perhaps after a bit of this you'll begin to think with organs other than your brain. Not a problem: the district is rife with bordellos and sleazy strip clubs.

Named for the ultimate Czech rabble rouser General Jan Žižka, who put fear into the Catholic armies, this area boasts an autonomous spirit you won't find in other Prague quarters. Czech cars abroad feature a 'CZ' sticker on the back. Roam around Žižkov and you'll see cars with a 'Ž' sticker, testifying their allegiance to this hallowed quarter.

Jan Žižka lords over the district, still riding his horse on top of Vítkov Hill. Right below his huge statue (pictured) is a pub whose name celebrates Žižka's most famous injury. **U vystřelenýho oka** ('The shot-out eye'; see page 161) is also one of the few pubs in Žižkov that is genuinely welcoming to non-Žižkovers. With dilapidated brown benches in its cigarette butt-strewn 'beer garden' and its headrests in front of the urinals offering a moment of solace to weary drinkers, it neatly embodies the area's many charms.

So does the **Akropolis** (see pages 129, 161 and 212), where quintessentially Žižkov artists like František Skála hang out and display their art, whether it's a cybernetic sculpture of found objects or a photo series of Gypsy subjects pulled in off the street.

Romanticised for centuries by Czech writers enraptured by the working-class feeling of the quarter, Žižkov has been the setting for many a Czech writer's tale, most recently the modern noir of Jáchym Topol's *A Trip to the Train Station*. It's not hard to see why. Streets that run into each other with cobblestones jutting out at unlikely angles; 30-year-old Ladas and Škodas lined up in rows or belching their black smoke from dying engines; the crumbling remains of buildings from the faded glory of the First Republic; and pubs, pubs and more pubs.

Clearly an essential literary role is played out here. What tale of Bohemia would be any good without rough, hard-edged characters to balance the princes and poets of Hradčany?

The cemetery extends from the Flora metro station to Jana Želivského, and includes a Garden of Rest, where the Red Army soldiers who died liberating Prague are buried in graves marked by sculptures of crossed machine guns.

Next door is the **Jewish Cemetery** (Židovské hřbitovy), where fans of Franz Kafka come to leave stones and pay their respects at his simple grave (follow the sign at the entrance by Želivského metro station; it's about 200m (660ft) down the row by the southern cemetery wall). The cemetery is in stark contrast to the cramped quarters of the Old Jewish Cemetery in Josefov. It was founded in 1890 and only a fraction of the graveyard has been used since World War II.

National Memorial

Národní památník
U památníku, Prague 3 (627 8452). Metro Florenc/133, 168, 207 bus. Map 8 C1.
One of the city's best-known and least liked landmarks. Looming above Žižkov, the massive, constructivist block and equally enormous equestrian statue high up on Vítkov Hill can be seen from around the city. It was built in 1925 by Jan Zázvorka

as a dignified setting for the remains of the legionnaires who fought against the Austro-Hungarian Empire in World War I. In 1953 the communist regime turned it into a mausoleum for Heroes of the Working Class. The mummified remains of Klement Gottwald, first communist president, were kept here, tended by scientists who unsuccessfully tried to preserve his body for display, Lenin-style, before the project was abandoned and the decaying body fobbed off on Gottwald's family in 1990.

No one is quite sure what to do with either memorial or the mausoleum. Opening times are unpredictable, but it doesn't really matter as most of what you might want to see can be seen from the outside. In front stands the massive equestrian statue of one-eyed General Žižka, scourge of 14th-century Catholics and the darling of the communists who adopted him in an effort to establish genuine Bohemian credentials.

Olšany Cemetery

Olšanské hřbitovy
Vinohradská/Jana Želivského, Prague 3. Metro Flora or Želivského. **Open** dawn-dusk daily. Map p311 D2
The overgrown yet beautiful Olšany Cemetery is the last resting place of two unlikely bed fellows:

The huge, thrusting, three-pillared television tower in Žižkov has been dubbed the Pražský pták or 'Prague Prick'. Seemingly modelled on a Soyuz rocket ready for blast-off, or maybe something out of *Thunderbirds*, it has been more of a hit with space-crazy visitors than with the locals. It was planned under the communists (who tore up part of the adjacent Jewish Cemetery to make room for it), completed early in 1989, and no sooner started operating in 1990 than it came under attack from nearby residents who claimed it was guilty of, among other things, jamming foreign radio waves and giving their children cancer. You can take a lift up to the eighth-floor viewing platform, or have a drink in the fifth-floor café, but in many ways standing at the base and looking up the 216m (709ft) of grey polished steel is even more scary. Views from the platform and the café are splendid, except at night, when they're obscured by reflections off the glass. More than 20 TV channels broadcast from behind the white plastic shielding that defends against the elements. Transmitters lower down deal with radio stations and emergency services.

Jižní Město & Háje

To the south and east of the city centre lies the wilderness of Prague 4. Though parts are very old and beautiful, the postcode has come to mean only one thing for Praguers: *paneláky*.

Panelák is the Czech word for a tower block made out of prefabricated concrete panels. These blocks sprouted like mushrooms throughout the 1960s and 1970s as a cheap solution to the post-war housing crisis. Jižní Město, or Southern Town, in Prague 4 has the greatest concentration of them, housing 100,000 people. Possibly the worst aspect of the *paneláky* is that they all look identical outside and in, although residents claim that even worse is the knowledge that they can't even be blown up and would have to be demolished the way they went up, panel by dreary panel.

Similar housing developments now ring the whole city, but Háje, the last metro stop on the red Line C, is as good a place as any to go to see the best of the worst. Before the big name change of 1989, Háje used to be known as Kosmonautů, a nod in the direction of the sister state's space programme and there's still a rather humorous sculpture of two cuddly cosmonauts outside the metro station. **Galaxie**, Central Europe's first multiplex cinema and perhaps the only place in the world that sells pork-flavoured popcorn, is nearby (*see page 197*), as is the popular swimming spot of **Hostivař Reservoir** (*see page 244*). Just beyond this new stab at capitalism is the odd combination of the Stodola Czech Country Bar, where the waitresses wear complete cowgirl kit, and the attached mega-bordello **Lotos** (*see page 232*).

the first communist president, Klement Gottwald, who died after catching a cold at Stalin's funeral, and the most famous anti-communist martyr, Jan Palach, the student who set fire to himself in Wenceslas Square in 1969. In death their fates have been strangely linked, as neither of their mortal remains have been allowed to rest in peace. Palach was originally buried here in 1969, but his grave became such a focus of dissent that the authorities disinterred his body and reburied it deep in the Bohemian countryside. In 1990 he was dug up and brought back to Olšany. His grave is just to the right of the main entrance. Gottwald is harder to locate, hidden away in Section 5 and sharing a mass grave with various other discredited party members. In 1990 his mummified remains were ejected from the National Memorial (*see page 112*) and returned to the family.

Žižkov TV Tower

Televizní vysílač
Mahlerovy sady, Prague 3 (6700 5778)). Metro Jiřího z Poděbrad/5, 9, 26 tram. **Open** *tower* 10am-11pm daily; *café* 11am-11pm daily. **Admission** 60Kč; children and students 30 Kč under-10s free. **Map** p311 C2.

Sightseeing

Museums

MiGs, Mozart, medieval portraiture, military models and Alfons Mucha surface from generations of fascinating clutter.

Prague's collection of museums is as rich, quirky and varied as you'd expect in a city where the nation's sense of self has changed so often. Revolution and restitution have taken their toll, and some collections remain homeless. Museums with foresight, finally freed from state control and galvanised into action by the need to be commercial, have begun mastering the contemporary arts of courting sponsors and making their collections accessible to the public. Still, with some exceptions – notably the revamped **Museum of Decorative Arts** (*see page 117*) and the **Jewish Museum** (*see page 118*) – you may well still gather an overall impression of benign neglect.

One positive influence was Prague's role as one of the European Cities of Culture 2000, which created various new venues and infused several older ones with much-needed cash.

NATIONAL GALLERY

All is in flux – or Fluxus – at the National Gallery. This fragmented institution, comprising five relatively small permanent collections, a modern art centre and a handful of exhibition spaces across the city including **Prague Castle Riding School**, **Wallenstein Riding School** and **Kinský Palace** (*for all, see page 204*), is thawing after a decade of shoddy leadership and shrinking finances. Conceptual artist Milan Knížák, formerly of the Fluxus movement, was appointed to head the gallery in 1999. This left the art scene gobsmacked – imagine a slightly older Damien Hirst becoming head of Britain's National Gallery – but Knížák has already streamlined the staff and set up a fund to compensate owners of works confiscated by Nazis and communists.

Knížák is busy reorganising three of the National Gallery's largest branches. The 19th-century Czech art from **St Agnes's Convent** (*see page 116*) is being moved to the **National Gallery Collection of 19th- & 20th-Century Art**, (*see below*) while art formerly in **St George's Convent** (*see page 116*) will have a suitably Gothic new home at St Agnes's. All this was under way at press time, so check the local papers or information offices to suss the current state of affairs, or call the venues or check the reasonably up-to-date English-language National Gallery website (www.ngprague.cz).

Things are looking up at the **National Gallery Collection of 19th- and 20th-Century Art**.

National Gallery Collection of 19th- & 20th-Century Art

Sbírka moderního a současného umění
Veletržní palác, Dukelských hrdinů 47, Holešovice, Prague 7 (2430 1111). Metro Vltavská/ 5, 12, 17 tram. **Open** 10am-6pm Tue, Wed, Fri-Sun; 10am-9pm Thur; closed Mon. **Admission** 90 Kč; 50 Kč concessions; 150 Kč family; free under-10s. **No credit cards. Map** p310 D2.

Public response to the country's newest modern art space has been overwhelmingly positive. The cubist sculpture of Otto Gutfreund, the moody take on impressionism typified by Jan Preisler and Antonín Slavíček, the perceptual explorations of Emil Filla and Bohumil Kubišta and even assorted surrealists fit in here so well you would think the place was purpose-built. (It opened as the Trade Fair Building in

1924.) Vincenc Kramář, the gallery's director during the First Republic, was among the first to recognise the importance of Picasso. His Parisian spending sprees in gave the Czech public a superb collection of French modern art. The corner devoted to Picasso and Braque here is a perfect introduction to cubism.

The collection starts with the founders of nationalist painting: Antonín Machek, a specialist in portraits of Czech intellectuals, and Antonín Mánes, known for romanticised landscapes. His son, Josef, a dominant figure of mid 19th-century painting, is most admired for his depictions of Czech legends and country life. The historical scenes fashionable at the time were executed most convincingly by Jaroslav Čermák and Mikoláš Aleš, and most laughably by František Ženíšek.

St Agnes's Convent

Klášter sv. Anežky české
U milosrdnůch 17, Staré Město, Prague 1 (2481 0628). Metro Náměstí Republiky/5, 8, 14 tram. **Open** 10am-6pm Tue-Sun; closed Mon. **Admission** 90 Kč; 50 Kč concessions; 150 Kč family; free under-10s. **No credit cards. Map** p306 J1.
At press time the gallery was preparing to receive the art from St George's Convent (*see below*) up to the 16th century, with a likely opening date of autumn 2000. This earlier art is the glory of the National Gallery collection, filled with the lyricism and humanity of Czech medieval art. During the reign of Charles IV (1346-78) Prague was in the forefront of European artistic development. The bronze statue of St George and the Dragon, for example, is so Renaissance in spirit that scholars still argue over its date. Czech artists were among the first to paint portraits, such as the compelling depictions of the Emperor and Archbishop Očko in the Votive Panel by Jan Očko of Vlašim. The panels by Master Theodoric show a similar interest in realism.

The outstanding artist of the end of the 14th century was the Master of Třeboň. His altarpiece featuring the *Resurrection of Christ* replaces realism with an atmosphere of mystery and miracle. His *Madonna of Roudnice*, is an example of the 'Beautiful Style' that prevailed until the outbreak of the Hussite wars. Gothic remained popular in Bohemia right up to the 16th century, as seen in the extraordinary wood carving by the monogrammist IP, depicting the skeletal, half-decomposed figure of Death brushed aside by the Risen Christ.

St George's Convent

Klášter sv. Jiří
Jiřské náměstí 33, Hradčany, Prague 1 (5732 0536/535 240). Metro Malostranská and up the Old Castle Steps./22, 23 tram. **Open** 10am-6pm Tue-Sun; closed Mon. **Admission** 90 Kč; 50 Kč concessions; 150 Kč family; free under-10s. **No credit cards. Map** p305 D2.
The impressive holdings of Bohemian painting and sculpture from the early Middle Ages to around 1600 were to be moved into St Agnes's Convent (*see above*), in 2000.

The remaining works include a handful of paintings that survive from the collections of Rudolf II (1576-1611). They include masterpieces by the Antwerp mannerist Bartholomaeus Spranger, whose sophisticated colours, elegant eroticism and obscure themes typify the style.

The baroque selection starts with Karel Škréta, who spent his youth as a Protestant exile in Rome, returning to Prague in 1638 as a convert ready to serve the Counter-Reformation. He was a down-to-earth painter, in contrast to the feverishly religious work of Michael Leopold Willmann and Jan Kryštof Liška. The tendency of baroque painting and sculpture to borrow from each other can be seen in the paintings of Petr Brandl, the most acclaimed Czech artist of the early 18th century. His work is displayed nearby that of the two great sculptors of the time, Mathias Bernard Braun and Ferdinand Maximilián Brokof.

Sternberg Palace

Šternberský palác
Hradčanské náměstí 15, Hradčany, Prague 1 (2051 4599/20514634-7). Tram 22, 23. **Open** 10am-6pm Tue-Sun; closed Mon. **Admission** 90 Kč; 50 Kč concessions; 150 Kč family; free under-10s. **No credit cards. Map** p304 C2.
Enlightened aristocrats trying to rouse Prague from provincial stupor founded the Sternberg Gallery here in the 1790s. The palace now houses the National Gallery's European Old Masters. Not a large or well-balanced collection, especially since some of its most famous works were returned to their pre-war owners, but some outstanding paintings remain, including a brilliant Frans Hals portrait and Dürer's *Feast of the Rosary*.

Zbraslav Chateau

Zámek Zbraslav
Zámek Zbraslav, Zbraslav (5792 1638). Metro Smíchovské nádraži/bus 129, 241, 243, 360 to Zbraslavské náměstí. **Open** 10am-6pm Tue-Sun; closed Mon. **Admission** 90 Kč; 40 Kč concessions; 150 Kč family. **No credit cards.**
This baroque pile at the southern tip of Prague, houses the National Gallery's surprisingly good collection of Asian art. The Chinese and Japanese holdings are particularly fine, especially the Han and Tang ceramic tomb figurines. There's also a smattering of Indian, Southeast Asian, and Islamic pieces, plus a handful of Tibetan *thangka* scrolls crawling with fire demons and battling monks. A 20-30 minute bus ride from the metro.

Other permanent collections

Bílek Villa

Bilkova vila
Mickiewiczowa 1, Hradčany, Prague 1 (2432 2021). Metro Hradčanská/18, 22 tram. **Open** *16 May-15 Oct* 10am-6pm Tue-Sun; closed Mon. *16 Oct-15 May* 10am-5pm Thu-Sun; closed Mon-Wed. **Admission** 50 Kč; 20 Kč concessions. **No credit cards. Map** p310 A3.

This must be the only building in the world designed to look like a wheatfield. Built in 1911-12 by mystic sculptor František Bílek as his studio and home, it still contains much of his work. Bílek went to Paris to study as a painter, but discovered that he was half colour-blind. He then turned to sculpture and illustration. The wheatfield, representing spiritual fertility and the harvest of creative work, was one of his many motifs. Others were his vision of light as an emanation of creative energy, and trees as signifiers of Man and the cycle of birth and decay. The results range from the sublime to the repellent. If the grouping of Hobbit-like wooden figures out front takes your fancy, have a look inside.

House of the Black Madonna
Dům U Černé matky boží

Celetná 34, Staré Město, Prague 1 (2421 1732). Metro Náměstí Republiky/5, 8, 14 tram. **Open** 10am-6pm Tue-Sun; closed Mon. **Admission** 35 Kč; 15 Kč concessions. **No credit cards. Map** p307 K3.

Worth a visit for the building alone, perhaps the finest example of Prague cubist architecture (*see page 33* **Origami in stone**). It's used by the Czech Museum of Fine Arts (*see page 202*) for a permanent exhibition of Czech cubism, featuring furniture design and architecture. The lower floors host temporary exhibitions of modernist and contemporary Czech artists.

House of the Gold Ring
Dům U Zlatého prstenu

Týnská 6, Staré Město, Prague 1 (2482 7022). Metro Náměstí Republiky/5, 8, 14 tram. **Open** 10am-6pm Tue-Sun; closed Mon. **Admission** 60 Kč; 30 Kč concessions; free under-6s. Free to all first Tue of month. **No credit cards. Map** p306 J3.

Run by the city of Prague, this showpiece space proves that the National Gallery isn't the only body willing to invest in the revival of Czech modern art. This Renaissance gem contains a broad spectrum of 20th-century Czech works. Clever curating – 'distorted figuration' and 'eurhythmy of the soul' are two themes – helps crack the code of some widely varied works. Fine basement exhibition space for up-and-coming artists.

Lapidárium
Výstaviště, Holešovice, Prague 7 (3337 5636). Metro Nádraží Holešovice/5, 12, 17 tram. **Open** noon-6pm Tue-Fri; 10am-6pm Sat, Sun; closed Mon. **Admission** 20 Kč; 10 Kč concessions. **No credit cards. Map** p310 D1.

This handsome gallery is officially the last resting place for sculptures rescued from demolished buildings or inclement weather. Unofficially, it is a testament to the city's swings in fortune. The collection includes the original baroque masterpieces from Charles Bridge; the Marian column from Old Town Square, erected in 1648 in gratitude for the defence of Prague from the Swedes; and a fine equestrian statue of Emperor Francis II. Particularly prized are the copies of Peter Parler's

14th-century sculpted heads, which are among the first examples of European portraiture. The originals remain tantalisingly out of view in St Vitus's Cathedral (*see page 71*).

Prague Castle Picture Gallery
Obrazárna Pražského hradu

Prague Castle (second courtyard), Hradčany, Prague 1 (2437 3531/www.hrad.cz). Metro Malostranská and up the Old Castle Steps/22, 23 tram. **Open** 10am-6pm daily. **Admission** 100 Kč; 50 Kč concessions; 150 Kč family; free under-6s. **No credit cards. Map** p304 C2.

Home of Giuseppe Archimboldo's infamous mannerist work *Vertumnus*, which cast Rudolf II as a Roman harvest god, this remnant of the eccentric emperor's private collection also includes works by Rubens, Titian, Veronese and lesser-known masters. Also worth a look are the unorthodox erotic depictions of scenes from antiquity, suggestive of the lifestyle of the Habsburg's family's wildest member.

Decorative arts

Mucha Museum
Muchovo muzeum

Kaunický palác, Panská 7, Nové Město, Prague 1 (628 4162/museum@mucha.cz/www.mucha.cz). Metro Můstek/3, 9, 14, 24 tram. **Open** 10am-6pm daily. **Admission** 120 Kč; 60 Kč students. **No credit cards. Map** p307 K4.

A property developer and the family of the artist collaborated to open this museum in 1998, dedicated to perhaps the most famous of all Czech visual artists, Alfons Mucha (1860-1939). Known for commercial work such as mass-produced decorative panels and posters for Sarah Bernhardt's theatre performances, Mucha exercised his greatest influence through his *Encyclopaedia For Craftsmen* (1902), a catalogue of art nouveau decorative elements, forms and designs. Mucha created a stained-glass window for St Vitus's Cathedral (*see page 71*) and the *Slavonic Epic*, a series of gigantic narrative oil paintings now residing in Moravský Krumlov castle, south-west of Brno. The museum also displays paintings, drawings, sketches, notebooks, and a video on his life.

Museum of Decorative Arts
Uměleckoprůmyslové muzeum

ulice 17. listopadu 2, Staré Město, Prague 1 (5109 3111/direct@anet.cz). Metro Staroměstská/17, 18 tram. **Open** 10am-6pm Tue-Sun; closed Mon. **Admission** 40 Kč; 20 Kč concessions; free under-10s. **No credit cards. Map** p306 G2.

Built between 1897 and 1900, this neo-Renaissance museum is itself a work of art, revelling in richly decorated halls, stained- and etched-glass windows, and intricately painted plaster mouldings. At press time the exhibit was to be completely overhauled to group objects according to material, and to bring the hitherto unseen 20th-century collection out of the storeroom. There should be ample space for the collections of modern glass and photography, which previously could be glimpsed only when on loan to other institutions.

The permanent collections document the craftsmanship, decorative styles and, occasionally, the hideous taste of previous centuries. The lavishly crafted pieces here include exquisite furniture, tapestries, pottery, clocks, books, a beautifully preserved collection of clothing, and fine displays of ceramics and glass. Bohemian glassmakers were highly inventive and perfected techniques such as engraving, facet-cutting and ruby-glass manufacture that their rivals found hard to match. (*See page 203* On the cutting edge.)

Historical museum at the Lobkowicz Palace

Lobkovický palác
Jiřská 3, Hradčany, Prague 1 (537 3641/537 218). Metro Malostranská/12, 18, 22, 23 tram. **Open** 9am-5pm Tue-Sun; closed Mon. **Admission** 40 Kč; 20 Kč concessions. **No credit cards. Map** p305 E2.
The prime attraction of this late 17th-century structure in the Castle complex is the two-floor perma-nent exhibition 'Treasures From the Nation's Past'. Although the English-language texts can be difficult to follow, it's worth a visit for the extensive collection of sculptures, coins, instruments of torture, armour, musical instruments, jewellery, furniture and scores of other items, including copies of the Czech coronation jewels. The gorgeously frescoed banquet hall is used for concerts and temporary exhibitions. Part of the sgraffitoed façade of the original Renaissance building can be seen from the courtyard café.

Komenský Pedagogical Museum

Pedagogické muzeum JA Komenského
Valdštejnská 20, Malá Strana, Prague 1 (5732 0039/www.pmjak.cz). Metro Malostranská/12, 18, 22, 23 tram. **Open** 10am-12.30pm, 1-4.30pm, Tue-Sat; closed Sun, Mon. **Admission** 6 Kč; 3 Kč concessions. **No credit cards. Map** p305 E2.
Jan Amos Komenský (Comenius), philosopher and Protestant pedagogue, remains a great source of Czech national pride whose influence on Western education is still felt. This museum traces his eventful life (1592-1670) during the turbulent times of the Bohemian Counter-Reformation, as well as his extensive European travels and mind-bogglingly large body of writing – Komensky published 132

The Jewish Museum

The museum was founded in 1906 to preserve the historical monuments of the former Jewish ghetto. By a gruesome irony, Hitler was responsible for today's comprehensive collections, though the story that he wanted a 'museum of an extinct race' is sometimes debated. Another suggestion is that Prague's German overlords allowed museum workers to catalogue and store the property of the 153 Czech Jewish communities, the better to plunder them. The loot remained here after the war because there was nobody to whom it could be returned.

The museum, comprising five different buildings and the **Old Jewish Cemetery** (pictured) is one of Prague's busiest tourist draws. It is also one of the costliest. You have to buy a ticket for all six components of the museum. You can buy a separate ticket for only the **Old-New Synagogue** (see page 98), not officially part of the Jewish Museum.

Tickets are sold at the **Klausen**, **Maisel**, **Pinkas** and **Spanish Synagogues** (below) and at Precious Legacy travel agency at Maiselova 16 (232 1951). English-language tours are conducted from Sunday to Friday from the **Maisel Synagogue** (below – call the Jewish Museum beforehand to check or reserve).

Groups and private guides in several languages are also available from **Precious Legacy** (see page 99) for higher rates.

Jewish Museum

Židovské Muzeum
Josefov, Staré Město, Prague 1 (231 7191/231 0302/www.jewishmuseum.cz). Metro Staroměstská/17, 18 tram. **Open** Apr-Oct 9am-6pm Sun-Fri; closed Sat. *Nov-Mar* (excluding Jewish holidays) 9am-4.30pm daily. **Admission** 480 Kč; 340 Kč students and 6-15-year-olds; 40 Kč more per person for guided tour. **No credit cards. Map** p306 H2-3.
The central address for the Jewish Museum complex, and the place to buy tickets for the other locations listed below.

Former Ceremonial Hall

Obřadní síň
U starého hřbitova 3a, Staré Město, Prague 1 (231 7191/231 0302). **Map** p306 H2.
Turreted and arched, the Romanesque details of this building at the exit of the cemetery make it appear as old as the gravestones. In fact, it was built in 1906 for the Prague Burial Society, which used the building for only 20 years. It currently houses an exhibition of Jewish

works during his lifetime, and a further 82 were published posthumously. The appealingly old-fashioned exhibits are in Czech, but the friendly attendants will provide visitors with an English-language information sheet, and perhaps even an enthusiastic tour.

Museum of the City of Prague

Muzeum hlavního města Prahy
Na Poříčí 52, Nové Město, Prague 1 (2481 6772).
Metro Florenc/3, 8, 24 tram. **Open** 9am-6pm Tue-Sun;
closed Mon. **Admission** 30 Kč; 15 Kč concessions;
under-10s free. Free to all first Thur of month. **No
credit cards. Map** p307 M2.
Antonín Langweil spent 11 years of the early 19th century building an incredibly precise room-sized paper model of Prague, which is now this museum's prize exhibit. It is the only complete depiction of what the city looked like before the Jewish ghetto was ripped down. The displays follow the city's development from pre-history through to the 17th century, with some English labels provided in the rooms devoted to medieval and later events. The upstairs galleries host temporary exhibitions and the original of the Josef Mánes painting reproduced below the Old Town Hall's astronomical clock.

Natural history & ethnography

Náprstek Museum

Náprstkovo muzeum
Betlémské náměstí 1, Staré Město, Prague 1 (2222 1416/2222 0017/www.aconet.cz/npm). Metro Můstek or Národní třída/6, 9, 17, 18, 22, 23 tram. **Open** 9am-noon, 12.45-5.30pm Tue-Sun; closed Mon. **Admission** 30 Kč; 10 Kč concessions; free under-6s. **No credit cards. Map** p306 G4/5.
The 19th-century nationalist Vojta Náprstek had two passions: modern technology and primitive cultures. While the gadgets he collected are now in the National Technical Museum (*see page 122*), the ethnographic oddities he acquired from Czech travellers are here in an extension to his house, an ungainly building that smells strongly of disinfectant. The displays concentrating on native peoples of the Americas, Australasia and the Pacific Islands are interesting and excellently arranged. More frustrating is any effort to match the items with the confusing explanations in the English-language binders. Still, enthusiasts of archaeology and primitive art shouldn't miss this impressive collection.

funereal items, including a set of naïve-style paintings showing the Burial Society's activities in the 18th century.

Klausen Synagogue

Klausová synagóga
U starého hřbitova 3a, Staré Město, Prague 1 (no phone). **Map** p306 H2.

The original was destroyed in the great ghetto fire of 1689, along with 318 houses and ten other synagogues. The existing synagogue, hastily constructed on the same site in 1694, has much in common with Prague's baroque churches, as some were built by the same craftsmen. Inside, a permanent exhibition details the place of religion in the daily lives of ▶

Sightseeing

National Museum

Národní muzeum
Václavské náměstí 68, Nové Město, Prague 1 (2449 7111/www.nm.cz). Metro Muzeum. **Open** *May-Sept* 10am-6pm daily. *Oct-Apr* 9am-5pm daily. Closed 1st Tue of mth. **Admission** 70 Kč; 35 Kč concessions; 60 Kč family; free under-6s. Free to all first Mon of month. **No credit cards. Map** p309 L6/7.

The city's grandest museum is also its biggest disappointment. The vast edifice dominates the top of Wenceslas Square, its neo-Renaissance flamboyance promising an intriguing interior. Instead it is filled with roomfuls of dusty fossils and stuffed animals. Apart from an introductory sheet in English for the prehistory, palaeontology, mineralogy, and zoology sections, all labelling is in Czech. If rocks are your thing, the 10,000 specimens on display (one of the largest collections in Europe) might impress. Elsewhere, the big woolly mammoth's head and skeleton of a fin whale are memorable.

The architecture is the most appealing feature. Designed by Josef Schulz and finished in 1890, it was a proud symbol of the Czech nationalist revival. Figures representing Bohemia flanked by Vltava, Elbe, Moravia and Silesia decorate the façade. Inside, murals by František Ženíšek and Václav Brožík depict scenes from Czech history.

Military & police

Aeronautical & Cosmonautical Exhibition

Letecké muzeum
Mladoboleslavská, Kbely, Prague 9 (2020 7504/2020 7505). Metro Vysočanská, then 185, 259, 280, 302 or 354 bus to Letecké muzeum. **Open** *May-Oct* 10am-6pm Tue-Sun; closed Mon. *Nov-Apr* closed. **Admission** 40 Kč; 25 Kč concessions. **No credit cards.**

It's a long haul out to Kbely airport, but it's your best chance to glimpse the other side of the Cold War. Three hangars house a huge collection of military and civil aircraft, ranging from World War I biplanes to a McDonnell-Douglas Phantom and a veritable squadron of MiG fighter jets. A small cosmonautical section, displaying space suits and segments of rockets, is popular with children, but the menacing collection of Russian tanks and military vehicles, right on up to mobile tactical missiles from the 1970s, is the real show-stopper.

Military Museum

Vojenské historické muzeum
Schwarzenberský palác, Hradčanské náměstí 2, Hradčany, Prague 1 (2020 2020). Metro Malostranská/12, 18, 22, 23 tram. **Open** *May-Oct*

▶ ## The Jewish Museum (continued)

the ghetto's former inhabitants. Accompanying texts explain the meaning, use and relevance of the Hebrew manuscripts and other artefacts on display. The best view of the synagogue is from the Old Jewish Cemetery, where the simple façade rises behind the ancient gravestones, topped by two tablets of the Decalogue engraved with a golden inscription. The tablets are echoed in the windows and in the decorative details on the balustrade.

Maisel Synagogue

Maiselova synagóga
Maiselova 10, Staré Město, Prague 1 (no phone). **Map** p306 H3.
Mordecai Maisel (1528-1601), mayor of the Jewish ghetto during the reign of Rudolf II, was one of the richest men in 16th-century Europe. Legend traces his wealth to a lucky intervention by goblins, but more realistic historians suggest that Rudolf II granted Maisel a lucrative trading monopoly. The original building on this site, funded by Maisel, was apparently the most splendid of all the quarter's synagogues, until it burned down along with most of the others in 1689. The present structure, sandwiched between tenement blocks, has a core dating to the 1690s; the rest was redone

between 1892 and 1905. It now houses an exhibition on the Jewish history of Bohemia and Moravia from the 10th to the 18th century.

Old Jewish Cemetery

Starý židovský hřbitov
Široká 3, Staré Město, Prague 1 (no phone). **Map** p306 H2.
The Old Jewish Cemetery, where all of Prague's Jews were buried until the late 1600s, is one of the eeriest remnants of the city's once-thriving Jewish community. The 12,000 tombstones crammed into this tiny, tree-shaded patch of ground are a forceful reminder of the lack of space accorded to the ghetto, which remained walled until the late 1700s. Forbidden to enlarge the burial ground, the Jews had to bury the dead on top of one another. An estimated 100,000 bodies were piled up to 12 layers deep. Above them, lopsided stone tablets were crammed on to mounds of earth.

Burials began here in the early 15th century, although earlier gravestones were brought in from a cemetery nearby. Among them was the oldest tombstone in the cemetery, that of Avigdor Kara, who died in 1439. (The original has been replaced by a copy). Kara was a boy during the Passover of 1389, when Christians rampaging through the quarter killed 3,000 people. He wrote an elegy of remembrance that is recited on Yom Kippur every year in the Old-

10am-6pm Tue-Sun; closed Mon. *Nov-Apr* closed.
Admission 40 Kč; 25 Kč concessions. Free to all Tue.
No credit cards. Map p304 C3.

Closed until spring 2001, when the opening hours given are supposed to come into force, but it might be worth checking them before setting out. A few metres from the main Castle gate, where sculpted Titans batter invaders, the Schwarzenberg Palace is an apt venue for a museum devoted to historical weaponry. Exhibits bristling with bloodthirsty implements chart Czech military campaigns from 13th-century battles against marauding Mongols to the end of World War I. The collection of scale models should please anyone who ever owned a set of toy soldiers. You can buy a new set in the shop just inside the main entrance.

Police Museum

Muzeum policie ČR
Ke Karlovu 1, Nové Město, Prague 2 (295 209/2413 5708/www.mvcr.cz/policie/muzeum.htm). Metro I.P. Pavlova/6, 11 tram. **Open** 10am-5pm Tue-Sun; closed Mon. **Admission** 20 Kč; 10 Kč concessions.; 40 Kč family. **No credit cards. Map** p309 K10.

A former convent attached to the Karlov Church is the incongruous home of Prague's surprisingly interesting Police Museum. Go beyond the cases of

uniforms for displays on crime detection techniques. Here you can take your own fingerprints or try to reconstruct events at a creepy scene-of-the-crime mock-up. The criminology section contains accounts of murder mysteries, illustrated with photographs, weapons and photo-fits. Kids love it, though be warned that some of the photographs are quite graphic. The final room contains an arsenal of home-made weaponry that would please James Bond: sword sticks, hand-made pistols, pen guns, even a converted lighter. Labelling is almost entirely in Czech.

Music & musicians

Dvořák Museum

Muzeum Antonína Dvořáka
Villa Amerika, Ke Karlovu 20, Nové Město, Prague 2 (298 214). Metro I.P. Pavlova. **Open** 10am-5pm Tue-Sun; closed Mon. **Admission** 30 Kč; 15 Kč concessions. **No credit cards. Map** p309 K8.

This small red and ochre villa was built by Kilian Ignaz Dientzenhofer in 1720 for Count Jan Václav Michna, then became a cattle market during the 19th century. It now houses the Dvořák Society's well-organised tribute to the most famous Czech

New Synagogue. The most prominent tombs, identified by their coverings of pebbles and messages, belong to Mordecaj Maisel and Rabbi Löw ben Bezalel (1512-1609).

Decorative reliefs on the headstones indicate the deceased's name or occupation: a pair of scissors, for example, indicates a tailor. The black headstones are the oldest, carved from 15th-century sandstone; the white ones, of marble, date from the 16th and 17th centuries. The graveyard is usually as full of chattering tourists as it is with teetering headstones.

Pinkas Synagogue

Pinkasova synagóga
Široká 3, Staré Město, Prague 1 (no phone). **Map** p306 H2/3.

The story goes that a Rabbi Pinkas founded this synagogue in 1479 after falling out with the elders at the Old-New. The building was enlarged in 1535, and a Renaissance façade added in 1625. In the 1950s, the names of 77,297 men, women and children of Bohemia and Moravia who died in the Holocaust were inscribed on the synagogue's walls as a memorial. In 1967, after the Six Day War, the Czechoslovak government expelled the Israeli ambassador and closed the synagogue for 'restoration'. In the ensuing 22 years, the writing decayed until indecipherable. Not until

1989 could the museum begin restoring the names, a job only recently completed.

The Pinkas also houses a powerful exhibition of drawings by children interned in **Terezín** (*see* chapter **Easy Day Trips**), the last stop en route to the death camps in the east. The drawings are both shocking and poignant: the mass dormitories and stormy skies of the camp stand next to idyllic recollections of fields and flowers.

Spanish Synagogue

Spanělská synagóga
Vězeňská 1, Staré Město, Prague 1 (no phone). **Map** p306 J2.

The Old Synagogue or Altschul, older still than the Old-New Synagogue, stood on this site as an island amid Christian territory, to which Jews could cross from the main ghetto only at certain times. It became a Reform synagogue in 1837, then the prospering congregation rebuilt it in 1868 in the then-fashionable Moorish style. After painstaking reconstruction the long-decrepit building reopened in 1998. Its lovely domed interior again glows with hypnotic floral designs traced in green, red, and faux gold leaf, lit by stained-glass windows.

> ► For more on **historic buildings in the Jewish Museum** see page 97.

Sightseeing

National Technical Museum – kid-pleaser.

composer. Memorabilia and photographs make up the ground floor display. Further exhibits and information on Dvořák's considerable musical output are upstairs, as is a recital hall, decorated with frescoes by Jan Ferdinand Schor, and used for concerts during the summer. CDs of Dvořák's works and an English-language translation of the exhibition's captions are available.

Mozart Museum

Bertramka, Mozartova 169, Smíchov, Prague 5 (543 893). Metro Anděl/4, 7, 9, 10 tram. **Open** *Apr-Oct* 9.30am-6pm daily. *Nov-Mar* 9.30am-5pm daily. **Admission** 90 Kč; 50 Kč concessions; free under-6s. **No credit cards.**

In a neighbourhood grimy and choked with traffic, the Villa Bertramka is a welcome refuge in its walled park. To find it, look for the garish Mövenpick Hotel next door. Mozart stayed here several times as a guest of the villa's owners, composer František Dušek and his wife Josefina. It was here, in 1787, that Mozart composed the overture to *Don Giovanni*, the night before its première in the Nostitz Theatre, now called the Estates Theatre (*see page 222*). Tranquillity is the villa's greatest asset – in mid-morning or late afternoon, it is possible to linger over cappuccino in the courtyard café relatively undisturbed by tour groups. Evening

recitals held on the terrace cash in further on the Mozart connection, when performers sometimes don period costumes. With the house and grounds restored to their 18th-century glory, the museum works better as a homage to Mozart's era than as a monument to the man himself.

Smetana Museum

Muzeum Bedřicha Smetany
Novotného lávka 1, Staré Město, Prague 1 (2422 9075). Metro Staroměstská/17, 18 tram. **Open** 10am-5pm Wed-Mon; closed Tue. **Admission** 40 Kč; 20 Kč students, OAPs; 5 Kč children. **No credit cards.** **Map** p306 G4.

The imaginatively revamped Smetana Museum displays an extensive collection of memorabilia from the life and works of Bedřich Smetana (1824-84). Only serious fans will care enough to match the English-language text found in the thick binder by the door to the items on display. Be advised that the staff will try to hit you up for a 30 Kč 'copyright' fee for taking pictures. The best plan is to browse for a few moments, then head for the rear of the museum, where a clever interactive display lets the visitor stand at an orchestra conductor's podium and point a baton at one of a dozen music stands, each devoted to a different Smetana composition. Aim well and press a little button on the wand to hear a snippet of the work.

Science & technology

City Transport Museum

Muzeum MHD Střešovice
Patočkova 4, Střešovice, Prague 6 (3332 2432). Tram 1, 8, 18. **Open** *Apr-Oct* 9am-5pm Sat, Sun; closed Mon-Fri. *Nov-Mar* closed. **Admission** 20 Kč; 10 Kč children. **No credit cards.**

Filled with a mesmerising collection of big shiny engines, and very popular with children and their fathers, this museum contains nearly every model of tram and trolley bus that ever ran the streets of Prague, polished and oiled to perfection. In summer you can take a trip on a historical tram to the city centre and back. A far cry from today's vehicles full of plastic seats and rampant advertising, the early 20th-century trams' wooden seats, dinging bells and spiffy red and tan paint jobs can make you feel like you've stepped back into history.

National Technical Museum

Národní technické muzeum
Kostelní 42, Holešovice, Prague 7 (2039 9111/ www.ntm.cz). Metro Hradčanská or Vltavská/1, 8, 25, 26 tram. **Open** 9am-5pm Tue-Sun; closed Mon. **Admission** 60 Kč; 20 Kč concessions. **No credit cards.** **Map** p310 C3.

Don't let the mundane name put you off: this is a fascinating collection, enjoyable for both kids and adults. The museum, one of few in Prague to use interactive displays, traces the development of technology and science in Czechoslovakia, which, until the communist era, was one of the most innovative and industrially advanced of European nations. The Transport Hall, with its steam trains, vintage motorcycles, racing cars and biplanes, stands in sharp contrast to the claustrophobic mine in the basement, where sinister coal-cutting implements are displayed in tunnels. Guided tours of the mine leave from the ticket office and are available in English. There's also an extensive photography and cinematography section, and a collection of rare astronomical instruments.

Toys

Toy Museum
Muzeum hraček
*Jiřská 4, Hradčany, Prague 1 (2437 2294/2437 1111).
Metro Malostranská/12, 18, 22, 23 tram.* **Open**
9.30am-5.30pm daily. **Admission** 40 Kč; 30 Kč students, OAPs; 20 Kč children; 60 Kč family; under-5s free. **No credit cards. Map** p305 E1.
Part of Czech émigré Ivan Steiger's large collection is displayed on the two floors of this museum on the Castle grounds. Brief explanatory texts accompany cases of toys, many adorable or ingenious, from wooden folk toys to an incredibly elaborate train set made of pure tin. Kitsch fans will love the

little robots and the enormous collection of Barbie and friends clad in vintage costumes throughout the decades. Good for a rainy day.

Wax

Prague Wax Museum
Pražské panoptikum
*Národní třída 25, Nové Město, Prague 1 (2108 5318).
Metro Národní třída/6, 9, 18, 22, 23 tram.* **Open**
10am-8pm daily. **Admission** 119 Kč; 59 Kč students;
49 Kč children, OAPs; free under-6s. **No credit cards.
Map** p306 H5.
In a dusty medieval library, alchemist Edward Kelley prepares a concoction as Rudolf II watches and a cauldron bubbles. Nearby, Tycho Brahe and Johannes Kepler gaze out of a window at a starry sky, while Franz Kafka haunts a corner in an eerily beautiful turn-of-the-century street scene. It's a uniquely visual journey through Bohemia's past and present, but there's little information other than simple name placards next to the figures. Miloš Forman, Václav Klaus and Václav Havel represent the post-socialist era. The movie offerings, labelled 'pseudoholography', feature tiny 3-D projections dancing through a tiny set – entertaining for five minutes, tops.

Rally of the dolls – peruse the First Republic's playthings at the **Toy Museum**.

Sightseeing

BUENOS AIRES

Buenos Aires Restaurant serves a variety of tempting dishes, featuring high quality Argentine steaks, T-Bone steaks, Ribs, tender and juicy, „Parrilla" - grilled to perfection.
And while favoring our juicy steaks enjoy one of our exclusive Argentine wines (Mendoza - Trapiche - Cabernet Savignon or Syrah), available only at our Restaurant.
The interior evokes Argentine atmosphere.

ARGENTINE RESTAURANT

Křemencova 7, Prague1
Open daily 11 a.m. - 12 p.m.
Reservations: 420-2-2491 3183, mobile: 0602-338 554
e-mail: buenosaires@buenosaires.cz, www.buenosaires.cz
All major credit cards welcome

Eat, Drink, Shop

Restaurants

Traditional Czech grub may still hold sway, but cosmopolitan cuisine is revitalising menus and American brunches abound.

When it comes to eating, Czechs are traditionalists. Any weekday lunchtime you'll see them lining up at the neighbourhood's last remaining *jídelna* – a style of cheap schnitzel and soup counter that dates back to the 1920s. Soup in fact inspires nationalist rhapsodies in the Czech lands – any proper meal must have it, you'll be told, and should also include at least one meat platter, plus *knedlíky*, or dumplings, to stick to your ribs. It's telling that '*Neslaný, nemasný* – 'Not salty, not fatty' – is a favourite Czech dis for an unsatisfying book or movie.

Thus, the opening of the borders in 1989 precipitated more of a trickle than a flood of international cuisine – and it certainly didn't reform Prague's infamously rude waiters much. Nor did the boom times of the mid-1990s, really. But pioneers like **Chez Marcel** (*see page 135*), **Kampa Park** (*see page 143*) and Sanjiv Suri's **Circle Line** (*see page 143*) have proved catalysts for change. They've inspired both Czech versions of more international concepts, like the Czech-Mex **Azteca** (*see page 131*), and genuine imports like the exciting new French wine bar and high-concept bistro **Trocadero** (*see page 137*). American-style brunches have been another hit in Prague, brought on by the American expat invasion – there are still more brunches on offer per capita in Prague than in any other city in Europe. *See page 142* **Top five Sunday brunches**.

But the upside of the preference for grandma's Bohemian recipes is that local restaurants do know what they're doing: sausage, *guláš*, *svíčková* (beef in a zingy cream sauce of veggie broth and lemon), and roast pork with *zelí* (sauerkraut) truly excel. Game is another classic local tradition, served up in sauces of rowanberry and wine with rosehips by places like **U modré kachničky** (*see page 127*). Even pubs do a respectable, if scaled-down job with duck and venison (*see page 131* **Pub dining**).

Heavy? To be sure. But Czechs don't seem to mind shaving years off their life expectancy for another tasty morsel of *staročeská bašta*, or 'Old Czech Grub' (a platter of at least three meats). They have a point, after all: Is there anything on earth that goes better with a half-litre of Pilsener?

Prague's not the most vegetarian-friendly of cities, but herbivores do reasonably well here by central European standards – largely because of all the new-fangled expat places. One gourmet restaurant that's sensitive to non-carnivores is **Le Bistrot de Marlene** (*see page 137*). **Lotos** (*see page 144*) does the city's most imaginative veggie menu, while **Radost FX Café** (*see page 144*) tries with mixed results. **Country Life** (*see page 146*) is a cheap and handy, if utilitarian, veggie resource. If out on a pub crawl or in any kind of basic Czech eaterie, you may well be restricted to *smažený sýr*, fried cheese, usually served with tartar sauce, or *knedlíky s vajíčkem*, dumplings with eggs, which sounds dreary but can actually be quite palatable with mustard or ketchup.

SERVICE WITH A SNARL

Communist-era service problems are in slow, but sure decline. Comically surly and/or glacial service is still not unusual, nor is a kitchen that closes at 9pm when the posted restaurant closing hour is midnight. Tables are often shared with other patrons who, like you, should ask '*Je tu volno?*' ('Is it free?') and may also wish each other '*dobrou chuť*' before tucking in. The national toast is '*na zdraví*'. Prague dines with an extremely relaxed dress code and reservations are necessary at only the fanciest spots in town.

When it comes to paying the bill, suspect maths skills remain pervasive at some places – or worse, two sets of menus, one reasonable, in Czech, and a much higher-priced one in English or German. Waiters record your tab on a slip of paper, which translates at leaving time into a bill. Pay the guy with the folding wallet in his waistband, not your waiter ('*Zaplatím, prosím?*' – 'May I pay, please?'). A small cover charge and extra charges for milk, bread and frightful accordion-playing are usual, as is tipping by rounding the tab up to the nearest ten crowns.

You should have little trouble making a phone reservation in English at swankier establishments, but elsewhere it may be easier to book in person.

Czech/Slovak

Expensive

Opera Grill

Karolíny Světlé 35, Staré Město, Prague 1 (2222 0518). Metro Národní třída/6, 9, 17, 18, 21, 22, 23 tram. **Dinner served** 7pm-2am daily. **Main courses** 500-800 Kč. **Credit** AmEx, MC, V. **Map** p306 G5.

The best) Restaurants

Stretch out at **Kampa Park** – arguably Prague's finest dining location.

For hole-in-the-wall haute cuisine
L'Equinoxe (see page 137).

For an idyllic riverside table
Kampa Park (see page 143).

For an emergency 4am pizza
Pizzeria Roma Due (see page 140).

**For non-traumatic
Czech pub dining**
U Radnice (see page 131).

For Prague's freshest fish
The Sushi Bar (see page 141).

For unpretentiously spicy food
Mailsi (see page 141).

For fusion with tassels
Mlynec (see page 145).

For steak while you wait
Jarmark (see page 129).

For baroque Thai dining
Delux (see page 144).

**For an authentic rude waiter
encounter**
Novoměstský Pivovar (see page 131).

A speakeasy fantasy fancied by seemingly every movie star on location in Prague. Locate the tarnished, unlit brass sign by the nondescript entrance to discover a plush little rose-tinted dining room. The Czech-international menu is short and to the point, with crispy roast Bohemian duck the house pride. Also good Moravian vintages at sensible prices. Booking essential.

U Maltézských rytířů

*Prokopská 10, Malá Strana, Prague 1 (5753 3666).
Tram 12, 22.* **Open** 11am-11pm daily. **Main courses** 260-540 Kč. **Credit** AmEx, MC. **Map** p305 E4.
A candlelit, Gothic cellar, once an inn for the eponymous Knights of Malta, that's justly proud of its venison chateaubriand. Mrs Černiková, whose

family runs the place, does a nightly narration on the history of the house, then harasses you to eat the incredible strudel. Booking essential.

U modré kachničky

*Nebovidská 6, Malá Strana, Prague 1 (5732 0308).
Tram 12, 22.* **Meals served** noon-4pm, 6.30-11.30pm, daily. **Main courses** 260-540 Kč. **Credit** AmEx. **Map** p305 E4.
On an obscure side street within strolling distance of Charles Bridge, set in a little Renaissance-era family house with strange wall collages, 'The Blue Duckling' caters to parliamentarians and visiting actors. Game is the speciality. Try roast pheasant, wild boar or roebuck haunch in rosehip wine sauce – with dumplings and sauerkraut, naturally.

O S *Ostroff* O F F

Italian restaurant Ostroff
Střelecký ostrov 336, Praha 1
Tel.: 2491 9235, Fax: 2492 0227
e-mail: ostroff@seznam.cz, www.ostroff.cz

Restaurant: 12 a.m.-2 p.m. - 7 p.m. - 11:30 p.m.
Bar: 6 p.m.- 3 a.m.
AmEx, MC, V

- Italian restaurant Ostroff dominates the Střelecký ostrov on the Vltava river.

- Italian cooks and pastry chef prepare culinary delights from the freshest, and fully authentic ingredients.

- Ostroff will open winter garden for taste of excellent view on Národní divadlo and enjoy italian speciality with Toscana's wines.

- The longest fashion cocktail bar in Prague can offer you 160 types of cocktails.

U MODRÉ KACHNIČKY

*N*estled in the quaint Malá Strana quarter of Prague 1, U Modré Kachničky (At the Blue Duckling), is one of the most beautifully decorated restaurants in the city. The wonderfully prepared duck and game dishes match the stunning interior. The restaurant has hosted such famous guests as Czech President, Václav Havel, Hungarian President, Arpád Gonez, German Chancellor Kobl, singer Phil Collins and actors Tom Cruise and Nicole Kidman to name a few. U Modré Kachničky welcomes you to Prague and invites you to enjoy a night you will treasure for a lifetime. Live piano music in the evenings.

Nebovidská 6, Praha 1, Open daily: 12-16, 18:30-23:30
Tel. 5732 03 08, Fax: 53 97 31, e-mail: modra.kachnicka@seznam.cz, www.umodrekachnicky.cz

U Patrona
Dražického náměstí 4, Malá Strana, Prague 1 (531 497). Metro Malostranská/12, 22 tram. **Open** Nov-Apr 6-11pm Mon-Fri, Sun; closed Sat. *May-Oct* 11am-2.30pm Mon-Fri, Sun; noon-11pm Sat. **Main courses** 260-540 Kč. **Credit** AmEx, MC, V. **Map** p305 E3.
Under the same ownership as Bellevue (*see p129*), Circle Line (*see p143*), Mlynec (*see p145*) and V Zátiší (*see below*), U Patrona has absolutely no difficulty meeting their high standards. The season-fresh menu, as at all of Sanjiv Suri's restaurants, goes with arty sauce arrangements on large white plates – sort of Czech nouvelle cuisine and lighter versions of traditional game dishes. Splendid view of the Charles Bridge.

V Zátiší
Liliová 1, Betlémské náměstí, Staré Město, Prague 1 (2222 1155/www.praguefinedining.cz). Metro Národní třída/6, 9, 18, 21, 22, 23 tram. **Meals served** noon-3pm, 5.30-11pm daily. **Main courses** 400-600 Kč. **Credit** AmEx, MC, V. **Map** p306 G4.
On a narrow cobbled lane and owned by the management of Bellevue and U Patrona (*above*), this is one of the city's most elegant dining rooms. The menu changes regularly and features everything from seasonal stuffed mushrooms to hand-stretched strudel stuffed with salmon. Expert preparation transforms common local ingredients into succulent delights while the daily special puts a deluxe spin on traditional Czech cooking. Formal but not oppressive.

Moderate

U Matouše
Preslova 17, Smíchov, Prague 5 (546 284). Metro Anděl/6, 9, 12 tram. **Open** 11am-11pm daily. **Main courses** 250-500 Kč. **No credit cards.**
A local favourite for lovers of traditional Czech food, with the inevitable tender duck with cabbage and dumplings and a definitively Old World, wood-heavy atmosphere. If in the mood for game bird, make sure to order it a day in advance.

U Kristiána
Smetanovo nábřeží Hollar, Staré Město, Prague 1 (9000 0601/9000 0639). Tram 17, 18. **Open** 11am-11pm daily. **Main courses** 100-200 Kč. **No credit cards.** **Map** p306 G4.
This dining room on a boat offers offers incomparable open-air Castle views to go with standard-issue Czech schnitzels and chicken steaks.

Koliba u pastýřky
Bělehradská 15, Nusle, Prague 4 (2256 0572). Tram 6, 11. **Open** 6pm-1am daily. **Main courses** 100-200 Kč. **Credit** AmEx, MC, V. **Map** p309 L8.
Highly romanticised Slovak village life is the theme at 'The Shepherdess's Cottage', with an open flame grill for any meat you can name, plus a nice, basic beer garden outside. Live cimbalom music completes the folk credentials.

U Ševce Matouše
Loretánské náměstí 4, Hradčany, Prague 1 (2051 4536). Tram 22. **Meals served** 11am-4pm, 6-11pm daily. **Main courses** 100-200 Kč. **Credit** MC, V. **Map** p304 A3.
Fish and chips and generous helpings of steak (in a dozen or so guises) are served up in this former shoemaker's workshop (it was once possible to get your boots repaired while lunching). Reasonable prices given the prime location.

U Supa
Celetná 22, Staré Město, Prague 1 (2421 2004). Metro Náměstí Republiky/5, 8, 14 tram. **Meals served** 11.30am-11 pm daily. **Main courses** 120-230 Kč. **Credit** AmEx, DC, MC, V. **Map** p306 J3.
Pork reaches its apotheosis in the traditional Czech pub interior of 'The Vulture,' where a whole roast pig, basted in beer and lard, is carved up at the table for a mere 3,000 Kč (order a day in advance). 'Lighter' fare of duck or beef, served with the ubiquitous dumplings and cabbage, is also available. Not for the faint-hearted.

Inexpensive

Akropolis
Kubelíkova 27, Žižkov, Prague 3 (2272 1026). Metro Jiřího z Poděbrad/11 tram. **Open** 4pm-2am Mon-Sat; 4pm-midnight Sun. **Main courses** 80-170 Kč. **No credit cards.** **Map** p311 B2.
Žižkov's young, hip, hard-smoking hangout. A bar and restaurant plus adjoining labyrinth of basement bars and concert hall (*see pages 159 and 212*), with decor that looks like de Chirico gone Tahitian. The Czech food, typically fried cheese or roast chicken, comes with bland Lobkowicz beer unless you specially request the award-winning Červený drak. *See chapter* **Beer**.

Bar Bar
Všehrdova 17, Malá Strana, Prague 1 (532 941). Tram 12, 22. **Open** noon-11pm daily. **Main courses** 80-140 Kč. **Credit** MC, V. **Map** p304 E5.
Pleasant and unpretentious but crowded local bar and restaurant on a picturesque Malá Strana backstreet. Though it serves open sandwiches, salads and grill dishes, the savoury crêpes are the real highlight. English-style dessert pancakes with lemon and sugar come for a mere 40 Kč. Staff are cool and reasonably flexible with substitutions.

Jarmark
Vodičkova 30, Nové Město, Prague 1 (2423 3733/www.jarmark.com). Metro Můstek/3, 9, 14, 24 tram. **Open** 11am-10pm daily. **Main courses** 70-140 Kč. **No credit cards.** **Map** p309 K6.
This shopping mall cafeteria, done up as a village covered in plastic ivy, is the Czech sensation of Wenceslas Square. Word has spread about what a fast, clean, cheap place this is, and customers now jostle for the thrill of telling a cook what kind of steak they want, then watching him fry it up.

Klub Architektů

Betlémské náměstí 169/5a, Staré Město, Prague 1 (2440 1214). Metro Národní třída/6, 9, 18, 21, 22, 23 tram. **Meals served** 11.30am-11pm daily. **Main courses** 70-140 Kč. **Credit** AmEx, DC, MC, V. **Map** p306 G5.

In the dim designer cellar of the Galerie Jaroslava Fragnera (*see p204*), which specialises in architectural exhibits, this place is better at style than fine cuisine. But the summer patio offers quiet respite, rare in Old Town, and low prices and decent vegetarian dishes keep this place packed to the gills. Cheapish Pilsner Urquell on tap.

U Sádlů

Klimentská 2, Staré Město, Prague 1 (2481 3874). Metro Náměstí Republiky/5, 14, 26 tram. **Open** 11am-1am daily. **Main courses** 120-230 Kč. **No credit cards.** **Map** p307 K2.

Medieval kitsch – but efficient, tasty and affordable medieval kitsch – can be a good laugh on a Friday night. Hoist a mead and choose from a variety of steak or game dishes – if you can work out the illuminated menu. Nice armour in the bar.

Pub dining

Na Kampě 15

Na Kampě 15, Malá Strana, Prague 1 (5753 1430). Metro Malostranská/12, 22 tram. **Open** noon-midnight daily. **Main courses** 90-200 Kč. **Credit** AmEx, DC, MC, V. **Map** p305 F4.

Forget about the pricey restaurant at this address and swing around the corner to the pub of the same name – goulash and dumplings for 90 Kč, fried mushrooms for 55 Kč and reasonably priced beer. Outdoor tables on the edge of Kampa Park are among the perks, and the waiters don't mind if you roam with drinks down to the bank of the Vltava a few metres away.

Novoměstský Pivovar

Vodičkova 20, Nové Město, Prague 1 (2223 2448). Metro Můstek/3, 9, 14, 24 tram. **Open** 10am-11.30pm Mon-Fri, 11.30am-11.30pm Sat, noon-10pm Sun. **Main courses** 120-230 Kč. **Credit** AmEx, MC, V. **Map** p308 J6.

This is one of surprisingly few brew pubs in Prague. The vast underground warren of rooms is fascinating to explore and they serve a remarkably good glass of beer. The addition skills of your waiter may prove even more remarkable, however, so do check the bill.

Pivnice u Pivrnce

Maiselova 3, Staré Město, Prague 1 (232 9404). Metro Náměstí Republiky/5, 8, 14 tram. **Open** 11am-midnight daily. **Main courses** 120-230 Kč. **No credit cards.** **Map** p306 H3.

Traditional Czech cooking done with above-average presentation right in the heart of the Jewish Quarter. *Svíčková* (beef in lemon-tinged cream sauce), duck with *zelí* (sauerkraut) and walls covered with crude cartoons, guaranteed to offend. Their Radegast is well-tapped and nicely priced.

Restaurace Pivovarský dům

corner of Lipová & Ječná, Nové Město, Prague 2 (9621 6666). Tram 4, 16, 22, 34. **Open** 11am-11.30pm daily. **Main courses** 70-140 Kč. **Credit** AmEx, DC, MC, V. **Map** p308 J8.

A brewer and chemist have joined forces to launch the city's newest and most fashionable brew pub, which offers a distinctive Pilsener of its own creation, plus such unlikely-sounding varieties as coffee beer and champagne beer. The wheat beer (*pšeničné*), generally a safer bet, is a true rarity in Prague, as is the surprisingly edible pub grub of smoked pork with dumplings or *utopenec* ('drowned man') – sausage immersed in vinegar.

U Radnice

U radnice 2, Staré Město, Prague 1 (2422 8136). Metro Staroměstská/17, 18 tram. **Meals served** 11am-11pm daily. **Main courses** 50-100 Kč. **Credit** AmEx, DC, MC, V. **Map** p306 H3.

One of the last places around Old Town Square with traditional food served at prices meant for locals. For lunch, tasty Czech specialities such as goulash and beef in cream sauce go for a pittance. Dark wood panelling and large communal tables create a comfortable pub atmosphere.

The world on your plate

Americas

Azteca

Říční 9, Malá Strana, Prague 1 (5732 7389). Tram 12, 22. **Open** 11am-11pm daily. **Main courses** 120-230 Kč. **Credit** MC, V. **Map** p305 E5.

As close to *comida autentica* as Czech-Mex gets. Hot tortilla soup and sizzling fajita plates come well enough, but reveal much about Czech spice phobia: they're padded with mild local peppers, which do double duty as quesadilla contents. But it's hard to knock the quiet Malá Strana location, tequila specials and moderate prices.

Barracuda

Krymská 2, Vinohrady, Prague 2 (7174 0599). Metro Náměstí Míru/4, 22 tram. **Open** 11am-11.30pm Mon-Fri; 5-11.30pm Sat, Sun. **Main courses** 130-270 Kč. **No credit cards.**

Judging by the inevitable dinner-hour rush, Prague has voted this little cellar in desert hues its best Mexican restaurant. No complementary tortilla chips, but the sizzling fajitas, unmatched elsewhere in the republic, go a long way to compensate, as do the overstuffed tacos.

Buffalo Bill's

Vodičkova 9, Nové Město, Prague 1 (2494 8624). Metro Můstek/3, 9, 14, 24 tram. **Meals served** noon-11.30pm daily. **Main courses** 150-300 Kč. **Credit** AmEx, MC, V. **Map** p308 J6.

Passable Tex-Mex fare and good service, but this place was long since surpassed by Barracuda (*see above*). The influence of bad westerns is apparent,

What's on the menu

Czech menus generally list two categories of dish: *minutky*, or cooked to order (which may take ages), and *hotová jídla*, theoretically ready-to-serve fare. Lunch dishes (*obědy*) are usually available until about 4pm; after this come more expensive dinner dishes (*večeře*). Usual accompaniments are rice, potatoes or fried béchamel dough (*krokety*), ordered separately. The closest thing to fresh veggies is often *obloha*, a garnish of pickles, and a tomato on a single leaf of lettuce. Surprisingly tasty appetisers are Prague ham with horseradish or rich soups, while dessert staples include *palačinky*, filled pancakes.

Meals (jídla)
snídaně breakfast; **oběd** lunch; **večeře** dinner.

Preparation (příprava)
bez masa or **bezmasá jídla** without meat; **čerstvé** fresh; **domácí** home-made; **dušené** steamed; **grilované** grilled; **míchaný** mixed; **na roštu** roasted; **pečené** baked; **plněné** stuffed; **smažené** fried; **špíz** grilled on a skewer; **uzené** smoked; **vařené** boiled.

Basics (základní)
chléb bread; **cukr** sugar; **drůbež** poultry; **karbanátek** patty of unspecified content; **máslo** butter; **maso** meat; **ocet** vinegar; **olej** oil; **omáčka** sauce; **ovoce** fruit; **pepř** pepper; **rohlík** roll; **ryby** fish; **smetana** cream; **sůl** salt; **sýr** cheese; **vejce** eggs; **zelenina** vegetables.

Drinks (nápoje)
čaj tea; **káva** coffee; **mléko** milk; **pivo** beer; **pomerančový džus** orange juice; **sodovka** soda; **víno** wine; **voda** water.

Appetisers (předkrmy)
boršč Russian beetroot soup (borscht); **chlebíček** open-faced mayo and meat sandwich; **hovězí vývar** beef broth; **jazyk** tongue; **kaviár** caviar; **paštika** paté; **polévka** soup; **uzený losos** smoked salmon.

Meat (maso)
biftek beefsteak; **hovězí** beef; **játra** liver; **jehně** lamb; **jelení** venison; **kanec** boar; **klobása** sausage; **králík** rabbit; **ledvinky** kidneys; **párek** sausage; **slanina** bacon; **srnčí** roebuck; **šunka** ham; **telecí** veal; **vepřové** pork; **zvěřina** game.

Poultry & fish (drůbež a ryby)
bažant pheasant; **husa** goose; **kachna** duck; **kapr** carp; **křepelka** quail; **krocan** turkey; **kuře** chicken; **losos** salmon; **pstruh** trout; **úhoř** eel.

Main meals (hlavní jídla)
guláš goulash; **sekaná** meat loaf; **řízek** schnitzel; **smažený sýr** fried cheese; **svíčková** beef in cream sauce; **vepřová játra na cibulce** pig's liver stewed with onion; **vepřové koleno** pork knee; **vepřový řízek** fried breaded pork.

Side dishes (přílohy)
brambor potato; **bramborák** potato pancake; **bramborová kaše** mashed potatoes; **hranolky**

with an eager young crew in American jeans and red cowboy kerchiefs slinging tacos beneath the watchful gaze of Duke Wayne.

Gargoyle's/Red Room
Křemencova 17, Nové Město, Prague 1 (2491 6047). Metro Národní třída/6, 9, 17, 18, 21, 22, 23 tram. **Open** *Gargoyle's* 11am-2pm, 6pm-10.30pm daily. *Red Room*, 11am-3am daily (meals served until 11 pm). **Main courses** *Gargoyle's* 250-500 Kč dinner, 150 Kč lunch. *Red Room* 130-270 Kč. **Credit** AmEx, MC, V. **Map** p308 G6.

Gargoyle's is the formal, French-California cuisine half that looks like a showroom for chefs in the market for elegant customers (they're lured by the five-course chef's choice, a delightful mystery concocted nightly by San Franciscan Thomas Ponder). Red Room, entrance around the corner, is where all the fun happens: much cruising, hellish lighting, funk soundtrack, vodka infusions, cold ginger soup, teriyaki burritos – and every single surface is painted blood red. The patio out back is a quiet spot for Red Room's excellent Sunday brunch.

Jáma
V jámě 7, Nové Město, Prague 1 (2422 2383). Metro Můstek/3, 9, 14, 24 tram. **Open** 11am-1am daily. **Main courses** 180-260 Kč dinner; 150 Kč lunch. **Credit** AmEx, MC, V. **Map** p309 K6.

American-owned and newly outfitted with a prime patio space out back and a bank of free Internet terminals by the door, Jáma still has the loud college vibe that made its name. Czech scenesters can be here by day and young business types by night. Lunch specials and happy-hour deals are a big draw, as is the Czech-Mex menu and well-poured Kozel. Their video-rental counter also does brisk business (*see also p200*).

Red Hot & Blues
Jakubská 12, Staré Město, Prague 1 (231 4639). Metro Náměstí Republiky/5, 14, 26 tram. **Open** 9am-11pm daily. **Main courses** 120-230 Kč. **Credit** AmEx, MC, V. **Map** p307 K3.

Expat institution with requisite blues player on a stool, Cajun chicken recipes and American-style brunch served on the patio. Reliable and relaxed, but avoid the overpriced drink specials.

chips; **kaše** mashed potatoes; **knedlíky** dumplings; **krokety** potato or béchamel dough croquettes; **obloha** small lettuce and tomato salad; **rýže** rice; **salát** salad; **šopský salát** cucumber, tomato and curd salad; **tatarská omáčka** tartar sauce; **zelí** cabbage or sauerkraut.

Cheese (sýr)

balkán a saltier feta; **eidam** hard white cheese; **hermelín** soft, similar to bland brie; **Madeland** Swiss cheese; **niva** blue cheese; **pivný sýr** beer-flavoured semi-soft cheese; **primátor** Swiss cheese; **tavený sýr** packaged cheese spread; **tvaroh** soft curd cheese.

Vegetables (zelenina)

česnek garlic; **chřest** asparagus; **cibule** onion(s); **čočka** lentils; **fazole** beans; **feferonky** chilli peppers; **hrášek** peas; **kukuřice** corn; **květák** cauliflower; **mrkev** carrot; **okurka** cucumber; **petržel** parsley; **rajčata** tomatoes; **salát** lettuce; **špenát** spinach; **žampiony** mushrooms; **zelí** cabbage.

Fruit (ovoce)

ananas pineapple; **banány** banana; **borůvky** blueberries; **broskev** peach; **hrozny** grapes; **hruška** pear; **jablko** apple; **jahody** strawberries; **jeřabina** rowanberries; **mandle** almonds; **meruňka** apricot; **ořechy** nuts; **pomeranč** orange; **rozinky** raisins; **švestky** plums; **třešně** cherries.

Desserts (moučník)

buchty traditional curd-filled cakes; **čokoláda** chocolate; **dort** layered cake; **koláč** cake with various fillings; **ovocné knedlíky** fruit dumplings; **palačinka/palačinky** crêpe/crêpes; **pohár** ice-cream sundae; **šlehačka** whipped cream; **zákusek** cake; **závin** strudel; **žemlovka** bread pudding with apples and cinnamon; **zmrzlina** ice-cream.

Useful phrases

May I see the menu? **Mohu vidět jídelní lístek?** Do you have...? **Máte...?** I am a vegetarian **Jsem vegetarián/vegetariánka** (m/f) How is it prepared? **Jak je to připravené?** Can I have it without...? **Mohu mít bez...?** No ketchup on my pizza, please **Nechci kečup na pizzu, prosím.** I didn't order this **Neobjednal jsem si to** How much longer will it be? **Jak dlouho to ještě bude?** Do all pork knees look like this? **Všechna vepřová kolena vypadají takhle?** The bill, please **Účet, prosím** I can't eat this and I won't pay for it! [use with extreme caution] **Nedá se to jíst a nezaplatím to** Takeaway/to go **S sebou** A beer, please **Pivo, prosím** Two beers, please **Dvě piva, prosím** Same again, please **Ještě jednou to samé, prosím** What'll you have? **Co si dáte?** Not for me, thanks **Pro mě ne, děkuji** No ice, thanks **Bez ledu, děkuji** He's absolutely smashed **Je totálně namazaný**

Grand Restaurant Septim

Rašínovo nábřeží 59, Nové Město, Prague 2 (298 559). Metro Karlovo náměstí/3, 6, 14, 18, 21, 22, 24 tram. **Open** 11am-midnight daily. **Main courses** 130-270 Kč. **No credit cards. Map** p308 G9.
American-style eats in a cheesily fancy setting attracts resident expats, while the video lounge encourages hanging out in grey winter. Bringing your own vids is fine with the laid-back owners.

Chinese

Čínské zátiší

Batelovská 120, Michle, Prague 4 (6121 8088). Metro Budějovická. **Open** 11.30am-10.30pm daily. **Main courses** 60-120 Kč. **No credit cards.**
On the ground floor of a communist-era block of flats, this is one of Prague's few good Chinese restaurants. Here the chef is not afraid of heat. The pork balls are seriously spicy and the hot and sour soup will make your eyes water.

Thanh Long

Ostrovní 23, Nové Město, Prague 1 (2491 2318). Metro Národní třída/6, 9, 18, 21, 22, 23 tram. **Meals served** 11.30am-3pm, 5-11pm daily. **Main courses** 100-200 Kč. **Credit** AmEx, V. **Map** p308 H6.
Distinguished mainly by its central location and blissfully kitsch trappings, such as the revolving 'Lazy Susan' tables and the pagoda lanterns and the huge moving-light painting in the back. Cuisine blanded down to suit Czech tastes.

Balkan

Dolly Bell

Neklanova 20, Vyšehrad, Prague 2 (2492 0782). Tram 3, 7, 16, 17, 21. **Open** 5-11pm daily. **Main courses** 130-270 Kč. **Credit** MC, DC, V.
An insider's favourite, with kooky upside-down furnishings on the ceiling, warm service, last year's prices and an impressive range of Balkan starters, lamb dishes and wines.

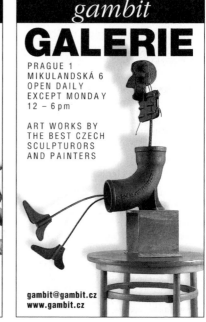

Modrá řeka

Mánesova 13, Vinohrady, Prague 2 (2225 1601).
Metro Muzeum/ 11 tram. **Open** 11am-11pm Mon-Fri,
5pm-11pm Sat, 3pm-11pm Sun. **Main courses** 130-
270 Kč. **No credit cards. Map** p311 A2.
Muhamed Londrc and his wife run this Vinohrady
hideout, where they welcome customers like prodi-
gal children and proceed to stuff them senseless
with homemade *somun* bread and *čevapčiči* finger
sausage served in piles of ten. *Šarena dolma*, lamb-
stuffed grape leaves in a sauce of peppers and
onions, do the job just as well.

Zlatá ulička

Masná 9, Staré Město, Prague 1 (232 0884). Metro
Náměstí Republiky/5, 8, 14, tram. **Open** 9am-
midnight daily. **Main courses** 80-170 Kč. **No credit**
cards. Map p306 J2.
Tiny place with excellent beef and veal-based
dishes defying the usual Czech bland-is-better atti-
tude. The veal stew with mashed potatoes is a
knockout, as is the *palačinka* (sweet pancake), big
enough for two. Kitsch decoration scheme based on
Prague Castle's eponymous Golden Lane.
Branch: Pizzeria Zlatá ulička, Petrská 21, Nové Město,
Prague 1 (231 7015).

Continental

Archiv

Masná 3, Staré Město, Prague 1 (2481 9297). Metro
Náměstí Republiky/5, 8, 14 tram. **Open** 10am-11pm
daily. **Main courses** 180-370 Kč. **Credit** AmEx, MC,
DC, V. **Map** p306 J2.
Czech goes Euro, with comfortably low-key antique
wood accents and a menu featuring crunchy bakes,
spinach tagliatelle, maraschino salmon filet and
stuffed quail with grapes. The patio out back is a
warm-weather blessing in overbuilt Old Town.

Bellevue

Smetanovo nábřeži 18, Staré Město, Prague 1 (2222
1438/www.praguefinedining.cz). Metro Národní
třída/17, 18 tram. **Open** noon-3pm, 5.30-11pm, Mon-
Sat; 11am-3pm (jazz brunch), 7-11pm, Sun. **Main**
courses 330-670 Kč. **Credit** AmEx, MC, V.
Map p306 G5.
Parnas was almost universally lauded as Prague's
finest restaurant prior to moving up the street and
changing its name to Bellevue. The pan-fried quail
in Drambuie sauce or veal tenderloin topped with
fresh truffles are winners and the service is generally head and shoulders above the competition.
Booking is essential.

David

Tržiště 21, Malá Strana, Prague 1 (5753 3109/
www.btcguide.cz/david). Tram 12, 22. **Open** 11.30am-
11pm daily. **Main courses** 360-700 Kč. **Credit**
AmEx, MC, V. **Map** p305 D3.
Frequented by touring rock stars, this family-run,
discreet little dining room knows how to pamper,
old club-style. The waiters seem more like butlers

as they whisk roast boar and port to your table. A
small vegetarian menu satisfies, though the strong
suit is definitive Bohemian classics like roast duck
with red and white cabbage or rabbit fillet with
spinach leaves and herb sauce. Booking essential.

Dynamo

Pštrossova 220/29, Nové Město, Prague 1 (294 224)
Metro Národní třída/6, 9, 18, 21, 22, 23 tram. **Open**
noon-midnight daily. **Main courses** 170-330 Kč.
Credit AmEx, MC, V. **Map** p308 H6.
Sleek designer diner that typifies the food and drink
renaissance sweeping through the area south of the
National Theatre. The steaks and pasta cuisine
doesn't quite keep up with the airstream decor, but
the collection of single-malt Scotches makes the bar
a connoisseur favourite.

Palffy Palác

Valdštejnská 14, Malá Strana, Prague 1 (5753
0522/www.czechreality.cz/palffy). Metro
Malostranská/12, 18, 22 tram. **Meals served** 11am-
3pm, 6pm-midnight daily. **Main courses** 130-270 Kč.
Credit MC, V. **Map** p305 E2.
Beautiful interior, fine service, brunch menu, fantastic terrace above a garden, but unpredictable
food. The aubergine lasagne is lovely but gone after
a few bites, and microwave defrosting has been
detected on a few desserts, but crêpes and salads
are generous and delicate affairs. With these surroundings, though, it's worth taking a chance as it's
excellent value for money.

French

Chez Marcel

Haštalská 12, Staré Město, Prague 1 (231 5676).
Metro Náměstí Republiky/5, 8, 14 tram. **Open** 8am-
1am Mon-Fri, 9am-1am Sat, Sun. **Main courses** 200-
350 Kč. **No credit cards. Map** p306 J2.
A thoroughly French brasserie with requisite brass
accents, *Le Monde* on a stick and views on to the Old
Town's most lovely cobbled square. The thickest
quiche in town goes well with the big baskets of
crispy fries, dappled with Dijon mustard. By night
it's a favourite rendezvous for Old Town clubbers
and by day it offers rare high chairs and a non-
smoking section for the kids.
Branch: Brasserie le Molière, Americká 20,
Vinohrady, Prague 2 (9000 3344).

Francouzká restaurace

Municipal House, Náměstí Republiky 5, Staré Město,
Prague 1 (2200 2777). Metro Náměstí Republiky/5, 8, 14
tram. **Open** noon-4pm, 6-11pm daily. **Main courses**
250-500 Kč. **Credit** AmEx, MC, V. **Map** p307 K3.
The aesthetics rarely get any better – the city's pre-
eminent shrine to art nouveau (and one of its top
concert halls – *see page 221*) has been painstakingly renovated with this dining room. The potato
soup's a treat – and a steal at the price – but otherwise it's an upmarket night out for rabbit and
French cheese plate. Service unpredictable.

Restaurants by area

Hradčany

Bazaar Mediterranée (Italian p139); **U Ševce Matouše** (Czech/Slovak p129).

Malá Strana

Aqua Bar & Grill (World/Fusion p145); **Azteca** (Americas p131); **Bar Bar** (Czech/Slovak p129); **Circle Line** (Seafood p143); **David** (Continental p135); **Kampa Park** (Seafood p143); **Na Kampě 15** (Pub dining p131); **Palffy Palác** (Continental p135); **U malířů** (French p137); **U Maltézských rytířů** (Czech/Slovak p127); **U modré kachničky** (Czech/Slovak p127); **U Patrona** (Czech/Slovak p129).

Nové Město

Buffalo Bill's (Americas p131); **Casablanca** (Middle Eastern p142); **Cicala** (Italian p139); **Delux** (Thai p144); **Dolly Bell** (Balkan p133); **Dynamo** (Continental p135); **Gargoyle's/Red Room** (Americas p132); **Grand Restaurant Septim** (Americas p133); **GyRossino** (Fast food p146); **Il Ritrovo** (Italian p139); **Indická restaurace** (Indian p141); **Jáma** (Americas p132); **Jarmark** (Czech/Slovak p129); **Koliba u pastýřky** (Czech/Slovak p129); **La Perle de Prague** (French p136); **Le Bistrot de Marlene** (French p137); **Le Gourmand** (Fast food p146); **L'Equinoxe** (French p137); **Marco Polo** (Italian p139); **Na rybárně** (Seafood p144); **Novoměstský Pivovar** (Pub dining p131); **Orso Bruno** (Italian p140); **Pizza Coloseum** (Italian p140); **Radost FX Café** (Vegetarian p144); **Řecká Taverna** (French p139); **Restaurace Pivovarský dům** (Pub dining p131); **Sports Café Cornucopia** (Fast food p146); **Thanh Long** (Chinese p133); **U Govindy Vegetarian Club** (Vegetarian p144); **U Rozvařilů** (Fast food p146).

Holešovice

U Cedru (Middle Eastern p142).

Nové Butovice

Čínské zátiší (Chinese p133).

Staré Město

Archiv (Continental p135); **Arsenal** (Japanese p141); **Barock** (Japanese p141); **Bellevue** (Continental p135); **Chez Marcel** (French p135); **Country Life** (Fast food p146); **Don Giovanni** (Italian p139); **Francouzká restaurace** (French p135); **Jewel of India** (Indian p141); **Jeruzalem Kosher Restaurant** (Kosher p141); **Kebab House** (Middle Eastern p142); **King Solomon** (Kosher p141); **Klub architektů** (Czech/Slovak p131); **Kogo Pizzeria & Caffeteria** (Italian p139); **La Brise** (French p136); **La Provence** (French p137); **Le Café Colonial** (French p137); **Le Petit Chablis** (French p137); **Le Saint-Jacques** (French p137); **Lotos** (Vegetarian p144); **Maestro** (Italian p139); **Mlynec** (World/Fusion p145); **Modrá Zahrada** (Italian p139); **Opera Grill** (Czech/Slovak p126); **Ostroff** (Italian p140); **Pivnice u Pivrnce** (Pub dining p131); **Pizzeria Roma Due** (Italian p140); **Praha Tamura/Japanese Bufet Dai** (Japanese p141); **Pravda** (World/Fusion p145); **Red Hot & Blues** (Americas p132); **Reykjavík** (Seafood p143); **Rybí trh** (Seafood p143); **Safir Grill** (Fast food p146); **Trocadero** (French p137); **U Bakaláře** (Fast food p146); **U Kristiána** (Czech/Slovak p129); **U Radnice** (Pub dining p131); **U Sádlů** (Czech/Slovak p131); **U Supa** (Czech/Slovak p129); **V Zátiší** (Czech/Slovak p129); **Zlatá ulička** (Balkan p135).

Smíchov

La Cambusa (Seafood p144); **The Sushi Bar** (Japanese p141); **U Matouše** (Czech/Slovak p129).

Vinohrady

Barracuda (Americas p131); **Grosseto Pizzeria** (Italian p139); **Modrá řeka** (Balkan p135).

Žižkov

Akropolis (Czech/Slovak p129); **Mailsi** (Indian p141); **Olympos** (Greek p137).

La Brise

Rybná 13, Staré Město, Prague 1 (2481 4909). Metro Náměstí Republiky/5, 8, 14 tram. **Meals served** noon-3pm, 6-10pm Mon-Sat; closed Sun. **Main courses** 270-530 Kč. **Credit** AmEx, MC, V. **Map** p307 K3.

Mediterranean French with an Asian flourish, expertly brought off in this easily overlooked Old Town eaterie. The white and blue interior acts as a neutral palette on which La Brise creates impressive little splashes of colour, spice and texture.

La Perle de Prague

corner of Rašínovo nábřeží & Resslova, Nové Město, Prague 2 (2198 4160). Metro Karlovo náměstí/17, 21 tram. **Open** 7pm-10.30pm Mon, noon-2pm, 7pm-10.30pm Tue-Sat, closed Sun. **Main courses** 500-1000 Kč. **Credit** AmEx, DC, MC, V. **Map** p308 G8.

This eyrie atop Frank Gehry's Fred and Ginger building (*see chapter* **Architecture**) was once king of the hill but bold plans to fly in different international chefs each month have now been scrapped and patrons are drifting away. Even the views are a bit disappointing – somehow cutting-edge design called for smallish recessed windows.

La Provence

Štupartská 9, Staré Město, Prague 1 (232 4801/ reservations 9005 4510-12). Metro Náměstí Republiky/5, 8, 14, tram. **Meals served** noon-midnight daily. **Bar open** 11am-2am daily. **Café open** 8pm-2am daily. **Main courses** 130-270 Kč. **Credit** AmEx, MC, V. **Map** p306 J3.

Billed as a 'restaurant, bistro and tapas bar' and sharing its premises with the Banana Bar (*see page 155*), this establishment suffers from just a wee identity crisis. The restaurant, with its rustic decor, offers good service, some decent wines and a nice cassoulet, but you have to elbow through a dense beefcake and hair-product mob to get there.

Le Bistrot de Marlene

Plavecká 4, Nové Město, Prague 2 (2492 1853). Metro Karlovo náměstí/3, 7, 16, 17, 21 tram. **Open** noon-3pm, 7-10.30pm Mon-Fri; 7-10.30pm Sat; closed Sun. **Main courses** 300-600 Kč. **Credit** AmEx, MC, V. **Map** p308 G10.

The chalkboard menus out front in French and Czech belie enchanting, market-fresh meals of fine traditional Franche-Comté cuisine in a small, wooden-shuttered room with rustic hues. The seasonal pheasant, venison and boar are the only things not imported and the expertly done mushroom flan in parsley sauce, *filets mignons* and *salades niçoises* have become a *cause célèbre* among Prague patrons. Attentive, vegetarian-friendly service.

Le Café Colonial

Široká 6, Staré Město, Prague 1 (2481 8322). Metro Staroměstská/17, 18 tram. **Open** 10am-midnight daily. **Main courses** 300-550 Kč. **Credit** AmEx, MC, V. **Map** p306 G3.

The café section has mini-quiches, duck, salads, big windows and a newspaper rack featuring *Le Monde*. More formal dining comes on the other side and there's designer veranda furniture in Matisse tones. Resolutely French.

Le Petit Chablis

Náprstkova 8, Staré Město, Prague 1 (2222 1019). Metro Národní třída/6, 9, 17, 18, 21, 22, 23 tram. **Open** 11am-midnight Mon-Sat; closed Sun. **Main courses** 400-800 Kč. **Credit** AmEx, MC, V. **Map** p306 G4.

A star of Prague's ever-growing French scene with a stylish but welcoming bar and a menu for gourmands. Small-scale, zesty creations fill out your five-course meal in this tiny Old Town dining room, with sauces a particular delight.

L'Equinoxe

Vojtěšská 9, Nové Město, Prague 1 (291 040). Metro Národní třída/6, 9, 18, 21, 22 tram. **Open** 11.30am-3pm, 6pm-1am Mon-Sat; closed Sun. **Café open** 7am-1am Mon-Fri, 10am-1am Sat; closed Sun. **Main courses** 120-230 Kč. **No credit cards. Map** p308 G6.

Prague's least pretentious French bistro specializes in meats and aromatic sauces with excellent value-for-money lunch deals. The wine list reveals the owner's Franco-Czech credentials, as does the engaging service.

Le Saint-Jacques

Jakubská 4, Staré Město, Prague 1 (232 2685). Metro Náměstí Republiky/5, 8, 14, tram. **Open** *Sept-June* noon-3pm, 6pm-midnight Mon-Sat; closed Sun. *July-Aug* 6pm-midnight Mon-Sat; closed Sun. **Main courses** 130-270 Kč. **Credit** AmEx, MC, V. **Map** p307 K3.

Around the corner from La Provence (*see above*), this excellent restaurant is too often overshadowed by its pricier, slicker neighbour. But Le Saint-Jacques has nothing to apologise for: the French proprietor personally lays out excellent fresh scallops, beef fondues and a pungent French onion soup. The decor resembles a Holiday Inn lobby, but the *tarte tatin* more than compensates.

Trocadero

Betlémská 9, Staré Město, Prague 1 (2222 0716/ trocadero_restaurant@hotmail.com). Metro Národní třída. **Open** 11.30am-3pm, 6pm-midnight daily. **Main courses** 260-540 Kč. **Credit** MC, V. **Map** p306 G5.

Designer French cuisine in Prague has just made several leaps forward with Trocadero, while affordability has stayed just about where it should. Chef Marco starts things off with rabbit pâté and pistachio nuts, then follows up with a phenomenal fricassee and tender duck cooked according to an old Nancy technique. With an interior by President Havel's decorator Bořek Šipek and an excellent wine collection priced in the 350-1000 Kč range, a sophisticated late-night crowd has gathered around this new Old Town haunt.

U malířů

Maltézské náměstí 11, Malá Strana, Prague 1 (5753 0000). Tram 12, 22. **Open** 11.30am-4pm, 6pm-11pm daily. **Main courses** 500-1000 Kč. **Credit** AmEx, MC, V. **Map** p305 E4.

Prague's most expensive restaurant by far lurks within a quaint 16th-century house with original painted ceilings. Authentic, quality French food but a clientele that likes to dine to impress. The seasonal menu runs from snails or pâté served with Sauternes to sea bass, lobster, lamb and pigeon. An excellent cheeseboard and wine list – although the price of a bottle will double the cost of your already ruinously expensive meal. Service is formal but not oppressive.

Greek

Olympos

Kubelíkova 9, Žižkov, Prague 3 (2272 2239). Metro Jiřího z Poděbrad/11 tram. **Open** noon-10pm daily. **Main courses** 130-270 Kč. **Credit** AmEx, MC, V. **Map** p311 B2.

Dressy Greek food in the pub mecca of Žižkov – the retsina here is likely the best wine in this beery district. The menu's rich in olive oil, aubergine and

Eat, Drink, Shop

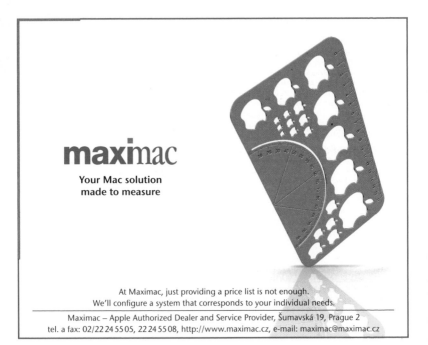

lamb with rosemary. Elegant without being fawning – a mix that's still unusual in Prague.

Řecká Taverna

Revoluční 16, Nové Město, Prague 1 (231 7762). Metro Náměstí Republiky/5, 8, 14 tram. **Open** 10am-midnight daily. **Main courses** 120-230 Kč. **No credit cards. Map** p307 K2.

Affordable, authentic Greek delights in a cheerily tacky tavern that somehow drifted far off course to Prague's Old Town and landed a block from the Roxy club (*see page 215*). Stuffed vine leaves in tzatziki, spinach pie and saganaki cheese lead the way to souvlaki and kebabs. Ouzo, retsina and cold frappé coffee are on hand to wash it down.

Italian

Bazaar Mediterranée

Nerudova 40, Hradčany, Prague 1 (9005 4510). Tram 12, 22. **Open** noon-midnight daily. **Main courses** 250-500 Kč. **Credit** AmEx, MC, V. **Map** p305 D3.

This surreal labyrinth of cellars and terraces presents overdone pasta as if it were the pride of the kitchen. Unfortunately, it is. The cellar bar trots out warped nightly entertainments ranging from drag shows to striptease, hoping to distract from your rapidly rising tab. Impressive terrace tables up top, though.

Cicala

Žitná 43, Nové Město, Prague 1 (2221 0375). Metro IP Pavlova/4, 6, 16, 22, 23 tram. **Open** 11.30am-11.30pm daily. **Main courses** 200-400 Kč. **No credit cards. Map** p308 J7.

Get the tip on which fresh Italian wonder the proprietor has driven in this week: it might be calamari or it might be figs; either way, it will be presented like a work of art. This subterranean two-room eaterie on an otherwise unappealing street is well worth seeking out as a bastion of home cooking and a mainstay of Prague's Italian community.

Don Giovanni

Karolíny Světlé 34, Staré Město, Prague 1 (2222 2060). Metro Staroměstská/17, 18 tram. **Open** 11am-midnight daily. **Main courses** 200-500 Kč. **Credit** AmEx, MC, V. **Map** p306 G5.

Grand but understated surroundings host some of the finest Italian dining in Prague. Owner Avelino Sorgato oversees the homemade fettucine, the Parma ham is the real stuff, the tiramisu is excellent, and there's a range of more than 30 different grappas. Nevertheless, the menu is conservative and the Italian wines not for those on a budget.

Grosseto Pizzeria

Francouzká 2, Vinohrady, Prague 2 (2425 2778). Metro Náměstí Míru/4, 16, 22, 23 tram. **Open** 11.30am-11pm daily. **Main courses** 100-200 Kč. **No credit cards. Map** p311 A3.

With two booming locations, Grosseto does flame-cooked pizzas, most notably the four-cheese version – beware imitations elsewhere using anything called *eidam* or *hermelin* (generic Czech cheeses).

The minestrone is a star too and the carpaccio in tomato sauce is perfect for sopping with the complementary fresh hot peasant bread.

Branch: Jugoslávských partyzánů 8, Dejvice, Prague 6 (312 2694).

Il Ritrovo

Lublaňská 11, Nové Město, Prague 2 (2426 1475). Metro IP Pavlova/4, 6, 11, 22, 23 tram. **Open** noon-3pm, 6-11pm, Mon-Sat; closed Sun. **Main courses** 130-270 Kč. **Credit** MC, V. **Map** p309 L8

Featuring 30 varieties of pasta, several home-made. Florentine proprietor Antonio Salvatore's most secret Tuscan sauces are only offered when you ask for them (eavesdrop on his visiting friends as they order to catch the hot tip for the day), but following the menu is by no means limiting. Try the antipasti bar, four-cheese linguine and ravioli in cream, sage and, if you fancy it, brandy. Just beware the gramophone collection of sentimental Italian ballads.

Kogo Pizzeria & Caffeteria

Havelská 27, Staré Město, Prague 1 (2421 4543). Metro Můstek/6, 9, 18, 21, 22 tram. **Open** *restaurant* 11am-11pm daily. *Café* 8am-11pm daily. **Main courses** 150-300 Kč. **Credit** MC, V. **Map** p306 J4.

For such an obvious hangout for the slick, this Old Town café and adjoining restaurant offer remarkably reasonable prices on outstanding pastas and sauces such as fusilli with Tuscan cheese and rucola. They stock a nice selection of Chiantis, too. The service is sharp and there are patio tables in a little-noticed, semi-enclosed shopping passage that dates from Renaissance times.

Maestro

Křižovnická 10, Staré Město, Prague 1 (232 0294). Metro Staroměstská/17, 18 tram. **Open** 11am-11pm Mon-Fri, 11pm-11pm Sat-Sun. **Main courses** 130-270 Kč. **Credit** AmEx, DC, MC, V. **Map** p306 G3.

It may not be authentic Italian, but the pizzas can hold their own against any in Old Town and service is several notches above the Prague average. Chicken cacciatore is a particularly strong suit, as is the baroque *trompe-l'oeil* decor.

Marco Polo

Masarykovo nábřeží 26, Nové Město, Prague 1 (2491 2900/24913853). Metro Národní třída/6, 9, 17 18, 21, 22, 23 tram. **Open** 11.30am-11pm daily. **Main courses** 130-270 Kč. **Credit** AmEx, MC, V. **Map** p308 G6.

Hidden under an extraordinary art nouveau entryway on the New Town embankment is this beloved neighbourhood secret. The generous Waldorf salad and *guláš* served in a round of peasant bread are standout starters, while the salmon in pastry with wild rice or a light canneloni do very well solo for lunch. Simple, classy presentation.

Modrá Zahrada

Pařížská 14, Staré Město, Prague 1 (232 7171). Metro Staroměstská/17, 18 tram. **Open** 11am-midnight daily. **Main courses** 70-140 Kč. **No credit cards. Map** p306 H2.

A classy bar perch, a decadent splurge and a perfect view, all come together at **Ostroff.**

Upstairs, a picture-window bar redolent of Howard Hawks; down below, a generous cellar with big wooden tables. Go for the big, acceptable pizzas rather than the fairly dodgy salads, all of which contain some kind of meat. It's a relaxing place, and cheap given the location. Service can be somewhat dizzy, though. Tables outdoors.
Branch: Vinohradská 29, Vinohrady, Praha 2 (2225 3829).

Orso Bruno
Za Poříčskou bránou 16, Karlín, Prague 8 (231 0178). Metro Florenc/8, 24 tram. **Open** 11am-3pm, 6pm-11pm Mon-Sat; closed Sun. **Main courses** 130-270 Kč. **Credit** MC, V.
Family-run authentic Italian pasta spot with subtle sauces and a daffy decor of teddy bear motifs. Great value and endearing service make it worth veering out of Old Town to the blighted next-door district.

Ostroff
Střelecký ostrov 336, Staré Město, Prague 1 (2491 9235). Tram 6, 9, 17, 18, 21, 22. **Open** *restaurant* 7pm-midnight daily. *Bar* 7pm-3am daily. **Main courses** 250-500 Kč. **Credit** AmEx, MC, V. **Map** p305 F5.
A perfect idyll, a classy bar perch and a decadent splurge, all rolled into one. Located on a Vltava

island, its bar can't be beat for sleek style and visuals while the vaulted cellar restaurant serves competent Sicilian and Tuscan fare. It's just a short walk across Most Legii (Legionnaire's Bridge) to Střelecký ostrov (Shooter's Island), an ideal setting for its rooftop terrace tables. Excellent brunch on Sundays; commanding Old Town view.

Pizza Coloseum
Vodičkova 32, Nové Město, Prague 1 (2421 4914). Metro Můstek/3, 9, 14, 24 tram. **Open** 11.30am-11.30pm daily. **Main courses** 100-200 Kč. **Credit** AmEx, MC, V. **Map** p308 J6.
Popular cellar joint just off Wenceslas Square that's a cut above the usual Prague pizzeria. Excellent bruschetta, flame-baked pizza, and big, saucy pastas complement well-stocked wine racks, an oil-heavy antipasti bar and a familiar range of dependable steak and fish dishes.

Pizzeria Roma Due
Liliová 18, Staré Město, Prague 1 (0606 287 943 mobile). Metro Staroměstská/17, 18 tram. **Open** 24 hours daily. **Main courses** 70-150 Kč. **No credit cards. Map** p306 G4.
Pizza that merits mention only because it's cheap, warm and available right around the clock. It's also

usefully within stumbling distance of the Roxy (*see p215*) and Chateau Rouge (*see p156*).
Branch: Jagellonská 19, Žižkov, Prague 3 (0606 225 930 mobile).

Indian/Pakistani

Jewel of India

Pařížská 20, Staré Město, Prague 1 (2481 1010). Metro Staroměstská/17, 18 tram. **Open** 11.30am-2.30pm, 5.30-11pm daily. **Main courses** 260-540 Kč. **Credit** AmEx, MC, V. **Map** p306 H2.
The sumptuous surroundings include a ground-floor bar and spacious cellar dining room with spicy though unadventurous Tandoori specialities. Service is typically Indian – a sort of teeming caste system of waiters – and British diners, at least, could probably live without their detailed explanation of every last item ('This is nan bread…'). The *nawabi* or *begumi khazana*, respectively meat and vegetarian, offer a little bit of everything.

Mailsi

Lipanská 1, Žižkov, Prague 3 (9005 9706). Tram 5, 9, 26. **Open** noon-3pm, 6pm-midnight daily. **Main courses** 120-230 Kč. **No credit cards. Map** p311 C1.
Not much atmosphere, just dirt-cheap Pakistani food, which goes down well in Žižkov, one of Prague's few ethnically mixed districts. Kebabs, dahl and other traditional dishes are expertly spiced and served up with fast and friendly gusto.

Indická restaurace

Štěpánská 63, Nové Město, Prague 1 (9623 6051). Metro Můstek/3, 9, 14, 24 tram. **Meals served** noon-10.30pm daily. **Main courses** 80-170 Kč. **Credit** AmEx, DC, MC, V. **Map** p309 K6.
For years this was the only place in the country where you could get tandoori chicken. Things have changed, but this shabby and friendly joint carries on as ever with highly unpredictable, dirt-cheap fare. Stick with the chicken and nans, though. Head for the snack bar right of the entrance, not the more expensive dining room.

Japanese

Arsenal

Valentinská 11, Staré Město, Prague 1 (2481 4099). Metro Staroměstská/17, 18 tram. **Open** 11.30am-2.30pm, 6.30-11.30pm daily. **Main courses** 300-600 Kč. **Credit** AmEx, DC, MC, V. **Map** p306 H3.
Expensive designer Thai and Japanese teppan fare geared toward customers who want to impress friends who've never tasted either. The furnishings and cruet sets, works of art by Bořek Šípek, thoroughly upstage the cuisine. A pity, since the chefs actually know what they're doing.

Barock

Pařížská 24, Staré Město, Prague 1 (232 9221). Metro Staroměstská/17, 18 tram. **Open** 8.30am-1am Mon-Wed; 8.30am-2am Thur, Fri; 10am-2am Sat; 10am-1am Sun; kitchen closed 4pm-6pm and 11pm. **Main courses** 250-500 Kč. **Credit** AmEx, MC, V. **Map** p306 H2.
Glam dining was never more overt. Gleaming steel bar, floor-to-ceiling windows, free drinks if you're a card-carrying model, and a credible sushi platter with suitably aesthetic *nigiri*. A reasonably priced breakfast menu of croissants, sandwiches and powerhouse latte attracts a contemplative morning crowd to the street tables.

Praha Tamura/Japanese Bufet Dai

Havelská 6, Staré Město, Prague 1 (2423 2056). Metro Můstek/6, 9, 17, 18, 22 tram. **Open** 11am-10.30pm daily. **Main courses** 500-1000 Kč. **Credit** DC, MC, V. **Map** p306 J4.
Arguably Prague's top-dog sushi establishment, Tamura is a full-on formal Japanese experience, while the recently added buffet is a nod towards backpacker budgets and Czech income levels. Just off the city's oldest market, it has tables laden with maki and curries – a measurable improvement to the city's reasonable lunch options.

The Sushi Bar

Zborovská 49, Smíchov, Prague 5 (9000 1517/www.sushi.cz). Tram 6, 9, 12, 22. **Open** 11am-10pm daily. **Main courses** 300-600 Kč. **Credit** DC, MC, V. **Map** p305 E5.
One of Prague's original seafood importers has opened this minimalist maki bar with maximal prices. The nigiri is served in small, beautiful portions on small, beautiful, enamel plates. Focus on the fine view of the old Savoy across the street rather than your mounting bill.

Kosher

King Solomon

Široká 8, Staré Město, Prague 1 (2481 8752). Metro Staroměstská/17, 18 tram. **Open** 11am-11pm Mon-Thur, Sun, 11am-90 minutes before sundown Fri; closed Sat. **Main courses** 200-500 Kč. **Credit** AmEx, MC, V. **Map** p306 H3.
Just a block from the Jewish Museum (*see p97*) an incongruous but solid addition to Prague's new wave of upscale kosher restaurants. An atrium in the back, a long and authoritative Israeli wine list and austere sandstone and iron decor clash with homey comfort food in generous servings: gefilte fish, chicken soup, carp with prunes.

Jeruzalem Kosher Restaurant

Břehová 5, Staré Město, Prague 1 (2481 2001/ www.jerusalem1.cz). Metro Staroměstská/17, 18 tram. **Open** 8am-11pm daily. **Main courses** 120-230 Kč. **No credit cards. Map** p306 H2.
Fast, informal and professional, this diner is also exactly where you need it when your feet swell from touring Josefov synagogues. Nondescript decor but an engaging right-to-left menu with sections in Hebrew, plus mushroom pancakes, kosher wines and a generous chocolate pudding that's unrivalled in Prague.

Eat, Drink, Shop

Middle Eastern

Casablanca

*Na příkopě 10, Nové Město, Prague 1 (2421 0519).
Metro Můstek/3, 9, 14, 24 tram.* **Open** 11am-midnight
daily. **Main courses** 250-500 Kč. **Credit** AmEx, MC,
V. **Map** p306 J4.

French-Moroccan tagines, harissa soups and home-
made sweetmeats exude sincerity, but this is decidedly a place of high production values. And it's
priced like one. For an evening of all-out indulgence
amid satin pillows, houkahs and the odd belly
dancer, however, it's hard to outdo.

Kebab House

*Perlová 1, Staré Město, Prague 1 (0606 268 871).
Metro Můstek/6, 9, 18, 21, 22, 23 tram.* **Open** 11am-
10pm daily. **Main courses** 60-160 Kč. **No credit
cards. Map** p306 J5.

Guess the house speciality. Friendly, bright, clean
little sit-down spot for a gyros or a quick plate of
meze. A refreshin oasis on Prague's main downtown drag for prostitution.

U Cedru

*Na hutích 13, Dejvice, Prague 6 (312 2974). Metro
Dejvická/20, 25, 26 tram.* **Open** 11am-11pm daily.
Main courses 150-300 Kč. **Credit** AmEx, DC, MC, V.

Top five · Sunday brunches

Gargoyle's/Red Room.

Gargoyle's/Red Room

Shield your bloodshot eyes from the sun in the
dim interior while a lovely server brings on a
spicy California-style omelette and an expertly
blended Bloody Mary. See page 132.

Red Hot & Blues

Massive veggie chili burritos and a potent cappuccino on the patio do wonders to nurse you
back to life. See page 132.

Angel Café

Soft classical tracks and a bright, sunny room in
which to linger over your buttermilk pancakes,

home fries, fresh juices or maybe a Jacob's
Creek Chardonnay. See page 149.

Palffy Palác

Romance made manifest in a faded baroque
palace setting populated by gracious, efficient
waiters bearing things like baked aubergine
lasagna and sparkling wine. See page 135.

Radost FX Café

Run into every Prague expat you were trying to
avoid while waiting for scrambled egg tostadas
and salsa (be patient – your cook and waitress
are as hungover as you are). See page 144.

Solid Middle Eastern fare in a small, unprepossessing Lebanese family restaurant out at the end of the green metro line. A good choice of familiar starters includes houmous and stuffed vine leaves, grilled meats and a small assortment of odd-sounding 'international' dishes. The mezes are the best value, offering five, seven or ten different starters at reasonable rates. Takeaway until midnight.

Seafood

Circle Line

Malostranské náměstí 12, Malá Strana, Prague 1 (5753 0021). Metro Malostranská/12, 22 tram. **Open** noon-11pm Mon-Fri; 11am-11pm Sat-Sun. **Main courses** 330-670 Kč. **Credit** AmEx, MC, V. **Map** p305 D3.

Fresh seafood in an elegant, high-ceilinged cellar or at street tables in summer. They lay on the luxury trappings a bit thick, but otherwise this place is hard to fault. Classy cruise ship theme decor with outstanding service, artful seasonal salads and main courses done up French- and Italian-style. Vegetarians are well-provided for and the wine list is good if you can afford to splash out.

Kampa Park

Na Kampě 8b, Malá Strana, Prague 1 (5731 3493/5731 3494/www.kampapark.com). Metro Malostranská/12, 22 tram. **Open** 11.30am-4pm, 6-1am daily; kitchen closes 11pm. **Main courses** 300-650 Kč. **Credit** AmEx, DC, MC. **Map** p305 F4.

Kampa Park's location is arguably the finest in Prague – in the shadow of Charles Bridge with a beautiful riverside terrace now encloseable for cool weather dining. Inside there's also a slick bar-room scene favoured by the business crowd, tasteful wood and glass accents and Nils Jebens' trademark Scandinavian sauces. The real joy, however, is a riverside table laden with oysters, swordfish and salad in summer. Service notably sharp.

Reykjavík

Karlova 20, Staré Město, Prague 1 (2222 1218). Metro Staroměstská/17, 18 tram. **Open** 11am-midnight daily. **Main courses** 250-500 Kč. **Credit** AmEx, DC, MC, V. **Map** p306 G4.

Smack-bang on the main tourist route to Charles Bridge, this comfortably elegant restaurant nevertheless boasts fresh seafood in abundance at reasonable prices. The Icelandic owner flies in fish and lobster and the crowds lap it up. Soups, starters, burgers and chicken are not quite as strong. There's a street terrace in summer, but the upstairs loft offers the quietest seating.

Rybí trh

Týn 5, Staré Město, Prague 1 (2489 5447). Metro Náměstí Republiky/5, 8, 14 tram. **Open** 11am-midnight daily. **Main courses** 200-500 Kč. **Credit** AmEx, MC, V. **Map** p306 J3.

A posh new seafood emporium in a sleek, cavernous space in the touristy Ungelt square, where the chefs will boil or grill a pike-perch, carp or eel, then present it with turmeric rice. In summer, grab a table on the courtyard but avoid the shellfish, as is usually the rule in Prague.

Eat, Drink, Shop

Heading for a colourful dining experience – **Kampa Park**, a mural idyll.

Polish fleas & liquid bread

Judging from the nearly identical menus posted outside most Prague restaurants that cater for locals, you might imagine that Czechs don't think much about food. But that's more old habits dying hard than any lack of passion for cuisine. Under the old regime a state-published cookbook, called *Teplé jidlo* ('Warm Meals'), dictated the menu at every restaurant in the republic – and incredibly, though no longer the law, still does at many.

But if you eavesdrop on any two Bohemians talking, whether they're playing, shopping or sitting at their desks, it won't be long before a food idiom crops up. Suppose one notices that their friend is getting a bit uppity. He may quickly bring him back to earth with *Co si myslíš? Pečení holuby ti budou lítat do huby?* – 'What do you think? Baked squabs will fly into your gob?'

If on their lunch hour, invariably appraising the soups on offer, one may sagely advise a foreign friend who's tagging along and vaguely hoping for some kind of salad: *Polívka je grunt, ostatní je špunt* – 'Soup is the foundation, everything else is frills'.

When visiting *maminka* for the weekend, even grown Czech children risk incurring her wrath if they ever stop eating: *Hlad a polské vši na vás!* – 'Hunger and Polish fleas on you!'

Safely back on the streets of Prague, two locals may well decide to take a liquid lunch at the local pivnice, reasoning, *Pivo je tekutý chléb* 'Beer is liquid bread'. Neither sleet nor rain will stop them, once their mind is set: *nejsme z cukru*, 'we're not made of sugar'. That pubbing should stand on equal footing with even the sacred midday *guláš* ritual should be no surprise. After all, *Hlad je převlečená žízeň* – 'Hunger is only thirst disguised'. *Mrkev zimě* – 'carrot in winter' – this is excellent Pilsener!

La Cambusa

Klicperova 2, Smíchov, Prague 5 (541 678). Tram 6, 12, 14. **Open** 7pm-midnight Mon-Sat; closed Sun. **Main courses** 700 Kč. **Credit** AmEx, DC, MC, V.
From an unlikely side street in the blue-collar Smíchov district, this French-Czech seafood specialist has built a name as a dependable source of the freshest tastes around. Decor is essentially a nautical afterthought, though at least they bothered to install fish tanks.

Na rybárně

Gorazdova 17, Nové Město, Prague 2 (2491 8885). Metro Karlovo náměstí/3, 6, 14, 17, 18, 22, 21, 24 tram. **Open** 11.30am-11.30pm Mon-Fri; 1pm-11.30pm Sat, Sun. **Main courses** 130-270 Kč. **Credit** MC, V. **Map** p308 G8.
A carefully kept neighbourhood secret was blown when Havel became president and let slip which place had been his favourite nosh joint. Notoriety hasn't set it back at all, however. It's still a good, unpretentious option for well-grilled local freshwater fish. Just remember: October is trout season; eel, carp and pike-perch are the other main options, but mind the bones.

Thai

Delux

Václavské náměstí 4, Nové Město, Prague 1 (9624 9444;www.delux.cz). Metro Můstek/3, 9, 14, 24 tram. **Open** 6pm-midnight daily. **Main courses** 170-330 Kč. **Credit** MC, V. **Map** p306 J5.
An incredible space, even by Prague standards, filled with baroque red and gold decor, live jazz and some of the city's best Thai food. Pad Thai is spicy and excellent, as is the tom yam soup and the onstage licks of the city's best jazz combos (*see page 216*). Thursday through Saturday the tables are whisked away after dessert to make way for dancing and DJ action.

Vegetarian

Lotos

Platnéřská 13, Staré Město, Prague 1 (232 2390). Metro Staroměstská/17, 18 tram. **Open** 11am-10pm daily. **Main courses** 130-270 Kč. **Credit** MC, V. **Map** p306 G3.
Though a few of the tofu-based creations, served amid pastel bunting and ambient classical music, have met with lukewarm responses, the banana ragout has a consistent winner. The grocery out front sells a limited range of organic fare.

Radost FX Café

Bělehradská 120, Nové Město, Prague 2 (2425 4776). Metro I.P. Pavlova/4, 6, 11, 16, 22, 23 tram. **Open** 11.30am-4am daily. **Main courses** 100-200 Kč. **No credit cards.** **Map** p309 L8.
Vegetarian eats in both in the gallery-like café at the front, and in the cosier bar section at the back, includes pastas, salads, falafel, spinach burgers, burritos and sandwiches, though somewhat lacking in zing. Still, it's open late and the Sunday brunch, served until 3pm, is an expat institution.

U Govindy Vegetarian Club

Soukenická 27, Nové Město, Prague 2 (2481 6631). Metro Náměstí Republiky/5, 8, 14, 26 tram. **Open** 11am-5pm Mon-Sat; closed Sun. **Main courses** 75 Kč. **No credit cards.** **Map** p307 L2.

Cheap although not so cheerful, offering a basic self-service vegetarian Indian meal for a mere 75 Kč, embellished with extras, such as pakora vegetables on a skewer, for another 30 Kč or so. At these prices you wouldn't expect much charm, but at least the ingredients are grown on the Krishnas' organic farm outside Prague.
Branch: Na Hrázi 5, Palmovka (683 7226).

World/Fusion

Aqua Bar & Grill

U Plovárny 8, Malá Strana, Prague 1 (5731 2578). Metro Malostranská/12, 18 tram. **Open** 7pm-1am daily. **Main courses** 500-1000 Kč. AmEx, MC, V. **Map** p306 G1.
A waterfront jewel of fine cuisine and imbibing. Aqua specializes in 'tastes' rather than platters, and an airy whitewashed space equipped with a phenomenal wine collection. Try a Robert Mondavi Cabernet Sauvignon and four or five dishes from their eclectic list, from duck spring rolls to tuna sushi or salmon with orange garnish and chili oil. Then shift gears for a dessert Sauternes and the intense chocolate fudge and filo pastry creation. Summer tables on the riverbank.

Mlynec

Novotného lávka 9, Staré Město, Prague 1 (2108 2208). Metro Staroměstská/17, 18 tram. **Open** 6pm-11pm daily. **Main courses** 400-800 Kč. **Credit** AmEx, MC, V. **Map** p306 G4.

The newest venture of Prague's star restaurateur Sanjiv Suri goes for the theatrical with a mix of traditional folk elements (including your server's costume) and global gumbo cuisine. Tuna steak in ginger and berry sauce is a typically novel treat, as is the view from this Vltava weir location. Handy for pre-clubbing as it's surrounded by no fewer than six neighbouring dancefloors.

Pravda

Pařížská 17, Staré Město, Prague 1 (232 6203). Metro Staroměstská/17, 18 tram. **Meals served** 11.30am-3pm; 6pm-11pm daily. **Main courses** 330-670 Kč. **Credit** AmEx, MC, V. **Map** p306 H2.
Owner Tommy Sjoo, who was instrumental in bringing fine dining to post-1989 Prague, presides over an airy multi-level establishment on fashionable Pařížská where chicken in Senegal peanut sauce goes up against Vietnamese nem spring rolls and borscht, all done credibly. Cool and graceful service from waitstaff in long black aprons.

Fast food

Fast food is the domain of both rich and poor in Prague, owing to the glacial service at even the city's best restaurants which often means your only chance of finishing in time for a movie or concert is to go the falafel route. Better still, these places stay up late and are lifelines in winter when waiting for a night tram to carry you home from clubbing.

Tommy Sjoo's **Pravda** – credible fine dining on fashionable Pařížská.

Eat, Drink, Shop

Country Life

Melantrichova 15, Staré Město, Prague 1 (2421 3366).
Metro Národní třída/6, 9, 18, 21, 22, 23 tram. **Open**
9am-8.30pm, Mon-Thur; 9am-6pm Fri; 11am-8.30pm
Sun; closed Sat. **Main courses** 50-100 Kč. **No credit
cards. Map** p306 H4.

Though this place has expanded from a shop with
salad bar (*see p174*) into a full-blown cafeteria
with seating and beautiful Old Town street
views, Country Life has managed to continue as a
low-key, dirt-cheap source of organically grown
vegetarian fare. Massive DIY salads, fresh carrot
juice, delectable lentil soups, wholegrain breads,
along with slightly disquieting mashed potato
casseroles. By all means avoid the lunchtime
crush, but be warned that there are salads and
sandwiches only before 11am Monday-Friday.
Branch: Jungmannova 1, Nové Město, Prague 1 (5704
4419).

Le Gourmand

*Vaclávské náměstí 18, Nové Město, Prague 1 (9624
8633). Metro Můstek/3, 9, 14, 24 tram.* **Open** 8am-
11pm daily. **Main courses** 60-120 Kč. **No credit
cards. Map** p307 K5.

Unbeatable hours have given rise to something
long believed impossible in this city: a fast, credible,
anytime salad on Wenceslas Square – and all this
for mere pocket change. The name, though, is a
hopeless exaggeration.

GyRossino

*Spálená 43, Nové Město, Prague 1 (290 232). Metro
Národní třída/6, 9, 18, 21, 22, 23 tram.* **Open** 8.30am-
3am daily. **Main courses** 40-75 Kč. **No credit cards.**
Map p308 H6.

Actually two places, side by side, separated by a
building entryway. The left half offers only roast
chicken and doesn't stay open late, the right serves
up falafel, kebabs and just-edible mini-pizzas until
supplies run out, usually at least 3am.

Safir Grill

*Havelská 12, Staré Město, Prague 1 (260 095). Metro
Můstek/3, 9, 14, 24 tram.* **Open** 10am-8pm Mon-Sat;
closed Sun. **Main courses** 40-100 Kč. **No credit
cards. Map** p306 J4.

Falafel, houmous and tahini counter with a pleasant, blond-wood sitting space. Perfect for refueling
after perusing the market stalls out front or for a
nibble on the run when heading for a Wenceslas
Square movie. Tables outdoors.

Sports Café Cornucopia

*Jungmannova 10, Nové Město, Prague 1 (2494 7742).
Metro Můstek/3, 9, 14, 24 tram.* **Open** 8.30am-10pm
Mon-Fri, 10am-8pm Sat, Sun. **Main courses** 60-160
Kč. **No credit cards. Map** p308 J6.

Soccer on Sky Sports is half the appeal of this
unpretentious and convenient little hole in the
wall. The other half is in the fast, custom-built
submarine sandwiches, Mexican food menu,
home-baked brownies, French toast and decent
Sunday brunch. *See also page 160.*

U Rozvařilů – classic caff, full of characters.

U Bakaláře

*Celetná 13, Staré Město, Prague 1 (2481 1870). Metro
Náměstí Republiky/5, 8, 14 tram.* **Open** 9am-6pm
Mon-Fri; closed Sat, Sun. **Main courses** 40-70 Kč. **No
credit cards. Map** p306 J3.

This convenient Old Town lunch buffet is a stal-
wart example of that pre-revolutionary classic, the
worker cafeteria. It's also a good standby for the
likes of toasted sandwiches, pancakes and soup.
Communal seating, friendly-ish service and way
too much salt in everything.

U Rozvařilů

*Na Poříčí 26, Nové Město, Prague 1 (2481 1736).
Metro Náměstí Republiky/5, 8, 14 tram.* **Open**
7.30am-7.30pm Mon-Fri; 7.30am-7pm Sat; 10am-5pm
Sun. **Main courses** 40-75 Kč. **No credit cards.**
Map p307 L3.

A chrome-covered, mirrored version of that pre-
revolutionary classic, the worker cafeteria. The
cast of characters, from servers in dirty white
aprons to harassed-looking customers in white
socks and sandals, all remain. So do the incredibly
cheap soups, *guláš*, dumplings and *chlebíčky* (open-
faced mayonnaise and meat sandwiches).

Cafés

From imperial elegance to American experiments, Prague has all manner of cafés and coffees. Many a mellow teahouse, too.

In Prague these days you can find anything from a Seattle-style double decaf and organic bagel to a Viennese melange with a white mountain of whipped cream on top. The collision between traditional *Mitteleuropäisch* coffeehouse culture and the new-fangled caffeine fads of the Americans who arrived here in the 1990s has led to a cornucopia of places to drink coffee, ways to order it, and snacks designed as accompaniment.

Cafés in Prague have long enjoyed the same esteem they do all over Europe as centres of intellectual life – and frequently of dissent. Well aware of this, the communists set about closing down as many venerable old-world cafés as they possibly could.

First on the casualty list were the bourgeois Viennese-style hang-outs left over from the Habsburg Empire: Franz Kafka's and Max Brod's old favourite, the Café Arco on Hybernská, was made into a cheesy bar with electric gambling machines; the legendary **Café Imperial** just up the street and **Café Montmartre** (said to be home to black masses during the swinging 1930s) simply went dark. By a terrible miscalculation, the

Slavia was allowed to carry on, giving theatrical dissidents like Václav Havel and Jiří Kolář a place in which to foment the Velvet Revolution. Then American property developers shut it down.

Fortunately, these last three have all come back to life, bringing with them a growing subculture of sunny, patio cafés with rich coffees and menus ranging from carrot cake, bagels and ciabatta sandwiches to full brunch. **Angel Café**, **Ebel Coffee House**, **Café Break** and **Café Orange** represent the newest wave.

In the void between pub floor and the heights of café culture, one wholly unique phenomenon has caught on recently with no signs of abating. The Prague tearoom combines the soundtrack, lighting, carpets, steeping methods and countless leaf varieties of traditional teahouses from Tunis to Shanghai via Kathmandu. Recommended escapes from all worldly cares include **Dobrá čajovna**'s two locations, the **Čajovna Duše** next door to the **Roxy** club, the noodle house-tearoom **Malý Buddha** near Prague Castle, and the best source of solace in restless Žižkov, the tearoom upstairs at the **U Vystřeleného oka** pub (*see page 161*).

Eat, Drink, Shop

Slavia – mother of all Prague cafés. *See p149.*

Malá Strana

Bohemia Bagel

Újezd 16, Prague 1 (530 921/www.bohemiabagel.cz).
Tram 12, 22. **Open** 7am-midnight Mon-Fri; 8am-
midnight Sat-Sun. **No credit cards. Map** p305 E5.
Glen Spicker of U Malého Glena (*see p155*) and
Delux club fame (*see p144 and 216*) created the
republic's first bagel café three years ago and it's
been packed ever since. Free refills, another break-
through idea in Prague, help wash down the fresh
muffins, breakfast bagels, and bagel sandwiches.
Service is as spaced-out as anywhere in Prague but
there's usually something of interest – courses,
places to rent, exhibitions – on the bulletin board.
Branch: Masná 2, Staré Město, Prague 1 (2481 2560).

Malostranská Kavárna

Malostranské náměstí 5, Prague 1 (533 092). Metro
Malostranská/12, 22 tram. **Open** 9am-11pm daily. **No**
credit cards. Map p305 E3.
The reopening of the Malostranská, founded in
1874, has gone a long way towards restoring
Prague's all but dead traditional café culture. Its
returning former clientele – a cross-generational
mix of pensioners, shoppers and students from the
neighbouring maths and physics university faculty – evidently approve of what the new owners
have done. An ideal rest stop for a very Central
European fix of coffee and cream cake.

Staré Město

Blatouch

Vězeňská 4, Prague 1 (232 8643). Metro
Staroměstská/17, 18 tram. **Open** noon-1am Mon-
Thur; noon-2am Fri; 2pm-2am Sat; 2pm-midnight Sun.
No credit cards. Map p306 J2.
Two sisters run this gentle, reasonably priced café,
a favourite of clean-cut Czech students and intellectuals. Jazz and soul waft through the narrow, high-
ceilinged space and up the metal stairwell to where
carpets and armchairs soften the room. The
wooden floors and bookcase add to the civilised
atmosphere. Salads and melted cheese amalgams
are available but can't be recommended.

Café Milena

Staroměstské náměstí 22, Prague 1 (2163 2602).
Metro Staroměstská/17, 18 tram. **Open** July-Aug
10am-8pm daily. *Sept-June* 10am-9pm daily. **Credit** V.
Map p306 J3.
Milena Jesenská was one of Kafka's lovers but it's
doubtful if the couple would have ever met at this sac-
charine-sweet dessert spot. Waiters in grey waist-
coats serve pancakes and ice-cream in the main room
opposite the Astronomical Clock (*see p91*), while the
Franz Kafka Society maintains an office upstairs.

Café Montmartre

Řetězová 7, Prague 1 (no phone). Metro Staroměstská/
17, 18 tram. **Open** 10am-1am daily. **No credit cards.**
Map p306 H4.
Gustav Meyrink, Jaroslav Hašek and Franz Werfel
all tippled here and word has it there were black
masses during the wild and wacky interwar days.
Pilsner Urquell and Velvet are on tap, but wine is better suited to the crowd of creative miscreants that
gather around the threadbare settees and battered
tables for late-night talks. Apple strudel is about the
only thing to eat.

Damúza

Řetězová 10, Prague 1 (2222 1749) Metro
Staroměstská/17, 18 tram. **Open** 11am-midnight
Mon-Fri; noon-11.30 Sat; noon-10pm Sun. **Credit** DC,
MC, V. **Map** p306 H4.
Just across from the Café Montmartre, this is the
official café of the Academy of Dramatic Arts,
whose Czech acronym is contained in the name. Six
kinds of beer are on tap, as are fairly substantial
steaks – an unusual option for Prague cafés. The
schedules on your table are for the irregular and
dubious theatre pieces and concerts in the downstairs cellar. Nice glass-roofed garden.

Ebel Coffee House

Týn 2, Prague 1 (2489 5788) Metro Náměstí
Republiky/5, 8, 14 tram. **Open** 9am-10pm daily.
Credit AmEx, DC, MC, V. **Map** p306 J3.
The Ebel touches the heights of the art of coffee
brewing. Journalist and designer Malgorzata Ebel
serves Prague's finest bean blends any way you
like, whether macchiato or melange, espresso or
cappuccino. More than 30 prime arabica coffees
from her neighbouring shop, Vzpomínky na
Afriku (*see page 176*), are available to go into your
cup. Passable quiches, bagels and brownies are
served as well, on tables in Prague's most fashionable Old Town courtyard.

Érra Café

Konviktská 11, Prague 1 (2423 3427). Metro Národní
třída/6, 9, 18, 21, 22, 23 tram. **Open** 10am-midnight
Mon-Fri; 11am-midnight Sat, Sun. **No credit cards.**
Map p306 G5.
It's as if a copy of Czech *Elle* exploded in an Old
Town cellar – even the menu parties and poses in
here: salads of smoked duck and artfully arranged
spinach leaves are a favourite lunch item, as are the
garlic-sesame chicken baguettes and rich banana
milkshakes. Gay-friendly scene by night.

Franz Kafka Café

Široká 12, Prague 1 (231 8945). Metro Staroměstská/
17, 18 tram. **Open** 10am-10pm daily. **No credit**
cards. Map p306 H2/3.
Surprisingly un-kitsch, this old-world coffeehouse
features dark, deep wooden booths, old engravings
of the Jewish Quarter and, naturally, loads of
Kafka portraits. Decent coffees and tables on the
street make it convenient when touring Josefov.

Káva Káva Káva

Národní třída 37, Prague 1 (268 409). Metro Národní
třída/6, 9, 18, 21, 22 tram. **Open** 9am-10pm Mon-Fri;
9am-10pm Sat, Sun. **Credit** MC, V. **Map** p306 H5.

Angel Café – buttermilk pancakes and a respectable brunch.

Prague's first full-blown coffee emporium is a kinder, gentler kind of Starbucks, with a quiet courtyard and a dozen varieties of bean on offer. Through a sweetheart deal with Bohemia Bagel, it also offers credible snacks. Carrot cake and a café latte go well with the parade of characters streaming by outside on busy Národní.

Kavárna Obecní dům

Náměstí Republiky 5, Prague 1 (2200 2763). Metro Náměstí Republiky/5, 14, 26 tram. **Open** 7.30am-11pm daily. **Credit** AmEx, MC, V. **Map** p307 K3.
The magnificently restored Municipal House (*see also p35, p91 and p219*) is one of Prague's most celebrated buildings. Its features include a stunning art nouveau concert space, galleries and a decent French restaurant but this café takes the cake. Replete with elaborate secessionist brass chandeliers, balconies, a pianist and, somewhat incongruously, a few Internet terminals, it's a memorable venue for an espresso.

Metamorphosis

Malá Štupartská 5, Prague 1 (2482 7058). Metro Náměstí Republiky/5, 14, 26 tram. **Open** 9am-1am Mon-Fri; 10am-1am Sat, Sun. **Credit** AmEx, DC, MC, V. **Map** p306 J3.
Sedate and capable, this family-run pasta café on the refurbished Ungelt Square has just one disadvantage: it's directly on a main tourist route to Old Town Square. The cellar restaurant within is enhanced by live jazz at night.

Slavia

Smetanovo nábřeží 2, Prague 1 (2421 8493). Metro Národní třída/6, 9, 17, 18, 22 tram. **Open** 9am-11pm daily **Credit** AmEx, MC, V. **Map** p306 G5.
The mother of all Prague cafés, where Karel Tiege, Jiří Kolář, and a struggling Václav Havel once tippled and plotted the overthrow of communism, the Slavia would hardly be recognized by its former customers today. The art deco fixtures and crisp service were overdue, but are not the stuff of Jaroslav Seifert's classic poem 'Café Slavia'. Still, it does offer the finest castle views in the city, a decent salmon toast and a fine Old Town respite just opposite the National Theatre.

Týnská literární kavárna

Týnská 6, Staré Město, Prague 1 (2482 6023). Metro Staroměstská/17, 18 tram. **Open** 10am-11pm daily. **No credit cards. Map** p306 J3.
A jumble of art students, smoke and bad coffee that leads onto a lovely hidden courtyard secreted behind the city of Prague's newest gallery of modern art, the House of the Gold Ring (*see p117*). The place to meet the next Czech art star.

Nové Město

Angel Café

Opatovická 3, Prague 1 (290 166/www.thecafe.cz). Metro Národní třída/6, 9, 18, 21, 22, 23 tram. **Open** 8am-10pm Tue-Fri; 10am-4pm Sat, Sun; closed Mon. **No credit cards. Map** p308 G6/H6.

Sofia Aziz and Matthew Smith have created one of the city's brightest lunch spots in this airy yellow room (and micro-patio out back) where they offer the likes of spicy chicken satay and Persian lentil soup, plus bakeshop delights such as butterscotch walnut brownies and lemon coconut cake. On weekdays, early risers enjoy Prague's finest buttermilk pancakes in the city, but it's brunch only at weekends, albeit a very respectable brunch. Genial service, sophistication and a light classical soundtrack further help Angel's case.

Café Break

Štěpánská 32, Prague 1 (2223 1065). Metro Můstek/3, 9, 14, 24 tram. **Open** 7.30am-11pm Mon-Sat; closed Sun. **No credit cards. Map** p309 K6.

Bright, lively and a lifeline for expats around Wenceslas Square. The owner camps out here all day, ensuring that everybody feels welcome, a practice all too rare in Prague. Window seats offer prime people-ogling while your formally polite waiter brings on fresh oysters, French table wine by the glass, a meal-sized salad or ciabatta sandwich at lunchtime. On Tuesdays chansons, lasagna and steaks come on with the evening.

The Globe Bookstore & Coffeehouse

Pštrossova 6, Prague 1 (2491 7230/www.ini.cz/globe). Metro Národní třída/6, 9, 18, 21, 22, 23 tram. **Open** 10am-midnight Mon-Thur, Sun; 10am-1am Fri, Sat. **No credit cards. Map** p308 G7.

The city's original expat bookstore café has been pegged from the outset as the literary heart of post-revolutionary Prague, blamed for encouraging all the wannabe Hemingways. The Globe carries its burden graciously, offering a cosy reading den and comfortable café surroundings to scribblers of both novellas and postcards to Ohio. Unpredictable pasta salads and such do for food, except during the great Sunday brunch, but the real star is the readings programme: Susan Sontag will show up one day, some expat's film treatment the next. The free Internet terminals are always busy.

Café Imperial

Na poříčí 15, Prague 1 (231 6012/ www.hostelimperial.cz). Metro Náměstí Republiky/ 5, 8, 14, 26 tram. **Open** 9am-1am daily. **No credit cards. Map** p307 L2.

Once the picture of decadence during Czechoslovakia's First Republic, the former Café Imperial has reopened with style after decades of neglect. Covered from floor to mosaic ceilings with art nouveau sculpted porcelain tiles, the Imperial exudes faded elegance and class.

Café Louvre

Národní třída 20, Prague 1 (297 665). Metro Národní třída/6, 9, 18, 22 tram. **Open** 8am-11pm daily. **Credit** AmEx, DC, MC, V. **Map** p306 H5.

A long, lofty café that somehow manages to get away with a garish cream and turquoise colour combination, perhaps because it leads to a fine back-room pool hall. Solid weekend breakfasts.

The Globe Bookstore and Coffeehouse.

French Institute Café

Štěpánská 35, Prague 1 (2223 2995). Metro Můstek/3, 9, 14, 24 tram. **Open** 9am-6pm Mon-Fri; closed Sat, Sun. **No credit cards. Map** p309 K6.

A crucial source of croissants and good, strong espresso before the opening of Chez Marcel (*see p135*) and Le Café Colonial (*see p137*). The French Institute carries on as a Gallic nerve centre with an unapologetically Francophile art gallery downstairs and free cinema adjoining. Elegant, prime posing with an open courtyard and a fair chance of starting an intellectual romance.

Le Patio Café

Národní třída 22, Prague 1 (2492 1060/2491 8136). Metro Národní třída/6, 9, 18, 21, 22, 23 tram. **Open** 8am-11pm Mon-Sat; 10am-11pm Sun. **Credit** AmEx, MC, V. **Map** p306 H5.

Possibly the best cheesecake in town, and a brilliant spying roost upstairs. The lovely wrought-iron and wicker furnishings, giant coloured candles and carved stone creations are also for sale in the gift shop at the back. Good breakfast option with a small list of salad-and-bread platters.

U Svatého Vojtěcha

Vojtěšská 14, Prague 1 (2491 0594). Metro Národní třída/6, 9, 17, 18, 22 tram. **Open** 10am-11pm Mon-Fri; 10am-10pm Sat; 10am-8pm Sun. *July, Aug* 10am-11pm daily. **No credit cards. Map** p308 G7.

Just behind the **National Theatre** (*see p237*) and largely untainted by non-Czechs, this quiet, unassuming café is frequented by actors and intellectual types who sit by the large window, have a leisurely smoke and leaf through the morning papers. No food to speak of.

Velryba

Opatovická 24, Prague 1 (2491 2391). Metro Národní třída/6, 9, 18, 21, 22, 23 tram. **Open** 11am-2am daily (kitchen closes at 11pm Mon-Sat; 10pm Sun). **No credit cards. Map** p308 H6.

Granddaddy of the young Czech hipster hangouts, the 'Whale' combines clamorous front-room dining on pastas and chicken steaks with backroom chess and a cellar gallery specialising in what looks suspiciously like art therapy. Curiously, the bar only serves bottled Gambrinus. The lack of air once prompted a no-smoking policy that lasted about a week before the nicotine-crazed clientele won the day. Avoid the healthy-sounding *tofu karbanátky* – it isn't anything of the sort.

Further afield

Holešovice

Caffé Dante

Dukelských hrdinů 16, Prague 7 (87 01 93). Metro Vltavská/1, 8, 14, 25 tram. **Open** 8am-10pm Mon-Fri; 11am-10pm Sat, Sun. **No credit cards. Map** p310 D2/3.

Handy if you're visiting the National Gallery Collection of 19th- and 20th-Century Art (*see p115*) up the street, this bright and brassy café serves basic grub with helpful service. The style-conscious Czech clientele makes for excellent people-watching.

Café Orange

Puškinovo náměstí 13, Prague 7 (no phone). Metro Dejvická/2, 20, 26. **Open** 9am-11pm Mon-Fri; 10am-11pm Sat, Sun. **No credit cards.**

Fresh juice, giant lattes and mozzarella ciabattas served to tables on the street. On a little square in the city's quiet embassy district, where children draw dragons on the asphalt in coloured chalk. The raspberry tarts attract all the old ladies in the neighbourhood out walking their dogs; the salmon walls, parquet floors, palm trees and seemingly perpetual Everything But the Girl soundtrack bring in the young, sleek and international.

La Crêperie

Janovského 4, Prague 7 (878 040). Metro Metro Vltavská/1, 8, 14, 25 tram. **Open** 11am-11pm Mon-Sat; 11am-10pm Sun. **No credit cards. Map** p310 D2.

French-owned niche serving the Francophone favourite flour-based delicacy. Generous crêpes, both sweet and savoury, go for a pittance in the comfortably closet-sized basement. Better than average wine list, too.

Vinohrady

Medúza

Belgická 17, Prague 2 (2251 5107). Metro Náměstí Miru/4, 22, 34 tram. **Open** 10am-1am Mon-Fri; noon-1am Sat, Sun. **No credit cards. Map** p309 M9.

Relaxed and friendly women-run café with good coffee and a limited menu of snacks and sandwiches. Comfortable old furniture, portraits and faded photos on the walls, and the classical music or old Czech chansons playing in the background make this a good place to chill.

Literární kavárna GPlusG

Čerchovská 4, Prague 2 (627 3332). Metro Jiřího z Poděbrad/11 tram. **Open** 10am-10pm daily. **No credit cards. Map** p311 B2.

A clean, well-lit place to catch a jazz trio or the opening of a Slovak Dadaist exhibition, all par for the

Spot the best cheesecake in town from **Le Patio Café**'s convenient spying roost. *See p150.*

course at this small press publisher cum coffee-house. A wide array of indie books and culture 'zines are available, plus wonderfully illustrated children's books. Everything is in Czech, but there's a very welcoming vibe.

Internet cafés

It's no longer necessary to choose between having a Staropramen and checking your email, since a growing number of bars have Internet access, often for free, such as **Kavárna Obecní dům** (*see page 149*), **The Globe Bookstore and Coffeehouse** (*see page 165*), **Jáma** (*see page 159*), and **Karlovy Lázně** (*see page 227*).

Hermes Internet Café

Nekázanka 10, Nové Město, Prague 1 (2423 9122/ www.hermescafe.cz). Metro Náměstí Republiky/5, 14, 26 tram. **Open** 24 hrs daily. **No credit cards.** **Map** p307 K4.

Just ten minutes from Wenceslas Square, open all night and actually passable as a café, Hermes is hard to beat. Checking messages is free if it takes less than five minutes, there's free coffee with one hour's Internet use and top games are installed on the 20 new terminals. Look up from time to time at the surrealist river in the ceiling or to order from the fine selection of brandies.

Internet Café Spika

Dlážděná 4, Nové Město, Prague 1 (2421 1521/ www.netcafe.spika.cz). Metro Náměstí Republiky/5, 8, 14 tram. **Open** daily 10am-10pm. **No credit cards.** **Map** p307 K4.

Curiously retro within, this open-plan Internet café offers 16 PCs on two levels. Large screens make reading easy on the eyes, and some monitors are placed to allow a modicum of privacy. A complicated price structure allows regular users to save money; the basic price is 25 Kč for 15 minutes.

Pl@neta

Vinohradská 102, Žižkov, Prague 3 (6731 1182). Metro Jiřího z Poděbrad/11 tram. **Open** 8am-11pm daily. **No credit cards.** **Map** p311 B3.

Friendly English-speaking staff, low-priced surfing and a minimum of coffee and libations. Like most Prague Internet cafés, it's more office than bar, but still the most relaxed around.

Terminal Bar

Soukenická 6, Nové Město, Prague 1 (2187 1223/2187 1224/technical support 2187 1666/www.terminal.cz). Metro Náměstí Republiky/5, 8, 14 tram. **Open** 10am-2am daily. **No credit cards.** **Map** p307 L2.

Cyber style takes precedence in Prague's most international Internet café, often to an annoying degree. But nobody else can touch Terminal's mix of expat interiors, outlandish interior decorating and Kahlua coffees. Multilingual technical advice during work hours, fast connections, battered terminals and a homey basement lounge also

Teahouses aren't boring – honest.

set it apart. The huge collection of Czech and foreign videos can be rented for home viewing or screened in the basement viewing room for 100 Kč plus 50 Kč per viewer.

Teahouses

When Luboš Rychvalský opened his first branch of **Dobrá čajnova** on a dark, stony Old Town mews called Boršov, it launched a tea-sipping revolution that has seen similar locations sprout throughout the republic. These days not even summer rockfests are complete without a tearoom and most feature all the appropriate rituals, piles of Persian rugs, half a dozen steeping methods and 40 or more teas.

Čajovna Duše

Dlouhá 33, Staré Město, Prague 1 (2482 7375). Metro Náměstí Republiky/5, 8, 14 tram. **Open** noon-midnight Mon-Sat ; 2pm-midnight Sun. **No credit cards.** **Map** p307 K2.

Prague's newest tearoom is nothing less than a harem tent strewn with pillows and teak, providing a perfect candle-lit counterpoint to the crazed goings-on at the Roxy next door.

Dobrá čajovna

Václavské náměstí 14, Nové Město, Prague 1 (2423 1480). Metro Můstek/3, 9, 14, 24 tram. **Open** 10am-9.30pm Mon-Sat; 3-9.30pm Sun. **No credit cards.** **Map** p306 J5.

The romanticised Asian fantasy setting was an early Prague *čaj* hit, with its dozens of Darjeelings, Assams, Algerian mint leaves and unpronounceable Chinese varieties. Ring the brass bell that comes with your menu to summon a serene, sandalled waiter. At the Boršov branch, pull the ringer to get in. **Branch**: Boršov 2, Staré Město, Prague 1 (269 9794).

Malý Buddha

Úvoz 46, Hradčany, Prague 1 (2051 3894). Tram 8, 22. **Open** 2-10.30pm Tue-Sun; closed Mon. **No credit cards.** **Map** p304 A3.

The 'Little Buddha' is a teahouse with a difference: great vegetarian spring rolls and noodle dishes go hand in hand with the dozens of teas brewed by the blissed-out owner, who's always on hand. Mellow doesn't half describe it. No smoking.

Pubs & Bars

Beer and loathing – visit ancient brew pubs and flash new cocktail bars, crawling through all kinds of establishment in between.

Chateau Rouge – a multinational college crowd ponders the pursuit of cheap sex. *See p156.*

Eat, Drink, Shop

From the 14th century when King Charles IV forbade the export of Bohemia's prize Žatec hops, Czechs have revelled in their destiny: to be the world's brewmasters.

But if the art of brewing is the Bohemian gift to lay alongside the printing press or penicillin, it's one most gladly received by the giver himself. It's a tradition so ingrained that neither World War II nor the central planners in Moscow could do much to change it – thus, a night at the corner pub feels and tastes (and smells) much the same as it always has.

Under balmy summer skies a Pilsener or six with your friends may well be the loveliest ritual in the world, but keeping pace with the locals is no picnic the rest of the year. Drinking is done in smoky pubs with stained tablecloths and surly servers with dodgy maths. Anything less than half a dozen half-litre mugs is suspect – if you can drink ten you can walk away with your pride intact. If you can walk at all.

> ▶ For a breakdown of the best **Czech brews**, see chapter **Beer**.

Czechs wouldn't have it any other way. That may explain why bars focusing on atmosphere, drink mixing or good wines are still somewhat thin on the ground. A few fortunate exceptions are **Hapu** (*see page 161*) and **Bugsy's** (*page 155*), and, in the Restaurants chapter, **Chez Marcel** (*see page 135*) and **Trocadero** (*page 137*).

For a taste of the authentic, try Žižkov's exemplary **U Houdků** pub, though any in this district will do. Pedigreed Old Town establishments include the **Radegast Pub**, **U medvídků** and **U krále Jiřího**. **Baráčnická rychta** and **U Černého vola** set the standard in Malá Strana and Hradčany.

For the wine-drinker, Moravian vintages aren't as refined as Bohemian brews but they're rebounding after years of official disdain for being bourgeois. Vineyards in Mikulov, Znojmo or Valtice yield increasingly drinkable whites such as **Rulandské bílé** and **Rulandské šedé**, (both pinots) and **Müller Thurgau**. More complex reds are **Svatovavřinecké** or the less reliable **Rulandské červené**, a pinot noir.

You can bring a plastic water bottle into any corner tavern marked *sudové víno* and take a chance on 'barrelled wine'. A litre costs 50-75 Kč.

Snack attack

Yes, the first priority for food in pubs is to soak up the beer, but the array of bar snacks you'll find in Prague truly demands consideration. There are the blackened filets that smoke up **Belle Epoque** and **Solidní nejistota**, but why eat fashionable food, especially when there are classics on hand like *utopenec*? The 'drowned man' is a particular favourite of pub denizens, who enjoy the taste that only marination in vinegar can impart to a sausage (pictured).

Zavináč, a dried herring speared on a toothpick, is presumably named for its shape, as it is also the Czech word for '@'. Then there's *pivní sýr*: stupefyingly smelly curd cheese, dabbed with hot mustard, sprinkled with paprika and mixed with onion. Try it once to test the loyalty of your friends (sardines optional).

Your second fishy option is *matesy:* cold, rolled herring, sour and more oily than *zavináč*. The ubiquitous schnitzel is *řízek*, usually made in the morning so that its corners are curling up by the time you order it that night. *Smažený sýr*, a strangely addictive breaded, fried cheese served with tartar sauce, is never difficult to find. It's what most Czech pubs take pride in offering as their '*vegetariánské*' option.

Hradčany

U Černého vola

Loretánské náměstí 1, Prague 1 (2051 3481). Tram 22. **Open** 10am-10pm daily. **No credit cards.** **Map** p304 B3.

One of the best pubs in Prague. The murals make it look like it's been here forever, but in fact the Black Ox was built after World War II. Its superb location, right above the Castle, made it a prime target for redevelopment in the post-1989 building frenzy, but the rugged regulars, in co-operation with the former Beer Party, bought it to ensure that local bearded artisans would have at least one place where they could afford to drink. The Kozel beer is perfection and, although the snacks are pretty basic, they do their job of lining the stomach for long sessions.

Malá Strana

Baráčnická rychta

Tržiště 23, Prague 1 (5753 2461). Metro Malostranská/12, 22 tram. **Open** noon-11pm daily. **No credit cards.** **Map** p305 D3.

Czech pub-goers complain that the tourist trade has all but killed the indigenous pub culture – immortalised in Jan Neruda's *Prague Tales* – that thrived in Malá Strana from the 19th century on. This place is one of few authentic remnants. Just off Nerudova, Baráčnická rychta eludes the mob behind a series of archways. Beyond these, it's split into two – a small beerhall frequented by hardcore *pivo* drinkers, both students and middle-aged, and a downstairs music hall that these days increasingly often features live stuff by local rock hopefuls. Obvious tourists may catch the occasional scowl, but in general this is a friendly place.

Blue Light

Josefská 1, Prague 1 (no phone). Metro Malostranská/12, 22 tram. **Open** 6pm-3am daily. **No credit cards.** **Map** p305 E3.

Cosy bar featuring occasional live jazz music, jazzy sounds on the stereo, and jazz posters all over the distressed walls. By day it's a convivial spot to sit with a friend, especially when there's room at the bar. At night it gets more rowdy and conversation becomes nigh impossible. Overpriced beers somehow fail to drive away the locals. Good selection of malt whiskies.

Café El Centro

Maltézské nám 9, Prague 1 (5753 3343). Metro Malostranská/12, 18, 22, 23 tram. **Open** 11am-midnight daily. **Credit** AmEx, MC, V. **Map** p305 E4.

Easily overlooked Malá Strana bar just a block off the main square that shines at tropical drink mixology and mambo soundtracks. Recent efforts to expand into a full restaurant specialising in paella aren't winning over the daiquiri lovers but the postage-stamp patio at the rear is a boon.

The best Bars

For 'contact sport' cruising
Chateau Rouge (see page 156).

For a thoroughly dry Martini
Hapu (see page 161).

For field-testing your brand-new gas mask
U krále Jiřího (see page 157).

For drinking yourself blind to help the sightless
U Černého vola (see page 154).

For doing a karaoke 'My Way' before passing out
Legends (see page 156).

Jo's Bar
Malostranské náměstí 7, Prague 1 (530 942). Metro Malostranská/12, 22 tram. Open 11am-2am daily. No credit cards. Map p305 E3.
Narrow bar crammed with backpackers. You can play chess, listen to loud rock, eat passable Mexican food, take coffee refills and get liquored quick on occasional drink specials. On a bad night it's like a mawkish American college reunion, but the cramped Gothic cellar dance space of Jo's Garáž below (just where are the fire exits?) can be a blast, with party people stripping off and dancing on the bar to Iggy Pop tunes until 4am. *See also p227.*

Petřínské Terasy
Seminářská zahrada 13, Prague 1 (9000 0457). Metro Malostranská/12, 18, 22, 23 tram. Open 11am-10pm daily. No credit cards. Map p304 C4.
New on the Petřín Hill, the Petřín Terraces offers exquisite dining of Prague Castle and the city and Krušovice, not necessarily in that order. An open-air grill tempts your appetite toward the full restaurant menu. Cover charge for occasional live music.

St Nicholas Café
Tržiště 10, Prague 1 (5753 0204). Metro Malostranská/12, 22 tram. Open noon-1am Mon-Fri; 4pm-1am Sat, Sun. Credit MC, V. Map p305 D3.
An atmospheric vaulted cellar decked out with steamer trunk tables, arches embroidered in red tempera and Pilsner Urquell on tap. A mellow but lively crowd gathers in the nooks for late evening conversation about nothing in particular. Also good for giving the brew a rest and taking up a glass of Havana Club rum, priced for a song.

U Malého Glena
Karmelitská 23, Prague 1 (535 8115). Metro Malostranská/12, 22 tram. Open 10am-2am daily. Credit AmEx, MC, V. Map p305 E4.

Two-level pub that has captured a chunk of the Malá Strana market by appealing to both tourists and Czech thirtysomethings, thirsty for a taste of imported brews and live music in a casual, upscale atmosphere. Upstairs is intimate without being suffocating, sporting wooden benches, Margaritas and light sandwiches. Downstairs a tiny bar hosts jazz and reggae shows (*see p216*).

Staré Město

Banana Bar
Štupartská 9, Prague 1 (232 4801). Metro Náměstí Republiky/5, 14, 26 tram. Open 8pm-2am daily. Credit AmEx, MC, V. Map p306 J3.
Upstairs from La Provence restaurant (*see p137*), this daft Euro-trash hangout features dated disco music, go-go dancers, a tiny dancefloor and bizarre entertainments, such as a woman in an improbable wig knitting on the bar. Worth one drink and a giggle on the way to somewhere else.

Belle Epoque
Křižovnická 8, Prague 1 (232 1926). Metro Staroměstská/17, 18 tram. Open noon-2am daily. No credit cards. Map p306 G3.
One of Prague's first grill bars, the Belle Epoque appeals to a mixed crowd of Czech Moderns bent on having a thoroughly western cocktail experience and willing to pay double the usual rate for it. Mobile-phone bearers can be seen gathered around Long Island ice teas amid the rough-hewn brick walls and candles. The staff are willing to slap anything you can name on to the barbecue.

Blatnička
Michalská 6, Prague 1 (2423 3612). Metro Můstek/6, 9, 18, 22 tram. Open 11am-11pm daily. No credit cards. Map p306 H4.
Hidden just off Karlova and away from the tourist hordes, this wine cellar masquerades as a tiny, smoke-filled bar that appears most unwelcoming. To the back and down the stairs, though, there's a snug little restaurant serving unimaginative Czech food to soak up the drinkable Moravian wines, on tap in half- and one-litre jugs.

Bugsy's
Pařížská 10, Prague 1 (entrance on Kostečná) (232 9943). Metro Staroměstská/17, 18 tram. Open 7pm-2am daily. No credit cards. Map p306 H3.
As swish as the street outside, offering a book-length drinks menu including 200 cocktails and bar staff good enough to mix them properly. Prices prohibit all but Czech yuppies, foreign businesspeople and babes waiting for some nice wealthy fellow to buy them a drink. The bar is fun to perch at; the tables less inviting. Packed in mid-evenings.

Café Konvikt
Bartolomějská 11, Prague 1 (2423 2427). Metro Národní třída/6, 9, 18, 21, 22, 23 tram. Open 9am-1am Mon-Fri; noon-1am Sat, Sun. No credit cards. Map p306 G5/H5.

Popular, well-lit Old Town spot at which to catch Prague's new generation of penniless creatives with a taste for bad wine. An edible strudel is served but it's really just about drink, talk and smoke here – all done in earnest.

Chateau Rouge

Jakubská 2, Prague 1 (no phone). Metro Náměstí Republiky/5, 14, 26 tram. **Open** *Winter* 4pm-4am daily. *Summer* 4pm-5am daily. **No credit cards.** **Map** p307 K3.

Multinational college crowds cram nightly into this loud and smoky epicentre of young Prague nightlife in search of contraband and cheap sex, both of which are indeed pretty easily arranged. Occasional DJs; rarely much room to breathe.

James Joyce

Liliová 10, Prague 1 (2424 8793). Metro Staroměstská/17, 18 tram. **Open** 11am-1am daily. **Credit** AmEx. MC, V. **Map** p306 G4.

The Hooray Henry hangout of the expat crowd. Few Czechs can afford the prices, and that is partly the purpose of this expat oasis. Such arrogance aside, it must be said that the braying hearties who come here do know how to have a piss-up. Irish stews and fry-ups are also well done amid an interior imported from a 19th-century Belfast church.

Kozička

Kozí 1, Prague 1 (2481 8308). Metro Náměstí Republiky/5, 8, 14 tram. **Open** noon-4am Mon-Fri; 6pm-4am Sat, Sun. **Credit** AmEx, MC, V. **Map** p306 J2.

Wall-to-wall crowds attest nightly to the can't-lose Prague formula of the moment: grill bars. Urban scene-making meets Czech meat-loving in an Old Town brick cellar. The 500-gram rumpsteaks go well with a mug of beer. A major meat market in other ways, too. Booking strongly advised.

La Casa Blů

Kozí 15, Prague 1 (2481 8270). Metro Staroměstská. **Open** 2pm-midnight daily. **No credit cards.** **Map** p306 J2.

Sarapes draped over hard-back chairs, Mexican street signs and tequila specials still pass for Latin culture in Prague. It's a pleasant break from the beer hall row, and is generally packed, but the film, music and art promised on the programme rarely come through. Try the buzzer even if the door is locked – people routinely wheedle their way in and carry on well past closing time.

Legends

Týn 1, Prague 1 (in the Ungelt Courtyard) (2489 5404). **Open** 10.30am-3am Mon-Thur, Sun; 10.30am-4am Fri, Sat. **No credit cards.** **Map** p306 J3.

A 'music and sports café' catering for the expat biz crowd. The place begins to fill from 3pm weekdays, when the three-hour happy hours start, and there isn't room to move during the silly Thursday theme parties (1960s karaoke, beach nights). Friday Ladies Nights endeavour to make it a major pickup joint. Small menu of atrocities.

Marquis de Sade

Templová 8, Prague 1 (no phone). Metro Náměstí Republiky/5, 14, 26 tram. **Open** 11am-2am daily. **No credit cards.** **Map** p307 K3.

The Old Town's crossover bar, featuring a little bit of everyone who's out and, despite nightly live jazz, enough peace and quiet for them to talk to each other. The splendid, large, picture-windowed room was the centrepiece of a lavish First Republic whorehouse. A new balcony bar has been installed at the rear, great for spying on other patrons. Good spot for hanging out, excellent location, mediocre but cheap salads and sandwiches.

The best Beer gardens

For blowing your holiday money in one dark, beery night
U Fleků (see page 160).

For stepping in something you don't want to identify
Letenský zámeček (see page 161).

For meeting a cute alcoholic biology student
U Holanů (see page 161).

For wishing you still could be a dissident
U vystřeleného oka (see page 161).

To take your mum to
Petřínské Terasy (see page 155).

The Garden Closes at 22:00

If you are out here after 22:00 you may have water poured on you by the neighbors.

Zahrádka se zavírá ve 22:00

Pokud zde zůstanete po 22:00 h.,může se Vám stát, že na Vás bude vylita voda od našich sousedů.

U mravence – quality spot for a late-night meet, but definitely best out of season.

Molly Malone's

U Obecního dvora 4, Prague 1 (534 793). Metro Náměstí Republiky/5, 14, 26 tram. **Open** noon-12.45am Mon-Thur, Sun; noon-1.45am Fri, Sat. **No credit cards. Map** p306 J2.

The archetype of Irish pubs everywhere: roaring log fire, mismatched chairs and tables constructed out of old beds and sewing machines, incessant Pogues in the background, 'traditional Irish food' and lots of backpackers and rowdy English businessmen. Much as you want to hate it, the place does have a certain charm. The bar is great for propping up, the Guinness is excellent, the food is decent, and in winter there's a warm and welcoming atmosphere. In summer, you risk an irate neighbour from this quiet corner of the Old Town throwing a plant pot at you if you stand outside after 9pm, but that's all part of the fun.

Radegast Pub

Templová 2, Prague 1 (232 8069). Metro Náměstí Republiky/5, 14, 26 tram. **Open** 11am-midnight daily. **No credit cards. Map** p307 K3.

One of the last typical Czech pubs to hang on in the Bermuda Triangle of expat drinking; its main draws are the excellent beer and pub food – you could pay an extra 200 Kč in a swank restaurant and not find a better goulash. The clientele are a mixture of Czechs, expats and backpackers who can't believe they've found such a cheap place to eat and drink right in the centre of Prague. Semi-enclosed snugs give an air of privacy, but the service is iffy – orders tend to get lost in the smoke.

U krále Jiřího

Liliová 10, Prague 1 (no phone). Metro Staroměstská/17, 18 tram. **Open** 11am-midnight Mon-Fri; noon-midnight Sat, Sun. **No credit cards. Map** p306 G4.

This narrow cellar pub is an insider's trump card with cheap Gambrinus 10-degree on tap in the heart of Old Town. Frequented by old-time locals, itinerant buskers and long-term expats, it's a funky, bare-bones hide-out for loud debates about the meaning of Velvet Underground lyrics.

U medvídků

Na Perštýně 7, Prague 1 (2422 0930). Metro Národní třída/6, 9, 18, 22 tram. **Open** 11am-11pm Mon-Sat; 11am-10pm Sun. **No credit cards. Map** p306 H5.

With five centuries as a beerhall behind it, The Little Bears brushed off communism as a passing fad. The only regime that counts here is the ritual of fine, cheap Budvar – and the half-litre mugs just keep on coming until you tell the waiter to stop. Don't be sidetracked by the modern bar to the left of the entrance; the real thing is on the right. The menu is a step up from pub grub, with pork in plum sauce and filets in dark beer. Feel free to dine in the hay-wagon if it's not occupied by the accordion band.

U mravence

U radnice 20, Prague 1 (no phone). Metro Staroměstská/17, 18 tram. **Open** 11am-midnight daily. **No credit cards. Map** p306 H3.

In the last location you'd expect to find a quality wine-sipping and gallery space, this Old Town Square bar consistently serves up cool ambient

Short, sharp shot treatment

Mixing harder stuff with Czech beer is risky alchemy, but at least the options are many and various, with an array of home-grown chasers on offer.

Becherovka, a ubiquitous sweetish yellow herb liqueur, is made to a secret recipe (of course) in Karlovy Vary. It's either drunk straight or cut with tonic, in which case it's known as *beton* – 'concrete'. **Fernet** – like a cross between Italy's Fernet Branca and Branca Menta – is more bitter. This too can be lightened with tonic water to make what is called, for some strange reason, *Bavorské pivo* – 'Bavarian beer'. The result is similar to Pimms, and quite refreshing. Both drinks are recommended as a hair of the dog and are even prescribed by some Czech doctors.

The cheapest ticket to oblivion, the one favoured by local drunks, is **Tuzemský Rum**, made from beets. With sugar, hot water and a slice of lemon it actually makes a good warming grog in winter. **Borovička** is a juniper brandy, more Slovak than Czech and not unlike Dutch Jenever, while **Slivovice** (plum brandy), if not

music and atmosphere. Tourist traffic does hamper The Ant in high season but a better grey weather spot for a late-night meet is not to be found.

U Zlatého tygra
Husova 17, Prague 1 (2222 1111). Metro Staroměstská/17, 18 tram. **Open** 3-11pm daily. **No credit cards. Map** p306 H4.
Once the headquarters of Prague's favourite writer, the famously crotchety Bohumil Hrabal (*see chapter* **Literary Prague**), this bar has lost virtually all its appeal since he fell to his death from a hospital window in 1997. Tourists still besiege the place, which may explain why the Pilsner Urquell is no bargain, but the remaining regulars are none too happy about all this and are likely to blow unfiltered cigarette smoke your way.

Žíznivý pes
Elišky Krásnohorské 5, Prague 1 (no phone). Metro Staroměstská/17, 18 tram. **Open** 11am-2am Mon-Fri; 2pm-2am Sat, Sun. **No credit cards. Map** p306 H2.

The Thirsty Dog is a shrine to the golden days of expat slacking, when its original location was still open and Nick Cave sat and wrote a song about the place. Nowadays it's burgers, Murphy's Stout and Lobkowicz with jubilantly cavorting Yanks and a handful of Czechs. Summer breezes waft through the Psi Bouda (Dog Kennel) patio out back.

Nové Město

Café Archa
Na Poříčí 26, Prague 1 (232 4149). Metro Náměstí Republiky or Florenc/3, 24 tram. **Open** 9am-10.30pm Mon-Fri; 10am-8pm Sat; 1-10pm Sun. **No credit cards. Map** p307 M2.
This glass fish tank, with long dangling lamps as bait, has hooked a young, laid-back clientele with cheap drinks, pristine surfaces and posters and photos from the theatre and rock worlds. You can stare out at the passers-by as you drink, though they're more likely to be staring in at you.

Becherovka and Fernet :
don't mix these drinks.

home-made, is smooth and goes down a treat. **Myslivecká** or 'Hunter's' is deceptively mild, a bit like weak bourbon, but should be treated with respect. **Griotte** is a cherry brandy, best in dessert sauces.

Absinthe, at a staggering 170 proof, has long been banned in most countries. It's a wormwood distillate, but contains a slightly smaller (and allegedly less brain-damaging) percentage of wood alcohol than the version

that once pickled the best minds of Paris. It's a translucent green liquid that tastes like alcoholic hair shampoo.

It's a grave *faux pas* not to observe the proper ritual. Take a spoonful of sugar and dunk it in the absinthe. Then set fire to the wet sugar, which will burn and caramelise. When the fire goes out, dump the spoonful back into the glass and stir.

Then close your eyes, take a glug, and try not to think about tomorrow.

Jágr's Sports Bar

Palác Blaník, Václavské náměstí 56, Prague 1 (no phone). Metro Můstek/3, 9, 14, 24, 52, 53, 55, 56, 58 tram. **Open** 11am-2am daily. **No credit cards. Map** p307 K5.
Comically epic basement shrine to Jaromír Jágr, the Czech ice-hockey star of the medal-winning Olympic team and later the Pittsburgh Penguins. There are wall-to-wall video screens on which to watch major sports events and matches from back home, including the Premiership on Sky. Food is overpriced (for Prague) red-blooded meat staples. The beer's expensive, too.

Jáma

V jámě 7, Prague 1 (2422 2383). Metro Můstek/3, 9, 14, 24 tram. **Open** 11am-1am daily (kitchen closes 10pm). **Credit** AmEx, V, MC. **Map** p309 K6.
Loud and collegiate year-round, this long bar with Mexican food is the choice of the local business crowd. The Arizonans who run it also sponsor the literary quarterly *Prague Revue*, but you'd never guess it from their loud and beery atmosphere,

their extensive cocktails (often on special), *faux* cacti, video counter or bank of Internet terminals. Decor is early Elvis Costello poster; service is above average. In summer 2000 they also added a beer garden in the back, offering a break from the noise within.

Jazz Café č. 14

Opatovická 14, Prague 1 (no phone). Metro Národní třída/6, 9, 18, 22 tram. **Open** 11am-11pm daily. **No credit cards. Map** p308 H6.
A crowd of local writers and arty types clearly considers this a cosy, if smoky winter hideaway, with its mismatched furniture, congenial service and jazz soundtrack. Oddly enough, there's never live music. The cold-pressed olive oils, groovy loose teas and honey on display in old hives are all for sale and make nice, cheap mementos.

Radost/FX Café

Bělehradská 120, Prague 2 (2425 4776). Metro I.P. Pavlova/4, 6, 11, 16, 22, 34 tram. **Open** 11am-4am

Letenský zámeček – nice beers under the trees, shame about the plastic cups. *See p161*.

daily. *Club* from 10pm Mon-Sat; closed Sun. **No credit cards. Map** p309 L8.
Back-room gallery, Sunday Beefstew poetry readings, downstairs disco with free video nights on Mondays, and a street-front vegetarian café with one of the city's mainstay Sunday brunches. Radost tries to be all things to all people – and succeeds reasonably well. The bulletin board is a critical link in the Prague housing and job food chain. Foreign residents moan but can never stay away for long. *See also p144 and p228*.

Sports Café Cornucopia

Jungmannova 10, Prague 1 (2494 7742).Metro Můstek/3, 9, 14, 24 tram. **Open** 8.30am-11pm daily. **No credit cards. Map** p306 J5.
Blaring Sky TV dominates, but the cheap buffet features Czech-Mex, custom sandwiches, breakfast French toast and crisp bacon. It fills with expats by mid-afternoon and there's standing-room only when *The Simpsons* comes on. *See p146*.

Solidní nejistota

Pštrossova 21, Prague 1 (2491 0593). Metro Národní třída/6, 9, 17, 18, 21, 22, 23, 21, 51, 52, 53, 54, 55, 56, 57, 58 tram. **Open** noon-3am Mon-Fri; 6pm-3am Sat, Sun. **No credit cards. Map** p308 G7.
A new shrine to posing and pickups, Solid Uncertainty comes equipped with the now standard blood-red interior and grill bar. Blues solos by Spider are a legitimate attraction and so is the, er, fresh meat if that's on your needs list.

U Fleků

Křemencova 11, Prague 1 (2491 5118). Metro Národní třída/3, 6, 14, 18, 24 tram. **Open** 9am-11pm daily. **Credit** AmEx, MC, V. **Map** p308 H7.

Prague's most famous pub has been brewing fine 13-degree dark beer on the premises for centuries. Though basic Bohemian meat and two veg is also available, you are automatically assumed to be here for the beer and will usually be treated like cattle – or rather like a nice, fleecy lamb when billing time rolls around. At the very least, don't accept the quadruple-priced Becherovka when it's suggested by your smiling waiter. The picturesque courtyard is shaded by cherry trees, enclosed by a sgraffitoed wall and leaded windows. Both inside and out, the long tables are invariably filled with hearty Germans swinging glasses to oom-pah music. Hardly the city's hippest venue, but the memorable beer is most definitely worth sampling.

U Kotvy

Spálená 11, Prague 1 (291 161). Metro Národní třída/6, 9, 18, 22 tram. **Open** 10am-10.30pm daily. **No credit cards. Map** p308 H6.
In winter, this smoky little hole-in-the-wall is inhabited by assorted intriguing mutants. In summer, the large garden hidden out back offers a leafy afternoon and evening haven. Slow service, passable food, and beware the toilets.

U Sudu

Vodičkova 10, Prague 1 (2223 2207). Metro Karlovo náměstí/3, 9, 14, 24 tram. **Open** 11am-midnight Mon-Fri; 3pm-midnight Sat, Sun. **No credit cards. Map** p308 J6.
Originally a small, dark wine bar on the ground floor, U Sudu has expanded down into two Gothic cellars and what seems to be somebody's spare room next door. The cellars have been claimed by students, while upstairs sees everyone from artists

to business types to little old ladies. The service is wonderful. The wine is nothing to shout about, except when the *burčák* (a half-fermented, traditional Czech wine punch) arrives in September.

Further afield

Holešovice

Letenský zámeček
Letenské sady 341, Prague 7 (in Letná Park) (3337 5604). Metro Hradčanská/1, 8, 25 tram. **Open** *Beer garden* 11am-10pm daily. *Restaurace Ullman* 11am-11pm daily. **Credit** *Restaurace Ullman* AmEx, MC, DC, V. **Map** p310 C3.

This leafy enclave on the hill above the Vltava is arguably the city's finest summer beer garden. A local crowd gathers under the chestnut trees for cheap Kozel beer in plastic cups late into the evening, every evening. Passable pizzas are served at the adjoining Restaurant Ullman, but the action is at the battered picnic tables with self-service for the beer kiosk. Great views of Old Town across the river; lots of roller-bladers and dogs.

Vinohrady

První Prag Country Saloon Amerika
Korunní 101, Prague 2 (2425 6131). Metro Náměstí Míru/16 tram. **Open** 11am-1am Mon-Fri; 5pm-midnight Sat; 6pm-11pm Sun. **No credit cards.** **Map** p311 B3.

A Czech cowboy's hoedown dream. Live country and western bands fiddle nightly while would-be Hosses and their gals crowd into hardwood seating, tuck into steaks and admire the animal skins on the walls. The hardcore (but incredibly friendly) crowd here risked jail under the old regime for collecting bits of Americana. (*See also p216.*)

U Holanů
Londýnská 10, Prague 2 (2251 1001). Metro Náměstí Míru/4, 6, 11, 16, 22, 34. **Open** 10am-11pm Mon-Fri; 11am-11pm Sat, Sun. **No credit cards.** **Map** p309 L7/8.

The Vinohrady district's most popular outdoor terrace pub for locals serves Gambrinus and Pilsner Urquell at local prices and the usual Czech meat-and-sauce staples to go with them. Note that it's *bez obsluhy* (without service) outside: you order indoors, then carry your order out to tables on the leafy, quiet street.

Žižkov

The Clown & Bard
Bořivojova 102, Prague 3 (2271 6453). Metro Jiřího z Poděbrad/5, 9, 26 tram. **Open** 8am-1am daily. **No credit cards.** **Map** p311 B2.

About as entertaining as hostel bars get, and that can be quite entertaining if you come on a night when one of the undiscovered bands that regularly

play here is actually any good. Otherwise, it's strictly backpacking, backgammon, cheap brews and comparing notes on the sights. *See also p64.*

Akropolis
Kubelíkova 27, Prague 3 (2272 1026/ www.spinet.cz/akropolis). Metro Jiřího z Poděbrad/5, 9, 26 tram. **Open** 10am-1am Mon-Fri; 4pm-1am Sat, Sun. **No credit cards.** **Map** p311 B2.

The current Prague hub of world music and its most happening concert space is a burgeoning labyrinth of bars. At last count there were four, plus a photo gallery, with themes ranging from proto-Alien (with fry-happy kitchen) to hayseed country and western (innermost cellar). They can't build them fast enough to satisfy the demand from hip Žižkov patrons, who carouse here late every night.

Hapu
Orlická 8, Prague 3 (no phone). Metro Flora/11, 16, 26, 51, 58 tram. **Open** 6pm-2am Mon-Sat; closed Sun. **No credit cards.** **Map** p311 C2/3.

The apotheosis of barmanship in the republic is remarkably free of the yuppie trappings sweeping the rest of Prague. This homey Žižkov drinking hole was opened by a couple who imagined their ideal bar, then created it for their friends. Fresh mint leaves adorn the rum Mojito; rum, cream, chocolate and more mint go into the house special, the *horká novinka* or 'hot news'. Shooters range from 30-60 Kč, while fru-fru short drinks and classic long ones abound. Dry martini lovers are catered to particularly well.

U Houdků
Bořivojova 110, Prague 3 (2271 1239). Metro Jiřího z Poděbrad/11 tram. **Open** 10am-11pm Mon-Sat; 11am-11pm Sun. **No credit cards.** **Map** p311 B2/C2.

Classic neighbourhood Žižkov pub with a blast of South Bohemia thrown in: Eggenberg and Budvar, both hearty brews from the Český Krumlov area, are served both light and dark, along with mounds of typical pub grub for pocket change. The picnic tables out back under the chestnut trees attract every student and worker still drinking in this trendifying neighbourhood.

U vystřelenýho oka
U božích bojovníků 3, Prague 3 (627 8714). Metro Florenc, then 135 or 207 bus. **Open** 3.30pm-1am Mon-Sat; closed Sun. **No credit cards.** **Map** p311 C1.

The Shot-Out Eye sits beneath the ominous giant statue of General Jan Žižka, the renowned warrior whose battle injury inspired the gory name. Žižkov has more pubs than any other area of Prague, but this is undoubtedly the best of the lot, and the only one that's genuinely welcoming to foreigners. A three-level outdoor beer garden serves bargain-basement Měšťan, while taps indoors flow non-stop to a soundtrack from local anarcho-rockers Psí Vojáci and to a backdrop of grotesque painting from Martin Velíšek. Upstairs is a quiet, Indian-style tearoom rather out of place amid the chaos, but inviting nonetheless.

Shops & Services

Designer malls and major labels march in, but Bohemian bargains and sassy souvenirs can still be snaffled up.

Prague shopping is not for the thin-skinned but treasures can be found, and not just on back streets and in dusty curio shops. The continuing invasion of the designer malls has transformed Wenceslas Square, Na Příkopě and Celetná beyond all recognition and the concept of the major sale is finally beginning to catch on. Prague fashion shops could never be mistaken for those of Paris or Milan (unless you notice last year's cast-offs from there on the racks) but the major labels are here in force. Since very few people can afford to buy them, a whole crop of second-tier design shops has sprouted, sometimes offering interesting stuff at discounted prices. Many of these are found in the newly opened **Černá růže** mall (*see page 180*) off Wenceslas Square.

Czech crystal and glass remains justly famous after centuries of skilled craftsmanship. Shops along the main tourist routes are bursting with such wares, mostly of reasonable quality, if not reasonable prices (*see page 172* **Lead-free luxury**). Meanwhile, on the quieter streets of Old Town, Czech fashion designers have never had as many places to show their work, while old bookshops and violin restorers remain where they have been since before communism. In these places you'll encounter old-fashioned pride and courtesy that you thought had disappeared forever – especially if you've already run the gamut of rudeness in the larger shops.

Pre-1989 Czechoslovakia, as one of the most hardline members of the East Bloc, had no private enterprise, so every shop clerk was a civil servant. And behaved accordingly. Sadly, most still do. You have to jump and shout to get their attention, they ring up the wrong price then look at your credit cards as though they were Monopoly money.

Prague shop clerks will ask '*Máte přání*' (Do you have a wish?) when you walk into a shop, and may ask '*ještě něco?*' (anything else?) or '*Všechno?*' (Is that all?) when they ring up your purchase. Ask *Kolik to stojí?* to find out what something costs. The polite custom is to say *Na schledano* as you leave, even if the clerk hasn't registered your presence.

A little strategic planning will assist in getting the most out of Prague's main shopping districts. The following may help you form the best plan. *See also page 164* **Shops by area**.

SHOPPING PRECINCTS

By and large, the shops in **Hradčany** and around Prague Castle carry only film, jester hats and postcards. For anything else, you'll need to head down the hill to **Malá Strana**. Though it's dominated by tourist shops, the artists, scribblers and pensioners living in the 'Little Quarter' require more than Bambino di Praga statuettes. Boutiques just south of the Charles Bridge on Saská offer an enticing taste, while antiques within a few blocks of Malostranské náměstí, especially along Nerudova, are rich in Old World atmosphere, if far too well-trafficked to offer bargains.

Staré Město is where you'll find the most active fashion boutiques and, along Na Příkopě, the most brazenly commercial pap. Otherwise it's a good area for antiquarian books and second-hand clothes.

Serious shopping gets done in **Nové Město**, whether it's filling the freezer or laying out for a new wardrobe. Just don't expect to find major bargains or charming, personal boutique experiences. Developers have built up most of New Town's shops, which means mass-produced fashions, as a rule. That said, the mysteries of the Havel family's pre-war enterprise, the Lucerna shopping passage, are ever intriguing. Otherwise, it's **Tesco** and the **Bontonland** music megastore. Bookstores here set the standard in Prague, though **The Globe Bookstore and Coffeehouse** remains the English-language literary epicentre.

Further afield, barrelled wine in Žižkov is an adventure, cut-rate CDs of questionable pedigree line the streets of Holešovice and lovely Vinohrady specialises in, well, mostly office space and cell phone stores.

Antiques

There may be few true antique shops in Prague, but there are numerous junk shops, selling everything from old irons and typewriters to prints by Alfons Mucha (*see page 117*). If an antiques shop is on a main tourist route, then you can be fairly sure that the prices are aimed at foreigners. For cheaper and more unusual items, seek out *bazar* stores, a better class of junk shop. Some are listed here, but more can be found in the *Zlaté stránky* (*Yellow Pages*).

Anagram Bookshop – a variety of reading for topical appetites. *See p164.*

Antique

Kaprova 12, Staré Město, Prague 1 (232 9003). Metro Staroměstská/17, 18 tram. **Open** 10am-7pm, Mon-Sat; 10am-6pm Sun. **Credit** DC, MC, V. **Map** p306 G3.
Expensive but rewarding. Check out the antique art deco watches – stylish and affordable.

Antique Ahasver

Prokopská 3, Malá Strana, Prague 1 (no phone). Metro Malostranská/12, 18, 22, 23 tram. **Open** 11am-6pm Tue-Sun; closed Mon. **Credit** V, MC. **Map** p305 E4.
Antique formal gowns, mother-of-pearl hairpins, beaded purses, brooches and trays of charming oddments. The English-speaking clerk is always ready to supply a story and help you decide.

Antique Anderle

Václavské náměstí 17, Nové Město, Prague 1 (2400 9166). Metro Můstek/3, 9, 14, 24 tram. **Open** 10am-7pm Mon-Sat; 10am-6pm Sun. **Credit** AmEx, DC, MC, V. **Map** p306 J5.
Very expensive shop with the city's best selection of above-par art and Russian icons (with export certificates). For serious collectors only.

Art Deco

Michalská 21, Staré Město, Prague 1 (261 367). Metro Staroměstská/6, 9, 18, 22 tram. **Open** 2-7pm Mon-Fri; closed Sat, Sun. **Credit** AmEx, MC, V. **Map** p306 H4.
The remains of a golden era when Prague was the fashion centre of eastern Europe. Vintage 1920-40s clothes, beaded hats and costume jewellery at fair prices. See the women's magazines for an interesting look at pre-war fashion.

Bazar v Dlouhé

Dlouhá 22, Staré Město, Prague 1 (232 0993). Metro Náměstí Republiky/5, 14, 26 tram. **Open** 10am-6pm Mon-Fri; 11am-4pm Sat; closed Sun. **No credit cards.** **Map** p306 J3.
Wall-to-wall antique furniture, walking sticks, watches, First Republic typewriters and entire ceramic ovens.

Bric á Brac

Týnská 7, Staré Město, Prague 1 (232 6484). Metro Staroměstská/17, 18 tram. **Open** 11am-7pm daily. **No credit cards.** **Map** p306 J3.
A quaint, eclectic mix of antiques and hand-sewn vintage clothes, plus quilts, odd little wooden jewellery boxes and groovy 1970s-style leather jackets. They also have a tiny shop around the corner stocked with every kind of timepiece imaginable.

Jan Huněk Starožitnosti

Pařížská 1, Staré Město, Prague 1 (2325 122). Metro Staroměstská/17, 18 tram. **Open** 10am-7pm daily. **Credit** AmEx, DC, MC, V. **Map** p306 H3.
Exquisite and expensive Czech glass from the 18th century to the 1930s. For dedicated collectors only.

Military Antique Army Shop

Křemencova 6, Nové Město, Prague 1 (no phone). Metro Národní třída/6, 9, 18, 21, 22, 23 tram. **Open** 11am-5pm Mon-Fri; closed Sat, Sun. **No credit cards.** **Map** p308 H6/7.
Just about everything you'd need to re-enact the Normandy landings. WWII flyer's headgear, goggles, bayonets, swords, badges and lots of those ever-so-handy ammo boxes.

Shops by area

Dejvice

Potraviny U Cedru (Food & drink p175).

Holešovice

Čínská restaurace Hong Kong (Food & drink p174); **McPaper & Co** (Stationery p184).

Malá Strana

Antique Ahasver (Antiques p163); **Candles Gallery** (Gifts p177); **Květinářství u červeného Iva** (Florists p174); **Mýrnyx Týrnyx** (Fashion p169).

Nové Město

234 (Music p181); **Academia** (Bookshops p164); **AM Optik Studio** (Opticians p183); **Antikvariát Kant** (Old books & prints p167); **Antique Anderle** (Antiques p163); **ART** (Shoes p173); **Austria Miniservis** (Shoe repairs p173); **AZ Foto** (Photography p183); **Baťa** (Shoes p173); **Black Market** (Fashion p169); **Bohemia Flowers** (Florists p174); **Bontonland (Supraphon)** (Music p181); **Bontonland Megastore** (Music p181); **Cellarius** (Wine p176); **Charita Florentinum** (Gifts p177); **Copy General** (Photocopying p183); **Čaj lepších časů** (Food & drink p174); **Černá růže** (Malls p180); **Česká tisková kancelář (ČTK)** (Photo developing p183); **Dája** (Dry cleaners p169); **Dobrá čajovna** (Food & drink p174); **Eiffel Optic** (Opticians p183); **Fleur de Nuit** (Lingerie p172); **Fotoplus** (Photo developing p184);

Fototechnika a video (Photography p183); **Fruits de France** (Food & drink p174); **Galerie bydlení** (Household p179); **Galerie Mody Heleny Fejkové** (Jewellery p170); **The Globe Bookstore and Coffeehouse** (Bookshops & newsagents p165); **Humanic** (Shoes p173); **Jan Ondrášek** (Shoe repairs p173); **Jan Pazdera obchod a opravna** (Photography p183); **Jarmark lahůdky** (Food & drink p175); **KDS** (Household p179); **Kenvelo Centre** (Malls p180); **Knihkupectví Jan Kanzelsberger** (Bookshops p165); **Krone/Julius Meinl** (Department Stores p169); **Ladana** (Costume & formal dress hire p173); **Le Patio** (Household p179); **Loco Plus** (Stationery p184); **Market at the Fountain** (Markets p181); **Match Kids Wear** (Children p170); **Military Antique Army Shop** (Antiques p163); **MPM** (Toys p184); **Music shop-antikvariát** (Music p181); **Myslbek Center** (Malls p180); **Pinito** (Children p170); **Potten & Pannen** (Household p180); **Praha Music Center** (Musical Instruments p182); **Ráj výtvarníků** (Art materials p184); **Rudolf Špičák Vetešnictví** (Antiques p163); **Šarm** (Hair & beauty p179); **Senior Bazar** (Fashion p170); **Simplicity** (Fashion p173); **Skiny** (Lingerie p172); **Tesco** (Department stores p169); **Trafika Můstek** (Newsagents p167); **Včelařské potřeby** (Gifts p178); **Vinotéka u Svatého Štěpána** (Wine p176); **White Dog** (Fashion p173).

Rudolf Špičák Vetešnictví

Ostrovní 26, Nové Město, Prague 1 (297 919). Metro Národní třída/6, 9, 18, 22 tram. **Open** 10am-5pm Mon-Fri; closed Sat, Sun. **No credit cards.** **Map** p308 H6.

A great junk shop in a damp basement. Among the old telephones, bashed violins and faded furniture you can find communist-era magazines and postcards, as well as the odd Stalin badge.

Bookshops & newsagents

English-language books in Prague are reasonably priced by Western standards, outrageous by local standards. If you're on a budget and none too picky, try one of the *antikvariáty* listed below. Most bookshops listed here can order new books, but there's a three- to five-week wait.

Academia

Václavské náměstí 34, Nové Město, Prague 1 (2422 3511/2422 3512). Metro Můstek. **Open** 9am-8pm Mon-Fri; 10am-8pm Sat, Sun. **Credit** MC, DC, V. **Map** p307 K5.

This friendly two-storey bookshop is handily located in the wonderfully restored Wiehl building on Wenceslas Square. Stock is predominantly Czech, but Academia also carries a wealth of English-language history, art and language texts, plus coffee-table books and culture magazines and journals with some English content. Well-lit café upstairs.

Anagram Bookshop

Týn 4, Staré Město, Prague 1 (2489 5737/ anagram@terminal.cz). Metro Náměstí Republiky/5, 14, 26 tram. **Open** 9.30am-7.30pm Mon-Sat; 10am-6pm Sun. **Credit** DC, MC, V. **Map** p306 J3.

This American-owned outlet has, in addition to a great selection of topical books on Prague and Central Europe, a great second-hand English-language rack, with an emphasis on health, fitness, philosophy, self-help and alternative medicine.

Big Ben Bookshop

Malá Štupartská 5, Staré Město, Prague 1 (2482 6565/www.bigbenbookshop.com). Metro Náměstí

Smíchov & Barrandov

Barrandov Studio, Fundus (Costume hire p173); **Ocean** (Food & drink p175).

Staré Město

Adelaide (Fashion p170); **Altamira** (Art materials p184); **Akant** (Photocopying p183); **Anagram Bookshop** (Bookshops p164); **Antikvariát Galerie Můstek** (Old books & prints p167); **Antikvariát Pařížská** (Old books & prints p167); **Antique** (Antiques p163); **Art Deco** (Antiques p163); **Association Club Sparta Praha** (Gifts p177); **Ateliér Kavka** (Florists p174); **Bakeshop Praha** (Food & drink p174); **Bazar** (Music p181); **Bazar v Dlouhé** (Antiques p163); **Benecel** (Photo developing p183); **Big Ben Bookshop** (Bookshops p164); **Blatnička** (Wine p176); **Botanicus** (Cosmetics & perfumes p169); **Bric á Brac** (Antiques p163); **Catwalk** (Fashion p169); **Chez Parisienne** (Lingerie p172); **CLU** (Fashion p170); **Česká lidová řemesla** (Gifts p177); **Country Life** (Food & drink p174); **De Gusto** (Food & drink p174); **Dětský dům** (Malls p180); **Dream Hair** (Hair & beauty p179); **Erpet** (Glassware p172); **ETS** (Gifts p178); **Global Ameritech** (Computers p167); **Golden Clean** (Dry cleaners p169); **GrandOptical** (Opticians p183); **Havelský Market** (Markets p180); **Hudební nástroje – Jakub Lis** (Musical instruments p182); **Ivre** (Toys p184); **James & Monika** (Hair & beauty p179); **Jan Huněk Starožitnosti** (Antiques p163); **Judita** (Lingerie p172); **Knihkupectví U Černé Matky Boží** (Bookshops p165); **Kondomerie** (Gifts p178); **Kotva** (Department stores p169); **La Bretagne** (Food & drink p175); **Makovský & Gregor** (Old books & prints p167); **Marks & Spencer** (Lingerie p172); **Maximum Underground** (Music p181); **McToy** (Toys p184); **Modes Robes** (Fashion p170); **Moser** (Glassware p172); **Music shop Trio** (Music p182); **Nostalgie** (Fashion p170); **Original Móda** (Fashion p170); **Pohodlí** (Music p182); **Prodejna U Salvatora** (Food & drink p176); **Sparky's Dům hraček** (Toys p184); **Šatna** (Fashion p170); **Sedin** (Rubber stamps p178); **Teuscher** (Food & drink p176); **U zlatého kohouta** (Musical instruments p182); **Vagabond** (Shoes p173); **Video Gourmet** (Video rental p184); **Vzpomínky na Afriku** (Food & drink p176).

Vinohrady

Atelier slunečnice (Hair & beauty p179); **Body Basics** (Cosmetics & perfumes p167); **Dionýsos** (Wine p176); **Macsource/ Compusource** (Computers p167); **Julius Meinl** (Supermarkets p176); **Le Delice Belges** (Food & drink p175); **Prague Laundromat** (Launderettes p169).

Republiky/5, 14, 26 tram. **Open** 9am-6.30pm Mon-Fri; 10am-5pm Sat, Sun. **Credit** AmEx, DC, MC, V. **Map** p306 J3.
This welcoming establishment has the standard books on Prague, several shelves of bestsellers, lots of English-language newspapers and magazines, plus the best children's books in English around. They'll gladly order for you and know their stock and writers better than most.
Branch: British Council, Národní 10, Nové Město, Prague 1 (2199 1200).

The Globe Bookstore and Coffeehouse
Pštrossova 6, Nové Město, Prague 2 (2491 7229/ www.globopolis.com). Metro Národní třída/6, 9, 18, 21, 22, 23 tram. **Open** 10am-midnight Mon-Thur; 10am-1am Fri, Sat; 10am-midnight Sun. **Credit** AmEx, V, MC. **Map** p308 G7.
The expat literary heart has moved from its first home in the Holešovice district to this multi-level, hardwired space in New Town. Fine second-hand paperbacks still line the walls, and it now has free Internet terminals, a sleek balcony and extra legroom. The list of international authors doing readings remains star-studded and the food remains, well, well-intentioned (*see p41 and 150*).

Knihkupectví Jan Kanzelsberger
Václavské náměstí 42, Nové Město, Prague 1 (2421 7335). Metro Můstek/3, 9, 14, 24 tram. **Open** 8am-7pm Mon-Sat; 9am-7pm Sun. **Credit** AmEx, MC, V. **Map** p307 K5.
Very central, with coffee-table books on Prague, a reasonably good selection of Czech fiction in translation and an odd assortment of guidebooks.

Knihkupectví U Černé Matky Boží
Celetná 34, Staré Město, Prague 1 (2421 1275). Metro Náměstí Republiky/5, 14, 26 tram. **Open** 9am-7pm Mon-Sat; 10am-7pm Sun. **Credit** AmEx, MC, V. **Map** p307 K3.
It's worth tracking down this arty bookshop just to gaze at the building's wonderful cubist exterior (House of the Black Madonna; *see p117*). The bookshop itself is good for gift-hunting, with hundreds of maps, art prints, T-shirts, translated Czech authors and coffee-table books and calendars.

Trafika Můstek

Václavské náměstí, Nové Město, Prague 1 (no phone).
Metro Můstek/3, 9, 14, 24 tram. **Open** 9am-8pm
daily. **No credit cards. Map** p306 J5.
Two green magazine stands at the bottom of
Wenceslas Square stocking everything from
Forbes to *Film Threat*. If you can't find a Western
periodical here, you can't find it in Prague.

Old books & prints

Prague's second-hand bookshops are known as
antikvariáty. For a one-of-a-kind Prague
souvenir, you couldn't do better than an old
communist coffee-table book or a dirt-cheap print
by a unknown Czech artist. *Antikvariáty* are also
the places to find second-hand novels in English.

Antikvariát Galerie Můstek

28. října 13, Staré Město, Prague 1 (268 058). Metro
Můstek/6, 9, 18, 22 tram. **Open** 10am-1pm, 2-7pm
Mon-Fri; 10am-2pm Sat; closed Sun. **Credit** AmEx,
DC, MC, V. **Map** p308 H6.
A discriminating *antikvariát* with fine antiquarian
books (19th-century natural history especially) and
a steady stream of major works on Czech art.

Antikvariát Kant

Opatovická 26, Nové Město, Prague 1 (2491 6376).
Metro Národní třída/6, 9, 18, 22 tram. **Open** 9am-
6pm Mon-Fri; 10am-3pm Sat; closed Sun. **Credit** MC,
V. **Map** p306 J3.
An eclectic mix of prints and dust-encrusted books.
There's an impressive selection of second-hand
titles in English, from *Jaws* to Germaine Greer.

Antikvariát Pařížská

Pařížská 8, Staré Město, Prague 1 (232 1442). Metro
Staroměstská/17, 18 tram. **Open** 10am-6pm daily.
Credit AmEx, MC, V. **Map** p306 H3.
Gorgeous prints and maps exclusively from the
16th to 19th centuries.

Makovský & Gregor

Kaprova 9, Staré Město, Prague 1 (no phone). Metro
Staroměstská/17, 18 tram. **Open** 9am-7pm Mon-Fri;
10am-6pm Sat; closed Sun. **Credit** AmEx, DC, MC, V.
Map p306 H3.
Dusty, crowded and dimly lit, this store is everything a good *antikvariát* should be. Stuffed with old
books, prints, engravings and coffee-table picture
books dating back to the 1950s. Second-hand novels in English for as little as 30 Kč.

Computers

Apple Macintosh was slow to enter the Czech
market and the choice of computers on offer
today is still limited. You'll be able to find PC

Shelf service at **The Globe Bookstore and
Coffeehouse**. *See p165.*

outlets on just about every street corner, and the
list of suppliers in the *Zlaté stránky* (*Yellow Pages*)
goes one forever. Pray that your computer
doesn't malfunction in Prague. In case it does, we
list a few places where you can get it fixed.
Typically, only one of the recommended
computer dealers and repair shops in the city
takes credit cards so do go armed with lots of cash
and even more patience.

Global Ameritech

Rytířská 10, Staré Město, Prague 1 (2421 1544/
www.gatc.com). Tram 4, 7, 9. **Open** 9am-4pm Mon-
Fri; closed Sat, Sun. **No credit cards. Map** p306 J4.
With helpful and English-speaking staff, this is an
authorised repair centre for both IBM and Compaq
computers. It's also the only repair centre in the
Czech Republic that can cope with handheld
Intermec computers. Repairs usually take less
than a week.
Branch: Pod Kavalírkou 18, Košíře, Prague 5
(5721 1450).

MacSource/CompuSource

Bělehradská 68, Vinohrady, Prague 2 (2251 5455/
www.compusource.cz). Metro I P Pavlova/6, 11 tram.
Open 9am-5pm Mon-Fri; closed Sat, Sun. **Credit**
AmEx, MC, V. **Map** p311 B2.
Probably the largest and best Macintosh outlet. But
even here, simple repairs can take half a day and
shipment of replacement components can sometimes take up to one month. The service is reasonable, but few of the consultants speak English. For
an extra fee, MacSource consultants will come to
your office or home.

Signet

Hanusova 9, Michle, Prague 4 (6121 8690). Metro
Pankrác. **Open** 8.30am-5pm Mon-Fri; closed Sat, Sun.
No credit cards.
Repairs Macs and all kinds of PCs in anything from
a few minutes to a few months.

Cosmetics & perfumes

In addition to the places listed below, most of the
department stores above have big-name cosmetic
booths on their ground floors.

Body Basics

Pavilon, Vinohradská 50, Vinohrady, Prague 2 (2423
3125 ext 105). Metro Náměstí Míru/11 tram. **Open**
9.30am-9pm Mon-Sat; noon-8pm Sun. **Credit** AmEx,
MC, V. **Map** p311 A3.
This shameless rip-off of the Body Shop has afford-
able, pleasant-smelling cosmetics that are guaran-
teed to be not tested on animals.
Branches: Pavilon, Vinohradská 50, Vinohrady,
Prague 2 (2423 3125 ext 105). Bílá labuť, Na Poříčí 23,
Nové Město, Prague 1 (0602 548 968 mobile); Koruna
Palace, Václavské náměstí 1, Nové Město, Prague 1
(2447 3072); Myslbek Center, Na příkopě 19/21, Staré
Město, Prague 1 (2423 6800); Ruzyně Airport, Ruzyně,
Prague 6 (2011 3595).

Botanicus

Týn 3, Staré Město, Prague 1 (2489 5445). Metro Náměstí Republiky/5, 14, 26 tram. **Open** 10am-8pm daily. **Credit** AmEx, MC, V. **Map** p306 J3.

An all-Czech hippy version of the Body Shop. Tons of soaps, shampoos, body lotions and creams infused with herbs and other natural ingredients, all lovingly wrapped in brown paper.

Branches: Bílá labuť, Na poříčí 23, Nové Město, Prague 1 (2170 5111); Lucerna, Štěpánská 61, Nové Město, Prague 1 (2422 1927); Michalská 2, Staré Město, Prague 1 (2421 2977); Mostecká 4, Malá Strana, Prague 1 (5731 5089); Havelská 20, Staré Město, Prague 1 (2422 9322).

Department stores

Kotva

Náměstí Republiky 8, Staré Město, Prague 1 (2480 1111). Metro Náměstí Republiky/5, 14, 26 tram. **Open** *Department store* 9am-8pm Mon-Fri; 9am-6pm Sat; 10am-6pm Sun. *Supermarket* 8am-8pm Mon-Fri; 10am-6pm Sat; 10am-8pm Sun. **Credit** AmEx, MC, V. **Map** p307 K3.

Ugly but well stocked. Work your way up past glossy cosmetics stalls, stationery, bed linen, fashion, sports gear, car accessories and end up with the fairly naff furniture and lighting. Shoe repairs in the basement, next to a glossy, split-level supermarket. Good for gourmet chocolates and French wines. Kids love the ramp escalator that takes the shopping carts from level to level.

Krone/Julius Meinl

Václavské náměstí 21, Nové Město, Prague 1 (2423 0477). Metro Můstek/3, 9, 14, 24 tram. **Open** 9am-8pm Mon-Fri; 9am-7pm Sat; 10am-6pm Sun. *Supermarket* 8am-9pm Mon-Fri; 9am-8pm Sat; 10am-8pm Sun. **Credit** MC, V. **Map** p307 K5.

The best thing here is the basement grocery, from which you can stagger directly into the metro with your carrier bags.

Tesco

Národní třída 26, Nové Město, Prague 1 (2422 7971-9). Metro Můstek or Národní třída/6, 9, 18, 22 tram. **Open** *Department store* 8am-8pm Mon-Fri; 9am-6pm Sat; 10am-6pm Sun. *Supermarket* 7am-8pm Mon-Fri; 8am-7pm Sat; 9am-7pm Sun. **Credit** AmEx, MC, V. **Map** p306 H5.

This is what became of Máj, the pride of communist Czechoslovakia's retail industry. Soon after the revolution it was sold to American chain K-mart, which revamped the shop and sold it to Tesco in 1996. Now has a nice mix of Czech and Western products, a popular supermarket with a good bakery, plus aisles of American peanut butter, tinned salsa and British biscuits.

Dry cleaners & launderettes

All launderettes in Prague charge roughly the same for washing and drying, so your choice chiefly depends on location.

Dája

V celnici, Nové Město, Prague 1 (2421 2787). Metro Náměstí Republiky/5, 14, 26 tram. **Open** 7am-7pm Mon-Fri; 8am-1pm Sat; closed Sun. **No credit cards.** **Map** p307 L3.

Alterations and dry cleaning.

Golden Clean

Dlouhá 27, Staré Město, Prague 1 (no phone). Metro Náměstí Republiky/5, 14, 26 tram. **Open** 8am-8pm daily. **No credit cards.** **Map** p306 J2.

British-owned chain claims to use the most modern technology to dry clean everything from furs and leathers to upholstery. More than 30 branches scattered throughout the city.

Prague Laundromat

Korunní 14, Vinohrady, Prague 2 (2251 0180). Metro Náměstí Míru/16 tram. **Open** 8am-8pm daily. **No credit cards.** **Map** p311 A3.

Self- and service washes and dry cleaning.

Fashion

Budget

Black Market

Petrské náměstí 1, Nové Město, Prague 1 (231 7033). Metro Náměstí Republiky/3, 5, 14, 24, 26 tram. **Open** noon-7pm Mon-Fri; 10am-5pm Sat; closed Sun. **No credit cards.** **Map** p307 L2.

Itsy-bitsy cotton tops and lycra dresses, catering to skinny-girl club queens – judging from the vast new basement space, there are armies of them out there. The prices are higher than at a lot of places in town, if normal for shops that stock silver lamé hot pants. Usually a bargain rack of cords, jeans and woollies at the back of the shop.

Catwalk

Husova 8, Staré Město, Prague 1 (no phone). Metro Národní třída/6, 9, 18, 21, 22, 23 tram. **Open** 11am-7pm Mon-Fri; noon-6pm Sat, Sun. **No credit cards.** **Map** p306 H4.

One of the city's original trendy second-hand shops, whose buyers obviously discriminate with taste. Leather trenches and stretchy hippie tops go with the club gear, most of which is new. Don't expect second-hand prices on any of it.

Mýrnyx Týrnyx

Saská ulička, Malá Strana, Prague 1 (297 938). Metro Malostranská/12, 22, 23 tram. **Open** 11am-7pm Mon-Wed; noon-7pm Thur-Sun. **No credit cards.** **Map** p305 E3.

Prague's hippest second-hand fashion shop doesn't waste any of its closet-sized space on boring togs. Day-glo 1960s vinyl hangs alongside feather boas and Homburg hats. Owner Mia Květná buys pieces from indie Czech designers. She also runs an 'alternative models agency' out of the shop, that does casting for commercials shooting in Prague. Prices reflect the creativity but you can always haggle – or swap something of your own.

Modes Robes

Benediktská 5, Staré Město, Prague 1 (2482 6016).
Metro Náměstí Republiky/5,14,26 tram. **Open** 10am-
7pm Mon-Fri; 10am-4pm Sat; closed Sun. **No credit
cards. Map** p307 K2.

A collective of seven local designers with classy,
not-too-outrageous-to-wear skirts, blouses and
suits, mostly for women. This is everything a
fringe fashion should be, with industrial
cable twisted into postmodern clothes racks and
walls pressed into service as canvasses for the
artists who run the place.

Original Móda

*Jilská 18 (entrance also at Michalská 19) Staré Město,
Prague 1 (2421 4626). Metro Můstek.* **Open** 10am-
6pm Mon-Sat; closed Sun. **Credit** AmEx, MC, V.
Map p306 H4.

Hand-made garments, ceramics and gifts by a collective of a dozen Czech artists and designers. For
genuine and stylish Prague crafts, you'll not find
better than the painted silk dresses, hand-stained
soufflé dishes and button-eyed children's toys.

Senior Bazar

*Senovážné náměstí 18, Nové Město, Prague 1 (2423
5068). Metro Náměstí Republiky/3, 5, 9, 14, 24, 26
tram.* **Open** 9am-5pm Mon-Fri; closed Sat, Sun. **No
credit cards. Map** p307 L4.

A Prague institution and one of the best second-
hand clothes shops in the city. Senior Bazar gets its
stock straight from Prague's most stylish citizens –
the octogenarians. Pick up a handmade 1950s summer dress or leather coat for peanuts. But get there
early, as the *Elle* and *Cosmo* girls who work nearby
do a clean sweep on their lunch breaks.
Branch: Karoliny Světlé 18, Staré Město, Prague 1
(2222 1067).

Šatna

*Jilská 18, Staré Město, Prague 1 (no phone). Metro
Národní třída/6, 9, 18, 21, 22, 23 tram.* **Open** 11am-7pm
Mon-Sat; closed Sun. **No credit cards. Map** p306 H4.

A friendly neighbourhood second-hand shop, run
by a North American proprietor with taste – this
joint actually wouldn't feel out of place in Chicago
or Berkeley and the great location in an Old Town
courtyard makes it ideal for that impulse-buy
accessory to reward yourself after a hard morning
of culture cruising at the galleries and museums
all around. Both men's and women's gear are
stocked and all at very reasonable prices, plus
there's a good selection of handbags at the back.
The leather jackets are more limited, as would be
expected in such a small shop space.

Children

Match Kids Wear

*Jungmannova 17, Nové Město, Prague 1 (no phone).
Metro Můstek/3, 9, 14, 24 tram.* **Open** 9am-6pm Mon-
Fri; 9am-noon Sat; closed Sun. **Credit** DC, MC, V.
Map p306 J5.

For the kid who won't be seen without his skate-
board logos and designer labels. Obligatory fashions moderately priced.

Pinito

*Na Příkopě 15, Nové Město, Prague 1 (7214 2320).
Metro Národní třída/6, 9, 18, 22 tram.* **Open** 9.30am-
8pm Mon-Sat; 10am-6pm Sun. **No credit cards. Map**
p308 H6.

All-grown-up kiddywear from Spain – suits and
dicky bows abound.

Designer

Adelaide

*Kaprova 8, Staré Město, Prague 1 (232 0972). Metro
Staroměstská/17, 18 tram.* **Open** 10am-7pm Mon-
Sat; closed Sun. **Credit** AmEx, MC, V. **Map** p306 H3.

Hand-painted clothes in rainbow hues. Everything
here is a mite hippy, bordering on twee, but is at
least unusual. The prices are more than fair, and dig
that pink, suede mini-skirt with the hand-painted
pussycat on the front.

CLU

*Konviktská 30, Staré Město, Prague 1 (2423 2521).
Metro Národní třída/6, 9, 18, 21, 22, 23 tram.* **Open**
10.30am-8pm Mon-Sat; noon-6pm Sun. **Credit** MC,V.
Map p306 G5/H5.

This new and oh-so-trendy Czech fashion shop
could almost be mistaken for a gallery – with art
gallery prices. Worth considering if you're determined to have all eyes on you when you make your
cocktail party entrance. The management make a
point of selling their simple, stylish pieces, ranging
from posh to casual, as 'New York fashions'. Might
be cheaper to get a ticket to New York.

Nostalgie

*Jakubská 8, Staré Město, Prague 1 (232 8030). Metro
Náměstí Republiky/5, 14, 26 tram.* **Open** 10.30am-
6.30pm Mon-Sat; closed Sun. **Credit** AmEx, MC, V.
Map p307 K4.

Flowing linen clothes in neutral shades designed by
Marie Fleischmannová. Classy and conservative in
the good sense, with truly lovely long winter coats.
Alterations for a nominal fee.
Branch: Husova 8, Staré Město, Prague 1 (2423 9622).

Jewellery & accessories

Galerie Módy Heleny Fejkové

*Lucerna passage, Štěpánská 61, Nové Město, Prague 1
(2421 1514). Metro Můstek/3, 9, 14, 24 tram.* **Open**
10am-7pm Mon-Fri; 10am-3pm Sat; closed Sun. **Credit**
AmEx, MC, V. **Map** p309 K6.

Look past the racks of so-so Czech clothes and you'll
find a great designer jewellery section at the back.
Getting up to the shop is tricky, though. Once you're

Mýrnyx Týrnyx – clothes to pose and
'alternative models'. *See p169.*

Lead-free luxury

Glassmaking is both an art and a craft in the Czech lands, studied at Prague's Academy of Decorative Arts and practised in age-old factories around the country. Glass blowing originated in monastery workshops in the 13th century. Czech glass, renowned for its clarity and toughness, eclipsed Venetian glass during the Renaissance and can still be seen in windows of royal palaces throughout Europe. Czech crystal, unlike its French or Waterford counterparts, contains no lead – something to consider if you want to keep brandy in a crystal decanter for 50 years.

Sadly, the glory days of Czech glass-making are over. There's still plenty of fine quartz in the earth of Bohemia, but the vast beech forests that supplied the potash for the mix and heat for the kilns are becoming depleted. More importantly, the master craftsmen were marginalised under the communists. Factories have been streamlined, privatised and modernised, but the level of work will never again be quite what it once was.

That said, a richer variety of glass and crystal wares would be difficult to find. Prague's main tourist routes are lined with glass shops, but the masterworks of Moser are sold only at the licensed Moser shop. For a potted history of Czech glassmaking and a list of shops,

museums, producers and artists, check out *A Guide to Czech and Slovak Glass* by Diane E. Foulds from Moser or a large bookshop. See also page 203 **On the Cutting Edge**.

Erpet

Staroměstské náměstí 27, Staré Město, Prague 1 (2422 9755/2421 5257/ www.erpet.cz). Metro Staroměstská. **Open** 10am-8pm daily. **Credit** AmEx, DC, MC, V. **Map** p306 J3
Not a whole lot of bargains here but an extremely wide and varied selection.

Moser

Na příkopě 12, Staré Město, Prague 1 (2421 1293-4/www.moser-glass.com). Metro Můstek/3, 9, 14, 24 tram. **Open** 9am-8pm Mon-Fri; 10am-6pm Sat. **Credit** AmEx, DC, MC, V. **Map** p307 K4.
Moser glass, made in Karlovy Vary since 1857, claims to be the 'King of Glass' and the 'Glass of Kings'. The lead-free formula produces a crystal of great brilliance and durability. As the only Czech crystal truly worth seeking out, it is very expensive. You could content yourself with a tiny ashtray for over 500 Kč.
Branch: Malé náměstí 11, Staré Město, Prague 1 (2161 1520/2161 1522).

in Lucerna Passage, look up, spot the shop, and then head up the cinema staircase. Turn right on the landing, and you're there. There's also a nice, quiet coffee shop from which you can gaze down upon the shoppers in the arcade below.

Lingerie

Chez Parisienne
Pařížská 8, Staré Město, Prague 1 (2481 7786). Metro Staroměstská/17, 18 tram. **Open** 10am-7pm Mon-Fri; 10am-6pm Sat; closed Sun. **Credit** AmEx, MC, V. **Map** p306 H3.
High-quality boxers, lingerie, T-shirts and pyjamas at sky-high prices. Oh, and vintage Triumph motorcycles. Honest!

Fleur de Nuit
Vojtěšská 1, Nové Město, Prague 1 (297 463). Metro Karlovo náměstí/3, 4, 6, 14, 16, 18, 22, 24, 34 tram. **Open** 10am-6pm Mon-Fri; 10am-2pm Sat; closed Sun. **Credit** MC, V. **Map** p308 G7.
No, it's not a Baudelaire poem. Rather it's your Prague source for super-sleek, sexy designer lingerie from Italy and France, but definitely not a place for the bargain hunter.

Judita
Jakubská 8, Staré Město, Prague 1 (9000 4847). Metro Náměstí Republiky/5, 14, 26 tram. **Open** 10am-6.30pm Mon-Fri; 10am-4pm Sat; closed Sun. **Credit** AmEx, MC, V. **Map** p307 K3.
All the major brands of bras, undies and tights. The nice, motherly ladies with tape measures are glad to help out, but they don't speak English. Only one changing room.

Marks & Spencer
Myslbek Center, Na příkopě 19/21, Staré Město, Prague 1 (2423 5735). Metro Můstek/3, 9, 14, 24 tram. **Open** 9am-8pm Mon-Fri; 9.30am-7pm Sat; 10.30am-6.30pm Sun. **Credit** DC, MC, V. **Map** p307 K4.
Can M&S become everyone's essential stop for underthings, just like in Britain? Probably.

Skiny
V Jámě 2, Nové Město, Prague 1 (0603 461 590 mobile). Metro Můstek/3, 9, 14, 24 tram. **Open** 10am-7pm Mon-Fri; 10am-3pm Sat; closed Sun. **No credit cards.** **Map** p309 K6.
A gloriously non-PC shop for sporty cotton lingerie and bodywear for women and men. Great quality and range of surprisingly practical layers.

Mid-range

Simplicity
Lazarská 5, Nové Město, Prague 1 (2494 7008) Metro Národní třída/6, 9, 18, 21, 22, 23 tram. **Open** 10am-7pm Mon-Fri; 10am-5pm Sat; closed Sun. **Credit** AmEx, MC, V. **Map** p308 H6/J6.

Anything but. Through an affiliation with the Czech edition of *Cosmo* and the other big time fashion glossies, Simplicity attracts every supermodel wannabe in town. It's as amusing to watch them squeezing their boyfriends dry in here as it is to try anything on yourself, if not more so. In a sleek (naturally) and minimalist space, all the picture windows an exhibitionist could want and prices as high as the ceilings. Good quality, though.

White Dog
Myslíkova 28, Nové Město, Prague 2 (295 707). Metro Karlovo náměstí/17 tram. **Open** 10am-7pm Mon-Fri; 10am-3pm Sat; closed Sun. **Credit** MC, V. **Map** p308 H7.

The place to find every young Czech with a board and some money to spend. Ball caps, baggies and Airwalks abound and the staff know about every upcoming skate championship in the republic. Don't be troubled by the resident pit bull – he's all snooze and no bite.

Shoes

ART
Štěpánská 33, Nové Město, Prague 1 (2421 5959). Metro Muzeum/3, 9, 14, 24 tram. **Open** 9.30am-7pm Mon-Fri; 9am-4pm Sat; closed Sun. **Credit** AmEx, MC, V. **Map** p309 K6.

Doc Martens and other big, clunky shoes.

Baťa
Václavské náměstí 6, Nové Město, Prague 1 (2421 8133). Metro Můstek/3, 9, 14, 24 tram. **Open** 9am-8pm Mon-Fri; 10am-6pm Sat, Sun. **Credit** AmEx, DC, MC, V. **Map** p306 J5.

The Baťa family, whose shoe-making operation was one of the world's first multinationals, saw trouble coming in 1938, fled the country and re-established their headquarters in Canada. The rump of the parent company was nationalised ten years later. Now back in the driving seat, the Baťa family has refurbished their original 1928 modernist store on Wenceslas Square, and stocks some of the best-quality bargain footwear in Prague.
Branches: Jindřišská 20, Nové Město, Prague 1 (2423 0254); Moskevská 27, Vršovice, Prague 10 (7717 21860).

Humanic
Národní třída 34, Nové Město, Prague 1 (2494 8811). Metro Můstek or Národní třída/6, 9, 18, 22 tram. **Open** 9am-8pm Mon-Fri; 9am-5pm Sat; 10am-6pm Sun. **Credit** MC, V. **Map** p306 H5.

Cheap and cheerful fashion shoes. Popular among trendy teenagers on a tight budget.

Vagabond
Pasáž Myslbek, Na příkopě 19. Staré Město, Prague 1 (2423 2234). Metro Můstek/3, 9, 14, 24 tram. **Open** 10am-7pm Mon-Sat; 11am-6pm Sun. **Credit** AmEx, MC, V. **Map** p307 K4.

One of the city's best options for cool shoes and summer sandals that won't break the bank. All the M&Ms colours represented.

Shoe repairs

There are shoe repair shops in **Baťa** (*see above*), and **Tesco** and **Kotva** supermarkets (*see page 169*); or you can try either of the places listed below. Failing that, look in *Zlaté stránky* (*Yellow Pages*) under *obuv-opravy*.

Austria Miniservis
Spálená 37, Nové Město, Prague 1 (2491 0822). Metro Národní třída/6, 9, 18, 22 tram. **Open** 9am-5pm Mon-Fri; closed Sat, Sun. **No credit cards. Map** p308 H6.

Jan Ondrášek
Navrátilova 12, Nové Město, Prague 1 (2223 1960). Metro Národní třída/3, 9, 14, 24 tram. **Open** 8am-6pm Mon-Fri; closed Sat, Sun. **No credit cards. Map** p308 J7.

Costume & formal dress hire

Every school and workplace holds its own *ples*, or ball, sometime between November and April – there are even annual balls for hunters, miners and Moravians. If you are invited to a ball, but have left your tux, evening gown or Napoleon outfit at home, try the places below. Make arrangements several days in advance, and take your passport as proof of identity.

Barrandov Studio, Fundus
Kříženeckého náměstí 322, Barrandov, Prague 5 (6707 2210). Metro Smíchovské nádraží, then 246, 247, 248 bus. **Open** 7am-3pm Mon-Fri; closed Sat, Sun. **No credit cards.**

Prague's main film studio rents everything from bear costumes to military uniforms from its extensive wardrobe of over 240,000 costumes and accessories, including 9,000 wigs. None of this comes cheap. Deposits start at around 4,000-8,000 Kč for an antique ballgown, including an 800 Kč fee for a one- to seven-day hire. No English spoken.

Ladana
Opatovická 20, Nové Město, Prague 1 (291 890). Metro Národní třída/6, 9, 18, 22 tram. **Open** *Sept-June* 9am-6pm Mon, Wed, Thur; noon-4.30pm Tue, Fri; closed Sat, Sun. *July-Aug* 9am-6pm Wed, Thur; closed Mon, Tue, Fri-Sun. **No credit cards. Map** p308 H6.

Small costume shop with some amusing dresses, period costumes and masks as well as wedding and bridesmaid dresses, Czech national costumes and dinner jackets. Very cheap, very friendly. Pay just 500 Kč for a Wizard costume for a one- to three-day hire, or 120-350 Kč for some less elaborate disguise. No deposit, although the staff may want to take your passport number.

Florists

There's no shortage of flower shops in Prague, but most are more or less the same. Your local corner *květinářství* is likely to be as good as the centrally located places listed below. When sending flowers out of the country, plan ahead as most florists require four or five days' notice.

Ateliér Kavka

Eliušky Krásnohorské 3, Staré Město, Prague 1 (232 0847). Metro Staroměstská/17, 18 tram. **Open** 9am-5.30pm daily. **No credit cards. Map** p306 H2.
Graceful and modern flower arrangements. Good dried flowers are also available, from as little as 150 Kč for a small bunch to 3,500 Kč for an urn-full.

Bohemia Flowers

Opletalova 22, Nové Město, Prague 1 (2272 0483/ www.flowers.cz). Metro Muzeum/3, 9, 14, 24 tram. **Open** 9am-7pm Mon-Fri; 9am-4pm Sat; closed Sun. **Credit** AmEx, MC, V. **Map** K6/L6.
A tiny, old-fashioned shop that can hand-deliver everything from name-day sprigs to wedding bouquets, delivered across Prague or anywhere else via Interflora. Little English spoken in the shop but telephone orders are answered by helpful multi-linguals.

Květinářství U červeného lva

Saská ulička, Malá Strana, Prague 1 (0604 855 286 mobile) Metro Malostranská/12, 22, 23 tram. **Open** 11am-7pm daily. **No credit cards. Map** p305 E3
The Red Lion is a photogenic little spot on a back street around the corner from the Charles Bridge. Sells fresh-cut flowers, charming ceramic pots and tasteful arrangements.

Food & drink

Food shopping in Prague has improved beyond all recognition in recent years. Western-style supermarkets are still a rarity outside the city centre, but most everyday shopping can be done in the local *potraviny* (grocery store) and *ovoce-zelenina* (greengrocer). Supermarket shoppers are expected to have a trolley at all times: those failing to observe this rule will be told off. If you want a plastic bag you will have to pay at least 2 Kč for it, so ask for a *tašku* before the cashier totals your bill.

Specialist

Bakeshop Praha

V Kolkovně 2, Staré Město, Prague 1 (2316 823) Metro Staroměstská/17, 18 tram. **Open** 7am-7pm daily. **No credit cards. Map** p306 J2.
Leading a revolution on the Prague baking scene is Anne Feeley's little shop of delightful quiches,

brioches, walnut-raisin bread and peanut butter cookies. Workers from all over Old Town duck in here at lunchtime. Most take away but there's always a pot of coffee warming and there's just enough counter space to nosh on site.

Čaj lepších časů

Národní třída 20, Nové Město, Prague 1 (2491 2230). Metro Národní třída/6, 9, 18, 22 tram. **Open** 8.30am-7pm Mon-Fri; 10am-4pm Sat; closed Sun. **No credit cards. Map** p306 H5.
Join in the Prague tea craze. Fresh uncut teas from Sri Lanka plus the shop's own brand of teabags.

Čínská restaurace Hong Kong

Letenské náměstí 5, Holešovice, Prague 7 (3337 6209). Metro Vltavská/1, 25, 26 tram. **Open** 11am-3pm Mon-Fri; 6pm-11pm Sat; closed Sun. **Credit** AmEx, MC, V.
Adjoining this favourite, if out-of-the-way, neighbourhood Chinese restaurant is a shop well stocked with glass noodles, chilli oils, ginger, soy sauces and a nice range of green and black teas.

Country Life

Melantrichova 15, Staré Město, Prague 1 (2421 3366). Metro Můstek. **Open** *Apr-Oct* 8am-7pm Mon-Thur; 8am-6pm Fri; 11am-6pm Sun; closed Sat. *Nov-March* 8am-7pm Mon-Thur; 8am-3pm Fri; 11am-6pm Sun; closed Sat. **No credit cards. Map** p306 H4.
A fully stocked health-food shop with cold-pressed oils, amaranth baked goods, corn meal and tofu. The buffet restaurant (*see p146*) has been serving soy burgers for years. Carrot soups are a cheap treat, and the DIY salads can't be beat. The owners have also opened an excellent soap and essence shop across the courtyard.
Branch: Jungmannova 1, Nové Město, Prague 1 (5704 4419)

De Gusto

Haštalská 10, Staré Město, Prague 1 (no phone). Metro Náměstí Republiky/5, 8, 14 tram. **Open** 8.30am-7.30pm Mon-Fri; 8.30am-2pm Sat; closed Sun. **No credit cards. Map** p306 J2.
This small but thoughtfully stocked Italian deli is the only place in Old Town for squid-ink fetuccini, mortadella, cheeses, baked sweets, Tuscan wines and marinated olives. The clerks treat you like lost family – but aren't out to get your inheritance.

Dobrá čajovna

Václavské náměstí 14, Nové Město, Prague 1 (2423 1480). Metro Můstek/3, 9, 14, 24 tram. **Open** 10am-9.30pm Mon-Sat; 3pm-9.30pm Sun. **No credit cards. Map** p306 J5.
More of a shrine than a tea shop, this place sells a daunting array of oriental teas that can be sampled in the dark, womb-like café. Also stocks everything you might need for a tea ceremony: tiny ceramic teapots and cups, joss sticks and Japanese tea strainers (*see p152*).

Fruits de France

Jindřišská 9, Nové Město, Prague 1 (2422 0304). Metro Můstek/3, 9, 14, 24 tram. **Open** 9.30am-6.30pm

Jarmark lahůdky – a cracking little Italian deli, just off Wenceslas Square.

Mon-Fri; 9.30am-1pm Sat; closed Sun. **No credit cards. Map** p307 K5.
Opened by an astute Frenchwoman in 1991 when Prague was still a gastronomic desert, today this remains a mouthwatering oasis of fruit, vegetables, olives, cheese, chocolate, oil and wine. Deliveries from France arrive weekly, but storage is good and everything remains in excellent condition. Such luxury does not come cheap, however: a block of mozzarella could set you back as much as 300 Kč. Two stand-up-and-eat tables at the rear of the shop allow for the service of quick deli snacks with wine. Fruits de France have also recently expanded into a more international range of equally high-quality stock at a second location in the New Town.
Branch: Bělehradská 94, Vinohrady, Prague 2 (9000 0339).

Jarmark lahůdky
Vodičkova 30, Nové Město, Prague 1 (2416 2619). Metro Můstek/3, 9, 14, 24 tram. **Open** 8am-8pm Mon-Fri; 9am-3pm Sat; closed Sun. **No credit cards. Map** p307 K5.
A cracking little Italian deli off Wenceslas Square with amaretto cakes, great jugs of cheapish Chianti, and hard-to-find peanut oil.

La Bretagne
Široká 22, Staré Město, Prague 1 (no phone). Metro Staroměstská/17, 18 tram. **Open** 10am-8pm Mon-Sat; closed Sun. **No credit cards. Map** p306 H2/3.
An impressive selection of fresh fish from squid to shark is always on ice at this friendly, family-run

fishmonger's. Pick up your French Chablis at the same time for a classy night in.

Le Delice Belges
Pavilon, Vinohradská 50, Vinohrady, Prague 2 (786 8063). Metro Náměstí Míru/11 tram. **Open** 9.30am-9pm Mon-Sat; noon-6pm Sun. **No credit cards. Map** p311 A3.
Handmade chocolates shipped in each week from Belgium. The Becherovka chocolates, made specially for the Czech market, have proved a big hit. Gift boxes and delivery possible.

Ocean
Zborovská 49, Smíchov, Prague 5 (9000 1517). Tram 6, 9, 12, 22. **Open** 10am-8pm Mon-Sat; closed Sun. **Credit** DC, MC, V.
Every Wednesday and Saturday a shipment of more than 35 types of fresh fish and seafood arrives from Belgium, France and Spain. Escargot, salmon at 49 Kč per 100g (3½ oz) and lobsters at 1,500 Kč each are snapped up weekly.

Potraviny U Cedru
Československé armády 18, Dejvice, Prague 6 (312 2119). Metro Dejvická. **Open** 7am-11pm daily. **No credit cards.**
Any grocery keeping these hours is a godsend in Prague, but one that stocks basmati rice, houmous, vine leaves and an assortment of other Lebanese delights? Definitely worth the trek to Dejvice. If you don't fancy cooking, go to their restaurant, U Cedru, one of the better quality Middle Eastern eateries in town (*see p142*).

Prodejna U Salvatora

Náprstkova 2, Staré Město, Prague 1 (2222 1161). Metro Národní třída/17, 18 tram. **Open** 10am-6pm Mon-Fri; closed Sat, Sun. **No credit cards. Map** p306 G4.

This sweet little store in the Old Town has more than 120 kinds of spices in paper packets or little glass jars. Ask the assistant for the English-language catalogue of wares.

Teuscher

Malá Štupartská 5, Staré Město, Prague 1 (2482 8050). Metro Náměstí Republiky/5, 8, 14 tram. **Open** 10am-8pm Mon-Thur; 9am-7pm Fri; 9am-6pm Sat; 10am-6pm Sun. **Credit** MC, V. **Map** p306 J3.

A handier source for a quality gift would be hard to find. Extraordinary Swiss chocolates from truffles and pralines to beautiful handmade creations.

Vzpomínky na Afriku

Rybná and Jakubská, Staré Město, Prague 1 (0603 544 492 mobile). Metro Náměstí Republiky/5, 14, 26 tram. **Open** 10am-7pm daily. **Credit** DC, MC, V. **Map** p307 K3.

The smell of dark, roasted African coffee beans hits you as soon as you step through the doors. If you can't make up your mind between the 30 or so beans on offer, you can always sit at the table and try a cup. Beans ground to any grade you request.

Supermarkets

In addition to the places below, there are centrally located supermarkets in the **Kotva** and **Tesco** department stores (*see page 169*).

Delvita

Sokolovská 14, Karlín, Prague 8 (232 7015). Metro Florenc/8, 24 tram. **Open** 7am-8pm Mon-Fri; 7am-7pm Sat; 9am-7pm Sun. **No credit cards.**

This well-stocked Belgian chain has good vegetables, meat and wine, but poor bread and very little seafood. There are ten branches: check *Zlaté stránky* (*Yellow Pages*) for your nearest.

Julius Meinl

Pavilon, Vinohradská 50, Vinohrady, Prague 2 (2423 3125). Metro Můstek/6, 9, 18, 22 tram. **Open** 8am-9pm Mon-Sat; noon-8pm Sun. **Credit** AmEx, MC, V. **Map** p304 J4.

This formerly state-owned supermarket has done an excellent job of transforming itself into a shiny Western-style grocery store. The prices tend to be a little higher than in a corner *potraviny*, but it's open late and is central.

Food delivery

Délicatesse

Kostelní 16, Holešovice, Prague 7 (2057 1775/0601 295 128/www.delicatesse.cz). Metro Vltavská/1, 3, 14, 25 tram. **Open** 9am-4pm Mon-Fri; closed Sat, Sun. **No credit cards. Map** p310 C3/D3.

A French bakery with an assortment of fresh-baked hot and cold sandwiches, quiches and salads available for delivery. Service extends only to some areas of central Prague, Holešovice, Dejvice and Žižkov. Minimum order 200 Kč with a 35 Kč charge for orders of less than 800 Kč.

Pizza Go Home

Sokolská 31, Nové Město, Prague 2 (8387 0000). Metro I P Pavlova/4, 6, 11, 16, 22, 23, 34 tram. **Open** 24 hours daily. **No credit cards. Map** p309 K7/8.

This won't win any international taste tests, but will quell the worst fit of 3am hunger pangs. With six outlets citywide, they're never far off. Delivery costs 50-150 Kč depending on district. A 32-cm (13-in) pizza is 100-180Kč, depending on toppings. **Branches:** Argentinská 1, Holešovice, Prague 7 (8387 0000); Ve Lhotce 814, Krč, Prague 4 (8387 0000); Mukařovského 1985, Stodůlky, Prague 5 (8387 0000); Trousilova 4, Kobylisy, Prague 8 (8387 0000).

Wine

Blatnička

Michalská 6, Staré Město, Prague 1 (2423 3612). Metro Národní třída/6, 9, 18, 22 tram. **Open** 10am-6pm Mon-Fri; closed Sat, Sun. **No credit cards. Map** p306 H4.

One of dozens of places around town to pick up cheap Moravian plonk or sample any of a dozen on the spot. '*Sudová vína*' signs indicate that the shop will fill your plastic bottle with local wine for next to nothing. The crowd here loves drink, even if they don't know a bouquet from Bo Diddley.

Cellarius

Lucerna Passage, Štěpánská 61, Nové Město, Prague 1 (2421 0979). Metro Můstek/3, 9, 14, 24 tram. **Open** 9.30am-9pm Mon-Sat; 3-8pm Sun. **Credit** AmEx, MC, V. **Map** p309 K6.

One of the first Prague shops to organise and collect Moravian wines and an excellent place to pick up some interesting vintages rarely available in Prague. Some international wines also sold.

Dionýsos

Vinařického 6, Vinohrady, Prague 2 (295 342). Tram 7, 18, 24. **Open** 10am-6pm Mon-Fri; closed Sat, Sun. **Credit** AmEx, MC, V. **Map** p308 H10.

A classy wine merchant patronised by Prague's élite, Dionýsos has a respectable range of foreign wines but specialises in top quality local produce, including older vintages. The staff know and love their wines and will guide you along the shelves.

Vinotéka u Svatého

Štěpánská 7, Nové Město, Prague 2 (2190 1160). Metro Muzeum/3, 9, 14, 24. **Open** 10am-7pm Mon-Fri; closed Sat, Sun. **Credit** MC, V. **Map** p309 K6.

Another new wine venture in New Town demonstrates the evolving Czech appreciation for something other than beer. The affordable international selection includes wines from France, Italy, Spain,

Austria, Hungary and Chile, as well as prime vineyard areas of South Moravia. Champagnes and malt whiskies also in abundance.

Gifts

Most expats have a nervous breakdown looking for gifts around Christmas time, so don't worry if you have difficulty locating that special something. The trick is to avoid the tourist tat, and go for the less obvious choices – it's just a question of knowing where to look. Czech CDs, both pop and classical, are always a good buy at approximately half the price of CDs back home, and most bookshops listed above (*see page 164*) stock beautiful calendars and Czech authors translated into English. For booze lovers, a bottle of Becherovka, that sweet, herby spirit famed as a 'medicine', will prove an eye-opener. Don't get bullied into buying one of those chicken toys flogged around Old Town Square. They're nothing more than half a loo roll on a string, and usually fall apart in the first ten minutes. Try our list of toy shops, instead (*see page 184*).

Association Club Sparta Praha

Na Perštýně 17, Staré Město, Prague 1 (no phone). Metro Národní třída/6, 9, 18, 22 tram. **Open** 10am-5pm Mon-Thur; 10am-4pm Fri; closed Sat, Sun. **No credit cards. Map** p306 H5.
Football paraphernalia, including lighters, beer mugs, beach balls, keychains, T-shirts, and hats

emblazoned with the name or red-star logo of Prague's biggest football team, Sparta Praha. Try to remember that Karel Poborský didn't actually come from this club but from its deadly rival across town, Slavia. The shop assistants here, ardent Sparta fans every last one, do not take kindly to this frequent mistake.

Candles Gallery

Újezd 31, Malá Strana, Prague 1 (0603 140 118 mobile). Metro Malostranská/12, 18, 22, 23 tram. **Open** 10am-7pm daily. **Credit** MC, V. **Map** p305 E5.
The creations of these wax sculptors adorn *le plus chic* restaurants in Prague. If your luggage is large enough, you can take home a lovely four-foot, four-wick, cornflower-blue wax candle or a sphere covered in Grecian architectural ornamentation.

Charita Florentinum

Ječná 2, Nové Město, Prague 2 (2492 0448). Metro Karlovo náměstí/4, 6, 16, 22, 34 tram. **Open** 8.30am-6pm Mon-Thur; 8.30am-5pm Fri, Sat; closed Sun. **No credit cards. Map** p308 J8.
Where Czech priests purchse their robes, incense burners and other gear. Incredibly cheap candles.

Česká lidová řemesla

Jilská 22, Staré Město, Prague 1 (2423 2745). Metro Můstek. **Open** 10am-6.30pm Mon-Thur; 10am-7pm Fri, Sat; 10am-6.30pm Sun. **Credit** AmEx, MC, V. **Map** p306 H4.
A chain selling touristy but attractive folk art, including straw nativities (around 1,000 Kč), a vast range of painted Easter eggs and willow twigs with

Caffeine addiction unmasked at **Vzpomínky na Afriku**. *See p176.*

The iron stamp of bureaucracy

Habsburgs and communists may come and go but bureaucrats will always be with us. Good news for those in the *razítko* business – the Czech word for rubber stamp, or more accurately 'seal', is virtually synonymous with officialdom.

It takes approximately 30 *razítka* of approval from various Prague ministries to convert your attic into an apartment. If you want to register a car you'll need half a dozen. Miss a day at work and you'd better have a stamp from your doctor. Your taxi fare receipt isn't valid without one. Your publican has one ever at the ready, and so does your barber and grocer.

During the Velvet Revolution, the general strike notices posted on Wenceslas Square were covered in the *razítka* of companies who were participating. These days you can request a rubber stamp ('you know, for my company') at any of the bordellos now lining the square and get a fully reimbursable, innocuous-looking receipt from your companion.

In Prague, if it isn't stamped, it doesn't exist. The Habsburgs brought bureaucracy to the Czech lands and today the Austrian firm Trodat dominates the *razítka* industry. The company has sold a million rubber stamps in the Czech Republic and Slovakia since displacing the former state monopoly Znak, and its products are the pride of every paper-pusher's desk.

The dry, lifeless stamps of the bad old days are gone forever, replaced by lively, springy models with coloured casing. Trodat makes dozens of varieties of stamps, the best-selling by far being the ones that imprint your office or business seal. Stationery stores are stocked with a dizzying array, from stately wooden-handled blotter-like stamps suitable for a minister to the utilitarian plastic press-down models on the desk of every bored functionary. If you really want to make an intimidating, Kafka-esque impression, it might be worth investing in a stately iron-handled stamp.

As for what your stamp will say, the possibilities are endless. Better stationery stores, such as the one listed below, will print anything for 350-500 Kč, up to six lines. Just bring in your imprint for scanning. One frustrated Prague expat, fed up with Town Hall clerks, finally got his revenge by getting his own stamps. He is now armed with razitka saying *Bohužel* and *zítra*, which he stamps on every form he's made to fill out. Translation: 'Unfortunately' and 'tomorrow', the two words most often heard from Czech officialdom.

Sedin

Rytířská 7, Staré Město, Prague 1 (2422 2072). Metro Můstek/3, 9, 14, 24 tram. **Open** 8.30am-6pm Mon-Thur; 8.30am-2pm Fri; closed Sat, Sun. **No credit cards. Map** p306 J4.

---

which to whack girls at Easter. The various branches have different specialities – for example, Jilská sells textiles and wooden toys.
Branches: Melantrichova 17, Staré Město, Prague 1 (2163 2411); Mostecká 17, Malá Strana, Prague 1 (5753 3678); Nerudova 23&31, Malá Strana, Prague 1 (5753 0080); Zlatá ulička 16, Hradčany, Prague 1 (2437 2292); Ruzyně Airport, Ruzyně, Prague 6 (2011 5344).

ETS (Electric Train Systems)

Týnská ulička 8, Staré Město, Prague 1 (232 6938). Metro Náměstí Republiky/5, 8, 14 tram. **Open** 10am-5.30pm Mon-Fri; 10am-3pm Sat; closed Sun. **Credit** AmEx, MC, V. **Map** p306 J5.

If your inner child is crying out, you could do a lot worse than a replica of a classic Czech steam train. Exercise some restraint, or you'll soon find yourself taking home entire stations, switching boxes and models of the Šumava mountains.

Kondomerie

Karoliny Světlé 9, Staré Město, Prague 1 (9000 1526/ www.kondomerie.cz). Metro Národní třída/6, 9, 18, 21, 22, 23 tram. **Open** 10am-6pm Mon-Fri; 11am-3pm Sat; closed Sun. **No credit cards. Map** p306 G5.

The gift that gives just once – but says it all. They're all here in flavours, shapes and humming musical tunes, accompanied by various jellies and oils. The friendly clerks cannot be embarrassed.

Včelařské potřeby

Křemencova 8, Nové Město, Prague 2 (293 668). Metro Karlovo náměstí/4, 6, 16, 22, 34 tram. **Open** 9am-5pm Mon-Thur; 9am-3pm Fri; closed Sat, Sun. **No credit cards. Map** p308 H6/7.

The Beekeeper's Store has everything you need to start your own hives business: gloves, headgear and manuals (in Czech). For the more casual bee fancier, there's bee shampoo, wine and dozens of fresh honey varieties.

Hair & beauty

Those after the simplest of cuts should be able to get a decent trim in any *kadeřnictví* (hairdressers) or *holičství* (barbershop) for around 100 Kč. Anyone looking for something more dramatic should enquire at one of the posh hotels, or try the following.

Atelier slunečnice
Vinohradská 53, Vinohrady, Prague 2 (2225 2547/2225 0028). Metro Jiřího z Poděbrad/11 tram. **Open** 7am-8pm Mon-Fri; 9am-3pm Sat; closed Sun. **Credit** MC, V. **Map** p311 B3.
Haircuts for men and women, manicures, pedicures, solarium and massages at this Western-style salon. Some of the staff speak English.

Dream Hair
Týn 2, Staré Město, Prague 1 (2489 5776). Metro Náměstí Republiky/5, 14, 26 tram. **Open** 9am-8pm Mon-Fri; 9am-3pm Sat; closed Sun. **No credit cards.** **Map** p306 J3.
A highly recommended salon, staffed mainly by English-speaking hairdressers. A ladies' cut will set you back around 450 Kč – at least twice the price of a cut by the average Czech hairdresser, but there's less risk involved.

James & Monika
Malá Štupartská 9, Staré Město, Prague 1 (2482 7373). Metro Náměstí Republiky/5, 8, 14 tram. **Open** 8am-8pm Mon-Fri; 8am-6pm Sat; closed Sun. **No credit cards.** **Map** p306 J3.
One of the hottest arrivals on the Prague fashion scene is this duo of truly international stylists and their crew. Dream cuts and makeovers are all in a day's work and the customer raves have spread throughout town. A cut costs between 500-1,000 Kč depending on the experience level of your hairdresser. Most of the staff speak English.

Šarm
Jungmannova 1, Nové Město, Prague 1 (2422 4814). Metro Můstek/6, 9, 18, 22 tram. **Open** 7am-9pm Mon-Fri; closed Sat, Sun. **No credit cards.** **Map** p306 J5.
A little more upscale than your average *kadeřnictví*, Šarm is still incredibly reasonable. More than 17 locations, a few listed below.
Branches: Dlouhá 1, Staré Město, Prague 1 (231 0133); Královdorská 12, Staré Město, Prague 1 (231 0772); Revoluční 25, Staré Město, Prague 1 (2482 6264).

Household

Galerie bydlení
Truhlářská 20, Nové Město, Prague 1 (231 2383). Metro Náměstí Republiky/5, 14, 26 tram. **Open** 9am-6pm Mon-Thur; 9am-5pm Fri; closed Sat, Sun. **Credit** AmEx, MC, V. **Map** p307 L2.
Wacky, surreal, fun furniture design. Well on the way to kitsch, though.

IKEA
Skandinávská 1, Zličín, Prague 5 (5718 6111). Metro Zličín. **Open** 10am-8pm daily. **Credit** MC, V.
When Swedish furniture giant IKEA opened its megastore in 1996, around 100,000 people – 8 % of the population of Prague – visited it in the first four days. IKEA is a byword for style in Prague, and has yet to meet with a serious competitor for quality and value for money. Riding the metro out this way on a Saturday and watching the hordes of excited shoppers on their way home with their IKEA bags is entertainment in itself.

KDS
Národní třída 43, Nové Město, Prague 1 (2421 2469). Metro Můstek or Národní třída/6, 9, 18, 22 tram. **Open** 9am-6pm Mon-Sat; closed Sun. **No credit cards.** **Map** p306 J5.
Stainless steel Czech knives in every size and shape. A modest outlay will provide interesting gifts for foodie friends.

Le Patio
Národní třída 22, Nové Město, Prague 1 (2491 8136). Metro Národní třída. **Open** 10am-7pm Mon-Sat; 11am-7pm Sun. **Credit** AmEx, DC, MC, V. **Map** p309 K6.
The Belgian owner has craftily married local ironworking skills with her own intriguingly romantic designs. Wrought-iron constructions from candleholders to bird cages are set off by the odd bunch of paper flowers or sculptural wooden bowl.
Branches: Pařížská 20, Staré Město, Prague 1; Ungelt 640, Staré Město, Prague 1 (2489 5773).

Obi
Výtvarná 3, Ruzyně, Prague 6 (302 5228). Bus 108, 225. **Open** 8am-8pm Mon-Fri; 8am-6pm Sat; closed Sun. **Credit** MC, V.
The biggest DIY store in the country now has three locations. None are anywhere near the centre.

Maximum Underground – *see p181.*

Eat, Drink, Shop

Branches: Ústřední 326, Štěrboholy, Prague 10 (702 488); Lhotecká 446, Modřany, Prague 4 (4447 2701).

Potten & Pannen

Václavské náměstí 57, Nové Město, Prague 1 (2421 4936). Metro Muzeum/3, 9, 14, 24 tram. **Open** 9.30am-8pm daily. **Credit** AmEx, DC, MC, V. **Map** p309 K6.

The last word in cookware – grinders, choppers, graters and squeezers, shining pots and pans. Also sells Calphalm aluminium saucepans from the US and Emile Henry oven-to-tableware, plus improbable Rosenthal Studio Haus kitchen tools.

Branch: Václavské náměstí 57, Nové Město, Prague 1 (2421 4936); Vodičkova 2, Nové Město, Prague 1 (2223 2525).

Key cutting & locksmiths

The best places to cut keys are the major supermarkets in town – they're more likely to speak English and less likely to rip you off. Try either Bílá labuť Tesco or at the bottom of the escalators at the entrance to the **Kotva** supermarket (*see page 169*). For a 24-hour locksmith, try one of the following.

Bon Express zámečnictví pohotovost

Tupolevova 515, Letňany, Prague 9 (858 6348/0604 266 266). **Open** 24 hrs daily. **No credit cards**.

KEY Non-Stop

Vazovova 3, Kamýk, Prague 12 (401 6616). **Open** *24 hrs daily.* **No credit cards**.

Malls

Prague's first malls employed marketing teams to explain the concept to Czechs and sold cheap potatoes in the basement to bring in the crowds. Czech teens have since grasped that their destiny is to spend Saturdays at the mall, and few young things would consider shoes from anywhere else. The latest downtown ventures, **Černá růže** and **Kenvelo Centre**, have revived a concept unknown in Prague since the 1930s: major sales.

Černá růže

Na příkopě 12, Nové Město, Prague 1 (2101 4111). Metro Můstek/3, 9, 14, 24 tram. **Open** 9am-8pm Mon-Fri; 9am-7pm Sat; 11am-7pm Sun. **Credit** AmEx, MC, V. **Map** p307 K4.

An easily overlooked entrance next to McDonald's leads from a main pedestrian drag into this three-level complex full of fashion boutiques, plus the odd shoe store, designer furniture outlet and wine shop. The Bonjour Bar patio café provides relief.

Dětský dům

Na Příkopě 15, Staré Město, Prague 1 (7214 2401). Metro Můstek/3, 9, 14, 24 tram. **Open** 9am-8pm Mon-Sat; 10am-8pm Sun. **Credit** AmEx, MC, V. **Map** p307 K4.

Once a communist centre for kids' gear, the Children's House has re-opened with a thoroughly capitalist 21st-century makeover. Packed with shops such as Bim Bam Bum, stocking Ralph Lauren for tykes, the mall also features occasional puppet shows and the odd fashion shop for mum.

Kenvelo Centre

Václavské náměstí 11, Nové Město, Prague 1 (2162 9702). Metro Můstek/3, 9, 14, 24 tram. **Open** 9am-9pm daily. **Credit** AmEx, MC, V. **Map** p306 J5.

The Kenvelo chain, having filled Wenceslas Square with cheap leather jackets, jumpers and stretchy separates for women, occupies this modern mall, affixing its label prominently to every item. This mall's makeover employs glass and chrome walkways, a 'food court' and an Argentine cellar steakhouse that serves beef udder.

Branches: Palác Koruna, Václavské náměstí 1, Nové Město, Prague 1 (2421 5904); Erpet, Staroměstské náměstí 25/26, Staré Město, Prague 1 (2163 2226); Shopping Park Praha, Skandinávská 15, Zličín, Prague 5 (651 8470); Centrum Černý Most, Chlumecká 765/6, Černý Most, Prague 9 (8191 8128).

Myslbek Center

Na příkopě 19/21, Nové Město, Prague 1 (2423 9550). Metro Můstek/3, 9, 14, 24 tram. **Open** 8.30am-8.30pm Mon-Sat; 9.30am-8.30pm Sun. **Credit** AmEx, MC, V. **Map** p307 K4.

You could be forgiven for thinking you're back in Britain. Clinique, Marks & Spencer, Next, Tie Rack, Mothercare, Kookai and Vision Express fill the swankiest and certainly most crowded mall in town. For a lesson in insensitive modern architecture, see how the back of the mall fails to relate to the surrounding Ovocný square outside. Some shops open and close at different times.

Markets

If you're looking for one of those fabled flea markets jam-packed with 1950s-era biker jackets and old vinyl, try some under the *bazars* listed under **Antiques**. Prague outdoor markets are mostly fruit 'n' veg affairs. Christmas and Easter markets spring up along the main tourist routes. If you catch one of the Christmas markets in Old Town Square, Václavské náměstí or Náměstí Republiky, warm yourself with a glass of steaming mulled wine – *svařené víno* or *svařák*.

Havelský Market

Havelská, Staré Město, Prague 1 (no phone). Metro Můstek or Národní třída/6, 9, 18, 22 tram. **Open** 7.30am-6pm Mon-Fri; 8.30am-6pm Sat, Sun. **No credit cards**. **Map** p306 J4.

Officially known as Staré Město Market, but universally referred to by its location, this is probably Prague's best market for greens and a taste of daily Bohemian life. Fresh fruit and vegetables are crammed alongside wooden toys, puppets, tourist trinkets and bad art. Good for gifts, and flowers are

Pensioners stretch their crowns at **Havelský Market** – fresh fruit, bad art. *See p180.*

a tremendous bargain. Best in the morning before the trinket hawkers take over three-quarters of the stalls. Havelská has recently become a prime pickpocket hunting ground – watch your purse.

Market at the Fountain

Spálená 30, Nové Město, Prague 1 (no phone). Metro Národní třída/6, 9, 18, 22 tram. **Open** 7.30am-7pm daily. **No credit cards. Map** p306 H5.

Excellent fruit and vegetable market just outside Tesco – usually cheaper, too.

Music

234

Bělehradská 120, Nové Město, Prague 2 (2425 2741). Metro I.P. Pavlova/6, 11 tram. **Open** 9.30am-7.30pm Mon-Fri; 11am-4pm Sat; 1pm-5pm Sun. **Credit** AmEx, DC, MC, V. **Map** p309 L8.

In the same building as the Radost nightclub, this small, CD-only shop specialises in techno, house and hip-hop. Owned by a member of the 1970s Czech band Garáž, it's an excellent place to find old Czech dissident rock. English-speaking staff.

Bazar

Karoliny Světlé 12, Staré Město, Prague 1 (2423 3467). Metro Národní třída/6, 9, 18, 21, 22, 23 tram. **Open** 10am-7pm Mon-Fri; closed Sat, Sun. **No credit cards. Map** p306 G5.

Loads of cheap second-hand CDs with a fair range of jazz and classical, many for only 150 Kč. The place to pick up Czech folk music or Karel Gott records without having to agonise over the price.

Bontonland Megastore

Palác Koruna, Václavské náměstí 1, Nové Město, Prague 1 (2422 6236). Metro Můstek/3, 9, 14, 24 tram. **Open** 9am-8pm Mon-Sat; 10am-7pm Sun. **Credit** AmEx, MC, V. **Map** p306 J4.

The first Western-style music megastore in Eastern Europe when it opened in 1996. Has stereo equipment, videos, CD-Roms, books, vinyl, posters, T-shirts, instore DJ, listening posts and a café – as well as CDs and cassettes of every genre. There's rock and pop aplenty, but stocks of world music and techno are limited. Good jazz section.

Bontonland (Supraphon)

Jungmannova 20, Nové Město, Prague 1 (2494 8718). Metro Národní třída or Můstek/3, 9, 14, 24 tram. **Open** 9am-7pm Mon-Fri; 9am-1pm Sat; closed Sun. **Credit** AmEx, DC, MC, V. **Map** p308 J6.

The former state recording company, now privatised and owned by Bonton, still has its own shop. To see what's in stock, flick through the files on the counter. Knowledgeable staff and an excellent selection of cheap Czech classical recordings.

Maximum Underground

Jilská 22, Staré Město, Prague 1 (628 4009). Metro Můstek, Národní třída or Staroměstská/3, 9, 18, 22 tram. **Open** 11am-7pm Mon-Sat; 1-7pm Sun. **No credit cards. Map** p306 H4.

Within a sort of alternative shopping mall that includes clothing stores, tattooing and piercing parlours, this friendly shop stocks mainly CDs, with some cassettes and vinyl. There's a good selection of techno, ambient and hardcore, and the staff seem to know their stuff.

Music shop-antikvariát

Národní třída 25, Nové Město, Prague 1 (2108 5221). Metro Národní Třída/6, 9, 18, 22 tram. **Open** 10.30am-7pm Mon-Sat; closed Sun. **No credit cards. Map** p306 H5.

A collectors' paradise, with hundreds of used CDs and LPs from the 1920s onwards. The selection includes jazz, blues, country, folk, Czech pop/rock, classical, a pricey stack of rarities and bootlegs, and long-deleted recordings from this country and the former East Germany.

Branch: Mostecká 4, Malá Strana, Prague 1 (no phone).

Music Shop Trio

U Radnice 5, Staré Město, Prague 1 (232 2583). Metro Staroměstská/17, 18 tram. **Open** 10am-7pm Mon-Fri; 10am-6pm Sat; closed Sun. **Credit** AmEx, DC, MC, V. **Map** p306 H3.

This shop, at the address where Kafka was born, specialises in Czech music and also stocks assorted staples from the standard classical repertoire. Due to the touristy location, the prices are slightly high, but service is attentive and knowledgeable.

Pohodlí

Benediktská 7, Staré Město, Prague 1 (2481 6627). Metro Náměstí Republiky/5, 14, 26 tram. **Open** 11am-6pm Mon-Fri; 10am-4pm Sat; closed Sun. **No credit cards.** **Map** p307 K2.

This tiny, family-run ethnic music store carries everything from Zimbabwean marimba music to Nusrat Fateh Ali Khan, plus a fair selection of Moravian folk music and Czech alternative music. The Polish owner is quite happy to let you listen to your chosen CD before purchasing. If you're lucky, you might even be offered a cup a tea.

Musical instruments

Hudební nástroje – Jakub Lis

Náprstkova 10, Staré Město, Prague 1 (2222 1110). Metro Můstek or Staroměstská/17, 18 tram. **Open** 10am-7pm Mon-Fri; 10am-5pm Sat; closed Sun. **No credit cards.** **Map** p306 G4.

Small, cheery shop with a selection of second-hand electric and acoustic guitars, violins, cellos and accordions, plus Indian and African drums and instruments. All this with all the usual musicians' paraphernalia – strings, rosin and reeds.

Praha Music Center

Soukenická 20, Nové Město, Prague 1 (231 3972). Metro Náměstí Republiky/5, 14, 26 tram. **Open** 9am-5pm Mon-Fri; closed Sat, Sun. **Credit** MC, V. **Map** p307 L2.

Caters admirably to plugged-in musicians. Has the standard equipment but is especially good for pick-ups, pedals and second-hand amps.
Branch: Revoluční 14, Staré Město, Prague 1 (231 1693); Klimentská 34, Staré Město, Prague 1 (231 3681).

U zlatého kohouta

Michalská 3, Staré Město, Prague 1 (2421 2874). Metro Můstek/3, 9, 14, 24 tram. **Open** 10am-noon; 1pm-6pm daily. **Credit** AmEx, MC, V. **Map** p306 H4.

Restorers of and dealers in fine old Bohemian string instruments, from violins to double basses, famed for the sound quality produced by resonant pine. How craftsmen of this high calibre survived the shoddy standards everyone else adopted in the decades before 1989 (and still seem to have trouble shaking) is a mystery.

Opticians

Frames and lenses can be incredibly cheap in Prague, making it possible to get a basic pair of glasses for around 1,500 Kč. Be aware, however, that the vast majority of opticians do not use shatterproof glass. The stores listed here are

Jan Pazdera obchod a opravna – Leicas like us, cameras for cognoscenti. *See p183.*

more upmarket than the average optician and stock high-quality lenses.

AM Optik Studio

Jungmannova 19, Nové Město, Prague 1 (2494 8451). Metro Národní třída/3, 9, 14, 24 tram. **Open** 8am-6pm Mon-Fri; closed Sat, Sun. **Credit** AmEx, MC, V. **Map** p308 J6.

A reasonably fashionable choice, though without much help for non Czech-speakers.

Eiffel Optic

Na příkopě 25, Nové Město, Prague 1 (2423 4966). Metro Můstek/3, 9, 14, 24 tram. **Open** 9pm-8pm Mon-Sat; 9.30am-6.30pm Sun. **Credit** AmEx, DC, MC, V. **Map** p307 K4.

This shop has a reputation for reliable, speedy service with a smile, and a small but better-than-average range of frames. A new pair of glasses is available for as little as 2,000 Kč, and there are coloured contact lenses if you need a quick and handy disguise. Free eye tests. The staff have difficulty with English.

Branches: Ječná 6, Nové Město, Prague 2 (2492 1487); Celetná 38, Staré Město, Prague 1 (2161 3301); Vodičkova 17, Nové Město, Prague 1 (2494 6850); Bělehradská 102, Nové Město, Prague 2 (2252 2272); Centrum Černý Most, Černý Most, Prague 9 (8191 6946).

GrandOptical

Myslbek Center, Na příkopě 19/21, Staré Město, Prague 1 (2423 8371). Metro Můstek/3, 9, 14, 24 tram. **Open** 9am-7pm Mon-Sat; 10am-6pm Sun. **Credit** AmEx, MC, V. **Map** p307 K4.

Owned and run by British chain Vision Express, GrandOptical is well-known for fast, precision lens crafting. Helpful English-speaking staff, but all of this comes at a premium.

Photocopying

Akant

Myslbek Center, Na příkopě 19/21, Staré Město, Prague 1 (2224 0031). Metro Můstek/3, 9, 14, 24 tram. **Open** 9am-6pm Mon-Fri; closed Sat, Sun. **No credit cards.** **Map** p307 K4.

Smaller than most, but central. English spoken.

Copy General

Senovážné náměstí 26, Nové Město, Prague 1 (2423 0020). Metro Náměstí Republiky/3, 5, 9, 14, 24, 26 tram. **Open** 24 hrs daily. **Credit** AmEx, MC, V. **Map** p307 L4.

This is the place to come if you suddenly need a colour photocopy at four in the morning. Or if you need binding, black-and-white digital printing, full-colour digital printing, pick-up and delivery services or print-outs from ZIP, CD or JAZ discs. Some assistants speak reasonable English. The other branches are open only 7am-10pm daily.

Branches: Vinohradská 13, Vinohrady, Prague 2 (2225 3011); Milady Horákové 4, Holešovice, Prague 7 (3337 0013); Na Bělidle 40, Smíchov, Prague 5 (5731 6653).

Photography

Camera shops & repairs

AZ Foto

Senovážná 8, Nové Město, Prague 1 (2421 3443). Metro Náměstí Republiky/3, 5, 9, 14, 24, 26 tram. **Open** 8.30am-6pm Mon-Fri; 9am-noon Sat; closed Sun. **Credit** AmEx, MC, V. **Map** p307 K4.

New and second-hand cameras and various accessories. Particularly strong on second-hand lenses.

Fototechnika a video

Vodičkova 36, Nové Město, Prague 1 (2423 2246). Metro Můstek/3, 9, 14, 24 tram. **Open** 8.30am-7.30pm Mon-Fri; 9am-5pm Sat; closed Sun. **Credit** AmEx, DC, MC, V. **Map** p308 J6.

One-stop shopping for the professional photographer: a wider range of film than any other store in the city, plus tripods, lights, enlargers, second-hand and new cameras. Prices tend to be a little bit higher than at smaller shops. At the back of the shop you can pick up an old Soviet or East German camera for around 500 Kč, or a black-and-white developer for under 4,000 Kč. This section is always crowded with the cognoscenti, so you'll need to assert yourself if you want to get served.

Jan Pazdera obchod a opravna

Lucerna passage, Vodičkova 30, Nové Město, Prague 1 (2421 6197). Metro Můstek/3, 9, 14, 24 tram. **Open** 10am-6pm Mon-Fri; closed Sat, Sun. **No credit cards.** **Map** p307 K5.

Used cameras, movie cameras, enlargers, filters, microscopes, telescopes, tripods and just about every other photographic accessory you can imagine. This excellent store stocks plenty of second-hand cameras from the former communist bloc, which are currently quite fashionable among photographers in the West. The staff also carry out simple camera repairs.

Photo developing

Photo shops have mushroomed all over the tourist areas, so finding a decent place to get your pictures developed should not be any problem whatsoever. Try also **Tesco** (*see page 169*).

Benecel

Celetná 36, Staré Město, Prague 1 (264 536). Metro Náměstí Republiky. **Open** 10am-6pm Mon-Fri; closed Sat, Sun. **No credit cards.** **Map** p306 J3.

One-hour developing.

Česká tisková kancelář (ČTK)

Opletalova 5-7, Nové Město, Prague 1 (2209 8353/2209 8237). Metro Muzeum/3, 9, 14, 24 tram. **Open** 8am-7pm Mon-Fri; 9am-1pm Sat; closed Sun. **No credit cards.** **Map** p309 K6.

One of the only places to get black-and-white photos developed 'quickly' – meaning a week, or three days if you fork out a 50% 'rush' fee. This is a

Eat, Drink, Shop

professional developing place in the same building as the country's leading news agency. Not really a place to bring mere holiday snaps.

Fotoplus

Na příkopě 17, Nové Město, Prague 1 (2421 3121). *Metro Náměstí Republiky/5, 14, 26 tram.* **Open** 9am-7.30pm Mon-Fri; 9am-7pm Sat; 10am-7pm Sun. **Credit** AmEx, MC, V. **Map** p307 K4.
One-hour developing. A little English spoken.

Stationery & art materials

The ubiquitous *papírnictví* shops sell everything from envelopes to toilet paper. If you can't find what you want in one, try **Kotva** (*see page 169*) or one of those listed below.

Altamira

Jilská 2, Staré Město, Prague 1 (2421 9950). Metro Národní třída/6, 9, 18, 21, 22, 23 tram. **Open** 9am-7pm Mon-Fri; 9am-4pm Sat; closed Sun. **No credit cards. Map** p306 H4.
A truly specialist art shop, crammed with stretchers, easels, canvases, paints, chalks and brushes. Not room for much else.
Branch: Skořepka 2, Nové Město, Prague 1 (2422 0923).

Loco Plus

Palackého 10, Nové Město, Prague 1 (2494 7732). Metro Národní třída or Můstek/3, 9, 14, 24 tram. **Open** 8.30am-6.30pm Mon-Thur; 8.30am-6pm Fri; 9am-noon Sat; closed Sun. **No credit cards. Map** p308 J6.
Masses and masses of good, cheap, local stationery and no overpriced imports.

McPaper & Co

Dukelských hrdinů 39, Holešovice, Prague 7 (3338 0002). Metro Vltavská/1, 3, 5, 8, 14, 25, 26 tram. **Open** 9.30am-4.30pm Mon-Fri; closed Sat, Sun. **No credit cards. Map** p310 D2.
Glossy German Berlitz products, including sketch pads, wrapping paper, jiffy bags and tableware.
Branch: Vršovická 70, Vršovice, Prague 10 (7173 6862).

Ráj výtvarníků

Truhlářská 12, Nové Město, Prague 1 (2423 1199). Metro Národní třída/6, 9, 18, 22 tram. **Open** 9am-6pm Mon-Fri; 10am-4pm Sat; closed Sun. **Credit** AmEx, MC, V. **Map** p306 H4.
Decorative Arts Paradise may not quite live up to its name but is nonetheless a well-stocked art shop bang in the centre of town, especially good for its selection of oil paints.

Toys

An invasion of Barbie dolls and Polly Pockets has hit Prague, but traditional Czech toys are managing to hold their own, at least among visitors. There is no shortage of places to buy all the old favourites – puppets, puzzles and pull-alongs. Meanwhile, Prague's department stores have large enough toy sections to please all but the pickiest kid.

Ivre

Jakubská 3, Staré Město, Prague 1 (232 6644). Metro Náměstí Republiky/5, 14, 26 tram. **Open** 10am-6pm Mon-Sat; 10am-5pm Sun. **Credit** AmEx, DC, MC, V. **Map** p307 K3.
Soft toys hand-sewn in the shape of moons, suns, puppets and pillows by Renáta Löfelmannová.
Branch: U Radnice 22, Staré Město, Prague 1 (2423 6865).

McToy

Jakubská 8, Staré Město, Prague 1 (232 2136). Metro Náměstí Republiky/5, 14, 26 tram. **Open** 10am-6.30pm Mon-Sat; closed Sun. **Credit** AmEx, MC, V. **Map** p307 K3.
Specialises in toy animals. Usually overcrowded.

MPM

Myslíkova 19, Nové Město, Prague 1 (292052). Metro Karlovo náměstí/3, 6, 14, 17, 18, 22, 24 tram. **Open** 9am-6pm Mon-Fri; 9am-1pm Sat; closed Sun. **Credit** MC, V. **Map** p306 H4.
A modeller's paradise with hundreds of kits: every make of aircraft, tank and ship, plus battalions of toy soldiers.

Sparky's Dům hraček

Havířská 2, Staré Město, Prague 1 (2423 9309/ info@sparkys.cz). Metro Můstek/3, 9, 14, 24 tram. **Open** 10am-7pm Mon-Sat, 10am-6pm Sun. **Credit** AmEx, MC, V. **Map** p306 J4.
If you need to tire your brood quickly with sensory overload, Sparky's House of Toys is the place to go. Thousands of playthings, from building blocks to plush toys that help tots identify their body parts. It's all top-of-the-line, so you won't get off cheaply, but there's little risk of not finding a child's dream acquisition here. All toys meet EU safety directives. A useful hint: the shop is near the bottom of Wenceslas Square, so a visit here may usefully serve as a bribe to get the kids quietly through the galleries and museums of the neighbouring Old Town.

Video rental

Other video rental outlets include **Jáma**, **Terminal Bar**, **Video To Go** and **Video Express** (*for all, see page 200*).

Video Gourmet

Jakubská 12, Staré Město, Prague 1(232 3364). Metro Náměstí Republiky/5, 8, 14 tram. **Open** 11am-11pm daily. **Credit** AmEx, MC, V. **Map** p307 K3.
Part of the Red, Hot & Blues restaurant in Old Town (*see p132*), this hip place stocks consistently cool videos, plus fresh things like Cajun chicken and carrot cake, packaged to take away. Rental videos available in both NTSC and PAL formats.

Arts & Entertainment

Feature boxes

By Season

Whether dressing warm to choose a carp or shedding everything to get on television, Praguers make the most of every season.

Prague seems a completely different place when the snow silently drifts through Old Town than when the sun, sandals and the microdresses come out. One of its most bewitching aspects is the city's total seasonal transformation – though winter always seems to win for sheer duration.

The Prague Spring festival has been heralding the first warm weather for half a century with world-class fanfare, of course. In May people stretch out and suit up for the Prague Marathon – and generally hurry to lose their pasty 'pub tans'. Jazz festivals begin moving into outdoor venues, spreading jubilance throughout the town.

With the hot days of June and July locals tend to clear out to avoid the flood of tourists (including the staff of most cultural institutions, which go dark until September) and head for the *kantry* (*see page 187* **Carry on *kempink***). If you can get an invitation, you may just get to experience the joy of the *chata* (*see page 60* **One room, nice view, no running water**) and blueberry picking. If not, the city bears its own

sweet fruit during the **Respekt** ethnic music fest and **Tanec Praha** modern dance recitals.

With autumn the symphony and opera return to town, and with them **Prague Autumn** – and not a little of the suspiciously mild drink known as **Burčák**. It's never long before winter returns, but the melancholy is tempered by ritual on **St Nicholas's Eve**, by carp-bashing at Christmas and by fireworks at **Silvestr**, as Czechs call New Year's Eve. And, of course, with the tourists finally gone, Praguers get their beautiful city back to themselves – just as it begins to fill with ice and smog. Even so, the spires of Old Town are an incomparable sight in the snow.

Spring

Easter Monday
Date Mar/April.
Men rush around the country beating women on the backside with willow sticks. Women respond by dousing the men with cold water. Then everyone gets gifts of painted eggs and shots of alcohol. This ancient fertility rite is these days rarely seen in Prague, but painted eggs and willow sticks are on sale all over the city.

Witches' Night
Pálení čarodějnic
Date 30 April.
Like Hallowe'en and Bonfire Night rolled into one, Witches' night marks the death of winter and the birth of spring. Bonfires are lit to purge the winter spirits, an effigy of a hag is burnt (a relic of historical witch hunts) and more daring observers of the custom leap over the flames. Most fires are in the countryside but there's occasionally a pyre in the capital, sometimes on Petřín Hill in Malá Strana.

May Day
Petřínské sady, Malá Strana, Prague 1. Metro Malostranská/12, 22 tram. **Date** 1 May.
Map p304 C5.
Czech lovers with their sap rising make a pilgrimage to the statue of Karel Hynek Mácha on Petřín Hill to place flowers and engage in a spot of necking. Mácha, a 19th-century romantic poet, gave rise to many myths, several bastards and the epic poem, *Máj* (May). It's actually a melancholy tale of unrequited love but nobody lets that minor detail spoil their fun. You might also get pulled underneath a lilac tree and energetically snogged to keep you from being 'dry' in the coming year.

Prague summer rolls around again.

Labour Day

Date 1 May.

There is no longer any danger of being run over by a tank in Wenceslas Square, but May Day is still a good excuse for a demonstration. The communists, in an attempt to keep the faith alive, usually have a small rally in Letná Park and encourage pensioners to moan about the rigours of the free market. Prague's anarchists sometimes hold an uncharacteristically orderly parade.

Prague Writer's Festival

Various venues (information 2425 7959/ www.pwf.globalone.cz). **Date** May.

Czech literary stars get together to read extracts and hob-nob with famous foreign writers imported specially for the occasion. Your chance to observe Ivan Klima's improbable hairdo and the quirks of other local literary lions.

VE Day

Date 8 May.

The Day of Liberation from Fascism is actually 9 May, the date on which the Red Army reached Prague in 1945. In their eagerness to be good Euro-citizens, the Czech government moved the celebration to 8 May, in line with the rest of the continent. Flowers and wreaths are laid on Soviet monuments such as Náměstí Kinských in Smíchov where a Soviet tank used to stand and the Garden of Rest at Olšany Cemetery (*see p112*).

Prague Spring Festival

Hellichova 18, Malá Strana, Prague 1 (530 293/533 474/www.festival.cz). Metro Malostranská/12, 22 tram. **Admission** varies according to venue. **Date** mid May-early June. **Map** p305 D4.

The biggest and best of Prague's music festivals begins on the anniversary of Smetana's death with a performance of his tone poem *Má Vlast* (*My Homeland*). The festival is very popular, so book in advance if possible. You can only do this up to one month before the first concert, as that's when the festival office opens. *See also p223.*

Prague Jazz Festival

Various venues (AghaRTA 2221 1275/ www.agharta.cz). **Date** May-Oct. **Admission** varies according to venue. **Map** p309 K7.

The AghaRTA club (*see p216*) that organises this event works hard to keep alive the flame of Prague's strong jazz tradition. The festival is small and sporadic, carrying on intermittently throughout the spring, summer and autumn. It can bring out excellent performances by top international acts both at the Lucerna Music Bar (*see p212*) and at various outdoor locations.

Prague International Marathon

Throughout the city (information 2491 9209/www.pim.cz). **Date** May. **Start fee** 100 Kč.

The biggest race of the year is also a city-wide street party, with bands 'serenading' runners en route. Those not up to the full distance are able to participate in various other events spread from spring to autumn: a bicycle race, a family run, an in-line skate race and a women's run, offering options as easy as 3km (2 miles). Star runners jet into town for the main event in May; participants pay a 100 Kč start fee.

Carry on *kempink*

When Prague families want to escape the summer heat and tourist hordes, they are likely to pack sleeping gear and head to the country for a spot of *kempink*. The custom is so popular that dozens of holiday camps have sprung up in recent years, many of them little more than parking lots off main roads, adorned with totem poles and 'Fort Apache' signs.

The tradition was established during the 1930s Depression, when Czechs unable to earn a crust in cities and towns went foraging in the countryside, like Steinbeck's drifters of the San Joaquin Valley. Naturally they required songs to fill the lonely nights.

For inspiration, drifters looked to the Wild West, as described in the romances of prolific German pulp novelist Karl May. Love of all things American, or at least of May's highly mythologised version of the American outdoors, blossomed in newly independent Czechoslovakia. Soon every mechanical

engineer and bored town-hall clerk yearned to play 'Red River Valley' on a beat-up guitar by a campfire under the stars. It was easy to forget that May's grizzled heroes had no dachshunds, bored children or complaining wives.

The appropriate gear must of course be American – or at least appear to be American. US Army camouflage is the preferred mode of dress, which lent the *kempink* tradition something of an oppositional character under communism. The gear was traded underground. These days it's much easier to get hold of, so don't be alarmed if your train out of Prague on a Friday evening is taken over by what looks like a lost commando of US Army rangers, all heading for the wilds of the Bohemian hills.

A home where the buffalo roam, it ain't. But you know, sometimes, under the stars, that ol' dachshund does sound just a little like a lonesome coyote.

Arts & Entertainment

Annual ethnic music highpoint – **Respekt!**

Summer

Tanec Praha

Various venues (information 2481 7886/ www.tanecpha.cz). Metro Florenc/8, 24 tram. **Date** June/July. **Admission** varies according to venue.

'Dance Prague' is an international gala of modern dance that has become one of the more successful performance festivals in Prague. International participants such as Martha Graham perform in major theatres and sometimes conduct workshops and symposia (*see p236*).

Respekt

Various venues (Rachot 2271 0050/060 3461 592 mobile). **Date** June. **Admission** varies according to venue.

The world and ethnic music high point of the year features Balkan folk and Gypsy music, plus local players such as Alom, the Prague masters of traditional Roma music. The organiser is Prague's main underground and ethnic music label, Rachot. Concerts are usually at the Akropolis (*see p212*).

Autumn

Prague Autumn

Various venues (information 627 8740/ www.pragueautumn.cz). **Date** mid-Sept. **Admission** varies according to venue.

The next best thing to Prague Spring, this festival annually attracts world-renowned talents to play at Prague's principal concert venues, such as the splendid Rudolfinum (*see p221*).

Burčák arrives

Date late Sept-early Oct.

Burčák, a cloudy, half-fermented, early-season wine, arrives in Prague sometime in the autumn. The stuff is a speciality of Moravia, where the locals perhaps haven't the patience to wait for it to finish fermenting. Served straight from the barrel into special jugs Czechs take to their local *vinárna* for the purpose, *burčák* looks like murky wheat beer, tastes like cherryade but will sneak up on you if you don't treat it with respect.

Festival of Best Amateur & Professional Puppet Theatre Plays

Various venues (Union of International Marionettists 4140 9293). **Date** Oct. **Admission** varies according to venue.

A festival that exploits Bohemia's long tradition of puppet-making (*see p239*). Some of the country's most innovative artists continue to use them, and a faculty at the university is devoted to the craft.

Anniversary of the Creation of Czechoslovakia

Date 28 Oct. Public holiday.

The nation no longer exists but the people still get a day off. Republicans spend the day in mourning, while various political factions hold demonstrations on Wenceslas Square.

All Souls' Day

Date 2 Nov.

Best time of year to visit any one of the city's cemeteries. Whole families turn out to light candles, lay wreaths and say prayers for the dead. The best place to go is the enormous Olšany Cemetery (*see p112*).

Anniversary of the Velvet Revolution

Národní třída & Václavské náměstí, Nové Město, Prague 1. Metro Můstek/3, 9, 14, 24 tram. **Date** 17 Nov. **Maps** p306 H5/p309 L6.

To commemorate the demonstration that began the Velvet Revolution, flowers are laid and candles lit in Wenceslas Square near the statue and on the memorial on Národní třída next to the passage by No.20.

Winter

St Nicholas's Eve

Around Charles Bridge & Staroměstské náměstí. Staré Město, Prague 1. Metro Staroměstská/17, 18 tram. **Date** 5 Dec. **Map** p306 G4/H-J3.

Grown men spend the evening wearing dresses, drinking large amounts of beer and terrorising small children. They wander the streets in threesomes, dressed as St Nicholas, an angel and a devil, symbolising confession, reward and punishment.

Undressed for the weather

Phew, what a scorcher!

If you need to know if the slopes will have decent snow in December or whether to pack an umbrella on your summer road trip, just ask any Czech at around midnight. They'll be able to tell you not only the high and low temperatures expected, but exactly what to wear. Or not.

You can thank *Počasíčko*. TV Nova's 'Little Weather' is watched nightly by almost every Czech with a working television. It could be that they're all obsessed with tomorrow's forecast. Or it could be because the weathercaster isn't wearing anything.

Since 1998, TV Nova has been winning the ratings battle between 10pm and midnight regardless of what low-budget American action series they happen to be airing. That's because viewers know that, in one of the programme breaks during those two hours, sultry music will sound and a strange disembodied window frame will appear. Through the window, a naked sex kitten or hunk of beefcake will appear, luxuriantly yawning as if they've just woken up. Then they'll begin to dress very slowly – or as slowly as *Počasíčko*'s one-minute airtime allows. If they put on enough clothes for cold

weather, you'd better bundle up. If they hardly dress at all, there's going to be fine weather.

Meteopress, which produces these weathercasts as well as fully-clothed versions for most Czech television stations, says it has never received a letter of complaint. That claim may be a bit exaggerated, but it isn't implausible. Czechs don't fret much about nudity, and aren't worried about their children seeing the naked human form. (They usually have more serious things to worry about, such as how to conceal income from the taxman).

Czech women often write in. Not that they're offended, mind; they just want *Počasíčko* to feature more naked men. And to keep them on screen longer. It was because of such letters that Meteopress included male presenters in what was originally an all-female cast.

The models are auditioned before going on air. About a dozen of them do the forecasts in rotation for six months, then *Počasíčko* appear with a new team.

And the actual weather forecast? Tomorrow's temperatures are superimposed on the scene. Not anywhere important, though.

invasion. His grave is adorned with candles and flowers all year round. Many people visit Olšany Cemetery (*see p112*) or the memorial to the victims of communism near the St Wenceslas statue (*see p102*) to lay a few more.

Out of town

Karlovy Vary International Film Festival

Hotel Thermal, IP Pavlova 11, Karlovy Vary (2423 5412/www.iffkv.cz). **Date** July. **Admission** varies.
This genteel spa town hosts the Czech version of Cannes. While hardly in the same league, the festival shows an interesting mix of foreign and home-grown features. *See also p200 and p250.*

Barum Rally

Start/finish line: Interhotel Moskva, náměstí Práce 2512, Zlín (information 067 320 04 mobile/www.rallysport.cz/barum). **Date** Aug. **Admission** free.
This is a classic road race dating back decades that still attracts drivers from across Europe. Moravian roads, generally pretty quiet, roar to life as amateur and pro drivers compete for the big *pohár*, the winner's cup. Autoklub Barum Zlín sponsors the event and an entry form in English can be downloaded from their website.

Velká pardubická Steeplechase

Pražská 607, Pardubice (040 6335 300/ www.pardubice-racecourse.cz). **Date** Oct. **Admission** 200 Kč-2,000 Kč. **No credit cards.**
The star steeplechase event in the annual calendar is also a controversial one: horses and riders are often injured on the difficult course. Celebrity horse people pour in from all over Europe, putting box seats at a premium. A full price list appears on the organisers' website, along with instructions for ordering an advance ticket.

Festival of Best Amateur & Professional Puppet Theatre Plays. *See p188.*

Rather than a red cloak, St Nicholas usually sports a long white vestment, with a white mitre and staff. The angel hands out sweets to children who have been good; the devil is on hand to dispense rough justice to those who haven't.

Christmas

Vánoce
In the week leading up to the holiday, the streets sport huge tubs of water filled with carp, the traditional Christmas dish. People buy them live and store them in the bathtub – otherwise, like most bottom-feeders, they taste of mud. The more squeamish get someone else to kill and gut the fish. The feasting and exchange of gifts happens on the evening of 24 December, when, apart from a midnight mass at St Vitus's Cathedral, pretty much everything closes down. Things don't start opening up again until the 27th.

New Year's Eve

Silvestr
Václavské náměstí and Staroměstské náměstí, Prague 1. Metro Můstek/3, 9, 14, 24 tram. **Maps** p307 K5/p306 H3.
At Silvestr the streets are packed with a rag-tag crowd of Euro-revellers, with much of the fun centred on Wenceslas Square and Old Town Square. Fireworks are let off everywhere and flung around with frankly dangerous abandon, then champagne bottles are smashed.

Anniversary of Jan Palach's death

Olšanské hřbitovy, Žižkov, Prague 3, & Václavské náměstí, Nové Město, Prague 1. Metro Flora & Muzeum. **Date** 16 Jan. **Maps** p311 D2/p309 L6.
Jan Palach set fire to himself on 16 January 1969 in Wenceslas Square as a protest against the Soviet

Gripe season

When Czechs want to complain about bad weather, they have a wealth of idiom at their command. Three favourites are: *chčije a chčije* ('it's pissing out'); *je zima, že by nevyhnal psa ven* ('it's so cold I wouldn't push the dog outside') and *mrzne, až praská* ('it's cold enough to hear it crack').

If those don't sum it up, you might try *padá jí čagany* ('it's raining canes'). But for totally miserable precipitation, the only real option is *padá jí trakaře* ('it's raining barrows').

As for sayings about good weather, there aren't any. It's not that the weather is always inclement, but Praguers are speechless when it's a beautiful day.

Children

What would a fairytale city be without lots of hidden treats for children?

Small and safe – Prague is an old-fashioned kid's world.

You can't push a stroller one block without a Czech stopping you to tickle your toddler's chin and make baby talk. When visiting a Czech home, your child will be stuffed with sweets and given grandpa's knee as all the picture books come out. Much as Czechs love children, though, public facilities for them are essentially limited to playgrounds – and these are shared with dogs no one bothers to clean up after.

Prague's reputation as a fairytale city is well deserved and its castles and museums should captivate any child with visions of princesses and knights. Visit any park in the city and you'll see, on the asphalt, children's chalk drawings of chivalrous scenes. But for those used to interactive museums and smart toys equipped with Pentium chips, the city's old-fashioned kids' world may take some getting used to. The historic centre is small, safe and well served by public transport and the city's larger parks are lovely. With a little imagination, Prague yields plenty of attractions to keep families occupied.

Increasingly modern shops with toys and kids' clothes are to be found throughout the city (*see* chapter **Shops & Services**).

Sightseeing & activities

Some common attractions, such as the **Astronomical Clock** (*see page 92*) and climbable towers such as **Petřín Tower** (*see page 89*), **Old Town Bridge Tower** (*see page 95*), and the **Powder Gate** (*see page 90*) are as suited to children as they are to adults.

Historic tram 91
312 3349/9612 4900. Apr-Oct hourly from 2pm-7pm. Nov-Mar not running. **Fare** 20Kč; 10Kč children. **No credit cards.**
A great sightseeing jaunt for tired feet, this quaint, wood-framed tram travels a loop from Výstaviště, trundling along the banks of Malá Strana, across the Legionnaires' Bridge to the National Theatre, up through Wenceslas Square and then back to Výstaviště via Náměstí Republiky. The antique vehicle can be joined at any stop along the route.

National Technical Museum
Národní technické muzeum
Kostelní 42, Holešovice, Prague 7 (2039 9111/www.ntm.cz). Metro Hradčanská or Vltavská/1, 8, 25, 26 tram. **Open** 9am-5pm Tue-Sun; closed Mon.

Admission 60 Kč; 20 Kč concessions. **No credit cards. Map** p310 C3.
Full of old vehicles, aircraft and gadgets, this museum is a sure hit with kids. A popular coal-mine tour tunnels through the basement. Special family rates available; English-speaking tours can be arranged in advance.

Prague Zoo

Zoologická zahrada v Praze
U Trojského zámku 3, Troja, Prague 7 (688 0480, 855 1752). Metro Nádraží Holešovice, then 112 bus. **Open** *May-Sept* 9am-7pm daily. *Oct-Apr* 9am-4pm daily.
Admission 50 Kč; 25 Kč children, students; free under-3s. **No credit cards.**
Built in 1931, Prague's zoo had become dilapidated and depressingly out-of-date by 1989. Thankfully, renovation has created more humane and 'natural' spaces for many of the animals, though some still inhabit cramped, barred cages. The lovely, sloping grounds are a fine place to stroll, and the chair lift provides a stunning views. A miniature train also enchants kids in the children's play area. An visit to the zoo can be easily combined with a walk through Stromovka park (*see page 195* **Park life**).

Toy Museum

Muzeum hraček
Jiřská 4, Hradčany, Prague 1 (2437 2294/2437 1111). Metro Malostranská/12, 18, 22, 23 tram. **Open** 9.30am-5.30pm daily. **Admission** 40 Kč; 30 Kč students, OAPs; 20 Kč children; 60 Kč family; under-15s free. **No credit cards. Map** p305 E1.
An interesting collection of antique and collectable toys from ancient Greece to the present day. The glass-enclosed exhibits were clearly created with children's viewing in mind, but there isn't much to play with. In one room, kid-level push-buttons activate elaborate displays of moving teddy bears.

Wax Museum

Pražské panoptikum
Národní třída 25, Nové Město, Prague 1 (2108 5318). Metro Národní třída/6, 9, 18, 22, 23 tram. **Open** 10am-8pm daily. **Admission** 119 Kč; 59 Kč students; 49 Kč 6-15-year-olds, OAPs; free under-6s. **No credit cards. Map** p306 H5.
Central Prague's wax museum displays life-size figures of international celebrities, figures from the pantheon of Czech history and 20th-century political leaders. A short special-effects film follows your trip through history.

St. Michael's Mystery

Michalská 27-29, Staré Město, Prague 1 (2421 3253). Metro Staroměstská/6, 9, 18, 22 tram. **Open** 10am-8pm daily. **Admission** 355 Kč. **Credit** MC, V. **Map** p306 H4.
A combination of haunted house, multimedia show and museum, St. Michael's features a creepy tour of talking file cabinets and all-seeing eyes, all billed as a Kafka-esque experience. You can take a jolting ride down a specially outfitted terror elevator. A stirring, completely over-the-top Hollywood-style summa-

tion of Prague history fills the main auditorium, followed by a photo exhibit on the city's changing fortunes. There are certainly cheaper and more subtle shows in Prague but this one is memorable.

Boating

A boat trip is a convenient and entertaining way to see central Prague. Rowing boats or paddleboats can be rented for 80-120 Kč per hour at Novotného lávka (just south of the Staré Město end of Charles Bridge), at Slovanský island (near the National Theatre), and on the Malá Strana side of the river between Charles Bridge and Mánes Bridge.

EVD

Central Wharf, south of Jirásek Bridge, Nové Město, Prague 2 (298 309). Metro Karlovo náměstí/3, 6, 14, 18, 21, 22, 24 tram. **Cruises** *May-Sept* 9.30am, 12.30pm, 3.30pm daily. *Mar 25-Apr 30* 9.30am, 12.30pm, 3.30pm Sat, Sun. *Oct-Mar 24* closed. Tickets 100 Kč. **No credit cards. Map** p308 G8.
This company's boats cruise north to the Prague Zoo from the Central Wharf three times a day, unhurriedly passing through the Vltava river's old lock system. Floating under the Charles Bridge is a thrill, and the façades of New Town are a visual feast to starboard. From the same pier, 75-minute tours also sail south past Vyšehrad before turning back, offering drink service along the way. More expensive trips include meals, music and night cruises. The simplest plan, though, is the 50-minute sightseeing tour (although half of that time is spent standing in a lock) that leaves hourly from Kampa Park between 11am and 8pm in summer.
Branches: Kampa Wharf, south of Charles Bridge, Malá Strana, Prague 1 (298 309); Čechův Wharf, east of Čechův Bridge, Staré Město, Prague 1 (298 309).

Entertainment & sport

For children's shows and events, check out the listings magazine *Kultura v Praze*, available in English at bookshops on Wenceslas Square, or the *Prague Post*. Be advised, though, that children's films from the West are usually dubbed into Czech.
Although there's a fair amount of children's programming on Czech television, including live-action fairytales and animated shorts, the language barrier may also prove a problem unless you happen upon one of the frequent *Tom & Jerry* broadcasts. Satellite television provides further options, including Cartoon Network.
Another option is to let children loose in the **Dětský dům** (*see page 180*). This recently modernised shopping mall caters specifically to kids, tempting them with toy and game shops plus occasional puppet shows in the basement, usually on weekends. The merry-go-round is always a hit and there's a café nearby.

Czech-American playtime in leafy Prague 6.

The **National Theatre** (*see page 237*) and **State Opera** (*see page 222*) stage matinées during the summer, for which families can book box seats for reasonable prices. Rarely in English, these are best suited to older children.

In the autumn, one circus or another is usually performing in Prague. A far cry from politically correct, high-tech three-ring western circuses, those that visit Prague tend to be rinky-dink one-ring affairs; nonetheless, many kids adore them.

There are plenty enough opportunities for swimming, skiing and skating (*see chapter* **Sport & Fitness**). The skating rinks sometimes have special hours for children. One hotel that excels at diverting the young ones is the **Hotel Praha** (*see page 62*), which is equipped with both swimming pool and bowling alley.

Hucul Club

Zmrzlík 1, Jinonice, Prague 5 (5796 0014). Metro Nové Butovice, then 256 bus. **Open** 9am-noon, 1.30-5pm Mon, Wed-Sun; closed Tue. **Rates** 280 Kč per hour; 800 Kč per month (four weekly lessons). **No credit cards.**
Though Czech horses tend to be very large and pretty wild, this stable is one of the few that has mounts suitable for children. Fees include riding and an instructor. Children's lessons by appointment only.

Divoká Šárka Koupaliště

Evropská, Nebušice, Prague 6 (368 022). Tram 20, 26 to end of line, then 5-minute walk north and west through the rocky valley. **Open** May-Sept 9am-7pm daily. *Oct-Apr closed.* **Admission** 25 Kč; 10 Kč children. **No credit cards.**
A lovely outdoor swimming area, quiet and shaded, with two pools fed by spring water. The smaller one is for paddling, the larger one shallow enough for young children to stand in. Swings and a slide are nearby and the spot is ideal for a picnic. There may be naturists in the vicinity.

Laser Game

Národní 25, Staré Město, Prague 1 (2422 1188). Metro Národní třída/6, 9, 17, 18, 21, 22, 23 tram. **Open** 10am-midnight daily. **Admission** 120 Kč for 20 minutes. **Map** p306 G5.

If family tensions are running high, work them out with cyberblast pulse guns. Children transform into Terminators in this dark basement labyrinth, shooting laser guns at sensor lights on your adversaries' belts to score a kill, while trying to dodge their shots at your sensor belt. A well-stocked amusement arcade awaits in the upper level (10 Kč per token, two tokens per game).

Diplomat Hotel Praha

Evropská 15, Dejvice, Prague 6, (2439 4111/ www.diplomat-hotel.cz). Metro Dejvická/2, 20, 26 tram. **Open** 6pm-2am Tue-Fri; closed Mon, Sat, Sun. **Rates** 200 Kč for 8 minutes. **Credit** AmEx, DC, MC, V.
In the basement of this respectable hotel is a miniature go-kart track where kids can roar around a serpentine course while you wait it out in the bar. The track is safe, well supervised and noisy as hell.

Puppet theatre

Puppet theatre has a rich history in Bohemia, and there are two child-orientated puppet theatres in Prague, the **Spejbl and Hurvínek Theatre** and the **National Marionette Theatre** (*for both, see page 239*). They usually feature performances in Czech, though **Opera Mozart** (*see page 223*) stages enchanting performance for foreigners on a regular basis during tourist season. Another option is the non-verbal multimedia performances at the **Magic Lantern** theatre (*see p239*), also aimed at foreigners.

You'll also see puppeteers in tourist areas such as Charles Bridge. High-quality puppet productions also tour the Czech Republic.

Eating out

You rarely see Czech parents eating out with their kids and after a little time in Prague restaurants you quickly understand why: high chairs, speedy service and non-smoking rooms are still very rare. That's why most parents end up in the brand-name burger and pizza chains, which at least make families feel welcome.

But things are improving. If you're a fan of Tex-Mex, **Buffalo Bill's** (*see page 131*) will also cater for your tykes with high chairs, crayons and scribble-ready placemats. The **Bohemia Bagel** (*see page 148*) branch in Old Town has a play area as well as healthy, kid-friendly food. If you just want the little ones out of your hair for an hour, consider the expensive noon lunch or 6pm dinner at the Restaurant Hradčany in the **Hotel Savoy** (*see page 47*). You can stow your offspring in a toy-filled room equipped with a babysitter.

In any restaurant, it's wise to avoid peak dining hours, when waiters may be too harassed to treat children with kid gloves and kitchens too busy to deliver food as promptly as your kids (and your sanity) demand.

Arts & Entertainment

Practicalities

Baby requirements

Disposable nappies and baby food are widely available, both at centrally located department stores such as **Kotva** and **Tesco** (*see page 169*) and at specialised stores, including the following:

Chicco

Ondřičkova 20, Žižkov, Prague 3 (627 6338). Metro Jiřího z Poděbrad/5, 9, 11, 26 tram. **Open** 9am-6pm Mon-Fri; 8am-noon Sat; closed Sun. **No credit cards.** **Map** p311 C2.

Kašpárek

Vítězné náměstí 1, Dejvice, Prague 6 (2432 1526). Metro Dejvická/20, 25, 26 tram. **Open** 9am-6pm Mon-Fri; 8am-noon Sat; closed Sun. **No credit cards.** **Map** p310 C2.
Also sells cribs, children's clothes, toys.

Childminding

The large hotels usually have a babysitting service. Otherwise, it can be hard to come by reliable childcare in Prague, unless through friends. Posting a notice at **Charles University** (*see page 285*) is as good an approach as any. For longer-term child-minding, try the following.

Au Pair Agency of Prague

Au Pair v Praze
Biskupský dvůr 9, Nové Město, Prague 1 (0603 889 016 mobile/5753 0122/info@au-pairprague.cz). Metro Muzeum/11 tram. **Open** 10am-6pm Mon-Fri; closed Sat, Sun. **No credit cards.** Map 307 M2.
Generally reliable and multi-lingual family help .

American Embassy Day Camp

International School of Prague, Nebušická 700, Nebušice, Prague 6 (Karel Rinda 5753 0663). Metro Dejvická then 161, 254, 312 bus. **Dates** June-Aug 8am-3pm daily. *Sept-May* closed. **Rates** 3,600 Kč per week. **No credit cards.**
Arts and crafts, field trips, sports, swimming and the occasional barbecue – all with professional supervision on the rambling campus of Prague's main school for American expat kids. Contact Karel Rinda for registration forms. Day attendance is possible too, but you still have to pay the weekly fee.

Health

Prague's water, though not especially appealing, supposedly conforms to international standards of cleanliness and safety. It is chlorinated but not fluoridated and its nitrate level is not considered safe for the developing respiratory systems of children and infants. Children up to 12 should get fluoride supplements. Bottled water is cheap and available everywhere – red caps usually indicate carbonated varieties.

Atmospheric pollution is also a problem. On some winter days the radio warns parents to keep children indoors. If you are planning to live in Prague, look for accommodation on the outskirts or on the hills of Prague 5 and Prague 6.

Tick-borne encephalitis is endemic throughout eastern Europe. If you intend to travel around the Czech countryside, it's advisable to get a vaccination before leaving home. If you're residing in Prague, **Na Homolce Hospital** (*see page 277*) and the **American Medical Centre** (*see below*) can provide the three-injection course of the vaccine. If ticks are found, they must be removed intact. Smother them in soap or Vaseline, then use tweezers to twist them off anti-clockwise. Then disinfect the area thoroughly. Occasionally the bite causes a red mark, leading to infection and fever, which should be treated immediately with antibiotics. If in doubt, see a doctor or get to an emergency clinic.

American Medical Centre

Americké Kulturní středisko
Janovského 48, Holešovice, Prague 7 (807 756). Metro Vltavska/1, 8, 17 tram. **Rates** $215 (£140) per consultation (non-members); $375 (£250) annual family membership. **Credit** AmEx, MC, V. **Map** p310 D2.
The yearly family membership includes a 30% discount on consultation, free complete annual examination and 24-hour house calls. The English-speaking general practitioners are variously from the USA, Canada and the Czech Republic; the English-speaking dentist is French. All work with children. A paediatrician visits every two weeks to care for newborns and infants.

Canadian Medical Centre

Veleslavínská 1, Veleslavín, Prague 6, (3536 0133/ emergency paediatrics 0603 212 320 mobile). Metro Dejvická then 20, 25, 26 tram. **Open** 8.30-5pm Mon-Fri; 9am-noon Sat; closed Sun. **Credit** AmEx, MC, V.
English-speaking staff experienced in serving the Prague expat parent community.

Národní Polyclinic

Národní třída 9, Nové Město, Prague 1 (2207 5120/ emergencies 0606 461 628 mobile/ poliklinika@narodni.cz). Metro Národní třída/ 6, 9, 17, 18, 21, 22, 23 tram. **Open** 8.30am-5pm Mon-Fri, by appointment only Sat, Sun. **Credit** AmEx, MC, V. **Map** p306 H5 .
Helpful and professional English-speaking staff.

Transport

Children up to six years old travel free on public transport. Those aged six to 15 go half price. When taking a pram on to a public bus or tram, signal to the driver as the vehicle pulls up. Most of the time he will wait long enough for you to lift the pram inside. People with prams must enter and exit by the rear door.

Park life

When you tire of the jostling city crowds and the overworked downtown tourist trails, there is always the park. You may not quite know your way around, but there's nothing foreign about rustling leaves and cool grass. Best of all, the little blighters can shout and run around as much as they want. Wheeeeeeeeee!

Stromovka

Metro Nádraží Holešovice/5, 12, 17 tram.
The sprawling expanse of Stromovka (pictured) used to function as Rudolf II's hunting grounds. Today, its hundreds of trees tower over a maze of paths, including a ring road perfect for biking or roller-skating. A wander through this huge park reveals flower gardens, bad communist sculpture, a man-made lake with ducks, a ruined château, picnicking families, young couples in clinches and pensioners walking their dogs. Star-gazing youngsters might enjoy shows at the city planetarium, just to the left of the main road some 50m (164 ft) from the park's entrance. Modest cafés and drink stands are sprinkled throughout the park, providing ice-cream for the children and cold beer for the grown-ups.

If your kids prefer roller-coasters to trees, follow the blaring techno music and the curving ring road back to **Výstaviště** (see page 109), the show grounds and funfair built for the 1891 Prague Exhibition. With metal-and-glass architecture straight from Dr Seuss, the grounds include the **Lapidárium** sculpture museum (see page 117), an outdoor cinema (Letní kino, operating irregularly on summer evenings), a ho-hum diorama of the Hussite defeat at the Battle of Lipany, and the Křižík fountains, which combine synchronised spraying with coloured lights and music (daily shows May-Sept). Towards the rear of Výstaviště's enclosure, **Lunapark** offers rides, including a ferris wheel, bumper cars, a pitiful excuse for a haunted house and a rickety but fun roller-coaster.

Petřín Hill

Tram 12, 22 to Újezd, then funicular railway.
A centrally located haven of green, Petřín Hill is above all a great place for a stroll. Even the funicular ride up there (9.15am-8.45pm daily) is fun in itself. Exit the funicular at the second and final stop, turn left, and you'll find yourself in a rose garden, overlooked by the **Štefánik Observatory** (see page 89). In there children can peer through telescopes, peruse an

exhibition of cosmic photographs and watch child-orientated films and slide shows. Some of the staff speak English.

Going to the right from the funicular station and following the path through an arch in the stone wall, you come to **Petřín Tower** (see page 89). Trudge up this mini-Eiffel's spiral staircase for a stunning view of the city. If you're feeling less ambitious, settle for an ice-cream in the café at the tower's base. With the tower behind at your back, you'll see several further buildings to the left. The Disneyesque pseudo-Gothic one, known as the **Mirror Maze** (see page 89), houses a none-too-disorientating labyrinth of mirrors, a boring diorama of the Thirty Years' War, and a fabulous room of distorting trick mirrors that will make even the grumpiest children (and adults) giggle madly.

The best thing to do on Petřín, though, is ramble. Various zigzag paths down the steep hillside lead to orchards, playgrounds, statues and **Strahov Monastery** (*see page 80*).

Best of the rest

Prague's other major parks are **Divoká Šárka**, **Obora Hvězda** and **Michelský les** (see page 243). Like Petřín, these are busy and popular. The ruins of **Vyšehrad** (see page 110) are dramatic and rewarding, while the more convenient Letná park, just opposite Old Town in Holešovice, is a good place for roller blading (see page 244).

Film

The multiplexes haven't quite yet chased the arthouses out of town,
but be careful not to fall foul of the cloakroom lady.

David Ondřiček's **Samotáři** – focussing on Prague relationships, drugs and hair-washing.

Like most culture in the modern history of the
Czech lands, great film has a tendency to flicker.
It wasn't until the late 1960s that Czech film won
any sort of international attention. The long
history of filmmaking here notwithstanding,
global audiences were only once before glued
to the screen for a Czech film – *Ecstasy* (1932)
featured cinema's first widely distributed nude
scene, courtesy of a young Hedy Lamarr. A few
stray science-fiction films also reached foreign
screens, including Karel Zeman's *The Fabulous
World of Jules Verne* (1958), but otherwise Czech
film has proven persistently difficult to export.

The rambling Barrandov complex in Prague's
southeast suburbs opened in 1933 as one of the
largest film studios in Europe, cranking out
dozens of Hollywood-influenced dramas and
comedies. During World War II, Barrandov
was seized by the Nazis to be used as a prime
propaganda factory, a role it kept under the
communist regime.

A brief thaw occurred between 1963 and 1968
when filmmakers such as Miloš Forman, Ivan
Passer and Jiří Menzel turned out several
touching and introspective films that signified
a Czech New Wave. The simple but stunning
works of this period can justly be placed
alongside the best of European cinema.

After the Russian tanks arrived in 1968, Czech
film had two more dark decades, during which
the most innovative directors were relegated to
the genres of fairy tales and animation – perhaps
explaining the national obsession with them.
Many talented feature filmmakers, including
Forman, managed to flee to Hollywood.

Post-1989, a new generation of filmmakers is
producing work that addresses the concerns of a
younger audience. David Ondřiček's *Samotáři*
(*Loners*), for example, doesn't touch on
politics, preferring to focus on modern Prague
relationships, drugs and obsessive hair-washing.
Slightly older filmmakers have been exploring

the recent past, such as Jan Svěřák, whose Oscar-winning *Kolja* presented a sentimental take on the last days of communism.

Meanwhile, Prague, with its incredible settings, inexpensive extras, modern studio space and skilled technicians, has become a magnet for foreign film production. *Mission: Impossible*, *Les Miserables* and *Plunkett & Macleane* have all shot on the streets of Prague, while the TV miniseries *Dune* used Barrandov resources to build its fantastic sets.

BUMS ON SEATS

Tickets at downtown and first-run cinemas average over 100 Kč. Neighbourhood theatres are much cheaper, but many are closing or reducing their hours. Except for **Galaxie Multiplex**, few cinemas have popcorn as we know it, but some downtown theatres (notably the **Lucerna**) have atmospheric cafés or bars. The stroppy coatcheck lady, demanding that you surrender your outer garments, is fast becoming an endangered species, but you may still get fuming looks from the elderly matrons when you snub the *šatna* (cloakroom).

Commercial Hollywood fare makes up the bulk of programming everywhere except at the art cinemas. There is generally a sign at the box office explaining what version the film is in. *Dabing* films are dubbed into Czech, but usually only children's films get this treatment. By and large, films are screened *s českými titulky*, or simply *č t* (with original soundtrack and Czech subtitles). Important Czech films are sometimes screened with English subtitles; look for *s anglickým titulky*.

Tickets have assigned seat numbers and you can usually pick your spot from a computer screen at the box office. Unless you want some latecomer to argue that you're in their place, be sure to find the row (*řada*) and seat (*sedadlo*) that are printed on the ticket. Most downtown theatres have upgraded their sound systems to some form of digital, but neighbourhood theatres are still equipped with squawky mono sound systems and wooden folding seats. Screening times can be erratic, but you can find basic listings in the *Prague Post*, the free large-format schedule *DoMěsta* (with translations in English), or on events posters around town.

Some nightclubs and cafés show videos of feature films, with **Rock Café** (*see page 212*) having the most consistent schedule.

Commercial cinemas

Kotva

Náměstí Republiky 8, Staré Město, Prague 1 (2481 1482). Metro Náměstí Republiky. **No credit cards.** **Map** p307 K3.

Medium-sized modern cinema next to a department store usually offering 11.30pm screenings of new films. Occasional salsa dancing in the café.

Galaxie Multiplex

Arkalycká 874, Háje, Prague 4 (6791 0616). Metro Háje. **No credit cards.**

Prague's first multiplex. Premières generally show in the large hall, which has a nicely sloped floor, big seats and a good sound system. Conditions diminish rapidly through the other seven halls, until you find yourself crammed into an oddly shaped cupboard where the screens look like they were borrowed from a geography class.

Kinokavárna Jalta

Václavské náměstí 43, Staré Město, Prague 1 (2422 8814). Metro Muzeum/3, 9, 14, 24 tram. **No credit cards.** **Map** p307 K6.

The cinema coffeehouse is a dying tradition. At one time they were relaxed, homey places where you could have a drink and a smoke while watching a movie, but this, the only *kinokavárna* still operating, is little more than informal seating around a small screen. It's a bit like watching a film in someone's basement. The cool thing is that this someone lives right on Wenceslas Square.

Lucerna

Vodičkova 36, Staré Město, Prague 1 (2421 6972/2421 6973). Metro Můstek/3, 9, 14, 24 tram. **No credit cards.** **Map** p307 K6.

In the Lucerna passage off Wenceslas Square, an art nouveau masterpiece that, while admittedly a little worse for wear, remains a true movie palace. Come early so you can clock its delightfully tatty decor while the lights are still up or hang out in the lobby bar. With a picture window overlooking the 1920s-era shopping arcade and occasionally featuring music from a live pianist, the bar is a prime spot for people-watching.

64 U Hradeb

Mostecká 21, Malá Strana, Prague 1 (535 006). Metro Malostranská/12, 22 tram. **No credit cards.** **Map** p305 E3.

Hidden down an alley next to a McDonald's is this large and comfortable theatre. The decor isn't as stunning as at some of the older movie palaces, but roomy seats and good sound do much to compensate. Near the Charles Bridge, this is one of the better places to catch a new movie.

Arthouse cinemas

Some of the venues below are film clubs, but you usually don't have to be a member to see a film; just buy a pass along with your ticket.

Aero

Biskupcová 31, Žižkov, Prague 3 (893 601). Tram 1, 9, 16. **No credit cards.**

This slightly hard-to-find neighbourhood theatre in the bleaker streets of Žižkov offers some of the

Intimate pleasures of inanimate objects

In a scene from Jan Švankmajer's *The Conspirators of Pleasure*, trembling hands pass over porno magazines and go at them with scissors. Breasts and buttocks are feverishly cut into strips and dipped into a pot of milky sludge by a nervous man. Above him, a severed chicken head is tacked to a cracked plaster wall, serving as inspiration. The man sticks the lurid strips to a large clay mould to create a pornographic, papier mâché... rooster.

'I like working with real, material objects that I have found somewhere and which have already been handled and touched by people,' says the surrealist stop-motion filmmaker. 'Living objects with a content and history of their own.' Jan Švankmajer has made more than 30 short films since 1964 – notably *Dimensions of Dialogue*, 1982, *Men's Games*, 1988, *Darkness, Light Darkness*, 1989, and *Food*, 1992. His four feature films, *Alice*, 1987, *Faust*, 1994, *The Conspirators of Pleasure*, 1996, and *Otesánek*, 2000, each employ a similar dream-like language of disturbing imagery, but always with different results. The power of Švankmajer's films to haunt a viewer's subconscious is due in large part to his choice of universal, archetypal materials and objects. Freed from their normal contexts, they are reinserted into new 'surrealities', giving them a

curious but familiar quality. Watching his films is a bit like dreaming about a long and revealing conversation with your toaster, and then being confronted with the actual object at breakfast.

His latest movie, *Otesánek*, is a dark comedy blending the Frankenstein myth with a Czech fairy tale about an insatiable infant carved from tree roots (pictured). Feeding time becomes problematic after the cupboards are stripped bare, but just about that time a hapless postman stops by, then a social worker ...

There's an agenda here, but even Švankmajer has to admit he's not entirely sure what it is. 'My aim,' he reckons, 'is to show that organic objects have content that brings another dimension to reality.' Clearly, this is a filmmaker with more on his mind than a hot chase in the third reel.

Characteristically, the puppet components of *Otesánek* at all the baby's growth stages were carved from tree stumps that Švankmajer himself selected from the woods around his studio in rural Knovíz. When the wood baby screams or giggles, no mechanics, latex or clay are involved, just a series of sawn-off, hollowed-out tree knots, replaced in order of size to produce an opening mouth. Real materials and their manipulation are central to the director's adherence to traditional stop-motion animation

best and most creative programming in the city. They show recent European art films, retrospectives and movie marathons, and Terry Jones and Terry Gilliam have both presented here. The battered lobby café encourages lingering and mixing.

British Council

Národní třída 10, Staré Město, Prague 1 (2199 1111). Metro Náměstí Republiky/5, 8, 14 tram. **No credit cards.** Map p306 H5.
For much of the year, one British film is shown every two weeks on Wednesday evenings. Offerings range from classic 1950s comedies up to relatively recent films, with the occasional mini-festival thrown in.

Dlabačov

Bělohorská 24, Střešovice, Prague 6 (311 5328). Tram 8, 22, 23. **No credit cards.**
Don't be scared off by this film club's mothership, the horrifying Hotel Pyramid. Ensconced in the basement and boasting a mammoth screen and decent sound quality, this cinema shows local and imported indies of reliable quality.

Evald

Národní třída 28, Staré Město, Prague 1 (2110 5225). Metro Národní třída/6, 9, 18, 22 tram. **No credit cards.** Map p306 H5.
Relatively small venue usually showing European art films, independent American films and Czech films with English subtitles. Advance booking recommended for new films. A pub restaurant is hidden away down the hall from the cloakroom.

MAT Studio

Karlovo náměstí 19, Staré Město, Prague 1 (2491 5765). Metro Karlovo náměstí/3, 4, 6, 14, 16, 18, 22, 24 tram. **No credit cards.** Map p308 H8.
Since installing digital sound, this small screening room has been mixing retrospective screenings of big-budget action fare with art films, Czech films subtitled in English and rare programming from the Czech TV vaults. It's a small place and invariably sells out so buy tickets in advance. If turned away, you can always wait for the next screening surrounded by cinemaphiles and old Czech movie posters in the bar.

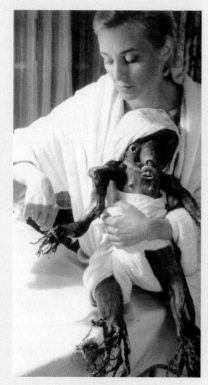

in all his films. Considerable patience and precision are required but the results are visible, as hammers wither away into piles of sawdust, leather shoes are ground through pencil sharpeners and rolling pins are transformed into peculiar new instruments by armies of nails.

Between 1973 and 1979 Švankmajer was 'retired' by the communists, who categorised his works as 'opposition' films. As he says: 'If the censors had been asked why they had banned them, their only possible response could have been, "Because they made people laugh". The censors had a far more fertile imagination than I do'.

His reaction was to turn inward, creating an encyclopedia of an alternate world, a lexicon of creatures and places pieced together into collages made from pieces of old medical magazines and books he found on the street. With his wife Eva, a surrealist painter, Švankmajer also produced a pantheon of ceramic creatures, using moulds taken from Czech puppets and socialist mass-produced sculptures. Some of these objects, including prints and drawings from both Švankmajers' prolific careers, are permanently on view and for sale along with many of their films on video, at the **Gambra Gallery** downstairs from the couple's apartment above Prague Castle (*see page 206*).

Ponrepo at Bio Konvikt

Bartolomějská 13, Staré Město, Prague 1 (no phone).
Metro Národní třída/6, 9, 18, 22 tram. **Annual membership** 150 Kč adults; tickets 30 Kč. **No credit cards. Map** p306 H5.
Screening venue for the Czech Film Archive, though they make it truly hard to see the films. You need a membership card with a photo, filling out the form takes at least five minutes, and if there is a queue, you'll likely miss the start of the film. The programme includes Czech and Slovak films, plus works by important world filmmakers from Eisenstein to John Ford. Make sure the film doesn't have a live Czech translation into the hall (denoted by *s překl.*) – torture for film-lovers who come expecting to enjoy a rare old gem.

Festivals & special events

The events listed below are pretty permanent; keep your eyes open, though, for occasional embassy-sponsored events such as The Days of Iranian Film or selections of recent German or Italian movies. Most of these offer English-subtitled copies when possible. The **Archa Theatre** (*see page 235*) occasionally has interesting mini-festivals and multimedia screenings including silent films with ambient live accompaniment.

Look out also for the summer outdoor cinemas (*Letní kino*) at **Výstaviště** (2010 2104, Map p310, C1) and on **Střelecký island** (0602 710 696, Map p305, F5). A drive-in also operates in **Stadium Strahov** on top of Petřín Hill (*see page 212*) during summer, but unpredictably so look out for posters advertising L&M Drive-In. Lawn chairs are put out for the many carless.

Days of European Film

2423 4875/www.eurofilmfest.cz. **Date** late March.
This (roughly) ten-day festival takes over the **Lucerna** and **64 U Hradeb** to screen co-productions and award-winning European films in their original language – usually with English subtitles. This is often the only chance to catch these films locally. Filmmakers sometimes come to introduce

their films and take questions afterward. The festival is organised by a number of European cultural centres; the number above is for the main organiser, the Austrian Cultural Institute.

Febiofest

2421 4254/www.febio.cz. **Date** late Jan.

Bigger and better every year, the week-long Prague version of this travelling festival shows all manner of film in traditional and non-traditional venues. Theatres such as Lucerna show the more mainstream Febio films, often months ahead of their official Czech release. Other venues show international art films, documentaries and cult stuff. Beware that some theatres pipe annoying live translations into the hall (denoted by *překl. do sálu*), while others have more discreet translations to headphones, (denoted by *překl. do sluch*).

Karlovy Vary International Film Festival

Info: Marek Brodsky, Pánská 1, Staré Město, Prague 1 (2423 5412/www.iffkv.cz). **Date** mid-July.

Centred at the Hotel Thermal but occupying practically every available space in this small spa resort (*see page 250*), this is the only film festival in the Czech Republic accredited by the FIAPF, the group that sanctions the Cannes, Berlin and Venice festivals. Gregory Peck, Lauren Bacall and Steve Buscemi have all put in appearances here and distribution deals are frantically made in the halls, but most attendees are content to party in and around the heated Hotel Thermal pool each night after the last screening. Sponsors have been trying to improve the organisation, but the best films still sell out quickly and the ticket distribution system is a nightmare. Nonetheless, film event of the year.

Project 100

www.artfilm.cz. **Date** Jan-Feb.

Film scholars pick ten diverse films from around the world each year to be included in this traveling retrospective that runs in Prague during January and February at **64 U Hradeb**, **Aero** and other theatres, before touring throughout the country. The films range from recent works to 1950s gems, and include some English-language selections.

One World Human Rights Film Festival

www.oneworld.cz. **Date** late April

Feature and documentary films focus on refugees, recent conflicts, basic freedoms and related topics. Venues include the **MAT Studio** and **Evald**. Most films are shown from videotape with the unfortunate effect that Czech subtitles added for the festival sometimes totally obscure the original English ones underneath.

FAMU Student Film Festival

FAMU, Smetanovo nábřeží 2, Staré Město, Prague 1 (2422 9468/www.f.amu.cz). Tram 9, 17, 18, 22. **Date** April.

Films on video

Several shops and two major bars rent imported videotapes, and this is often the only way to see English-language versions of less commercial films and foreign films with English subtitles.

Jáma

V Jámě 7, Staré Město, Prague 1 (0606 406 741 mobile). Metro Můstek/3, 9, 14, 24 tram. **Open** noon-11pm daily. **Membership** 100 Kč. **Rental** 60-80 Kč. **No credit cards.** **Map** p307 K6.

Popular expat bar stocking hundreds of English-language movies and TV shows in PAL format. VCRs can be rented, but not TVs.

Terminal Bar

Soukenická 6, Staré Město, Prague 1 (2187 1999). Metro Náměstí Republiky/5, 8, 14 tram. **Open** 11am-1am daily. **Rental** 120 Kč. **No credit cards.** **Map** p307 K2.

Rents a wide variety of films including some classic Czech films with English subtitles and all sorts of horror, sci-fi, action and cult movies. Some are in NTSC format, but most are in PAL. Films can be viewed in the downstairs video room for an extra 100 Kč per person. Taking tapes home requires refundable deposit. Bring some ID.

Video Express

Žitná 41, Staré Město, Prague 1 (2221 1425). Metro IP Pavlova/4, 6, 11, 22, 23 tram. **Open** 11am-11pm daily. **Membership** 400 Kč. **Rental** 50 Kč. **No credit cards.** **Map** p307 K7.

The only place in Prague to offer tape delivery service. Selection includes English-language and English-subtitled tapes in NTSC and PAL format.

Video to Go

Vítězné náměstí 10, Dejvice, Prague 6 (312 4096). Metro Dejvická/20, 25, 26 tram. **Open** 10am-10pm daily. **Membership** 500 Kč. **Rental** 150-180 Kč. **No credit cards.**

Prague's largest selection of English-language tapes – though much of it old and uninspiring – can be found at this store's two locations, both of which have 24-hour tape drop boxes. Also rents TVs, multisystem VCRs and DVD players. **Branch:** Čelakovského sady 12, Nové Město, Prague 2 (2423 5098).

Grand Restaurant Septim

Rašínovo nábřeží 59, Staré Město, Prague 2 (298 559). Metro Karlovo náměstí/3, 6, 14, 18, 21, 22, 24 tram. **Open** 11am-midnight daily. **No credit cards.** **Map** p308 G9.

This restaurant's comfortable back room has a TV and VCR that can be booked in advance, or you can try your luck at finding it free. There's a small selection of tapes, but you're welcome to bring your own.

Galleries

Regimes and empires may rise and fall, but Czech art still clings to its muted colours, spritual yearnings and dogged sense of irony.

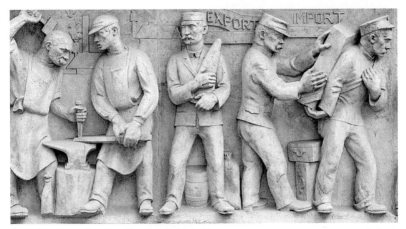

Art under communism – another regrettable legacy.

Czech artists, though often short of patrons and physically remote from the creative centres, have striven with some success to keep up with the big boys elsewhere. At their best, they marched at the head of the parade, most recently during the interwar First Republic. Four decades of communism were a grim interlude, but, since 1989, Prague's artists and curators have energetically reintegrated themselves into the international art network.

Amid all this activity, it's easy to forget that the roots of today's Czech art lie deeper in the national psyche than the 1948 communist putsch. Over the centuries, Czech artists have continually returned to muted colours, spiritual yearnings and a sense of irony. Forty years of insularity did not blunt the sensibility that gave rise to visionary medieval court painters, erotic mannerist allegory, cubist architecture and the art nouveau splendour of Alfons Mucha.

A regrettable legacy of communism was the top-heavy administration of arts institutions, which until recently survived all attempts at modernisation. But even under communism, abstract painter Adriena Äimotová, printmaker Jiří Anderle and documentary photographer Josef Koudelka were able to produce original and provocative work from the 1960s onwards. There are still fresh ideas out there; the trick is to track

them down at the handful of adventurous public spaces and private galleries. You might even find them in bars and bookstores. The city is also scattered with small, intriguing spaces such as the villa of visionary artist František Bílek, designed to resemble a wheatfield. See page 116.

The Modernist heirs of Bílek – Josef Čapek, Emil Filla and František Kupka – and his contemporary successors are no less ardent in their pursuit of the transcendent. Of the first such post-war generation, those banned before 1989, Vladimir Kokolia is most representative. A painter and singer with the underground band E, Kokolia employs soothing colours to portray the meditative worlds of atoms and living cells.

Václav Stratil's 'Hu haba' school of Brno, named after a nonsensical outburst overheard from a street drunk, has given rise to suitably abstract and chaotic sculpture and paintings. František Skála is more of a surrealist, inclined toward cybernetic metals, processed natural materials and melting effects – his designs adorn the Akropolis bar (see page 161). Martin Mainer, formerly an unpredictable painter of icons, has lately moved toward stripped-down surrealism and geometric abstraction.

A second wave has grown up unfettered in the arts vacuum that followed 1989. Jiří Příhoda has emerged from the void with installations,

Lukáš Rittstein's Oči – elastic forms.

including a sensational collaboration with Brian Eno, that make use of structural elements and inner lighting to rethink physical form. Petr Kvícala favours vibrant colour abstractions on canvas in tense geometric patterns and woven strands. The work of Kateřina Vincourová is characterised by ghostly, luminescent wedding dresses, huge sperm-shaped balloons and other transformations of sexual icons. Veronika Bromová and Lukáš Rittstein represent the state of digital art in Prague. Bromová uses high-tech imagery to portray the body as an elastic form, while Rittstein's sculptures meld body and space into a new hyperreality.

Prague's place on the international circuit makes it a great city in which to catch travelling exhibitions by noteworthy foreign artists. The gallery scene further benefited from Prague's selection as one of the nine European Cities of Culture 2000. Some choice projects are in prospect, including a permanent home on Kampa Island for the Jan and Meda Mládek collection of modern Czech and other Central European art, to open late in 2000. Another is a collection of children's drawings in the old Dům U Zelené Náby (Green Frog House) on U Radnice west of Old Town Square. In the offing for 2001 is a comprehensive, four-site summer exhibition, The Glory of Baroque Prague.

This chapter covers the principal public exhibition spaces and the more interesting commercial galleries. For permanent art collections, *see chapter* **Museums**.

INFORMATION

For information on exhibitions, consult the *Prague Post, Culture in Prague* (*Kultura v Praze*) – a white listings booklet available from newsstands, in English at some central locations – or *Atelier*, a Czech fortnightly broadsheet with an English summary and listings of all exhibitions in the country.

Most galleries and museums are closed on Mondays, and some private spaces take a holiday in August, but it's always best before setting out to check that the one you want to visit hasn't closed 'temporarily'.

Exhibition spaces

Temporary exhibition spaces come and go, but the main organising bodies are the National Gallery, Prague Castle and the city of Prague. Their shows are increasingly large-scale, though sometimes curated without much cohesion.

State-curated exhibitions are generally devoted to reappraising Czech artistic heritage. Previous ones have covered the national fixation with surrealism, the photographic expressionism of František Drtikol, the inter-war avant-garde and socialist realism.

The Belvedere

Belvedér
Letohrádek královny Anny, Hradčany, Prague 1 (2437 2327). Metro Hradčanská/22, 23 tram. **Open** Apr-Oct 10am-6pm Tue-Sun (during shows); closed Mon. *Nov-Mar* closed. **Admission** 80 Kč; 40 Kč children; 120 Kč family. **No credit cards. Map** p305 E1.
Stunning Renaissance-style space within the Castle complex (*see page 69*) for large touring shows.

Carolinum

Výstavní síň Karolinum
Železná 9, Staré Město, Prague 1 (2449 1111/2449 1635). Metro Můstek/5, 8, 14 tram. **Open** 10am-5pm Tue-Sun; closed Mon. **Admission** 20 Kč; 10 Kč concessions. **No credit cards. Map** p306 J4.
With a vaulted ground floor and a labyrinth of subterranean rooms, this is an excellent space for touring exhibitions and shows by Czech artists.

Czech Museum of Fine Arts

České muzeum výtvarných umění
Husova 19-21, Staré Město, Prague 1 (2222 0218). Metro Staroměstská/17, 18 tram. **Open** 10am-6pm, Tue-Sun; closed Mon. **Admission** 20 Kč; 10 Kč concessions; free under-6s. **No credit cards. Map** p306 H4.
In an elegant Renaissance townhouse, this organisation mostly exhibits 20th-century Czech art, but sometimes stretches itself to stage international exhibitions and retrospectives of foreign artists.

Galerie Hollar

Smetanovo nábřeží 6, Staré Město, Prague 1 (2423 5243). Metro Národní třída/17, 18 tram. **Open** 10am-1pm, 2-6pm, Tue-Sun; closed Mon. **Admission** 10 Kč; 5 Kč concessions. **No credit cards. Map** p306 G5.
The gallery of the Union of Czech Graphic Artists, on the ground floor of Charles University's Faculty of Sociology. The building faces the river but is rather swamped by traffic noise from the busy embankment. Apart from monthly exhibitions – normally of Czech or Slovak artists – there are large racks of prints to browse through or buy.

On the cutting edge

Czech glassmakers have been at the forefront of their craft since Slavic tribes produced beads and rings in the fifth and sixth centuries. Their techniques served glassmakers until the 17th century, when the chemical recipe for what would become known as Bohemian Crystal was developed. This new glass, stronger and clearer than that traditionally used in Murano, (the Venetian capital of glass production) quickly established Bohemia as the new seat of fashionable tableware, and crystal became *de rigueur* in the royal households of Europe. Techniques normally applied to gem cutting were first applied to glass in Kamenický Šenov. The delicate images and decorations that resulted are mirrored in the baroque-style offerings along the tourist arteries of Old Town. For a glimpse of the original quality and craftsmanship, make a visit to the **Museum of Decorative Arts** (*see page 117*). There you can view the largest collection of glass in the Czech Republic, along with a sampling of styles developed in other countries.

At the turn of the 20th century, the curvilinear forms and flowing lines of art nouveau rippled their way into vessels and ornaments, from vases to chandeliers – sometimes with exquisite results. The Joseph Loetz glass works of Klášterský Mlýn won the greatest renown for the newly ornate glass, providing stiff competition for the US-based Tiffany. Loetz creations, wrought by Czech craftsmen and Viennese designers, are still on view at the **Šumava Museum** (0187 922 505, *May-Oct* Tue-Sun 9am-5pm; closed Mon. *Nov-Apr* 10am-2pm Sat; closed Mon-Fri, Sun) in Kašperské Hory near the Austrian border.

Under communism, glass makers, like other artisans, were compelled to create works of Aesthetic Realism, forcing creative glassmaking indoors. Out of view, and making the most of its status as an unaccepted art form, the craft began quietly to sow the seeds of its own rebirth. In the 1960s, subversive professors such as Stanislav Libenský at the Academy of Applied Arts sought to keep students technically and conceptually abreast of developments beyond the Iron Curtain. His experimental approach helped produce today's strong crop of glass artists.

The work of these artists is hard to come by – most of the glass trade in Prague centres around cheap knock-offs and factory-made knick-knacks. The most deservedly well known are the husband and wife team of **Libenský and Jaroslava Brychtová**, whose thick, luminous, colour-saturated glass-cast forms have dominated the international glass scene since 1989. Libenský draws his subtle, simple, yet increasingly massive designs on large pieces of paper tacked to a wall, then Brychtová transforms these two-dimensional impressions into three-dimensional forms, using plaster and clay. From Brychtová's sculptures moulds are made, into which the glass is then melted. Their studio, in the town of Železný Brod, two hours northeast of Prague by car on Route 10, is in the middle of the most concentrated area of glass production in the Czech Republic, with ten large-scale glass works and countless smaller studios and shops.

Another husband and wife team of the next generation has vastly different interests. **Marian Karel** uses huge sheets of plate glass to reflect and mix ambient light surrounding landscape and architecture. His wife **Dana Zámečníková** stacks the sheets together to create figurative paintings with multiple levels of depth and obscured expression. For a ready-to-hand look at Czech glass engraving, pick up the work of Prague's premier engraver, **Jiří Harcuba**, working in a rather different medium – the five-crown coin.

Art of glass – unbroken Czech tradition.

Arts & Entertainment

Galerie Jaroslava Fragnera

Betlémské náměstí 5a, Staré Město, Prague 1 (2222 2157). Metro Národní třída/6, 9, 18, 21, 22 tram. **Open** 10am-6pm Tue-Sun; closed Mon. **Admission** free. **No credit cards. Map** p306 H4.

This gallery devoted to modern architecture and urban planning occupies a renovated Gothic space beneath the Bethlehem Chapel.

Galerie Rudolfinum

Alšovo nábřeží 12, Staré Město, Prague 1 (2489 3309/2489 3205). Metro Staroměstská/17, 18 tram. **Open** 10am-6pm Tue-Sun; closed Mon. **Admission** 90 Kč; 45 Kč concessions; free under-15s, art students. **No credit cards. Map** p306 G2.

Budget cuts have dulled the edge of what started out in the mid 1990s as the city's best space for international contemporary art. The occasional top touring show (Nan Goldin, for one) still drops in. Upcoming Czech artists get massive exposure in this set of grand rooms in the 19th-century Rudolfinum concert building (*see page 221*).

Kinský Palace

Palác Kinských

Staroměstské náměstí 12, Staré Město, Prague 1 (2481 0758). Metro Staroměstská/17, 18 tram. **Open** 10am-6pm Tue-Sun; closed Mon. **Admission** 90 Kč; 50 Kč concessions; 150 Kč family; free under-10s. **No credit cards. Map** p306 J3.

The renovated Kinský Palace has shifted gears after hosting 320,000 drawings and graphics from the Middle Ages. A few of these may still be seen, including works by Veronese, Breughel, Spranger, Petr Brandl, 19th-century Czech landscape artists, portrait miniatures from the 17th-19th centuries, plus Cézanne, Gauguin, Kupka and Váchal. Also goes in for exhibits by such topical artists as David Černy, who once painted a Soviet tank pink.

House of the Stone Bell

Dům U kamenného zvonu

Staroměstské náměstí 13, Staré Město, Prague 1 (2482 7526). Metro Staroměstská/17, 18 tram. **Open** 10am-6pm Tue-Sun; closed Mon. **Admission** 50-120 Kč; half price concessions. **No credit cards. Map** p306 J3.

This Gothic sandstone building on the east side of Old Town Square features a gorgeous baroque courtyard surrounded by three floors of exhibition rooms, some with their original vaulting. It also hosts concerts (*see page 222*).

Imperial Stables

Císařská konírna

Prague Castle (second courtyard), Hradčany, Prague 1 (2437 3312). Metro Malostranská and up the Old Castle Steps/22, 23 tram. **Open** 10am-6pm Tue-Sun; closed Mon. **Admission** 60 Kč; 30 Kč concessions; 90 Kč family. **No credit cards. Map** p304 C2.

Rudolf II would probably be pleased to find that his stables are now an art gallery. A recent exhibition on Egyptian tapestries was typically well-curated and laid out.

Municipal House Exhibition Hall

Obecní dům výstavní sál

Náměstí Republiky 5, Staré Město, Prague 1 (2200 2674). Metro Náměstí Republiky/5, 8, 14 tram. **Open** 10am-6pm daily. **Admission** 60-120 Kč. **Credit** AmEx, MC, V. **Map** p307 K3.

Exhibition space producing extended shows on broad themes like the relationship between crafts and their surroundings. It lies within the art nouveau **Municipal House** (*see p35, p149 and p221*). A ticket to an art show or concert is the only way to see the gorgeous upper floors.

Municipal Library

Městská knihovna

Mariánské náměstí 1 (entrance on Valentinská), Staré Město, Prague 1 (231 0489/231 3357). Metro Staroměstská/17, 18, tram. **Open** 10am-6pm Tue-Sun; closed Mon. **Admission** 50 Kč; 20 Kč concessions. **No credit cards. Map** p306 H3.

A modern art (usually Czech stuff) exhibition space since 1945, the extensive layout of large, well-lit rooms rivals the National Gallery's spaces.

Prague Castle Riding School

Jízdárna Pražského hradu

U Prašného mostu 55, Hradčany, Prague 1 (2437 3232). Metro Malostranská and up the Old Castle Steps/22, 23 tram. **Open** 10am-6pm Tue-Sun; closed Mon. **Admission** 60-100 Kč; half price concessions. **No credit cards. Map** p304 C1.

This and the Wallenstein Riding School (*see below*) are the National Gallery's principal exhibition venues. It was built in 1694 to designs by Jean-Baptiste Mathey and restored by Pavel Janák after World War II. The book stall is a good source of current and remaindered catalogues on Czech art.

Wallenstein Riding School

Valdštejnská jízdárna

Valdštejnská at Klárov, Malá Strana, Prague 1 (536 814). Metro Malostranská/12, 18, 22, 23 tram. **Open** 10am-6pm Tue-Sun; closed Mon. **Admission** 60-100 Kč; half price concessions. **No credit cards. Map** p305 D2.

Part of the Wallenstein Palace, this space has established itself as host to Prague's most experimental and thought-provoking exhibitions. These range from explorations of technology and social questions to baroque sculpture and romantic landscape.

Commercial galleries

Prague has a thriving commercial scene, best viewed at a smattering of small galleries. Exhibitions vary widely in quality, but a number of spaces show consistently good work. Outstanding galleries such as **Galerie Jiří Švestka** and **Galerie Nová síň** show tantalising artworks, as do contemporary breeding grounds **Galerie Behémót** and **Galerie MXM**. Artists to watch out for include Václav Stratil, Viktor Pivovarov, Jiří David, František Skála and Petr Nikl.

Vaulted, much-vaunted, **Galerie MXM** is Prague's oldest private gallery.

Galerie Behémót

Elišky Krásnohorské 6, Staré Město, Prague 1 (231 7829). Metro Staroměstská/17, 18 tram. **Open** 11am-6pm Tue-Sat; closed Sun-Mon. **No credit cards.** **Map** p306 H2.

Owner Karel Babíček considers display conditions to be as important as the original creative act and thus favours installation. The resulting exhibits are some of the most interesting and dynamic shows in Prague. The artists are mostly young, Czech and Slovak; their more portable work upstairs can be viewed upon request. The days of bargain hunting for good contemporary art are fading fast. A tiny daub of paint by hot young artist Martin Mainer will set you back 25,000 Kč.

Galerie Jiří Švestka

Jungmannova 30, Nové Město, Prague 1 (9624 5025). Metro Národní třída/6, 9, 18, 21, 22, 23 tram. **Open** noon-6pm Tue-Fri; 11am-6pm Sat; closed Sun, Mon. **No credit cards.** **Map** p308 J6.

Curator Jiří Švestka operates a shop in the former Mozarteum concert hall that specialises in bold, internationally recognised modern art. Top-quality solo and group installations of work from the likes of Dan Graham and Bořek Šípek.

Galerie Jiřího a Běly Kolářových

Betlémské náměstí 8, Staré Město, Prague 1 (2222 0689). Metro Národní třída/6, 9, 17, 18, 21, 22, 23 tram. **Open** 10am-7pm daily. **No credit cards.** **Map** p306 H5.

The world knows Jiří Kolář as the master of collage, autocollage, anticollage, rolage, assemblage – he and his wife Běla do them all. Czechs also revere

him as an influential poet of the 1950s. Here you can view – and buy for around 50,000 Kč and up – a montage or collage of your own, such as a shovel made of newspaper. Worth exploring; this is art that will stick with you.

Galerie MXM

Nosticova 6, Malá Strana, Prague 1 (531 564). Metro Malostranská/12, 22, 23 tram. **Open** noon-6pm Tue-Sun; closed Mon. **No credit cards.** **Map** p305 E4.

Conceived in 1990 to represent Czech artists, this small vaulted space in the heart of Malá Strana is the oldest private gallery in Prague and remains one of the most influential. Only Czech artists are shown. Exhibitions are consistently good and recent ones have included works by Petr Nikl, Jiří David, Karel Malich and Tomáš Cisařovský. Ring bell for entry.

Galerie Na Jánském vršku

Jánský vršek 15, Malá Strana, Prague 1 (533 9271/538 257). Metro Malostranská/12, 22, 23 tram. **Open** 10.30am-5.30pm Tue-Sun; closed Mon. **No credit cards.** **Map** p304 C3.

Focusing on Czech artists who translate the traditional Bohemian medium of glass from craft into modern art, this tiny, respected gallery specialises in fresh perspectives. Artists to look out for include Dana Zámečníková, Václav Cigler, František Vizner and Vladimír Kopecký.

Galerie NO.D

Dlouhá 33, Staré Město, Prague 1 (2482 8285). Metro Náměstí Republiky/5, 8, 14 tram. **Open** 2-8pm Tue-Sun; closed Mon. **No credit cards.** **Map** p307 K2.

Sharing premises with the Roxy club (*see p215*) is this newish space for occasional shows of experimental and digital work by young and otherwise obscure pioneers. You might just discover the next Nam June Paik here.

Gambra

Černínská 5, Hradčany, Prague 1 (2051 4527). 22, 23 tram. **Open** *Mar-Oct* noon-6pm Wed-Sun; closed Mon-Tue. *Nov-Feb* noon-6pm Sat, Sun; closed Mon-Fri. **No credit cards.** **Map** p304 A2.

Tucked away in a beautiful Hradčany street is one of the city's most interesting exhibitions. It's the gallery of the Czech surrealist movement and is part-owned by the cult hero of animated filmmaking, Jan Švankmajer (*see page 198* **The intimate pleasures of inanimate objects**). He has always said that his films are only a small part of his work as a surrealist: here you can see his other side, in lithographs and ceramics. The gallery emphasises group work, however, and equal importance is given to other members of the movement, classic and contemporary, such as Eva Medková, Karel Baron and Švankmajer's wife, Eva.

Gandy Galerie

Školská 7, Nové Město, Prague 1 (9623 3066). Metro Můstek/3, 9, 14, 24 tram. **Open** 1.30-6.30pm Tue-Fri; 10am-noon Sat; closed Sun, Mon. **No credit cards.** **Map** p308 J6.

Deals in known western artists, especially French ones, as it's owned by a Frenchwoman. Also hosts minor exhibitions by not-so-minor names such as Lydia Lunch and Nan Goldin.

Czech Fund for Art Foundation

The following galleries have exhibitions sponsored by this organisation (Nadace Český fond umění), always of contemporary artists. The quality of the work varies enormously, but entry tends to be cheap and the venues are usually worth a visit. Direct purchases from the artists can usually be arranged through the galleries.

Galerie Václava Špály

Národní třída 30, Nové Město, Prague 1 (2494 6738). Metro Národní třída/6, 9, 18, 21, 22, 23 tram. **Open** 10am-1pm, 2-6pm, Tue-Fri; 1pm-6pm Sat, Sun; closed Mon. **Admission** 20 Kč; 10 Kč students. **No credit cards.** **Map** p306 H5.

This gallery has been going for 40 years in its present incarnation. It comprises two floors of exhibition space, plus a basement for young artists. Group shows, such as a recent one by the satirical political collective, Podebal, are a speciality.

Nová síň

Voršilská 3, Nové Město, Prague 1 (292 046). Metro Národní třída/6, 9, 18, 21, 22, 23 tram. **Open** 11am-6pm Tue-Sun; closed Mon. **Admission** 20 Kč; 10 Kč students. **No credit cards.** **Map** p308 H6.

A single bright, clean room tucked away in a building close to Národní třída. The excellent lighting makes it a great place to view work by contemporary Czech artists. Samplers of their output, along with the latest issues of art magazines *Umělec* and *Divus*, crowd the rack at the entrance.

Výstavní síň Mánes

Masarykovo nábřeží 250, Nové Město, Prague 1 (295 577). Metro Karlovo náměstí/17, 21 tram/176 bus. **Open** 10am-6pm Tue-Sun; closed Mon. **Admission** 25 Kč; 15 Kč concessions; children free. **No credit cards.** **Map** p308 G7.

The largest and most important of the foundation's galleries is also a beautiful piece of functionalist architecture built by Otakar Novotný in 1930. This riverside gallery, home to the Mánes Graphic Artists Society, usually hosts two exhibitions at the same time, anything from international travelling shows to those of classic and contemporary Czech artists. If present trends continue, the gallery will again become the vibrant centre it used to be. Be sure to look up at the cubist ceiling frescoes on the lower ground floor.

Photography galleries

In photography, the long and admirable Czech tradition is carried on today by practitioners such as Josef Koudelka and Jindřich Streit. The **Czech Photography Centre** and **Prague House of Photography** regularly show the best of the lot.

Czech Photography Centre

České centrum fotografie
Náplavní 1, Nové Město, Prague 2 (296 587). Metro Karlovo náměstí/17, 21 tram. **Open** 11am-7pm daily. **Admission** 60 Kč **No credit cards.** **Map** p308 G7.

A fairly small but well-lit space with consistently compelling work by such diverse talents as Manhattan newshound Bedřich Grunzweig, Czech parodists of American billboards and early Russian silver plate pioneers.

Josef Sudek Gallery

Úvoz 24, Hradčany, Prague 1 (5753 1489). Tram 22, 23. **Open** 10am-noon, 1-6pm, Tue-Sun; closed Mon. **Admission** 10 Kč; 5 Kč students. **No credit cards.** **Map** p304 B3.

The father of Czech photography almost seems to be hanging about the corners in this, his former studio. It is now an exhibition space for his still lifes, diffracted light studies and classic Prague vignettes.

Prague House of Photography

Pražský dům fotografie
Haštalská 1, Staré Město, Prague 1 (2481 0779). Metro Náměstí Republiky/5, 8, 14 tram. **Open** 11am-6pm daily. **Admission** 20 Kč. **No credit cards.** **Map** p306 J2.

The peripatetic PHP seems to have settled in an Old Town courtyard. With luck, it may recreate its early 1990s glory days, when it helped publicise Czech photography through shows and workshops.

Gay & Lesbian

Prague's gay scene is either hardcore orgy or tea and sympathy.
There ain't no middle ground.

Prague's queer scene is not terribly visible to the
untrained eye – but then it's rare for Czechs of
any persuasion to parade their personal side
in public. This old habit dates back to the city's
history of oppression and repression: standing
out in any way was to ask for trouble before 1989.
These days a traditional macho beerhall ethic
prevails on the face of things, certainly, but
no one is stamping down on anything except
the dancefloor. Thus the city's gay and lesbian
awakening, like most things important to
Praguers, grows steadily just out of the limelight.
You must press buzzers on heavy doors to
get into many of the city's gay venues, but once
inside the vibe is mellow and raucous.

GOING DOWN

Of course there are other things going on behind
these doors than mere social drinking. A number
of clubs are pretty hardcore, such as Drake's,
Escape to Paradise and Tunel, and all are
involved in male prostitution, some with little
else to offer. The age of consent in the Czech
Republic is 15 and no one is doing much about the
growing number of German sex tourists being
serviced by Prague street kids.

More sophisticated and subtle (though not *too*
subtle) gay scenes are to be found at most of the
other venues listed below. The only significant
lesbian venue is Žižkov's **A Club**, but a number
of social and support groups orbit around it.

Tasteful, mixed, gay-friendly venues include
the **Érra Café** (*see page 148*), and anything else
by restaurateur Roman Řezníček, whose heavily
stylised **Palffy Palác** (*see page 135*), and
Mecca (*see page 228*) have an easy-going and
loyal clientele.

Begin exploring the Prague gay scene at
**www.gayguide.net/Europe/Czech/
Prague**. This online newsletter, classifieds
serviceand booking agent is up-to-date on
gay accommodation, tours and general city
information. They claim to reply to every email
within 48 hours.

Once in town, look for the monthly gay guide
Amigo, with classified ads in Czech and other
languages. Amigo also publishes *Maxxx*, a
monthly 'gay erotický magazín' with hundreds
of personal ads, all in Czech. *Promluv* and *Alia*
are general-interest lesbian magazines,
irregularly published, available at A Club.

Accommodation

Arco Guesthouse

*Voroněžská 24, Vršovice, Prague 10 (7174
0734/www.gayguide.net/praha/Arco). Metro Náměstí
Míru/4, 16, 22, 23 tram.* **Rates** 950 Kč-1,400 Kč
double. 1,700-1,900 Kč apartments. **Open** *Reception*
8am-midnight daily. *Restaurant* 8am-midnight Mon-
Fri; 2pm-midnight Sat, Sun. **Main courses** 200-300
Kč. **No credit cards**.

Just on the edge of Vinohrady, the city's centre of
gay life, the helpful Arco places guests in private
apartments that it maintains. The restaurant is one
of the best in town. Reservations advised.

Ron's Rainbow Guesthouse

*Bulharská 4, Vršovice, Prague 10 (0604 876 694
mobile/www.gayguide.net/praha/Ron). Metro Národní
třída/6, 9, 18, 21, 22, 23 tram.* **Rates** 1,850-2,400 Kč
double. **No credit cards**.

The Rainbow comprises four comfortable apartments in residential Prague bordering Žižkov, one
with whirlpool – and Ron is always at your service.
Reservations required.

AIDS

ČSAP

*Dům Světla, Malého 3, Karlín, Prague 8 (2481
4284/helpline 2481 0702/web.telecom.cz/AIDS-pomoc).
Metro Florenc/8, 24, 52 tram.* **Open** 8am-6pm Mon-Fri;
closed Sat, Sun.

ČSAP is the Czech Organisation for AIDS preven-
tion and for the support of people with HIV and
AIDS. They also operate the Lighthouse project,
which administers to the same community.

KHS

Krajská hygienická stanice
*Dittrichova 17, Nové Město, Prague 2 (0800 144
4444). Metro Karlovo náměstí/3, 7, 10, 14, 16, 17
tram.* **Open** *Helpline* 1pm-6pm Mon-Fri. *HIV tests*
8am-noon Mon-Fri; closed Sat, Sun. **Map** p308 G8.
Free and anonymous HIV tests and condoms.

Nemocnice Bulovka AIDS Centrum

*Budínova 2, Libeň, Prague 8 (6608 2629). Tram 12,
14, 24.* **Open** *Testing* 8am-noon Mon-Fri; closed Sat,
Sun. **No credit cards**.

State hospital with a dedicated AIDS ward and
clinic. Anonymous testing and English-speaking
doctors, though not necessarily staff. Temporary
health insurance, available through the Central
Health Insurance Office (*see p279*) is accepted.

Hands up who wants to be **Friends**. *See p209.*

Associations

The **Lesbian Klub Lambda Prague**, **Promluv** and **Kruh A Klub** are lesbian organisations all based at A Club, and offer various degrees of support, exchange, resources and socialising.

Project Šance

Ve Smečkách 28, Nové Město, Prague 1 (222 11 797/ 0602 229 395 mobile). Metro Můstek/3, 9, 14, 24 tram. **Open** 4-8pm Tue. **Map** p309 K6.
Outreach project for male prostitutes that's always in need of donations.

SOHO

Sdružení organizací homosexuálních občanů v ČR
Senovážné náměstí 2, Nové Město, Prague 1 (2422 3811/0601 213 840 mobile/www.gay.cz/soho). Metro Náměstí Republiky/5, 8, 14 tram. **Open** only by appointment. **Map** p307 L4.
The Association of Organisations of Gay Citizens in the Czech Republic brings together 30 gay organisations from all over the country. *Gaycko* magazine lists activities throughout the country. SOHO also organises several special events.

Bars, pubs & clubs

Many of these bars claim to be 'members only' in order to keep out undesirables but are not about to turn away good customers. Just look in the know, and you'll be let in.

A Club

Milíčova 25, Žižkov, Prague 3 (2278 1623/www.mrfetish.cz/aclub). Tram 5, 9, 26, 55, 58/Bus 133, 207. **Open** 7pm-3am daily. **Admission** free Mon-Thur; 25Kč Fri; 50Kč Sat. **No credit cards. Map** p311 C1.
'A' for effort. This rose-hued lesbian bar with a microscopic dancefloor hosts women-only nights on Fridays and occasional poetry readings and performances. Lots of girl-power art on the walls.

Alcatraz

Bořivojova 58, Žižkov, Prague 3 (no phone). Metro Jiřího z Poděbrad/11, 55, 58. **Open** 9.30pm-4am Tue-Sun; closed Mon. **Admission** 100Kč. **No credit cards. Map** p311 B2/C2.
Modern sex club. Uniforms, rubber and leather.

Club Stella

Lužická 10, Vinohrady, Prague 2 (2425 7869). Metro Náměstí Míru, 4, 22, 23, 34, 57 tram. **Open** 8pm-5am daily. **Admission** free. **No credit cards. Map** p311 B3.
Candle light and second-hand sofas. Very cosy place to hang out at night. You have to be buzzed through one of those security doors.

Drake's

Petřínská 5, Smíchov, Prague 5 (534 909). Metro Anděl/6, 9, 12, 22, 57, 58 tram. **Open** 24 hrs daily. **Admission** 500Kč. **No credit cards.**
A Prague sex industry veteran. The high admission, good for 24 hours, makes this a venue for

tourists rather than locals. It features 20 booths with videos and more in a downstairs equipped with glory holes. Daily strip shows at 9pm and 11pm. Escort service.

Escape to Paradise

V Jámě 8, Nové Město, Prague 1 (0602 403 744 mobile). Metro Můstek/3, 9, 14, 24 tram. **Open** *Restaurant* 7pm-3am daily. *Disco* 10pm-5am daily. **Admission** free before 9pm, then 70 Kč. **No credit cards.** Map p309 K6.

Recently opened in a former straight bordello off Wenceslas Square, this passable restaurant leaves nothing to subtlety: strip shows, go-go dancers, sex shows and an escort service are on the menu.

Fajn Bar

Dittrichova 5, Nové Město, Prague 2 (2491 7409). Metro Karlovo náměstí/3, 7, 10, 14, 16, 17 tram. **Open** 1pm-1am Mon-Fri, 2pm-1am Sun; closed Sat. **Admission** free. **No Credit cards.** Map p308 G8.

A throwback to Prague of the 1970s, both musically and in terms of its no longer so young clientele. A place to meet Czech gays with a sense of humour.

Friends

Náprstkova 1, Staré Město, Prague 1 (2163 5408/ www.friends-prague.cz). Metro Národní třída/6, 9, 18, 21, 22, 23, 51, 54, 57, 58 tram. **Open** 4pm-3am daily. **Admission** free. **No credit cards.** Map p306 G4.

This comfortable stone-walled cellar video bar, operated by a Czech-American couple, is a good place to network and make friends. A relaxing favourite of many Prague visitors and expats.

Piano Bar

Milešovská 10, Žižkov, Prague 3 (6275 467). Metro Jiřího z Poděbrad/11, 51 tram. **Open** 5pm-3am daily. **Admission** free. **No credit cards.** Map p311 C2.

A low-key place with cheapish cold cuts and a piano no one ever seems to play. It's wall-to-wall with patrons all week and there's normally no overtly naughty activities.

Projdejna & Kafírna U českého pána

Kozí 13, Staré Město, Prague 1 (2328 283). Metro Staroměstská/17, 18 tram. **Open** 11am-10pm Mon-Fri; 2pm-10pm Sat, Sun. **No credit cards.** Map p306 J1/2.

Small bar in the centre of town that's very popular with Czech gays. This may be the best spot to gain an insight into Czech gay life.

Tunel

Plzeňská 41, Smíchov, Prague 5 (no phone). Metro Anděl/4, 7, 9, 10, 58 tram. **Open** 9.30pm-4am Tue-Sat; closed Mon, Sun. **Admission** 50 Kč minimum consumption. **No credit cards.**

Wannabe hardcore scene that targets leather, uniform and rubber fiends. Unfortunately, most of the clientele just wear street clothes while gawking at the video screens. You can leave as much of your clothing as you like at the coat check. At the back are toilets and a dark room with several beds.

U Střelce

Karolíny Světlé 12, Staré Město, Prague 1 (2423 8278). Metro Národní třída/6, 9, 18, 21, 22, 23, 51, 54, 57, 58 tram. **Open** 9.30pm-2am Wed, Fri, Sat; closed Mon, Tue, Thur, Sun. **Admission** 100-500 Kč. **No credit cards.** Map p306 G5.

Home of the city's star transvestite show of the moment, the 'Butterflies', this is as much a place for straight couples looking for a laugh as for gays. Every other Thursday SOHO puts on a 'culture evening' with performances by Czech actors.

Cruising

Skate punks aren't the only ones practising their moves near the Metronome sculpture in Letná park (*see page 244*). Cruising also goes on after dark in the bushes by the Hanovský Pavilon restaurant at the south end of the park.

Petřín Hill is an amorous (and dark) park, for both straights and gays. There are plenty of remote bushes, but not that much activity. Hlavní nádraží, the railway station, is a magnet for male prostitution, especially in the Fantova kavárna, the coffee shop above the central passage. But trade here is scary-looking. Divoka Šárka park's naturist area by the lake, just north of the terminus of the 22 and 25 trams, is a popular, and more innocent, meeting scene.

Dance clubs

Gejzír

Vinohradská 40, Vinohrady, Prague 2 (2251 6036). Metro Náměstí Míru/11 tram. **Open** 6pm-4am Tue, Wed, Thur; 9pm-5am Fri, Sat; closed Sun, Mon. **Admission** free Tue, Wed, Thur and until 10.30pm Fri, Sat, then 100Kč minimum consumption. **No credit cards.** Map p309 M6/7.

The city's largest gay club is always crowded, and one of the best spots. Thursdays, Fridays and Saturdays are dancefloor nights with DJs, two bars and usually a show. Darkrooms downstairs.

Tom's Bar

Pernerova 4, Karlín, Prague 8 (2481 3802/ freeweb.coco.cz/tomsbar/index.htm). Metro Křižíkova/3, 24, 52 tram. **Open** 9pm-4am Fri, Sat; closed Mon-Thur, Sun. **No credit cards.**

Men-only bar and disco. The cellar houses a dancefloor, video room and a cavernous darkroom.

Restaurants

U starého songu

Štítného 27, Žižkov, Prague 3 (2278 2047). Tram 5, 9, 26, 56, 58. **Open** 6pm-midnight Mon-Thur; 6pm-2am Fri, Sat; closed Sun. **Main courses** 200-300 Kč. **No credit cards.** Map p311 C1.

A friendly neighbourhood restaurant in the Žižkov district that makes a brave stab at mixing Czech and Indonesian cuisine – with mixed results.

Arts & Entertainment

Just another 'culture evening' at **U střelce**. *See p 209.*

U kapra

Žatecká 7, Staré Město, Prague 1 (2481 3635). Metro Staroměstská/17, 18 tram. **Open** 11am-11am daily. **Main courses** 250-350 Kč. **No credit cards.** **Map** p306 H3.

A comfortably upmarket Czech kitchen, U Kapra is frequented by a regular clientele of gays and straights. The unobtrusive music, summer garden and wine cellar are popular and mean reservations are usually necessary.

Saunas

Sauna Babylonia

Martinská 6, Staré Město, Prague 1 (2423 2304). Metro Národní třída, Můstek/6, 9, 18, 21, 22, 51, 54, 57, 58 tram. **Open** 2pm-3am daily. **Admission** 200 Kč. **No credit cards.** **Map** p306 H5.

Popular large sauna with steam rooms , whirlpool, fitness equipment, videos and private cabins.

Sauna Marco

Lublaňská 17, Nové Město, Prague 2 (292 307). Metro IP Pavlova/4, 6, 11, 16, 22, 34, 51, 56, 57 tram. **Open** 2pm-3am daily. **Admission** 180 Kč. **No credit cards.** **Map** p309 L8/10.

Not very crowded, but recommended. A good place if you like it hot and steamy.

Shops

City Fox

Seifertova 3, Žižkov, Prague 3 (6284 756). Metro Hlavní nádraží/3, 22 tram. **Open** 11am-10pm daily. **No credit cards.** **Map** p311 B1.

All the usual videos and paraphernalia.

Lambda City Man

Krakovská 2, Nové Město, Prague 1 (9623 0015). Metro Muzeum and Můstek. **Open** 2pm-8pm daily. **No credit cards.** **Map** p309 K6/7.

Videos, toys and gels just off Wenceslas Square.

Special Events

Aprilfest

Various venues (information aprilfest@post.cz). **Date** April.

The republic's biggest lesbian gathering. Workshops, discussions, films, exhibition and more.

Candlelight March

Various venues (information 2422 3811/0601 213 840 mobile/www.gay.cz/soho). **Date** June-Aug.

Several times every summer since 1989, candlelight vigils have been held by an international gathering of gays at different places in the Czech Republic. Organised by SOHO.

Gay Men of the Czech Republic

Various venues (information 2422 3811/0601 213 840 mobile/www.gay.cz/soho). **Date** June-Aug.

The year 2001 will mark the tenth anniversary of this annual gathering of gay groups from all over the country. Films, exhibitions, workshops and more. Organised by SOHO.

Parník

Central Wharf, south of Jirásek Bridge, Nové Město, Prague 2 (information 6846 548/ 0602 641 274 mobile/www.amigo.cz). **Date** June-Sept. **Map** p308 G8.

The good ship lollipop of the Prague gay scene holds semi-regular party cruises down the Vltava, organised by *Amigo*.

Arts & Entertainment

Music: Rock, Roots & Jazz

Folk-influenced jazz or rocking Roma sounds, digital breakbeats or Czech golden oldies – live music in Prague is defiantly diverse.

While Prague is no hotbed of live rock, there's an undeniable soulfulness to the sounds you'll hear in cellar clubs all over town. Slavic folk ballads inform and inspire sax solos while Romany influences are increasingly sprinkled throughout Prague rock. This process is being helped along by increasingly regular Roma music festivals, the biggest of which is Respekt (respekt.inway.cz; *see page 188*), and the popularity of Gypsy folk group Alom. Meanwhile the old stalwarts of Czech rock – once dissident, now merely broke and obscure – play on as they always have: Už jsme doma, Filip Topol (brother of the once *samizdat* now merely broke writer Jáchym) and a whole array of jazzmen tend to produce introspective, moody sounds punctuated with squawks of pain – it makes a night out something to savour.

The digital revolution found its way to Prague and is having a huge impact. This after Czech rock, so long underground, found itself little changed after the Velvet Revolution – and was still kept off the racks by the same Czech pop that had been tolerated under communism, but now also had to compete with the Red Hot Chili Peppers and Pet Shop Boys too.

The search for alternatives led to digital solutions that have sparked up the whole scene. These days home-grown, and often home-recorded, tracks can be heard on the floor of **Roxy**, **Radost** (*see pages 144, 159 and 228*), the new **CZ Beat** (*see page 225*) and state-of-the-art **Futurum** (*see page 225*). Their producers can man the decks, meet Dave Angel, and gather an overnight following of Czechs and foreigners who have no problem making out their lyrics. Two of the republic's more interesting digital dance acts are Ecstasy of St Theresa, who have been signed by EMI, and Ohm Square (*see page 214* **Ohm sweet Ohm**). Both of these bands appear on the soundtrack of *Samotáři* (*Loners*), Prague's indie film hit of 2000.

Crowds have responded to the new flavour by turning out in greater force than anyone's seen since the First Republic party days. Year-round raves, the most epic of which are promoted by Radio 1 DJ Josef Sedloň's busy Lighthouse Promotions (*see page 230* **Lighthouse & heavy techno**), take over underground parking lots in winter and meadows in summer.

Czech jazz has never brought in huge crowds, though it's had a stellar reputation for such a small country ever since the early days, when the RA Dvorský band heated up little cabarets all over Old Town. Posters from pre-war times show big and little bands at a dozen venues throughout the city, all boasting 'Americký' music delivered by real black players. The scene today is a pale shadow of what it was then, having been suppressed until 1989 as an insidious virus from the decadent West. But Saturday all-night sessions at **U Staré Paní** get hot and the **AghaRTA Jazz Festival** brings world-class talents such as Hiram Bullock or Maceo Parker to the **Lucerna Music Bar** in spring and summer.

Prague is also a great place to catch foreign rock, as the city's mystique attracts everyone from John Cale to Public Enemy and its cramped venues allow you to get up close and personal – but get your tickets early for big concerts.

To see what's coming up, check flyers at Roxy or Radost, or pick up *Think* magazine or *The Prague Post* (www.praguepost.cz).

Tickets & information

Tickets should be booked in advance for big-name concerts. For the smaller, funkier ones you'll need to buy directly from the venue.

Ticketpro

Old Town Hall, Staroměstské náměstí, Staré Město, Prague 1 (14051/www.ticketpro.cz). Metro Staroměstská. **Open** 9am-7pm Mon-Fri; 9am-6pm Sat-Sun. **Credit** AmEx, MC V. **Map** p306 H3/J3.
Advance booking for major commercial concerts and numerous smaller events. The automated toll-free number above works for all branches (when it works at all – it doesn't with old Czech analogue phones), which can be found at Prague Information Service offices and hotels citywide.
Branches: Štěpánská 61 (Lucerna passage), Nové Město, Prague 1 (14051); Rytířská 31 Staré Město, Prague 1 (2161 0162); Salvátorská 10, Staré Město, Prague 1 (2481 4020).

Venues

Enormous gigs

Prague's largest venue is **Stadium Strahov**, graced in the past by President Havel's mates, the Rolling Stones, as well as Pink Floyd and Billy Idol. Shows are far more frequent at **Výstaviště** (good enough for Bowie), though the sound quality at both is appalling.

Congress Centre

Kongresové centrum
5. května 65, Vyšehrad, Prague 4 (6117 1111). Metro Vyšehrad.
The former Palace of Culture has changed its name in an effort to make over its past as a Communist Party convention facility. It has also installed better sound and lights, but concerts here still tend to feel institutional – in the main hall, overstuffed seats allow no room for dancing.

Stadium Strahov

Diskařská 100, Břevnov, Prague 6 (539 951-9). Tram 22 to Újezd, then cable car, or 132, 143, 149, 176 bus. **Map** p304 A5.
Prague's largest stadium can take a staggering 200,000 people. Special bus services for big gigs.

Výstaviště Sportovní hala

U Výstaviště, Holešovice, Prague 7 (2010 3111). Metro Nádraží Holešovice/5, 12, 17 tram. **Map** p310 D1.
Officially known as the Sport Hall, this barn has all the acoustics you'd expect from such. Only indoor spot in Prague that can accommodate thousands.

Small to middling gigs

Akropolis

Kubelíkova 27, Žižkov, Prague 3 (2271 2283/www.spinet.cz/akropolis). Metro Jiřího z Poděbrad/5, 9, 11, 26, 55, 58 tram. **Open** *concerts start* 7.30pm. **Admission** 100-250 Kč. **No credit cards.** **Map** p311 B2.
This club's Jazz Meets World series promotes a rich array of world beat, dub, roots and avant-garde acts, from Algerian nomad music to the Klezmatics. The downstairs *divadelní* (theatre) bar offers nightly DJs and MCs free of charge. The main basement stage, a tatty former cinema, has lights and sound as good as any in Prague to accommodate groups you won't find anywhere else. New bars keep opening downstairs in a kind of subterranean labyrinth of drinking and a greasy spoon operates at street level (*see also p129 and 159*).

Lucerna Music Bar

Vodičkova 36, Nové Město, Prague 1 (2421 7108). Metro Můstek/3, 9, 14, 24, 52, 53, 55, 56 tram. **Open** *concerts start* 9pm. **Admission** *concerts* 60-300 Kč. **No credit cards.** **Map** p307 K5.
In the faded 1920s Lucerna passage off Wenceslas Square, this bar and concert space attracts big-time

jazz masters such as Wynton Marsalis but also books such local 'Louie Louie' bands as Brutus, who can't hit a straight note. Wood-panelled balconies and white tablecloths remain from its pre-war days of Josephine Baker shows.

Lucerna Great Hall

Vodičkova 36, Nové Město, Prague 1 (no phone). Metro Můstek/3, 9, 14, 24, 52, 53, 55, 56 tram. **Open** *concerts start* 8pm. **Admission** 200-700 Kč. **No credit cards.** **Map** p307 K5.
Run independently of the Lucerna Music Bar (*above*), this vast underground performance hall hosts big-time acts from Lou Reed to The Cardigans. Its art nouveau balconies, marble stairs and wooden floors add a palatial feel to rock shows. Acoustics are lousy but, though it feels big, you're always in reasonably close contact with the band. It has no regular box office hours.

Kumštát

Řetězová 3, Stare Město, Prague 1 (602 276 562). Metro Můstek/3, 9, 14, 24 tram. **Open** 11am-11pm daily. **Admission** 100-500 Kč. **No credit cards.** **Map** p306 H4.
This 'centre for mystic and ritual art' is actually a trippy patio venue for Renaissance troubadours, baroque lute concerts and, naturally, beer. The House of the Lords of Kunštát and Poděbrady (*see p94*) has important Romanesque caverns but the main appeal is live music at 8pm in the garden. You won't find this place accidentally – look for the gate as you amble down the narrow Old Town street.

Malostranská beseda

Malostranské náměstí 21, Malá Strana, Prague 1 (539 024). Metro Malostranská/12, 22, 57 tram. **Open** 2pm-1am daily. *Concerts start* 9.30pm. **Admission** 40-80 Kč. **No credit cards.** **Map** p305 E3.
Surprisingly classy rock and roots bands grace this faded glory, plus the occasional retro jazz act. Bottled beer is the only drawback to an otherwise welcoming, well-worn bar and adjacent dance room. Battered wood surfaces and windows overlooking Malá Strana's main square add appeal. Well-stocked jazz and alternative CD shop.

Meloun

Michálská 12, Staré Město, Prague 1 (2423 0126). Metro Můstek/3, 9, 14, 24, 51, 52, 53, 54, 55, 56, 57, 58 tram. **Open** 11am-3am daily; *concerts start* 9pm. **Admission** 60-100 Kč. **No credit cards.** **Map** p306 H4.
Mixing blues, disco, cover bands and occasional film screenings, this rambling cellar pub covers all bases. The serviceable garden pub offers traditional Czech schnitzels and the like.

Rock Café

Národní třída 20, Nové Město, Prague 1 (2491 4416/www.radio.cz/rock-cafe). Metro Národní třída/6, 9, 18, 22, 51, 54, 57, 58 tram. **Open** 10pm-3am Mon-Fri; 8pm-3am Sat, Sun. **Admission** 60-300 Kč. **No credit cards.** **Map** p306 H5.

Lucerna Music Bar. *See p212.*

Ohm sweet Ohm

Prague's hottest drum 'n' bass act are not often be found playing live – so if you see **Ohm Square** on a flyposter anywhere, drop your other plans for that evening and get to the gig.

Their album *Scion* is heard often enough, though. In summer 2000, all you needed to do to catch its lead track, 'Jam #3', and the sassy MCing of Charlie 1 (aka Charlotte Fairman, *pictured*, an expat Essex girl) was to tune into Radio 1 (91.9FM). Meanwhile the work of her bandmate Jan 2 (or Čechtický to his mum) is audible on any of the steady string of hits to stream out of the East Authentic studio in Žižkov. Ohm Square's other programmer, Dušan Only 1, is also a busy remixer and guitarist about town.

But collectively, with keyboards/bass man Jan 5, the band members are mostly just seen by each other, in the studio. They spend most of their time mixing up tight digital rhythms with Charlie 1's spooky lyrics. Then hunting for inspiration in grotty pubs or on night trams.

Ohm Square bridge the gap between expat bands, who tend to be upbeat and are usually modelled on distant Western icons, and Czech bands, who tend to brood and grope in introspective darkness. By contrast, Ohm

Square has both upbeat, danceable qualities and a kind of noir ethos of disorientation, melancholy and angst.

That's one reason they're in such demand, with two movie soundtrack deals just in the first six months of 2000. *Scion*, Ohm Square's most recent album, mixed at London's Strange Weather Studios, built on a following they had established in 1997 with their first album *Ohmophonica*.

The band got its start in 1995 when Czech jungle stars Ecstasy of St Theresa came across Fairman doing her act with Wubble U in London. Her rough but girlish voice sounded like just the touch that Ecstasy's friends back in Prague were looking for in getting a new group started. So Fairman moved to the Czech capital.

The instincts of Ecstasy programmer Jan P Muchow, himself a veteran of several Prague indie film soundtracks, proved spot on. Don't despair completely of catching them, though. Even if you don't happen upon Ohm Square members DJing at hardwired clubs like Futurum (see page 225) their two albums (both on the hardworking Next Era label) are always stocked at Bontonland (see page 181) on Wenceslas Square.

Ohm Square's Charlie 1.

Baroque around the clock at **Delux,** plus Czech jazz, Latino DJs and Thai curries. *See p216.*

Once a post-revolution rock pioneer, these days more of a backpacker hangout. Features daily rock documentaries and Czech 'revival' bands. Not much in the way of atmosphere.

Roxy

Dlouhá 33, Staré Město, Prague 1 (2481 0951). Metro Náměstí Republiky or Staroměstská/5, 14, 17, 18, 26, 51, 53, 54 tram. **Open** from 8pm daily. **Admission** *live acts* 150-350 Kč; *DJs* 80-250 Kč. **No credit cards. Map** p306 J3.

The crumbled Roxy is, along with Futurum (*see p225*), one of Prague's two crucial destinations for house, dub, and jungle. A refreshing stream of live acts from The Disciples to Wubble U also make appearances, while the cyber Gallery NO.D (*see p205*) and rock festivals like the Alternativa fill the subterranean labyrinth with art and fringe jazz. *Poupelka* (girls free) and Climax parties with local DJs such as Loutka or Chris Sadler pack the place with kids that probably should be in school. Sometimes closed on Mondays.

Jazz & blues

Prague's jazz history stretches back to the 1930s, when Jaroslav Ježek led an adored big band while colleague RA Dvorský established a standard of excellence that survived Nazi and communist oppression. Karel Velebný, of the renowned Studio 5 group, continued that tradition postwar, while Czech-Canadian novelist Josef Škvorecký chronicled the eternal struggle of Czech sax men in book after book.

These days, the jazz scene occupies a lower echelon of the club world, but a corps of talented players works the city circuit – to such an extent that you'll find the same half-dozen top combos in any venue you choose. A handful have managed to release original works on CD through the **AghaRTA** label and club. 'Creative isolation' is a favoured phrase among those who perpetually jam at **U staré paní** but seem unable to get far beyond the borders.

Arts & Entertainment

Blues is a relative newcomer to Prague but has quickly acquired a dedicated contemporary following. Concerts by the likes of BB King invariably fill the city's biggest halls. Among local 12-bar practitioners watch out for guitarman Spyder and Luboš Andršt, both of whom play frequent gigs around town.

AghaRTA

Krakovská 5, Nové Město, Prague 1 (2221 1275). Metro Muzeum or IP Pavlova/4, 6, 16, 22, 34 tram. **Open** *July-Aug* 7pm-1am daily. *Sept-June* 5pm-midnight daily; *concerts start* 9pm. **Admission** around 80 Kč. **No credit cards. Map** p306 K6.

Named after Miles Davis's most controversial LP, this club off Wenceslas Square is one of Prague's best spots for modern jazz and blues. A fairly even mix of Czechs and foreigners mingle in the relatively small but comfortable space – perfect for sitting back and enjoying solo performances from artists such as flautist Jiří Stivín. As at many Prague jazz clubs, there's a CD shop selling local recordings for 150-400 Kč. Look for releases on the club's own ARTA label.

Delux

Václavské náměstí 4, Nové Město, Prague 1 (9624 9444/www.delux.cz). Metro Můstek/3, 9, 14, 24 tram. **Open** 6pm-midnight Mon-Wed; 6pm-2am Thu-Sat; 6pm-midnight Sun. **Admission** 100 Kč (free with dinner). **No credit cards. Map** P306 J5.

Deep under Wenceslas Square, one of the city's best jazz holes is hidden away in what looks like an imperial bedroom. The baroque red and gold setting frames a little stage on which local jazzmeisters such as Najponk jam a dinner featuring some of the city's finest Thai cuisine (*see p144*). Afterwards, DJs take over entertainment duties until the wee hours, going Latin on Fridays and Saturdays. A trip, to say the least.

Jazz Club Železná

Železná 16, Staré Město, Prague 1 (no phone). Metro Můstek. **Open** 3pm-midnight daily. **Admission** 70 Kč. **No credit cards. Map** p306 J3.

The music at Jazz Club Železná is finally catching up with its prime location off Old Town Square. This is a fun cellar, with low prices and an excellent CD shop. Sunday 'Ethno' nights fill the space with conga beats and reggae while Latino nights spice up the more traditional midweek jazz programme with salsa rhythms.

Reduta

Národní třída 20, Nové Město, Prague 1 (2491 2246). Metro Národní třída/6, 9, 18, 22, 51, 54, 57, 58 tram. **Open** 9pm-midnight daily; *box office* 3-9pm Mon-Fri; 5-9pm Sat; 7-9pm Sun. **Admission** 120 Kč. **No credit cards. Map** p306 H5.

That Bill Clinton once played sax here to entertain Václav Havel hardly makes up for the steep cover, bland repertoire and dreary interior. Even so, some of the best musicians in town often sit in with the evening's band.

Sputnik

Pařížská 6, Staré Město, Prague 1 (2481 3605). Metro Staroměstská/17, 18 tram. **Open** 6pm-1am daily; *concerts start* 9pm. **Admission** 90 Kč. **Map** p306 H3.

Warehousey basement blues bar awash in cheap Pilsner Urquell. Local bands test their mettle here, so you take your chances. The sandwich board out front, just a few metres east of Old Town Square, signals the hidden entrance.

U Malého Glena

Karmelitská 23, Malá Strana, Prague 1 (535 8115). Metro Malostranská/12, 22, 57 tram. **Open** 10am-2am daily. **Admission** 100 Kč. **No credit cards. Map** p305 D4.

Intimate jazz trios somehow sound wonderful in the closet-sized basement beneath the rowdy main floor café (*see p155*). This despite a terrible sound system, about six tables, rock-hard seats and noise from above. Veteran Czech players such as Roman Pokorný, along with rising stars, here meld impressive grooves with a minimum of pretension.

U staré paní

Michalská 9, Staré Město, Prague 1 (264 920/267 267). Metro Můstek. **Open** 7pm-4am daily; *concerts start* 9pm. **Admission** 160 Kč. **Credit** AmEx, MC, V. **Map** p305 H4.

Doubling as a decent restaurant, this Old Town hotel is a late-night favourite with top local players. After performing for the tourists, they come here for informal all-night jams on Saturdays. Though the high cover charge alienates most locals, this remains a top spot for serious jazz.

Ungelt Jazz & Blues Club

Týn 2 (enter from Týnská ulička), Staré Město, Prague 1 (2489 5748). Metro Můstek/3, 9, 14, 24 tram. **Open** noon-midnight daily. **Admission** 100-150 Kč, 50-100 Kč students. **No credit cards. Map** p306 J3.

Prague's newest jazz club is a bit too close to Old Town Square to get very near the musical edge, but is nonetheless an appealingly relaxed cellar in which to catch a session and a Pilsener.

Folk/country & western

Folk and C&W connect with the Czech rural heritage. The 'trampers'– avid practitioners of hiking and camping – romanticise the American cowboy lifestyle (*see page 187* **Carry on kempink**). Those consigned to block housing and jobs five days a week come alive on Friday night to act out their Marlboro Man fantasies.

První Prag Country Saloon Amerika

Korunní 101, Vinohrady, Prague 2 (2425 6131). Metro Náměstí Míru/16 tram. **Open** 6pm-11pm Mon; 11am-midnight Tue-Sat; 5pm-11pm Sun. **Admission** free. **No credit cards. Map** p311 B3.

The place for an all-Czech cowboy fiddle jam. Ranch house benches, big ol' steaks and six-shooters on the waiting staff add up to a hootenanny of an evening. No music on Sundays.

Music:
Classical & Opera

Talented orchestras, incomparable settings and an awful lot of Mozart.

The Czech Philharmonic under Vladimir Ashkenazy, highlight of the **Prague Spring Festival**.

With three full-time opera theatres, four major orchestras and countless smaller ensembles, Prague should be able to offer an incredible range of classical options on any given night. A reluctance to take risks, however, leaves the repertoire limited to traditional Czech fare, albeit one performed by top quality musicians.

The shining exception, offering a vast range of both performers and pieces, is the **Prague Spring Festival**, easily the concert high point of the year. The event attracts the likes of Kurt Masur and the New York Philharmonic along with the best of a considerable array of Czech talents. The **Czech Philharmonic**, under the baton of **Vladimir Ashkenazy**, is a perennial star of the festival. Its recordings grow more

impressive each year, and lure guest conductors of the calibre of **Kent Nagano**.

The no less capable **Prague Symphony Orchestra** has a wider repertoire embracing 20th-century and non-European music, as well as a strong commitment to Russian symphonic works – **Maxim Shostakovich**, the composer's son, is an annual guest conductor.

Prague's third major ensemble, the **Radio Prague Symphony Orchestra**, lacks the notoriety of the above two but generally produces more than creditable performances of contemporary works. The **Prague Chamber Philharmonic**, founded and conducted by Prague Symphony Orchestra conductor **Jiří Bělohlávek**, is an excellent ensemble of

Arts & Entertainment

younger players that has recently risen to fame with a mix of the classics and the little-known.

Czech conductors such as Bělohlávek and **Libor Pešek** have established themselves on the international circuit, as have divas **Eva Urbanová, Dagmar Pecková** and **Magdalena Kožená**. All are likely to come home for the Prague Spring Festival.

If you happen to be hitting the city outside the festival's May-to-June dates, you've still got the autumn and winter seasons in which to catch the above orchestras at the same stunning performance venues used during the festival – the **Municipal House, Rudolfinum** and **National Theatre** are treats in themselves. This last, where Smetana scored the Czech national awakening with his opera *Libuše*, composed for the opening of the theatre in 1881, is a cultural cornerstone of the republic.

Don't be taken in by summer concert packages: every major symphony, orchestra and opera company shuts down at the end of June and goes on a two-month vacation just when audience potential is at its greatest.

The one company willing to perform in the summer is the small troupe that stages open-air opera in the **Lichtenstein Palace**. Their shows often sell out. Otherwise, it's strictly chamber recitals – though very good ones, as a rule – that are left for summer visitors.

Prague opera is, appropriately, dominated by histrionics as the two principal venues vie for attention. Increasing rivalry between the National Theatre and the **State Opera** often results in two different productions of the same opera on the same night, a strange extravagance in a city where state funding has decreased dramatically. Business sense is only slowly being learned in ensembles still operated by the state, where it was once unnecessary to think of the bottom line. To date, only the **Estates Theatre** has the acumen to rent itself out during the summer hiatus – to the **Opera Mozart** company, which fills the house with commercial productions of *Don Giovanni*.

Corporate sponsorship is catching on, however, filling concert programmes with portraits of company directors. Many small Prague ensembles, meanwhile, have become so good at making profits that they've inundated the city with cliché renditions of *A Little Night Music* and *The Four Seasons*, performed in every vacant church or palace in town – usually at prices above those for major concerts by any of the principal orchestras.

Works by Czech musical giants **Bedřich Smetana** and **Antonin Dvořák** are both regularly heard in the performance halls of Prague, particularly their celebrations of Bohemian folk traditions. The bolder, more

modern **Leos Janáček** and **Bohuslav Martinů** aren't so well represented, although Janáček's operas are given increasingly frequent airings at the National Theatre. **Josef Suk**, Dvořák's son-in-law and a late romantic, is another talented Czech composer, though only known in the West for the *Asrael* symphony. His heir, a violin virtuoso also named Josef, often performs and records in Prague. **Zdeněk Fibich**, a contemporary of Smetana and Dvořák, is another discovery whose lyrical piano pieces have been released extensively on the Czech classical label Supraphon. Several contemporary composers, such as **Petr Eben**, are also finding their voice, though performances of their work are more commercially risky and therefore infrequent.

Other little-known Czech composers were well-established long before the première of *Don Giovanni* in Prague in 1787 (the one landmark in Czech musical history that everyone seems to know). **Zelenka, Mysliveček, Benda, Černohorský** and **Brixi** are just a handful of those slighted by history. Ongoing research continues to uncover material from archives.

Tickets & information

As **Ticketpro** doesn't book for the biggest classical venues and most agencies that do hike prices dramatically for foreigners, it's best to buy directly from the venue's box office if you're already in Prague. Touts buy up all the remaining seats for popular shows so don't worry if something is 'sold out' – just wait around the entrance until the last minute when the touts have to sell or lose their investment. Prices for concerts vary and some (in the smaller churches) are free, but the cost is usually between 250 Kč and 600 Kč.

Information can be haphazard, but **Bohemia Ticket International** has an online calendar prepared months in advance and is willing to take your telephone order and credit card payment from abroad. Prague has a tradition of subscription evenings, so you may find certain glittering occasions difficult to get into.

Ticket agencies

Bohemia Ticket International

Malé náměstí 13, Staré Město, Prague 1 (2422 7832/fax 2161 2126/www.csad.cz/bti). Metro Můstek or Náměstí Republiky. **Open** 10am-7pm Mon-Fri; 10am-5pm Sat; 10am-3pm Sun. **Credit** AmEx, MC, V (fax orders only). **Map** p307 K4.

Best non-travel agency for buying tickets in advance from abroad for opera and concerts at the National Theatre, Estates Theatre and State Opera, plus other orchestral and chamber events. **Branch**: Na příkopě 16, Nové Město, Prague 1 (2421 5031).

High standards, stunning surrounds: **Rudolfinum**. *See p221.*

Čedok

*Na příkopě 18, Nové Město, Prague 1 (2419
7411/2419 7203). Metro Můstek or Náměstí
Republiky.* **Open** 9am-7pm Mon-Fri; 10am-2pm Sat;
closed Sun. **No credit cards. Map** p307 K4.
Tickets for various events, with some concerts.
Branches: Václavské náměstí. 53 Nové Město,
Prague 1 (2196 5240); Rytířská 16, Prague 1 (263 697).

Ticketpro

*Old Town Hall, Staroměstské náměstí, Staré
Město, Prague 1 (14051/www.ticketpro.cz). Metro
Staroměstská.* **Open** 9am-7pm Mon-Fri; 9am-6pm Sat,
Sun. **Credit** AmEx, MC V. **Map** p306 H3/J3.
Advance booking for major concerts and various
smaller events. The automated toll-free number
works for all branches – mostly found at Prague
Information Service offices and hotels.
Branch:, Štěpánská 61 (Lucerna passage), Nové
Město, Prague 1 (14051); Rytířská 31 Staré Město,
Prague 1 (2161 0162); Salvátorská 10, Staré Město,
Prague 1 (2481 4020).

Wolff Travel Agency

*Na příkopě 24, Nové Město, Prague 1 (2422 9153
2421 1964/fax 2422 8849). Metro Můstek or Náměstí
Republiky.* **Open** 9.30am-6.30pm Mon-Fri; 9am-1pm
Sat; closed Sun. **No credit cards. Map** p307 K4.
Tickets for the opera and chamber concerts.

Principal concert halls

Municipal House

Obecní dům
*Náměstí Republiky 5, Nové Město, Prague 1 (2200
2336/2200 2100). Metro Náměstí Republiky/5, 14, 26
tram.* **Open** box office 10am-6pm daily. **Tickets** 200-
1100 Kč. **Credit** AmEx, MC, V. **Map** p307 K3.
A stunning example of Czech art nouveau, the
Municipal House is built around the Smetana Hall,
home to the Prague Symphony Orchestra. The
orchestra launches the Prague Spring Festival here
every year, as it has for over half a century. Listen to
Smetana variations on folk tunes while gazing at
the ceiling mosaics of old Czech myths for an
authentic Bohemian national cultural experience.
(See also p34, 121 and 221.)

Rudolfinum

*Alšovo nábřeží 12, Staré Město, Prague 1 (2489 3352).
Metro Staroměstská/17 tram.* **Open** box office mid
Aug-mid July 10am-6pm Mon-Fri; closed Sat, Sun.
Mid July-mid Aug closed. **Tickets** 200-1,100 Kč.
No credit cards. Map p306 G2.
One of the most beautiful concert venues in Europe,
built in neo-classical style at the end of the 19th
century, the Rudolfinum has two halls: the Dvořák
Hall for orchestral works and major recitals, and
the Suk Hall for chamber, instrumental and solo
vocal music. Opinions are divided about the
acoustics of the Dvořák Hall, but the grandeur of
the building's interior – plus the high standard of
musicianship – make an evening here eminently
worthwhile. *See also p99.*

Other venues

Venues for chamber music and instrumental
recitals are legion. Practically every church and
palace offers concerts. Programming is mainly
from the baroque and classical repertoire, with
the emphasis on Czech music. The quality of
performance is usually of a high standard.

Basilica of St James

Bazilika sv. Jakuba
*Malá Štupartská 6, Staré Město, Prague 1 (no phone).
Metro Náměstí Republiky/5, 14, 26 tram.* **Open** 9am-
4pm daily. **Tickets** 200-400 Kč. **No credit cards.**
Map p306 J3.
A prime example of Czech baroque architecture,
with resounding organ acoustics and an over-the-
top façade of The Fall above the entrance. In
addition to large-scale sacred choral works, music
for Sunday mass (usually 10am) is impressive.

Bertramka

*Mozartova 169, Smíchov, Prague 5 (5731 8461).
Metro Anděl/4, 7, 9 tram.* **Open** 9.30am-6pm daily.
Tickets 350-550 Kč. **No credit cards.**
The house where Mozart stayed when in Prague is
now a museum devoted to him *(see page 122)* that
puts on regular concerts. Nearly all include at least
one work by the Austrian who has been all but
adopted into the Czech musical pantheon.

Chapel of Mirrors

Zrcadlová kaple
*Klementinum, Mariánské náměstí, Staré
Město, Prague 1 (2166 3111 ext 331). Metro
Staroměstská/5 tram.* **Open** 9am-4.30pm daily.
Tickets 200-500 Kč. **No credit cards. Map** p306 G4.
A pink marble chapel in the vast Clementinum com-
plex, featuring all manner of romantic, baroque and
original chamber recitals. Seemingly an age away
from the tourist hordes outside.

Church of St Nicholas

Chrám sv. Mikuláše
*Malostranské náměstí, Malá Strana, Prague 1 (536
983). Metro Malostranská/12, 22 tram.* **Open**
May-Sept 9am-4.30pm daily; Oct-Apr 9am-4pm
daily. *Concerts start* 6pm daily. **Tickets** 250-450 Kč.
No credit cards. Map p305 D3.
One of Prague's most celebrated churches, with a
stunning baroque interior. Irregular choral concerts and organ recitals are as grand as the setting
(see p32 and p83).

Church of St Nicholas

Kostel sv. Mikuláše
*Staroměstské náměstí, Staré Město, Prague 1 (no
phone). Metro Staroměstská.* **Open** 9am-6pm daily;
concerts start 8pm. **Tickets** 200-400 Kč. **No credit
cards. Map** p306 H3.
St Nicholas's hosts regular organ, instrumental
and vocal recitals, with an emphasis on baroque
music. A somewhat plain setting, having been
looted once or twice too often.

Church of St Simon & St Jude

Kostel sv. Šimona a Judy
Dušní and U Milosrdných, Staré Město, Prague 1
(232 1068). Metro Staroměstská/17 tram. **Open**
10am-6pm daily. **Tickets** 200-450 Kč. **No credit**
cards. Map p306 H2.

Renovated with cunning *trompe-l'oeil* work, this
deconsecrated church is a full-time venue for chamber music. The Prague Symphony Orchestra,
which also promotes selected ensembles, is responsible for the programming.

House of the Stone Bell

Dům U kamenného zvonu
Staroměstské náměstí 13, Staré Město, Prague 1
(2481 0036). Metro Staroměstská. **Open** 10am-6pm
Tue-Sun; closed Mon. **Tickets** 200-450 Kč. **No credit**
cards. Map p306 J3.

One of the oldest Gothic halls in Prague books concerts that range from Gregorian chants to contemporary music. *See also p31 and p92.*

Lobkowicz Palace

Lobkovický palác
Jiřská 3, Hradčany, Prague 1 (537 364/537 306).
Metro Malostranská/22 tram. **Open** 9am-5pm
Tue-Sun. **Tickets** 200-600 Kč. **No credit cards.**
Map p72.

Concerts of baroque and romantic chamber works
are held in the imposing banquet hall, with frescoes
by Fabián Harovník. (*See p77 and p118.*)

Lichtenstein Palace

Lichtenštejnský palác
Malostranské náměstí 13, Malá Strana, Prague 1
(5753 4205). Metro Malostranská/12, 22 tram.
Open 11am-7pm daily. **Tickets** 450-1500 Kč.
No credit cards. Map p305 E3.

Home of the Czech Academy of Music. Regular concerts are given in the Gallery and in the Martinů
Hall but the real star is the summer open-air series
of popular operas in the courtyard.

St Agnes's Convent

Klášter sv. Anežky české
U milosrdných 17, Staré Město, Prague 1 (2481
0828/2481 0835). Metro Staroměstská or Náměstí
Republiky/5, 14, 26 tram. **Open** 10am-6pm Tue-Sun;
closed Mon. **Tickets** 250-550 Kč. **No credit cards.**
Map p306 J1.

The acoustics in St Agnes's Convent are not without their critics, but the Gothic atmosphere and
high standard of chamber music – usually from the
classical, romantic and 20th-century repertoire,
with an emphasis on Smetana, Dvořák and Janáček
– makes this venue worth a visit. (*See also p31.*)

Opera

Estates Theatre

Stavovské divadlo
Ovocný trh 1, Staré Město, Prague 1 (info 2422
8503/box office 2421 5001). Metro Můstek. **Open** box
office mid Aug-mid July 10am-6pm Mon-Fri; 10am-

12.30pm, 3-6pm Sat, Sun. *Mid July-mid Aug* closed.
Tickets 690-1950 Kč. **No credit cards. Map** p306 J4.

A shrine for Mozart lovers, this is where *Don
Giovanni* and *La Clemenza di Tito* were first performed. The theatre was built by Count Nostitz in
1784; its beautiful dark blue and gold auditorium
was almost over-renovated after the Velvet
Revolution. The theatre began as the Prague home
of Italian opera, but in 1807 became the German
opera with Carl Maria von Weber as its musical
director (1813-17). Today much of the programming is given over to theatre but there is still regular opera here – including, of course, *Don Giovanni*.
(*See p32, p222 and p236.*)

National Theatre

Národní divadlo
Národní 2, Nové Město, Prague 1 (2491 3437/2490
1520). Metro Národní třída/6, 9, 17, 18, 22 tram.
Open box office Sept-June 10am-6pm Mon-Fri; 10am-
12.30pm, 3-6pm, Sat, Sun. July, Aug closed. **Tickets**
200-600 Kč. **No credit cards. Map** p308 G6.

Smetana was a guiding light behind the establishment of the National Theatre, a symbol of Czech
nationalism that finally opened in 1883 with a performance of his opera *Libuše*. In keeping with tradition, the theatre concentrates on Czech opera, the
core of the repertoire being works by Smetana and
Dvořák (including lesser known works such as
Dvořák's *The Devil and Kate* and Smetana's *The
Kiss*), together with some Janáček. Operas by non-Czech composers and some impressive ballets are
also performed – generally three major new productions a year. (*See p34, p109 and p237.*)

State Opera

Státní Opera
Wilsonova 4, Nové Město, Prague 2 (2422 7693/box
office 265 353). Metro Muzeum. **Open** box office mid
Aug-mid July 10am-5.30pm Mon-Fri; 10am-noon,
1-5.30pm Sat, Sun. *Mid July-mid Aug* closed. **Tickets**
200-600 Kč. **No credit cards. Map** p309 L6.

The State Opera (then the German Theatre) opened
in 1887. Music directors and regular conductors
included Seidl, Mahler, Zemlinský, Klemperer and
Szell, and the theatre was regarded as one of the
finest German opera houses outside Germany until
World War II. After the war it changed its name to
the Smetana Theatre and became the second house
of the National Theatre. Today it's a separate
organisation and presents the occasional bold contemporary opera alongside standards from the
Italian, German, French and Russian repertoires.

Festivals

The major event in the calendar is the **Prague
Spring Festival**, which runs from May to
June. Since the Velvet Revolution it has a much
stronger international flavour and ranks with
the Edinburgh Festival or the Proms in its ability
to attract first-class international performers.
Traditionally, the festival opens with Smetana's

Mozart touts: 'Quick, put your wig straight, there's another Japanese tour group coming.'

patriotic cycle of symphonic poems, *Má Vlast* (*My Country*), and concludes with Beethoven's Ninth. Many of the major events sell out quickly. It's best to obtain tickets from the **Prague Spring Festival Office**, rather than from agencies, which add a hefty mark-up. The office opens one month before the festival and there are two price ranges – one for tickets sold in Prague and one for those booked from abroad. If possible, get a Czech friend to buy them for you or wait until you get here.

Opera Mozart is Prague's best-promoted collection of tourist-orientated classical events. It has two components. **Mozart Open** takes over the Estates Theatre during the summer for a big-budget Mozart opera performed by foreigners (tickets cost a withering 690-1,950 Kč), and **The Best of Mozart** brings costumed arias, duets and snippets year-round to the **Smetana Museum** (*see page 122*).

Several summer festivals are held out of town, in popular spots like **Karlovy Vary** (*see p251*), **Mariánské Lázně** and **Český Krumlov** (*see p258*). Litomyšl and Hukvaldy, the respective birthplaces of Smetana and Janáček, celebrate

their music with summer galas. For more information contact PIS, the Prague Information Service (*see page 288*).

Prague Spring Festival Office

Hellichova 18, Malá Strana, Prague 1 (530 293/ 533 474/fax 536 040/www.festival.cz). Metro Malostranská/12, 22 tram. **Open** *Apr* 9am-6pm Mon-Fri; closed Sat, Sun. *May-Mar* closed. **Credit** AmEx, MC, V. **Map** p305 D4.
Buy your tickets here in person and save a fortune from agents' mark-ups. The office is only open in the month before the festival.

Opera Mozart

Žatecká 1, Staré Město, Prague 1 (232 2536/232 4189/www.mozart.cz). Metro Staroměstská/17, 18 tram. **Open** 9am-7pm daily. **Credit** MC, V. **Map** p306 H3.
Tickets for the Mozart Open and Best of Mozart events, and also for the **National Marionette Theatre**'s year-round puppet productions of *Don Giovanni* and *Yellow Submarine* (*see p239*) and the **Magic Theatre of the Baroque World**'s puppet theatre classics for foreign kids. Performances are at the Theatre on the Balustrade (*see p239*).

Arts & Entertainment

Nightlife

Discos and gambling dens, late-night pubs and budget bordellos, techno clubs and cellar lounge bars – enough to amuse even the most jaded of nighthawks.

Nobody looking for a good time late into the night should go unsatisfied in Prague. Dancing and bar-hopping options have multiplied in recent years, often at places that do double or triple duty as eateries and live music venues. **Mecca**, **Radost/FX** (*see pages144 and 159*) and **Delux** (*see pages 144 and 216*) all do a bit of everything, while the **Lucerna Music Bar** (*see page 212*) is split between DJs, rock and jazz bands.

Diversifying is probably wise, considering the state of nightlife politics. Opening a club is a risky business anywhere, but in Prague it's further complicated by the crowded architecture of the city centre: the only hope of finding enough dance space is to burrow underground or choose a site in a remote industrial district, as Mecca has done. Early-rising neighbours also hold much sway in the city, as it's very easy to call out the city's army of inspectors to truss up a club owner with municipal red tape. Thus you'll find music sometimes stopping dead at 10pm as managers plead with the audience to go on drinking quietly.

The nightlife venues listed here favour DJs more than live music; the bars included keep notably longer hours than those listed in *chapter* **Pubs & Bars**.

The places to find local star DJs, plus a sprinkling of international names, are Radost/FX, Mecca, **CZ Beat**, **Futurum**, and the **Roxy** (*see page 215*). **Karlovy Lázně** is the juggernaut DJ club of Prague, with a capacity exceeding 2,200 – a bit deceptive, as they have to divide themselves among four floors, each featuring a different dance genre.

Smaller holes featuring more out-there sounds include **Wakata** and the Divadelní bar of the **Akropolis** club (*see pages 129, 159 and 212*). Old Town's eerie back streets conceal some of the best hideaways in the city, such as **Železné dveře**, which take groovy atmosphere as seriously as they do their drink selection.

Clearly not everyone is looking for well-mixed Martinis and sounds: the Czech sex industry is growing bigger every year, fuelled mostly by German tourists. In mid-2000 a campaign was begun to have German border guards provide drivers entering the Czech Republic with leaflets on child pornography and prostitution problems in Prague. The sex clubs listed here are adults-only (on both sides of the business). They operate openly but are technically on the fringes of the law.

La Comedia – Latino dance parties, fierce action, and lessons during the day. *See p227.*

Futurum – best house in Bohemia.

Another legal point to consider is the absurd Czech drug laws: police have the discretion to arrest anyone in possession of 'more than a little' of some controlled substance. It then seems to take them forever to bring charges, let alone bring people to trial. The jails are full of people yet to be convicted of anything at all.

High rollers will find Wenceslas Square teeming with casinos, though none as classy as the **Palais Savarin**. Fans of lowlife, on the other hand, will feel comfortable in Prague's ubiquitous *herna* bars, smoky dives lined with electronic one-armed bandits.

When planning your night out, remember that any tram numbered in the 50s is a night tram.

Clubs

Bílý koníček
Staroměstské náměstí 20, Staré Město, Prague 1 (2422 0947). Metro Staroměstská/17, 18, 51, 54 tram. **Open** 5pm-4am daily. *Disco* 9pm-5am daily. **Admission** 30 Kč. **No credit cards. Map** p306 J3.
Billed as 'Prague's oldest disco', the White Horse is a supposedly 12th-century cellar on Old Town Square. It's invariably full of young German tourists dancing to piss-poor pop techno, with the occasional go-go dancer getting her kit off. It can be fun for few minutes, if you're in the mood.

CZ Beat
Balbínova 26, Prague 2, Vinohrady (2225 2504/ www.beat.cz). Metro Muzeum/11, 51, 57 tram. **Open** 7pm-5am Mon-Sat; 7pm-midnight Sun. *Shows* 9pm Mon-Sat. **Admission** free-120 Kč. **No credit cards. Map** p309 M7.
The city's newest club hosts digital mixology with renowned local DJs such as Josef Sedloň, Chris Sadler and Krejdl. The owners know what they're doing and its smallish, cyber-flavoured interior also attracts the city's most fashionable club kids, though it's not that expensive a place.

Delta
Vlastina 887, Vokovice, Prague 6, (3331 2443/ delta@noise.cz). Tram 20, 26, 51/night bus 501. **Open** 7pm-1am Thur-Sat; closed Mon-Wed, Sun. **Admission** 60-120 Kč. **No credit cards.**

The best Nightclubs

For freestyle genre-hopping
Karlový Lázně (see page 227).

For surfing the edge of techno
CZ Beat (see below).

For intimate all-night breakbeats
Wakata (see page 228).

For factory-sized fun
Mecca (see page 228).

For pop, pop and still more pop
Fromin (see below).

For mambo lessons
La Comedia (see page 227).

For a 3am California roll
Železné dveře (see page 230).

For 'bopping' with a backpacker
Jo's Garáž (see page 227).

This fringe rock refuge amid suburban apartments on the city's western border attracts a local crowd that's young, bored and aching to break out. This translates into a steady supply of uncommercial, once-banned live bands such as Filip Topol, the MCH Band and Echt!. Worth the trip to see what the old regime was trying to stamp out.

Fromin
Václavské náměstí 21, Nové Město, Prague 1 (2423 5793). Metro Můstek/3, 9, 14, 24, 52, 55, 56, 58 tram. **Open** 9pm-3am daily. *Disco* 10pm Wed-Sat. **Admission** 100 Kč. **No credit cards. Map** p306 J5.
If you have to experience a Wenceslas Square disco, this is as good as any. Penthouse views, overpriced drinks and escorts go with the top-40 sounds. In April the Italian students who tramp all over Old Town in formation land here at night. Still, the cappuccino is hot and so is the action. Comfortable chill space on the terrace, where meals are served.

Futurum
Zborovská 7, Smíchov, Prague 5 (5732 8571/ futurum@netforce.cz). Metro Anděl/6, 9, 12, 58 trams. **Open** 8pm-3am daily. *Shows* 9pm Mon-Sat. **Admission** 60-100 Kč. **No credit cards.**
The best of house and techno in Bohemia today. The basement of an old communist 'community house' has been gloriously packed with banks of monitors, a tilework bar that looks like part of a swimming pool, and little cocktail tables lit from within. The city's biggest and brightest DJs and dance acts come here for the sound and light systems and the connoisseurs follow.

Arts & Entertainment

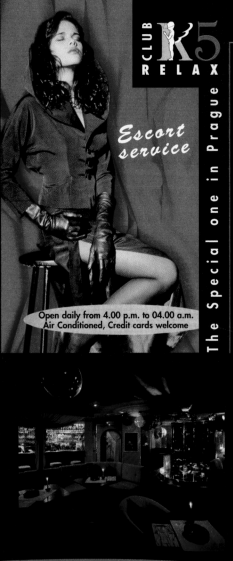
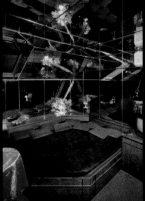

Jo's Garáž

Malostranské náměstí 7, Malá Strana, Prague 1 (530 942). Metro Malostranská/12, 22, 57 tram. **Open** 9pm-5am daily. *Shows* 10pm Thur-Sun. **Admission** free. **No credit cards. Map** p305 E3.

Gothic cellar adjunct to the backpacker's first-stop, Jo's Bar (*see p155*). This rock and funk cave plays predictable DJ rock tracks, eagerly lapped up by crowds of the young and budget-conscious. It's cheap, infectious and packed with booty-shaking and shouted monosyllabic conversation. When that line of communication fails, suggestive gestures are generally understood, particularly by the frequent bar-top dancers.

Karlovy Lázně

Novotného lávka 1, Staré Město, Prague 1 (2222 0502). Metro Staroměstská/17, 18 tram. **Open** *Dance clubs* 9pm-5am daily. *MCM café* 10am-5am daily. **Admission** 40-100 Kč. **No credit cards. Map** p306 G4.

The long-awaited megaclub has arrived with a bang. In a former bathhouse next to the Charles Bridge, the four levels of Karlovy Lázně cover every base: techno on the fourth floor, 1960s-'80s hits on the third, radio pop on the second floor and, on the ground floor, the MCM café, for sitting more than dancing, also books fashionable jazz and funk combos. The café is the only part of the club open by day and sports banks of free Internet terminals and a decent cappuccino bar. Getting down in a drained pool is amusing and lights and sound are as up-to-date as they get in Prague.

Klub Lávka

Novotného lávka 1 Staré Město, Prague 1 (2222 2156/2108 2278/lavka@magicware.cz). Metro Staroměstská/17, 18, 51, 54 tram. **Open** *Bar* 24 hrs daily. *Disco* 10pm-5am Mon-Wed; 10pm-6am Thur-Sat; 10pm-5am Sun. **Admission** 50 Kč. **Credit** AmEx, MC, V. **Map** p306 G4.

An old standby for brainless fun within spitting distance of the Charles Bridge. No challenging digital music here, just disco, go-go dancers, black light and a lovely riverside terrace.

La Comedia

Malá Štupartská 7, Staré Město, Prague 1 (2482 8046). Metro Náměstí Republiky/5, 8, 14, 52, 53, 56 tram. **Open** 11am-3am daily. **Admission** free. **No credit cards. Map** p306 J3.

This Old Town hole in the wall has emerged as the salsa centre of Prague, with nightly Latino dance parties at 9pm on a small, invariably jammed dancefloor. Daiquiris and such from the capable, if equally tiny, bar cool your heels. Those new to the steps can learn from the staff by day – a lesson you'll not regret when you see the fierce action at night.

Mánes

Masarykovo nábřeží 250, Staré Město, Prague 1 (299 438). Tram 17, 18, 51, 54. **Open** 11am-11pm daily. *Shows* 9pm-4am Fri. **Admission** 50 Kč. **No credit cards. Map** p308 G7.

This classy 1930s functionalist gallery is more than living art history. It's also an increasingly popular riverside dance venue with an international

Make a pilgrimage to **Mecca** – disused factory turned dance palace. *See p228.*

flavour. 'Tropicana' nights on Friday and Saturday bring out some of the city's most serious mambo dancers. Stick to the edge of the dancefloor unless you know your stuff. The terrace café is nice for cooling off, but closes around 11pm.

Mecca

U průhonu 3, Holešovice, Prague 7 (8387 0522/8387 1520/www.mecca.cz). Metro Vltavská/1, 3, 12, 25, 54 tram. **Open** 7pm-2am daily. *Shows* 11pm Fri, Sat. **Admission** free-120 Kč. **No credit cards. Map** p310 E1.

A great example of what's possible on the former East Bloc party scene: a disused factory transformed into a large, welcoming dance palace with respectable restaurant service early in the evening and dancing 'til dawn when the tables are stacked away. A bit inconvenient but worth the trek to Holešovice, especially for DJs Loutka or Braun.

Music Park

Francouzská 4, Vinohrady, Prague 2 (2251 5825). Metro Náměstí Míru/4, 22, 34, 57 tram. **Open** 9pm-5am Tue-Thur; 9pm-6am Fri, Sat; closed Sun, Mon. **Admission** 50 Kč. **No credit cards. Map** p311 A3.

Prague's undisputed centre of Euro-trash disco culture – a great place to show off your leather jacket that says something stupid in big letters on the back, have cheery conversations with the po-faced bouncers and pick up a girl in a denim mini-skirt.

Punto Azul

Kroftova 1, Smíchov, Prague 5 (no phone). Tram 6, 9, 12, 58. **Open** 8pm-2am daily. **Admission** 40 Kč. **No credit cards.**

Nothing Spanish about it but the name, but this little Smíchov hideaway is on every wirehead's map. The techno dance space is about the size of a circuit board and half of the club is a routine student drinking dive. A consistent groove is laid down by the city's more avant house DJs.

Radost/FX

Bělehradská 120, Nové Město, Prague 2 (2425 4776/www.techno.cz/radostfx). Metro IP Pavlova/4, 6, 11, 16, 22, 34, 51, 56, 57 tram. **Open** 11am-5am daily. *Shows* 10pm Mon-Sat. **Admission** 50-250 Kč. **No credit cards. Map** p309 L8.

A survivor from the club scene's baby days, probably because it continues to offer the best all-night mix of enticements in the city. A creative veggie café, a spaced-out backroom lounge and art gallery, a small but slick downstairs club featuring absurdly glam theme parties and endless fashion shows, a steady supply of the local stars of house and techno and, to revive you after all this, a classic Sunday brunch (*see p144 and 160*).

Rock Café

Národní třída 20, Nové Město, Prague 1 (2491 4416/www.rockcafe.cz). Metro Národní třída/6, 9, 18, 22, 51, 54, 57, 58 tram. **Open** 10pm-3am Mon-Fri; 8pm-3am Sat, Sun. **Admission** 50-100 Kč. **No credit cards. Map** p306 H5.

Once a fairly respected rock 'n' roll joint, since bequeathed to tourists and out-of-touch Czechs, but the interior is still worth a look. It tends to attract Czech 'revival' bands who cover everyone from ABBA to the Velvet Underground. Endless screenings of rock documentaries by day.

Spiral

Lublaňská 48, Nové Město, Prague 2 (no phone/ www.spiral-club.cz). Metro IP Pavlova/4, 6, 11, 22, 23, 51 58 tram. **Admission** free. **No credit cards. Map** p309 L8.

This new club around the corner from Radost is a cheap alternative with a respectable line-up of house DJs, very long hours and a bar with just the basics. 'After party' sessions sometimes carry on until noon the next day.

Újezd

Újezd 18, Malá Strana, Prague 1 (no phone). Metro Malostranská/9, 12, 22, 58 tram. **Open** 6pm-4am daily. **Admission** free. **No credit cards. Map** p305 E5.

Once known as Borát, this three-storey madhouse was back then an important alternative music club. Today it's home to some loud and badly amplified Czech rock tracks, battered wooden chairs in the café upstairs and shouted conversation in the bar below. Still packed, though.

U zlatého stromu

Karlova 6, Staré Město, Prague 1 (2222 0441). Metro Staroměstská/17, 18, 51, 54 tram. **Open** *Restaurant* 24 hrs daily. *Club* 8pm-6am daily. *Shows* 9pm-5am daily. **Admission** 50 Kč. **Credit** AmEx, MC, V. **Map** p306 G4.

One of the strangest combinations in Old Town: a non-stop disco, striptease, bar, restaurant and hotel a few metres from Charles Bridge. Descend into the stone cellar labyrinth of bad pop and strippers, and you could end up in a peaceful outdoor garden or a nook for conversing. The upstairs café has a full menu plus coffee and drinks, but it's 100 per cent tourist and the staff are often unwelcoming.

Wakata

Malířská 14, Holešovice, Prague 7 (2225 2504/ AbdulRahman@hotmail.com). Metro Vltavská/1, 8, 25, 26, 51, 56 tram. **Open** 5pm-5am daily. *Shows* 11pm daily. **Admission** free. **No credit cards. Map** p309 L8.

Strictly speaking this is a bar, but it's a bar with such a strong tradition of all-night parties that it qualifies as a club. The international crew that run Wakata make it a sort of work in progress at which to test their welding and drink-mixing experiments: You could, for example, sample an ořechovka (walnut liqueur) while perched on a motorcycle-seat barstool.

Late bars

For late-night watering holes other than those listed here, try also **Banana Bar** (*see page 155*), **Chateau Rouge**, **Kozička** or **Marquis de Sade** (*for all, see page 156*).

Radost/FX – small, slick, spaced-out.
See p228.

Bar-Herna non-stop

Královodvorská 9, Staré Město, Prague 1 (231 6239). Metro Náměstí Republiky/5, 14, 26, 53 tram. **Open** 24 hrs daily. **No credit cards. Map** p307 K3.

Catering to gambling machine addicts and obliterated exiles from the nearby Taz bar, this non-stop joint provides a sobering glimpse of authentic Prague nocturnal low-life. A good place to research social aberration.

Battalion Rock Club

28 října 3, Staré Město, Prague 1 (2010 8148). Metro Můstek/3, 6, 9, 14, 18, 22, 51, 52, 54, 55, 56, 57, 58 tram. **Open** 24 hrs daily. **No credit cards. Map** p306 J5.

Grubby, throbbing with generic hip-hop, packed with teenage skate punks and offering an intriguing decor of tree limbs and beat-up vinyl sofas.

Ostroff

Střelecký ostrov 336, Staré Město, Prague 1 (2491 9235). Tram 6, 9, 17, 18, 21, 22. **Open** *Restaurant* 7pm-midnight daily. *Bar* 7pm-3am daily. **Main courses** 250-500 Kč. **Credit** AmEx, MC, V. **Map** p305 F5.

With an enviable location on Shooter's Island, this phenomenally well-stocked bar features views no one can touch. Ostroff's Italian barmen run an affable, sophisticated show in a setting of blond wood, designer seating and late-night *limoncello*. If you go by tram, get off before Legionnaires' Bridge (*most Legií*) then walk across it. *See also p140.*

Železné dveře

Michalská 19, Staré Město, Prague 1 (0603 717 842 mobile). Metro Můstek/6, 9, 18, 22, 51, 54, 57, 58 tram. **Open** 6pm-6am daily. **No credit cards. Map** p306 H4.

Bridging the gap between the backpacker mecca of Chateau Rouge (*see p156*) and the strictly expense-account Bugsy's (*see p155*), the Iron Door is a sort of lounge cave offering a comfortably retro vibe with overpadded vinyl booths, passable late-night sushi, a well-made dry Martini and ultra-cool funk and groove sounds.

Studio A Rubín

Malostranské náměstí 9, Malá Strana, Prague 1 (9000 1905). Metro Malostranská/12, 22, 57 tram. **Open** 5pm-2am daily. **No credit cards. Map** p305 E3.

Popular with young Czechs, this cellar pub maintains a consistently great vibe, sometimes so irresistible that even the bar staff end up on the dancefloor. Local, affordable and not bad fun.

ZanziBar

Lázeňská 6, Malá Strana, Prague 1 (no phone). Metro Malostranská/12, 22, 57 tram. **Open** noon-3am Mon-Sat; 5pm-3am Sun. **Map** p305 E3.

If you've just spent half your salary on Italian boots and a Joe Camel expedition jacket, you won't find a better place to show them off – nor more competition. Crowds of revellers orbit around the drink specials lists while grooving to James Brown. Nobody seems to mind the steepest prices in town for clumsily mixed drinks.

Late-night eating

Bistro Flip

Havlíčkova 2, Nové Město, Prague 1 (no phone). Metro Náměstí Republiky/5, 14, 24, 26, 52, 53, 56 tram. **Open** 9am-11pm daily. **Map** p307 L3.

Desperate hunger has been known to drive men to cannibalism or, worse, to this Masarykovo Nádraží train station buffet where the fried cheese has the flavour of dirty socks. Yum.

Lighthouse & heavy techno

Josef Sedloň – beacon of beats.

As in most cities, DJ culture has been exploding in Prague – and the biggest detonations are the work of crew called **Lighthouse**, headed by Radio 1 DJ Josef Sedloň. Every large-scale house and techno event since 1995 has been the work of this three-man party agency.

In their biggest blowout to date, 6,000 partiers descended on a little-used area of Prague's Ruzyně airport in early 2000 for a heavy all-nighter with Derrick May and David Holmes plus a host of local talent. Before that 5,000 rocked the ČKD tram works in an industrial district of Prague. And at least 2,500 revelled beneath the gigantic equine statue of Jan Žižka inside the Vítkov monument in Žižkov at one of Lighthouse's first big raves – filling what was once the most sacred communist memorial in the republic with blissed-out kids

Rebecca

Olšanské náměstí 8, Žižkov, Prague 3 (627 6920).
Metro Flora/5, 9, 26, 55, 58 tram. **Open** 24 hrs daily.
No credit cards. Map p311 D2.
This so-called 'non-stop' in Žižkov fills up with
clubbers, who trek from miles around to sit in the
narrow, hideously purple setting and eat stale food.
Officially open 24 hours daily, but the management
is known for closing for cleaning on Friday morn-
ings – unless they feel like doing so all day Saturday
or all day Sunday.

U Havrana

Hálkova 6, Nové Město, Prague 2 (9620 0020). Metro
IP Pavlova/4, 6, 16, 22, 34, 51, 56, 57 tram. **Open**
9am-6pm Mon-Fri; 6pm-6am Sat, Sun. **No credit**
cards. Map p309 K7.
Near Radost/FX, Music Park and AghaRTA (*see*
p216) this all-night pub is clean, serves good food
and beer, and has service varying from attentive to
surly, depending on which waitress you get.

Gambling

Gambling is big business in Prague, and seems to
get bigger every year. First came the *hernas*
('gambling halls' – bars full of one-armed bandits).
Then came the bigger casinos that now line
Wenceslas Square. Most casinos in Prague are
legit (with a few obvious Wenceslas Square
exceptions). Being geared towards tourists, they
encourage small-time betting and have fairly
relaxed atmospheres. The *hernas* cater mostly to
locals, pay out a maximum of 300 Kč for a 2 Kč
wager, and operate on a legally fixed ratio of
60 to 80 odds.

Casinos

Palais Savarin

Na příkopě 10, Nové Město, Prague 1 (2422 1648).
Metro Můstek/5, 14, 26, 53 tram. **Open** 1pm-4am
daily. **Credit** DC, MC, V. **Map** p307 K4.
Easily the classiest gambling operation in town,
with sterling candelabras and baroque frescoes, the
Savarin is a world apart from most of the betting
rooms on Wenceslas Square. Just about worth a
look even if you don't like to play the tables.
American roulette and stud poker are offered along
with all the traditional games of chance. Bets from
20-5,000 Kč.

Herna bars

Herna Můstek

Můstek metro station, Nové Město, Prague 1 (no phone).
Metro Můstek/3, 9, 14, 24, 52, 53, 55, 56, 58 tram.
Open 9am-11pm daily. **No credit cards. Map** p307 K5.
Most *herna* bars are pretty seedy places, but this
one inside Prague's main metro interchange is rela-
tively unthreatening.

Poker club

Václavské náměstí 7, Nové Město, Prague 1 (no phone).
Metro Můstek/3, 9, 14, 24, 52, 53, 55, 56, 58 tram.
Open 24 hrs daily. **No credit cards. Map** p306 J5.
A particularly dark non-stop on the main avenue.

Reno

Vodičkova 39, Nové Město, Prague 1 (2494 8679).
Metro Můstek/3, 9, 14, 24, 52, 53, 55, 56, 58 tram.
Open 11am-4am daily. **No credit cards. Map** p308 J6.
Patronised by nervous types deep into the night.
Light food served.

Arts & Entertainment

slurping from plastic beer cups. This in a city
where the largest permanent dancefloor has
space for only a few hundred.

Such is the level of excitement about
Lighthouse parties that urban myths are
already growing up around them: 'First Working-
Class President' Klement Gottwald hasn't lain
in the Vítkov crypt for decades, but most of the
city's clubbers believe to this day that one of
their number made off with his arm on the night
of the Lighthouse party.

Which is just fine with Sedloň, whose
operation is gaining momentum every year. It's
a fair indication of how DJ culture is taking off in
Prague that he's able to attract the biggest
names from Chicago to Berlin for megagigs,
while simultaneously expanding Lighthouse
from a party organiser into an agency and label

(downloadable MP3 samples can be found on
the company website, www.lighthouse.cz).

Not one to let notoriety go to his head, Sedloň
keeps up his three shows on Radio 1, Prague's
most progressive station, plus residencies at
two of Prague's top venues for mixing
connoisseurs: Ritemix nights twice monthly at
Radost FX and Democrazy at Futurum. At the
latter, no commercial sponsorship is permitted
– something without which the epic Lighthouse
parties couldn't hope to get off the ground.

Given the economic circumstances, it's a
reasonable enough compromise, Sedloň
reckons: if blanketing Gottwald's former tomb
with banners bearing enormous cigarette logos
allows kids from all over Europe to party to big-
name DJs without paying sky-high admission,
where's the harm?

Adult entertainment – anything the free market can bare.

Late-night shops

Agip
Olbrachtova 1, Michle, Prague 4 (692 1465). Metro Budějovická/504, 505 bus. **Open** 24 hours daily. **No credit cards.**
A 24-hour petrol station with a weird assortment of gourmet and snack foods.

Potraviny-Lahůdky
Národní třída 37, Staré Město, Prague 1 (2421 4968). Metro Národní třída/6, 9, 18, 22, 23, 51, 54, 57, 58 tram. **Open** 6am-midnight Mon-Fri; 8am-midnight Sat, Sun. **No credit cards. Map** p306 H5.
Last-chance groceries before the ride home from the nearby night tram terminus on Lazarská. Like most such places, prices are relatively steep.

Samoobsluha
Uhelný trh 2, Staré Město, Prague 1 (2421 0548). Metro Můstek or Národní třída/6, 9, 18, 22, 23, 51, 54, 57, 58 tram. **Open** 6.30am-11pm Mon-Fri; 8am-11pm Sat; 9am-11pm Sun. **No credit cards. Map** p306 H5.
Potraviny (grocery store) near Old Town Square with a large food selection.

Adult clubs

Prostitution is theoretically illegal in the Czech Republic but in practice it goes on openly – one bordello, **Hanka Servis** (*see below*), even advertises on the sides of trams. Most bordellos officially operate as strip clubs and customers are generally not pressured to go any further than the bar – which usually commits price robbery sufficient to satisfy the house.

Goldfingers
Václavské náměstí 5, Nové Město, Prague 1 (2419 3856). Metro Můstek/3, 9, 14, 24, 52, 53, 55, 56, 58 tram. **Open** 9pm-4am daily. **Admission** 450 Kč. **Credit** AmEx, MC, V. **Map** p306 J5.

Viva Prague's Vegas. The original king of skin, with drinks named for James Bond foils, a theatrical setting and a dozen dancers, almost as dizzying as the drink prices. Oddly enough, though, this is not actually a bordello.

Cabaret Atlas
Ve Smečkách 31, Nové Město, Prague 1 (9622 4260/9622 4262). Metro Muzeum/4, 6, 16, 22, 34, 51, 56, 57 tram. **Open** 7pm-7am daily. **Admission** 200 Kč. **Credit** MC, V. **Map** p309 K6.
Striptease for the price of a drink and whirlpools at a mere 3,500 Kč an hour.

Hanka Servis
Bulharská 10, Vršovie, Prague 10 (7172 0102). Bus 135, 139, 213. **Open** 24 hrs daily. **Admission** 200 Kč. **Credit** MC, V.
An unremarkable sex joint with relatively cheap prices and a high-profile marketing campaign.

Lotos
Kupeckého 832, Háje, Prague 4 (791 6825). Metro Háje. **Open** 24 hours. **Admission** 200 Kč. **Credit** AmEx, MC, V.
Prime practitioners, known here and abroad, but certainly not for the bargain-hunter. Prague's biggest hedonistic spectacle.

Nancy
Krakovská 25 Nové Město, Prague 1 (2221 0796/2221 1816/www.nancy.cz). Metro Muzeum/11, tram. **Open** 7pm-6am daily. *Shows start* 9pm daily. **Admission** 200 Kč. **Credit** DC, MC, V. **Map** p309 K6.
The newest club off Wenceslas Square is not for the timid – it specialises in live sex shows.

Satanela
Vilová 9, Vršovice, Prague 10 (781 6618). Metro Strašnická/7, 19, 26, 51, 55 tram. **Open** 10pm-4am Mon-Sat; 10pm-2am Sun. **Admission** free. **No credit cards.**
Whips and chains, lab coats and fetish.

Arts & Entertainment

Theatre & Dance

From black light or puppet shows to expat dramatics, there's no shortage of theatre in the Czech capital, while modern dance faces off against folkloric footwork.

Sleeping Beauty at the **National Theatre.** *See p237.*

The first thing that strikes you about theatre in Prague is how very much of it there is. Every quarter of the city has at least one playhouse of its own, supported by a die-hard local audience. As a result, the scene is very diverse, sometimes to a fault. On a given night, Czech-language Tennessee Williams may have to compete with *Evita*, which goes up against a 'free adaptation' of *Yellow Submarine* in black-light theatre.

Part of the Prague obsession with theatre is an appreciation of its role in the development of the modern Czech nation. The 1783 inscription above the Estates Theatre's portal, *Patriae et musis* – 'The Homeland and the Muses' – was a thumbing of the Czech nose at the dominant German culture of the period. An even grander gesture was the construction of the **National Theatre** in 1868, funded entirely by patriotic donations collected over 38 years.

The First Republic enjoyed a golden age of theatre and film following independence in 1918. Then the Nazis brought the house down. After the war, Czech theatre was largely shunted offstage in favour of the communist preference for pan-Slavic conceptions that embraced Russian brotherhood. But native theatre persisted. A new generation of actors, directors and playwrights, including Václav Havel, enjoyed a brief moment in the sun during the Prague Spring of 1968. The international reputation they gained back then sustained them until the Velvet Revolution validated their work two decades later.

After 1989, theatre aficionados were on tenterhooks awaiting the next wave of Czech theatrical brilliance. They are, for the most part, still waiting. Those lights that burned so brightly through the gloom of totalitarianism flicker only faintly in a democratic free market.

The scope of this loss is difficult to grasp, both for visitors and the new generation of more worldly theatre-goers. For these audiences, surely the most willing to buy tickets to new, risk-taking productions, there's the city's small English-language theatre scene.

Of the several troupes to come and go in this micro-community, only two survive. Once the dominant player, the international theatre company **Black Box** has had a mostly non-speaking role in recent years. New director Cathy Meils took the helm in 1999, with plans to turn Black Box into a vital community-based theatre; it is now the most likely theatre to find boundary-skating drama.

A new creative director for the competing **Misery Loves Company**, Daniel Fleischer-Brown, has injected this veteran troupe with energy, productivity and increasingly tough standards. The company performs new international works, and its growing repertoire of original, non-verbal performances have been a hit with wider audiences. Misery has also gained credibility at the annual Summer Shakespeare Festival, performing at **Globe Výstaviště**. The company is currently homeless; audiences can catch their performances in various performing spaces around town. For information call 2400 5229 or 9614 1179 (voicemail).

Tickets & information

Many box offices have at least a rudimentary command of English, but you might be better off buying tickets through one of the central agencies listed below (though they are likely to charge a commission). They accept credit cards, unlike most venues. You can easily book your theatre tickets via these agencies' websites or by telephone, where English-speaking operators will assist you. They also have numerous outlets throughout the city.

Ticket touts tend to cluster at the National Theatre, **Estates Theatre** and **State Opera**, so you can often get into sold-out (*vyprodáno*) performances, though at a price. Wait until the last bell to get the best deal.

Ticketpro
Old Town Hall, Staroměstské náměstí, Staré Město, Prague 1 (14051/www.ticketpro.cz). Metro Staroměstská. **Open** 9am-7pm Mon-Fri; 9am-6pm Sat-Sun. **Credit** AmEx, MC V. **Map** p306 H3/J3.
Advance booking for major concerts and many smaller events. The automated toll-free number above works for all branches, found at Prague Information Service offices and hotels citywide. **Branches**: Štěpánská 61 (Lucerna passage), Nové Město, Prague 1 (14051); Rytířská 31 Staré Město, Prague 1 (2161 0162); Salvátorská 10, Staré Město, Prague 1 (2481 4020).

Bohemia Ticket International
Malé náměstí 13, Staré Město, Prague 1 (2422 7832/fax 2161 2126/www.csad.cz/bti). Metro Můstek or Náměstí Republiky. **Open** 10am-7pm Mon-Fri; 10am-5pm Sat; 10am-3pm Sun. **Credit** AmEx, MC, V (fax orders only). **Map** p307 K4.
The best non-travel agency for buying tickets in advance from abroad with a credit card for opera and concerts at the National Theatre, Estates Theatre and State Opera, plus many other orchestral and chamber concerts. But, inexplicably, you can't use a credit card if you turn up at their office. Maybe Prague still is eastern Europe, after all. **Branch**: Na příkopě 16, Nové Město, Prague 1 (2421 5031).

Czech theatres

Committed theatre buffs determined to see a Czech performance should take heart – many Prague productions are adaptations of familiar works. If you are willing to be patient and appreciative, take the opportunity to see work by contemporary local playwrights. Otherwise, try the frequent 'entertainment experiences' and multimedia rock operas.

Adria Theatre
Palác Adria
Jungmannova 31, Nové Město, Prague 1 (2209 1966). Metro Národní třída or Můstek/3/3, 6, 9, 14, 18, 22, 23 tram.. **Box office** Sept-June 10am-1pm, 1.30-6pm Mon-Fri; closed Sat, Sun. *July, Aug* closed. **Tickets** 200-600 Kč. **No credit cards. Map** p308 J6.
Home to Divadlo Bez zábradlí (Theatre Without a Balustrade), this venue presents classics by such as Chekhov, Molière and Hrabal, plus newer international works. Current stars include the latest generation of the famed Hrušinský family. In summer the theatre is sometimes rented to other companies, who usually present tourist-friendly fare.

Alfred ve dvoře Theatre
Divadlo Alfred ve dvoře
Františka Křížka 36, Holešovice, Prague 7 (2057 1584). Metro Vltavská/1, 5, 8, 12, 17, 25, 26 tram. **Open** box office only for advertised shows. **Tickets** 200 Kč. **No credit cards. Map** p310 D3.
Founded by experimental theatre artist, mime, director and teacher Ctibor Turba in 1996, this innovative theatre is facing death due to lack of funding. It could go belly-up anytime, but continues to present fine, if irregular, alternative and non-verbal performances, mostly with guest touring companies.

Archa Theatre
Divadlo Archa
Na Poříčí 26, Nové Město, Prague 1 (232 7570/reservations 232 8800/ www.archatheatre.cz). Metro Náměstí Republiky or Florenc/3, 24 tram. **Open** box office 10am-6pm daily. **Tickets** 200-600 Kč. **No credit cards. Map** p307 M2.

Archa Theatre – spotlight on the avant garde.

Prague's hippest and most daring theatre brings international avant-garde luminaries of dance, theatre and musical performance to its versatile and well-equipped space. Features the cream of the Czech avant-garde crop – such as Filip Topol, Petr Nikl and Agon orchestr – as well as international acts like Min Tanaka, Einstürzende Neubauten and the Royal Shakespeare Company.

Celetná Theatre
Divadlo v Celetné
Celetná 17, Staré Město, Prague 1 (2326 843). Metro Náměstí Republiky/5, 14, 26 tram. **Open** *box office* 9am-7.30pm daily. **Tickets** 100-300 Kč. **No credit cards.** Map p306 J3.
Small, charming theatre run by Jakub Špalek, mastermind of the talented Kašpar group of actors. It currently hosts performances by students and recent graduates of DAMU, Prague's leading drama school, and showcases Kašpar's own high-energy productions. The box office is the theatre's Gaspar Kašpar café.

Estates Theatre
Stavovské divadlo
Ovocný trh 1, Staré Město, Prague 1 (2421 5001). Metro Můstek/3. **Open** *box office* 10am-6pm Mon-Fri;

National Theatre – Slavic ode. *See p237.*

10am-12.30pm, 3pm-6pm Sat, Sun; and half an hour before performances. **Tickets** 300-1,200 Kč. **No credit cards.** Map p306 J4.
Opened in 1783, the Estates was envisioned as a sanctuary for Czech theatre amid the dominant German culture of the time. It was here in 1834 that the song later to become the national anthem, Josef Tyl's 'Kde domov můj?', was first performed. The

In the mood for dancing?

Though classical ballet prevails in Prague, through the National Ballet performances at the National Theatre, the Estates Theatre and the State Opera, modern dance is slowly making inroads, thanks to the international exposure of festivals like **Tanec Praha** and troupes such as **Deja Donné** (*see below*).

Bohemian folk dancing is still vital in many parts of the country, and you can catch a glimpse even in the big city. Folklore shows combine live music, high-energy dance, colourful, elaborate costumes, and athletic ensembles of male and female dancers. For the best traditional dancing, head for the folk festivals held throughout Bohemia and Moravia during summer.

Dance venues

Duncan Centre
Branická 41, Radlice, Prague 4 (4446 1810). Tram 3, 16, 17, 21. **Open** varies. **Tickets** 200-1,200 Kč. **No credit cards.**
Contemporary dance school doubling as the home performance space for Deja Donné Productions, the international company run by Lenka Flory and Simone Sandrone. Sometimes presents exciting student productions and hosts a good array of touring foreign artists.

Ponec
Husitská 24A, Žižkov, Prague 3 (2481 7886/2481 3899). Metro Florenc, then 133 bus. **Open** varies. **Tickets** 80-100 kč. **No credit cards.** Map p311 B1.
This converted cinema was still under renovation at press time following its acquisition by the non-profit organisation Tanec Praha (*see below*). In future it will be hosting Czech and international contemporary dance productions.

Dance festivals

Progressive European Dance Theatre Festival
Info: Duncan Centre (*see above*). **Date** October.
The annual autumn festival that brings in performers from all over the world to present wildly diverse recitals in dance and dance theatre. Performances are followed by seminars given by the artists.

Tanec Praha
info: Ponec (*see above*). **Date** June/July.
Every summer, Dance Prague (Tanec Praha) stages an international dance and movement theatre festival that attracts Czech artists, such

theatre is more famous, however, for hosting the premiere of Mozart's *Don Giovanni*. The Estates is well aware of its appeal, drawing tourists keen to see Mozart, but it's also home to ballet and more modern dance. If only for its history and architectural beauty, it's worth a visit.

Globe Výstaviště

Výstaviště, Holešovice, Prague 7 (2271 1515). Metro Holešovice/5, 12, 17, 25. **Open** *May-Sept* varies; *Oct-April* closed. **Performances** at 7.30pm. **Tickets** 100-250 Kč **No credit cards.**

This replica of Shakespeare's Globe Theatre is Prague's most evocative summer venue, where Czech and English-language theatre companies perform the Bard in something approximating their original setting. The carnival lights and smells of Výstaviště, the city's main exhibition grounds and summer funfair in Holešovice, makes the vibe somehow even more authentic.

National Theatre

Národní divadlo
Národní třída 2, Nové Město, Prague 1 (2491 2673). Metro Národní třída/6, 9, 18, 17, 22, 23 tram. **Open** *box office* 10am-6pm Mon-Fri; 10am-12.30pm, 3-6pm

Sat, Sun. **Tickets** 250-1,200 Kč. **No credit cards.** **Map** p308 G6.

This architectural ode to Slavic myth, first completed in 1881, is a crowning achievement of the Czech National Revival. It reopened following a fire in 1883 to the strains of Smetana's opera *Libuše*, commissioned for the occasion, based on the tale of the prophet who envisioned Prague. The repertoire includes drama, ballet and operas in their original language, with Czech subtitles. Nearly as many visitors are drawn to see the playhouse itself. Tours are available daily. Weekdays, call the National Theatre at 2491 4153; weekends, call Prague Information Service at 544 444.

Spiral Theatre

Divadlo Spirála
Výstaviště, Holešovice, Prague 7 (3337 8449). Metro Nádraží Holešovice/5, 14 tram. **Open** 10am-6pm Mon-Fri; closed Sat, Sun. **Tickets** 200-400 Kč. **No credit cards.** **Map** p310 C1/D1.

Located in Prague's exhibition grounds, this venue takes its name from the conical arena which allows plenty of seating for popular shows, such as neverending runs of *Evita* in Czech. Shows tend to be overproduced.

---

as Jan Kodet and Mirka Eliášová, as well as international stars like the Martha Graham Dance Company. The festival aims to establish contact with foreign artists, stimulate public interest in contemporary dance, and encourage innovation among Czech choreographers and dancers. So far, it's doing just that.

Folklore performances

Since 1989, Czechs, Moravians and their Slovak neighbours have been aggressively reclaiming their roots. Traditional Slavic dress, music and celebrations were cautiously encouraged under the communist regime; today's traditionalists can approach their heritage with lighter hearts.

In summer, folklore festivals occur almost weekly in the countryside. Check local media and the internet (www.folklor.cz) for details.

Municipal Library

Městská knihovna
Mariánské náměstí 1, Staré Město, Prague 1 (684 01 02, 688 54 16). Metro Staroměstská/17, 18 tram. **Tickets** 300-450 Kč. **No credit cards. Map** p306 H3.

Performances at the library's folklore festivals every July are energetic, if long and pricey. That

the dancers and musicians do the same routine nightly begins to show after the first week. Still, these are professional entertainers.

Restaurace U Marčanů

Veleslavínská 14, Veleslavín, Prague 6 (3536 0623). Tram 20, 26. **Open** 7-11pm daily. **Tickets** 650 Kč. **Credit** MC, V.

Prague's version of dinner theatre includes a folklore show of live music, song and dance, along with a traditional Czech three-course meal, aperitifs, wine and coffee – all at a reasonable price.

Theatre at the Fire Brigade

Divadlo u hasičů
Římská 45, Vinohrady, Prague 2 (2251 6910/2251 5657). Metro Náměstí Míru/4, 11, 16, 22, 34 tram. **Open** *box office* 1-6pm Mon-Fri; 10am-1pm Sat; closed Sun. **Tickets** 250 Kč. **No credit cards. Map** p309 M7.

Decent folklore shows from June to September.

Tradition International Folklore Festival

Mezinárodní Folklor Festival Tradice
(040 38210/ales@folklor.cz). **Date** October. This annual celebration of folk traditions of Bohemia, Moravia and Silesia is one of the best. Takes place in Pardubice, south of Prague.

timeout.com

The World's Living Guide

Theatre on the Balustrade

Divadlo Na zábradlí

Anenské náměstí 5, Staré Město, Prague 1 (2222 2026/ dnz@volny.cz). Metro Staroměstská/17, 18 tram. **Open** 2pm-7pm Mon-Fri; closed Sat, Sun. **Tickets** 100-300 Kč. **No credit cards. Map** p306 G4.

Founded in 1958, this theatre lay the groundwork for Czech Theatre of the Absurd. It was the focus of much secret police attention prior to 1989, when it harboured such dissidents as Václav Havel and New Wave filmmaker Jiří Menzel. Havel's celebrated play *The Garden Party* premiered here, and his works are still part of the repertoire. Czech theatre suffered a serious loss in 1999 when artistic director Petr Lébl took his own life.

Black Light theatre

The puppetry tradition in which performers dress in black velvet so as to be invisible against a black background has been all the rage in Prague since Czech performers blew the audience away at the World Expo '58 in Brussels. Modern practitioners with the tourist trade in mind have added fluorescent paint, black lights, and a large dose of kitsch. 'Black Light' is sometimes referred to as 'Magic Lantern' theatre, after the Prague venue that helped popularise it (*see below*).

Black Light Theatre of Jiří Srnec

Černé divadlo Jiřího Srnce

Celetná 17, Staré Město, Prague 1 (5792 3397). Metro Náměstí Republiky/5,14, 26 tram. **Open** *box office* 9am-7.30pm daily. **Tickets** 600 Kč. **No credit cards. Map** p306 J3.

Founding father of Czech black-light theatre and co-author of Laterna Magika's Kouzelný Cirkus, Jiří Srnec's show moves from theatre to theatre, but at press time had set up camp at the Celetná. His *Ahasver: Legends of Magic Prague* is a classic.

Magic Lantern

Laterna Magika

Nová Scéna, Národní třída 4, Nové Město, Prague 1 (2222 2041) Metro Národní třída/6, 9, 18, 22, 23 tram. **Open** *box office* 10am-3pm, 3.15pm-8pm daily. **Tickets** 600 Kč. **No credit cards. Map** p306 G5.

Famous for pioneering the Magic Lantern style, this company's glossy, high-tech multimedia productions are professional, though no longer at the cutting edge. Their home is the Nová Scéna, the brutalist glass addition to the National Theatre designed by Karel Prager in 1983 (*see page 37*).

Ta Fantastika

Karlova 8, Staré Město, Prague 1 (2222 1366). Metro Staroměstská/17, 18 tram. **Open** *box office* 11am-9.30pm daily. **Tickets** 390 Kč. **No credit cards. Map** p306 G4.

The best of black-light theatres, and the place to recapture the pristine wonder of the medium. Its well-choreographed productions are done with a sense of humour, to music of a high standard.

Puppet theatre

Puppetry is not just for children in the Bohemian lands, having formed an intrinsic part of the Czech National Revival in the 1800s. Though much puppet theatre is aimed at tourists, high quality Czech puppeteers and productions appear frequently. The **Dragon Theatre** (Divadlo Drak) and **Buns and Puppets** (Buchty a Loutky) troupes put on inspired and entertaining shows that should not be missed. The theatres listed below regularly present puppet performances.

National Marionette Theatre

Národní divadlo marionet

Žatecká 1, Staré Město, Prague 1 (232 2536). Metro Staroměstská/17, 18 tram. **Open** *box office* 10am-8pm daily. **Tickets** 390-490 Kč. **No credit cards. Map** p306 H3.

This touristy company presents long and artistically inferior productions of *Don Giovanni* and *Yellow Submarine* set to recorded music. The puppets and scene design can be mildly interesting.

Spejbl and Hurvínek Theatre

Divadlo Spejbla a Hurvinka

Dejvická 38, Dejvice, Prague 6 (2431 6784). Metro Hradčanská/2, 20, 25, 26 tram. **Open** *box office* 10am-2pm, 3-6pm Tue-Fri; 1pm-5pm Sat, Sun; closed Mon. **Tickets** 60-120 Kč. **No credit cards.**

Spejbl and Hurvínek, a father and son duo, are among Bohemia's most famous puppet characters. Created by Josef Skupa in the inter-war period, their subject matter is mostly aimed at children.

Festivals

Mezi ploty Festival

Areál PL Bohnice-Ústavní 91, Bohnice, Prague 8 (8401 6111/www.meziploty.cz). Metro Nádraží Holešovice, then 152 or 200 bus. **Date** late May.

This annual two-day theatre, music and art festival is staged on the grounds of the Bohnice mental hospital on the outskirts of Prague. It features performances by top Czech theatre companies and bands, plus productions by Bohnice's patients.

Next Wave Theatre Festival

Various venues; information from Theatre on the Balustrade (2222 2026). **Date** October.

This annual alternative festival includes theatre, puppetry and dance performances.

Four Days in Motion Festival

Box office: Ekomuzeum, Papřrenská 6, Bubeneč, Prague 6 (2480 9116). Hradčanská then 131 bus. **Date** November.

An excellent festival of dance and visual theatre, usually held every two years, that brings prominent practicioners of international movement theatre to an assortment of venues around Prague for four exciting days.

Sport & Fitness

The national football and ice hockey teams can compete with the best, while Prague's sporting facilities now cover all bases.

Two things helped Czechs deal with the country's economic recession of the late 1990s – beer and international sporting success.

Though the Czech football team disappointed at Euro 2000, having reached the finals in 1996, they set a record by winning all ten of their qualifying matches – an impressive feat even in a relatively weak group. In the country's other favourite sport, ice hockey, Czechs have been dominant in recent years, winning World Championships in 1996, 1999 and 2000, plus gold at the 1998 Nagano Olympics.

A measure of the significance of these performances was the way rabid street parties followed each victory – remarkable for the normally introspective Czechs.

Of participant sports, football remains the most popular. Tennis and golf are fashionable, but relatively high prices make them essentially yuppie pursuits in Prague. The only time Praguers run is to catch a tram, but once a year Prague streets turn into one of the world's most hazardous running tracks for the **Prague International Marathon** (*see page 187*) when over 30,000 runners from around the world jet in to show how it's done.

Spectator sports

Football

Internationally, Czech clubs have enjoyed some success in the European tournaments, with Sparta advancing to the second group phase of the Champions' League and Slavia reaching the UEFA Cup quarter finals in the 1999-2000 season. The country is still digesting the poor Czech showing in Euro 2000 that followed its record-breaking streak of qualifying victories. Domestically, the fierce and ancient rivalry between Sparta and Slavia, Prague's two top clubs, remains the lifeblood of spectator sport in the Czech Republic.

SK Slavia Praha
Stadion SK Slavia Praha, Vršovice, Prague 10 (6731 1102). Tram 4, 7, 22, 24. **Admission** *League games* 50-90 Kč. *European games* 100-160 Kč. **No credit cards**.
The only club capable of giving Sparta a run for their money, Slavia have long endured being second-best. Their only league title of the last decade, in 1996,

Prague International Marathon – hazardous.

when Sparta blinked, came after a generation without silverware. Traditionally the club with university-educated, rather than working-class, support.

FC Sparta Praha

Stadion Sparta, Milady Horákové 98, Holešovice, Prague 7 (2057 0323). Metro Hradčanská/8, 25, 26 tram. **Admission** *League games* 40-100 Kč. *European games* 150-600 Kč. **No credit cards. Map** p310 B2.
Historically the most successful Czech club, Sparta faltered somewhat in the 1990s. Sparta are still pretty dominant in local competitions, but some regrouping is needed before they'll be troubling European opposition again. Currently an asset of Vltava-Labe-Press, a German-owned publishing group, they play in claret and white. Their working-class fan base is the republic's largest.

FK Viktoria Žižkov

Stadion TJ Viktoria Žižkov, Seifertova 130, Žižkov, Prague 3 (2272 2045). Tram 5, 9, 26. **Admission** *league games* 40-70 Kč. **No credit cards. Map** p311 B2.
A rundown local club in a rundown locality, blessed with loyal, local working-class support and atmosphere but few other assets either on the field or off.

Horse racing

It's not Epsom Downs, but the Chuchle race track on the outskirts of Prague offers regular chances to spend a day at the races. For an unusual treat, hold out for the **Velká Pardubice steeplechase**, longest in the world, held at **Dostihový spolek** (*see below*) in late October – but leave your animal-rights activist friends at home, as the jumps are among the most dangerous in Europe.

Betting works in a similar way to the British system, with two agents accepting minimum bets, of 20 Kč and 50 Kč, respectively. You can bet to win (*vítěz*) or place (*místo*) as well as on the order (*pořadí*). Handicapper's information is in the programme.

There's outdoor seating and indoor monitors, with a selection of dilapidated bars and restaurants for inter-race libations.

Chuchle

Radotínská 69, Radotín, Prague 5 (5794 1171/9000 1703). Metro Smíchovské nádraží, then 129, 172, 241, 244 bus. **Admission** 30 Kč adults; 10 Kč children. **No credit cards.**
Races start at 2pm Sundays.

Dostihový spolek

Pražská 607, Pardubice, 110km (68 miles) east of Prague (040 633 5300/www.pardubice-racecourse.cz). Metro Florenc, then ČSAD bus to Pardubice. **Race meets** Saturdays in May-October. **Admission** 40 Kč. **No credit cards.**
The Velká Pardubická Steeplechase (*see p190*) is held here on the second Sunday in October.

Fierce and ancient rivalry: **Sparta** versus **Slavia**.

Ice hockey

Sport can never fully compensate for history, but Czech triumphs in the 1999 and 2000 World Championships, in Norway and Russia, came pretty damned close.

HC Sparta Praha

Za elektárnou 419, Holešovice, Prague 7 (2423 2251). Trams 5, 12, 17. **Admission** 40-90 Kč. *European games* 150 Kč. **No credit cards. Map** p310 B2.
Sparta's home ice resembles Wembley, both architecturally and acoustically. A well-financed team with a passionate following.

Slavia Praha

Stadion SK Slavia Praha, Vršovice, Prague 10 (6731 1415). Tram 4, 7, 22, 24. **Admission** 30-50 Kč. **No credit cards.**
Stuck out in working-class Vršovice, Slavia has to work harder than Sparta to get respect, but fans are still willing to freeze their bottoms during games on the stadium's uncomfortable worn-out seating.

Active sports

Bungee jumping

They string you up. You jump. You don't hit the ground. In theory, at least.

KI Bungee Jump

Hvězdova 2, Pankrác, Prague 4 (4140 1637/0602 250 125 mobile). Metro Pankrác/134, 188, 193 bus. **Open**

The Golden City salutes Olympic Gold: **ice hockey** fans, 1998. *See p241.*

office 9am-3pm Mon-Fri; closed Sat, Sun. *Jumps* May-Oct 11am-5pm Sat, Sun; closed Mon-Fri. *Nov-Apr* closed. **Cost** 700-800 Kč. **No credit cards.**
Jumps are made from Zvíkovské podhradí, a bridge over the Vltava.

Canoeing

Central European Adventures

Old Town Hall, Staroměstské náměstí 1, Staré Město, Prague 1 (2328 879/1051/www.ticketpro.cz). Metro Staroměstská/17, 18 tram. **Tours** *Apr-Oct* Sat, Sun (depending on weather); closed Mon-Fri. *Nov-Mar* closed. **Cost** 810 Kč. **No credit cards. Map** p306 H3.
Price includes canoe rental (with paddle and life jacket), English-speaking guide, coach, lunch and transport from and back to Prague. Rowers take on the Berounka river 20 minutes' drive south of the city – mild stream water for beginners, though fun. Show up at Old Town Hall at 8.30am on the day you'd like to go. Booking via fax is necessary for groups. Groups of four to eight people get a 5% discount, eight or more get 10% off.

Cycling & mountain biking

Beware of biking in Prague – if the fumes don't kill you, the cars will do their best. Perhaps for this reason, bike rentals are rare, except through tour agents such as the one below. If you make it outside the city limits, you'll find a network of reasonably maintained bike trails. Bike maps are available at most bookstores.

   Central European Adventures *(see above)* run bicycle tours around Karlštejn Castle *(see page 254)* with all arrangements, including bike, handled by the friendly folks at the agency. The 30-km (20-mile) tour starting at Karlštejn rambles on to Koněpruské jeskyně, the caves south of Prague, and Sv. Jan pod Skalou, a lovely hilly, rural spot.

Bike Ranch

Palackého náměstí 2, Nové Město, Prague 2 (294 933). Metro Karlovo náměstí/3, 4, 7, 16, 17, 34 tram. **Open** 9am-noon, 1-7pm Mon-Thur; 9am-noon, 1-6pm Fri; 9am-noon Sat; closed Sun. **No credit cards. Map** p308 G9.
Just bicycle sales and repairs, but good work, done fast. Some of the staff speak English.

Sport S-cyclo

Korunní 19, Vinohrady, Prague 2 (2251 6800). Metro Náměstí Míru/11, 16 tram. **Open** 10am-6pm Mon-Fri; 9am-noon Sat; closed Sun. **No credit cards. Map** p311 B3.
Sells and repairs bikes.
Branch: Plzeňská 61, Smíchov, Prague 5 (5732 2817).

Fishing

River fishing is allowed from mid-June to mid-August. The Czech Fishing Association makes it very tough for foreigners to procure even temporary licences, but if you are serious, they will give you the necessary paperwork and advice.

Czech Fishing Association

Český rybářský svaz
Nad Olšinami 31, Strašnice, Prague 10 (7811 7513). Tram 22, 26. **Open** 7am-3pm Mon, Tue, Thur; 7am-4pm Wed; 7am-2pm Fri; closed Sat, Sun. **Licence** *With trout* 1,200 Kč a year. *Without trout* 1,000 Kč a year. **No credit cards.**

Golf

Though not exactly world-renowned for its golfing facilities, the Czech Republic has 13 courses. Only four are 18-hole, but two of these are in dramatic settings at **Karlštejn** *(see page 254)* and **Karlovy Vary** *(see page 250)*. Prague is poorly served.

Erpet Golf Centrum

*Strakonická 510, Smíchov, Prague 5 (548 086). Metro
Smíchovské nádraží/12 tram.* **Open** 8am-11pm daily.
Rates 150 Kč per hour. **Membership** 15,000 Kč per
year. **Credit** AmEx, DC, MC, V.
The only '18-hole course' in Prague is restricted to
members. Full-swing golf simulators offer a choice
of ten courses, and there's an indoor putting green
and pitching course. The shop has some brochures
(in English) with details of other courses in the
Czech Republic.

Golf Club Karlštejn

*Běleč 280, Karlštejn (0311 684 716/www.golf.cz).
30km (19 miles) south-west of Prague on the E50-D5;
leave at exit 10 and follow signs for Karlštejn.*
Open *Apr-Oct* 8am-8pm daily. *Nov-Mar* closed.
Rates 1,000 Kč per round Mon-Fri; 1,800 Kč per
round Sat, Sun. **Membership** *Lifetime* 220,000 Kč,
plus 19,000 Kč annually. *One year* 50,000 Kč. *Two
years* 80,000 Kč. **Credit** AmEx, MC, V.
On the edge of Karlštejn, this course makes up in
convenience what it lacks in beauty – it can add a
nice reward to an otherwise dull trip to the castle
(*see p254*). Minimum handicap 36. Free use of
course with membership.

Golf Club Praha

*Plzeňská 215, Smíchov, Prague 5 (5721 6584).
Metro Anděl, then 4, 7, 9 tram.* **Open** 8am-dusk daily.
Rates 900 Kč per day Mon-Fri; 1,000 Kč per day Sat,
Sun. **No credit cards.**
A nine-hole course and driving range on a hilltop.
The course can get very dry in the summer, a handy
excuse for poor form.

Golf Resort Karlovy Vary

*Pražská 125, Karlovy Vary (017 333
1101/www.golfresort.cz). 131km (81 miles) west of
Prague on E48.* **Open** *Apr-Oct* 8am-8pm daily.
Nov-Mar closed. **Rates** 1,100 Kč per round Mon-Fri;
1,300 Kč per round Sat, Sun. **Membership** *Lifetime*
170,000 Kč per person, 250,000 Kč couples, plus 12,000
Kč a year. **Credit** AmEx, MC, V.
On the edge of Karlovy Vary, resort-style golfing
in the hill country around this traditional spa town
(*see p250*). This is a more roomy and scenic course
than any near Prague. Free use of course with
membership.

Horse riding

Most stables will be more than willing to seat
you on the steed of your choice and let you loose
in the open plain. So for your own sake, don't
exaggerate your experience.

TJ Žižkov Praha

*Císařský ostrov 76, Holešovice, Prague 7 (878 181/878
476).* **Open** 9am-5pm daily. **Rates** 400 Kč per hour
(with instructor). **No credit cards.**
Good facilities, plus a show-jumping arena and
dressage ring. Not the best place for absolute beginners as there are no structured classes, but all riders

are accompanied. For a 300 Kč supplement you can
ride on trails in Stromovka park (*see p243*), a far
more enjoyable setting. Reserve in advance.

Ice skating

Though you can no longer skate on the Vltava,
the reservoirs at Hostivař and Divoká Šárka (*see
below*) come alive in December with skaters and
grog vendors. Most indoor facilities operate from
October to April, and are inexpensive.

Krasobruslařský Stadion

*Sámova 1, Vršovice, Prague 10 (no phone). Tram 6, 7,
24.* **Open** *Sept-June* 10am-noon Mon-Fri; closed Sat,
Sun. *July-Aug* closed. **Admission** 20 Kč.
No credit cards.
Big and institutional, this old hall attracts serious
athletic skaters and teams when it's not given over
for public skating.

Sportovní hala HC Sparta

*Za elektrárnou 419, Holešovice, Prague 7 (872
7443). Tram 5, 12, 17.* **Open** *Sept-Mar* 3.15-5.15pm
Sat, Sun; closed Mon-Fri. *Apr-Aug* closed. **Admission**
20 Kč. **No credit cards.** Map p310 D1.
The most convenient place to skate, just on the edge
of Stromovka park (*see p243*) in Holešovice.

Vokovice

*Za lány 1, Dejvice, Prague 6 (362 759). Metro Dejvická,
then 26 tram.* **Open** *Sept-Mar* 3.30-5.45pm Sun;
closed Mon-Fri. *Apr-Aug* closed. **Admission** 20 Kč.
No credit cards.
A favourite rink of the expat kids attending the
nearby International School of Prague.

Jogging

Jogging, even in the parks of central Prague, is
the aerobic equivalent of smoking a pack a day –
no joke. But if you must get your running shoes
out, try one of the following, which are far enough
from the pollution to make the endeavour less
than harmful. No park is safe from menacing
dogs, which snap at your heels as their owners
stand by laughing.

Divoká Šárka

*Nebušice, Prague 7. Metro Dejvicka then 20, 26 tram
or 119, 216, 218 bus.*
'Wild Šárka' lives up to its name, with bulbous
rock formations and forests so thick you'll think
you've left all civilisation far behind. There are
challenging, hilly trails for joggers. Šárka is most
easily accessible from Evropská, heading towards
the airport.

Michelský les

Krč, Prague 4. Metro Roztyly.
Avert your gaze from the hideous tower block at the
base of the hill and head for the green hills behind.
You'll quickly forget you're anywhere near a city.

Obora Hvězda

Břevnov, Prague 6. Tram 8, 22/179, 191 bus.
All trails are designed to wind you back to the park's centrepiece, the stunning Hvězda Hunting Lodge (*see p32*).

Stromovka

Holešovice, Prague 7. Metro Nádraží Holešovice, then 5, 12 or 17 tram. **Map** p310 B1.
The most central of Prague's large parks. After the initial sprint to avoid the Výstaviště crowds (*see p109*), you can have the woods to yourself. The park was developed by Rudolf II, who was keen on communing with nature (*see p108*).

Skateboarding

To get a glimpse of local talent, check out the concrete pavilion next to the **National Theatre** ticket office (*see page 237*) or the area around the giant metronome in Letná Park.

Mystic Skates

Štěpánská 31, Nové Město, Prague 1 (2223 2027). Metro Muzeum/3, 9, 14, 24 tram. **Open** 10am-7pm Mon-Fri; 10am-3pm Sat; closed Sun. **Credit** MC, V. **Map** p309 K6.
The best skate shop in Prague. A good place to link up with the underground graffiti artists.

Skiing & snowboarding

Serious ski buffs head for the Tatra mountain range in Slovakia (*see p265*). If you don't want to cross the border, the Krkonoše mountains are your best bet for downhill skiing. Stock up in Prague at one of the places listed below and head for the mountains.

Snowboardel

Husitská 29, Žižkov, Prague 3 (627 9900). Metro Florenc, then bus 133, 207. **Open** 10am-6pm Mon-Fri; 9am-1pm Sat; closed Sun. **Credit** MC, V. **Map** p311 B1.
A huge selection of new and used snowboards, sold by goatee-wearing aficionados. Good selection of stylish snowboardwear.

Sport Slivka

Újezd 40, Malá Strana, Prague 1 (5700 7231). Tram 12, 22. **Open** 10am-6pm Mon-Fri; 9am-noon Sat; closed Sun. **Credit** MC, V.
Good, reasonable rentals for skiers – a wise idea as resorts often have little to offer.

Squash

Squash is becoming increasingly popular in the Czech Republic, especially in winter, when it's not unheard of to reserve more than a month in advance. The courts listed below rent out playing space and equipment by the hour. See also **Fitness Forum International** (*p246*) and **Erpet Golf Centrum** (*p243*).

Squash Centrum Strahov

Strahov 1230, Malá Strana, Prague 6 (2051 3609). Metro Dejvická, then 132, 143, 149, 219 bus. **Open** 7am-11pm Mon-Fri; 8am-11pm Sat, Sun. **Rates** 170-370 Kč per hour. **No credit cards.**
One of the city's oldest squash centres. Often mobbed with students from the adjacent dorm.

Squashové centrum

Václavské náměstí 15, Nové Město, Prague 1 (2423 2752). Metro Můstek/3, 9, 14, 24 tram. **Open** 7am-11pm Mon-Fri; 8am-11pm Sat, Sun. **Rates** 190-420 Kč. **No credit cards.** **Map** p306 J5.
Three courts and a central location.

Swimming

As the winter is long and the summer fickle, an indoor pool is your most reliable bet. But choose with care: many of Prague's pools are thick with chlorine, hysterical children or amorous teenagers who pointedly ignore the designated areas for lap-swimmers. If you prefer open-air swimming, dam reservoirs (*see below*) are even dirtier, but wildly popular. See also **Fitness** (*see page 246*) for hotels with pools.

Areál Strahov Stadion

Olympijská, Malá Strana, Prague 6 (2431 4188). Tram 22/132, 143, 149, 217 bus/funicular from Újezd to top of Petřín Hill, then 5min walk. **Open** *Sept-June* 6am-8pm Mon, Thur, Fri; 6am-5pm Tue; 6am-5pm, 7-8pm Wed; 8am-2pm Sat; closed Sun. *July-Aug* closed. **Admission** 30 Kč. **No credit cards. Map** p304 A5.
A large indoor pool that serves as a training site for competitive Czech swimmers. The sauna facilities are a rare bonus.

Divoká Šárka

Nebušice, Prague 6 (368 022). Tram 26, then 5min walk. **Open** *May-mid Sept* 9am-7pm daily. *Mid Sept-Apr* closed. **Admission** 20 Kč; 10 Kč children. **No credit cards.**
Follow the other swimmers or the red and white striped trail up the valley to find this outdoor pool. The setting is idyllic and the lawned sunbathing area gets more crowded than the water.

Džbán Reservoir

vodní nádrž Džbán
Vokovice, Prague 6 (2056 2368). Tram 26. **Open** *May-Sept* 9am-7pm daily. *Oct-Apr* closed. **Admission** 20 Kč; 10 Kč children. **No credit cards.**
This is a large and popular reservoir and naturist beach, close to the tram stop. Volleyball and table tennis as well as swimming.

Hostivař Reservoir

vodní nádrž Hostivař
Hostivař, Prague 10 (no phone). Metro Skalka, then 147, 154 bus/22, 26 tram; or Metro Háje, then 165, 170, 212, 213 bus/22, 26 tram, then 10min walk through woods. **Open** *May-Sept* 10am-7pm daily. *Oct-Apr* closed. **Admission** 20 Kč. **No credit cards.**

Coming unstrung

Czechs have become accustomed to international success in tennis through such stars as Martina Navrátilová, Ivan Lendl and, more recently, Petr Korda and Jana Novotná. Not any more.

The Czech tennis scene has in recent years been wracked by doping scandals and suffered a new indignity in the summer of 2000: the indefinite postponement of the only regular ATP stop in the former East Bloc, the Czech Open.

The reason: plain lack of sponsorship. But the funding crisis of the Czech Tennis Association, which wrought the postponement, is more symptom than cause, to hear it from Korda himself. Lendl's would-be heir, who was suspended for a year after testing positive for steroids at Wimbledon in 1998, believes that fear has been the powerful motive behind his record of successes.

'My generation grew up under communism,' Korda has said. 'We knew that only success would open doors abroad – if we had failed, [the communists] would take our passports away from us.' Today, that fear is gone, and with it the drive to win at all costs.

Some also say the Czech victories in the Grand Slam games of the 1990s hurt the development of the sport back home by rendering taboo any negative discussions about looming problems.

'We couldn't talk about any crisis while Korda and Novotna were achieving success,' says former Davis Cup captain Vladislav Šavrda. Now general manager of the Czech Lawn and Tennis Club in Prague, Šavrda reckons: 'It was clear that they were approaching the end of their careers and there was no one to continue the strong showings.'

As the talent pool was evaporating, so were the sources of funding that might have refilled it. 'We all understand the importance of the Czech Open, but we can't take the money from other funds,' laments ČTA marketing director Tomáš Petera. 'Otherwise, no junior would be able to travel to tournaments abroad.'

One year ago Petera warned that that the demise of the Czech Open 'would be the real end of tennis in this country'. Ominously, he does not expect that the star event will be returning anytime soon.

Larger and deeper than Džbán, and with more activities, including rowing, wind-surfing, tennis, volleyball, water slide and naturist beach.

Hotel Axa
Na Poříčí 40, Nové Město, Prague 1 (232 3967). Metro Florenc or Náměstí Republiky/3, 5, 14, 24, 26 tram. **Open** 7am-10pm Mon-Fri; 9am-9pm Sat, Sun. **Admission** 1 Kč per minute. **No credit cards. Map** p307 M2.
The pool in this hotel is a good length and stays free of shrieking children in the morning. There are decent sauna facilities, too.

Podolí
Podolská 74, Podolí, Prague 4 (4143 3952). Tram 16, 17, 32. **Open** 6am-10pm (last entry 9pm) Mon-Fri; 8am-8pm (last entry 7pm) Sat, Sun. **Admission** *Indoor* 60 Kč for 3 hours. *Outdoor* 80 Kč per day; 20 Kč children under 125cm (49in). **No credit cards.**
Watch the struggle between overexcited kids and massive quantities of chlorine. It's quite a pick-up joint for tanned young singles, as well as being a notorious centre of male prostitution.

SK Slavia
Stadion SK Slavia Praha, Vladivostocká 2, Vršovice, Prague 10 (7273 4800). Tram 4, 7, 22, 24. **Open** *Indoor* Sept-Apr 6am-8pm Mon-Fri; 9am-7pm Sat, Sun; Mar-Aug closed. *Outdoor* May-Sept 6am-8pm daily. Oct-Apr closed. *Sauna* 10am-10pm Mon-Fri; 10am-6pm Sat, Sun. **Admission** *Indoor* 30 Kč per hour; 20

Kč children. *Outdoor* 60 Kč per day; 40 Kč children. *Sauna* 90 Kč for 2 hours. **No credit cards.**
The Slavia complex has indoor and outdoor pools, both of a respectable size. On hot days the outdoor pool gets far too crowded for real swimming.

YMCA
Na Poříčí 12, Nové Město, Prague 1 (2487 2220). Metro Náměstí Republiky/5, 14, 26 tram. **Open** 6.30am-12.30pm, 4.30-10.30pm Mon, Wed, Fri; 6.30am-12.30pm, 4.30pm-5.30pm, 6.30pm-10.30pm Tue, Thur; 8.30am-12.30pm, 4.30pm-10.30pm Sat, Sun. **Admission** 1 Kč per minute. **No credit cards. Map** p307 L3.
Though the tiny Nautilus rooms get claustrophobic if more than a handful of people are using them, the pool is more spacious, and is frequented by some reasonably serious swimmers.

Tennis

The Czech Republic has long been renowned for its tennis stars – notably Ivan Lendl and Martina Navrátilová. Although both defected to the West, they're still national heroes. Czech success at the 1996 Olympics and Jana Novotná's Wimbledon triumph in 1998 helped boost the game. More recent woes, however, could make for a difficult future (*see above* **Coming unstrung**).

1. ČLTK

Ostrov Štvanice 38, Holešovice, Prague 7 (232 4601/2481 0272). Metro Florenc or Vltavská. **Open** *Apr-Oct* 6am-11pm daily *Nov-Mar* closed. **Rates** 400 Kč per hour (before 1pm); 800 Kč per hour (after 1pm). **No credit cards. Map** p310 E3.

These six outdoor floodlit courts, the setting for the now defunct Czech Open ATP games, are on an island in the Vltava. Booking essential.

Tenis Club

Střelecký ostrov, Staré Město, Prague 1 (2492 0136). Tram 6, 9, 22. **Open** *Apr-Oct* 8am-9pm daily; *Nov-Mar* closed. **Rates** 150 Kč per hour 8am-3pm Mon-Fri; 200 Kč per hour 3pm-9pm Mon-Fri, 8am-9pm Sat, Sun. **No credit cards. Map** p305 F5.

Outdoor courts on a Vltava island. Not for the shy.

Tenisový klub Slavia Praha

Letenské sady 32, Holešovice, Prague 7 (3337 4033). Tram 1, 8, 25. **Open** *Apr-Oct* 7am-8pm daily. *Nov-Mar* (indoor) 7am-9pm daily. **Rates** *Outdoor* 200 Kč per hour. *Indoor* 600 Kč per hour. **No credit cards. Map** p310 B3.

Eight floodlit outdoor clay courts on Letná Hill. The courts are in good condition and the outdoor café is convivial, but facilities are otherwise shoddy. Book at least a day ahead in summer; call after 4pm.

TJ Vyšehrad

V Pevnosti 6, Vyšehrad, Prague 2 (427 578). Metro Vyšehrad. **Open** 10am-7pm daily (in good weather). **Rates** 250 Kč per hour Mon-Fri; 150 Kč per hour Sat, Sun 7am-noon; 200 Kč per hour Sat, Sun noon-7pm. **No credit cards.**

An excellent outdoor complex of clay courts, nestled in sunken red-brick castle walls. The public is allowed in only when the courts are not in use by members – phone to discover when that might be.

Shooting

Czechs gave the world the word 'pistol' and over 40,000 people in Prague alone own a gun. Many love to practise at the city's noisy, surprisingly friendly ranges. Forgot yours? No worries. You can rent a piece by the hour.

Rambo Shooting Range

Za poříčskou branou 7, Karlín, Prague 8 (231 3712). Metro Florenc. **Open** 9am-noon, 1-6pm daily. **Admission** 60 Kč for 30 minutes; 500 Kč for 10 visits. **No credit cards.**

Indoor range with paper targets and a wide range of handguns available.

Fitness

As the city grows increasingly body-conscious, fitness centres are sprouting to meet the demand, but there's still no central, modern, fully equipped gym. The places listed below have knowledgeable, helpful staff. There are also facilities at Erpet Golf Centrum (*see page 243*).

Body Island

Uruguayská 6, Vinohrady, Prague 2 (2251 7955). Metro Náměstí Míru/4, 22, 34 tram. **Open** 8am-10pm Mon-Thur; 8am-9pm Fri; 9am-7pm Sat; 2pm-9pm Sun. **Admission** *Sauna* 150 Kč per hour; 250 Kč per two hours. *Classes* 60 Kč. **Membership** 3-month (12 visits) 580 Kč; 10-month (48 visits) 2,400 Kč. **No credit cards. Map** p309 M9/p311 A3.

The Nautilus machines are nothing to write home about, but this complex meets most bodily needs with a wide range of aerobics and dance classes, plus sauna, masseur and hairstylist.

Fitness Centre Hilton

Pobřežní 1, Karlín, Prague 8 (2484 2713). Metro Florenc/3, 24 tram. **Open** *Gym* 6pm-10pm Wed; closed Mon, Tue, Thur-Sun. *Swimming* 6.30am-10pm daily. *Tennis* 7am-10pm daily. **Admission** *Gym* 220 Kč (including one-hour sauna or swimming afterwards). *Swimming* (no time limit) 280 Kč. *Tennis* 660 Kč per hour; 400 Kč members. **Membership** *tennis* 9,000-11,000. **Credit** AmEx, MC, V.

The Hilton's small luxury fitness centre offers rowing machines, Airsteppers and Soloflex, plus a warm, if rather small, pool. Good English-speaking assistance and a poolside juice bar.

Fitness Club Intercontinental

Náměstí Curieových 43, Staré Město, Prague 1 (2488 1525). Metro Staroměstská/17 tram. **Open** 5.30am-11pm Mon-Fri; 8am-11pm Sat, Sun. **Admission** *Gym* 180 Kč per hour. *Pool, sauna and jacuzzi* 300 Kč per two hours. *Solarium* (10 minutes) 180 Kč. **Credit** AmEx, MC, V. **Map** p306 H1.

Popular among the rich and moderately famous. Come flex with the movers and shakers (and runners and lifters) of Prague's business community. Good cardiovascular machines and an eager staff of trainers. TVs in front of the treadmills.

Fitness Forum International

Kongresová 1, Vyšehrad, Prague 4 (6119 1326). Metro Vyšehrad. **Open** 7am-10pm Mon-Fri; 9am-10pm Sat, Sun. **Admission** *Gym* 150 Kč per hour. *Swimming & sauna* 250 Kč per hour. *Gym, swimming & sauna* 3000 Kč for 10 visits. **Credit** DC, MC, V.

This 25th-floor fitness centre has squash courts, aerobics and a small but useful assortment of training equipment. Treat yourself to a sauna, cold dip or tanning session, or slob out in a white robe by the small pool and enjoy the panoramic view.

Holiday Inn Prague

Koulova 15, Dejvice, Prague 6 (2439 3838). Tram 20, 25. **Open** 7am-10pm Mon-Fri; 9am-8pm Sat, Sun. **Admission** *Gym* 80 Kč. *Sauna* 70 Kč per hour (call ahead). *Solarium* 5 Kč per minute. **No credit cards.**

The machines at this well-equipped fitness centre show how far things have come at what was formerly the Hotel International, pride of communist-era Prague. These days the red star atop the spire out front has been replaced by a green one and the bench presses and exercise bicycles are relatively underused due to the remote location. All the better for those who make the trip. Good value, too.

Arts & Entertainment

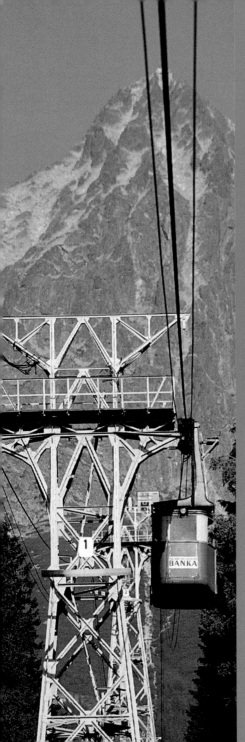

Trips Out of Town

Getting Started

Spa towns, romantic castles, mountain retreats, ski slopes, cave systems
– if you can't find it within a few hours of Prague, you're simply not trying.

Prague may be one of the world's most beautiful cities, but even this gem can at times be hard to tolerate. The antidote to its noise, exhaust fumes and stress is just a few hours and a few hundred crowns away in the charming villages and towns of Bohemia, Moravia, Slovakia and Germany.

The trains of the former East Bloc are an excellent resource: a survivor of communist times, they may be somewhat shabby and overheated, but they're cheap, efficient, scenic and go just about everywhere. Cars can be rented for around 500 Kč a day if you shop around (*see page 272*) and buses, also very cheap, go everywhere that the trains don't. Any of these modes of transport will immerse you in the heartlands of Central Europe and expose you to people and places that seem a world apart from Prague. You'll learn far more about modern Czech life by joining the natives and hiking through the countryside or pottering around a small town for an afternoon than you could ever glean from Old Town tours, Mozart concerts and kitschy beer halls.

Our suggested excursions are divided into the following categories. Day trips are places perfectly feasible to get to even if you had one too many beers the night before and don't make it out of bed until mid morning. As well as some stunning towns, we've included a selection of Central Bohemian castles (*see page 250*). Overnighters are places worth spending a bit more time on – both for the journey to get to them, and for how much there is to see and do when you get there. We've divided these into trips to other towns (*see page 256*) and excursions into the countryside (*see page 262*). Most destinations have been included with ease of access by public transport in mind. We've also suggested a couple of trips abroad: Dresden in Germany is a three-hour train ride from Prague, and a beautiful one, too. A jaunt to the Tatra mountains in Slovakia offers excellent skiing and a look at what was once the Czech Republic's other half (*see page 264*).

If you want to get out of town with minimal effort, try one of the trips to Terezín, Karlštejn, or Karlovy Vary available through the travel agents Precious Legacy Tours (*see page 118* **The Jewish Museum**) and Čedok (*see page 288*). Rafting and cycling trips are also a breeze when the logistics are left to an agency (*see page 242*).

If you're thinking of staying overnight at any of these destinations, the tourist offices listed in the following chapters should be able to help you book accommodation. Private houses all over the country also offer rooms, and this can be a good way to taste something of authentic Czech life.

A TOUR OF THE COUNTRY

Divided into the provinces of Bohemia in the north-west and Moravia in the south-east, the terrain of the Czech Republic is surprisingly diverse. Riddled with vineyards and undulating hills, Moravia is prettiest in autumn, where a leisurely week could be spent vineyard-hopping, combing through the region's caves, and getting your music and culture fix in Brno, the Czech Republic's second city.

Northern Bohemia, though it features a sad legacy of pollution from heavy industry, also offers the bizarre and beautiful **Český ráj** (Czech paradise; *see page 262*), a playground for hikers and clean-air addicts. Here striking sandstone cliffs line the banks of the Labe (Elbe) river.

Southern Bohemia, with its carp ponds and dense woods, is heavily trafficked in the summer, both by tourists basking in the medieval charm of Český Krumlov and by Czechs chilling out at the family *chata* (*see page 60* **One room, nice view, no running water**). In western Bohemia, the landscape around the famed spa towns is dramatically verdant, with rolling hills and spruce forests.

Getting out of town

By bus

Many intercity bus services depart from **Florenc coach station** (*see page 268*). Bus services are more frequent in the morning. It's worth checking the return times before you leave, as the last bus back may leave disappointingly early (often before 6pm). The bus information line (in Czech) is on 1034 and operates between 6am and 6pm, Monday to Friday. A few buses also leave from **Nádraží Holešovice** (*see page 268*). Most destinations are covered by the state bus company ČSAD, although a number of private services now offer competitive prices and times. One of the largest of these is Čebus Ke štvanici (2481 1676).

Castle in the air – the highlight of a visit to the tiny town of **Český Krumlov**. *See p258.*

By car

There are just a few motorways in the Czech Republic, although more are planned, so drivers are often confined to A roads. Petrol stations (some marked by a big sign saying *benzína*) are not that frequent, so if you see one it's a good idea to fill up. Petrol comes in two grades, super and special; the latter is recommended for most West European cars. Unleaded is called *natural* and diesel is *nafta*. The speed limit is 60kph (37mph) in built-up areas, 110kph (68mph) on motorways, and 90kph (56mph) everywhere else. If you have an accident call the Emergency Road Service on 154. Prices for car hire vary widely depending on whether you're renting from an international or local company.

By train

Trains often follow more scenic routes than buses, but cover less ground and usually take longer. There are four main railway stations in Prague (*see page 268*) but no fixed pattern as to which destinations or even part of the country they serve. **Hlavní nádraží** is the most central station and one of two principal departure points

for international services, as well as some domestic services. Timetables can be obtained at the state railways (ČSD) information office at the station, and there are English-speaking operators on their info-line (2422 4200/2461 4030). **Nádraží Holešovice** is also principally used for international services. **Masarykovo nádraží** (Metro Náměsti Republiky) serves most destinations in northern and eastern Bohemia. Domestic routes to the south and west leave from **Smíchovské nádraží**. Travel is priced by the kilometre and, despite recent enormous price hikes, is still a resounding bargain by West European or American standards.

Hitch-hiking

The usual rules of courtesy and common sense apply to hitch-hiking within the Czech Republic. It's a time-honoured method of transport, particularly among students and soldiers. As in any country, position yourself just outside the city limits and brandish a sign bearing your destination of choice. Offer to help with petrol money, though your money will most likely be waved away. Be wary of accepting rides from German-speakers with Playboy air-fresheners hanging from their rear-view mirrors.

Trips Out of Town

Day Trips

Ossuaries, film festivals, concentration camps, spas and a collection of medieval castles are all within easy striking distance of Prague.

Promenade your ailments at **Karlovy Vary**, Bohemia's oldest and most grandiose spa town.

Karlovy Vary

Far and away the most touristed of Bohemia's spa towns, Karlovy Vary is also the oldest, largest and most grandiose. The midsummer **Karlovy Vary Film Festival** (*see pages 190 and 200*), is probably the best time to visit, when the town hosts a non-stop orgy of screenings and celebrity-spotting. At other times of year there are classical music festivals (*see page 251*).

Karlovy Vary began its ascent to fame in 1358 when one of Charles IV's hunting hounds leapt off a steep crag in hot pursuit of a more nimble stag. The unfortunate dog fell to the ground and injured its paw, then made a miraculous recovery as it limped through a pool of hot, bubbling water. Experts were summoned to test the waters and declared them beneficial for all kinds of ills. From that moment, Karlovy Vary's future was ensured.

The river Ohře runs through the centre of town and disappears beneath the hulking Hotel Thermal – a fascinating symbol of the

communist notion of luxury, especially when contrasted with the gracious elegance of the **Grand Hotel Pupp**. The garish boutiques and inescapable wafer shops may not be your idea of relaxation – but you can always retreat to the parks, adorned with busts of some of the spa's more famous guests, or down a few Becherovkas – the herbal liqueur that works magic with its base of the region's pure spring water. If you fancy a cheaper splash than the hotels offer, try the **Vojenský State Baths**.

Vojenský State Baths

Mlýnské nábřeží 7 (017 311 9111). **Open** 7am-3.30pm Mon-Fri; closed Sat, Sun. **Admission** 90 Kč. **No credit cards.**

Where to stay & eat

Grand Hotel Pupp

Mírové náměstí 2 (017 310 9111). **Open** 7am-10am; noon-3pm; 6pm-10pm daily. **Main courses** 250-550 Kč. **Credit** AmEx, DC, MC, V.
If you splurge on this lavish hotel – said to be the finest in the country – ask for a room that has not yet

been refurbished; several have been unsympathetically 'modernised'. The elegant restaurant is worth a visit if you're feeling flush.

Promenáda
Tržiště 31 (017 322 5648). **Open** noon-11pm daily. **Main courses** 150-300 Kč. **Credit** AmEx, V.
Karlovy Vary is notorious for its lack of acceptable restaurants. If you can't afford the Pupp's dining room, try this – a cut above the usual goulash-and-dumplings places – with reasonably quick service, freshwater trout and steaks.

Getting there

By bus
Buses run at least every hour from Prague's Florenc station, starting at 5.30am. The journey takes about two and a half hours.

By car
130km (81 miles) west of Prague on E48.

By train
Trains leave Prague's Hlavní nádraží three times a day. The journey takes about four hours.

Tourist information

Tur-Info
Vřídelní kolonáda (017 322 9312/322 4097). **Open** 7am-5pm Mon-Fri; 8am-3pm Sat, Sun.
In the big glass complex built around the main spring. Staff are helpful. Karlovy Vary hosts a number of arts festivals, including the annual international film festival held in July and several classical music festivals.

Čedok
Dr Davida Bechera 21 (017 322 2994). **Open** 9am-5pm daily. **No credit cards**.
Information and tickets for festivals and concerts.

Kutná Hora

Kutná Hora's short-lived wealth but lasting fame began with the discovery of silver ore here in the late 13th century. A Gothic boom town was born, and for 250 years Kutná Hora was regionally second in importance only to Prague.

Don't be put off by the blighted concrete flatblocks when you get off the train in Sedlec. The UNESCO-designated old centre is only a couple of kilometres to the south-west and well worth the hike. But first you might see Sedlec's incredible bone chapel, where 40,000 skeletons have been used as ornate and somewhat morbid decoration. The Cistercian Abbey, founded in 1142 and now housing a tobacco factory, established the ossuary a few hundred metres north of the church on Zámecká.

It's a long walk or a short bus ride through Sedlec's industrial ugliness to reach Kutná Hora's centrepiece, the **Cathedral of St Barbara**. Designed in Peter Parler's workshop, it is a magnificent building dating from 1388, with an exterior outclassing that of Parler's St Vitus's Cathedral in Prague. St Barbara was the patron saint of silver miners and the emblems of their guilds decorate the ceiling. For an idea of life in a medieval mine, head to the Hrádek on Barborská. Here, the **Czech Silver Museum**, housed in a late Gothic fort, kits you out in protective white suits and hardhats for a trip into the tunnels.

Cathedral of St Barbara
Kostel sv. Barbory
Open *Apr, Oct* 9-11.30am, 1-4pm daily. *May-Sept* 9am-5.30pm daily. *Nov-Mar* 9-11.30am, 2-3.30pm, Tue-Sun; closed Mon. **Admission** 30 Kč; 15 Kč children. **No credit cards**.

Czech Silver Museum & Medieval Mine
Muzeum a středověké důlní dílo
Barborská 28 (0327 512 159). **Open** *Apr, Oct* 9am-5pm; *May-June, Sept* 9am-6pm; *July-Aug* 10am-6pm Tue-Sun; closed Mon. Last entry 90 minutes before closing time. *Nov-Mar* closed. **Admission** 100 Kč; 50 Kč children. **No credit cards**.
If you want to see the mine, a guided tour is compulsory. Booking is advisable.

Cathedral of St Barbara – silver setting.

The Ossuary

Kostnice
Zámecká (0327 561 143). **Open** *Apr-Sept* 8am-6pm
daily. *Oct* 8am-noon, 1-5pm daily. *Nov-Mar* 9am-noon,
1pm-4pm daily. **Admission** 30 Kč; 15 Kč children.
No credit cards.
If the Ossuary is closed, the key may be collected
from the vegetable shop at Zámecká 127.

Where to eat

Harmonia

Husova 105 (0327 512 275). **Open** 11am-11pm daily.
Main courses 180 Kč. **No credit cards**.
Beautiful terrace overlooking a picturesque lane.

Getting there

By bus

Buses leave five times a day from outside Želivského
metro, and once daily from Florenc bus station. The
journey takes about 75 minutes.

By car

70km (44 miles) from Prague. Head out through Žižkov
and follow signs to Kolín to get on to Route 12; then
change to road 38 to Kutná Hora. A scenic alternative is
Route 333 via Říčany, further south.

By train

Trains run from Hlavní nádraží or Masarykovo
nádraží, and take 50 minutes. The main Kutná Hora
station is actually located in Sedlec. Local trains meet
express trains coming from Prague and take visitors
into Kutná Hora proper.

Tourist information

Tourist Information Kutná Hora

Palackého náměstí 377 (0327 515 556). **Open**
Summer 9am-6.30pm Mon-Fri; 9am-5pm Sat, Sun.
Winter 9am-5pm Mon-Fri; closed Sat, Sun.
Staff can book accommodation in private houses.

Mělník

In the heart of verdant grape-growing country,
Mělník is a sleepy little town just 33km (20 miles)
north of Prague with a fine castle, a bizarre
ossuary and spectacular views over the
surrounding countryside. It is also the home of
Ludmila wine, the beverage Mozart supposedly
drank while composing *Don Giovanni*.

The main sights are concentrated near the
lovely castle, now more château than
stronghold. It occupies a prime position on a
steep escarpment overlooking the confluence
of the Vltava and Labe rivers.

Although a settlement has existed here
since the tenth century, it was Charles IV who

introduced vines to the region from his lands in
Burgundy in the 14th century. He also
established a palace for the Bohemian queens,
who would come here to escape Prague until the
end of the 15th century.

The castle was rebuilt during the 16th and
17th centuries. Recent restitution laws have
returned it to the Lobkowicz family, some of the
most powerful magnates in Bohemia before they
were driven into exile by the communists.

You can take a tour around the castle's
interior and, even better, another one round the
splendidly gloomy wine cellars. Here a lesson
in viticulture is followed by a chance to sample
some of the end product and also to walk over a
bizarre arrangement of tens of thousands of
upturned bottles.

Opposite the castle is the **Church of Sts
Peter and Paul** (sv. Petr a Pavel), a late
Gothic structure with a 60m (197ft) tower. The
onion-shaped cupola was added in the 16th
century. The ossuary in the church's crypt
consists of skulls and bones piled to the ceiling
– a weird experience. Two speakers precariously
balanced on top of a stack of femurs broadcast a
breathless English commentary delivered in
Hammer horror style, accompanied by liberal
doses of Bach organ music.

The site was established as a burial place for
plague victims in the 16th century and sealed off
for the next few hundred years. However, in 1914
a social anthropology professor from Charles
University cracked open the vault and brought in
his students to arrange the 15,000 skeletons he
found within. The end result includes the Latin
for 'Behold death!' spelled out in skulls, and a
cage displaying the remains of people with
spectacular physical deformities.

The main square below the castle, **Náměstí
Míru**, is lined with typically Bohemian baroque
and Renaissance buildings. The fountain dates
from considerably later.

The Castle

Svatováclavská 19 (0206 622 127). **Open** *Mar-Oct*
10am-5pm daily. *Nov-Feb* 11am-4pm Mon-Fri; closed
Sat, Sun. **Admission** *Castle tour* 50 Kč; 40 Kč children.
Wine-tasting tour 110 Kč. **No credit cards**.

The Ossuary

Kostnice
Church of Sts Peter & Paul (0206 621 2337). **Open**
English-language tours 10.30am, 1pm, 3pm, 5pm daily.
Admission 30 Kč; 15 Kč children. **No credit cards**.

Where to eat

Castle vinárna

Svatováclavská 19 (0206 622 121). **Open** 11am-6pm
Wed-Sun; closed Mon, Tue. **Main courses** 250 Kč.
No credit cards.

There are two restaurants inside the castle, and at press time two more were due to open. This is the swankiest: the crockery is embossed with the Lobkowicz insignia, the vaulted walls are painted peach and it's one of the best places in Bohemia to splash out on an expensive meal.

Restaurace Stará škola

Na vyhlídce 159 (no phone). **Open** 11am-11pm daily. **Main courses** 190 Kč. **No credit cards**.
This basic restaurant, close to the Church of Sts Peter and Paul, does steak and chips. The terrace has a stunning view over the surrounding countryside and the Vltava/Labe confluence.

Getting there

By bus

There are roughly ten departures a day from Prague's Florenc station. The trip takes around 50 minutes.

By car

33km (21 miles). Head north out of Prague on route 608; follow signs to Zdiby, then Mělník on Route 9.

Tourist information

Náměstí Míru 30 (0206 627 503). **Open** *May-Sept* 9am-5pm daily. *Oct-Apr* 9am-5pm Mon-Fri; closed Sat, Sun.

Terezín: 'Work makes you free.'

Terezín

Terezín, originally known as Theresienstadt, was built as a fortress town in 1780 on the orders of Emperor Joseph II, to protect his empire from Prussian invaders.

Its infamy dates from 1941, when the entire town became a holding camp for Jews en route to death camps further east. Of 140,000 men, women and children who passed through Terezín, 87,000 were sent east, mainly to Auschwitz. Only 3,000 returned alive. Another 34,000 people died within the ghetto of Terezín itself.

The town atmosphere is still distinctly eerie, with lifeless, grid-pattern streets. The Nazis expelled the native population, few of whom chose to return after the war.

The **Ghetto Museum** screens documentary films of wartime life here in several languages. Easily the creepiest contains clips from the Nazi propaganda film *The Führer Gives a Town to the Jews*, part of the sophisticated strategy to hoodwink the world. Red Cross officials visited the camp twice and saw a completely staged self-governing Jewish community with a flourishing cultural life.

The ground-floor exhibition of harrowing artwork produced by the children of Terezín has been removed to Prague's **Pinkas Synagogue** (*see page 121*). Upstairs is a well laid out exhibition on the Nazi occupation of Czechoslovakia. Decrees of discriminating measures against Jews are detailed – including the certificate that a customer in a pet shop intending to buy a canary had to sign, promising that the pet would not be exposed to any Jewish people.

A 15-minute walk back down the road towards Prague brings you to the **Small Fortress**, built at the same time as the larger town fortress. The Gestapo established a prison here in 1940, through which 32,000 political prisoners passed. Some 2,500 died within its walls.

The approach to the Small Fortress passes through a cemetery containing 10,000 graves of Nazi victims, most marked simply with numbers. In the middle stands a giant wooden cross – an insensitive memorial considering the tiny percentage of non-Jews buried here.

The whole fortress is now a museum and a free map (available from the ticket office) assists exploration of the Gestapo's execution ground and of courtyards and cells, some of which held more than 250 inmates at a time. The former SS commander's house is now a museum with displays detailing the appalling physical condition of the inmates.

Trips Out of Town

Ghetto Museum

Komenského 411, Terezín (0416 782 577). **Open** *Oct-Apr* 9am-6pm daily. *May-Sept* 9am-5.30pm daily. **Admission** 130 Kč; 100 Kč children, students. *Joint ticket for museum and Small Fortress* 150 Kč; 110 Kč children, students. **No credit cards.**

Small Fortress

Malá pevnost
Malá pevnost, Terezin (0416 782 577). **Open** *Oct-Apr* 8am-4.30pm daily. *May-Sept* 8am-6pm daily. **Admission** 130 Kč; 100 Kč children, students. *Joint ticket for fortress and Ghetto Museum* 150 Kč; 110 Kč children, students. **No credit cards.**
Guided tours for groups of ten or more.

Where to eat

Light meals and snacks can be had in the former guards' canteen just inside the entrance to the Small Fortress.

Hotel Salva Guarda

Mírové náměstí 12, Litoměřice (0416 732 506). **Open** 8am-10pm daily. **Main courses** 150 Kč. **Credit** AmEx, DC, MC, V.
The best hotel and restaurant in the area.

Restaurace u Hojtašů

Komenského 152, Terezín (0416 782 203). **Open** 10am-10pm daily. **Main courses** 150 Kč. **No credit cards.**
The best bet for a bite within Terezín town.

Getting there

By bus

Buses leave Florenc station about once every two hours. The journey takes 60-75 minutes.

By car

50km (31 miles) from Prague. Join Route 8 or the E55 at Holešovice, via Veltrusy.

Tourist information

Náměstí čs armády 85, Terezín (0416 782 369). **Open** *Apr-Sept* 9am-4pm Sun-Fri; closed Sat. *Oct-Mar* closed.

Castles

Karlštejn

Fantastically shaped and without a doubt the Czech Republic's most trafficked castle, Karlštejn is situated on a lush bend of the Berounka river. This 14th-century stronghold, former home to the royal jewels, is indeed impressive from afar. The approach, however, is overrun by pricey snack bars and hawkers of postcards, crystal and lace. Inside, the Holy Rood Chapel, its walls adorned

Chapel of the Holy Rood at **Karlštejn** Castle.

with semi-precious stones and painted wooden panels by Master Theodoric, plus an altar with a diptych by Tomaso da Modena, is the star of the show. The remaining rooms can't match this splendour. Karlštejn is an easy and convenient trip, but be prepared for throngs of tourists.

The Castle

0311 681 617. **Open** *Mar* 9am-noon, 1-3pm daily. *Apr, Oct* 9am-noon, 1-4pm daily. *May-June, Sept* 9am-noon, 1-5pm daily. *July-Aug* 9am-noon, 1-6pm Tue-Sun; closed Mon. Last tour one hour before closing. *Nov-Feb* closed. **Admission** *First tour* 200 Kč; 100 Kč children, students. *Second tour* 600 Kč; 200 Kč children, students.
The tours are available in English, but are thoroughly tedious in any language. The second and more expensive tour includes the chapel.

Where to eat

U Janů

Karlštejn 90 (0311 681 210). **Open** 11am-10pm Tue-Sun; closed Mon. **Main courses** 170Kč. **No credit cards.**
A cosy old-fashioned place with antlers hanging from the ceiling, a pleasant terrace garden and assorted schnitzels and goulash.

Koruna

Karlštejn 13 (0311 681 465). **Open** 10am-10pm Tue-Sun; closed Mon. **Main courses** 190Kč. **Credit** AmEx, MC, V.
A local fave populated by village beer drinkers.

Getting there

By car

30km (19 miles) south-west of Prague. Take the E50-D5 or Route 5 towards Plzeň, then leave the motorway at exit 10 and follow signs for Karlštejn.

By train

Trains leave Prague's Smíchovské nádraží or Hlavní nádraží for Karlštejn about every hour. The trip takes about 40 minutes. It's a ten-minute walk from the station up to the village, and a further 15 minutes from there up to the castle.

Konopiště

Other castles may showcase tapestried bedrooms, tranquil gardens or rows of stuffy portraits, but at Konopiště, taxidermy is the main attraction. This castle, which dates back to the 1300s, was refurbished by the Habsburgs as a hunting lodge to satisfy the passions of its most famous occupant, Archduke Francis Ferdinand. He resided here with his Czech wife Sophie, who was also shot when the Archduke was assassinated in Sarajevo in 1914, triggering World War I. Ferdinand never acceded to the throne to which he was heir, but as you meander through his decadent digs it will become apparent that he did damage enough, even so. Brace yourself for the accusing, glassy stares of hundreds of stuffed animal heads and thousands of sawn-off antlers. Ferdinand slaughtered nearly every kind of fauna imaginable and the taxidermy on display represents only one per cent of the total collection.

The Archduke supposedly felled an average of 20 animals a day, every day for 40 years. The fearsome-looking hunting weapons on display testify to the seriousness with which the Habsburgs approached this recreation. The tour lets you down gently with sedate rooms featuring collections of wooden Italian cabinets and Meissen porcelain. A second tour of the castle, requiring a separate ticket, takes you through the Archduke's private chambers, the chapel and a Habsburg-era version of a gentlemen's club.

The castle has large grounds in which the peacocks and pheasants aren't affixed to a wall. Bears pace incessantly in the dry moat, oblivious to their unluckier brethren within.

Konopiště's popularity is second only to that of Karlštejn, so expect lots of coach parties.

The Castle

0301 721 366. **Open** *Apr, Oct* 9am-noon, 1-3pm Tue-Fri; 9am-noon, 1-4pm Sat, Sun; closed Mon. *May-Aug* 9am-noon, 1-5pm daily. *Sept* 9am-noon, 1-4pm daily. *Nov* 9am-noon, 1-3pm Sat, Sun. **Admission** 120 Kč; 70 Kč students, children. **Credit** DC, MC, V.

Getting there

By bus

Buses leave from Florenc bus station nearly every 45 minutes; the trip lasts a little over an hour.

By car

35km (22 miles) from Prague. Go south on the D1 and exit near Benešov, following the signs for Konopiště.

By train

Hourly trains to Benešov from Hlavní nádraží take about one hour. The castle is a two-kilometre (1.25-mile) walk from the station, or you can catch one of the infrequent buses.

Křivoklát

This Gothic fortress is the perfect counterpoint to overtrafficked Karlštejn. Just inconvenient enough to remain peaceful, Křivoklát features one of the finest interiors in the country, thanks to devoted restoration. The drive there is lovely too, along the Berounka river, past fields, meadows, and a forested hill before the castle dramatically appears before you, perched upon a lofty promontory.

Křivoklát was originally a Přemyslid hunting lodge, later converted into a defensible castle at the beginning of the 12th century by King Vladislav I. But the bulk of the rebuilding was done by the Polish King Vladislav II Jagiellon, whose trademark 'W' can be seen throughout the Castle. A fine Gothic altarpiece in the Castle Chapel portrays Christ surrounded by sweet-looking angels holding medieval instruments of torture. A more varied selection awaits in the dungeon: a fully operational rack, a thumbscrew, the Rosary of Shame (a necklace made of lead weights) and the Iron Maiden. The Castle's enormous Round Tower dates from 1280. English alchemist Edward Kelley was locked up here after Rudolf II tired of waiting for him to succeed at turning base metals into gold.

The Castle

0313 558 120. **Open** *June-Aug* 9am-noon, 1-5pm daily. *May, Sept* 9am-noon, 1-4pm daily. *Mar, Apr, Oct* 9am-noon, 1-3pm Tue-Sun; closed Mon. **Admission** *Long tour* 120 Kč; 60 Kč students, children. *Short tour (tower only)* 70 Kč; 40 Kč students, children. **No credit cards.**

Two English-language tours run every half hour up to one hour before closing. Minimum five English-speakers (or those willing to pay for five tickets).

Where to eat

Hotel u Dvořáků

Roztoky 225, Křivoklát (0313 558 355). **Main courses** 150 Kč. **No credit cards.**
The only real place to eat near the castle, with decent menu of the usual Czech fare.

Getting there

By car

45km (28 miles) from Prague. Take the E50-D5 in the direction of Beroun. Turn off at junction 14 and follow the Berounka valley west, as if going to Rakovník.

By train

Direct trains to Křivoklát are infrequent, so take one to Beroun, which leave from Smíchovské nádraží or Hlavní nádraží about every half hour (journey time around 45 minutes), and change at Beroun for Křivoklát (a further 40 minutes).

Town & Village Overnighters

Brno bounces to an avant-garde beat, Tábor offers a take on Hussite history, Telč and Český Krumlov just sit there and look beautiful.

Brno

The capital of Moravia, the Czech Republic's sunnier eastern half, has been a bustling centre of trade and culture almost as long as Prague has, but always marched to its own tune. While Protestant soldiers were fighting off papal armies in Bohemia, Brno was erecting splendid Catholic cathedrals and monasteries.

Capping the pedestrianised old town centre is the vertiginous **Petrov** cathedral. Though a bit of a disappointment inside, it balances atop a suitably dramatic hill in defiance of the heretics. Its noon bells sound at 11am, a tradition that originated during the Swedish siege of Brno, when the town was supposedly saved by an ingenious monk: the attackers had decided to fight only until noon, and then give up and move on.

The **Capuchin Crypt**, just below Petrov and adjoining the former coal market, Zelný trh, features a sobering confrontation with the hereafter. Through the action of constant draughts, several nobles and monks buried here have mummified and are now on display, many still in their original garb. More lugubrious sights await in the fortress of **Špilberk**, on a hill even higher than Petrov's, across Husova from the old centre. Here you can visit the labyrinth of dungeons, the *kasematy*, where Emperor Joseph II had prisoners suspended on walls in the lightless dank.

Back in the fresh air, Brno's streets revive you with engaging walking possibilities: centuries-old pubs such as **Pegas**, the produce market on Zelný trh and half a dozen impressively ornate baroque cathedrals within strolling distance of the main square, náměstí Svobody. A sight that almost every tourist sees

Hip, but unpretentious hangout – Brno's **Spolek** bookstore café. *See p258.*

Bittová provocateur

More laid back and more assured than artists in Prague, the contemporary music makers, DJs and painters centred on Brno constitute a vital part of the Czech art world. The best-known Brno musician is **Iva Bittová** (pictured), the violin-playing, toy-squeaking warbler of nonsense noises and poetic lyrics with a voice like little bells. That may sound thoroughly annoying, but Bittová uses clownery to break down an audiences' defences until she has their hearts in her small, capable hands.

From the time of Bittová's first big break, the 1975 musical love story *Balada pro banditu* ('Ballad for a Bandit') she has played the provocateur both on stage and in the studio. Performing at the Brno theatre Na provázku (and later on film) as Eržika, the lover of a Carpathian Robin Hood and bearer of his child, the half-Romany Bittová pushed the boundaries of accepted social situations in Czech culture.

Her later collaborations with Pavel Fajt, a major counter-culture influence of the 1980s from the Brno area, produced daring albums that soon became required listening for every dissident. Bittová's mid-'90s efforts, *Pustit musíš* ('You Have to Let Go') and the double album *Bílé Inferno* ('White Inferno') brought in the distinctive moody bass and guitar sound of Vladimír Václavek, another Brno musician. That project also mixed in the children's choir of Lelekovice, the village near Brno where Bittová lives. The performer founded the ensemble on the principle that every child has the ability to make music. *Bílé Inferno*, released on the Brno label Indies, proved an unqualified hit.

The more recent *Čtyřicet Čtyři Duet pro Housle* ('Forty-four Duets for Violin'), with Dorothea Kellerová, in which the pair freely reinterpret Béla Bartók sketches, adding vocal improvisations, did even better. The Prague label Rachot created its most expensive packaging ever for the CD, each copy including a red feather from Bittová's costume, and was obliged to charge an unprecedented 600 Kč. It sold out in double-quick time and still can't be found today.

Bittová likes touring so it's possible to catch her in Prague and at alternative rock festivals. The best bet is to seek out the most progressive venues and line-ups: there's an even chance that Bittová will be on the roster. The Akropolis (*see page 212*) is a likely spot – but book early.

---

is the Dragon of Brno – actually an overstuffed crocodile – hanging outside the tourist information bureau. It is said to be the gift of a Turkish sultan who rather exaggerated its status – hence the name.

These days Brno is a bit more culturally savvy. In fact, a steady stream of Prague's more innovative musicians and artists flows westward from this part of Moravia (*see above* **Bittová provocateur**). You might run into a local rocker or performance artist at **Spolek**, the city's newest bookstore café. This is a prime spot to try Moravia's best claim to fame and distinction from Bohemia: delectable white wines. The owners also operate a popular pool hall pub, Mýdlo, around the corner.

Capuchin Crypt

Kapucínská krypta

Kapucínské náměstí (05 4221 3232). **Open** 9am-noon, 2pm-4.30pm Mon-Sat; 11am-11.45am, 2pm-4.30pm Sun. **Admission** 40 Kč; 20 Kč students, children under 6. **No credit cards**.

Castle Špilberk

Špilberk 1 (05 4221 4145). **Open** *May-June, Sept* 9am-5.15pm Tue-Sun; closed Mon. *July-Aug* 9am-5.15pm

daily. *Oct-Apr* 9am-4.15pm Tue-Sun; closed Mon.
Admission *Castle and dungeon* 60 Kč; 30 Kč students,
children under 6. *Dungeon only* 20 Kč; 10 Kč students,
children under 6. **No credit cards.**

Petrov

Biskupská and Petrská streets (05 4323 5030).
Open 9am-6pm daily. **Admission** 30 Kč; 15 Kč
students, children under 6. **No credit cards.**

Where to eat

Restaurant Pegas

Jakubská 4 (05 4221 0104). **Open** 9am-midnight
daily. **Main courses** 150 Kč. **Credit** DC, MC, V.
A classic, grand-scale beerhall with its own brew,
served in wheat and cinnamon varieties.

Šermířský klub LAC

Kopečná 50 (05 4323 7068). **Open** 11am-midnight
Mon-Fri; 5pm-midnight Sat, Sun. **Main courses** 150
Kč. **No credit cards.**
Ye olde Moravian inn, with waiters in medieval
tunics serving massive stuffed potato pancakes. It is
also the headquarters of the local historic sword-
fighting club.

Spolek

Orlí 22 (05 4221 9002). **Open** 10am-10pm daily. **No
credit cards.**
A short walk from the bus station, this bookstore
café is a hip but unpretentious hangout.

Nightlife

Charlie's Hat

Kobližná 12 (05 4221 0557). **Open** *Bars* 5pm-4am
Mon-Thur; 5pm-5am Fri; 6pm-5am Sat; 6pm-4am Sun.
Garden 11am-11pm Mon-Thur; 11am-midnight Fri;
noon-midnight Sat; 3pm-11pm Sun. **No credit cards.**
Handy labyrinth of bars and a patio with DJ action
and local bands.

Where to stay

Hotel Royal Ricc

*Starobrněnská 10 (05 4221 9262/fax 05 4221
9265/www.romantichotels.cz).* **Rates** (including
breakfast) single 2,500-3,000 Kč; double 2,800-3,200
Kč; suite 4,500 Kč. **Credit** AmEx, MC, V.
Those staying at the Royal Ricc can enjoy its
luxurious Renaissance-era quarters with timbered
ceilings, stained-glass windows and pampering
staff. Modern amenities, too.

Hotel Amphone

*Třída kapitána Jaroše 29 (05 4521 1783/fax 05 4521
1575/amphone@brn.czn.cz).* **Rates** (including
breakfast) single 950 Kč; double 1,390 Kč.
Credit AmEx, MC, V.
The most convenient and friendly accommodation
in Brno, although it is not situated in a particularly
enchanting building.

Getting there

By bus

Buses leave every two hours on weekdays, less
frequently on weekends, from Florenc station,
platform 10. Trip takes around two and a half hours.

By car

Take the E50/65 motorway directly to Brno.

By train

Trains leave from Hlavní nádraží 11 times a day and
take about three and a half hours.

Tourist information

Tourist Information Brno

*Radnická 8 Brno (4221 1090/4221 0758/
www.kultura-brno.cz).* **Open** 8am-6pm Mon-Fri;
9am-5pm Sat, Sun.
Staff can book rooms at hotels and pensions.

Český Krumlov

In 1992 the tiny south Bohemian town of Český
Krumlov so impressed UNESCO with its beauty
that it was declared second in importance only
to Venice on the World Heritage list. A castle and
fantastic pink Renaissance tower rise high above
the town, idyllically positioned on a double loop
of the Vltava river on the eastern edge of the
unspoilt, forested Šumava region. It's almost
impossible not to be impressed and charmed
by Český Krumlov. The streets are a labyrinth
of tiny cobbled alleyways and almost every
building is an architectural gem.

The Castle is one of the most extensive
complexes in Central Europe, with 40 buildings
in five courtyards. Founded before 1250, the
fortress was adopted by the Rožmberk clan in
1302. As their wealth and influence increased, it
was transformed into the palace you see today.

Cross the dry moat to enter, noting the bored
bears that roam below. The tower was redone as
a whimsical pink and yellow Renaissance affair
in 1591, topped with marble busts and gold
trimmings. The five-tiered Plášťový Bridge is
equally spectacular, linking sections of the palace
perched on two steep escarpments. For the best
view descend to the Stag Gardens (Jelení zahrada)
and look upwards. The extensive formal gardens
host a **summer music festival** featuring
everything from costumed period performances
to Roma music.

The highlights of the castle tour include a
gilded carriage built in 1638 to convey presents
to the Pope, and the Mirror and Masquerade
Halls, both triumphs of the art of stucco and
trompe l'oeil painting.

Český Krumlov Castle – founded before 1250, built around five courtyards.

On the opposite side of the Vltava from the Castle district (Latrán) is Nové město (New Town), laid out a mere seven centuries ago. On Horní street, you'll notice the impressive Church of St Vitus, circa 1439, the long slender tower of which is visible from all parts of town.

It's not just a tourist town. Residents work in graphite mining, at the Eggenberg Brewery or at the nearby paper mills. Before World War II, Český Krumlov was part of the predominantly German-speaking Sudetenland, so was annexed by Hitler in 1938. The majority of the region's German-speaking inhabitants were then expelled in 1945 and the town's centuries-old bicultural life came to an end.

The Castle

0337 711 687/711 465. **Open** *Apr, Oct* 9am-noon, 1-3pm daily. *May, Sept* 9am-noon, 1-4pm daily. *June-Aug* 9am-noon, 1-5pm Tue-Sun; closed Mon. *Nov-Mar* closed. **Admission** 130 Kč; 65 Kč children. **No credit cards.**
The only way to see the castle is to take an hour-long tour. Last entrance is one hour before closing time.

Český Krumlov International Music Festival

Various venues (Auviex 6126 3700/www.auviex.cz) **Date** August. **Admission** varies according to venue.

Where to eat & stay

Hospoda Na louži

Kajovská 66 (0337 711 280). **Open** 10am-11pm daily. **Main courses** 200 Kč. **No credit cards.**
A good place to sample some Southern Bohemian cuisine. This is a central pub with traditional food and atmosphere.

Hotel Růže

Horní 154 (337 711 141/fax 337 711 128/hotelruze@ck.ipex.cz). **Rates** 1,820-3,800 Kč single;

2,580-4,780 Kč double; 3,260-7,290 Kč suite. **Main courses** 350-700 Kč. **Credit** AmEx, MC, V.
A restoration of this towering Renaissance pile, a former Jesuit college, has helped to create one of the country's most luxurious hotels. The carved wood furnishings, ceiling beams, cellar wine bar and amazing views fit the town perfectly. The modern attractions feel almost out of place: a sleek fitness centre and pool, business amenities, top-notch service and a disco. Its three restaurants will keep you well fed.

Pension Ve věži

Pivovarská 28 (0337 711 742). **Rates** (including breakfast) 1,000 Kč double. **No credit cards.**
Call well ahead to reserve one of the four rooms inside this fortress tower with metre-thick walls.

Getting there

By bus

Two buses a day leave from Roztyly bus station in the afternoon. The trip takes about four hours.

By car

Either leave Prague on the Brno motorway (D1-E50) and then take the E55 at Mirošovice past Tábor and České Budějovice, then the 159 road; or go via Písek leaving Prague on Route 4, towards Strakonice.

By train

The trip from Hlavní nádraží takes five hours and includes a change at České Budějovice.

Tourist information

Tourist Information Český Krumlov

Náměstí Svornosti 1 (0337 711 183). **Open** *July, Aug* 9am-8pm daily. *Sept-June* 9am-6pm daily. **No credit cards.**
Staff can book canoe and boat tours down the Vltava. Trips range from a one-hour jaunt to an eight-hour expedition.

Egon Schiele's revenge

Egon Schiele and Český Krumlov never had a terribly healthy relationship. The moody young artist stayed here for a few months in 1911, and the town gave him inspiration – mostly in the form of adolescent nude girls, whom he portrayed in some of his best Expressionist gouaches. But the town's price was to run him out on a rail, abruptly ending his fruitful stay.

It's not surprising that a turn-of-the-century Czech mountain town, even one with such rich a history of art and architecture, should have looked askance at a morose young Viennese painter who wanted to explore their daughters' forms. After his eviction by folk he regarded as simple, Schiele never returned to the Czech town where his mother was born.

Even his paintings of Český Krumlov show some revulsion for the place, clearly vying with an appreciation of its beauty. Such turmoil was par for the course for the tortured Austrian, who

Egon Schiele: self portrait.

died at 28 of Spanish flu. His last painting, a haunting image of his wife, was completed one day before she died, six months pregnant, of the same flu.

It's ironic but typical that the town's most significant modernist collection – and a reasonable source of revenue – is the **Egon Schiele Art Centre**. His former studios just west of the main square on Široká were adapted in 1993 into an exhibition space, showing 80 of his works on permanent loan from private American collectors. The limited collection may be disappointing to diehard Schiele fans, but its presence testifies in a bittersweet way to the eventual victory of genius over provincialism.

Egon Schiele Art Centre

Široká 70-72 (0337 704 011). **Open** *Apr-Oct* 10am-6pm daily. *Nov-Mar* 11am-5pm daily. **Admission** 120 Kč; 60 Kč students. **Credit** AmEx, DC, MC, V.

Tábor

If you're a bit nonplussed by the sleepy streets of Tábor, bear in mind that things haven't really been hopping in this town for over 600 years. Its beginnings were steeped in drama. A band of religious radicals founded Tábor in 1420 following Jan Hus's execution (*see page 8*). Led by the one-eyed general Jan Žižka, 15,000 Taborites battled the Catholic forces for nearly 15 years. Their policies of equal rights for men and women and common ownership of property did not endear them to the ruling classes and the Taborites were eventually crushed by moderate Hussite forces under George of Poděbrady. A statue of Žižka sits astride a hill overlooking Prague; Tábor honours him with a more modest sculpture in its main square.

Bone up on more details of Hussite history at the town's **Hussite Museum**. A highlight is Žižka's unusual military innovation, a crude sort of tank consisting of cannons balanced on a wagon. The museum also runs tours of a section

of the underground passages, used as stores and refuges, that snake under much of the centre. Most of the town's other bona fide points of interest are also on the main square, Žižkovo náměstí, from which the city's many labyrinthine streets and alleys radiate. Their confusing layout is not due to *ad hoc* medieval building, but was a deliberate ploy to confuse the town's enemies. The square is also adorned with a fountain statue of a Hussite, and two stone tablets believed to have been used for religious services.

Hussite Museum

Žižkovo náměstí 1 (0361 254 286). **Open** *Apr-Oct* 8.30am-5pm daily. *Nov-Mar* 8.30-5pm Mon-Fri; closed Sat, Sun. **Admission** 40 Kč; children 20 Kč. *Tunnel tours* 40 Kč; children 20Kč. **No credit cards**.

Where to stay, eat & drink

Beseda

Žižkovo náměstí (no phone). **Open** 10am-10pm daily. **No credit cards**.
Beerhall within the town hall on the main square.

Černý leknín
Příběnická 695 (0361 256 405). **Rates** (including breakfast) 1,290 Kč single; 1,550 Kč double. **No credit cards.**
A Gothic villa. The best accommodation in Tábor.

Getting there

By bus
Two or three buses depart Prague's Florenc station for Tábor daily. The trip takes around two hours.

By car
82km (51 miles) south of Prague. Take the D1 south-east towards Jihlava and Brno, exiting at junction 21 to highway 3 south.

By train
Trains to Vienna from Prague stop in Tábor. The journey lasts just under two and a half hours.

Tourist information

Infocentrum
Žižkovo náměstí 2 (0361 486 230). **Open** *May-Sept* 8.30am-7pm Mon-Fri; 9am-1pm Sat; 1-5pm Sun. *Oct-Apr* 9am-4pm Mon-Fri; closed Sat, Sun.

Telč

The tiny town of Telč, with its immaculately preserved Renaissance buildings, still partly enclosed by medieval fortifications and surrounded by lakes, undoubtedly deserves its place on UNESCO's World and Natural Heritage list. Its centrepiece is a large rhomboid central square dating back to the 14th century, with a delicate colonnade running along three of its sides. That feature, along with the photogenic gabled houses, were added in the 16th century by Zacharía of Hradec. A trip to Genoa and a fortuitous marriage to Katerina of Wallenstein gave this Renaissance man the inspiration and means to rebuild the town following a devastating fire in 1530. Each of the pastel-hued buildings has a different façade adorned with frescoes, sgraffito or later baroque and rococo sculptures.

The narrow end of the square is dominated by the onion-domed bell towers of the 17th-century Jesuit church on one side and the **Renaissance castle** on the other. In 1552 Zacharía decided to turn his 14th-century family seat into his principal residence. At his invitation Italian architect Baldassare Maggi arrived with a troupe of master masons and stuccodores and set to work transforming the Gothic fort into the Italianate palace you see today. The coffered ceilings of the Golden Hall and of the Blue Hall, and the monochrome *trompe l'oeil* decorations that cover every inch of plaster in the Treasury are among the finest Renaissance interior decorations in Central Europe. The Marble Hall exhibits fantastic armour for knight and steed, while the African Hall is a collection of hunting trophies.

The castle also houses a small municipal museum with an unusual 19th-century mechanical nativity crib. There is a permanent exhibition of works by Moravian surrealist Jan Zrzavý (1890-1977). After you've exhausted the interior possibilities, relax in the peaceful gardens that stretch down to the lake.

The Castle
Náměstí Zachariáše z Hradce (066 724 3943). **Open** *Apr, Sept, Oct* 9-11.30am, 1-4pm (last tour 3.30pm) daily. *May-Aug* 9-11.30am, 1-5pm (last tour 4.15pm) Tue-Sun; closed Mon. *Nov-Mar* closed. **Admission** *Castle* 120 Kč; 60 Kč children. *Gallery* 20 Kč; 10 Kč children. **No credit cards.**
Tours are conducted in Czech but you can pick up a detailed English text at the ticket counter.

Where to eat & stay

Hotel pod kaštany
Štěpnická 409 (066 721 3042). **Rates** 500Kč single; 850 Kč double. **Credit** MC, V, AmEx.
Past its prime, perhaps, but a friendly place.

Pension Privát Nika
Náměstí Zachariáše z Hradce 45 (066 724 3104). **Rates** 350 Kč single; 700 Kč double. **No credit cards.**
Comfortable and good value.

Šenk pod věží
Palackého 116 (066 724 3889). **Open** 11am-10pm daily. **Main courses** 150 Kč. **No credit cards.**
Of the various restaurants in Telč, this is the most charming. It serves good Czech fare, has friendly staff and a terrace.

Getting there

By bus
Buses leave five times daily from Florenc bus station and once per afternoon from Roztyly. The journey takes just under four hours.

By car
150km (93 miles) south-east of Prague. Head out of Prague in the direction of Brno on the E50/D1 motorway. At Pávov follow signs to Jihlava; at Třešť follow signs to Telč.

Tourist information

Tourist Information Telč
Náměstí Zachariáše z Hradce 10 (066 724 3145). **Open** *July-Aug* 8am-6pm Mon-Fri; 9am-6pm Sat, Sun. *Sept-June* 8am-5pm Mon-Fri; 9am-5pm Sat, Sun. **No credit cards.**
Staff can book accommodation, plus fishing, horse riding and hunting expeditions.

Trips Out of Town

Country Overnighters

Camp in the Czech Paradise or spelunk in the Moravian Karst.

Český ráj

Český ráj literally means 'Czech Paradise', and it certainly is one when compared to the industrial pollution of the surrounding region. Český ráj is a peaceful haven of densely forested hills, giant rock formations and ruined castles that constitute a protected national park. For many Czechs, donning walking boots and venturing into the great outdoors does indeed come close to paradise (*see page 187* **Carry on *kempink***). Though the area is accessible by road, the best way to explore it is on foot; even reluctant amateurs can cross the region in two days. The neighbouring towns of Jičín and Turnov provide a good base from which to begin your exploration, as signposted trails can be followed almost from the centres of the towns. A great way to see Český ráj is to get the train to one town and hike over to the other for the return train journey.

The greatest concentration of protruding rocks is to be found around Hrubá skála: follow any of the marked footpaths from the village and you'll soon find yourself surrounded by these pockmarked giants. The Hotel Zámek and Hotel Štekl (*for both, see page 266*) make the best bases for exploring the region. The most useful map is the *Český ráj Poděbradsko*, available at any decent Prague bookshop.

Supreme among ruined castles in the area is **Trosky** (the name means 'ruins'). Its two towers, built on dauntingly inaccessible basalt outcrops, form the most prominent silhouette in the region.

The taller, thinner rock goes by the name of Panna (Maiden), while the smaller one is Bába (Grandmother). In the 14th century, Čeněk of Vartemberk undertook a monumental feat of medieval engineering by building a tower on each of the two promontories, and interconnecting ramparts between them.

The towers remained virtually impregnable, as they could only be reached by an ingenious wooden structure that could be dismantled in times of siege, leaving invaders with the choice of scaling the impossibly steep rocks or, more likely, beating a hasty retreat. In the 19th century Trosky Castle became a favourite haunt of Romantic poets, painters and patriots. Now you too can climb to the base of the tower on Panna for outstanding views of the countryside.

From 1 April until 31 October climbers can scale the sandstone pinnacles in the region. Simply pay the 40 Kč entry fee at any park attendants' booth.

Trosky Castle

Troskovice-Rovensko (0436 313 925).
Open *May-Aug* 8am-5pm Tue-Sun; closed Mon. *Sept* 9am-5pm Tue-Sun; closed Mon. *Oct-Apr* 9am-4pm Sat, Sun, public holidays; closed Mon-Fri.
Admission 20 Kč; 10 Kč children. **No credit cards**.

Where to eat & stay

Places close to every main tourist sight offer filling, if uninspiring, Czech fare. If you want to sleep out there are several campsites, but most people just seem to pitch their tent on any appealing plot of land.

Český ráj – peaceful haven of forested hills and giant rock formations.

Hotel Štekl

Hrubá skála (0436 391 684). **Rates** 490 Kč single; 750 Kč double (including breakfast). **Open** *Restaurant* 10am-8pm daily. **Main courses** 150 Kč. **Credit** MC, V. Resembles an alpine resthouse and has views over the surrounding valleys. Decent dining room.

Hotel Zámek

Hrubá skála castle (0436 391681). **Rates** 850 Kč single; 1,120 Kč double. **Open** *Restaurant* 11am-7.30pm Wed-Sun; closed Mon, Tue. **Main courses** 250 Kč. **Credit** AmEx, MC, V. Fabulous location, good prices and fantastic views from the ivy-covered turret rooms.

Getting there

By bus

Four buses a day go to Malá skála from Holešovice bus station. A private bus line leaves each morning from Palmovka metro for Jičín. Call 6631 1040 for information. It's roughly a two-hour ride.

By car

About 90km (56 miles) north-east of Prague; follow signs to Mladá Boleslav and join the E65 or Route 10 to Turnov. Jičin is 23km (14 miles) south-west of Turnov. Hrubá skála and Trosky are both just off Route 35 – the Turnov-Jičin road.

By train

Eight trains a day leave Hlavní nádraží for Turnov. There are local connections from Turnov to Hrubá skála and Malá skála. A local train goes between Jičin and Turnov.

Moravian caves

The east of the Czech Republic is riddled with caves (*jeskyně*), the most notable of which are north of the Moravian capital of Brno. Caving in this country is not for spelunkers alone: it's common to see busloads of children and even pensioners (the rarefied air is touted as a cure for allergies and asthma). Guided tours through the limestone caves are a welcome respite in the summer. But bring a sweater.

The Moravský kras ('Moravian karst'), a series of 400 holes, is by far the most concentrated and accessible network of caves in the Czech Republic. They are best visited as a day trip from Brno (*see page 256*). All of these are limestone caves, created over 350 million years by slightly acidic rain water and underground streams. The Kateřinská, Sloupsko-Šošůvské and Balcarka caves are all within easy reach of Brno.

If you're looking to do all your caving in one go, your best bet is the **Punkevní jeskyně**, the largest cave in the country. Some three kilometres (two miles) of the caves' 12km (7.5-mile) length is

open to the public. Passages of stalactites give way to the colossal Macocha Abyss. 140m (459ft) deep, it was formed in part by the collapse of the ceiling of a cave farther below. The tour then sends you down the narrow tunnels by boat. The passages are barely wide enough for the boats, and you'd likely be impaled by a stalactite if you stood up.

Arrive early in peak season as tours can sell out by mid morning. It's even better to reserve a place by phone, as queues can be long.

There are other attractions within easy reach by car. The most popular is the spectacular Gothic castle of **Pernštejn**; others include the Napoleonic battlefield of **Austerlitz** (Slavkov) and the **Alfons Mucha Museum** at the Renaissance château of Moravský Krumlov.

Moravský kras

Skalní mlýn (0506 413 575). **Open** *Punkevní jeskyně* 8.20am-3.50pm daily. *All other caves* Apr-Aug 8.30am-3.30pm daily; Sept-Mar closed. **Admission** *Punkevní jeskyně* 75 Kč adults, 30 Kč students, children (includes chairlift to cave entrance and boat ride). *Other caves* 40 Kč adults; 20 Kč students; free under-6s. **No credit cards.**

Where to eat & stay

Hotel Skalní Mlýn

Skalní Mlýn (0506 418 113). **Rates** 690 Kč single; 940 Kč double. **Open** *Restaurant* 9am-11pm. **Main courses** 150 Kč. **Credit** AmEx, MC, V. A popular place but the best base for the caves – and with a reasonable restaurant.

Getting there

By bus

Buses run roughly every hour between Brno and Prague. Journey time is two and a half hours.

By car

202km (126 miles) south-east of Prague. The D1 motorway runs all the way to Brno. The caves are 22km (14 miles) north-east of Brno.

By train

Hourly trains to Brno from Prague take between three and four hours. A dozen trains a day leave Brno for the nearby town of Blansko. Local buses then run to the caves. A tourist train travels between the Punkevní and the centre of Skalní Mlýn, from which the other three caves are accessible.

Tourist information

Tourist information Brno

Old Town Hall, Radnická 8, Brno (05 4221 1090). **Open** 8am-6pm Mon-Fri, 9am-5pm Sat, Sun. **No credit cards.** Can book rooms as well as providing maps, brochures and other information.

Trips Out of Town

Trips Abroad

Hike in the High Tatras or contemplate culture in dynamic Dresden.

Dresden

The transformation of the capital of Saxony from living ruin to cultural centre is proceeding at an almost disorienting pace. The cranes that stalk every city of the former East Germany punctuate the skyline here too, albeit more sparingly than at any time since 1989. Thanks to their work, evidence of the city's devastation during World War II, with which the city marketed itself to tourists just a few years ago, is visibly making way for designer shops, trendy cafés and a lively club and music scene.

Those art and architectural treasures that survived Allied bombing balance the new with a rich complement of historic buildings and great paintings dating back to the Gothic era.

The famous bombing raids of February 1945 caused huge firestorms killing up to 100,000 people, mostly refugees from the Eastern Front. But it wasn't the first time Dresden was destroyed by flames: Altendresden, on the bank of the Elbe, was consumed by fire in 1685. Augustus III did much to rebuild, then lost to Prussia in the Seven Years War (1756-63). Frederick the Great destroyed much of the city in that war, although not the **Brühlsche Terrassen** in the old part of the city. A victorious Napoleon ordered the demolition of the city's defences in 1809.

Dresden's main attractions are the surviving buildings from the reign of Augustus the Strong (1670-1733), Augustus III's predecessor. The Hofkirche (Am Theaterplatz 1), the **Zwinger**, a garden containing one of Germany's best art museums, and the Grünes Gewölbe, a collection of Augustus' jewels and knick-knacks in the **Albertinum**, all have the flavour of the city's baroque exuberance. They can be reached via the Hauptbahnhof's Prager Straße exit and the mall that takes you into Altstadt, the old centre of town along the west bank of the Elbe.

Across the river stands the Neustadt. This new hub of Dresden nightlife and fashion has sprung up on and around Hauptstraße, with hip venues like the **Hostel Mond Palast** rock club and the tapas restaurant **El Espanol** all within walking distance. Dozens of alternative entertainments fill the back pages of *Sax* magazine, available at any newsstand. It's a far cry from communist times, when this part of Germany, shut off from

Western media by the Saxon hills, was known as *'Tal der Ahnungslosen'* ('Valley of the Clueless').

After World War II, Dresden's destruction was lamented far and wide. The city was twinned with Coventry and Benjamin Britten's *War Requiem* was given its first performance in the Hofkirche by musicians from both towns. Kurt Vonnegut's novel *Slaughterhouse Five*, based on his experiences as an American POW in Dresden during the bombing, became a cult hit. Reconstruction, erratic under the GDR, has come so far that even the **Frauenkirche**, on Neumarkt in the Altstadt district, which stood in rubble for 50 years as the symbol of Dresden's suffering, is nearly complete. The **Semperoper**, named after its architect Gottfried Semper (1838-41), is another delight now restored to its earlier elegance.

Other surviving cultural treasures are on show in the **Gemäldegalerie Alte Meister** in the Zwinger. The building features a superb collection of Old Masters, particularly Italian Renaissance and Flemish, as well as exhibitions of porcelain from nearby Meißen, plus armour, weapons, clocks and scientific equipment.

Industrialisation also produced some impressive buildings: the **Rathaus** (1905-10) at Dr-Külz-Ring; the **Hauptbahnhof** (1892-95) where your Prague train arrives; the **Yenidze** cigarette factory (1912) in Könneritzstraße, designed to look like a mosque and now home to a cheap rooftop restaurant; and the grandiose **Landtagsgebäude** (completed to plans by Paul Wallot in 1907) at Heinrich-Zille-Straße 11. Massive rebuilding of the **Schloß** and buildings throughout the Altstadt should see Dresden in its best light for its 1,000th anniversary in 2006.

The **Striezelmarkt** (named after the savoury pretzel you will see everyone eating), is held on Altstädtermarkt every December. At the colourful Christmas market you can sample *Gluhwein* and find *Stollen*, a German variety of yuletide cake. Dresden's is said to be the best.

Note: dial 00 49 351 before the numbers below when calling from outside Germany.

Albertinum

Brühlsche Terrasse, Altstadt (491 4622).
Open 10am-6pm Mon-Wed, Fri-Sun; closed Thur.
Admission DM7; DM4 concessions.
No credit cards.
The Albertinium houses two major collections of paintings and treasures, the Gemäldegalerie Neue Meister and the Grünes Gewölbe.

Dresden – architectural treasure. *See p264.*

Semperoper
Altstädter Wache, Theaterplatz, Altstadt (484 2323/ 491 1730/www.semperoper.de). **Open** noon-5pm Mon-Fri; 10am-1pm Sat; closed Sun. **Tickets** DM9-DM75; DM8 concessions. **No credit cards.**
The Altstädter Wache is the box office for the Semperoper. The season is complemented by tours of the opera house and performances in summer.

Gemäldegalerie Alte Meister
in the Zwinger at the Theaterplatz, Altstadt (491 4619/www.staatl-kunstsammlungen-dresden.de). **Open** 10am-6pm Tue-Sun; closed Mon. **Admission** DM7; DM4 concessions. **No credit cards.**

Where to eat & drink

El Espanol
An der Dreikönigskirche 7, Neustadt (804 8670/ www.espanol.de). **Open** 10am-1am Mon-Thur; 10am-2am Fri, Sat; 10am-1am Sun. **Main courses** DM15. **Credit** AmEx, MC, V.
Summer dining on the street under torchlight with spicy tapas and courteous service.

Yenidze
Weißeritzstraße 3, Altstadt (490 5990). **Open** 11am-midnight daily. **Main courses** 10DM. **Credit** AmEx, MC, V.
Mosel wine and nosebleed views at this terrace restaurant, atop a *faux* mosque and former factory.

Where to stay

Hotel Classic Restaurant
Winckelmannstraße 6, Südvorstadt-West (478 500/fax 478 5099/www.hotel-classic.de). **Rates** (including breakfast) DM 140-180 single; DM 170-210 double; DM 295 suite; DM 30 extra bed; DM 20 children 7-12; free for children under 6. **Credit** AmEx, MC, V.
Quaint old family house-cum-hotel one block south of the main rail station.

Hostel Mond Palast
Katherinenstrasse, Neustadt (804 6061). **Rates** DM25 per person. **No credit cards.**
Serviceable hostel in a former industrial space that's a mecca for the new Dresden counterculture, with bar, pool tables and live rock.

Getting there

By car
Take the E55 to Dresden, about a three-hour drive.

By train
Trains from Hlavní nádraži leave for Dresden three times daily. The trip takes 3 hours, with beautiful riverside scenery along the way.

Tourist information

Tourist office
Prager Straße, Altstadt (491 920/www.dresden-tourist.de). **Open** 10am-6pm Mon-Fri; 10am-2pm Sat, Sun.
There's an English-speaking service at two tourist offices, both of which can book hotel rooms. The Dresden Card is available for DM27. It allows free travel on public transport and also free or reduced admission to museums for one adult and child. It's valid for 48 hours.
Branch: Neustädter Markt, Neustadt (491 920).

The Tatra mountains

It's a long haul from Prague to the mountains of Slovakia, but if skiing, climbing or serious hiking is on your agenda, don't be swayed when Praguers' recommend the Bohemian hills. The Tatras have what you're looking for.

Though it's a small range just 20 kilometres (12.5 miles) long, the Vysoké Tatry ('High Tatras') together with the Nízké Tatry ('Low Tatras') in northern Slovakia offer a wealth of jutting rock, alpine lakes and challenging trails. The tallest mountain is Gerlachovský štit, at 2,655 metres (8,710 feet). In the wooded valleys leading up to the peaks, it's not unusual to spot marmots, foxes or even brown bears – these last are generally harmless if left alone. Tiny alpine

Trips Out of Town

Take a scenic Slovak hike in the **High Tatras**.

blooms of primrose, gentian and mountain orchids dot the peaks well into June.

Though policing is patchy, hiking season often does not officially open until well into June and closes at the end of October. More worrisome than the chance of a fine are the sudden and violent summer storms of the region. But the mountain rescue service is experienced (call 0969 442 2820 or 0969 442 2855 24 hours) and thousands of hikers each year enjoy the stunning views and mountains without a hitch. Villages invariably feature a cheap and basic pension; a few have classy rustic hotels with saunas.

Despite their name, the Low Tatras offer the better skiing, on the slopes of Chopok, and climbing, on Ďumbier. Both are most easily accessed from the town of Jasná.

The High Tatras are far more easygoing, if no less scenic, hiking and crawl with tourists in warm weather. Slovak cuisine is hearty and meaty, though *halušky*, a kind of gnocchi with sour cream, is delightful. Plum brandy, or *slivovice*, takes more getting used to.

Note: dial 00 421 before telephone numbers when calling from outside Slovakia; from within the towns listed, leave off the local area code. Prices are given in Slovak crowns, worth a little less than their Czech counterparts.

Where to stay & eat

Grand Hotel

Demenovská dolina Jasná (0849 559 1441). **Open** *Restaurant* 7am-10am, noon-3pm, 6pm-10pm daily. **Main courses** 200-300 SK. **Rates** (including breakfast) 1,910 SK single; 2,650 SK double; 4,000 SK suite. **Credit** AmEx, MC, V.
You could spend a lot less but the comfort might be appreciated after a day on the scree.

Bilíkova chata

Hrebienok, Starý Smokovec (0969 442 2439). **Open** *Restaurant* 7.30am-7.30pm daily. **Main courses** 100-120 SK. **Rates** (including breakfast) 1,010 SK single; 1,802 SK double; 1,912 SK triple; 3,398 SK suite; 308 SK extra bed. **No credit cards**.
Friendly little pension in the woods near the top of the Starý Smokovec chair lift.

Getting there

By car

Take the E50/E65 motorway to Brno, then continue on the E50 when it branches off as a dual-carriageway via Trenčín and Žilina. The trip takes at least seven and a half hours.

By train

Trains from Hlavní nádraží leave five times a day and take around eight and a half hours to reach Liptovský Mikuláš, the stop for the Low Tatras. Poprad, the stop for the High Tatras, is about an hour further. From Liptovský Mikuláš, change to a local bus for Jasná from opposite the train station. From Poprad, change to a local train for Starý Smokovec.

Tourist information

Informačné centrum mesta Liptovský Mikuláš

Námestie mieru 1, Liptovský Mikuláš (0849 16 186/ www.lmikulas.sk). **Open** *Jun 16-Sept 15, Dec 15-Mar* 8am-7pm Mon-Fri; 8am-2pm Sat; noon-6pm Sun. *Apr-June 15, Sept 16-Dec 15* 9am-6pm Mon-Fri; 8am-noon Sat; closed Sun. **No credit cards**.
Can provide information and accommodation in Liptovský Mikuláš and the Low Tatras.

Popradská informačná agentura

Námestie sv Egídia 2950, Poprad (092 772 1700/16186/www.poprad.sk). **Open** *May-Sept* 8am-6pm Mon-Fri; 9am-1pm Sat; closed Sun. *Oct-Apr* 8.30am-12.30, 1pm-5pm Mon-Fri; 9am-1pm Sat; closed Sun. **No credit cards**.
Can help with information and accommodation in Poprad and the High Tatras or book you into cottages above Starý Smokovec.

T-ski Travel

Starý Smokovec 46 (0969 442 3200). **Open** 9am-6pm daily. **Credit** MC, V.
Staff can book rooms and hire out skis and bikes.

Trips Out of Town

Directory

Directory

Getting Around

By air

Prague's only airport, the recently expanded and modernised Ruzyně, is located about 20 kilometres (12.5 miles) north-west of the centre, and is not directly accessible by metro or tram. Some of the more expensive hotels provide a pick-up service from the airport if you book ahead and there is a regular public bus service.

For information in English on arrivals and departures call 2011 3314; for other airport information call 2011 3321.

CONNECTIONS TO THE CITY

Airport taxis are regulated but often charge illegally high prices. The ride, which should take about 20 to 25 minutes, should cost around 300 Kč to the centre. Check at the airport information kiosk for the going rate to your destination. For a more honest taxi driver you could try taking your luggage to the customs depot (where people accept air-freighted shipments from abroad) and phone one of the local taxi services to fetch you (*see page 271*). They will not pick you up at the regular arrivals/departures area, though.

EXPRESS AIRPORT BUS

Two express buses run every half hour from the airport into town, first stopping in Prague 6 at Dejvická metro – the end station on the green Line A – and then at Revoluční třída in Prague 1. The Welcome Touristic bus runs from 8.30am to 7pm and the Čeda bus 4.30am to 11.30pm daily.

The express bus service is quick and cheap at 15 Kč for the 20-minute ride to Dejvická and 30 Kč for the 35-minute ride to Revoluční třída. Out of hours, night bus 510 goes from the airport to Divoká Šárka, from where you can catch night tram 51 to the centre.

LOCAL BUS

Three local buses run from the airport to metro stations about every 20 minutes from 5am to midnight. Bus 119 runs from the airport to Dejvická metro (green Line A), bus 108 goes to Hradčanská metro (green Line A) and bus 179 goes to Nové Butovice metro (yellow Line B). This is the cheapest, slowest and most crowded alternative. If you have a lot of luggage, you will need to buy extra tickets for your bags. The buses depart from the stands in front of the arrivals hall. There you'll find orange public transport ticket machines (you'll need change). There are also ticket machines and an information office in the airport lobby. For ticket details, *see page 269*.

By rail

International trains arrive at the Main Station (Hlavní nádraží, sometimes called Wilson Station or Wilsonovo nádraží) and Holešovice Station (Nádraží Holešovice) – both on the red Line C of the metro. It's easy to get off at Holešovice thinking that it is the main station. If your train stops at both, wait for the last stop.

The centrally located Main Station is a beautiful art nouveau building with communist-period lower halls. It has several food stalls and

a PIS information office in the main hall and showers and a 24-hour left luggage area below in the lower hall.

It's never a good idea to hang around in the small park near the station – locals have nicknamed it Sherwood Forest because so much illegal redistribution of wealth goes on here.

24-hour rail infoline
2422 4200/2461 4030.
National and international timetable info. English is spoken. For ticket prices, call 2461 5249 (8am-7pm daily).

Hlavní nádraží
Main Station
Wilsonova, Nové Město, Prague 2 (2422 4200/2461 4030). Metro Hlavní Nádraží/12, 25 tram. **Map** p307 M5.

Masarykovo nádraží
Masaryk Station
Hybernská, Nové Město, Prague 1 (2461 4030/2422 4200). Metro Náměstí Republiky/3, 5, 14, 24, 26 tram. **Map** p307 L3.

Nádraží Holešovice
Holešovice Station
Vrbenského, Prague 7 (2461 5865). Metro Nádraží Holešovice/12, 25 tram. **Map** p310 E1.

Smíchovské nádraží
Smíchov Station
Nádražní, Prague 5 (2461 7686). Metro Smíchovské nádraží/12 tram.

By coach

Florenc coach station may be the least pleasant place in Prague. Perhaps its best feature is that it is on two metro lines (yellow Line B and red Line C) so you can make a quick getaway. Late arrivals can take the night tram or a taxi or stay in one of the hotels on Na Poříčí, the main street in front of the station. The easiest place to buy coach tickets is Čedok (*see page 288*).

Kingscourt Express

Havelská 8, Staré Město, Prague 1 (2423 4583/2423 3334). Metro Můstek. **Open** 8am-6pm Mon-Fri; 9am-1pm Sat; closed Sun. **No credit cards.** Kingscourt Express is the biggest company running coach services to and from the UK.

Getting around Prague

Walking is the best way to see the relatively compact centre of Prague. Every twist of the city's ancient streets reveals some new curiosity. The centre is full of intriguing alleys, sudden broad squares, covered arcades and pedestrian-only precincts. Walking is also often faster than hailing a taxi or using public transport.

Greater Prague is a different story, spreading out into a sprawl of distant tower blocks. But the city has an excellent, inexpensive and pretty much 24-hour integrated public transport system that will get you pretty much anywhere you want to go to.

Driving in Prague takes some getting used to, and it really isn't worth the bother on a short visit. Taxis are ubiquitous but unreliable – pretty cheap if you find an honest driver; ruinous if you let one rip you off.

Because the communists dammed the Vltava so thoroughly, there isn't any real freight or passenger traffic on the river – just pleasure cruises. An assortment of eccentric conveyances – including horse-drawn carriages, bike-taxis and an electric train that takes tourists up to the Castle and back – can all be found in Old Town Square.

Public transport

The places in Prague that you can't get to by using a combination of metro, tram, bus and occasionally train are

places that you wouldn't want to go to anyway.

There are bus and/or tram connections and usually taxi stands at every metro station, and all of Prague's railway stations except Masaryk are connected to the metro network.

Public transport runs around the clock. Regular day service is from about 5am to midnight daily. Peak times are 5am to 8pm Monday to Friday. From about midnight to 5am, night buses and night trams take over.

Metro, tram and bus lines are indicated on most city maps, but note that roadworks often cause unpredictable stoppages or detours, especially during the summer months.

Timetables can be found at every tram and bus stop. The times posted apply to the stop where you are – which is highlighted on the schedule. If your destination is listed below the highlighted stop, you are in the right place.

Prague Public Transit Company (DP) Information Offices

Muzeum metro station, Nové město (2264 0103). **Open** 7am-9pm daily. **Map** p309 L6.

Můstek metro station, Nové město (2264 6350) Open 7am-9pm daily. **Map** p306 J4; p307 K5.

Nádraží Holešovice metro station, Holešovice (806 790). **Open** 7am-9pm daily.

Karlovo náměstí metro station, Nové město (294 682). **Open** 7am-6pm Mon-Fri; closed Sat, Sun. **Map** p308 H8. Employees usually have at least a smattering of English and German and are unusually helpful. They provide free information booklets and sell tickets, maps, night transport booklets and individual tram and bus schedules (cash only).

TICKETS

Tickets (*jízdenky*) are good for any mode of transport (metro, bus, tram, even the funicular). In 1996, the city introduced transit zones – two inside Prague city limits and four outside. Most locals have passes (which is why you don't see them punching tickets). Buying a pass is probably the

easiest option for you, too – if only to avoid the rigmarole at ticket machines.

The machines have control panels covered with buttons, but only two ticket types need concern you. An 8 Kč ticket entitles the buyer to a single 15-minute ride on any transport above ground, or one ride of up to four stops on the metro. It is not valid for use on night transport, the Historical Tram or the funicular. A 12 Kč ticket lasts for 60 minutes at peak times (5am-8pm Mon-Fri) and 90 minutes at slow times (8pm-5am Mon-Fri and during Sat-Sun), allowing unlimited travel throughout Prague, including transfers between metros, buses and trams.

Babies in carriages, children under six, handicapped people, small bags and skis ride free. Children aged six to 15, large items of luggage and other sizeable items need a half-price ticket. Enormous luggage and 'items that stink or look disgusting' aren't allowed on Prague public transport at all. Check with the nearest DP (Prague's public transport authority) office or read the posted information for details.

The orange ticket machines are marvels of Czechnology. They have buttons marked with prices. Press once for the ticket you want, twice if you want two tickets (and so on), and then press the 'enter' button. Insert the total amount in coins (the machines give change) and wait an agonisingly long time for the machine's screeching mechanism to print out each ticket individually.

If you're here for anything other than a quick visit it's worth stocking up on tickets in advance. They can be bought at most tobacconists, DP information offices (*see below*) and PIS offices (*see page 288*), or anywhere where you see the red-and-yellow DP sticker in the window.

Buy your ticket in advance and stamp it (face up in the direction of the arrow) in a machine as soon as you board a bus or tram or as you enter the 'paid area' of the metro. There are no guards or gates, but plain-clothes inspectors (*revizoři*) carry out random ticket checks. They'll flash a shiny red and yellow badge at you and spot-fine you 200 Kč if you're travelling without a valid ticket. The guard should also, on your request, show you his or her photo ID badge and make out a receipt for the fine. Playing the dumb foreigner usually doesn't work.

TRAVEL PASSES

At most of the places listed above, you can also buy transit passes, which allow unlimited travel on the metro, trams and buses. During working hours, metros with a DP window also sell individual tickets, short-term passes for tourists and long-term passes for residents. Only the 24-hour pass is available at automatic ticket machines.

You must first fill in your full name and date of birth on the reverse side of short-term passes and then stamp them as you would an ordinary ticket. The pass is valid from the time it was stamped. It is invalid if the information on the reverse side is not filled in – even if it is stamped. A 24-hour pass costs 70 Kč, a three-day pass 200 Kč, a seven-day pass 250 Kč and a 15-day pass 280 Kč.

Residents usually have long-term passes. All you need to get one is a recent photo and some ID. They are available at the DP windows and at the Můstek metro station. Passes must be filled in with your full name and 'rodné číslo' or passport number. Coupons inserted in the pass are valid for one day before and three days after the month or other time period shown on the coupon and are not stamped. Long-term passes

cost 420 Kč for one month, 1,150 Kč for three months and 3,800 Kč for a year.

THE METRO

The Prague metro network, with a total length of 43.6 kilometres (27 miles) running between 46 stations along three lines, is a little copy of the grandiose Moscow metro. The stations are well lit and clearly signposted; trains are clean and frequent. A digital clock on each platform informs you of the time elapsed since the last train came along (admittedly the due time of the next arrival would be more useful).

The Prague metro consists of three lines: the green Line A (Skalka-Dejvická); the yellow Line B (Černý most-Zličín); and the red Line C (Nádraží Holešovice-Háje). A fourth line is due to open sometime in the next decade.

Transfers (*přestup*) are possible at three stations: Muzeum (between the green Line A and the red Line C), Můstek (between the green Line A and the yellow Line B) and Florenc (between the yellow Line B and the red Line C).

The metro runs from 5am to midnight daily. At peak times, expect trains every two minutes; at other times it will be more like every five or ten minutes.

TRAMS

An electric *tramvaje* service began in Prague in 1891 and trams have been the preferred method of transport for most Praguers ever since, as they are the most picturesque and convenient of the city's transport services.

Twenty-three daytime tram lines stop at 606 stations along 494 kilometres (309 miles) of tram track between 4.30am and midnight daily – after which eight night trams take over (*see below*). Trams come every six to eight minutes at peak times and every ten to 15 minutes at other times. With the newer, boxier

trams, you may find you need to open the doors by pressing the green button.

The best tram lines for seeing the city are the 22, which runs from the Castle to Národní třída and beyond, and the Historic Tram (number 91), which runs from the Výstaviště in Prague 7 through Malá Strana, across to National Theatre, through Wenceslas Square, Náměstí Republiky and back to Prague 7. The Historic Tram runs on Saturdays, Sundays and holidays from Easter to the middle of November and leaves Výstaviště every hour from 2pm to 7pm. The complete ride takes 40 minutes, and tickets cost 20 Kč for adults and 10 Kč for children. *See also page 191.*

BUSES

Since 1925, *autobusy* in Prague have provided transport to places where no other means of public transport dare to go. There are 196 daytime bus lines stopping at 2,060 stations along a 697.5-kilometre (435-mile) network. Buses run from about 5am to midnight, after which ten night bus lines take over (*see below*). Buses run every five to 18 minutes during peak times and every 15 to 30 minutes at other times.

Bus infoline

1034 Czech-language only. **Open** 6am-8pm Mon-Fri; 8am-4pm Sat, Sun.

NIGHT TRAMS & BUSES

Night buses and trams run about every 40 minutes from midnight to approximately 4.30am. Every night tram (they all have numbers in the 50s) stops at Lazarská crossroads on Spálená. Night buses (501-512) don't have one central stop, but many stop at the top of Wenceslas Square (near Muzeum metro) and around the corner from IP Pavlova metro. You can buy a guide to night transport – showing all lines, times and stations – at the DP information offices (*see page 269*) for about 10 Kč.

DISABLED ACCESS

There are lifts at the following metro stations: Dejvická; Skalka on the green Line A; Zličín, Stodůlky, Luka, Lužiny, Hůrka on the yellow Line B; Nádraží Holešovice, Hlavní nádraží, Florenc, IP Pavlova, Pankrác, Roztyly, Chodov, Opatov and Háje on the red Line C. At some, you'll need help to operate the lift.

There are two bus routes served only by kneeling buses. The 109B starts in Černý most and runs via Florenc, Náměstí Republiky and IP Pavlova to Jižní město. The 118D runs from Zličín via Hradčanská, Náměstí Republiky and Nádraží Holešovice to Sidlistě Ďáblice.

All of the newer, boxier trams kneel also, but there's no counting on when one is going to come along. You can find out which tram lines are using the newer cars at DP information offices (*see page 269*).

FUNICULAR RAILWAY

The funicular (*lanovka*) runs for half a kilometre from the bottom of Petřín hill at Újezd (around the corner from the tram stop of the same name), stopping midway at Nebozízek (at the pricey restaurant of the same name) and continues to the top of Petřín hill. It runs every ten or 15 minutes between 9.15am and 8.45pm daily and costs 12 Kč for adults and 6 Kč for children, or if you already have a day ticket or tram pass you can use it here.

Taxis

The appalling reputation of Prague's taxi drivers has caused Prague City Hall to introduce strict guidelines. Even so, the odds are high that you will still get ripped off. The drivers waiting at ranks in obvious tourist locations are all crooks, so avoid them. Hail a moving cab or call one of the services listed below. Make sure that you are using an authorised taxi (it should be clearly marked,

with registration numbers and fares printed clearly on the doors and a black and white checked stripe along the side). If the driver doesn't turn on the meter, insist he does. If he won't, get out immediately or agree a fee to your destination. Do neither, and the driver will likely demand a ruinous fare at the end of your journey – and maybe even resort to violence to collect it.

Ideally, your taxi experience should go something like this: the driver does not turn on the meter (*taximetr*) until you enter the cab. When he does, 30 or 25 Kč appears as the initial amount. While you are driving inside Prague, the rate is set at '1' and should never be more than 22 or 20 Kč per kilometre.

When your ride is over, the driver provides you with a receipt (*účet* or *paragon*) that must include the name and address of the taxi company, the taxi registration number, the date of your journey, the times and places of departure and arrival, the rate per kilometre and total mileage, the price of the trip and the driver's name and signature. If the driver does not provide this receipt or if the information on it is incorrect, you are theoretically not required to pay the fare.

In reality, few drivers will provide a receipt unless you request one. Honest cabbies will then print one out on the agonisingly slow machine attached to the meter. Rip-off merchants will write you one out on a pad.

FARES

At the time of writing, the maximum rates for taxi service were 30 Kč (if you stop them on the street) or 25 Kč (if you call them) for entering the cab (irrespective of the number of passengers), 4 Kč a minute for waiting (because of a passenger request or heavy traffic) and no more than 22Kč (if you stop them on the street) or 20 Kč (if

you call them) per kilometre for normal rides. However, they were scheduled for a slight increase.

Taxi companies

AAA
1080/312 2112.

Acro Taxi
1088.

ProfiTaxi
1035/2213 5551.

Taxi complaints
Prague City Hall, Department of Local Revenues (Magistrát hl. m. Prahy), Mariánské náměstí 2, Staré Město, Prague 1 (2448 1111). **Map** p306 H3. You could also try the Taxi Guild on 2491 6666.

On foot

It is generally safe to walk anywhere in Prague at anytime – using common sense and appropriate caution in the wee hours, of course. Prague does not (yet) have any 'bad' areas that you should avoid (*see page 284*). Beware of bad drivers, though – they'll often try to run you down even if you are on a zebra crossing (crosswalk).

By bicycle

Cycling in Prague is hellish. There are no bike lanes, drivers are oblivious to your presence and pedestrians yell at you if you ride on the pavement. Mountain bikes are best, as the wide wheels shouldn't get stuck in the tram tracks. Prague does, however, have acres of parkland inside and outside the centre. On public transport, bicycles are allowed in the last car of metro trains only, and your bike is expected to purchase and stamp its own 6 Kč ticket.

By boat

The Prague Steamship Company (Pražská paroplavební služba) had a

Directory

Road emergencies

Autoklub Bohemia Assistance
Dial 1240 for ABA's 24-hour emergency road service.

Central Automobile Club
Ústední automotoklub
Call 1230 for the 'Yellow Angel' 24-hour emergency service.

Service 24
24-hour emergency road service for lorries. Call 6110 4477.

monopoly on river traffic way back in 1865 – and still provides the most boat services on the river today. You'll find these, other boat companies plying sightseeing and booze cruises, and rowing boats for hire (*see page 192*) along the right bank of the Vltava.

Prague Steamship Company
Pražská paroplavební služba Rašínovo nábeži, Nové Mésto, Prague 2 (298 309/293 803). Metro Karlovo námĕsti/3, 16, 17 tram. Map p308 G9.

Driving

One of the first things the Nazis did after occupying the country in 1939 was to switch traffic flow from the left to the right side of the street. Czechs have been driving on the right side ever since.

The worst driving days are Friday and Sunday, when people who don't know the difference between the clutch and the brake pack their families into old Škodas for a weekend trip to their summer cottage, or *chata*. Czech drivers tend to stop in the middle of intersections on a red light and, since they don't usually bother to stop for pedestrians on a zebra crossing, pedestrians unsurprisingly don't usually bother to use them.

RULES & REGULATIONS
Traffic regulations in the Czech Republic are similar to those in most European countries.

There is zero tolerance for drinking and driving, though – drivers are not allowed to drink any alcohol at all before driving. Ditto for drugs. Use of seat belts is required in the front and – if the car is equipped with them – in the back seat as well. Children under the age of 12 or anybody shorter than 150 centimetres (5 foot 1 inch) may not ride in the seat next to the driver. Small children must be in approved child safety seats. Trams, which follow different traffic lights to cars, always have the right of way. You must stop behind trams when passengers are getting on and off at a stop where there is no island, and you should avoid driving on tram tracks unless the road offers no alternative.

The maximum speed limits permitted for cars and buses are 90 kilometres an hour (56 miles an hour) on roads, 110kph (69mph) on highways and 60kph (37mph) in villages and towns.

Motorcyclists and their passengers are required to wear helmets, and the maximum speed limit for motorcycles is 90 kilometres and hour (56 miles an hour) on roads and highways and 60kph (37mph) in villages and towns.

You are required to notify the police of any accident involving casualties or serious damage to a car. If you are driving your own car, you will need to have international proof of insurance (known as a Green Card – *see below*) and

you must pay an annual toll for using the Czech roads. If you rent a car, insurance and toll should be taken care of for you. The toll sticker – which should be displayed on the windscreen – costs 400 Kč and can be bought at post offices, most border crossing points and petrol stations. For caravans and other vehicles weighing 3.5-21 metric tons, the cost is 1,000 Kč.

Car hire

Renting a car can be a pretty expensive business in Prague, with many Western firms charging higher rates than they would back home. It is definitely worth shopping around, as many small local firms charge far less than the big boys. When renting a car, be sure to bring your driving licence, passport and credit card with you. The agency should provide you with a green insurance card that permits you to drive across the border. It is also wise to arrange your rental a few days in advance to be sure that you get the car you want.

In addition to the places listed below, American Express (*see page 283*) and Čedok (*see page 288*) can arrange car rental.

A Rent Car
Washingtonova 9, Nové Mĕsto, Prague 1 (2421 1587). Metro Muzeum. **Open** 7am-9pm daily. **Rates** 2,360 Kč-4,400 Kč per day. **Credit** AmEx, DC, MC, V. **Map** p307 L5.
Branch: Ruzynĕ Airport, Prague 6 (2011 4370/24281053).

Avis
Klimentská 46, Staré Mĕsto, Prague 1 (2185 1225). Metro Florenc/3, 8 tram. **Open** 7am-7pm daily. **Rates** from 3,780 Kč for 1 day; 5,080 Kč for 2 days. **Credit** AmEx, DC, MC, V. **Map** p307 M1.
Branch: Ruzynĕ Airport, Prague 6 (2011 4270).

Budget
Čistovická 100, Řepy, Prague 6 (302 5713/302 2272/www.budget.cz).

Tram 8, 22. **Open** 8am-4.30pm Mon-Fri; closed Sat, Sun. **Rates** from 800 Kč-900 Kč per day. **Credit** AmEx, DC, MC, V. **Map** p306 H1.
Branches: Ruzyně Airport, Prague 6 (2011 3253); Hotel Intercontinental, Staré Město, Prague 1 (231 9595).

European Inter Rent/National Car Rental

Pařížská 28, Staré Město, Prague 1 (2481 0515/2481 1920). Metro Staroměstská/17, 18 tram.
Open 8am-8pm daily. **Rates** from 2,700 Kč per day. **Credit** AmEx, DC, MC, V. **Map** p306 H2.
Branches in most of the major cities in the Czech Republic.

Hertz

Karlovo náměstí 28, Nové Město, Prague 2 (2223 1010/www.hertz.cz). Metro Karlovo náměstí/3, 4, 6, 14, 16, 18, 22, 24, 34 tram.
Open 8am-8pm daily. **Rates** from 2,300 Kč for 1 day; 4,200 Kč for 2 days. **Credit** AmEx, DC, MC, V. **Map** p308 H7.

Ren Auto

Černá růže Na příkopě 12, Staré Město, Prague 1 (2101 4630/0602 339 902). Metro Můstek/3, 9, 14, 24 tram. **Open** 9am-8pm daily. **Rates** 1,500 Kč-3,000 Kč for 1 day. **Credit** AmEx, DC, MC, V. **Map** p307 K4.
The best option for a cheap and reliable Škoda.
Branch: Pivovarská 3, Žižkov, Prague 3 (536 354).

Car insurance

To drive your own car in the Czech Republic you need a Green Card as international proof of insurance. This should be issued by your usual insurer at home before you go. Should the Green Card expire, you can buy short-term insurance from the Czech insurance agency Česká pojišťovna (5732 2371) for 3,000 Kč a month. For long-term insurance, you'll need to register your car with the Czech authorities (paying something like half the cost of the car in duties and tax), get *technický průkaz* registration papers and sign up for *Povinné ručení* – the minimum legal insurance.

Česká pojišťovna

Spálená 16, Nové Město, Prague 1 (2405 1111/fax 2405 2220/infoline

0800 133 666 toll-free). Metro Národní třída/6, 9, 18, 22 tram. **Open** 8am-6pm Mon-Fri; 9am-1pm Sat, Sun. **No credit cards. Map** p308 H6.

Czech motoring clubs

See also page 272 Road emergencies.

Central Automobile Club Prague

Ústřední automotoklub
Na strži 9, Michle, Prague 4 (6110 4111). Metro Budějovická, then 118, 121, 124, 205 bus. **Open** 8am-4.30pm Mon-Fri; closed Sat, Sun. **No credit cards.**
Call 1230 or 6122 0220 for the 'Yellow Angel' 24-hour emergency road service.

Autoklub Bohemia Assistance

Autoklub České republiky
Opletalova 29, Nové Město Prague 1 (2423 0506). Metro Hlavní nádraží. **Open** 8am-6pm Mon-Fri; closed Sat, Sun. **No credit cards.**
Call 1240 for 'ABA': 24-hour, seven-day-a-week emergency road service.

Petrol & service

An increasing number of petrol filling stations are now staying open for 24 hours a day, seven days a week. Leaded fuel (octane 90) is called Special, leaded fuel (octane 96) is known as Super and unleaded fuel (95D) is called Natural. Super Plus 98 and diesel fuel are also widely available. A booklet listing all the petrol and service stations (and also including information on selected car parks) in Prague is available from PIS offices (*see page 288*).

Parking

Parking can be a nightmare in Prague, as it is in all large cities in the Czech Republic. Watch out particularly for special zones (usually of one to five parking spaces) that are reserved for area residents and businesses. If you park illegally in one of these, your car can be towed away (call 158 to get it back) or clamped – both of which are a major pain. It

could cost around 1,000 Kč to retrieve your vehicle, more if you can't retrieve it immediately.
Don't be surprised if you are ripped off by the parking authorities. If you're new in town, the easiest and safest option is to leave your vehicle in a car park, ideally one that has 24-hour security.

PARKING METERS

Parking meters dispense tickets that should be placed face up on the dashboard and be visible through the windscreen. There are three parking zones – orange, green and blue. The orange zone is for stops of up to two hours and costs a minimum of 10 Kč for 15 minutes and 40 Kč for one hour. The green zone is for stays of up to six hours. It costs 15 Kč for 30 minutes, 30 Kč for an hour and 120 Kč for six hours.
Parking is free in green zones from 6pm to 8am and on Sundays (Saturdays, too, in some areas). The blue zone only permits long-term parking for residents and businesses. Ignore the restrictions at your peril.

Park & ride car parks

All car parks listed have direct metro access

GREEN A LINE

Dejvická
Vítězné náměstí (Prague 6)

Hradčanská
Milady Horákové (Prague 6)

Skalka
V Rybníčkách (Prague 10)

Strašnická
V Olšinách (Prague 10)

YELLOW B LINE

Nové Butovice
Bucharova (Prague 5)

Radlická
Radlická (Prague 5)

RED C LINE

Opatov
Hrnčiská (Prague 4)

Directory

Resources A-Z

Resources & organisations

British Embassy Commercial Section

Na příkopě 21, Nové Město, Prague 1 (2224 0021/fax 2224 3622). Metro Můstek. **Open** 9am-noon; 2pm-5pm Mon-Fri; closed Sat, Sun. **Map** p307 K4.

Czechinvest

Štěpánská 15, Nové Město, Prague 2 (9634 2500/fax 9634 2502). Metro Můstek/3, 9, 14, 24 tram. **Open** 9am-4.30pm Mon-Fri; closed Sat, Sun. **Map** p307 L5.
This Czech government agency encourages large-scale direct foreign investment and assists in joint ventures. Staff can research Czech contacts in fields of interest.

Economic Chamber of the Czech Republic

Hospodářská komora ČR
Seifertova 22, Žižkov, Prague 3 (2409 6111/fax 2409 6222/hkcrinf@ traveller.cz). Metro Hlavní nádraží, then 5, 9, 26 tram. **Open** 8am-10.30am, noon 4.30pm Mon-Thur; 8-10.30am Fri; closed Sat, Sun. **Map** p311 B1.
Provides background information on Czech industrial sectors, companies and economic trends and establishes trade contacts.

Enterprise Ireland

Tržiště 13, Malá Strana, Prague 1 (5753 1617/fax 5731 2224). Metro Malostranská/12, 22 tram. **Open** 9am-1pm, 2-5pm Mon-Fri; closed Sat, Sun. **Map** p305 D3.

Prague Stock Exchange (PX)

Rybná 14, Staré Město, Prague 1 (2183 1111/www.pse.cz). Metro Náměstí Republiky. **Open** 8am-8pm Mon-Fri; closed Sat, Sun. **Map** p307 K3
PX trades about 50 companies in its top-tier listing. The big banks are among several dozen brokerages that can place orders. Liquidity is good, though insider trading has been a problem.

US Embassy Foreign Commercial Service

Tržiště 15, Malá Strana, Prague 1 (5753 1162/fax 57531165). Metro Malostranská/12, 22 tram. **Open** 8am-4.30pm Mon-Fri; closed Sat, Sun. **Map** p305 D3.

Banking

Anyone can open a bank account in the Czech Republic, although some banks will require a minimum deposit. Corporate bank accounts require special paperwork. Banks generally charge high fees and current accounts do not bear interest. Most banks have some English-speaking staff. Service is improving, but still expect long queues, short opening hours and lots of burdensome paperwork – even on relatively simple transactions. Czech banks usually cater to individual account holders, while foreign banks are largely geared to corporate accounts. The four main Czech banks are Česká spořitelna (*see below*), Československá obchodní banka (ČSOB), Komerční banka and Živnostenská banka (*for all, see page 284*). All provide a similar range of services.

About 30 international and foreign banks are represented in the Czech Republic. Many offer at least some traditional banking services, although most cater exclusively to wealthier private clients or corporate accounts, or offer only consulting or other secondary services.

Česká spořitelna

Rytířská 29, Staré Město, Prague 1, (2410 1111). Metro Můstek. **Open** 8am-5pm Mon-Thur; 8am-4pm Fri; closed Sat, Sun. **Map** p306 J4.

Geared toward domestic savings accounts. Operates a large cashpoint (ATM) network throughout the city.

Bank Austria

Revoluční 15, Staré Město, Prague 1, (2285 4114). Metro Náměstí Republiky. **Open** 8.30am-noon, 1-4.30pm Mon-Thur; 8.30am-2pm Fri; closed Sat, Sun. **Map** p307 K2.

Citibank

Evropská 178, Dejvice, Prague 6 (2430 4111). Tram 20, 26. **Open** 9am-3pm Mon-Fri; closed Sat, Sun.

Hypobank

Štěpánská 27, Nové Město, Prague 1 (2209 1911). Metro Můstek. **Open** 9am-noon, 1-4pm Mon-Thur; 9am-12.30pm Fri. **Map** p309 K6.
A full range of banking services in a growing number of branches around the country.

Accounting firms

The 'Big Six' international accounting firms are well established and can offer a full range of services. There are also hundreds of local companies offering basic book-keeping and payroll services. All operate standard business hours (9am-5pm Monday to Friday).

PriceWaterhouse Coopers

Karlovo náměstí 17, Nové Město, Prague 2 (2190 5111www.twc global.cz). Metro Karlovo náměstí/4, 6, 16, 22, 34tram. **Map** p308 H7.
Accounting specialists whose auditors have a good reputation.

Deloitte & Touche

Týn 4/641, Staré Město, Prague 1, Prague 1 (2489 5500). Metro Náměstí Republiky. **Map** p306 J3.

Emergencies

The following emergency numbers are toll-free.

First aid	155
Czech police	158
Prague City Police	156
Fire	150
Road accidents	0123, 0124

Mr Hedgehog & his pals

No matter how dizzying becomes Prague's transformation into a go-ahead postmodern metropolis, Czechs will never be able to stray very far from their roots in the storybook villages of Bohemia.

It isn't so much that they're spiritually connected to rural life. It's more like they're branded. Surnames featuring barnyard animals or woodland creatures are the Czech equivalents of Smith, Mason or Cooper.

This can lend a surreal dimension to Czech institutions precisely when they're trying to be at their most stately and dignified. On the floor of Parliament, for example, the speaker may address the Right Honourable Mr Duck (Káchyně). And then the chair might yield to the esteemed Mr Rabbit (Zajíc).

This absurdist aspect is only heightened by the Czech obsession with titles, an old habit dating back to Habsburg days. Just try not to giggle while enunciating such statements as the following furry formality: 'We would be ever so grateful for a brief moment of your time, Mr Doctor Engineer Squirrel [Vávra].'

Not even the Church can provide sanctuary from this legacy of four-legged family names. The flock of a recent Prague archbishop might be forgiven for a getting a mite edgy, knowing their spiritual leader, Father Vlk, was really a wolf in priest's clothing.

When foreign investment in the Czech Republic began to flag in the mid-1990s, the business community was frantic to know why. Could it have been that skittish international capital had finally discovered that the Prague Stock Exchange was being run by one Tomáš Ježek, aka Mr Hedgehog?

And animal surnames aren't the only rural relic in the field of Czech personal nomenclature. Lovers of symphonic music groan loudly when they see a cheesy TV commercial for a brand of particularly rich, thick yoghurt. It's set to a jingle adapted from one of Bedřich Smetana's national hymns.

Why oh why, they'll sigh and tut to each other, did the ancestors of Czech classical music's preeminent composer have to acquire the moniker Cream?

KPMG

Jana Masaryka 12, Vinohrady, Prague 2 (691 0194). Metro Náměstí Míru. **Map** p309 M10.
Smaller and more personal than the other agencies, KPMG is known for its financial planning and technical expertise.

Computer rental & leasing

See also page 167.

APS

Opletalova 33, Nové Město, Prague 1 (2421 5147/apscorp@mbox.vol.cz). Metro Hlavní nádraží. **Open** 9am-1.30pm-5pm, 2pm-5pm Mon-Fri; closed Sat, Sun. **No credit cards**. **Map** p307 L4.
Flexible PC leasing options.

MacSource/ CompuSource

Bělehradská 68, Nové Město, Prague 2 (2251 5455/fax 2251 5456). Metro I P Pavlova/6, 11. **Open** 9am-5pm Mon-Fri; closed Sat, Sun. **Credit** AmEx, MC, V. **Map** p309 L10.
Both PC and Macintosh equipment are available for leasing and rental, both short and long term.

Couriers/messengers

DHL

Aviatická 1048/12 Airport Ruzyně, Prague 6 (0800 103 000/2030 0111/www.dhl.cz). **Telephone bookings** 24 hrs daily. **Credit** AmEx, MC, V.
Offers a daily pick-up service until 6pm on weekdays, 3pm on Saturdays.

Express Parcel System (EPS)

Patočkova 3, Dejvice, Prague 6 (2031 6111). Tram 2, 18. **Telephone bookings** 7.30am-11pm daily. **No credit cards**.
Cycle couriers. One-hour collection and two-hour delivery on local jobs. Also delivers outside Prague.

FedEx

Olbrachtova 1 Prague 4 (4400 2200/www.fedex.com). Metro Budějovická. **Telephone bookings** 8am-7pm Mon-Fri; 8am-1pm Sat; closed Sun. **Credit** AmEx, MC, V.

Estate agents

Finding reasonably priced and adequate office space can be challenging. Estate agents

tend to push more expensive properties in order to maximise their commission. Make sure that any space has adequate (ie modern) phone lines and isn't due for noisy or disruptive repairs. If parking is important, choose a space out of the centre.

Apollo

Záhřebská 33, Vinohrady, Prague 2 (2151 1100). Metro Náměstí Míru. **Open** 9am-5.30pm Mon-Fri; closed Sat, Sun. **Map** p309 M9.
Lease and sale of commercial and private real estate. Provides financial and development consulting.

Nexus

Belgická 36, Vinohrady, Prague 2 (2251 3419). Metro Náměstí Míru. **Open** 9am-5.30pm Mon-Fri; closed Sat, Sun. **Map** p309 M9.
Serves small and medium-sized businesses.

Interpreting & translating

Prague has dozens of translation companies, with most offering services in all the

Directory

major European languages and many languages further afield. Translation rates are usually determined by the page (there are reckoned to be 30 lines per page at 60 characters per line).

SkyWalker
Dlouhá 16, Staré Město, Prague 1 (2481 7315). Metro Staroměstská/17, 18 tram. **Map** p306 J2.
Claims (somewhat improbably) that it can translate all languages. Operates a freelance pool of about 1,500 translators.

Interlingua
Spálená 17, Nové Město, Prague 1 (2490 9250). Metro Národní třída. **Map** p308 H6.
Specialises in legal and financial documents.

Law firms

There are dozens of local and international law firms that can help establish a company and provide the standard range of legal services. Local firms tend to have a better grasp of arcane bits of Czech law, while international firms offer better linguistic skills and more polish (at a much higher price). For a referral to local lawyer, contact the Czech Chamber of Commercial Lawyers.

Czech Chamber of Commercial Lawyers
Senovážné náměstí 23, Nové Město, Prague 1 (2414 2457). Metro Náměstí Republiky. **Open** 8am-4pm Mon-Fri. **Map** p307 L4.

Altheimer & Gray
Platnéřská 4, Staré Město, Prague 1 (2481 2782). Metro Staroměstská. **Map** p306 H3.
Offers advice on privatisation, acquisitions and foreign investment.

Cameron McKenna
Husova 5, Staré Město, Prague 1 (2424 8518/fax 2424 8524). Metro Staroměstská. **Map** p306 H4.
Cameron McKenna claims to have the largest network of law offices in Central Europe.

Čermák, Hoejš & Vrba
Národní třída 32, Nové Město, Prague 1 (9616 7401). Metro Národní třída. **Map** p306 H5.
Local firm specialising in patent and other types of corporate law.

Office hire

Chronos
Václavské náměstí 66 (entrance at Mezibranská 23), Nové Město, Prague 1 (2422 6612). Metro Muzeum. **Open** 8am-6pm Mon-Fri; closed Sat, Sun. **Map** p309 K6.
Offers temporary office space, phone services and secretarial help.

Regus
Klimentská 46, Staré Město, Prague 1 (2185 1055). Metro Náměstí Republiky; closed Sat, Sun. **Map** p307 L1.
Can provide short-term offices and conference rooms, as well as access to the Internet and email.

Photocopying

See page 183.

Recruitment agencies

Finding good employees in Prague can be challenging given the city's booming economy and the general shortage of English-speakers.

AYS
Žitná 8, Nové Město, Prague 2 (2499 3137). Metro Karlovo náměstí. **Open** 8.30am-5pm Mon-Fri; closed Sat, Sun. **Map** p309 J7.
Specialises in secretarial and administrative support.

Helmut Neumann International
Národní třída 10, Nové Město, Prague 1 (2495 1530). Metro Národní třída. **Open** 8am-6pm Mon-Fri; closed Sat, Sun. **Map** p306 H5.
One of several international head-hunting agencies. Fills positions in all sectors of the economy.

Work Plus – Inter Staff
Vodičkova 33, Nové Město, Prague 1 (2494 9212). Metro Můstek. **Open** 9am-6pm Mon-Fri: closed Sat, Sun. **Map** p308 J6.
Provides a range of temporary office support staff.

Customs

There are no restrictions on the import and export of Czech currency, but if you're carrying more than 200,000 Kč out of the country, you must declare it at customs. The allowances for importing goods are:

● 200 cigarettes or 100 cigars at 3g each or 250g of tobacco;
● 1 litre of liquor or spirits and 2 litres of wine;
● Medicine in any amount for your own needs.
    If you want to export an antique, you must have a certificate stating that it is not important to Czech cultural heritage. Every once in a while, and usually without warning or much reason, EC countries limit the import of some Czech foodstuffs – even for personal consumption.

Customs Office
Celní editelství pro Prahu a Středočeský kraj Washingtonova 11, Nové Město, Prague 1 (6133 1111). Metro Muzeum. **Open** 8am-4pm Mon-Fri. **Map** p309 L6.
Branch: Ruzyně Airport (2011 4380).

Disabled access

According to law, all buildings constructed after 1994 must be barrier-free. Reconstructed buildings, however, need not provide wheelchair access, but many do voluntarily. Even so, it is no picnic to be in Prague in a wheelchair. There are few ramps. Most hotels provide no wheelchair access and only five railway stations in the entire country are wheelchair-friendly. The guidebook *Accessible Prague* (Přístupná Praha), available from the Prague Wheelchair Association, maps hotels, toilets, restaurants, galleries and theatres that are wheelchair-friendly. For travel information for the disabled, *see page 271.*

Prague Wheelchair Association
Pražská organizace vozíčkářů Centre for Independent Living (Centrum samostatného života), Benediktská 6, Staré Město, Prague 1 (2482 7210/ www.pov.cz). Metro Náměstí Republiky. **Open** 10am-5pm Mon-Thur; 10am-3pm Fri. **Map** p307 K2.
This organisation is run by the disabled for the disabled. In addition

to its *Accessible Prague* guidebook, it provides helpers and operates a taxi service and an airport pick-up service for the disabled. Service is limited and should be ordered as far in advance as possible. It can also rent wheelchairs if people have any problem with theirs.

Electricity

Electricity is 220 volts with two-pin plugs almost everywhere. Bring continental adaptors or converters with you, as they are expensive here when they are available at all.

Embassies

All embassies and consulates are closed on Czech holidays (*see page 289*) as well as their own national holidays. For other embassies, you will need to consult the *Zlaté stránky* (*Yellow Pages*) under 'Zastupitelské úřady'.

American Embassy

Tržiště 15, Malá Strana, Prague 1 (5753 0663/emergency number 5753 2716). Metro Malostranská/12, 22 tram. **Open** 8am-noon Mon-Fri; closed Sat, Sun. **Map** p305 D3.

Australian Trade Commission & Honorary Consulate

Na Ořechovce 38, Střešovice, Prague 6 (2431 0743/2431 0071). Metro Dejvická/132, 216 bus. **Open** 8.30am-5pm Mon-Thur; 8.30am-2pm Fri; closed Sat, Sun.

British Embassy

Thunovská 14, Malá Strana, Prague 1 (5753 0278/duty officer 0602 217 700). Metro Malostranská/12, 22 tram. **Open** 9am-noon Mon-Fri; telephone enquiries 2-5pm Mon-Fri; closed Sat, Sun. **Map** p305 D3.

Canadian Embassy

Mickiewiczova 6, Dejvice, Prague 6 (7210 1800/fax 7210 1890). Metro Hradčanská/18, 22 tram. **Open** 8.30am-12.30pm Mon-Fri; closed Sat, Sun. **Map** p310 A3.

Health

Prague isn't a very healthy place to live. The Czech diet is fatty, pork-laden and low on fresh vegetables. The Czechs top world beer-consumption charts and are unrepentant smokers. The city also has serious smog problems and nitrate-infested water to deal with (*see also page 194*).

Prague is a great place for hypochondriacs. The damp climate creates a haven for various moulds that can be hell for anyone with allergies. Summer is the time for treating yourself to salmonella-infected ice-cream and a nice trip to the countryside, which could be preceded by a visit to the doctor for inoculations against tick-borne encephalitis and other horrible things that might be lurking in trees.

But if you really do get ill, the semi-privatised ex-socialist healthcare system means you'll be smothered with attention whenever you go to the doctor. If you have health insurance, the doctors will try to rack up points for the care they give – sometimes overdoing it – which they redeem for money from the health insurance companies. If you pay cash you'll get even better treatment than the locals.

GENERAL HEALTHCARE

Medical facilities are usually open from 7.15am to 6pm on weekdays only. It's usually best for expats to find a GP (*rodinný* or *praktický lékař*), dentist (*zubní lékař*) and paediatrician (*dětský lékař*) close to your home or workplace. Many Czech doctors will speak English or German, especially at larger facilities like hospitals (*nemocnice*) and medical centres (*poliklinika*) and in the larger cities.

Emergency

First Medical Clinic of Prague

Tylovo náměstí, 3/15 Nové Město, Prague 2 (2425 1319/emergency 0603 555 006/ppz-fmc@mbox.vol.cz). Metro IP Pavlova/4, 6, 16, 22, 34 tram. **Credit** AmEx, MC, V. **Map** p309 L8.
Highly recommended, with professional international staff, it honours Central Health Insurance Office temporary insurance (*see p279*).

Motol Hospital

Fakultní nemocnice v Motole V úvalu 84, Smíchov, Prague 5 (2443 3681/2443 1111/emergency 2443 1007-8/155 toll-free). Metro Hradčanská/ 167, 174, 179, 180 bus. **Open** 24 hours daily. **Credit** AmEx, MC, V.
Emergency treatment, plus a hospital department dedicated to care of foreigners.

Na Homolce Hospital

Nemocnice Na Homolce Roentgenova 2, Smíchov, Prague 5 (5727 1111/paediatrics 5727 2025/emergencies 5727 2043/www.homolka.cz). Tram 4, 7, 9/167 bus. **Open** *Emergency* 24 hours daily. *Paediatric department* 8am-4pm daily. **Credit** AmEx, MC, V.
Provides English-speaking doctors and 24-hour emergency service. Care can be excellent but given the state of the Czech public healthcare system, a private clinic is more advisable. Home visits are possible if needed.

Helplines & crisis centres

Helplines generally run around the clock, but you have a better chance of catching an English-speaker if you call during regular office hours. For AIDS crisis helplines, see page 207.

Alcoholics Anonymous

Na Poříčí 16, Nové Město, Prague 1 (2481 8247). Metro Florenc or Náměstí Republiky. **Sessions** (for English speakers) 7.30pm Tue, Wed; 12.30pm Fri; 5.30pm Sun. **Map** p307 M2.
Twelve-step programmes. Anyone with alcohol problems is welcome to call or attend. English spoken.

Crisis Intervention Centre

Centrum krizové intervence – Psychiatrická léčebna Bohnice Ústavní 91, Prague 8 (8401 6666). Metro Nádraží Holešovice, then 102, 177, 200 bus. **Open** 24 hours daily.
The biggest and best-equipped mental health facility in Prague. Runs lots of outreach programmes.

Drop In

Karolíny Světlé 18, Staré Město, Prague 1 (tel/fax 2222 1431/dropin@ecn.cz). Metro Národní třída. **Open** 9am-5.30pm Mon-Thur; 9am-4pm Fri. **Map** p306 G5.
Focusing on problems related to drug addiction, including HIV testing and counselling, this is an informal clinic. Call or just drop in 24 hours a day.

Directory

Finding a flat to rent

So you've finally met the endless list of requirements for a residence permit. Brilliant. But you may not quite be out of the woods yet. Apartment space is in Prague is so tight that many divorced couples still live together. Before you begin your search, you should be aware of a few of the realities of life for the local population. Under the old regime, there was a 20-year waiting list for flats in the town centre and at least a ten-year wait in the outlying districts. Divorced couples often had to continue living together; newlyweds had to live with one set of parents; and families fought over who would get granny's flat decades before her death.

It's perhaps not surprising, then, that the average Czech simply cannot understand foreigners' demands for luxuries like a fully equipped kitchen, a washing machine, a telephone and parking. You should be happy just to have a roof over your head. This gap in expectations can cause problems when looking at flats. Whatever your requirements, the landlord or estate agent will show you somewhere completely unsuitable, far away from the centre, devoid of public transport connections and furnished with the ugliest stuff you've ever seen in your life – and tell you that it's the only place available in your price range. This is unlikely to be true. There are good flats on the market, but you have to be patient, lucky and persistent to find one.

LEGAL RIGHTS

Landlord-tenant rights have not been legally defined in the new free market economy. Even after restitution, which restored property to those who owned it before the communist nationalisation, many apartments in Prague are still state-owned. This means that people often find themselves renting a black-market apartment. To meet the increasing demand, families rent out their flats to foreigners at ten times the average rent of 1,000 Kč a month without bothering to declare their presence to the state authorities. Consequently, any lease you sign won't be legally binding, leaving you with no legal rights if you have any problems. You're best off finding a privately owned flat and signing a legally binding lease that can

Non-emergency clinics

First Medical Clinic of Prague

Tylovo Náměstí, 3/15 Nové Město, Prague 2 (2425 1319/emergency 0603 555 006/ppz-fmc@mbox.vol.cz). Metro IP Pavlova/4, 6, 16, 22, 34 tram. **Credit** AmEx, MC, V. **Map** p309 L8

Motol Hospital

Fakultni nemocnice v Motole V úvalu 84, Motol, Prague 5 (general information 2443 1111/foreigners' department 2443 3681/emergency 2443 1007-8/0602 271 697/155 toll-free). Metro Hradčanská/167, 174, 179, 180 bus. **Credit** AmEx, MC, V.

Pharmacies

Many central pharmacies (*lékárna* or *apothéka*) have been doing business in exactly the same place for centuries and have gorgeous period interiors that are worth a visit even if you don't need any aspirin.

Over-the-counter medicines are only available at pharmacies, which are usually open 7.30am to 6pm on weekdays, though some operate extended hours. All pharmacies are supposed to post directions to the nearest 24-hour pharmacy in their window, though this information will be in Czech. Ring the bell for after-hours service, for which there will usually be a surcharge of approximately 30 Kč.

24-hour pharmacies

Belgická 37, Vinohrady, Prague 2 (2251 9731). Metro Náměstí Miru. **Map** p309 M9.
Štefánikova 6, Smíchov, Prague 5 (5732 0918). Metro Anděl/6, 7, 12, 14 tram.

Women's health

Dr Kateřina Bittmanová

Mánesova 64, Vinohrady, Prague 2 (office 627 1951/0603 551 393/home 793 6895). Metro Jiřiho z Poděbrad/11 tram. **Map** p311 B3. Dr Bittmanová speaks fluent English. She runs a friendly private practice

and is on call 24 hours a day. Her fee for a general examination is 900 Kč; a smear costs an additional 450 Kč.

Bulovka Hospital

Budínova 2, Libeň, Prague 8 (6608 3239/6608 3240). Tram 12, 14. Housed within a huge state hospital complex, the privately run MEDA Clinic here is favoured by British and American women. Prices are reasonable, the gynaecologists speak English and facilities are clean and professional. Contraception and HIV testing available. Multilingual staff.

Podolí Hospital

Podolské nábřeží 157, Podolí, Prague 4 (4143 0349 ext 315). Tram 3, 16, 17. The Podoli Hospital has obstetricians/gynaecologists who speak English. With modern facilities and neo-natal care, it handles most births to expats.

RMA Centrum

Dukelských hrdinů 17, Holešovice, Prague 7 (3337 8809). Tram 4, 12, 14, 17, 26. **Map** p310 D2. An alternative medicine centre that offers clients homeopathy, acupuncture and acupressure, traditional Chinese medicine and massage as well as gynaecology and mammography. There's even a sauna and beauty salon.

protect you from being evicted at the whim of your landlord, though how much protection this really affords you is open to conjecture.

There is no consistency in rent prices for foreigners. The price you pay (generally in dollars or marks) depends on who you are negotiating with, the security of the lease and how rich the landlord thinks you are. An executive on a generous allowance may pay US$2,500 a month for an apartment in the Old Town Square, while an English-language teacher may live in the same size flat in the same building for US$400 a month.

FLAT-HUNTING

There are three basic ways to find a flat in Prague.

1. Word of mouth

Both the most effective and the most elusive method. Hang out at the well-known expat bars and restaurants – such as Jo's Bar (see page 155), Radost/FX Café (page 160) and the Globe Bookshop & Café (page 150) – and tell as many people as possible that you're looking for a flat. Keep an eye on the

noticeboards in these places, too, and post your own 'flat wanted' card.

2. Advertising

Scour the rental section in *Annonce*, the classified ads paper that comes out three times a week. Also have a look through the classifieds section of the *Prague Post*, which occasionally lists flats available.

3. Estate agents

If you are not on a tight budget, getting an agent can be the most painless way to find a flat (see page xxx). Like the property market itself, agents are inconsistent. They usually charge a success fee of between one and two months' rent for finding you somewhere to live.

Agentura Kirke

Moskevská 25, Vršovice, Prague 10 (7172 0399). Metro Náměstí Míru/4, 22 tram. **Open** 8.30am-5pm Mon-Fri.
Run by British expat Nicholas Kirke, this respected estate agency offers long-term rentals on flats (minimum lease two years). Shorter rentals are available on houses.

Insurance

Non-residents entering the Czech Republic are required to have proof of having internationally recognised health insurance, unless they are nationals of a country with which the Republic has a reciprocal emergency healthcare agreement. These countries are the United Kingdom, Greece and most of the republic's former allies in the ex-Warsaw Pact countries. If you do need to take out your own insurance, or have an annual policy, make sure that it covers Central and Eastern European countries.

Once inside the country, foreigners can take out temporary health insurance for as long as 90 days, which will be good for treatment at any state hospital and many private Prague clinics as well. This is usually cheaper than

maintaining a home policy, and expats are recommended to consider it, especially as it covers more than just emergency medicine. Note however that there have been a number of scandals in the banking and insurance industries since regulations in both sectors were eased. It's much safer to go with the formerly state-run Central Health Insurance Office or with a trusted international firm than to use a smaller company, no matter how stable they may seem or who recommends them.

Central Health Insurance Office

Všeobecná zdravotní pojišťovna Tyršova 7, Nové Město, Prague 2 (2197 2111). Metro IP Pavlova/4, 16, 22 tram. **Open** 8am-6pm Mon-Thur; 8am-4pm Fri; closed Sat, Sun. **Map** p309 L9.
Known as the VZP, this is the main provider of health insurance in the Czech Republic, offering reasonable rates for short-term coverage, issued in terms of 30-day periods.

Branch: Na Perštýně 6, Staré Město, Prague 1 (2166 8111).

Property insurance

Insuring personal belongings is always wise and should be arranged before leaving home.

Internet

Only a few of the newer and more expensive hotels provide dataports, so unless you're one of the lucky few to have one or can do clever things with your mobile phone, your best bet is to set up a web-based email account before you leave and autoforward your mail to it. You can then pick it up from an Internet café (*see page 152*).

If you do have access to a modem line, ask your ISP before you leave home whether it has a Prague dial-in or a reciprocal arrangement with a local provider. Alternatively, if you are a frequent traveller or plan

Directory

on a long stay, you could set up an account locally. The number of companies offering Internet access here is growing and services are improving. The standard rate for individual accounts, including browsing time and e-mail, starts at about 500 Kč a month. Corporate and leased lines are also available and rates rise according to the connection speed and number of accounts.

The main Internet providers in Prague are listed below. Alternatively, a good list of Czech providers is kept at sgi.felk.cvut.cz/~prikryl/providers.html. You can check out this and other sites at one of Prague's growing number of Internet cafés.

Telenor/Nextra
Václavské náměstí 4, Nové Město, Prague 1 (9615 9411/www.ti.cz). Metro Můstek/3, 5, 9, 14, 24 tram. **Open** 11am-1am Mon-Fri; 11am-3am Sat, Sun. **Map** p307 L2.
Born as the humble Terminal Bar (*see p152*), the ISP side of the business was bought up and separated from the wirehead's caffiene and video stop. Now the market leader, offering dial-up services, web hosting and design. Standard rates, generally friendly and reliable (but occasionally rather flaky) service.

Language

The Czech language was exiled from officialdom and literature, in favour of German for much of the history of Bohemia until the national revival of the 19th century. Today Czech is spoken throughout Prague, though most places of business at least in the centre should have some English-speaking staff. German may help you in speaking to older Czechs, and many younger ones speak Russian, which was taught compulsorily in schools before the Velvet Revolution.

Czech is a difficult but rewarding language to learn in that it helps penetrate the wall put up by rather shy Czechs. They invariably light up upon hearing even an attempt at their

mother tongue by a foreigner. For essential vocabulary, *see page 292*.

Left luggage

There are left luggage offices/lockers at Hlavní nádraží and Nádraží Holešovice stations and Florenc bus station (*for all, see page 268*).

Libraries

For a full list of Prague's libraries, ask at the National Library or look in the *Zlaté stránky* (*Yellow Pages*) under 'knihovny'. Admission rules vary; generally, you don't need to register to use reading rooms, but you do to borrow books, and for this you'll need your passport and sometimes a document stating that you are a student, teacher, researcher or Prague resident. Most libraries have restricted opening hours or close in July and August.

British Council
Národní třída 10, Nové Město, Prague 1 (2199 1111). Metro Národní třída. **Reading room open** *Sept-June* 9am-7pm Mon-Thur; 9am-4pm Fri; closed Sat, Sun. *July, Aug* 9am-4pm Mon-Fri; closed Sat, Sun. **Library open** noon-7pm Mon-Thur; 9am-1pm Fri; Sat; closed Sun & July, Aug). **Map** p306 H5.
The light and airy reading room has a cheap, excellent café and free Internet terminals. The downstairs library is packed with materials and aids for TEFL and TESL teachers, but virtually no literature. The video selection is eclectic, and the free screenings can be excellent. The library is open to everyone. Membership entails providing solid proof of your status as either a teacher or a student.

City Library
Městská knihovna v Praze Mariánské náměstí 1 (2211 3338/232 8208). Metro Staroměstská. **Open** *July, Aug* 9am-6pm Tue-Fri; closed Mon, Sat, Sun. *Sept-June* 9am-8pm Tue-Fri; 10am-5pm Sat; closed Mon, Sat. **Map** p306 H3.
The freshly renovated main branch of the City Library is now spacious, calm and state of the art. You'll find an excellent English-language literature section, a handful of English-language magazines, fine music and audio

collections and plenty of comfortable spaces for studying, scribbling and flipping through tomes.

National Library
Národní knihovna v Praze Klementinum, Křížovnické náměstí 4, Staré Město, Prague 1 (2166 3331/fax 2166 3261/www.nkp.cz). Metro Staroměstská. **Open** 9am-7pm Mon-Sat; closed Sun. **Map** p306 G4.
A comprehensive collection of just about everything ever published in Czech and a reasonably good international selection, housed in a confusing warren of occasionally gorgeous halls. Hours vary somewhat depending on which reading room you want to use. It is possible to take books out but you'll need to show your passport and a residence permit.

Lost property

Most railway stations have a lost property office (*Ztráty a nálezy*). If you lose your passport, contact your embassy (*see page 277*).

Central Lost Property Office
Karoliny Světlé 5, Staré Město, Prague 1 (2423 5085). Metro Národní třída/6, 9, 17, 18, 22 tram. **Open** 8am-noon, 12.30-5.30pm Mon, Wed; 8am-noon, 12.30-4pm Tue, Thur; 8am-noon, 12.30-2pm Fri; closed Sat, Sun. **Map** p306 G5.

Media

Business/news publications (English)

Business Central Europe
A monthly economics and business magazine from *The Economist*. Covers the whole of Central Europe and the former Soviet Union with regular stories on the Czech Republic.

Central European Business Weekly
Prague-based business weekly with full coverage of Central and Eastern Europe.

Central European Economic Review
A monthly regional overview published by the *Wall Street*

Journal that tends to focus its coverage on finance, banking and capital markets.

The Fleet Sheet

A daily one-page digest of the Czech press offering good coverage of major political and financial events. Sent out as a fax each morning.

Newsline/Radio Free Europe

www.rferl.org
Dry but highly informative daily overview of events in Eastern Europe and the former Soviet Union. Produced in co-operation with Prague-based Radio Free Europe/Radio Liberty. The information is available as an email service or from RFE's comprehensive website.

Prague Business Journal

www.pbj.cz
Weekly business newspaper that focuses on Prague and the Czech Republic. Highly informative.

The Prague Post

www.praguepost.cz
Weekly newspaper with good coverage of business, banking and capital markets. Highlights and major stories available free on its website.

The Prague Tribune

Glossy, bilingual Czech-English monthly mag with an emphasis on business, social issues and features.

Radio Prague E-News

www.radio.cz
Czech state radio offers free email copy of daily news bulletins in English, Czech and other languages. Informative website with links to other Internet-based info sources.

Resources

www.resources.cz
Resources is a comprehensive and practical directory of business contacts in Prague and Bratislava.

General interest (English)

The New Presence

This is the English-language version of *Nová přítomnost*, a journal dating back to inter-war Bohemia that offers a liberal and stimulating selection of opinion writings, some translated from their original Czech, by both local and international writers. Not easy to find, but worth seeking out for an in-depth look at the Czech Republic. Try the Globe Bookstore (*see page 165*) or Big Ben Bookshop (*page 164*).

Prague Post

www.praguepost.cz
Among younger Prague types, the *Prague Post* often gets a bad rap for being dull and lifeless. Its local news is steady (if perhaps overly heavy on the party politics) but rarely seems to do more than scratch the surface of Czech life. Still, as competitors fall by the wayside, the *Post* – with its useful cultural listings, business focus and entertainment features – is still around after all these years. Editor-in-chief Alan Levy's self-promoting 'Prague Profile' column is loved by many and hated by many.

Think

A free 'zine with the look of a ransom note but an authoritative list of club events and parties, plus occasionally useful website tips, hidden among conspiracy theory rants and silly stabs at counter-culture. Find it at Radost (*see p181*) or U Malého Glena (*see p155*).

Czech newspapers

Blesk

The extremely popular *Blesk* ('Lightning') is a daily tabloid full of sensationalised news, celebrity scandals, UFO sightings and busty page-three girls.

Hospodářské noviny

The Czech equivalent of the *Financial Times*, this respected daily brings news of capital markets, exchange rates and business transactions. *Hospodářské noviny* is required reading for Czech movers and shakers.

Lidové noviny

An underground dissident paper in the communist days, *Lidové noviny*'s finest hour came in the early 1990s. Today, the paper is still respected in some right-wing and intellectual circles, but commercialism has taken its toll.

Mladá fronta Dnes

A former communist paper, *Dnes* has been the country's leading serious newspaper for several years. It now offers fairly balanced domestic and international news, and a reasonable level of independence. The reporting and editing, however, are often inexcusably poor.

Právo

The former communist party newspaper (the name means 'Justice'; it used to be *Rudé Právo* – 'Red Justice') is now a respectable, left-leaning daily with an equally respectable circulation.

Respekt

A weekly newspaper, *Respekt* takes a close look at the good, the bad and the ugly effects of the Czech Republic's transformation to a market economy. Not only does it ask the questions other newspapers don't but it also has some cutting-edge cartoons.

Sport

Daily sports paper, and you don't need Czech to figure out the results it publishes from home and abroad. Predictably heavy on European football, ice hockey and tennis coverage. *Sport* also lists results from the NBA and NFL.

Czech periodicals

Cosmopolitan/Elle

Cosmopolitan fails to stand up against its Western counterparts, but Czech *Elle* appeals to both teens and middle-aged women with flashy fashion spreads, decor and interviews.

Reflex

Reflex is a popular, low-rent style weekly with glossy format, some interesting editorial and some very boring design.

Živel

A cool cyberpunk mag with an interesting design and a sub-cultural editorial slant – like a cross between *The Face* and *Wired*. Hip, small circulation and more likely to be found in bookshops than at newsagents. Was quarterly but now only publishes irregularly.

Listings

Annonce

A classified ad sheet into which bargain-hunting Czechs delve to find good deals on second-hand washing machines, TVs, cars, etc. *Annoce* is also a good apartment-hunting tool. Place your ad for free, then wait by the phone – it's a proven-success formula.

Culture In Prague

A privately run monthly alternative to *Kulturní přehled* (*see below*) covering all major cultural events; available in English at bookstores around Wenceslas Square.

Do města

'Downtown' is a tall-format entertainment freesheet in Czech with English translations. It's good for weekly listings of galleries, cinemas, theatres and clubs. New edition every Thursday. You'll find it lying around in bars, cafés and clubs.

Kulturní přehled

A reliable monthly listing of cultural events in Prague. It's in Czech only but not hard to understand and it gives schedules for the main cultural venues, including theatres, operas, museums, clubs and exhibitions.

Týdeník

A weekly guide to what's on TV. If you're looking for the occasional English-language movie with Czech subtitles, better to check the listings in the *Prague Post* (*see page 281*).

Literary magazines

Though many have folded over the past few years, a whole pile of literary magazines is still published in Prague, in both Czech and English. You should be able to track down most of them at the Globe Bookstore (*see page 165*) or Big Ben Bookshop (*page 164*). The Czech-language *Revolver Review*, supposedly published quarterly (but distinctly irregular), is a hefty periodical with samizdat roots. The RR presents new works by well-known authors along with lesser-known pieces by pet favourites such as Kafka. *Labyrint Revue*, a monthly magazine, and *Literární noviny*, a weekly, are the other two main Czech publications offering original writing and reviews of new work. *Labyrint* also has music and art reviews.

English publications tend to come and go. The best and most widely known is *Trafika*, a 'quarterly' showcase for international writers that tends to lapse into an 'occasionally'. Although it has recently been out of action, *Trafika*'s editors now look to be reviving this early pioneer.

The *Prague Review*, formerly the *Jáma Review*, is a slim quarterly of plays, prose and poetry from Czechs and Czech-based expats. Its editors – who

have included such Czech literary heavyweights as Bohumil Hrabal, Ivan Klíma and Miroslav Holub – generously subtitle the volume 'Bohemia's journal of international literature'.

Optimism

A more-or-less monthly literary mag that's a forum for Prague's English-speaking expatriate community, its content ranges from the intriguing to hopelessly trite but is genuinely open to young, unproven writers.

Foreign press

Foreign newspapers are available at various stalls on and around Wenceslas Square and at major hotels. The *International Guardian*, *International Herald-Tribune* and the international *USA Today* are available on the day of publication. Most other papers arrive 24 hours later.

Television

ČT1/ČT2

The two national public channels. ČT1 tries to compete with TV Nova (*see page 283*), but is out of its depth financially. ČT2 serves up serious music (including frequent spotlights on the jazz greats), theatre and documentaries to the small percentage of the population that tunes in. ČT2 sometimes broadcasts English-language movies with Czech subtitles; Woody Allen flicks are popular, as are Monty Python classics. It also airs *Euronews*, an English-language pan-European programme, on weekdays at 8am and on weekends at 7am.

Prima TV

A Prague-based regional broadcaster that lamely follows the lead of TV Nova (*see page 283*) but is slowly being revamped by new foreign partners from the West.

TV Nova

One of the first national private television stations in Eastern Europe. Initially funded by Ronald Lauder, son of Estée, Nova TV looks like US television with lots of old Hollywood movies and recycled sitcoms dubbed into Czech. Appallingly successful.

Radio

BBC World Service (101.1 FM)

English-language news on the hour plus regular BBC programming, with occasional Czech and Slovak news broadcasts. For 30 minutes a day around teatime it transmits local Czech news in English, courtesy of Radio Prague.

Limonádový Joe (90.3 FM)

Lemonade Joe pumps out nothing but corny old Czech hits from the 1960s and '70s, plus an Elvis song here and there. Named after a classic Czech parody of American westerns, Joe is worth tuning in to if just for a giggle.

Radio Free Europe

Prague is now the world headquarters for RFE. It still beams the same old faintly propagandist stuff to Romania, Ukraine and other former Soviet republics. The station is based at the former Czechoslovak Federal Assembly building, next to the National Museum.

Radio Kiss (98.0 FM) Radio Bonton (99.7 FM) Evropa 2 (88.2 FM)

Pop music, pop music and more pop music.

Radio 1 (91.9)

Excellent alternative music station that plays everything from Jimi Hendrix to techno. Evening calendar listings have everything the hip party goer needs to know.

Radio Prague (92.6 FM & 102.7 FM)

Daily news in English, plus interviews, weather and traffic. Nothing too inspired, but a well-established and connected source with some history behind it.

Money

CURRENCY

The currency of the Czech Republic is the Česká *koruna* or Czech crown (abbreviated as Kč). One crown equals 100 hellers (*haléřů*). Hellers come as small, light 10, 20 and 50 coins. There are also 1, 2, 5, 10, 20 and 50 Kč coins in circulation. Notes come in denominations of 20, 50, 100, 200, 500, 1,000 and 5,000 Kč.

At the time of going to press, the exchange rate was approximately 62,5 Kč to the pound, or around 37,8 Kč to the US dollar. It's obviously impossible to predict exchange rates, but recently they have been fluctuating, largely downwards, so it's probably wise only to cash only as many crowns as you need.

The crown was the first fully convertible currency in the former Eastern Bloc. A bizarre indicator of its viability is the number of convincing counterfeit Czech banknotes in circulation. If someone stops you in the street asking if you want to change money, it's a fair bet that he'll be trying to offload dodgy notes.

CASH ECONOMY

The Czech Republic has long been a cash economy, and such conveniences as cash machines (ATMs), credit cards and cheques, travellers' cheques included, are not nearly as ubiquitous here as they are in EC countries or the US, though they are becoming more common. However, the situation is changing and, particularly in Prague, it's not

difficult to find ATMs that will pay out cash on the major credit and charge card networks such as Maestro, Cirrus and Delta. Looks for the symbol that matches the one on your card and use your usual PIN number. Many of the classier restaurants and shops, especially around Wenceslas Square and the Old Town, also accept credit cards and travellers' cheques.

Banks & currency exchange

Exchange rates are usually the same all over, but banks offer a better rate of commission (usually one to two per cent). Unfortunately, they are only open during regular business hours (usually 8am-5pm Monday to Friday).

Bureaux de change usually tend to charge higher rates of commission for changing cash or travellers' cheques, although some (such as those at the Charles Bridge end of Karlova) may only take one per cent. Bear in mind that this means little if you're getting a poor exchange rate.

OPENING AN ACCOUNT

The high toll of bank failures recently appears to have improved service at the survivors. At some, such as ČSOB, there is no minimum requirement to open an account and foreign currency accounts are also available without the outlandish fees once charged.

MONEY TRANSFER

To get money fast, try the American Express office or, in the case of a serious emergency, your embassy. The Na příkopě branch of ČSOB processes transfers faster than other Czech banks.

American Express

Václavské náměstí 56, Nové Město, Prague 1 (2421 9992). Metro Můstek or Muzeum/3, 9, 14, 24 tram. **Open** 9am-7pm daily. **Map** p307 K5. Cardholders can send and receive their mail and faxes here.

Directory

Československá obchodní banka (ČSOB)

Na příkopě 14, Nové Město, Prague 1 (2411 1111). Metro Můstek or Náměstí Republiky/3, 5, 9, 14, 24 tram. **Open** 8am-5pm Mon-Fri; closed Sat, Sun. **Map** p307 K4.
Specialises in international currency transactions.

Komerční banka

Na příkopě 33, Nové Město, Prague 1 (2243 2111/2424 8110). Metro Můstek or Náměstí Republiky/3, 5, 9, 14, 24 tram. **Open** 8am-5pm Mon-Fri; closed Sat, Sun. **Map** p307 K4.
The country's largest full-service bank, with a large network of branches throughout the country. The ATM network accepts international credit cards and is a Mastercard (Eurocard) agent. Its card emergency number is 2424 8110.

Živnostenská banka

Na příkopě 20, Nové Město, Prague 1 (2412 1111). Metro Můstek or Náměstí Republiky/3, 5, 9, 14, 24 tram. **Open** 8.30am-5pm Mon-Fri; closed Sat, Sun. **Map** p307 K4.
This old trading bank, housed in one of the most beautiful buildings in Prague, has long experience in working with foreign clients, and English is generally spoken by tellers. Represents Visa. For lost or stolen Visa cards phone 2412 5311/5313/5314 or 00 1 410 581 3836 (for the US).

Numbers

Dates are written in the following order: day, month, year.

When writing figures, Czechs put commas where Americans and Britons would put decimal points and vice versa, thus ten thousand Czech crowns is written as 10.000 Kč.

Opening hours

Standard opening hours for most shops and banks are from 8am or 9am to 5pm or 6pm Monday to Friday. Many shops are open a bit longer and from 9am to noon or 1pm on Saturday. Shops with extended hours are called *večerka* (open until 10pm or midnight) and 'non-stop' (open 24 hours daily). Outside the centre, most shops are closed on Sundays and holidays. Shops frequently close for a day or two for no

apparent reason; some shops close for an hour or two at lunch; and many shops and theatres close for a month's holiday in August. Most places have shorter opening hours in winter (starting September or October) and extended hours in summer (starting April or May). Castles and some other attractions are only open in summer.

Police & security

Police in the Czech Republic are not regarded as serious crimefighters or protectors of the public and are just barely considered keepers of law and order. Their past as pawns for the regime, combined with a present reputation for corruption, racism and incompetence, has prevented them from gaining much in the way of respect. If you are the victim of crime while in Prague, then don't expect much help – or even concern – from the local constabulary.

LEGALITIES

You are expected to carry your passport or residence card at all times. If you have to deal with police, they are supposed to provide an interpreter for you. Buying or selling street drugs is illegal, and a controversial new law has outlawed the possession of even small quantities. The legal drinking age is 18, but nobody here seems to pay any attention.

Prague's pickpockets concentrate in tourist areas like Wenceslas Square, Old Town Square, Charles Bridge and the Castle. Keep an eye on your handbag or wallet, especially in crowds and on public tranport. Seedier parts of Prague include parts of Žižkov, parts of Smíchov, the park in front of Hlavní nádraaži, the main station, and the lower end of Wenceslas Square and upper end of Národní třída.

For emergencies, call the Czech police on 158

Post

Stamps are available from post offices, newsagents, tobacconists and most places where postcards are sold. Postcards cost 7 Kč within Europe and 8 Kč outside Europe; regular letters cost 9 Kč within Europe and 11 Kč airmail elsewhere. Packages should be wrapped in plain white or brown paper. Always use black or blue ink or a snippy clerk will refuse to accept your mail. Even oddly shaped postcards have been refused by the rule-obsessed Czech Post.

Post offices are scattered all over Prague. Though they are being thoroughly modernised, many have different opening hours and offering varying degrees of service and all are confusing. Indeed, the system designating what's on offer at which window is perplexing, even for some Czechs.

The Main Post Office on Jindřišská in Nové Město, Prague 1 offers the most services, some of them available 24 hours a day. Fax, telegram and international phone lines are located in the annex around the corner at Politických vězňů 4. Some services, such as poste restante (general delivery) and EMS express mail are theoretically available at all post offices, but are much easier to use at the main Post Office branch on Jindřišská Street.

You can buy special edition stamps and send mail overnight within the Czech Republic and within a few days to Europe and the rest of the world via EMS – a cheaper but less reliable service than commercial couriers.

PACKAGES

To send or collect restricted packages or items subject to tax or duty, you must go to the Customs Post Office (*see page 285*). Bring your passport, residence permit and any other ID. For incoming packages, you will also need to pay duty and tax. The biggest queues at the Customs Post Office form between 11am and 1.30pm.

Outgoing packages should be wrapped in plain white or brown paper. If they weigh more than two kilogrammes (4.4 pounds), are valued upwards of 30,000 Kč or contain 'unusual contents' such as medicine or clothing, they must officially be cleared through the Customs Post Office, but in practice this is not usually necessary.

Uninsured packages of up to two kilos don't need to be declared and can be sent from any post office – they're treated as letters (250 Kč to the UK; 593 Kč to the US), and you don't need your passport. Up to four kilos and the consignment is treated as a package, but if you don't want to insure it, it doesn't usually need to be declared and can be sent from a post office (457 Kč-505 Kč to the UK; 715 Kč-881 Kč to the US). If the package is heavier or you would like to insure it, take it to the Customs Post Office and declare it. Take your passport.

Note that the export of antiques is strictly restricted.

USEFUL POSTAL VOCABULARY

letters: *příjem – výdej listovin*
packages: *příjem – výdej balíčků*
          or *balíků*
money transactions: *platby*
stamps: *známky* – usually at
          window marked *Kolky*
          a ceniny
special issue stamps:
          filatelistický servis
registered mail: *doporučeně*

Main Post Office

Hlavní pošta
Jindřišská 14, Nové Město, Prague 1 (2113 1445/232 0837). Metro Můstek/3, 9, 14, 24 tram. **Open** 7am-8pm daily. **No credit cards.** **Map** p307 K5.

Non-Stop Post Office

Masarykovo nádraží, Hybernská 15, Nové Město, Prague 1 (2224 0271). Metro Náměstí republiky. **Open** 12.15am-11.15pm daily. **Map** p307 L3.

Customs Post Office

Plzeňská 139, Smíchov, Prague 5, (5701 9105). Metro Anděl, then 4, 7, 9 tram. **Open** 7am-3pm Mon, Tue, Thur, Fri; 7am-6pm Wed; closed Sat, Sun. **No credit cards.**

Religion

Services in English are held at only a handful of Prague churches, listed below.

Anglican Church of Prague

Kostel U Klimenta, Klimentská, Nové Město, Prague 1 (231 0094). Metro Náměstí Republiky. **Services** 11am Sun. **Map** p307 L4.

Church of St Joseph

Sv Josef
Josefská 4, Malá Strana, Prague 1 (5753 2100). Metro Náměstí Republiky. **Services** 4pm Thur (in French). **Map** p307 K3. Catholic services.

International Baptist Church of Prague

Vinohradská 68, Žižkov, Prague 3 (2425 4646). Metro Jiřího z Poděbrad. **Service** 11am Sun. **Map** p311 B3.

International Church of Prague

Vrázova 4, Smíchov, Prague 5 (5731 9839). Metro Anděl. **Services** 11.15am Sun.

Prague Christian Fellowship

Ječná 19 (entry at back of house), Nové Město, Prague 2 (5753 0020/2431 5613). Metro Karlovo Náměstí. **Services** 2pm Sun. **Map** p308 J8.

Smoking

Smoking is not allowed on public transport in Prague but that's about the only place people don't light up. One or two restaurants now have non-smoking areas but by and large people around you will freely light up, even if they are sharing the table with you at a pub and you are eating a meal.

Street names

When addressing an envelope, put the street name first, followed by street number,

with the post code following on the next line before the Prague district number, like this:

Jan Novák
Václavské náměstí 56
11 326 Praha 1
Czech Republic

Study

Charles University courses

Founded in 1348 by King Charles IV, Charles University (Universita Karlova) is the oldest university in Central Europe, and the undisputed hub of Prague's student activity. Its heart is the Carolinum, a Gothic building on Ovocný trh near the Estates Theatre, which houses the central administration offices. Other university buildings are scattered all over the city.

Several cash-hungry faculties now run special courses for foreigners. Contact the relevant dean or the International Relations Office during the university year (October to May) for information on courses and admissions procedures.

Below is a selection of the more popular offerings. For courses outside Prague, contact the British Council (*see page 280*).

Charles University

International Relations Office, Universita Karlova Rektorát, Ovocný trh 3-5, Staré Město, Prague 1 (2449 1310/fax 2422 9487). Metro Staroměstská or Můstek. **Open** 8am-4pm Mon-Fri; closed Sat, Sun. **Map** p306 J4.

FAMU

Smetanovo nábeží 2, Staré Město, Prague 1 (2422 0955/fax 2423 0285). Metro Staroměstská or Národní třída. **Open** 9am-3pm Mon-Fri; closed Sat, Sun. **Map** p306 G4.
Famous for turning out such Oscar-winning directors as Miloš Forman, Prague's foremost school of film, TV and photography runs several English courses under its Film For Foreigners (3F) programme, including summer workshops, six-month and one-year courses in aspects of film and TV production and a BA in photography.

Directory

Institute of Language & Professional Training

Ústav jazykové a odborné přípravy *Universita Karlova, Vratislavova 10, Nové Město, Prague 2 (2499 0420/ fax 2499 0440). Metro Karlovo náměstí/3, 16, 17, 21 tram.* **Open** 9-11am, 1-3pm Mon, Wed; 9-11am Tue, Fri; 1-3pm Thur; closed Sat, Sun. **Fees** six-week session 15,900 Kč; intensive semester 51,100 Kč; two-semester school year 100,000 Kč; individual lesson 500 Kč per 45 minutes. **No credit cards.**

Aimed at preparing foreign nationals who want to embark on degree courses at Czech universities, this branch of Charles University offers Czech-language training in the form of six-week summer courses, semester-long intensive courses and pricey individual lessons.

School of Czech Studies

Filosofická fakulta, Universita Karlova, náměstí Jana Palacha 2, Staré Město, Prague 1 (2161 9280/www.ff.cuni.cz). Metro Staroměstská. **Open** Oct-May 10.30am-6pm Mon-Fri; closed Sat, Sun & June-Sept. **Fees** $2,010 (74,400 Kč) per two-semester year. **No credit cards.** Map p306 G3.

Runs year-long courses during the school year, offering a mix of language instruction and lectures in Czech history and culture. Classes are available for beginner, intermediate and advanced speakers of Czech.

Summer School of Slavonic Studies

Filosofická fakulta, Universita Karlova, náměstí Jana Palacha 2, Staré Město, Prague 1 (tel/fax 231 9645). Metro Staroměstská. **Fees** 17,000 Kč (course fee only); 36,300 Kč (includes dorm accommodation & meals). **No credit cards.** Map p306 G3.

This one-month summer course, held yearly in August, is designed for professors and advanced students in Slavonic studies. It's best to correspond by mail. A registration deadline of 1 May is recommended, but not enforced.

Other courses

Anglo-American College

Lázeňská 4, Malá Strana, Prague 1 (5753 0202/www.aac.edu). Metro Malostranská/12, 18, 22, 23 tram. **Open** 9am-5pm Mon-Fri. **Fees** 33,000 Kč per five-course semester; 9,000 Kč per one-course semester. **No credit cards.** Map p305 E3/4.

A private college offering Western-style degree courses in business, economics, the humanities and law.

While the entire syllabus and all classes are in English, the student body is a mix of Czechs, Slovaks and foreign nationals. Limited course offerings during the summer session.

Language courses

Many schools offer Czech-language instruction. If you prefer a more informal approach, place a notice on one of the boards at the Charles University Faculty, the Globe Bookstore (*see page 165*), Radost (*see page 181*) or anywhere else where young Czechs and foreigners meet. Many students and other young people are happy to offer Czech conversation in exchange for English conversation. But since Czech grammar is difficult most serious learners need systematic, professional instruction to master the basics.

Accent

Bítovská 3, Kačerov, Prague 4 (420 595/fax 422 845/www.akcent.cz). Metro Budějovická. **Fees** intensive 5,200 Kč; standard 7,800 Kč; individual lesson about 500 Kč 45mins. **No credit cards.**

A co-operative run and owned by the senior teachers, both Czech and foreign, this school has a good reputation for standards and quality. Choose a one-month intensive course (two hours daily instruction) or a more relaxed 'standard' five-month course (four hours weekly). All classes have a maximum size of six. A bit out of the way, but worth the travel.

Angličtina Expres Office

Korunní 2, Nové Město, Prague 2 (2251 3040). Metro Náměstí Míru. **Fees** 30-hour course 4,300 Kč (including books and tapes). **Open** 8am-8pm Mon-Thur; 8am-4pm Fri. **No credit cards.** Map p311 A3.

Well-established Czech-run school originally set up to teach the locals English but now with years of experience in teaching rudimentary Czech to expats. Instructors use materials developed in-house. The 30-hour course runs every weekday for four weeks in classes of eight or less.

Berlitz

Hybernská 24, Nové Město, Prague 1 (2212 5555-6/fax.2212 5558/www. berlitz.com). Metro IP Pavlova. **Open** 8am-8pm Mon-Fri; closed Sat, Sun.

Fees 40-minute lesson 600 Kč. **No credit cards.** Map p307 L3.

The staggering cost of lessons is testament, supposedly, to the efficiency of the Berlitz method, which emphasises speaking drills and discourages systematic grammar teaching and note-taking. With an internationally standardised method of teaching and branches all over the world (several in Prague alone), Berlitz is the McDonald's of language schools, and it gets results.

Lingua Viva

Spálená 57, Nové Město, Prague 1 (2492 0675/fax 2492 1051/www.lingua viva.cz). Metro Národní třída/6, 9, 18, 21, 22, 23 tram. **Open** 9am-7pm Mon-Thur; 9am-noon Fri; closed Sat, Sun. **Fees** 72-hour course (5 months) 4,950 Kč; intensive 64-hour course (1 month) 3,990 Kč; individual lesson 420 Kč 45mins; 500 Kč 60mins. **No credit cards.** Map p308 H6.

This small independent school is an upstart, with better rates and more informal instruction than most.

State Language School

Státní jazyková Škola Školská 15, Nové Město, Prague 1 (Slavonic languages & Czech for foreigners 2223 2238/fax 2223 2236/summer courses 297 114/www.sjs.cz). Metro Můstek or Národní třída. **Open** 12.30-3.30pm Tue; 12.30-6.30pm Wed; 12.30-3.30pm Thur, Fri; closed Mon, Sat, Sun. **Fees** intensive 14,760 Kč; standard 4,065 Kč; summer 7,000 Kč. **No credit cards.** Map p308 J6.

The largest and cheapest language school in Prague is state run and teaches just about every language under the sun. The Czech for Foreigners department offers both intensive courses (16 hours weekly for five months) and standard courses (four hours weekly for five months) during the normal school year, as well as shorter intensive summer courses (20 hours weekly for one month). Classes tend to start very large, but many students drop out over the course of the term, leaving a smaller, more dedicated, but still dead cheap class.

Student travel

CKM

Jindřišská 28, Nové Město, Prague 1 (268 532/2423 0218/fax 268 623). Metro Můstek. **Open** 10am-6pm Mon-Thur; 10am-4pm Fri; closed Sat, Sun. **No credit cards.** Map p307 K5.

Specialises in cheap travel in and outside the Czech Republic for young people, students and teachers. ISIC cards are very liberally issued; just

---

Stats entertainment

Try catching a bus somewhere in the Czech Republic – the country around Prague is lovely and easily accessible.

But don't forget to bring along a statistician.

Bus timetables, like much else in Bohemia, are virtually incomprehensible for all their rows of dates, hours, footnotes and exceptions. But be reassured, if that's the word: even Czechs who've spent their lives with such schedules can be seen at any bus stop, frantically trying to figure out what's coming when.

On vacation, Czechs tote guide books filled with measurements. They may not tell you about the delectable seafood, but you can rest assured they'll report how deep the sea is. Ask any Czech what's beautiful about Slovakia's highest mountain and they'll be stuck for a reply. But they'll tell you in an instant that Gerlachovský štít is 2,655 metres (8,710 feet) above sea level. Or that the *Rukopis*

královédvorský, a major historical document, was discovered in 1817. What the damn thing meant is anybody's guess.

One of Prague's largest state-sector employers is the CzechStatistical Office, where hundreds of clerks churn out thousands of charts and publish them in fat books such as the *Numeri Pragensis*. This 167-page tome reveals how much money the average Praguer spends on meat as opposed to vegetables, and analyses 'deaths by selected causes per 100,000 inhabitants'. This last discloses that in 1999, 10.6 out of 100,000 Praguers died from genito-urinary diseases, while 73.9 expired from 'injury, poisoning and suicide'.

For all its wealth of data, one calculation is notably missing from the work of these busy bean-counters: just how many of those suicides are down to depression caused by charts and measurements.

show a letter from your university vouching that you are studying in Prague, pay 180 Kč, hand over a passport photo and – bingo! – you're a bona fide student. (No fact-checking has ever been witnessed.)
Branch: Mánesova 77, Vinohrady, Prague 2 (2224 1137).

GTS

Ve Smečkách 27, Nové Město, Prague 1 (9622 4301/fax 2221 0478). Metro Museum or Můstek. **Open** 9am-6pm Mon-Fri; 10am-2pm Sat; closed Sun. **No credit cards. Map** p309 K6.
The best place for ISIC card-holders to find cheapo student fares. Especially good international flight bargains, as well as occasional deals on bus and train travel. GTS also offers travel insurance and issues ISIC cards.
Branch: Lodecká 3, Nové Město, Prague 1 (2481 2770).

Telephones

Virtually all of the public coin telephones that still take 2 Kč coins are broken; the rest run on telephone cards, which come in denominations of 50 to 150 units and can be bought at newsstands, post offices and anywhere you see the blue and yellow Telecom sticker. Local calls cost 3,20 Kč for one unit (lasting two minutes from 7am-7pm weekdays, and four and

half minutes from 7pm-7am weekdays, all day weekends and public holidays and Sundays). International calls, which are horrendously expensive, can be made from any phone box or a private booth at the Main Post Office (*see page 285*).

The international dialling code to the Czech Republic is 420 and the city code for Prague is 2 (02 within the republic). To call abroad, dial the prefix 00, the country and the area codes (for UK area codes omit the 0) and then the number. The prefix for the United Kingdom is 44, for America and Canada it's 1 and for Australia 61. On local numbers, eight digits indicate that the number is on a digital switchboard while a four-, five-, six- or seven-digit number indicates an analogue board. Czech Telecom is rapidly digitalising the entire system.

The phone system could never be described as any better than bad, and it's noticeably worse when it's raining and the underground lines get wet. It often takes several attempts to get through, and you may get a

disconnected tone even when a number is in service.

SPT Czech Telecom

Olšanská 6, Žižkov, Prague 3 (0800 123 456). Metro Želivského/5, 9, 16, 19 tram. **Open** 9am-3pm Mon, Wed; 9am-6pm Tue, Thur; closed Fri-Sun. **Map** p311 D2.

Net Master

Rumunská 1, Vinohrady, Prague 2 (9618 1818/fax 9618 7780). Metro Míru Náměstí. **Open** 9am-5pm Mon-Fri; closed Sat, Sun. **Map** p309 K8.
A provider of a cheap Internet-routed phone calling service through Net Master 'smartcalls'.

Faxes & telegrams

You can send faxes and telegrams from the Main Post Office (*see page 285*) and major hotels. A fax costs the same per minute as a phone call; telegrams are usually 30 Kč plus 2.50 Kč per word (up to ten letters) within the Czech Republic, 22,60 Kč per word to the UK and 30,60 Kč per word to the US. Faxes marked clearly with your name can be sent to the Main Post Office (fax 2423 0303/2421 5146). There is a modest charge.

Directory

Mobile phones

Competition has led to improved services and lower rates in the Czech Republic but it sometimes seems that more energy goes into marketing mobile phones than providing good service and coverage. The two main companies are listed below – they offer different payment schemes and coverage areas, so it's best to get details of before deciding. They are also the only people in town who rent out phones short-term – for exorbitant sums.

Both companies use both the 1,800 MHz and 900 MHz wavebands, which means that owners of all standard UK mobiles can use them as long as they have a roaming facility (which may need to be pre-arranged). As in the rest of Europe, US cell phones will not work in the Czech Republic.

EuroTel

Sokolovská 225, Vysočany, Prague 9 (6701 6711/www.eurotel.cz). Metro Českomoravská/8 tram. **Open** 8am-6pm Mon-Fri; closed Sat, Sun.
The leading provider of mobile phone services and a subsidiary of telephone monopoly SPT Telecom.

Radiomobil

Londýnská 57-59, Vinohrady, Prague 2 (0603 603 603/0603 0604 0604). Metro IP Pavlova. **Open** 9am-4pm Mon-Fri; closed Sat, Sun. **Map** p309 M8.
The newer mobile phone provider, under the label Paegas, charges prices generally lower than at Eurotel, but the coverage (especially outside of Prague) may not be as extensive. The welcome arrival of this new phone company should precipitate a price war that will bring down the prohibitive cost of cell services.

Time

The Czech Republic is on Central European Time (CET), one hour ahead of the UK, six ahead of New York and nine ahead of Los Angeles, and uses the 24-hour clock. The Czechs are prompt, and you should never be more than 15 minutes late for a meeting.

Tipping & VAT

Czechs tend to round up restaurant bills, often only by a few crowns, but foreigners are more usually expected to leave a ten per cent tip. If service is bad, however, don't feel obliged to leave anything. Service is often added on automatically for large groups. Taxi drivers expect you to round the fare up, but, if you've just been ripped off, don't give a heller.

A value-added tax of 22 per cent has been slapped on to retail purchases for years in the Czech Republic but only as recently as 2000 was a system set up to reimburse non-resident foreigners' VAT payments at the border or airport. You'll need your shop receipt, passport and a VAT refund form, which staff can supply. Purchases of over 1,000 Kč are eligible if taken out of the country within 30 days of sale.

Toilets

Usually called a 'WC' (pronounce it 'veh-tseh'), the word for toilet is *záchod* and the usual charge for using one is 3 Kč. Calls of nature can be answered in all metro stations from at least 8am to 8pm, and at many fast-food joints and department stores. 'Ladies' is *Dámy* or *Ženy*, and 'Gents' is *Páni* or *Muži*.

Tourist information

The English-language weekly newspaper *Prague Post* carries entertainment sections along with survival hints. Monthly entertainment listings mags are the pocket-sized *Exit* (in Czech), *Kulturní přehled* (in Czech), *Kultura v Praze* and its shorter English equivalent *Culture in Prague*. (*See also above* **Media**.) The Prague Information Service (PIS) also publishes a free monthly entertainment listings programme in English.

The use of the international blue and white 'i' information sign is not regulated, so the places carrying it are not necessarily official.

The best map for public transport or driving is the widely available *Kartografie Praha Plán města* (a book with a yellow cover), costing about 100 Kč, though for central areas the co-ordinates are sometimes far too vague. Check you've got the latest edition. For central areas the free map from Prague Information Service (*see below*) is very useful.

Čedok

Na příkopě 18, Nové Město, Prague 1 (2419 7642/2419 7615/262 904). Metro Můstek or Náměstí Republiky. **Open** 9am-6pm Mon-Fri; 10am-3pm Sat; 10am-2pm Sun. **Map** p307 K4.
The former state travel agency is still the biggest in the Czech Republic. A handy place to obtain train, bus and air tickets and information.

PIS (Prague Information Service)

Pražská informační služba Na příkopě 20, Nové Město, Prague 1 (264 022/general info 187/544 444/www.prague-info.cz). Metro Můstek or Náměstí Republiky. **Open** *Apr-Oct* 9am-7pm Mon-Fri; 9am-5pm Sat, Sun. *Nov-March* 9am-6pm Mon-Fri; 9am-3pm Sat; closed Sun. **Map** p307 K4.
After decades of truly awful service, the PIS woke up and started to do what it was always supposed to do – provide free information, maps and help with a smile.
Branches: Hlavní nádraží (Main Station), Wilsonova, Nové Město, Prague 1 (2423 9258); Old Town Hall, Staroměstské náměstí, Staré Město, Prague 1 (2448 2202); Charles Bridge – Malá Strana-side Tower (summer only; 536 010).

Visas

Requirements can change frequently, but at press time citizens of the US, Canada, New Zealand, Ireland, EU members and most other European countries did not need a visa to enter the Czech Republic for stays of up to 30 days – just a valid passport with at least six months to run by the end of their visit. Under a new law aimed at preventing illegal residence by foreigners, however, border crossings can get complicated if you don't prepare. Foreigners who do require a visa to enter the Czech Republic, including Australians and South Africans, can no longer get theirs at the border but must apply at a Czech embassy outside the Czech Republic (but not necessarily in their home country). The process may take three months or longer, so early planning has become critical.

Even visitors who don't require a visa may now be asked for proof that they have sufficient finances, pre-arranged accommodation in the Czech Republic and international health insurance. Americans may now legally stay only 30 days, Canadians and UK citizens up to six months, and EU citizens are generally allowed up to 90 days, as are Irish and New Zealanders.

Automated, extremely confusing visa information is available in English at the Foreigner's Police in Prague (*see below*). You are technically required to register at the local police station within 30 days of arriving (if you are staying at a hotel this will be done for you). If you are from one of the countries whose residents are allowed only 30 days in the Czech Republic, you must obtain an extended visa (confusingly called an exit visa, or *vyjezdní vízum*) from the Foreigners Police office to allow you up to 90 days in total.

LONGER STAYS

The other option to stay longer is a residence permit (*občanský průkaz*), which isn't easy to get (*see page 291*) and must be obtained from a Czech embassy – they can no longer be arranged from within the Czech Republic.

The Czech police conduct periodic crackdowns on illegal aliens. They're usually aimed at Romanians, Ukrainians, Vietnamese and other nationals considered undesirable, though

a few Brits and US citizens usually get caught. Even so, many expatriates reside here illegally. Some avoid dealing with the above requirements by leaving the country every month to three months. Border police are getting wise to the trick, however, and it may not work for much longer. If you choose this option, be sure to get the required stamp in your passport as you leave by saying 'razítko prosím'.

Foreigners Police

Cizinecká policie, Olšanska 2, Praha 3, Žižkov (6144 1119). Metro Želivského/ 5, 9, 26 tram. **Open** 8am-3pm Mon, Tue, Thur; 9am-5pm Wed; 8am-2pm Fri; closed Sat, Sun. **Map** p311 D2.

Weights & measures

The Czechs use the metric system, even selling eggs in batches of five or ten. Things are usually measured out in decagrams or 'deka' (10 grams) or deciliters or 'deci' (10 centilitres). So a regular glass of wine is usually two deci (abbreviated dcl), and ham enough for a few sandwiches is 20 deka (abbreviated dkg).

When to go

That Prague is such a beautiful city helps to make up a little for its lousy weather.

SPRING

The best season in Prague – and surely the most awaited. The city comes out of hibernation from a long, cold, cloudy winter. While it is not unheard of for there to be snow lingering on as late as 1 May, temperatures are often perfect for strolling.

Averages

March 0°C to 7°C (five hours' sun a day, 65mm of rain the month)
April 3°C to 12°C (6 hours' sun, 78mm rain)
May 8°C to 17°C (8 hours' sun/63mm rain)

SUMMER

Prague citizens usually abandon the city to the tourist hordes by heading for their summer cottages (*chatas*) or to the seaside. Summers are pleasant, warm (rarely hot) and prone to thundery showers. The days are long, and it stays light until 10pm.

Averages

June 12°C to 21°C (nine hours' sun daily, 50mm rain the month)
July 13°C to 23°C (nine hours' sun/25mm rain)
August 14 to 22°C (eight hours' sun/50mm rain)

AUTUMN

This can be the prettiest time of year, with crisp cool air and sharp blue skies, but can also be the wettest. September is a good month to visit the city. The streets are once again jammed with cars, the parks full of children, and the restaurants full of local business people plotting their next move. The days grow shorter alarmingly quickly. By the end of October, the sun sets at around 5.30pm.

Averages

September 10°C to 17°C (six hours' sun daily, 55mm rain the month)
October 5°C to 14°C (four hours' sun, 100mm rain)
November 1°C to 5°C (two hours' sun, 110mm rain)

WINTER

Street-side carp sellers and Christmas markets help break the monotony of the long, cold, grey winter. When it snows, Prague is so beautiful and white that you forget for a few minutes the winter-long gloom that blankets the city. Sadly, bright, white snows are rarely accompanied by clear blue skies. Many Prague residents still burn coal for heating, and by midwinter the smog is so bad, you can't see across the river.

Directory

Averages

December 2°C to 0°C (one hour's sun a day, 76mm rain the month)
January 5°C to 0°C (two hours' sun, 62mm rain)
February 4°C to 1°C (three hours' sun/73mm rain).

Public holidays

New Year's Day
1 Jan
Easter Monday
Labour Day
1 May
Liberation Day
8 May
Cyril & Methodius Day
5 July
Jan Hus Day
6 July
Independence Day
28 Oct
Christmas holidays
24-26 Dec

Women

If you ask an expatriate what they like best about living in Prague, and the expatriate you ask happens to be male, 'Czech girls' will be near the top of the list. Springtime in the city is not only heralded by the blooming of lilacs and the arrival of Italian tourists, but also by a glazed look in the eyes of the city's male residents, due no doubt to the shedding of bulky winter clothing by the city's female population. Short skirts and big shoes can be seen in great numbers even in wintertime, but with the arrival of spring, the hemlines rise even farther and the men can be seen bumping into lampposts all over town. Milan Kundera writes of the Russian invasion in 1968: 'they must have felt that they had landed on a planet of stunning women who paraded their scorn on beautiful long legs the likes of which had not been seen in Russia for the last five or six centuries.'

If you ask a female expatriate what she likes best about living in Prague, you are highly unlikely to hear the response 'Czech men'. While innumerable expat men, delighted with Czech women's supermodel looks and acceptance of traditional gender roles, are dating Czech women, the number of expat women dating Czech men is minuscule. When confronted with the traditional gender-role expectations of Czech men, foreign women opt mostly to brave the cutthroat competition involved in trying to date foreigners, rather than get stuck doing a boyfriend's laundry. This may also have something to do with the male national hairdo, the shameless mullet.

FEMINISM? NOT

Foreign women here have a unique oppurtunity to see what happens in a society where feminism has never, ever been taken seriously. In the workplace, she will see her boss being brought his coffee by a snug-skirted secretary. She, however, is likely to be shown where they keep the Nescafé. In the pubs, she can expect to hear comments like 'Women just aren't cut out to be politicians' bandied about with no dissent whatsoever – after all, didn't the ODS party just choose a former beauty queen as their spokeswoman, with one of the reasons given that she has a nice smile? A foreign woman visiting a Czech doctor may find her health complaints are taken rather less than seriously, and a foreign male who goes to dinner at a Czech friend's can expect to be met with sincere surprise or even shock if he offers to help with the washing-up.

The disdain for feminism can be explained in part by the fact that the communists talked an awful lot about women's rights. In practice, this meant that women were to add full-time tractor maintenance to their duties of full-time housework and full-time childcare. Traditional attitudes about home duties are still prevalent, leaving many Czech women holding down full-time jobs as well as shouldering all the responsibility for chores and the kids. Women in positions of power in Czech business are becoming more and more visible, but the idea of 'women's work' is still very much in place – you are very unlikely to see a male secretary, nurse or schoolteacher anywhere below university level, and if you visit a Czech office a male secretary will certainly not be bringing you your coffee.

HARASSMENT

Prague is generally a pretty safe town to be female in, and walking around late at night is safer than in most European cities, but it's the little daily interactions that make it clear that women are considered rather differently than in some other countries. What is considered sexual harassment in the west is often considered 'just kidding around' here, and there will occasionally be a news magazine report on how women who dress provocatively are just asking for trouble if they are attacked.

WOMEN'S RESOURCES

Though feminism is still not taken very seriously, women's organisations do exist. They tend to emphasize women's rights as an integral part of human rights, rather than get caught up in the debate about that tricky word 'feminism'.

Ženské Centrum in Prague 5 (5732 4604) consists of four organizations: proFem, proMluv, La Strada and the Centre for Gender Studies, as well as the Gender Studies Library, which has some materials in English. The bilingual magazine *One Eye Open* acts as a forum for women's writing, publishing essays and interviews relevant to women's issues. Find it at any English-language bookstore.

Working in Prague

According to the law, you can't work unless you have a work permit and the necessary residency permit (confusingly termed a 'Temporary Visa for over 90 Days'). Unless you already have the residency permit, only available from Czech embassies outside the republic, usually after a months'-long wait, there isn't much hope of finding legal work.

If you do have the residency permit, and are to be employed by a Czech company, the company needs to obtain a work permit for you. You'll need to give evidence of qualifications and in some cases proof of relevant work experience, all accompanied by official notarised translations.

Expatriate Prague

Say what you will about Prague's English-speaking community, but it is largely thanks to such expatriates that the city is as welcoming and lively a place as it is.

Shortly after the Velvet Revolution, adventurous Westerners trickled into Prague and discovered Bohemia, in the manner of Columbus discovering the New World and its inhabitants. Among these intrepid explorers were artistic types, entrepreneurs and no shortage of aspiring journalists determined to find a city lousy with dharma bums. Their prophecy that Prague would be a sort of Club Med for the latest lost generation proved to be self-fulfilling.

Much has changed since those early days when, at least according to a clever advert, a pair of Levi's could be traded for a car. The cost of living, while still very low by Western standards, has since skyrocketed and Prague loses a little more mystery with the opening of each new McDonald's. The expatriate community has changed as well. Compared with the first wave of backpackers, today's expat is much more likely to be employed, married and washed.

Nonetheless, slackers are far from extinct, even if they have undergone a dramatic evolution. For one, today's expats are continually plugged in. Although hand-held devices such as Palm Pilots have yet to take off, most expats carry mobile phones and are seldom far away from an internet café. Establishments such as Terminal Bar (see page 152) are constantly filled with customers communicating with distant lands. Web surfing is also on the menu at Bohemia Bagel (page 148) and at the Globe (page 150), but has yet to replace the face-to-face chatting that have made these establishments the expat hubs that they are.

Today's expats are also more concerned about work than their predecessors in the early '90s were. Although a few are content to simply stay until whatever savings they brought with them are gone, most are eager to find gratifying and well-paying employment, although changes in the foreigners' law that went into effect on 1 January 2000 have made living and working legally in Prague more challenging thanks to endless restrictive bureaucracy. Expats are increasingly starting up their own businesses.

Some aspects of the expat life are likely never to change, however. Generally speaking, expats have an abundance of free time and fill it much the way they would have in their native land – spending money. Given their transient nature, they seldom spend it on durable goods such as televisions or cars. Rather, expat cash is spent on having a good time. Hence, Prague's party scene shows no sign of slacking. The club scene has finally blossomed, giving international bright young things multiple opportunities to follow their bliss all night long. Yet the pre-eminent party zones are the ones that have endured. Clubs such as the Roxy (see page 215) and Radost/FX (page 228) are still the favourites, and expat institutions such as Radost's weekly Beefstew open-mic, while not nearly so groovy as Radost's other activities, continues to draw a crowd of literary types.

Numerous peculiarities persist among Prague expatriates, such as the absence of surnames. Expats prefer to distinguish each other either by land of origin (Kiwi Rachael), hanging-out partner (Julie-and-Anthony Julie) or distinguishing physical characteristics (Little Glenn). And despite their general affluence, expats are loath to spend more than 30 crowns on a glass of beer.

Among the old guard it is remarked that there are many who attribute the noun 'expatriate' to themselves, but few who are willing to do the same with the verb. Yet for every Prague-weary expat who returns home or ventures further afield there is another fresh face waiting to take his place in line at the internet cafe working that hotmail account.

Directory

Vocabulary

For food and drink vocabulary, *see page 132*.

Pronunciation

a	as in gap
á	as in father
e	as in let
é	as in air
i, y	as in lit
í, ý	as in seed
o	as in lot
ó	as in lore
u	as in book
ú, ů	as in loom
c	as in its
č	s in chin
ch	as in loch
ď	as in duty
ň	as in onion
ř	as a standard r, but flatten the tip of the tongue making a short forceful buzz like ž
š	as in shin
ť	as in stew
ž	as in pleasure
dž	as in George

Handy words & phrases

Czech words are always stressed on the first syllable.

hello/good day	dobrý den
good evening	dobrý večer
good night	dobrou noc
goodbye	na shledanou
yes	ano (often abbreviated to no)
no	ne
please	prosím
thank you	děkuji
excuse me	promiňte
sorry	pardon
help!	pomoc!
attention!	pozor!
I don't speak Czech	Nemluvím česky
I don't understand	Nerozumím
do you speak English?	mluvíte anglicky?
sir	pán
madam	paní
open	otevřeno
closed	zavřeno
I would like...	chtěl bych...
how much is it?	kolik to stojí?
may I have a receipt, please?	účet, prosím
can we pay, please?	zaplatíme, prosím

where is... ?	kde je... ?
go left	doleva
go right	doprava
straight	rovně
far	daleko
near	blízko
good	dobrý
bad	špatný
big	velký
small	malý
no problem	to je v pořádku
who are you rooting for?	máš rád(a)?
cool shades!	máš dobře vychytaný brejle!
It's a rip-off	to je zlodějina
I'm absolutely knackered	jsem úplně na dně
the lift is stuck	výtah zůstal viset
could I speak to Václav?	mohl bych mluvit s Václavem?

Street names, etc

In conversation, as in this Guide, most Prague addresses are referred to by their name only, leaving off ulice, třída and so on.

avenue	třída
bridge	most
church	kostel
embankment	nábeží or náb
gardens	sady or zahrada
island	ostrov
lane	ulička
monastery, convent	klášter
park	park
square	náměstí or nám.
station	nádraží or nádr.
steps	schody
street	ulice or ul.
tunnel	tunel

Numbers

0	nula
1	jeden
2	dva
3	tři
4	čtyři
5	pět
6	šest
7	sedm
8	osm
9	devět
10	deset
11	jedenáct
12	dvanáct
13	tináct
14	čtrnáct
15	patnáct
16	šestnáct
17	sedmnáct
18	osmnáct
19	devatenáct
20	dvacet
30	třicet
40	čtyřicet
50	padesát
60	šedesát
70	sedmdesát
80	osmdesát
90	devadesát
100	sto
1,000	tisíc

Days of the week

Monday	pondělí
Tuesday	úterý
Wednesday	středa
Thursday	čtvrtek
Friday	pátek
Saturday	sobota
Sunday	neděle

Months & seasons

January	leden
February	únor
March	březen
April	duben
May	květen
June	červen
July	červenec
August	srpen
September	září
October	říjen
November	listopad
December	prosinec
Spring	jaro
Summer	léto
Autumn	podzim
Winter	zima

Pick-up lines

What kind of music do you listen to?
Jakou posloucháš hudbu?
I lost my keys to my flat. Is there any room for me at your place?
Ztratily se mi klíče od bytu. Nemáš u sebe místečko pro mě?
Do you want to take a look at my butterfly collection?
Chceš se podívat na moji sbírku motýlů?
I love you   Miluju Tě

Put-down lines

Don't make me laugh!	Ty mě chceš rozesmát!
Kiss my arse!	Polib mi prdel
Shit your eye out!	Vyser si oko!
That pisses me off!	To mě sere!
You jerk!	Ty vole!
You bitch!	Tý děvko!
Jump into a toilet!	Běž do hajzlíku!

Directory

Further Reference

Books

Literature & fiction

Brierley, David
On Leaving A Prague Window
Readable but dated thriller set in post-communist Prague.

Buchler, Alexander (ed)
This Side of Reality
Absorbing anthology of modern Czech writing.

Chatwin, Bruce
Utz
Luminous tale of a Josefov porcelain collector.

Hašek, Jaroslav
The Good Soldier Švejk
Rambling, picaresque comic masterpiece set in World War I, by Bohemia's most bohemian writer.

Havel, Václav
The Memorandum; Three Vaněk Plays; Temptation
The President's work as playwright. The Memorandum is his ground-breaking absurdist work.

Hrabl, Bohumil
I Served The King Of England
The living legend's most Prague-ish novel tracks its anti-hero through a decade of fascism, war and communism.

Klima, Ivan
Love And Garbage
Reflections on the lives of intellectuals as street-sweepers.

Kundera, Milan
The Joke; The Book Of Laughter And Forgetting; The Unbearable Lightness Of Being
Called smug by some and disliked by Czechs, his tragi-comic romances are still the runaway bestselling sketches of Prague.

Leppin, Paul
Others' Paradise/Severin's Journey Into The Dark
Recently translated work from pre-War Prague German writer, both in beautiful editions from Twisted Spoon Press.

Meyrink, Gustav
The Golem
The classic version of the tale of Rabbi Loew's monster, set in Prague's Jewish Quarter.

Neruda, Jan
Prague Tales
Wry and bitter-sweet stories of life in 19th-century Malá Strana, from Prague's answer to Dickens.

Šimečká, Martin M
The Year Of The Frog
Award-winning debut about dissidence in Bratislava.

Škvorecký, Josef
The Engineer of Human Souls
The magnum opus of the eternal chronicler of Czech jazz and skirtchasers.

Topol, Jáchym
Sister City Silver
A long-awaited translation of three noir novellas by one of the city's leading young writers, set in corrupt contemporary Prague.

Wilson, Paul (ed)
Prague: A Traveller's Literary Companion
Excellent collection, from Meyrink to Škvorecký, organised to evoke Prague's sense of place.

Kafka

Kafka, Franz
The Castle; The Transformation & Other Stories; The Trial
Worth re-reading, if only to note how postmodern Prague has completely lost all sense of Kafkaesque menace.

Kafka, Franz
Contemplation
Observations, vignettes and reflections in a beautiful illustrated edition from Twisted Spoon Press.

Anderson, Mark M
Kafka's Clothes
Erudite, subtle and unconventional book encompassing Kafka, dandyism and the Habsburg culture of ornament.

Brod, Max
Franz Kafka: A Biography
The only biography by anyone who actually knew the man.

Hayman, Ronald
K: A Biography of Kafka
Widely available, dependable, but a bit boring.

Hockaday, Mary
Kafka, Love And Courage: The Life Of Milena Jesenská
Best biography of Kafka's lover, and excellent on Prague.

Karl, Frederick
Franz Kafka: Representative Man
Hefty for a holiday read, but a thorough and thoughtful account of the man, his work, and the Prague he inhabited.

History, memoir & travel

Brook, Stephen
The Double Eagle: Vienna, Budapest & Prague
Fussy but entertainingly detailed travelogue of the Habsburg capitals in the early 1980s.

Demetz, Peter
Prague in Black and Gold
Thoughtful exploration of prehistoric to First Republic life in the Czech lands.

Fermor, Patrick Leigh
A Time Of Gifts
Evocative 1930s travelogue, culminating in inter-war Prague.

Garton Ash, Timothy
The Magic Lantern: The Revolution of 1989 Witnessed in Warsaw, Budapest, Berlin And Prague; History of the Present
The Oxford academic's on-the-spot 1989 history, and his look back a decade later, painfully explore the morality of the Velvet Revolution.

Pynsent, Robert B
Questions of Identity: Czech and Slovak Ideas of Nationality and Personality
Witty, erudite and incisive look at Czech self-perception.

Rimmer, Dave
Once Upon a Time in the East
Communism seen stoned and from ground level.

Ripellino, Angelo Maria
Magic Prague
Mad masterpiece of literary and cultural history, mixing fact and fiction as it celebrates the city's sorcerous soul.

Sayer, Derek
Coasts of Bohemia
Phenomenally well-researched and witty account of the millennium-long Czech search for identity.

Shawcross, William
Dubček
Biography of the Prague Spring figurehead, updated to assess his role in the 1989 Velvet Revolution.

Directory

Essays & argument

Čapek, Karel
Towards The Radical Centre
Selected essays from the man who coined the word 'robot'.

Klima, Ivan
The Spirit of Prague
Thought-provoking essays, of which the title piece is highlight.

Havel, Václav
Living In Truth/Letters To Olga/Disturbing The Peace
His most important political writing, his prison letters to his wife, and his autobiographical reflections.

Miscellaneous

Iggers, Wilma A
Women Of Prague
Fascinating – the lives of 12 women, across 200 years.

Sís, Peter
Three Golden Keys
Children's tale set in Prague, with wonderful drawings.

Putz, Harry
Do You Want To Speak Czech?
If the answer is yes, this is the book (and the cassette).

Various eds
Prague: 11 Centuries of Architecture
Solid, substantial and not too stodgy.

Film

The following can be viewed on video at Terminal Bar (*see page 200*) or found periodically at film festivals or video stores with a strong international selection.

Ecstasy (Extáze)
Gustav Machat (1932)
Known primarily for its groundbreaking nude scene with the nubile actress who would later be known as Hedy Lamarr, this imagistic film depicts a girl frustrated with her relationship with an older man, and the strange triangle of desire that emerges.

The Long Journey (Daleká cesta)
Alfred Radok (1949)
Banned by the Communists for 20 years, this film uses innovative lighting and camera techniques to depict the deportation of Jews to concentration camps.

The Fabulous World of Jules Verne (Vynález zkázy)
Karel Zeman (1958)
A unique film, also called *The Invention of Destruction*, that tries to capture the look of the original engravings used to illustrate Verne's books. Animated flying machines and submarines are joined to live action scenes in this story of a mad inventor.

The Great Solitude (Velká samota)
Ladislav Helge (1959)
One of the few pre-new wave movies that goes deeper than farm-tool worship, this film focuses on how tough it is to be a rural party official.

Ikarie XB 1 (Voyage to the End of the Universe)
Jindřich Polák (1963)
Even in the badly re-edited and dubbed English-language version, this spaced-out thriller set on a lost rocket ship in the 25th century shows flashes of brilliance. The secret mission known only to the ship's computer pre-dates Kubrick's *2001*.

The Shop on Main Street (Obchod na korze)
Ján Kádár & Elmar Klos (1964)
Set during World War II in the Nazi puppet state of Slovakia, it's about an honest carpenter who must act as the person 'Aryanising' a button shop run by an old Jewish woman. Winner of the 1966 Oscar for Best Foreign Film.

Intimate Lighting (Intimní osvítlení)
Ivan Passer (1965)
Possibly the most delightful film of the Czech new wave, *Intimate Lightning* tells about the reunion of two old friends after many years of living very different lives, only to discover the musical ensemble in which they used to play is as tuneless as it ever was.

Larks on a String (Skřivánci na niti)
Jiří Menzel (1969)
This tale of forced labour in the steel mills of industrial Kladno deals with politics a bit, but love – and libido – somehow always triumph. Banned soon after its release, the film was not shown again until 1989 when it won the Berlin Film Festival's Golden Bear.

The Ear (Ucho)
Karel Kachyňa (written by Jan Procházka) (1970)
The full force of surveillance terror and paranoia is exposed in this chilling film, whose origins go further back than the communists to Kafka. Banned instantly, of course.

Buttoners (Knoflíkáři)
Petr Zelenka (1997)
Sardonic, schizophrenic flick that shuffles the lives of several disparate characters, all vaguely connected through the bombing of Hiroshima. Sassy and clean-paced enough to have nabbed a few international awards.

Pelišk y (Cozy Dens)
Jan Hřebejk (1999)
A bittersweet look at the lives of neighboring families from Christmas 1967 to 21 August 1968, the day that Russian tanks rolled in. One family supports the communist regime, one doesen't and their kids are embarrassed by it all.

Otesánek
Jan Švankmajer (2000)
Employing his usual alchemy of still animation and live action, Švankmajer updates a classic Czech myth about a childless couple who adopt a baby made from tree roots, which proceeds to eat the local populace.

Music

Ivá Bittová: Bilé Inferno (Indies)
One of the most listened-to double albums on the post-1989 scene, the *White Inferno* showcases the best of the Brno sound.

Hypnotix: New World Order (EMI)
The dub stars of Prague, led by the polemical Bourama Badji, mix up language and fat beats to formulate Prague's idea of a Jamaican session.

Ecstasy of St Theresa: In Dust 3 (EMI)
Jan P Muchow creates a textured digital background for the provocative vocals of Kateřina Winterová on the album most cherished as a lifestyle choice by clubby Praguers, circa 2000.

Various: Future Sound of Prague (Intellygent)
This anthology of house and trip hop presents the best of Significant Other, Southpaw, Garden Zitty and other acts on the Bohemian club circuit at the turn of the millennium.

Richard Müller (B&M Music)
The Slovak classic rocker sits in with an improbably wide range of singers, from the avant-garde Ivá Bittova to the vintage chanteuse Hana Hegerová. Funky keyboards and bass underscore this poppy all-Czech top seller.

Directory

Homegrown classics

Below we select eight excellent domestic recordings. All feature music by Czech composers or performances by outstanding Czech musicians.

Jan Ladislav Dusík: Piano Concerto, Sonatas

Jan Novotný, Prague Chamber Philharmonic, conducted by Leoš Svárovský (Panton)
The Prague Chamber Philharmonic delivers the energy and spontaneity that has set it apart from the city's larger orchestras in these excellent recordings of Dusík's Concert Concerto for Piano and Orchestra in E flat major, Op 70 and two of his more lyrical sonatas, the F Sharp minor, Op 61 and the A flat major, Op 64. Novotný's playing is particularly expressive.

Vítěslav Novák: Slovácko Suite, Melanchoy Songs of Love, Serenade in F

Jana Tetourová, Prague Chamber Philharmonic, conducted by Jií Bělohlávek (Supraphon)
One of the most unjustly overlooked Czech composers is rendered with crystal clarity by the rising-star soprano Tetourová, who seems to have a special feeling for the restrained heartbreak contained in Novák's pieces.

Chopin: The Piano Concertos, No 1&2

E Leonskaja, Czech Philharmonic, conducted by Vladimir Ashkenazy (Teldec)
A prize recording of the Czech Philharmonic, which works very well with the renowned Russian pianist, trading off with her in the execution of powerful passages, but also giving her the space to caress an emotive softer stanza when needed. Leonskaja shows an incredible range in her interpretation on this double CD.

Krzystof Penderecki: Works for Clarinet (Sharon Kam Meets Krzystof Penderecki)

Sharon Kam, Krzystof Penderecki, Czech Philharmonic, conducted by Vladimir Ashkenazy (Teldec)
One of the Czech Philharmonic's proudest recent accomplishments is this magnificent duo. Original, rarely heard works from the modern avant-garde composer Penderecki are a rewarding, surprising treat.

Messiaen, Pärt, Dvořák, Saint-Saéns: Reflections

Jií Bárta (Supraphon)
Arguably the Czech Republic's top cellist, Bárta performs works ranging from plaintive to glowing in his usual intense and rich style. Among the big-name composers whose short works have inspired Bárta is the virtually unknown Zemek-Novák Sonata No 2 and Cantus rogans by Kopelent, neither ever recorded before.

Bohuslav Martinů: The Spectre's Bride, Nipponari, Magic Nights

Kühn Mixed Chorus, Prague Symphony Orchestra, conducted by Jií Bělohlávek (Supraphon)
Three unjustly neglected works by one of the giants of 20th-century Czech classical music are performed with sensitivity. Magic Nights, a setting of three Chinese poems from the same anthology that Mahler used for Das Lied von der Erde, is a gem.

Websites

Central Europe Online
www.centraleurope.com
A flashy and popular website offering news, business and special reports on the Czech Republic and other Central European countries. Crisply designed pages, but somewhat dry content.

Charles University
www.cuni.cz
The official site of Charles University, much of it in English, with links to a university-run news service (available via e-mail), the university library, departments and courses for foreigners.

Czech-English Dictionary
www.foreignword.com
Thousands of words translated from Czech or dozens of other languages into English or back.

Czech Info Centre
www.muselik.com/czech/index.html
Popular bulletin board for meeting Czechs looking for work or travel deals.

Czech Railways
idos.datis.cdrail.cz/Conn.asp?tt=2
Searchable online train timetables for every city and town in the Czech Republic with a rail connection.

Czech Techno
www.techno.cz
All the party and club news in the Czech Republic with links to techno-favouring clubs and promoters and the bands that rock them.

Czech and Slovak Yellow Pages
users.aol.com/mpgrego/private/title.htm
Hundreds of well-arranged topics on all things Czech and Slovak, from the environment to art events, are packed in and easy to navigate.

Globopolis
www.globopolis.cz
This expat bookstore and coffeehouse has expanded into a searchable regional culture and events site. Well hyped and probably worth it, once the search bugs are worked out.

Praha Interactive
http://test.cech.cesnet.cz/praha/
Street index and metro maps of Prague on an interactive, zoomable format.

The Prague Post
www.praguepost.cz
Prague's main English-language weekly features useful online tourist information pages, plus classifieds, movie listings, pub and restaurant reviews and feature and news articles. A must-stop for surfers who plan to visit the city, it offers a goldmine of tips on the Golden City, from medical and safety issues to accommodation and restaurant reviews.

Prague Information Service
www.prague-info.cz
Comprehensive source for city addresses with well-organised pages of general tourist information from embassy addresses to concert links.

Praha Interactive Street Index
http://cech.cesnet.cz/cgi-bin/st
Find where your hotel is located by looking it up on this complete online map of Prague.

Radio Free Europe/ Radio Liberty
www.rferl.org/newsline/
News, maps, facts and figures and lots on Czech society.

Seznam
www.seznam.cz
A fast Czech-language search engine with data on all things Czech.

Terminal Bar
www.terminal.cz
The heart of Prague's cyber scene with virtual views of the bar, cool links and a list of the Terminal Video library.

Time Out Prague Guide
www.timeout.com
Shameless self-promotion it may be, but here's where you'll find the online version of the best guide available.

Directory

Index

Advertisers' Index

Maps

Place of Interest and/or Entertainment	
Railway Stations	
Metro Stations	Ⓜ
Parks	
Pedestrian Zones	
Churches	✚
Steps	
Area Name	JOSEFOV
Tram Routes	—

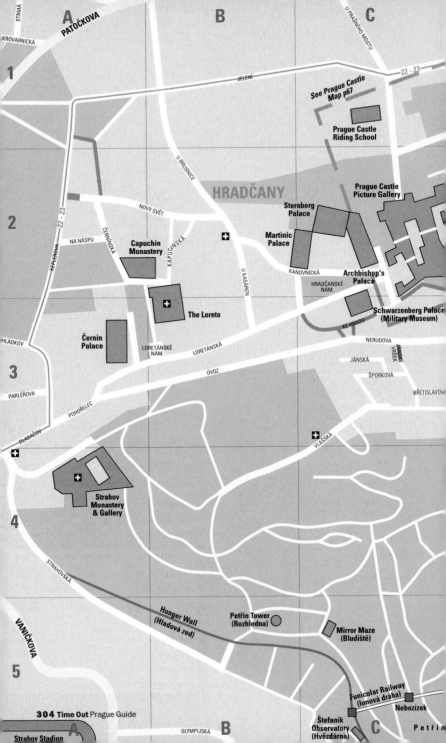

STRMÁ

PATOČKOVA

KROVARNICKÁ

1

JELENÍ

U PRAŠNÉHO MOSTU

22 - 23

See Prague Castle
Map p67

Prague Castle
Riding School

U BRUSNICE

HRADČANY

Prague Castle
Picture Gallery

NOVÝ SVĚT

Sternberg
Palace

KEPLEROVA

22 - 23

NA NÁSPU

ČERNINSKÁ

KAPUCÍNSKÁ

Capuchin
Monastery

2

Martinic
Palace

U KASÁREN

KANOVNICKÁ

Archbishop's
Palace

HRADČANSKÉ
NÁM.

The Loreto

Černin
Palace

Schwarzenberg Palace
(Military Museum)

KE HRADU

HLÁDKOV

LORETÁNSKÉ
NÁM.

LORETÁNSKÁ

NERUDOVA

JÁNSKÝ
VRŠEK

JÁNSKÁ

ŠPORKOVA

3

ÚVOZ

PARLÉŘOVA

BŘETISLAVOV

POHOŘELEC

DLABAČOV

VLAŠSKÁ

Strahov
Monastery
& Gallery

4

STRAHOVSKÁ

VANIČKOVA

Hunger Wall
(Hladová zed)

Petřin Tower
(Rozhledna)

Mirror Maze
(Bludiště)

5

Funicular Railway
(lanová dráha)

Nebozízek

304 Time Out Prague Guide

Strahov Stadion

OLYMPIJSKÁ

Štefaník
Observatory
(Hvězdárna)

Petřín

A   B   C

MARIÁNSKÉ HRADBY

TYCHONOVA

K BRUSCE

Chotkovy sady

1

Royal Gardens
(Královská zahrada)

The Belvedere

CHOTKOVA

POD BRUSKOU

U BRUSKÝCH KASÁREN

NÁBŘ. EDVARDA BENEŠE

Ball Game
Court

18 - 22 - 23 - 57

NA OPYŠI

Stag Moat

STARÉ ZÁMECKÉ SCHODY
(Old Castle Steps)

KLÁROV

**Prague
Castle**

Golden Lane

Toy
Museum

Historical
Museum

St George's
Basilica

Ledeburg Gardens
(Ledeburská zahrada)

12

U ŽELEZNÉ LÁVKY

KOŠÁRKOVO NÁBŘEŽÍ

2

St Vitus's
Cathedral

Old Royal
Palace

U ZLATÉ STUDNĚ

Komenský
Pedagogical
Museum

VALDŠTEJNSKÁ

Malostranská

M

Wallenstein
Palace

Gardens on the Ramparts
(Zahrada na Valech)

VALDŠTEJNSKÉ
NÁM.

Wallenstein Gardens
(Valdštejnské zahrady)

KLÁROV

18

MÁNESŮV
MOST

ZÁMECKÉ SCHODY
(Castle Steps)

THUNOVSKÁ

SNĚMOVNÍ

TOMÁŠSKÁ

LETENSKÁ

Church of
St Thomas

*Vojan's Gardens
(Vojanovy sady)*

3

ZÁMECKÁ

NERUDOVA

Church of
St Joseph

JOSEFSKÁ

U LUŽICKÉHO SEMINÁŘE

CIHELNÁ

See
Page 306

BŘETISLAVOVA

Church of
St Nicholas

MALOSTRANSKÉ
NÁM.

MIŠEŇSKÁ

**MALÁ
STRANA**

TRŽIŠTĚ

MOSTECKÁ

DRAŽICKÉHO
NÁMĚSTÍ

CHARLES BRIDGE
(Karlův most)

ÚJEZDSKÁ

SASKÁ

Church of Our Lady
Beneath the Chain

Kampa
Wharf

Church of Our
Lady Victorious
(Il Bambino di Praga)

KARMELITSKÁ

PROKOPSKÁ

MALTÉZSKÉ
NÁM.

John Lennon
Wall

HROZNOVÁ

NA KAMPĚ

4

Buquoy
Palace

HARANTOVA

NEBOVIDSKÁ

NOSTICOVA

**KAMPA
ISLAND**

ČERTOVKA

12 - 22 - 57

HELLICHOVA

U SOVOVÝCH MLÝNŮ

Michna Palace
(Tyrš Sport & Physical
Training Museum)

0   200 m

0   200 yds

© Copyright Time Out Group 2000

VŠEHRDOVA

*Střelecký
ostrov*

5

U LANOVÉ DRÁHY

Funicular Railway
(lanová dráha)

ÚJEZD

ŘÍČNÍ

ŠEŘÍKOVA

BOROVSKÁ

NÁBŘ.

MALOSTRANSKÉ

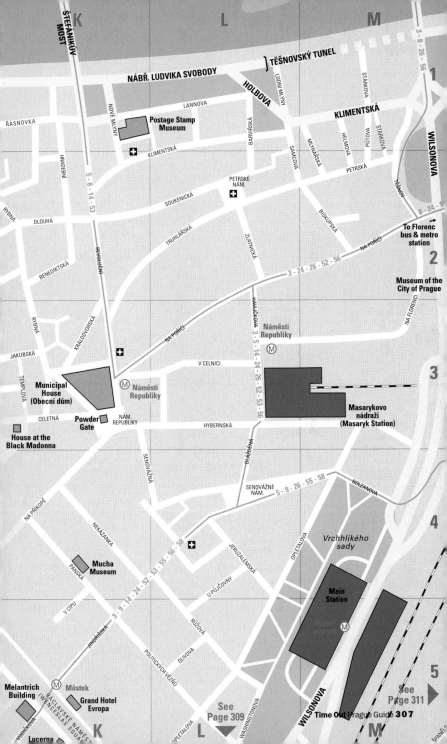

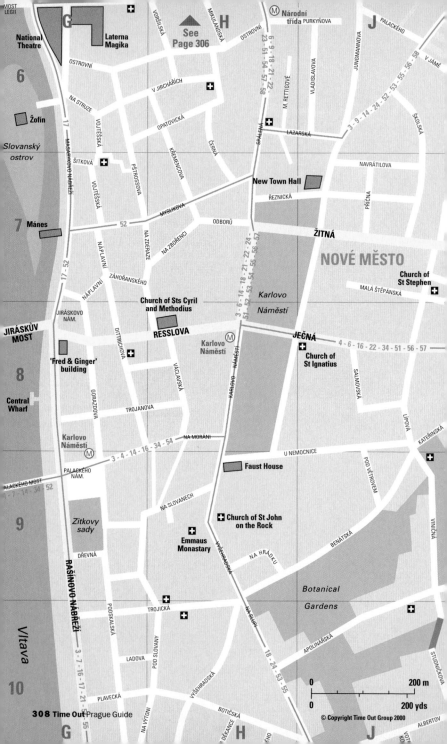

National Theatre

Laterna Magika

See Page 306

Národní třída PURKYŇOVA

MOST LEGII

G

H

J

6

Žofin

Slovanský ostrov

7 Mánes

JIRÁSKŮV MOST

8

'Fred & Ginger' building

Central Wharf

Karlovo Náměstí

9

Zitkovy sady

Vltava

10

OSTROVNÍ

NA STRUZE

V JIRCHÁŘÍCH

VODIČKOVA

MIKULANDSKÁ

OSTROVNÍ

23 - 51 - 54 - 57 - 58

6 - 9 - 18 - 21 - 22 -

M. RETTIGOVÉ

VLADISLAVOVA

JUNGMANNOVA

PALACKÉHO

V JÁMĚ

55 - 56 - 58

3 - 9 - 14 - 24 - 52 - 53 -

ŠKOLSKÁ

OPATOVICKÁ

ČERNÁ

ŠPÁLENÁ

LAZARSKÁ

NAVRÁTILOVA

KŘEMENCOVA

PŘÍČNÁ

New Town Hall

ŘEZNICKÁ

ŽITNÁ

NOVÉ MĚSTO

Church of St Stephen

MALÁ ŠTĚPÁNSKÁ

17

MASARYKOVO NÁBŘEŽÍ

VOLTĚŠSKÁ

ŠITKOVÁ

PSTROSSOVA

VOLTĚŠSKÁ

MYSLÍKOVA

ODBORÚ

52

NÁPLAVNÍ

NA ZDERAZE

ZÁHOŘANSKÉHO

NA ZBOŘENCI

3 - 6 - 14 - 18 - 21 - 22 - 24 -

51 - 53 - 54 - 55 - 56 - 57

Karlovo Náměstí

25

17

NÁPLAVNÍ

JIRÁSKOVO NÁM.

DITTRICHOVA

Church of Sts Cyril and Methodius

RESSLOVA

Karlovo Náměstí

JEČNÁ

4 - 6 - 16 - 22 - 34 - 51 - 56 - 57

Church of St Ignatius

SALMOVSKÁ

LIPOVÁ

GORAZDOVA

VÁCLAVSKÁ

TROJANOVA

NA MORÁNI

U NEMOCNICE

POD VĚTROVEM

KATEŘINSKÁ

3 - 4 - 14 - 16 - 34 - 54

PALACKÉHO NÁM.

Faust House

ALACKÉHO MOST

4 - 7 - 14 - 34 - 52

NA SLOVANECH

Church of St John on the Rock

VINIČNÁ

BENÁTSKÁ

DŘEVNÁ

RAŠÍNOVO NÁBŘEŽÍ

3 - 7 - 16 - 17 - 21 -

PODSKALSKÁ

TROJICKÁ

Emmaus Monastary

VYŠEHRADSKÁ

NA HRÁDKU

NA SLUPI

Botanical Gardens

STUDNIČKOVA

LADOVA

POD SLOVANY

APOLINÁŘSKÁ

VYŠEHRADSKÁ

18 - 24 - 53 - 55

ALBERTOV

55

PLAVECKÁ

NA VÝTONI

BOTIČSKÁ

DĚKANCE

VOTO KO

0   200 m

0   200 yds

© Copyright Time Out Group 2000

G

H

J

K

Lucerna

V JÁMĚ

ŠTĚPÁNSKÁ

VE SMEČKÁCH

L

See
Page 307

VÁCLAVSKÉ NÁMĚSTÍ
(WENCESLAS SQUARE)

OPLETALOVA

WASHINGTONOVA

WILSONOVA

**St Wenceslas
Statue**

Ⓜ **Muzeum**

M

ŠPANĚLSKÁ

HELÉNSK

6

NA SMETANCE

MÁNESOVA

LEGEROVA

**State
Opera**

KRAKOVSKÁ

MEZIBRANSKÁ

**National
Museum**

*Čelokovského
sady*

VINOHRADSKÁ

VINOHRADY

11

See
Page 311 ▶

7

ŽITNÁ

**Rotunda of
St Longinus** ✚

NA RYBNÍČKU

V TŮNÍCH

HÁLKOVA

SOKOLSKÁ

ANGLICKÁ

MIKOV-
COVA

VOCELOVA

BĚLEHRADSKÁ

ŘÍMSKÁ

RUBEŠOVA

LONDÝNSKÁ

BALBÍNOVA

ITALSKÁ

ŘÍMSKÁ

IBSENOVA

ŠUBER

**Church of
St Ludmila** ✚

NÁMĚSTÍ
MÍRU

JEČNÁ

Ⓜ I. P. Pavlova

JUGOSLÁVSKÁ

— 4 - 16 - 22 - 34 - 51 - 57

Ⓜ

*Náměstí
Míru*

8

LEGEROVA

LUBLAŇSKÁ

TYLOVO
NÁM.

RUMUNSKÁ

BĚLEHRADSKÁ

AMERICKÁ

URUGUAYSKÁ

KATEŘINSKÁ

KE KARLOVU

**Dvořák
Museum**

NA BOJIŠTI

TYRŠOVA

KOUBKOVA

BRUSELSKÁ

LONDÝNSKÁ

BELGICKÁ

ZÁHŘEBSKÁ

9

FÜGNEROVO
NÁM.

SOKOLSKÁ

LEGEROVA

APOLINÁŘSKÁ

KE KARLOVU

WENZIGOVA

6 - 11 - 56

ŠAFAŘÍKOVA

U ZVONAŘKY

JANA MASARYK

POD
NUSELSKÝMI
SCHODY

10

K

**Police
Museum**

STUDNIČK

✚ **Na Karlově**

L

*Park
Folimanka*

LUBLAŇSKÁ

POD ZVONAŘKOU

Time Out Prague Guide **309**

M

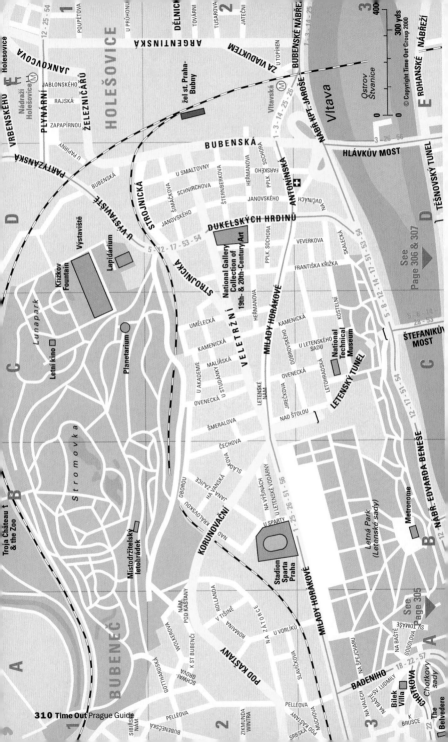

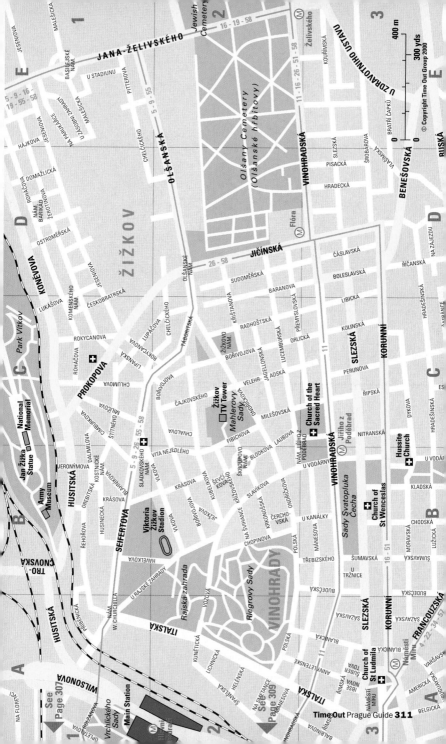

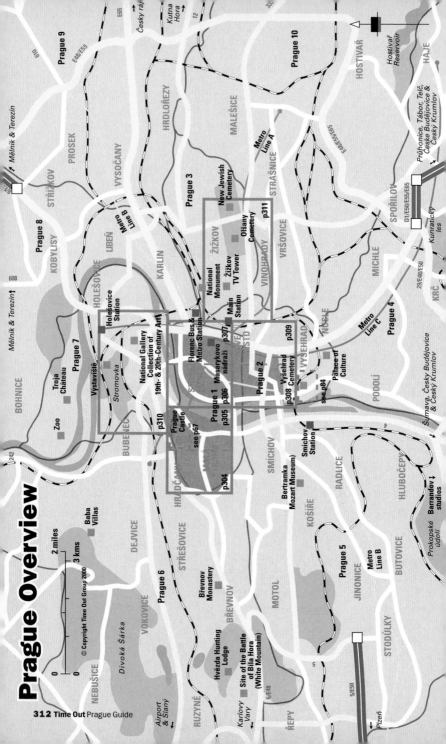

Prague Overview

2 miles

3 kms

© Copyright Time Out Group 2000

Prague 9

Prague 10

HOSTIVAŘ

Hostivař
Reservoir

HÁJE

Mělník & Terezín

Český ráj

Kutná Hora

E65

12

Průhonice, Tábor, Telč,
České Budějovice &
Český Krumlov

SPOŘILOV

D1/E50/E55/E65

STŘÍŽKOV

PROSEK

VYSOČANY

610

E48/E55

HRDLOŘEZY

Metro
Line A

STRAŠNICE

Kunratický
les

MALEŠICE

KOBYLISY

Prague 8

UBEŇ

Metro
Line B

KARLÍN

New Jewish
Cemetery

Prague 3

ŽIŽKOV

Olšany
Cemetery

p311

VRŠOVICE

VINOHRADY

MICHLE

29/E48/E50

KRČ

Metro
Line C

Prague 4

E48/E55/E65

HOLEŠOVICE

Holešovice
Station

National
Monument

Žižkov
TV Tower

Main
Station

Mělník & Terezín

608

BOHNICE

Troja
Château

Zoo

Výstaviště

Stromovka

National Gallery
Collection of
19th- & 20th-Century Art

Prague 7

BUBENEČ

p310

Florenc Bus &
Metro Station

Masarykovo
nádraží

Prague 1

Prague
Castle
see p67

p305

p306

p304

p307

Prague 2

Vyšehrad
Cemetery

p308

p309

NUSLE

Palace of
Culture

PODOLÍ

see p84

SMÍCHOV

Smíchov
Station

Bertramka
Mozart Museum)

KOŠÍŘE

Prokopské
údolí

HLUBOČEPY

Barrandov
studios

Prague 5

RADLICE

BUTOVICE

Metro
Line B

JINONICE

STODŮLKY

MOTOL

BŘEVNOV

Břevnov
Monastery

STŘEŠOVICE

Baba
Villas

DEJVICE

Prague 6

VOKOVICE

Divoká Šárka

NEBUŠICE

Hvězda Hunting
Lodge

Site of the Battle
of Bílá Hora
(White Mountain)

RUZYNĚ

ŘEPY

Airport
& Slaný

Karlovy
Vary

6/E48

5/E50

Plzeň

242

Šumava, České Budějovice
& Český Krumlov

0

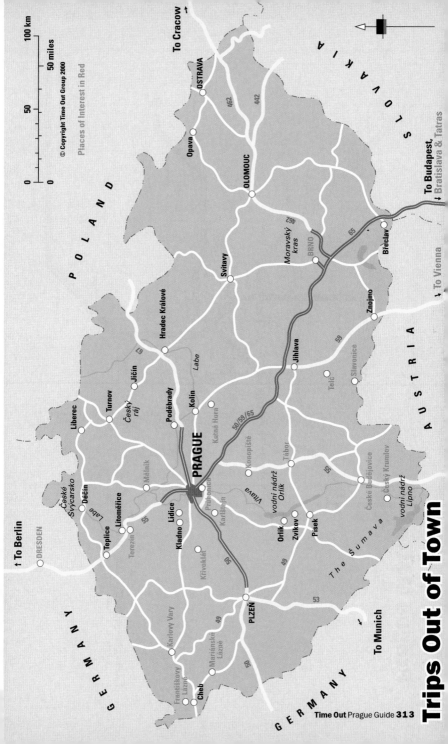

Trips Out of Town

Prague Metro

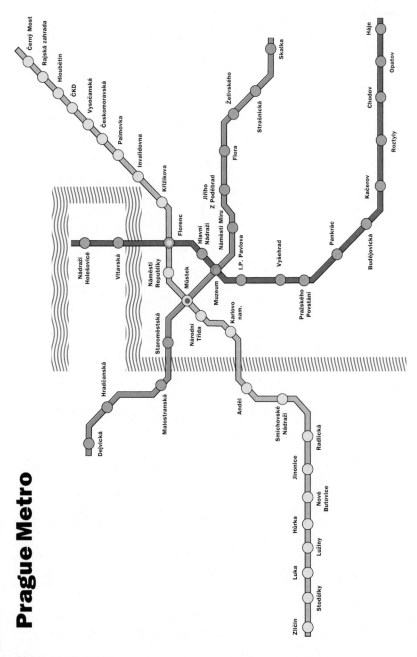

Street Index

TimeOut Prague Please let us know what you think

Visit Time Out's website at **www.timeout.com**
or email your comments to **guides@timeout.com**
(FOURTH EDITION)

About this guide...

1. How useful did you find the following sections?

	Very	Fairly	Not very
In Context	☐	☐	☐
Accommodation	☐	☐	☐
Sightseeing	☐	☐	☐
Eat, Drink, Shop	☐	☐	☐
Arts & Entertainment	☐	☐	☐
Trips Out of Town	☐	☐	☐
Directory	☐	☐	☐
Maps	☐	☐	☐

2. Did you travel to Prague...?

Alone ☐   With children ☐
As part of a group ☐   On vacation ☐
On business ☐   To study ☐
With a partner ☐   I live here ☐

3. How long was your trip to Prague? (write in)

_____ days

4. Where did you book your trip?

Time Out Classifieds ☐
On the Internet ☐
With a travel agent ☐
Other (write in) ☐

5. Where did you first hear about this guide?

Advertising in Time Out magazine ☐
On the Internet ☐
From a travel agent ☐
Other (write in) ☐

6. Is there anything you'd like us to cover in greater depth?

_____

7. Are there any places that should/ should not* be included in the guide?
(*delete as necessary)

_____
_____
_____
_____
_____
_____

8. How many other people have used this guide?

none ☐   1 ☐   2 ☐   3 ☐   4 ☐   5+ ☐

9. What city or country would you like to visit next? (write in)

_____

About other Time Out publications...

10. Have you ever bought/used Time Out magazine?

Yes ☐   No ☐

11. Have you ever bought/used any other Time Out City Guides?

Yes ☐   No ☐

If yes, which ones?
_____

12. Have you ever bought/used other Time Out publications?

Yes ☐   No ☐

If yes, which ones?
_____

About you...

13. Title (Mr, Ms etc):
First name: _____
Surname: _____
Address: _____
_____
Postcode: _____
Email: _____
Nationality: _____

14. Date of birth: ☐☐/☐☐/☐☐

15. Sex: male ☐   female ☐

16. Are you...?
Single ☐
Married/Living with partner ☐

17. What is your occupation?

_____

18. At the moment do you earn...?

under £15,000 ☐
over £15,000 and up to £19,999 ☐
over £20,000 and up to £24,999 ☐
over £25,000 and up to £39,999 ☐
over £40,000 and up to £49,999 ☐
over £50,000 ☐

☐ Please tick here if you'd like to hear about offers and discounts from Time Out and relevant companies.

Time Out Guides

FREEPOST 20 (WC3187)
LONDON
W1E 0DQ